AF587542

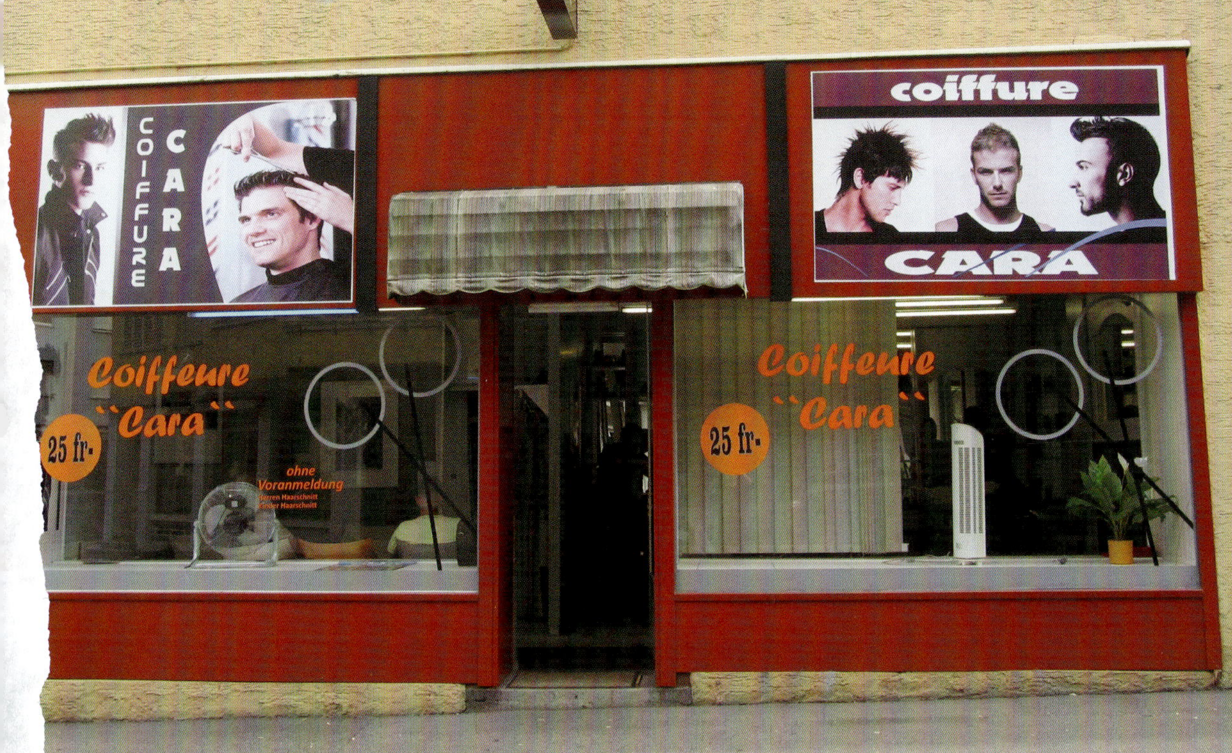
COIFFURE
CARA
coiffure
CARA
Coiffeure
``Cara``
25 fr.-
ohne
Voranmeldung
Coiffeure
``Cara``
25 fr.-

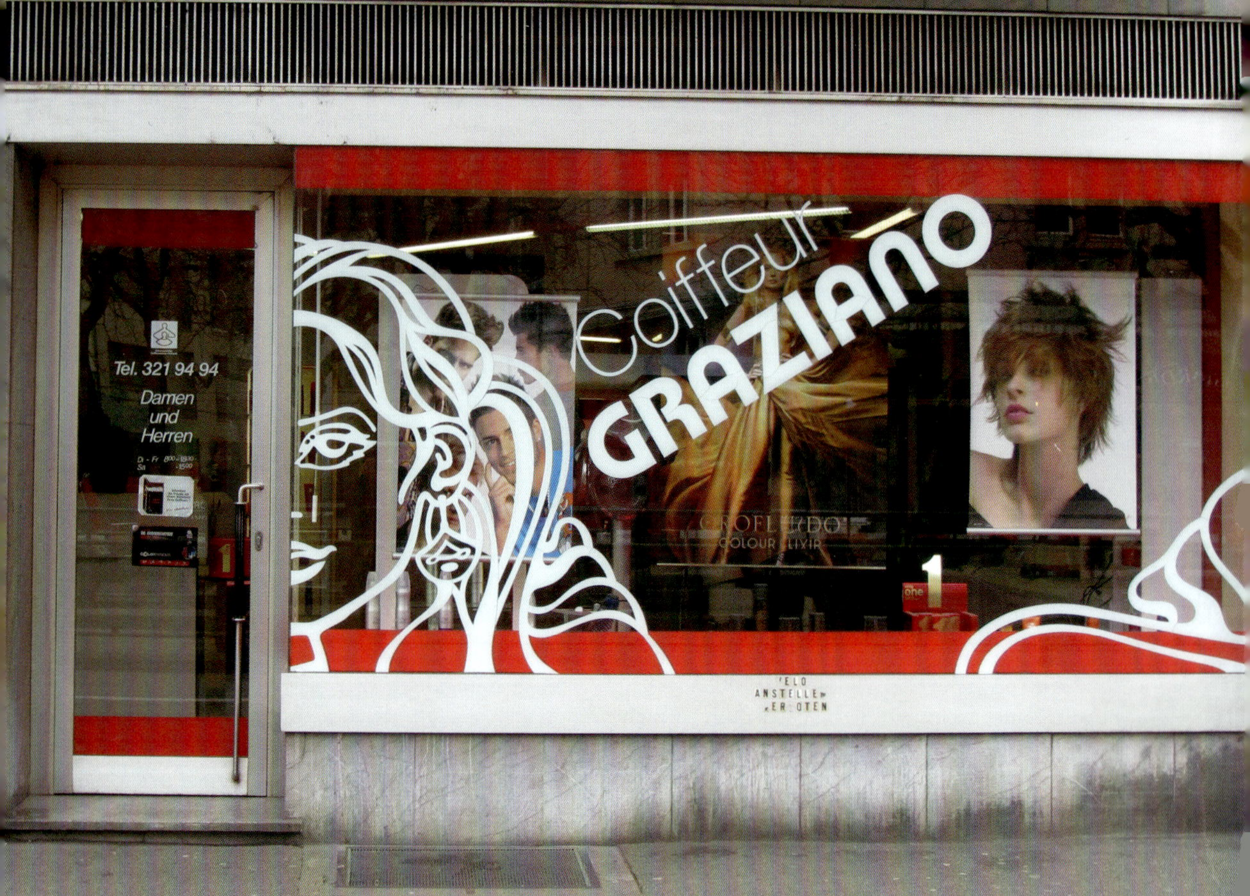
Coiffeur
GRAZIANO
Tel. 321 94 94
Damen
und
Herren

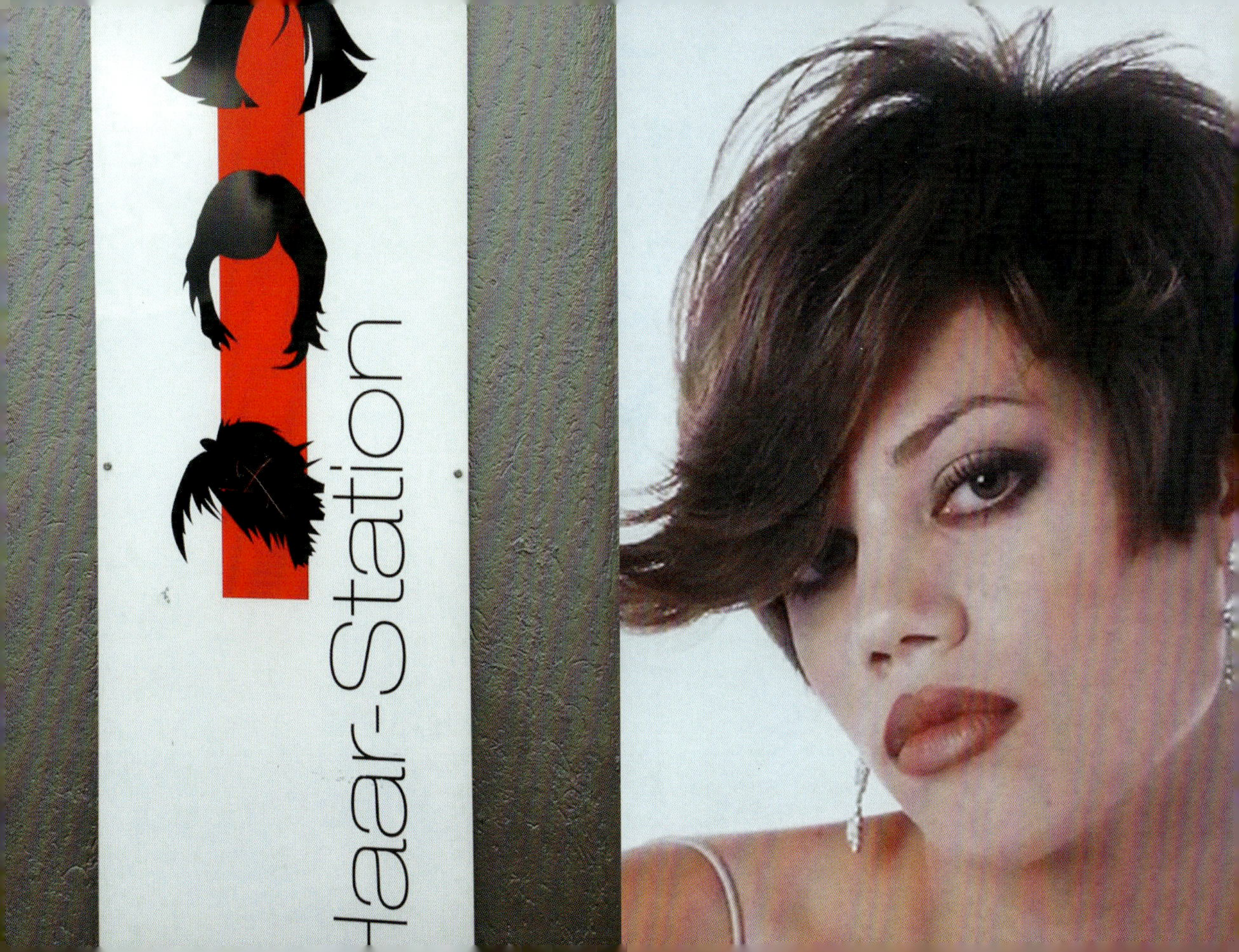
Haar-Station

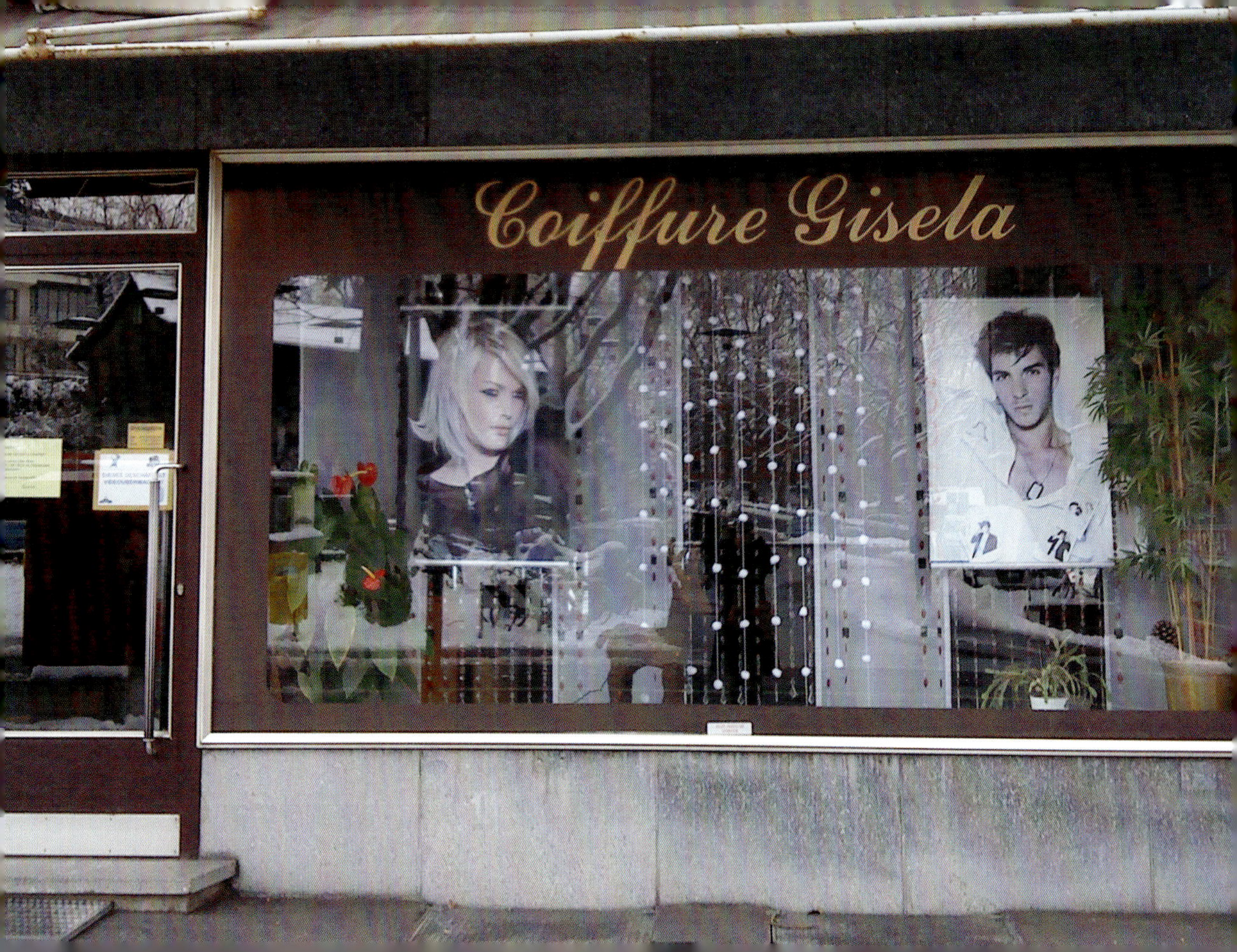
Coiffure Gisela

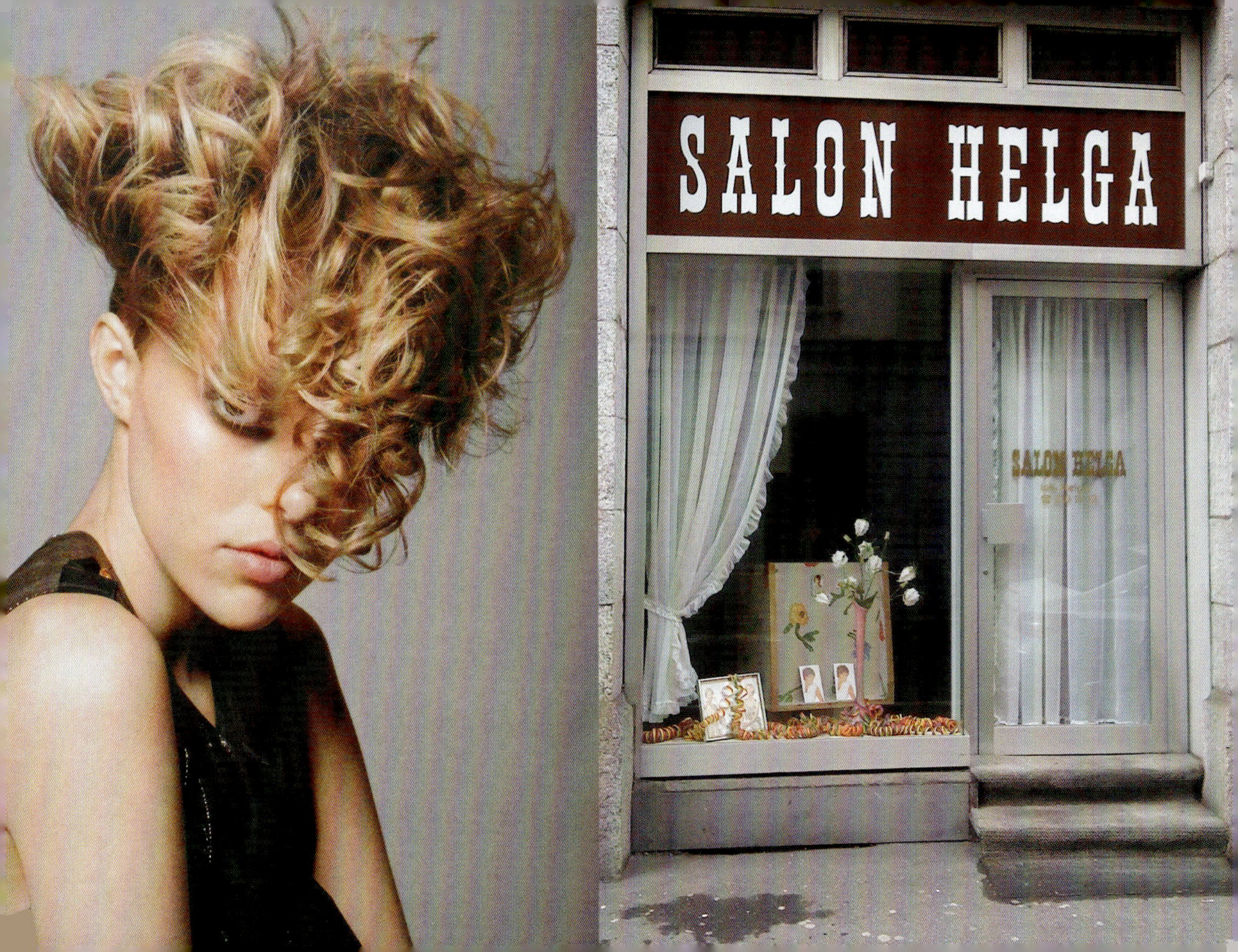
SALON HELGA
SALON HELGA

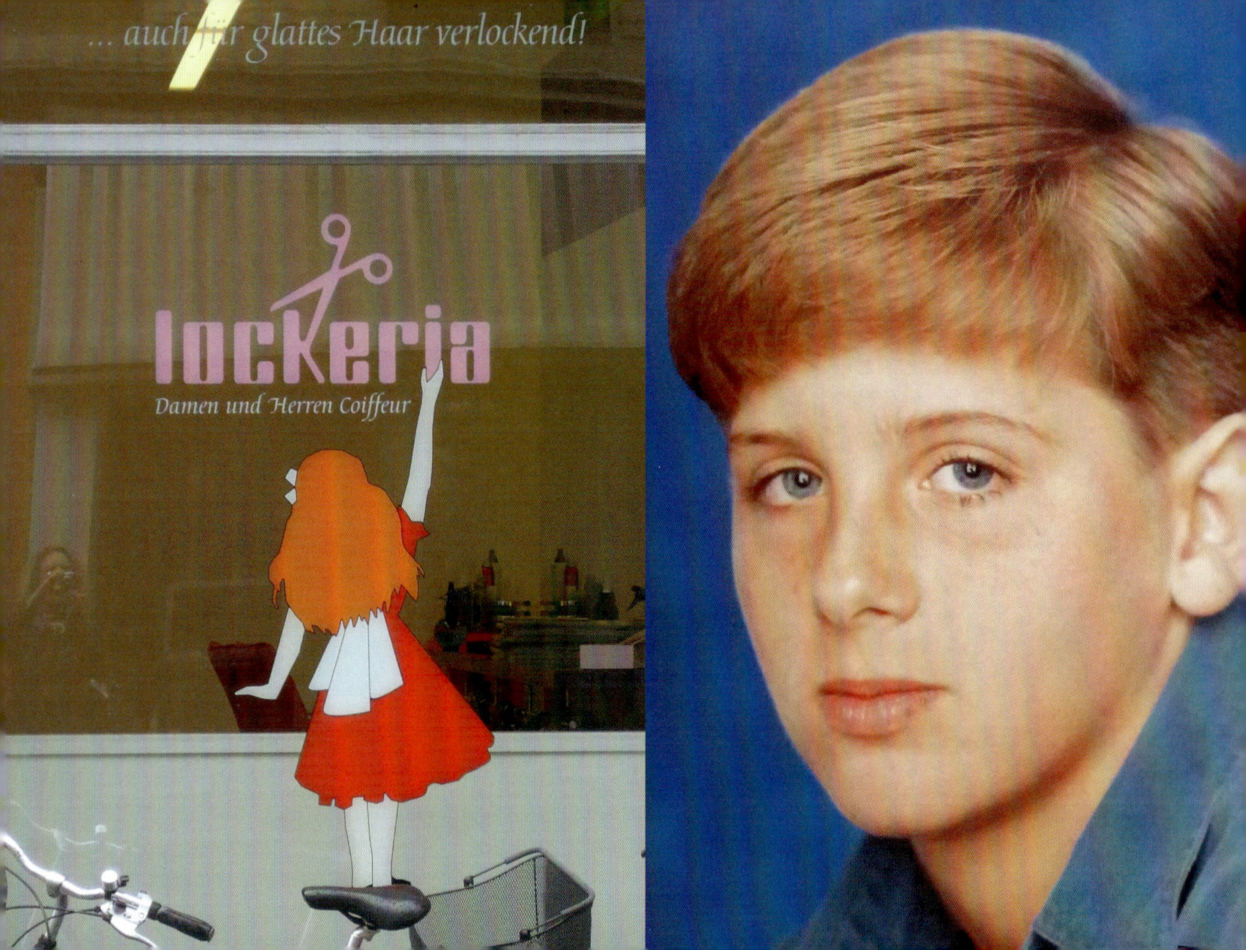
... auch für glattes Haar verlockend!
lockeria
Damen und Herren Coiffeur

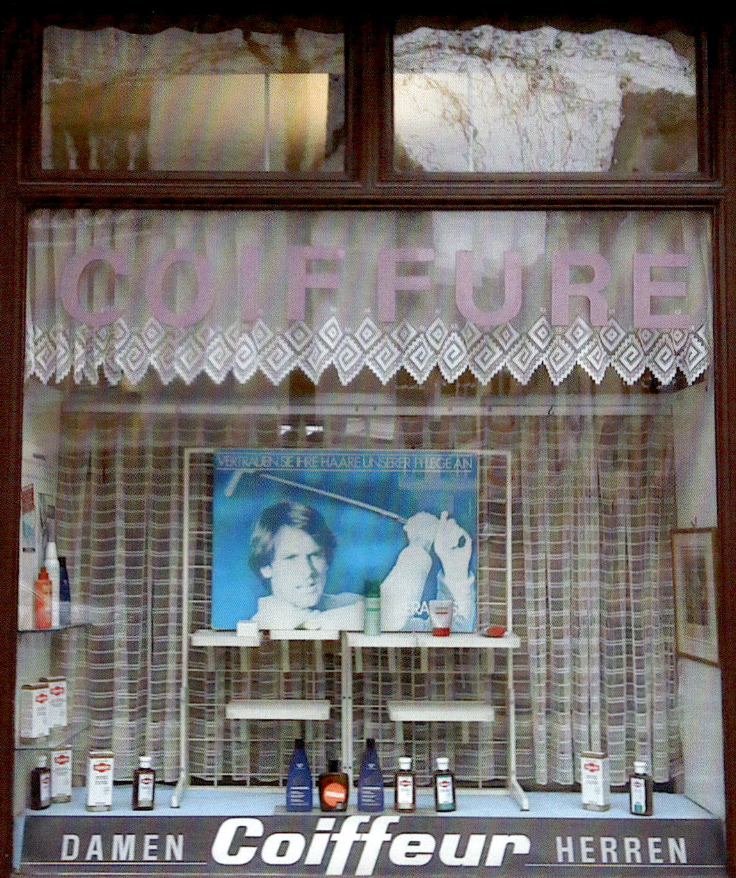
COIFFURE
VERTRAUEN SIE IHRE HAARE UNSERER PFLEGE AN
DAMEN
Coiffeur
HERREN

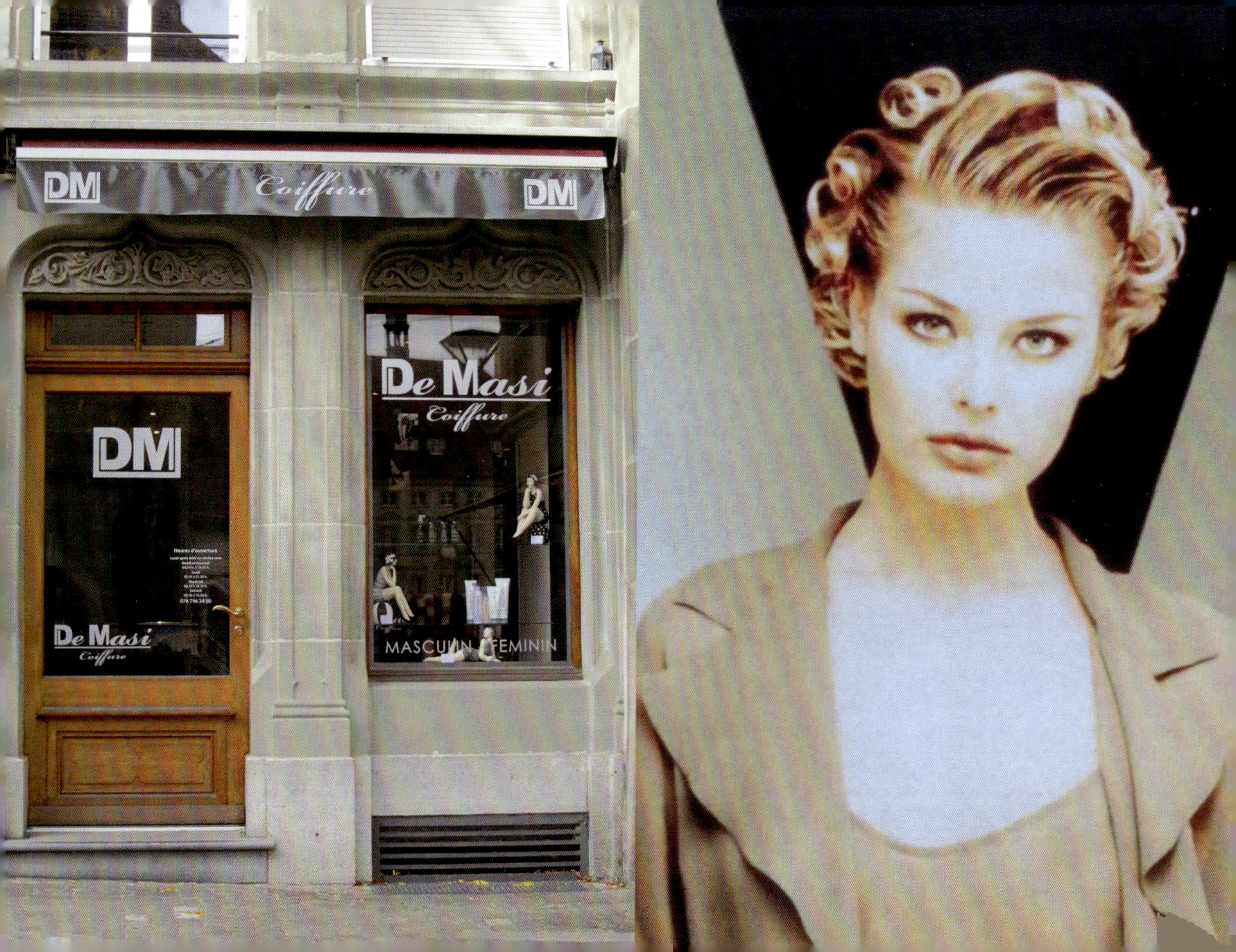
DM
Coiffure
DM
DM
De Masi
Coiffure
De Masi
Coiffure
MASCULIN FEMININ

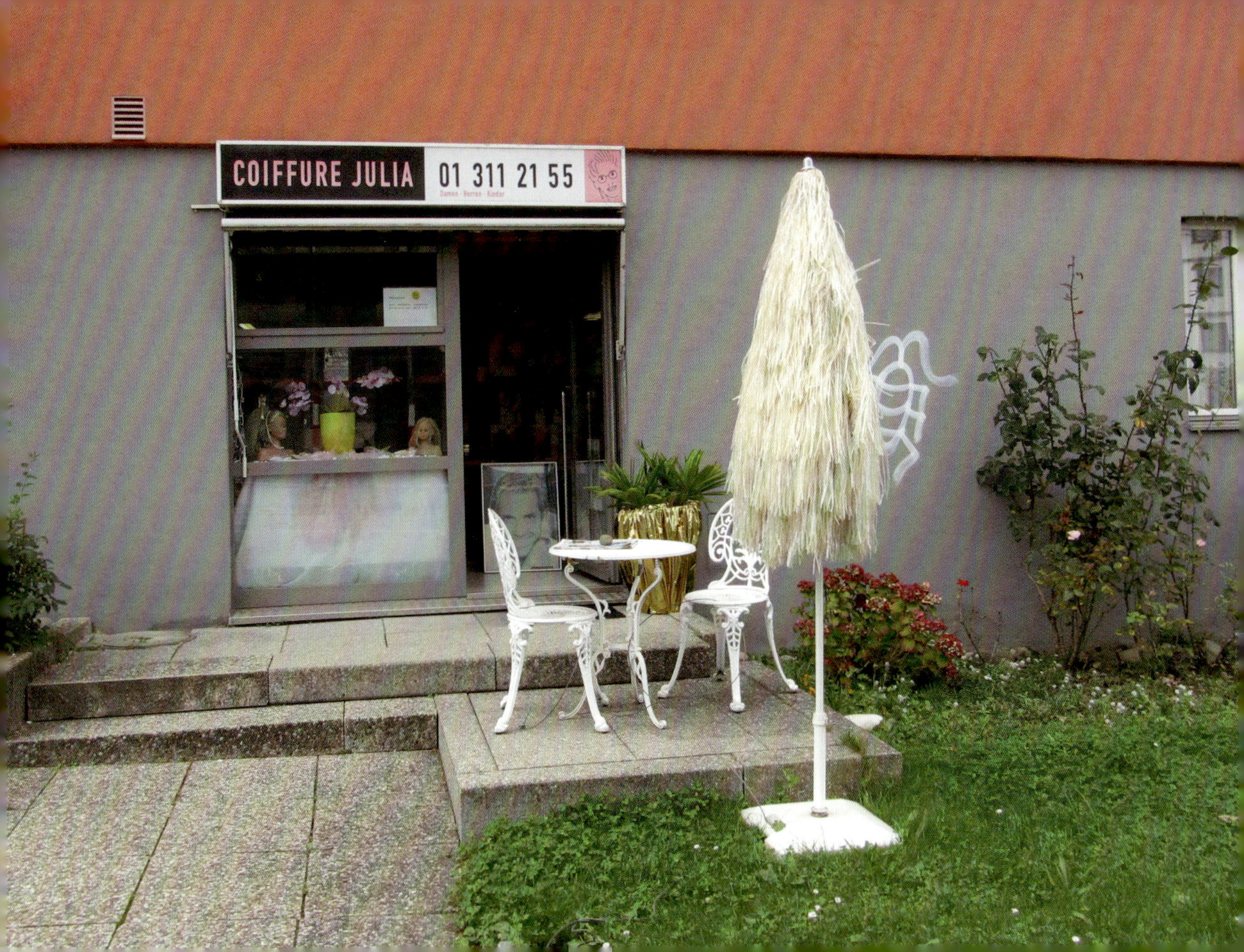
COIFFURE JULIA
01 311 21 55

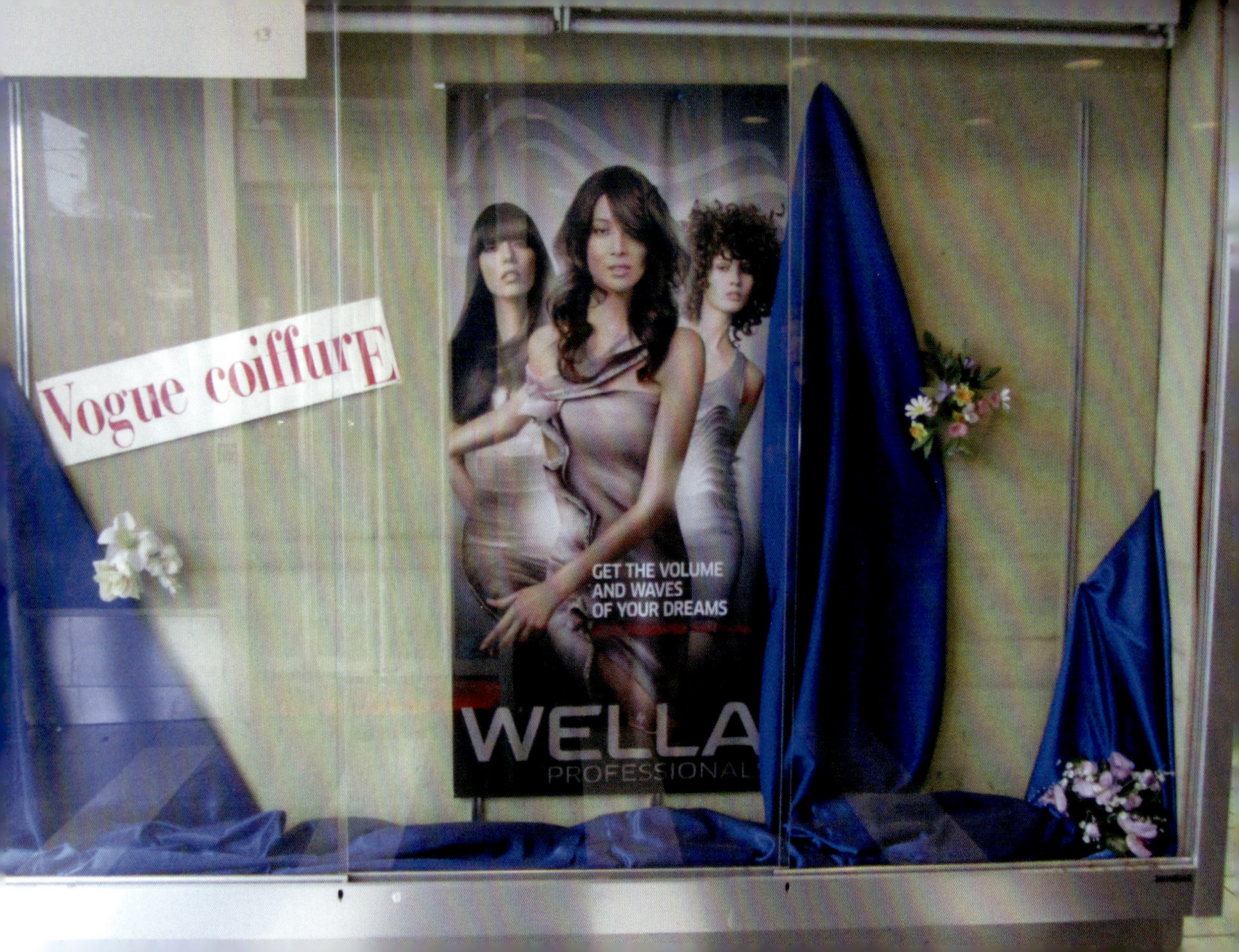

Vogue coiffurE
GET THE VOLUME
AND WAVES
OF YOUR DREAMS
WELLA
PROFESSIONAL

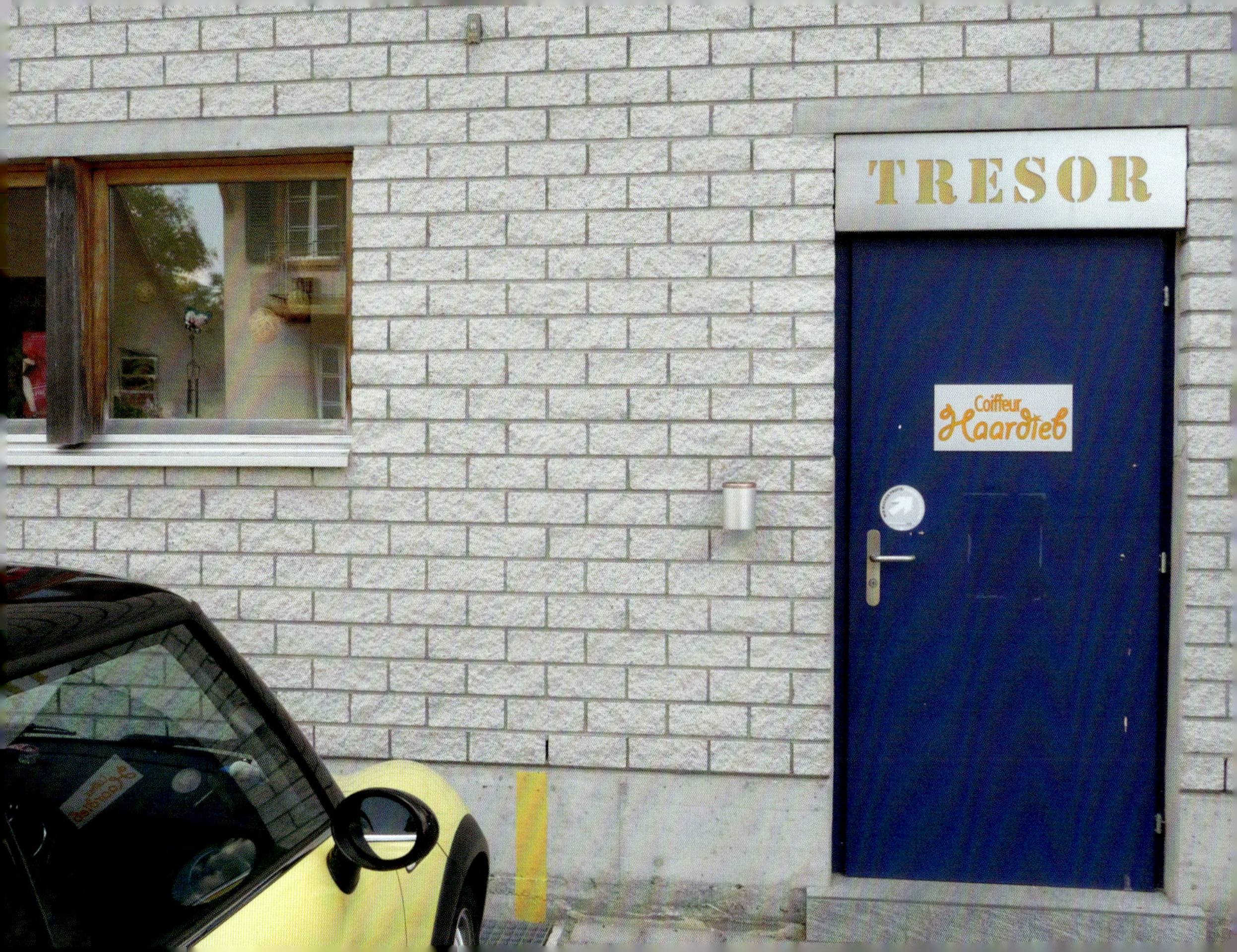
TRESOR
Coiffeur
Haarlieb

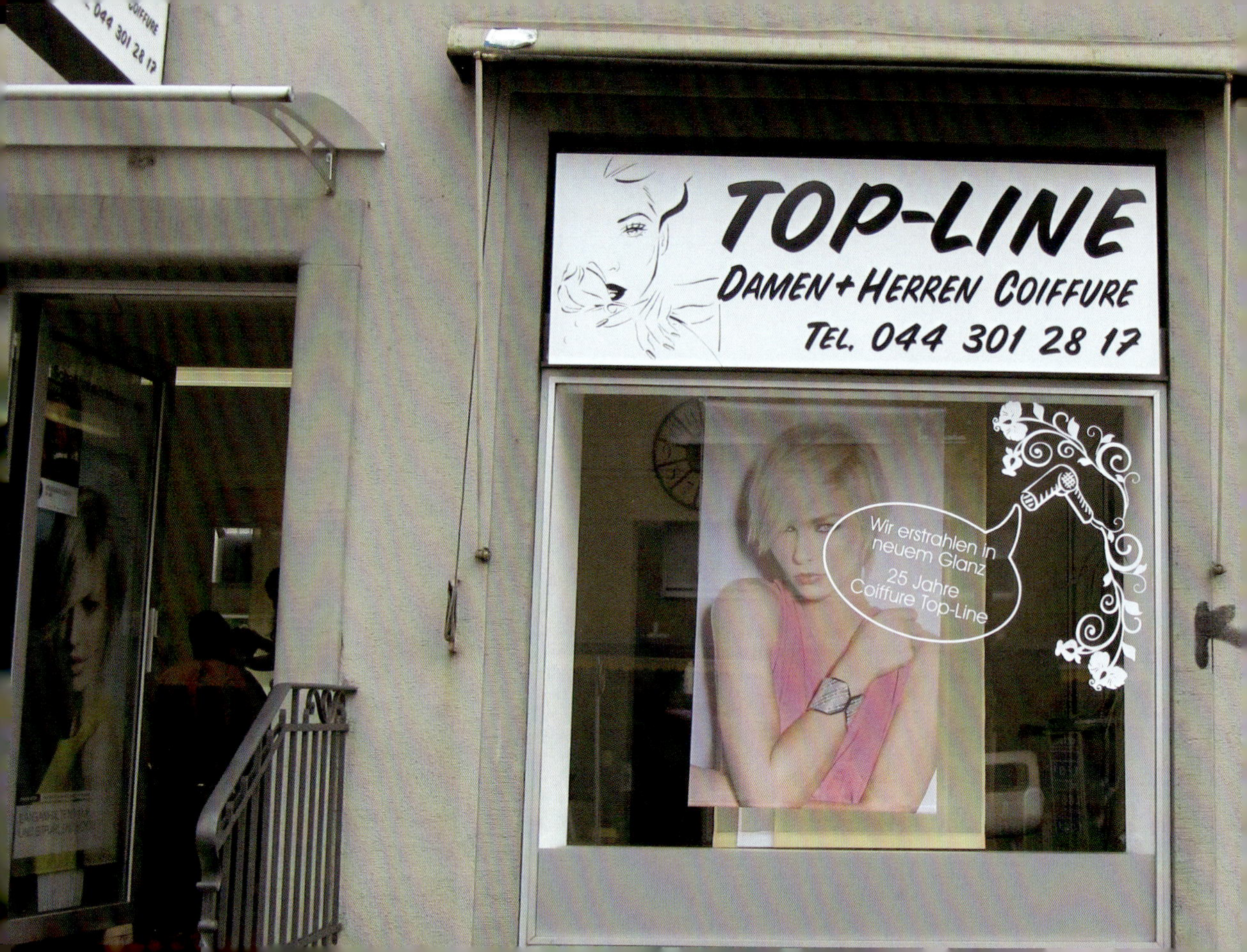

TOP-LINE
DAMEN + HERREN COIFFURE
TEL. 044 301 28 17
Wir erstrahlen in neuem Glanz
25 Jahre Coiffure Top-Line

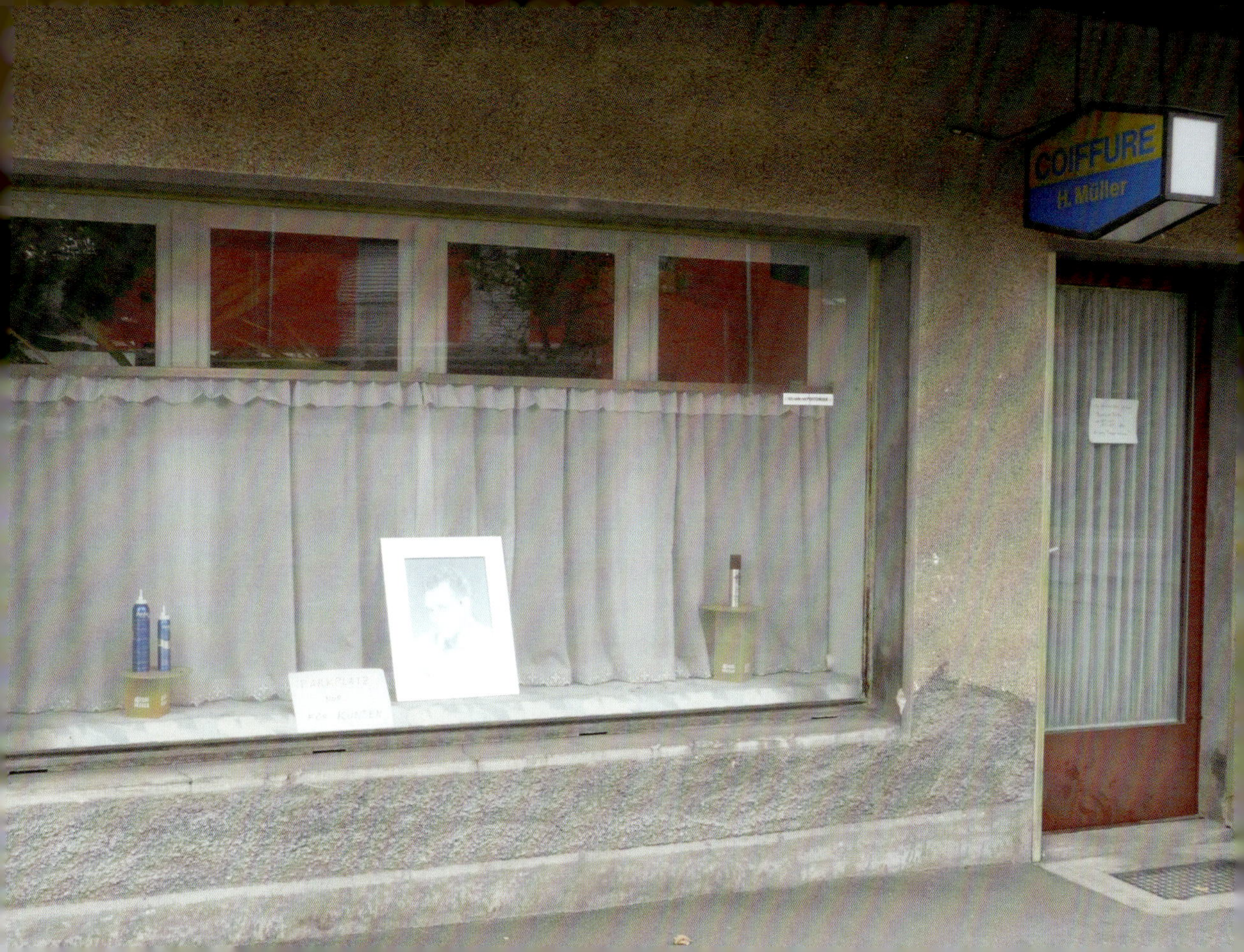
COIFFURE
H. Müller

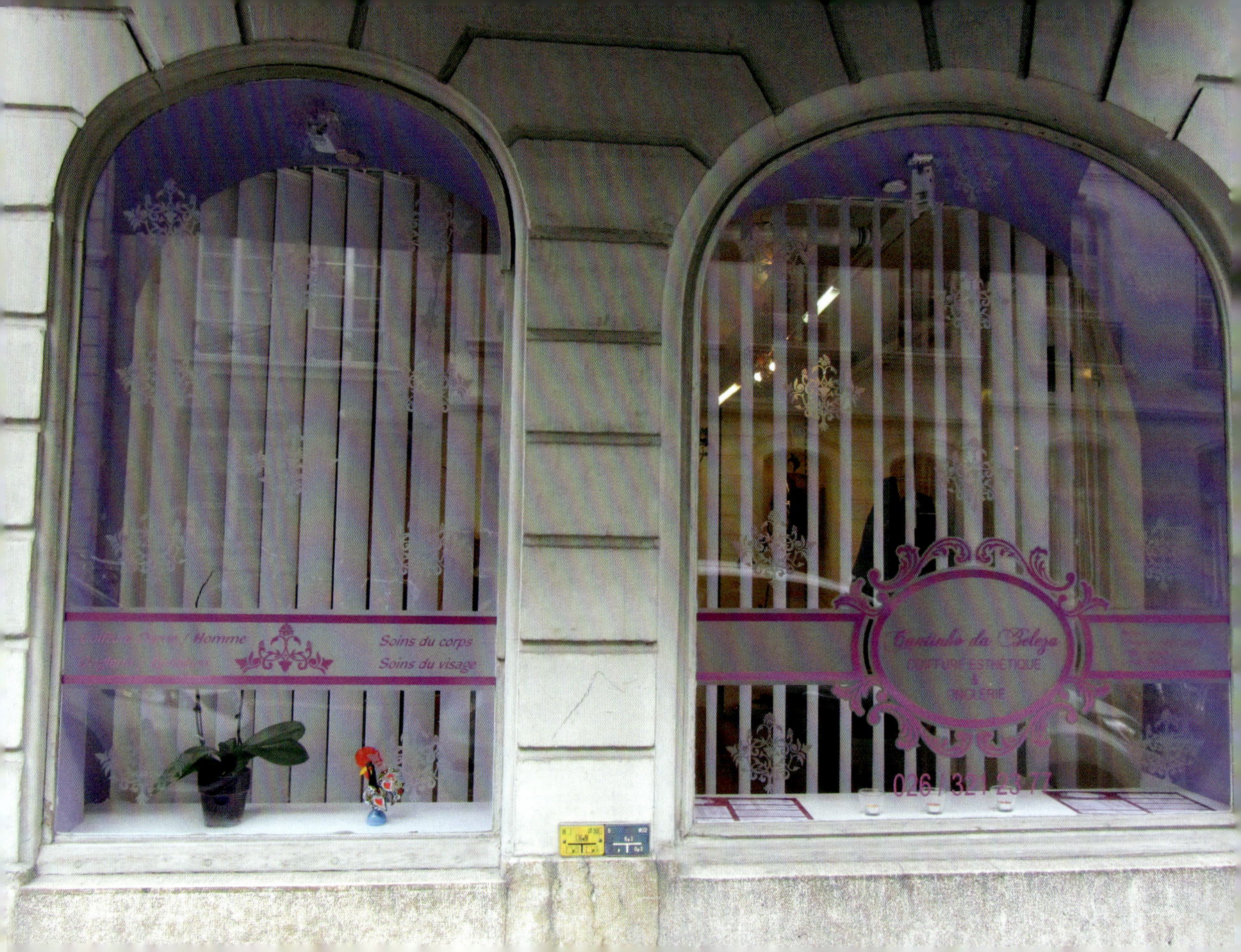
Soins du corps
Soins du visage
026 / 321 23 77

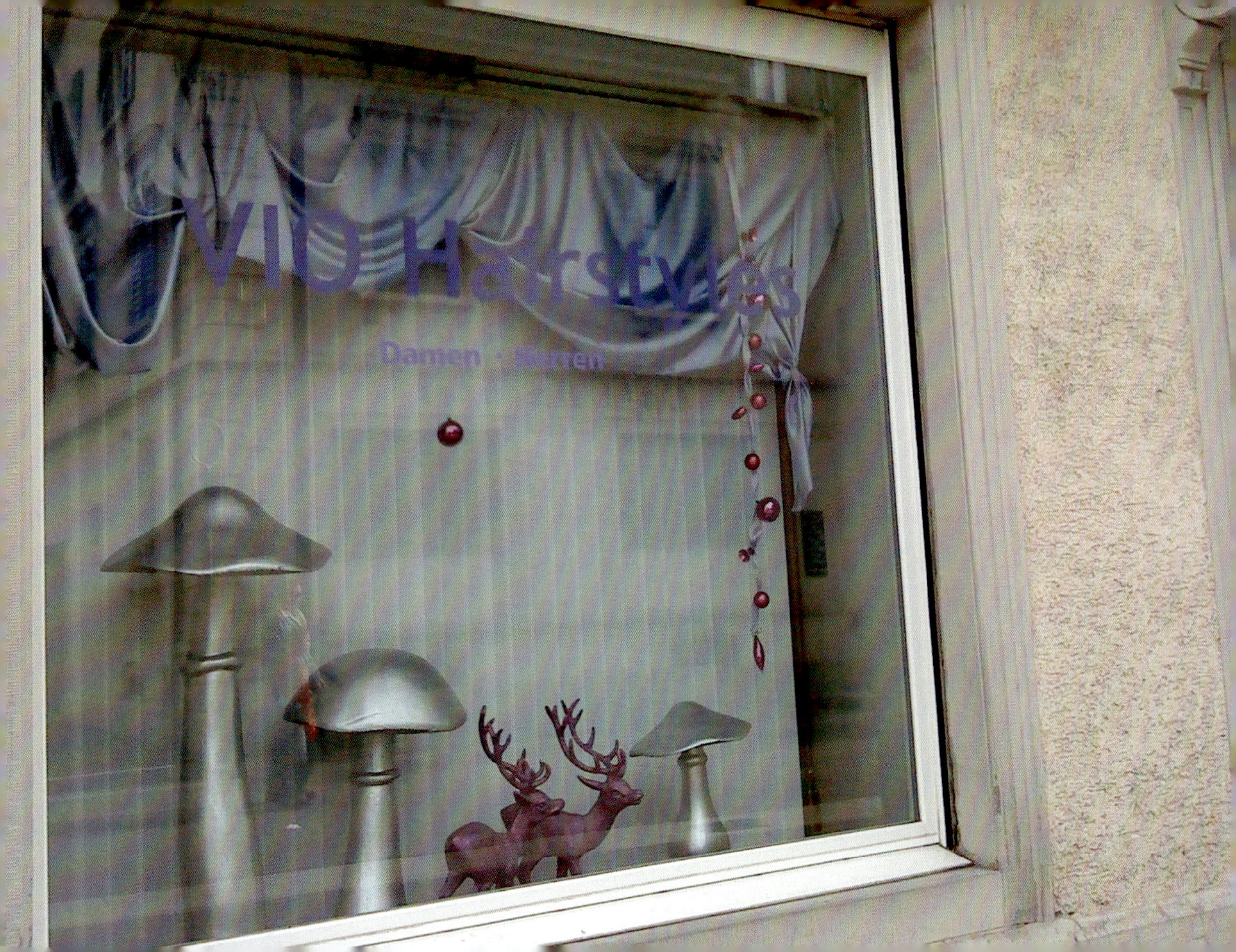
VIO Hairstyles
Damen · Herren

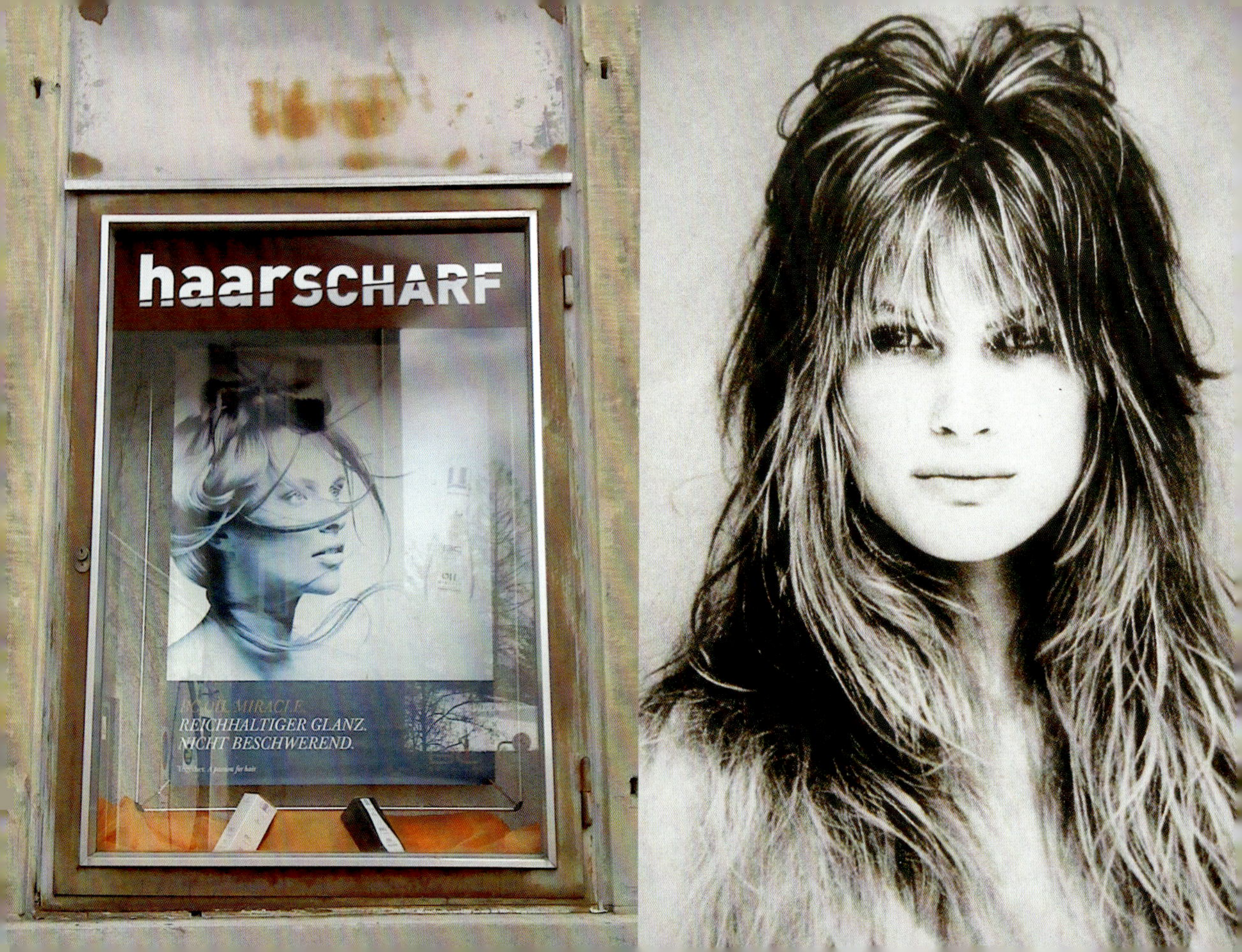

haarSCHARF
MIRACLE
REICHHALTIGER GLANZ.
NICHT BESCHWEREND.

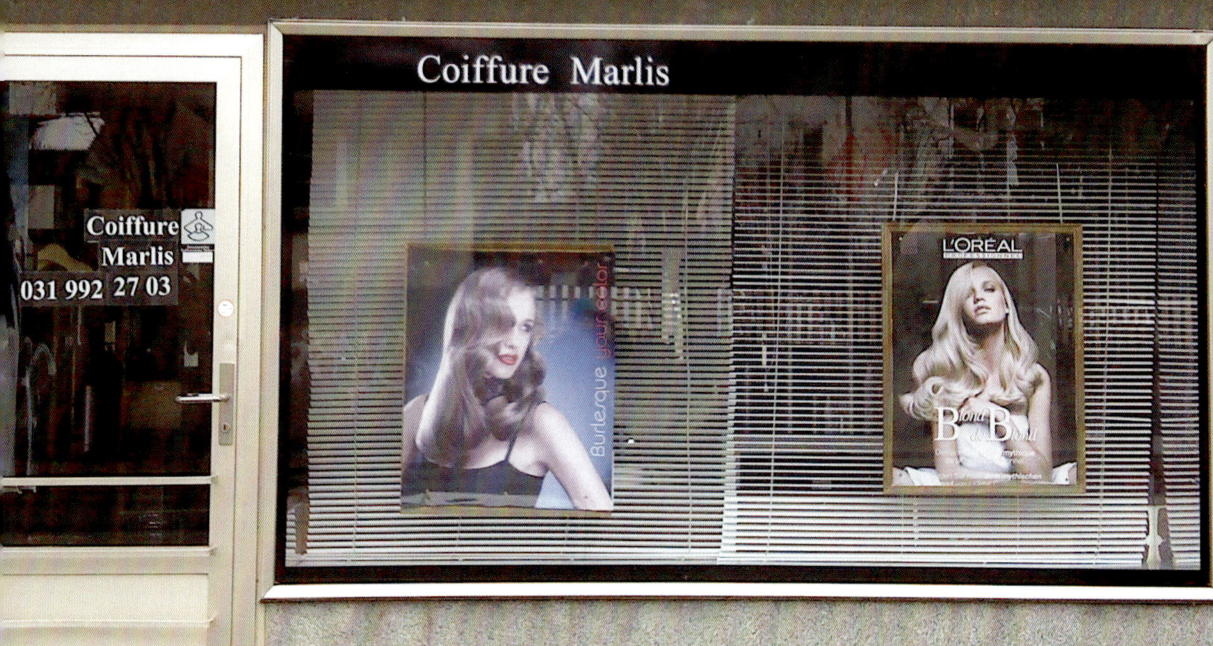
Coiffure Marlis
Coiffure
Marlis
031 992 27 03
Burlesque your color
L'ORÉAL
Blond de Blond

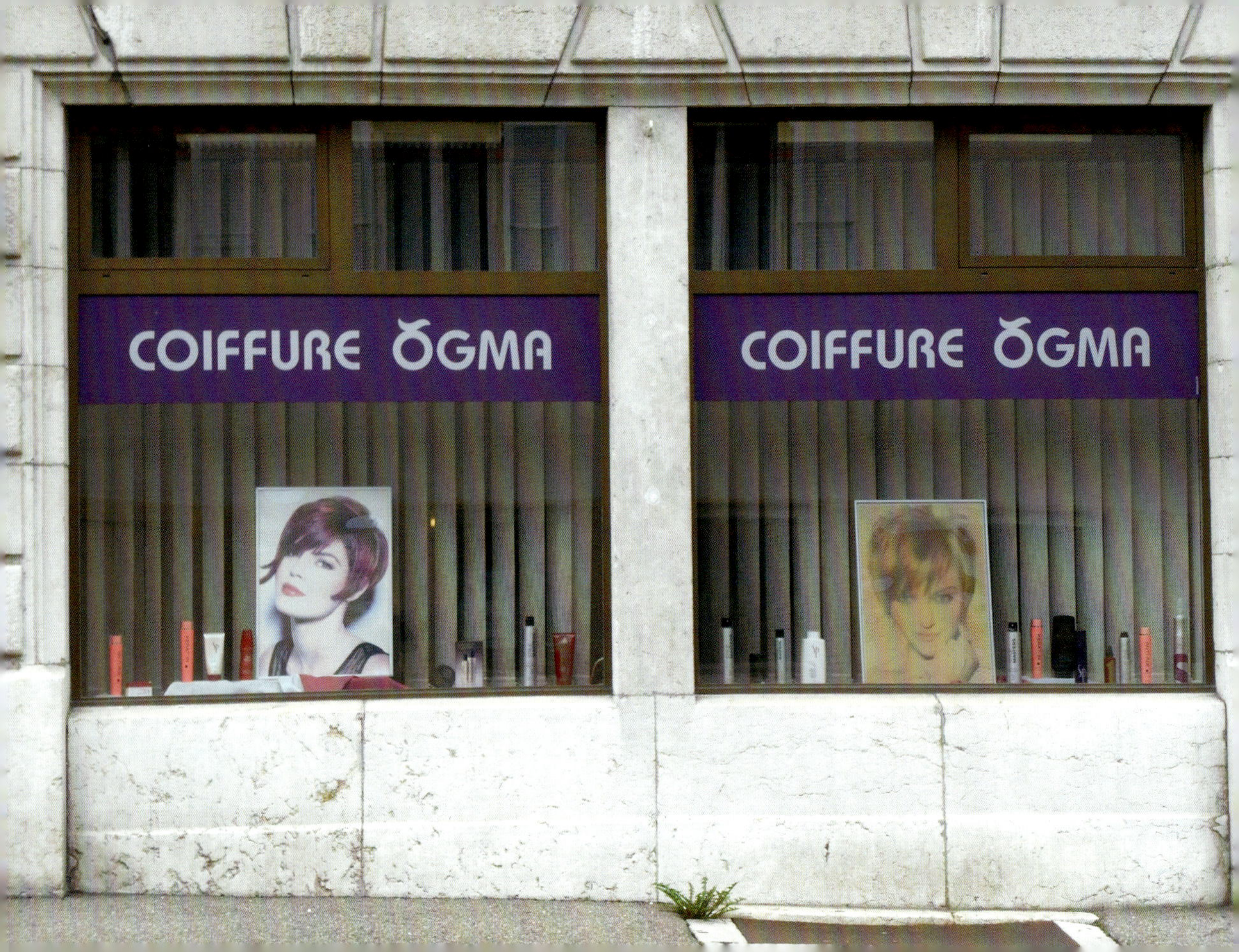
COIFFURE ÕGMA
COIFFURE ÕGMA

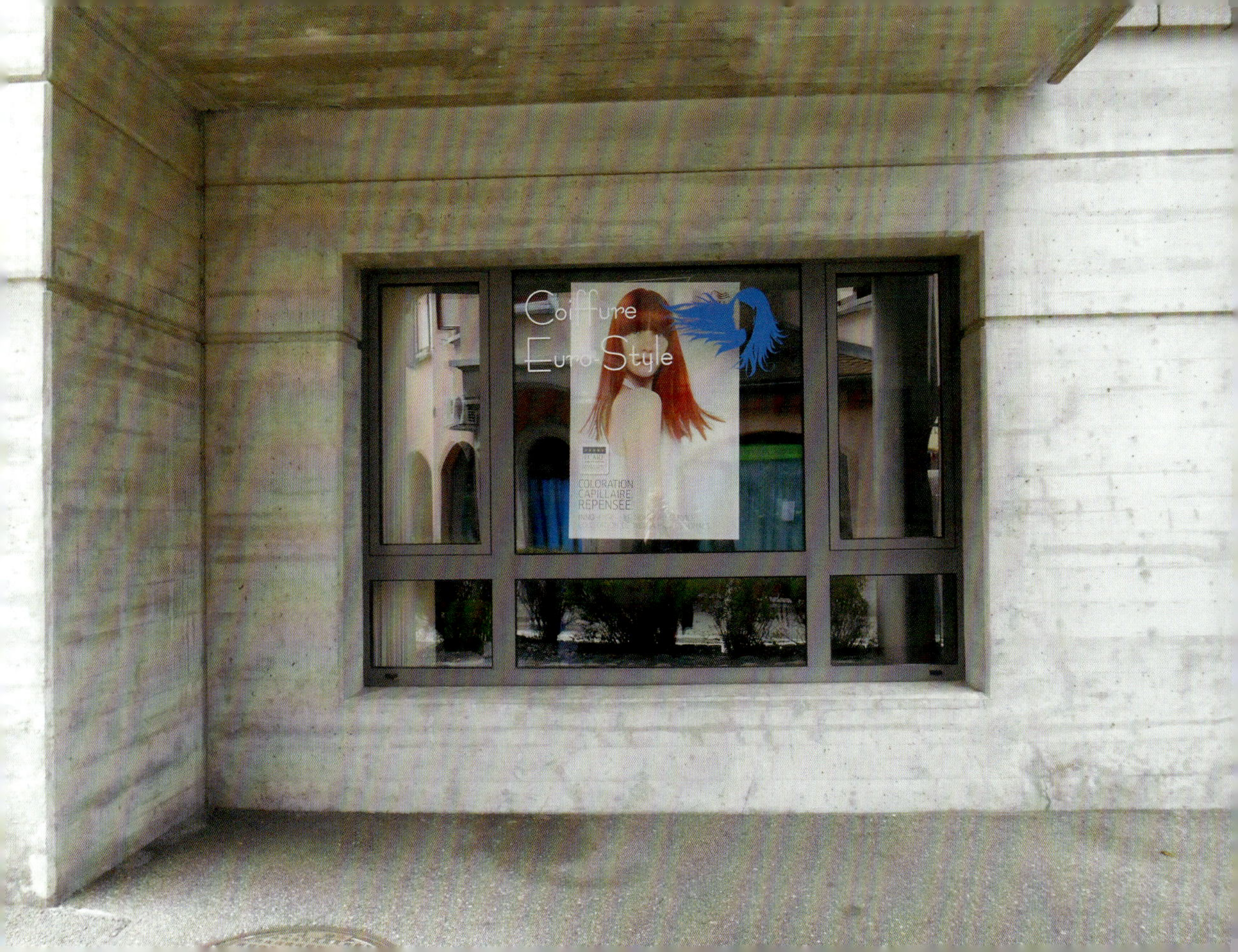
Coiffure
Euro-Style
COLORATION
CAPILLAIRE
REPENSEE

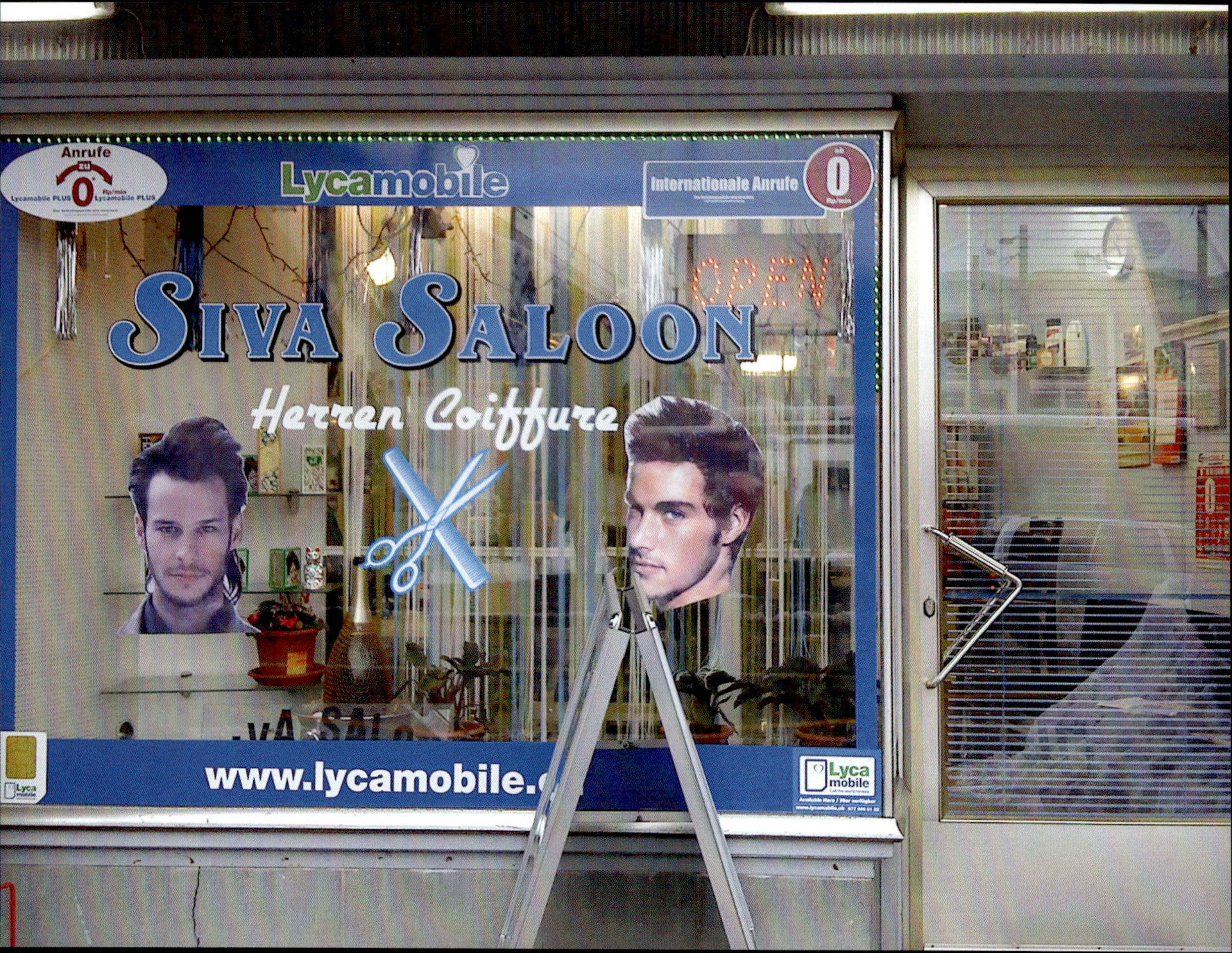
Anrufe
0
Lycamobile
Internationale Anrufe
0
OPEN
SIVA SALOON
Herren Coiffure
www.lycamobile.c
Lyca mobile

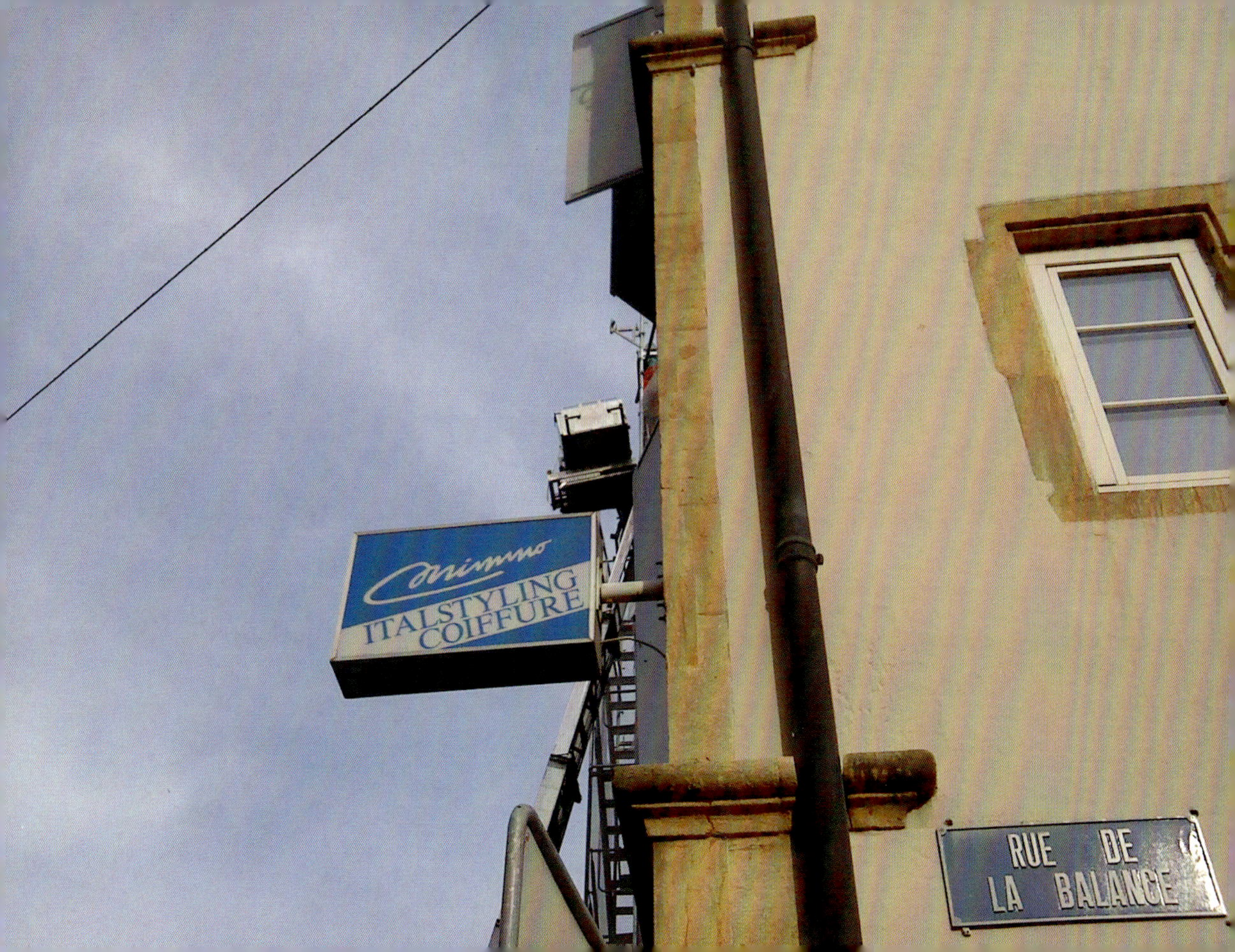
Mimmo
ITALSTYLING
COIFFURE
RUE DE
LA BALANCE

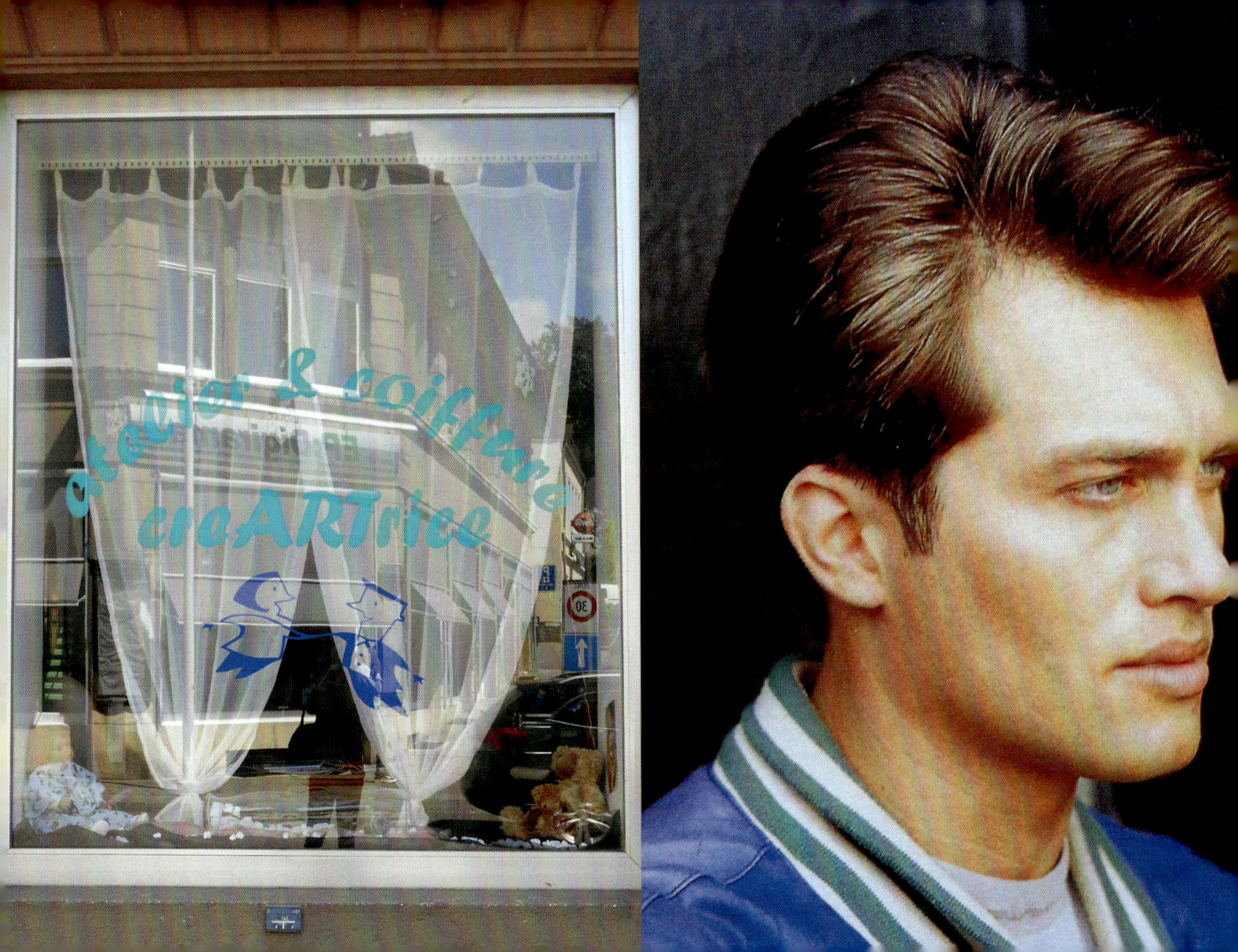
atelier & coiffure
creARTrice

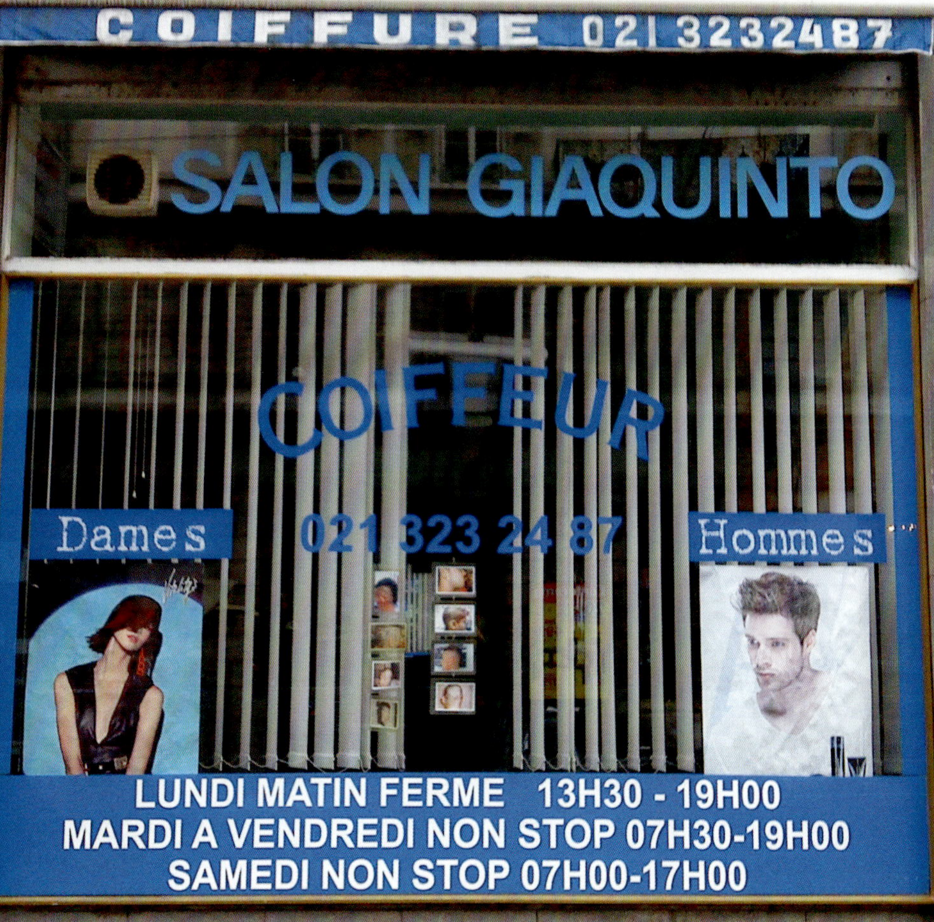
COIFFURE 021 3232487
SALON GIAQUINTO
COIFFEUR
Dames
021 323 24 87
Hommes
LUNDI MATIN FERME 13H30 - 19H00
MARDI A VENDREDI NON STOP 07H30-19H00
SAMEDI NON STOP 07H00-17H00

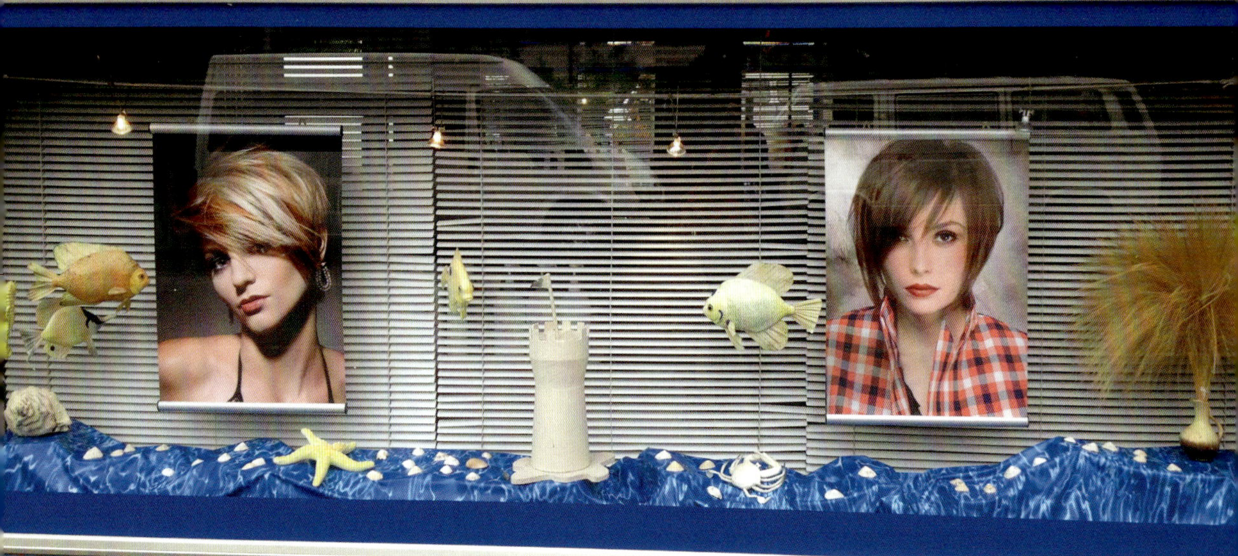
Coiffure Daniela

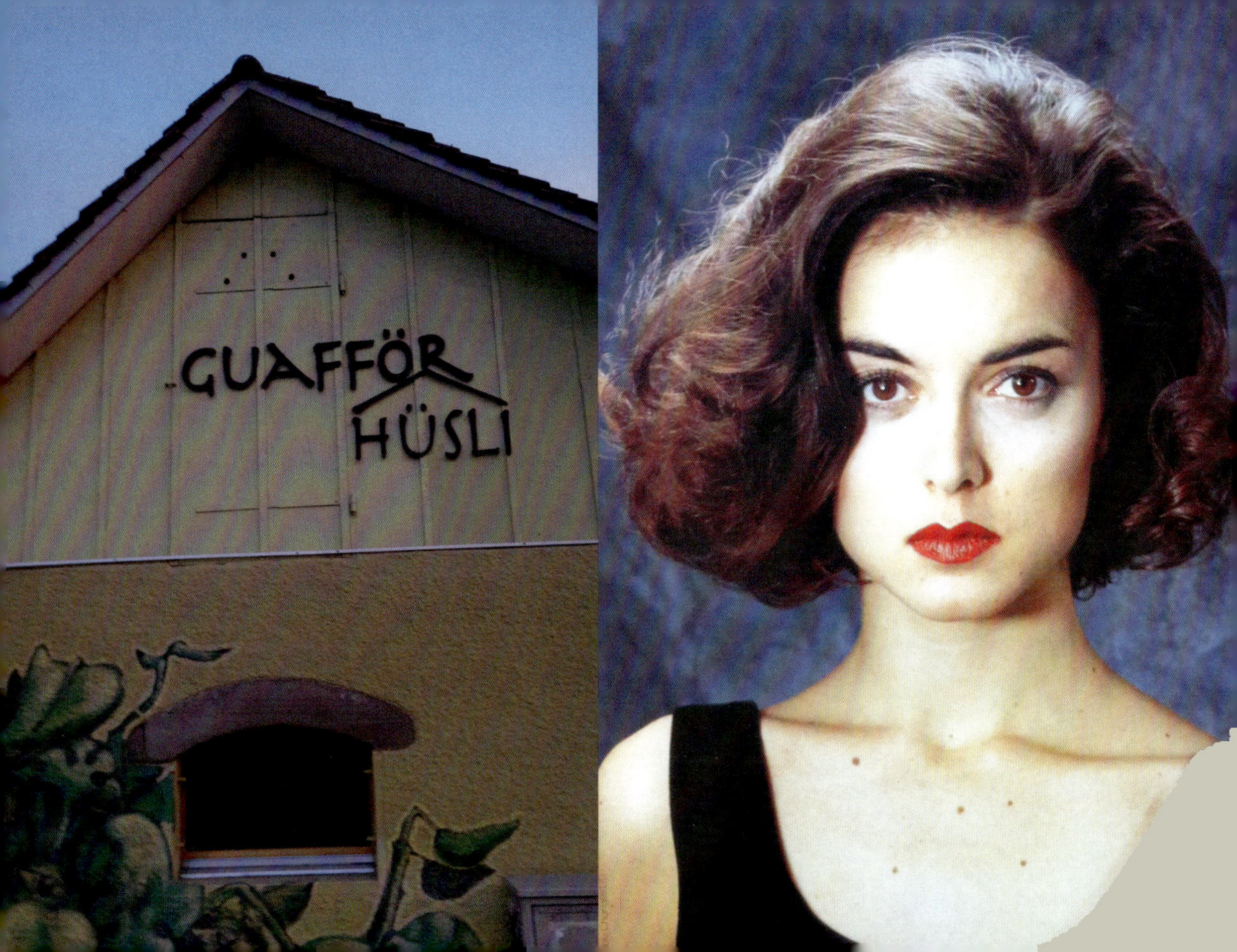
GUAFFÖR
HÜSLI

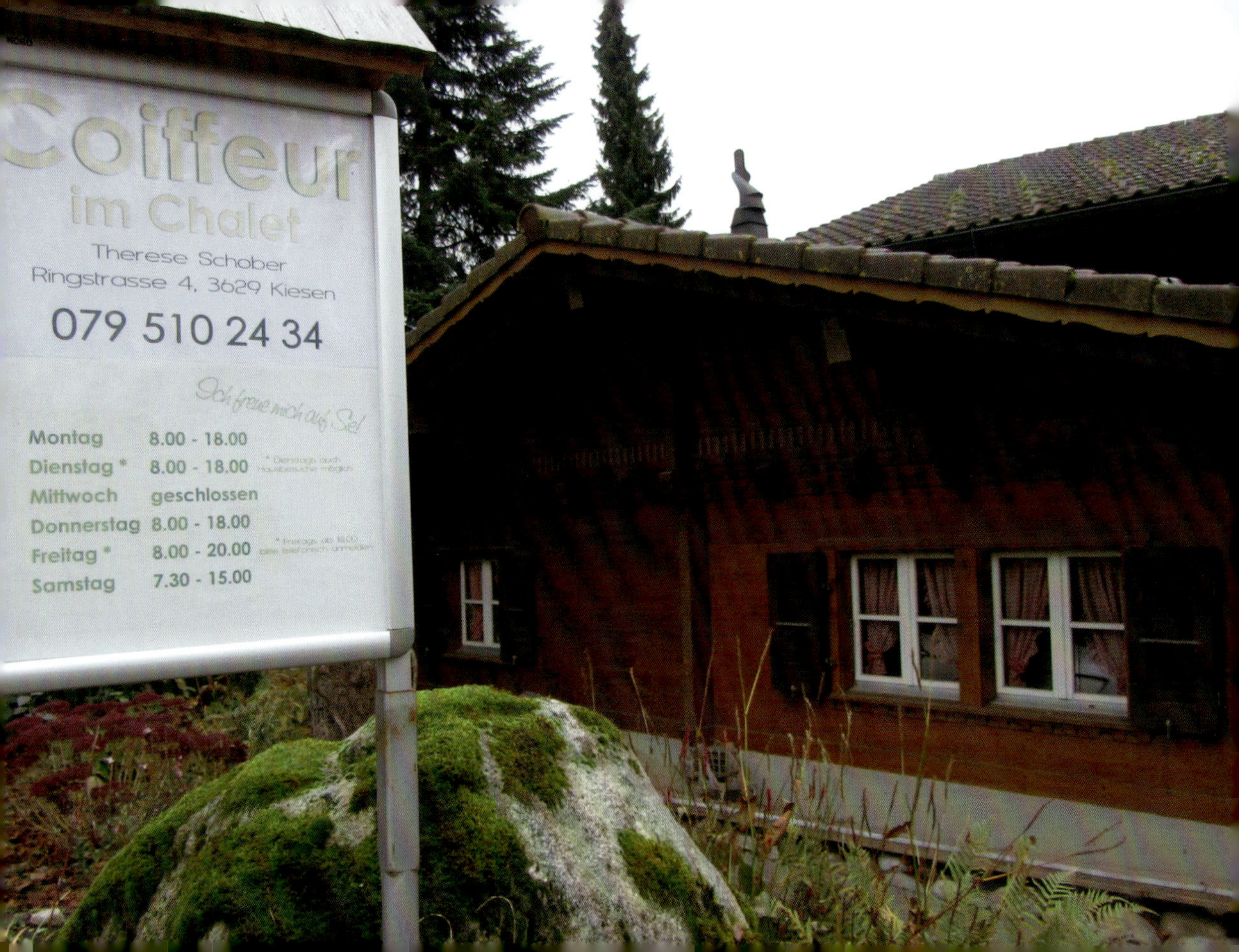
Coiffeur
im Chalet
Therese Schober
Ringstrasse 4, 3629 Kiesen
079 510 24 34
Ich freue mich auf Sie!
Montag 8.00 - 18.00
Dienstag * 8.00 - 18.00
Mittwoch geschlossen
Donnerstag 8.00 - 18.00
Freitag * 8.00 - 20.00
Samstag 7.30 - 15.00

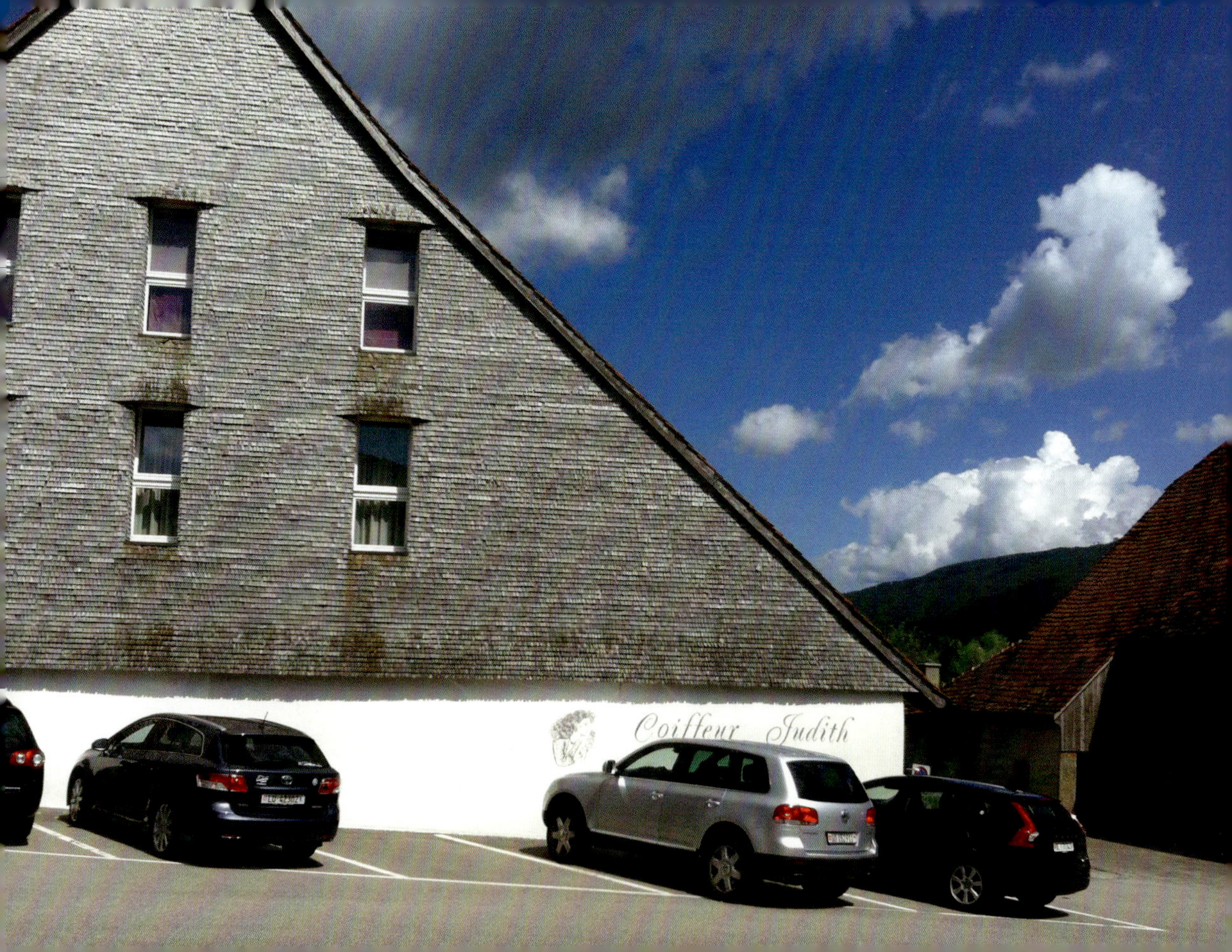
Coiffeur Judith

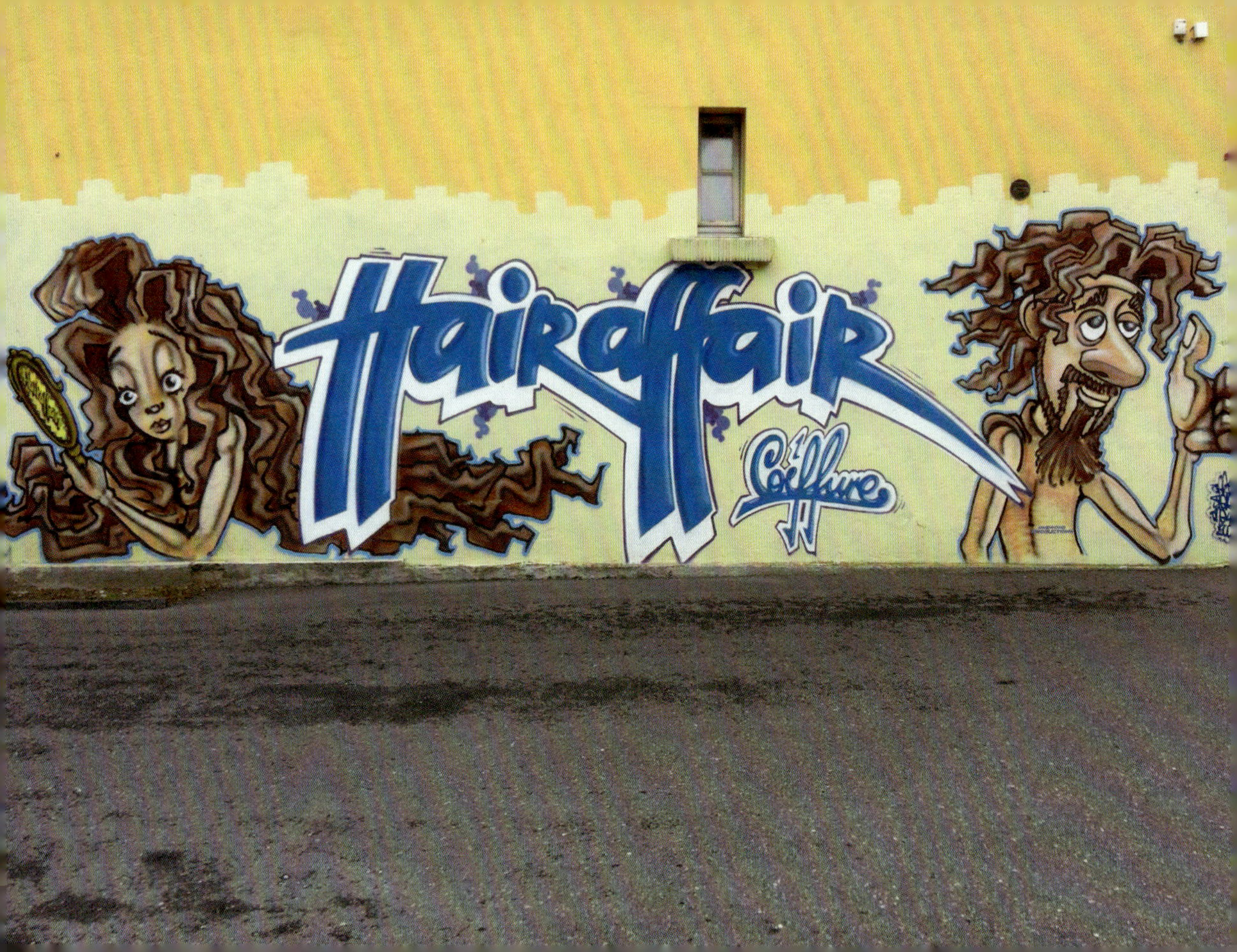
Hairaffair
Coiffure

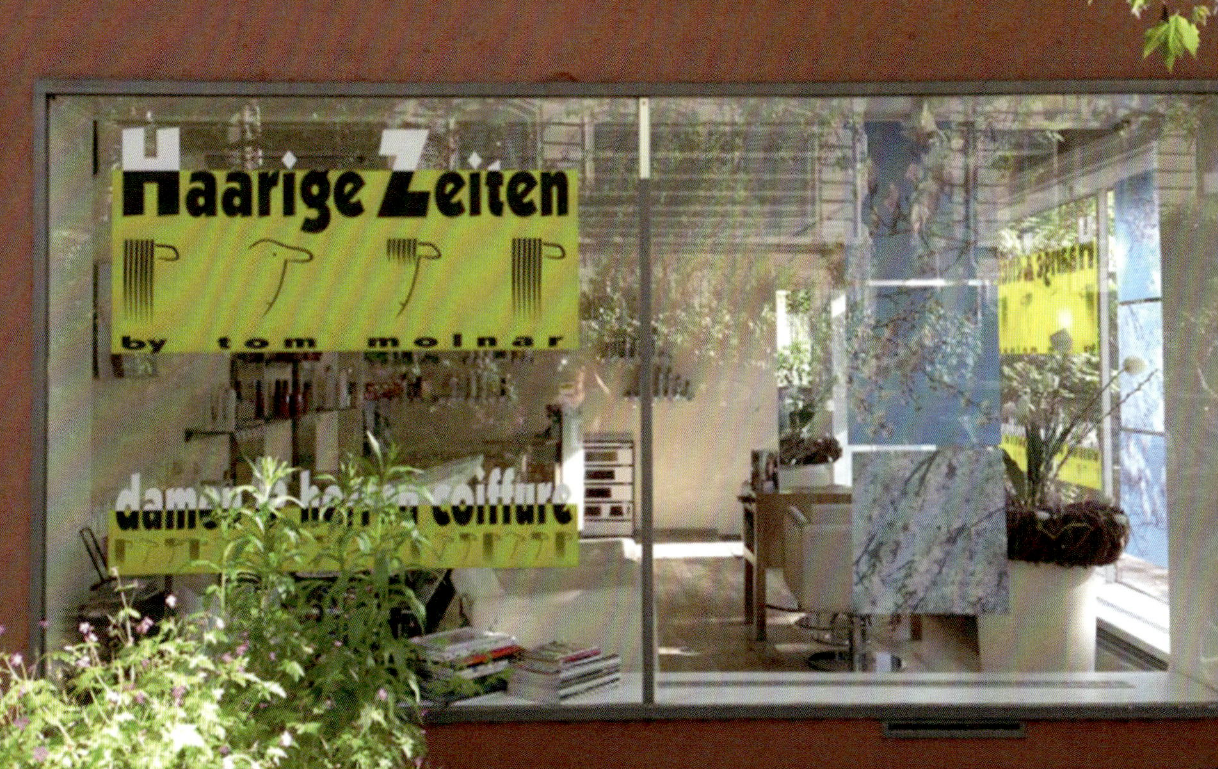
Haarige Zeiten
by tom molnar
coiffure

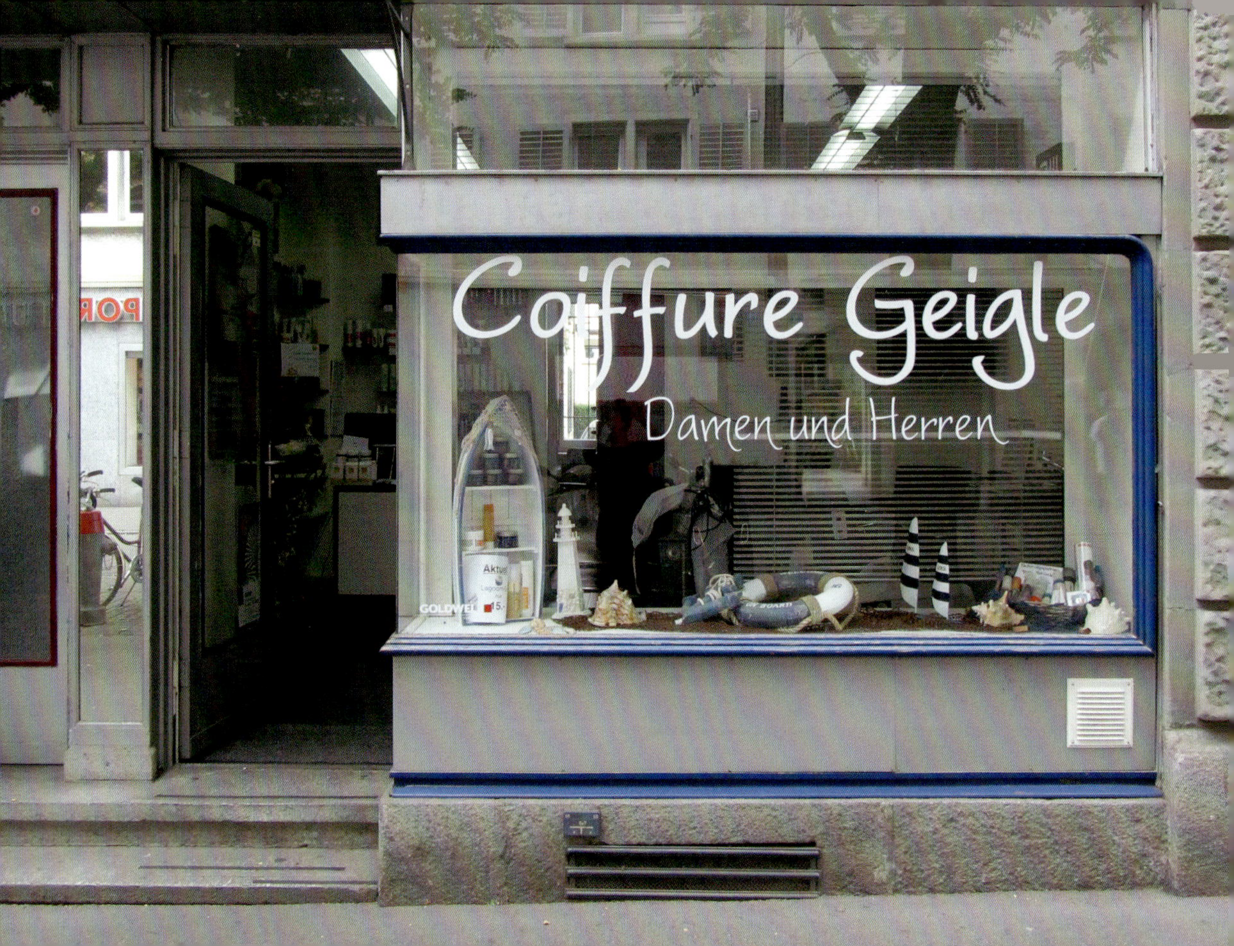
Coiffure Geigle
Damen und Herren

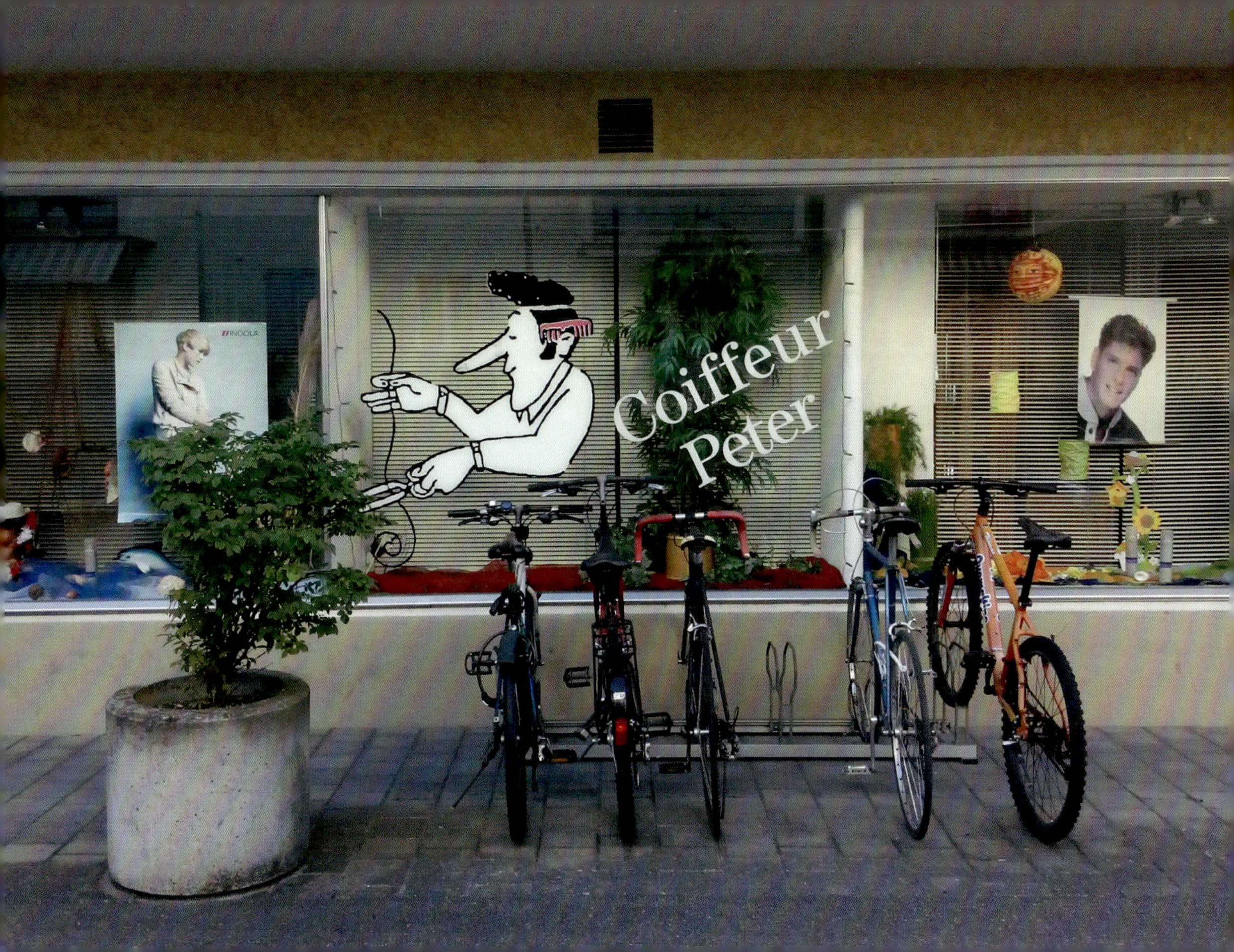
INDOLA
Coiffeur
Peter

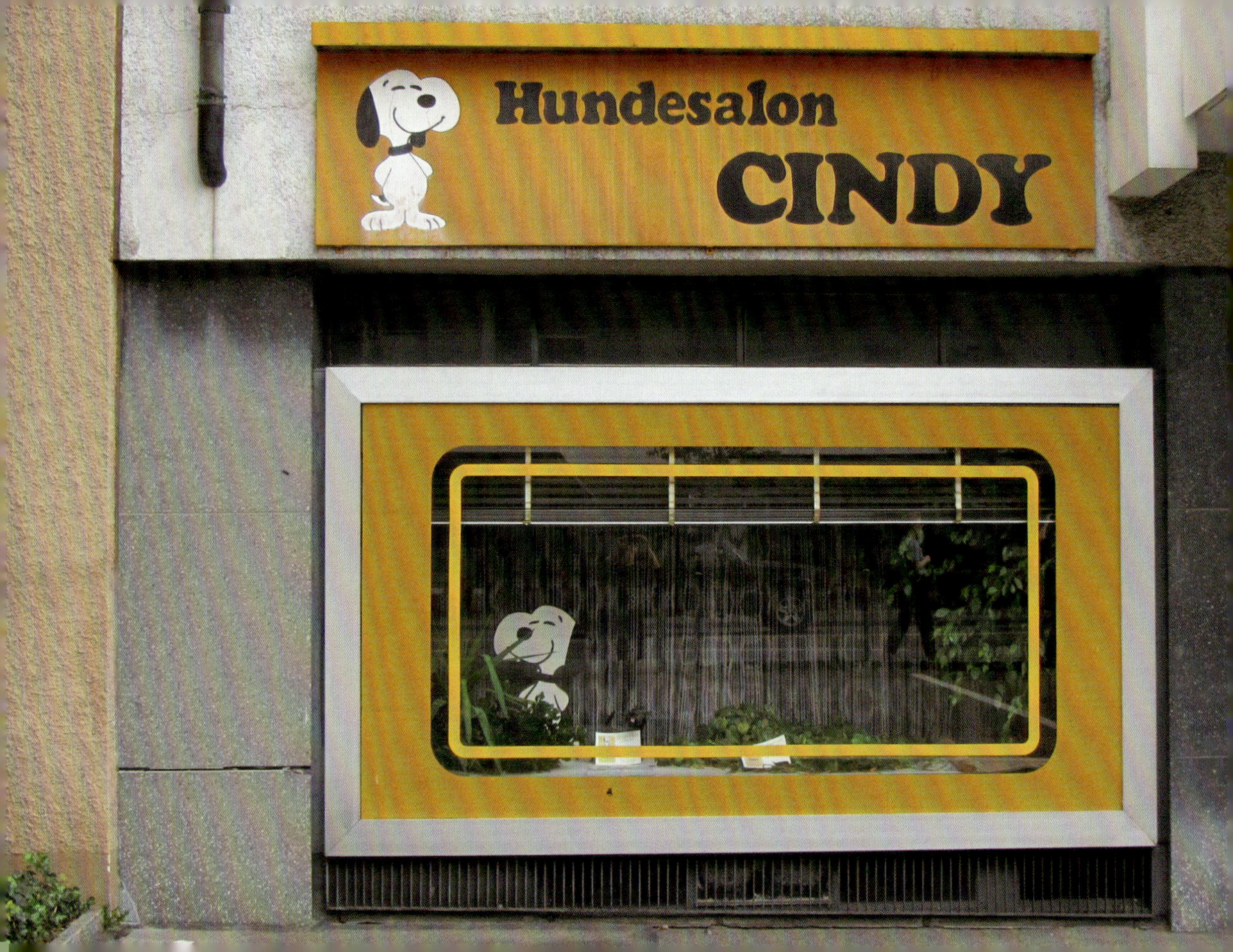

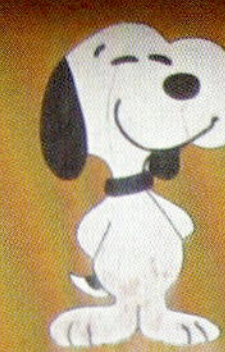
Hundesalon
CINDY

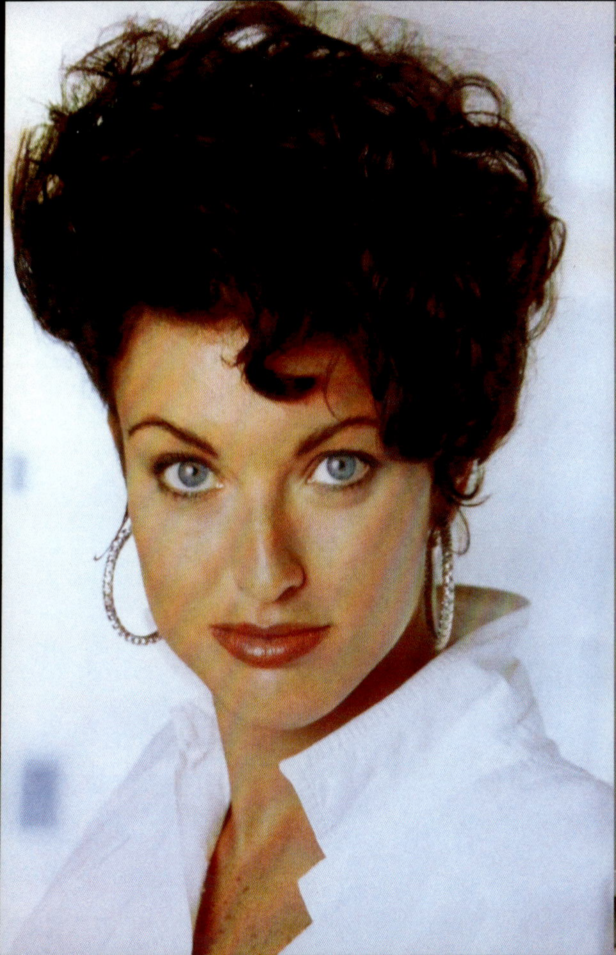

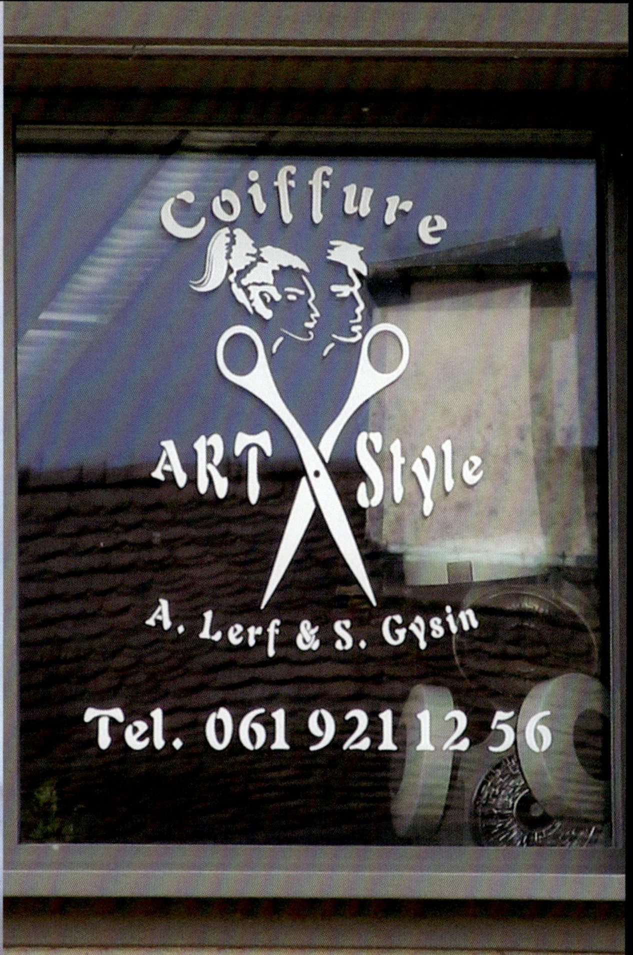

Coiffure
ART Style
A. Lerf & S. Gysin
Tel. 061 921 12 56

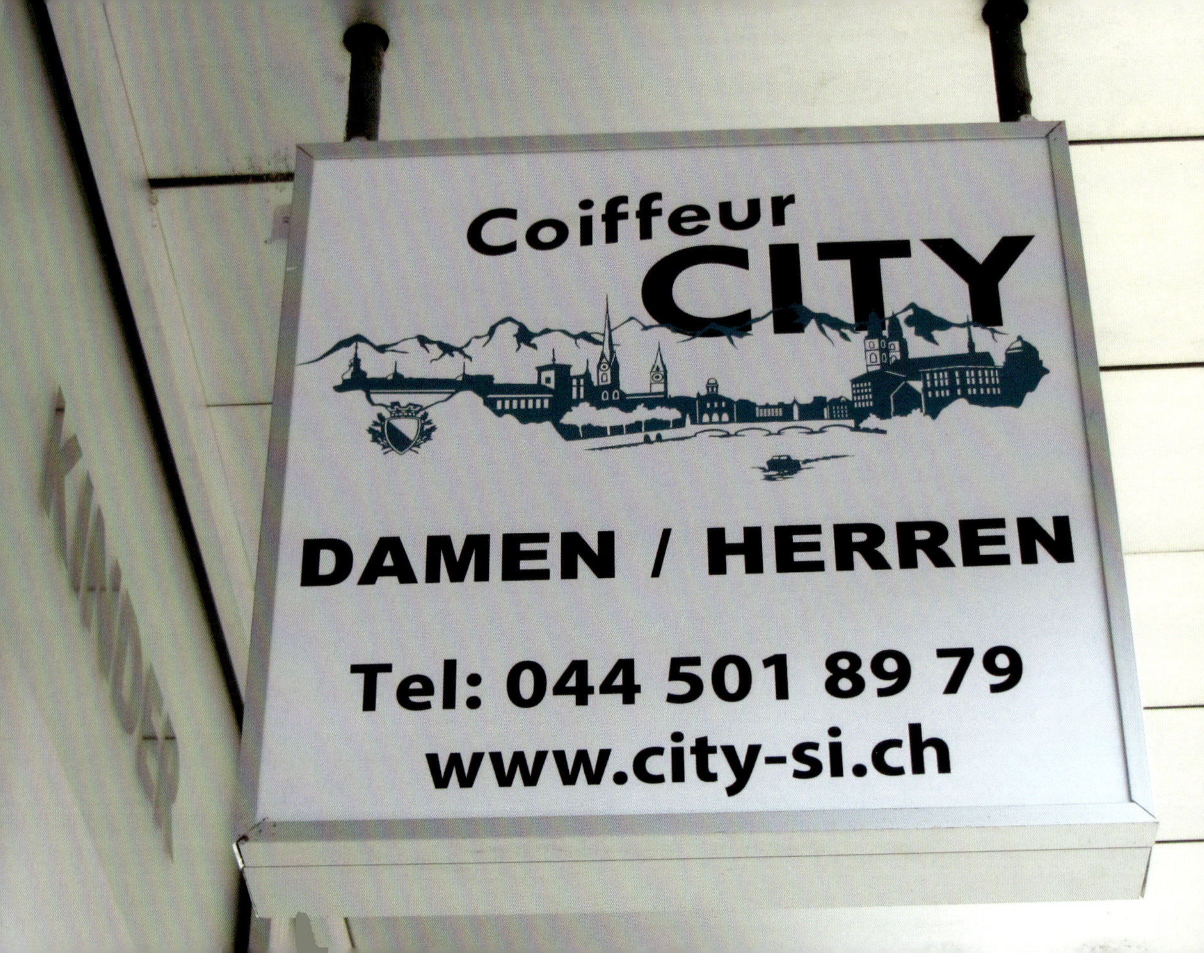
Coiffeur
CITY
DAMEN / HERREN
Tel: 044 501 89 79
www.city-si.ch

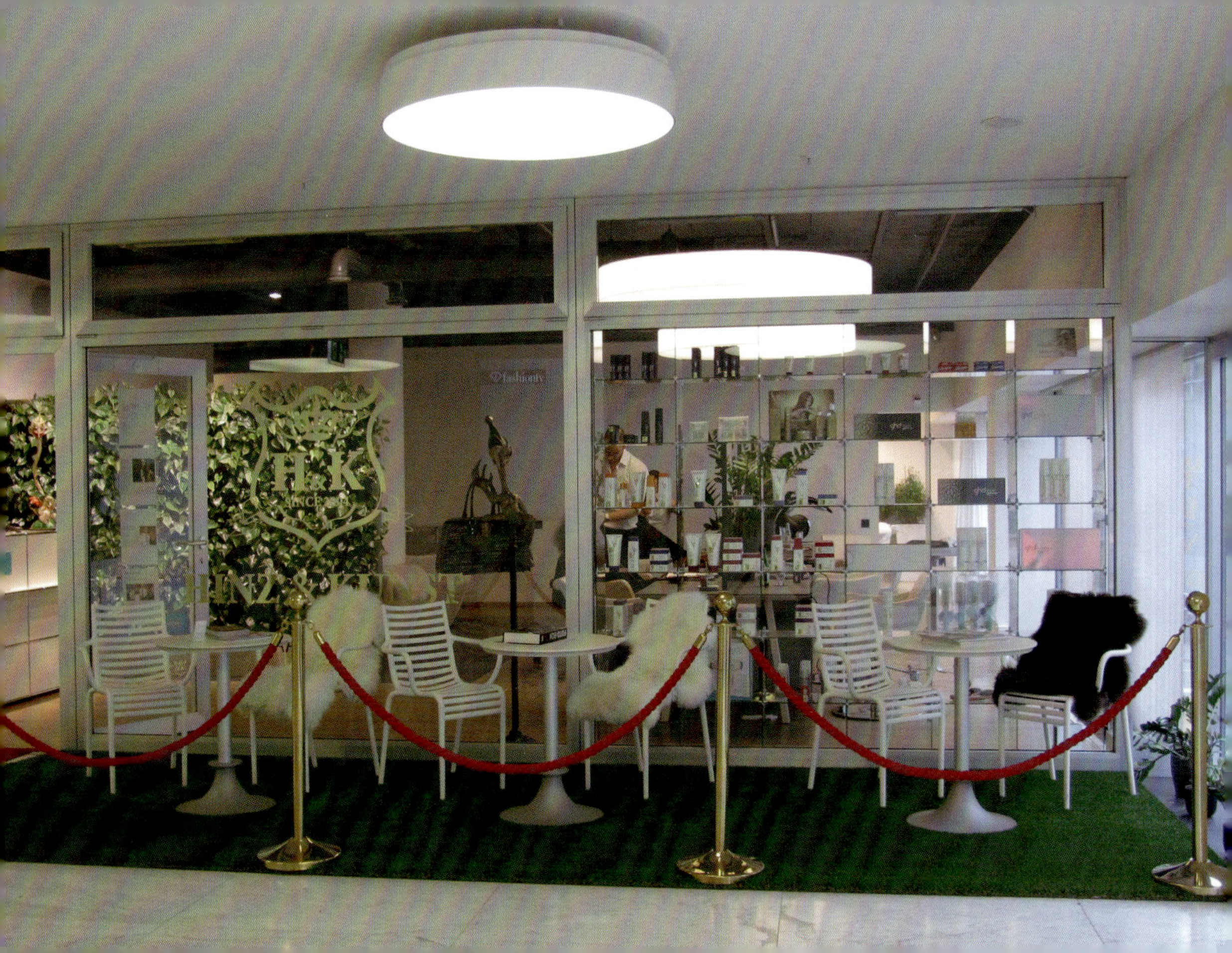
H&K

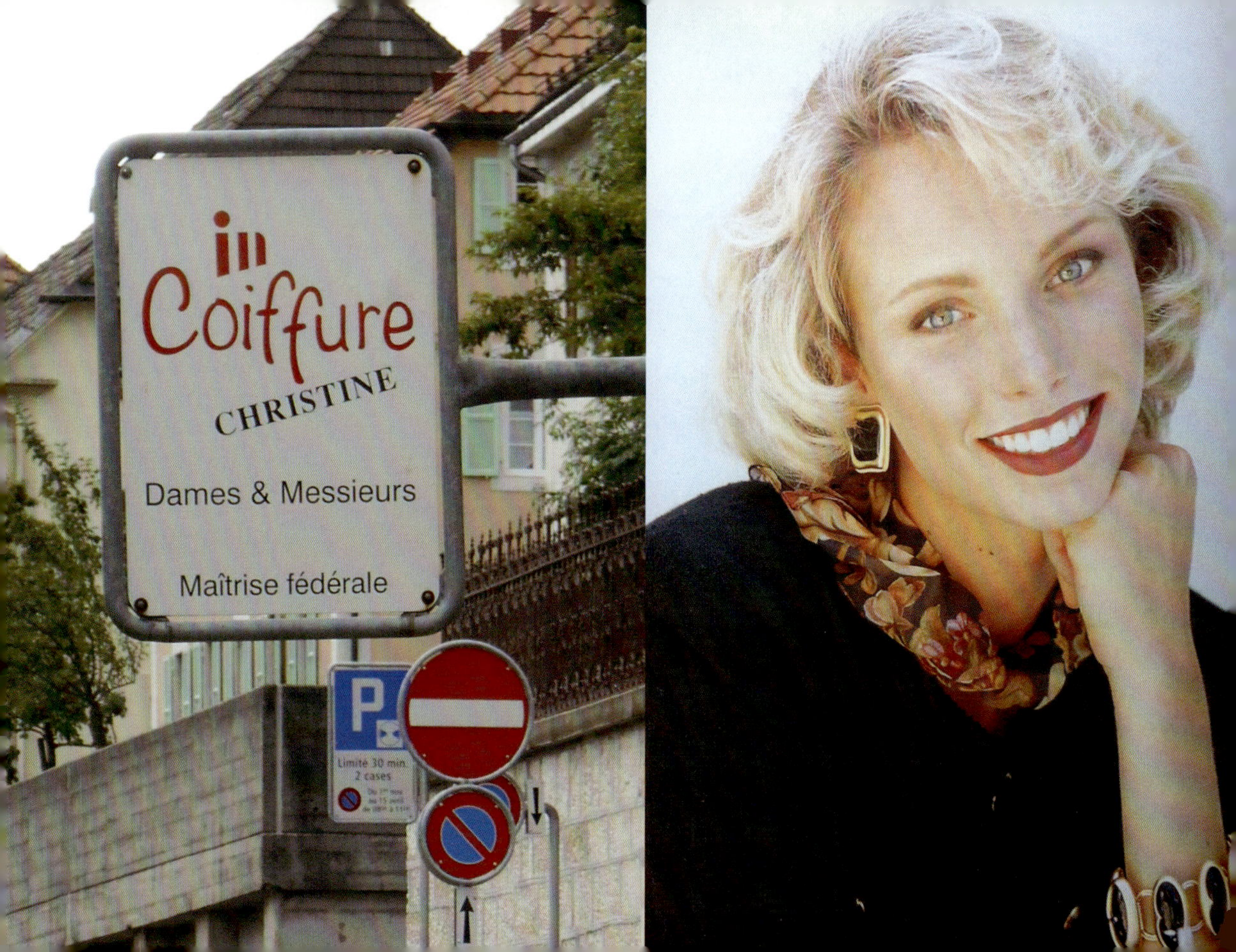
Coiffure
CHRISTINE
Dames & Messieurs
Maîtrise fédérale
P
Limité 30 min.
2 cases

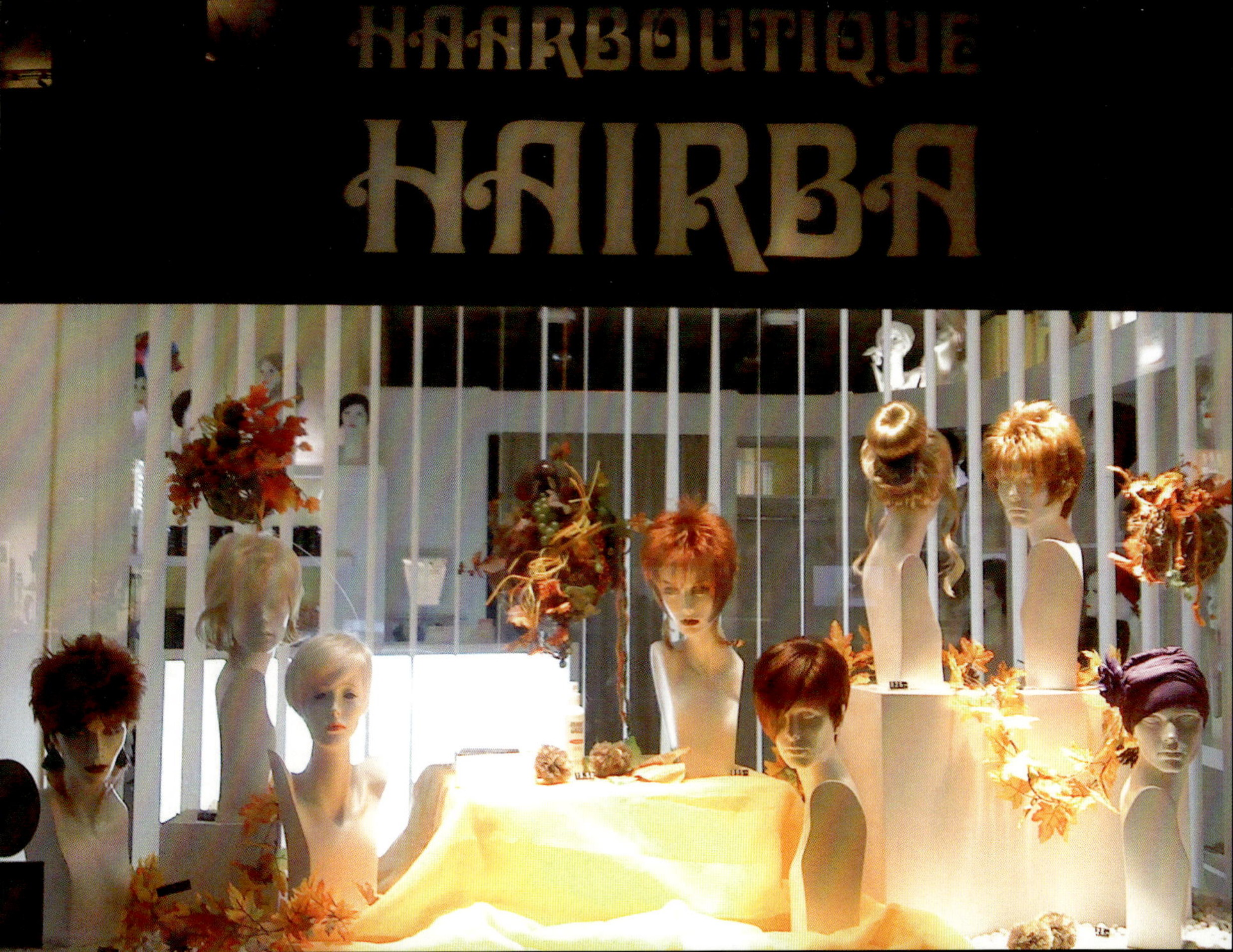

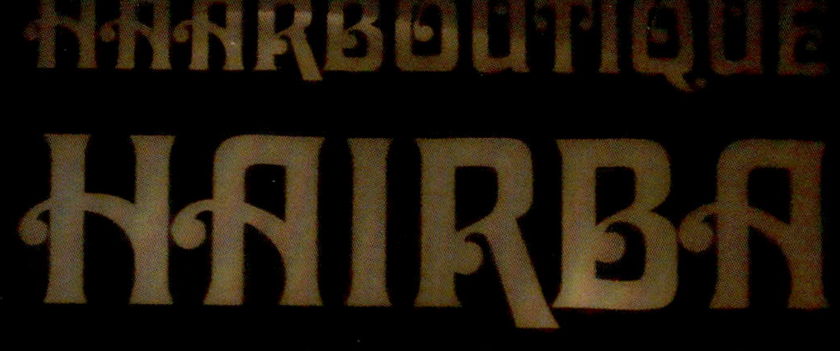
HAARBOUTIQUE
HAIRBA

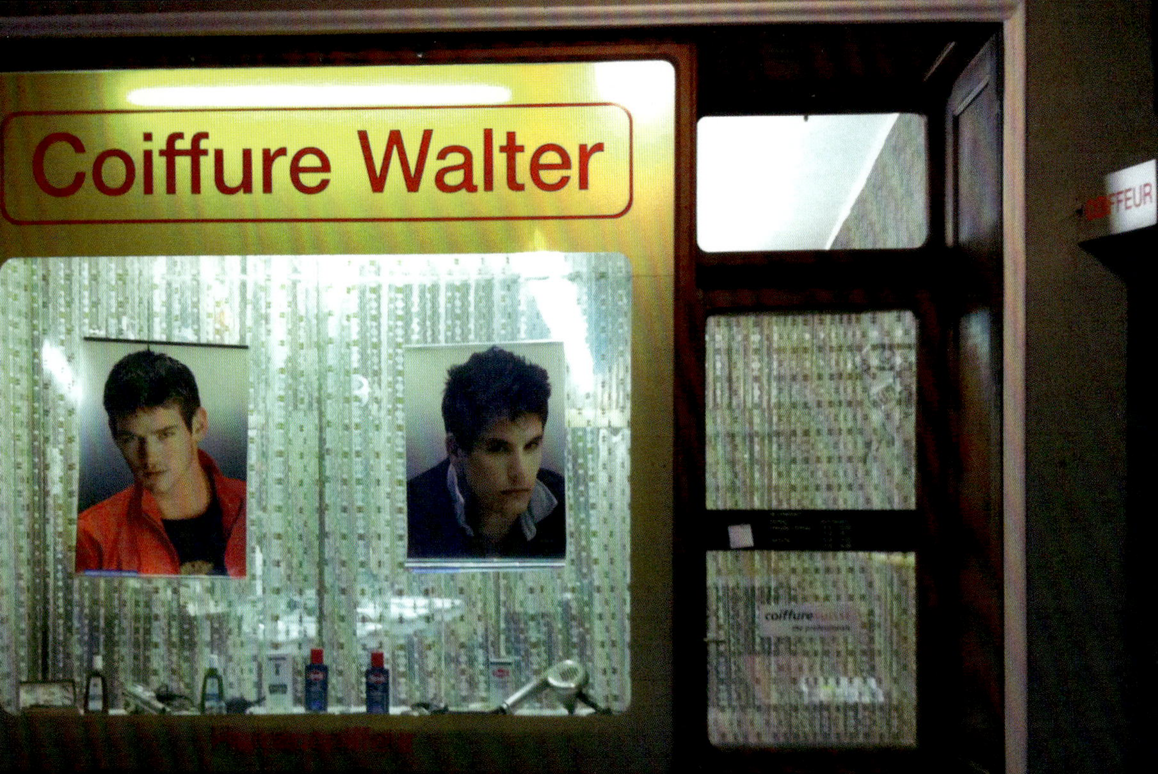

Coiffure Walter

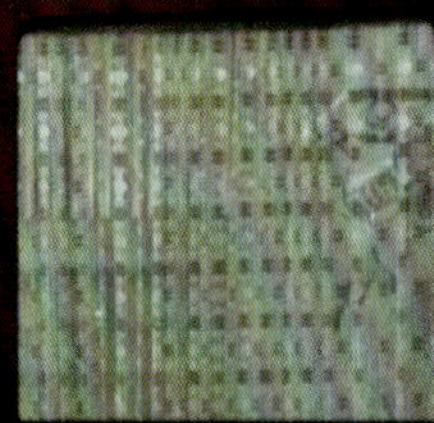

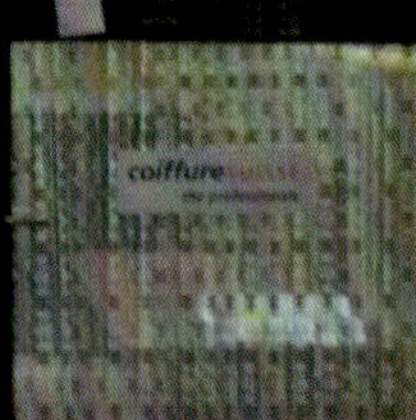
coiffure

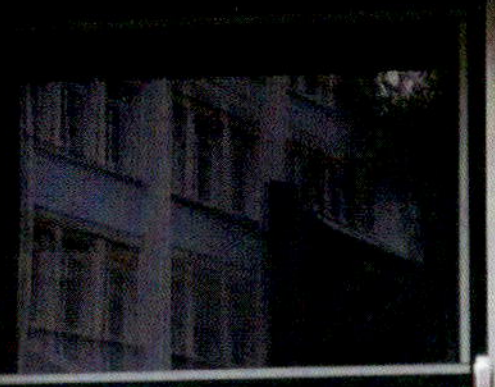

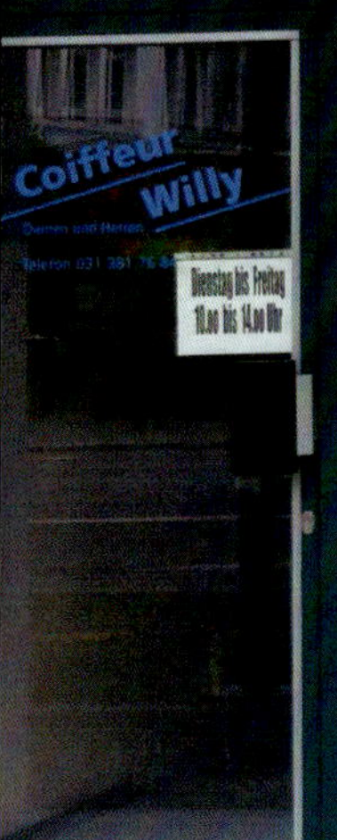
Coiffeur
Willy
Dienstag bis Freitag
10.00 bis 14.00 Uhr

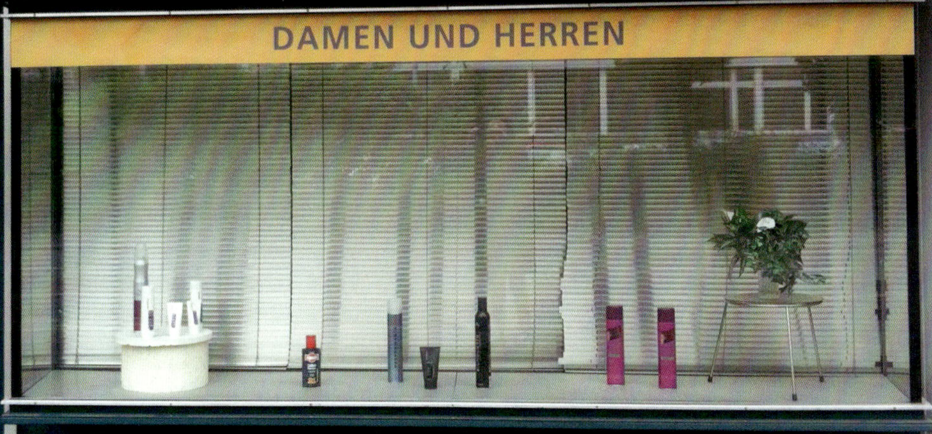
COIFFEUR
DAMEN UND HERREN

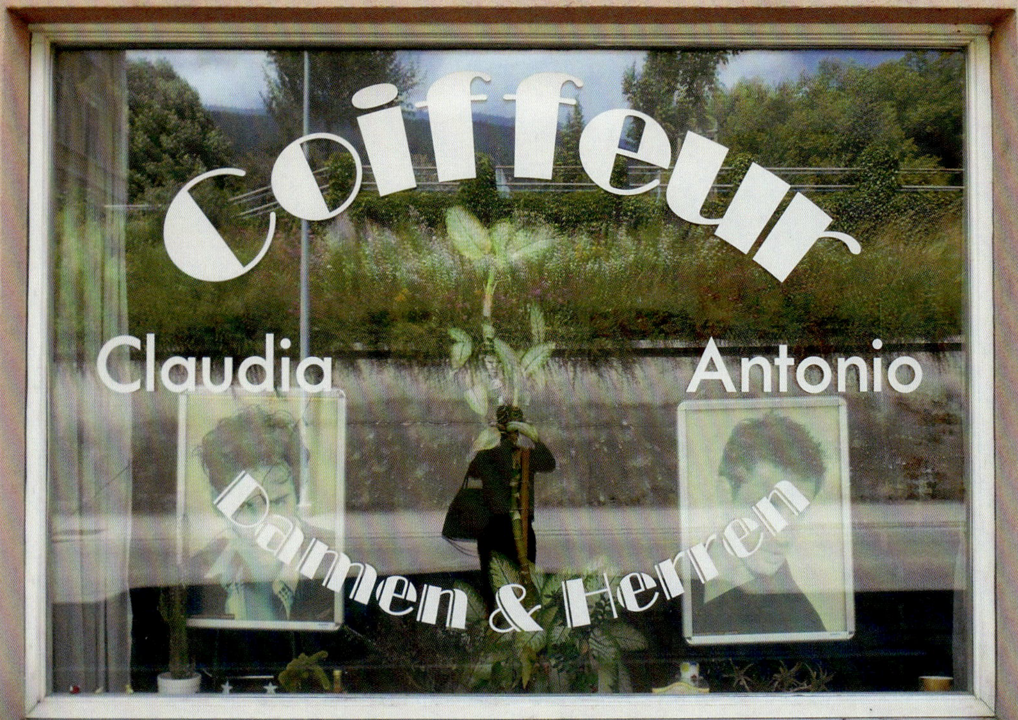
Coiffeur
Claudia
Antonio
Damen & Herren

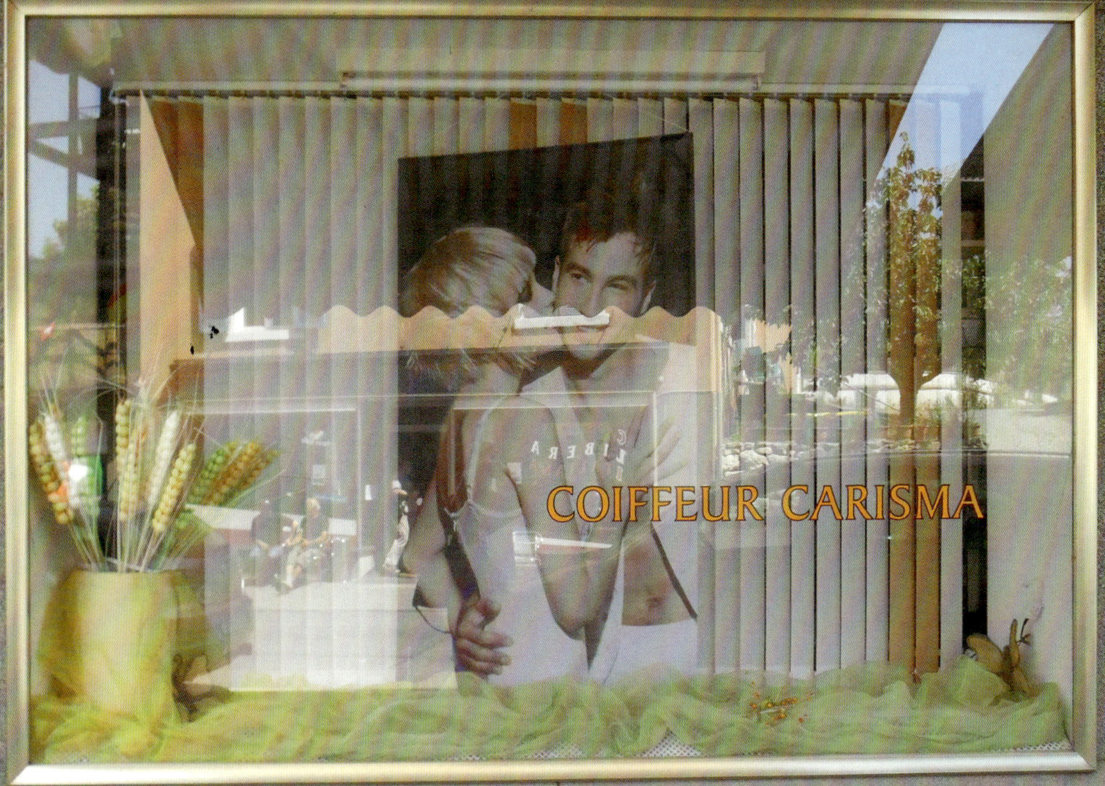
COIFFEUR CARISMA

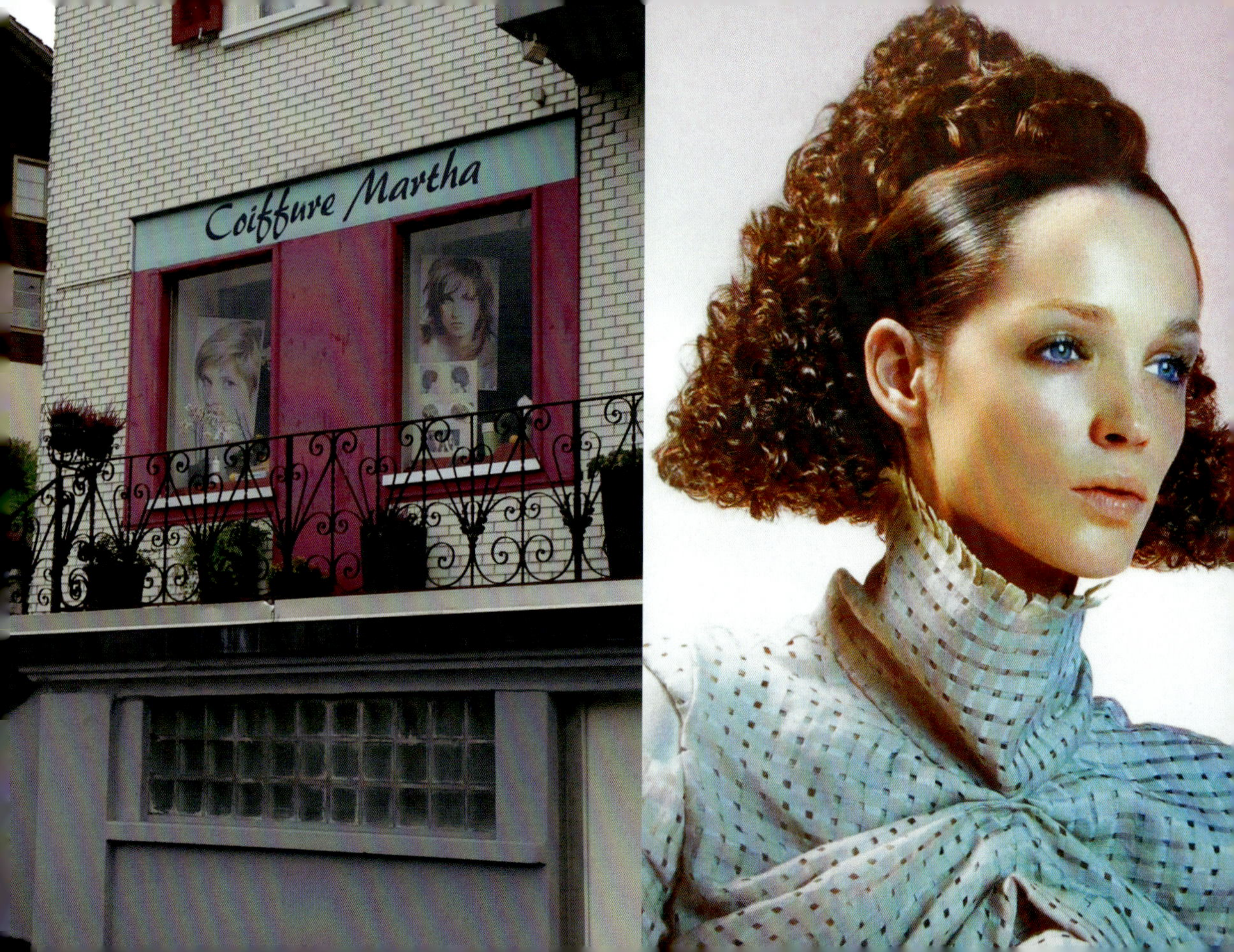
Coiffure Martha

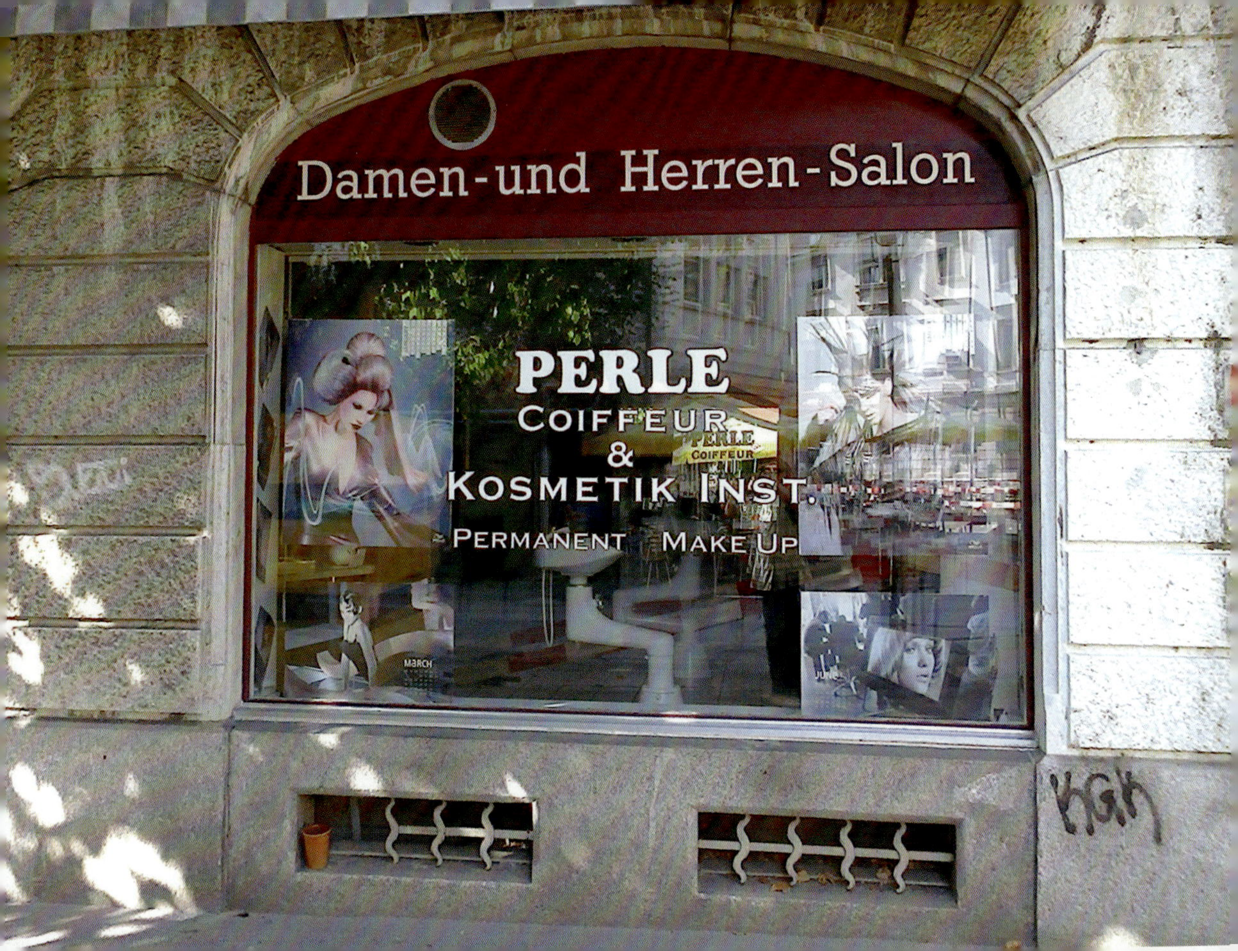
Damen-und Herren-Salon
PERLE
COIFFEUR
&
KOSMETIK INST.
PERMANENT MAKE UP

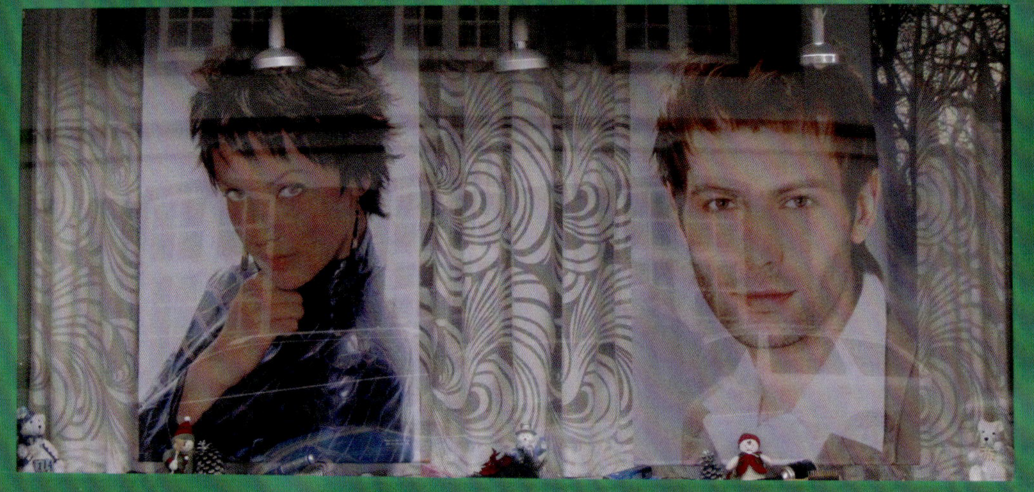
Coiffure Claudia
DAMEN
HERREN

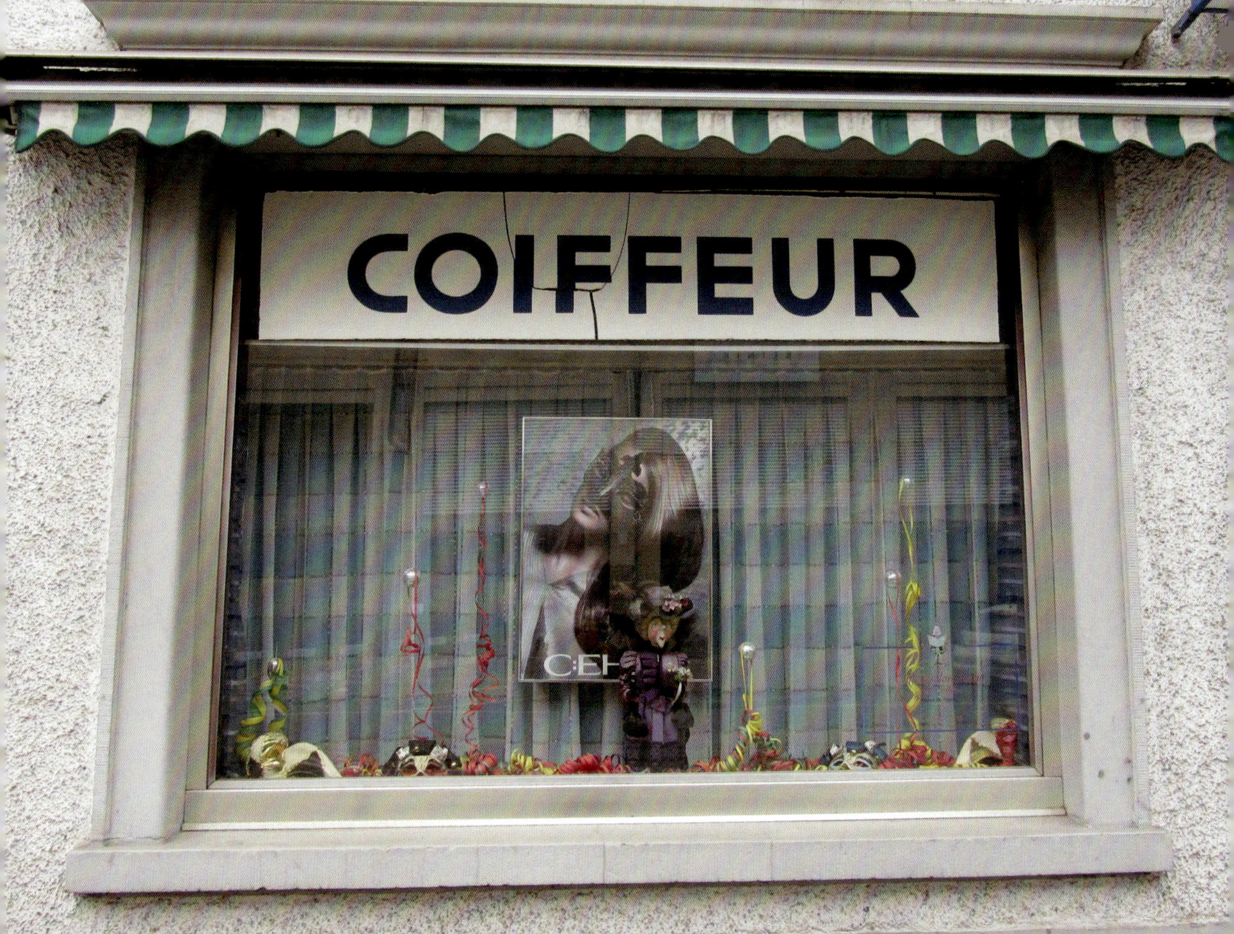
COIFFEUR
C:EH

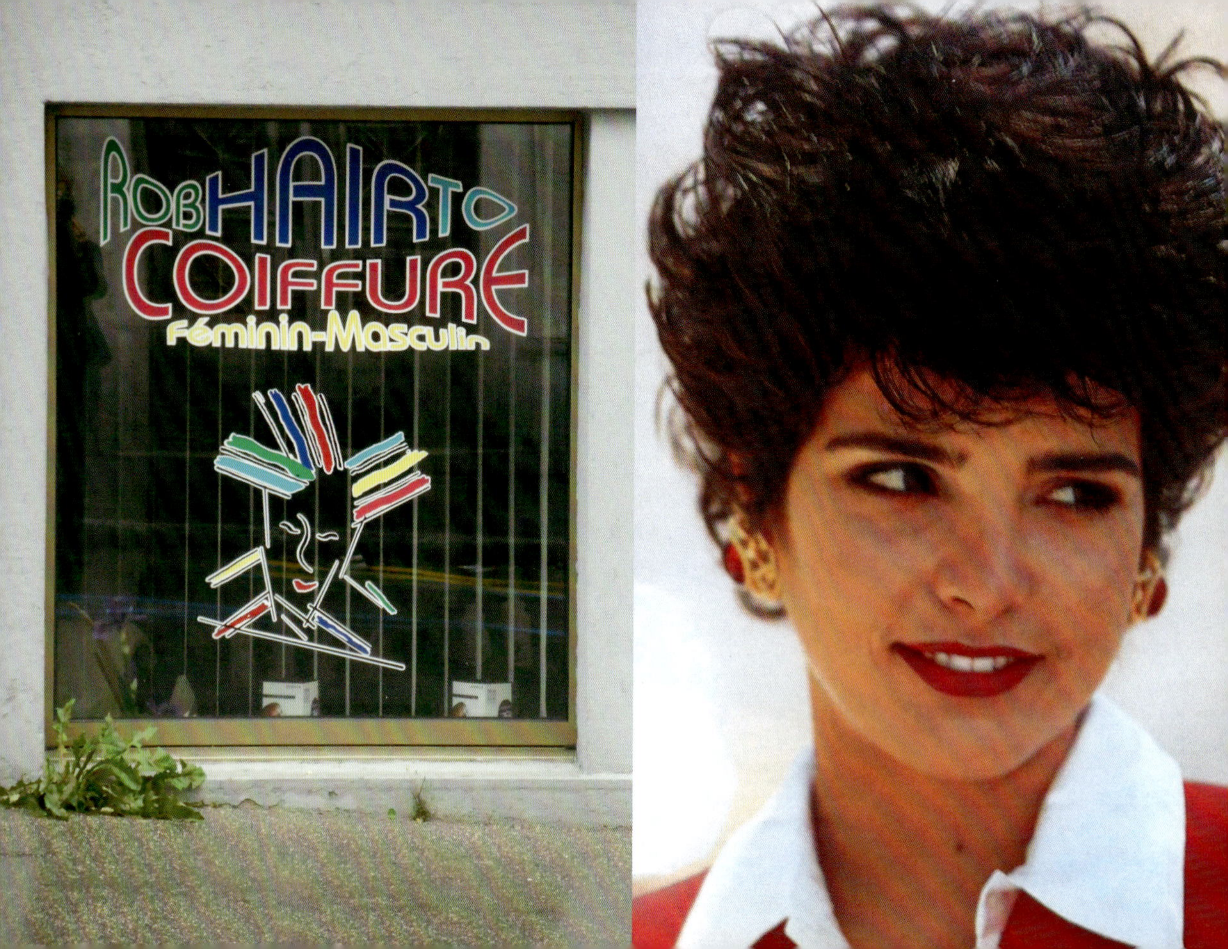
RobHAIRto
COIFFURE
Féminin-Masculin

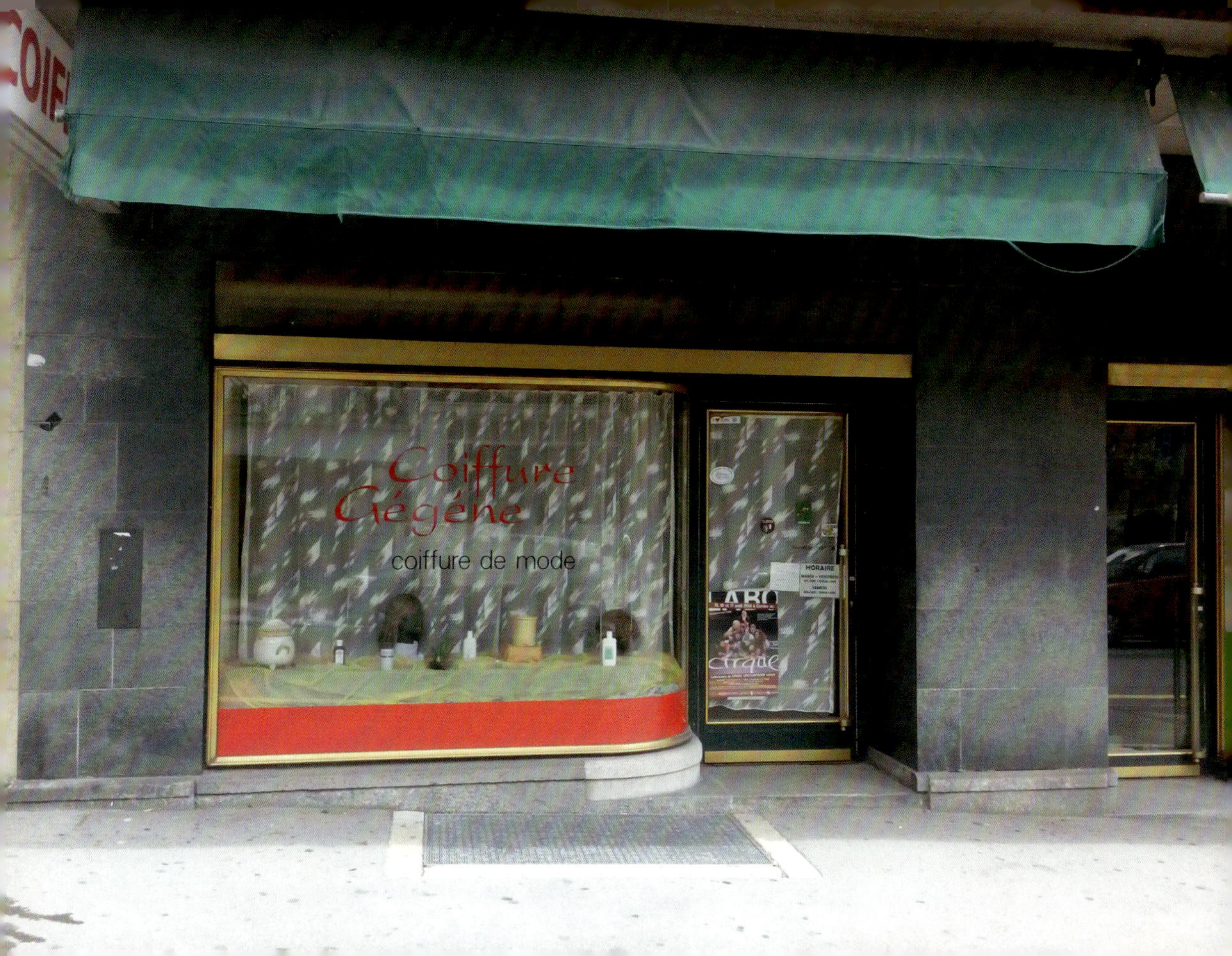
Coiffure
Gégène
coiffure de mode
HORAIRE
cirque

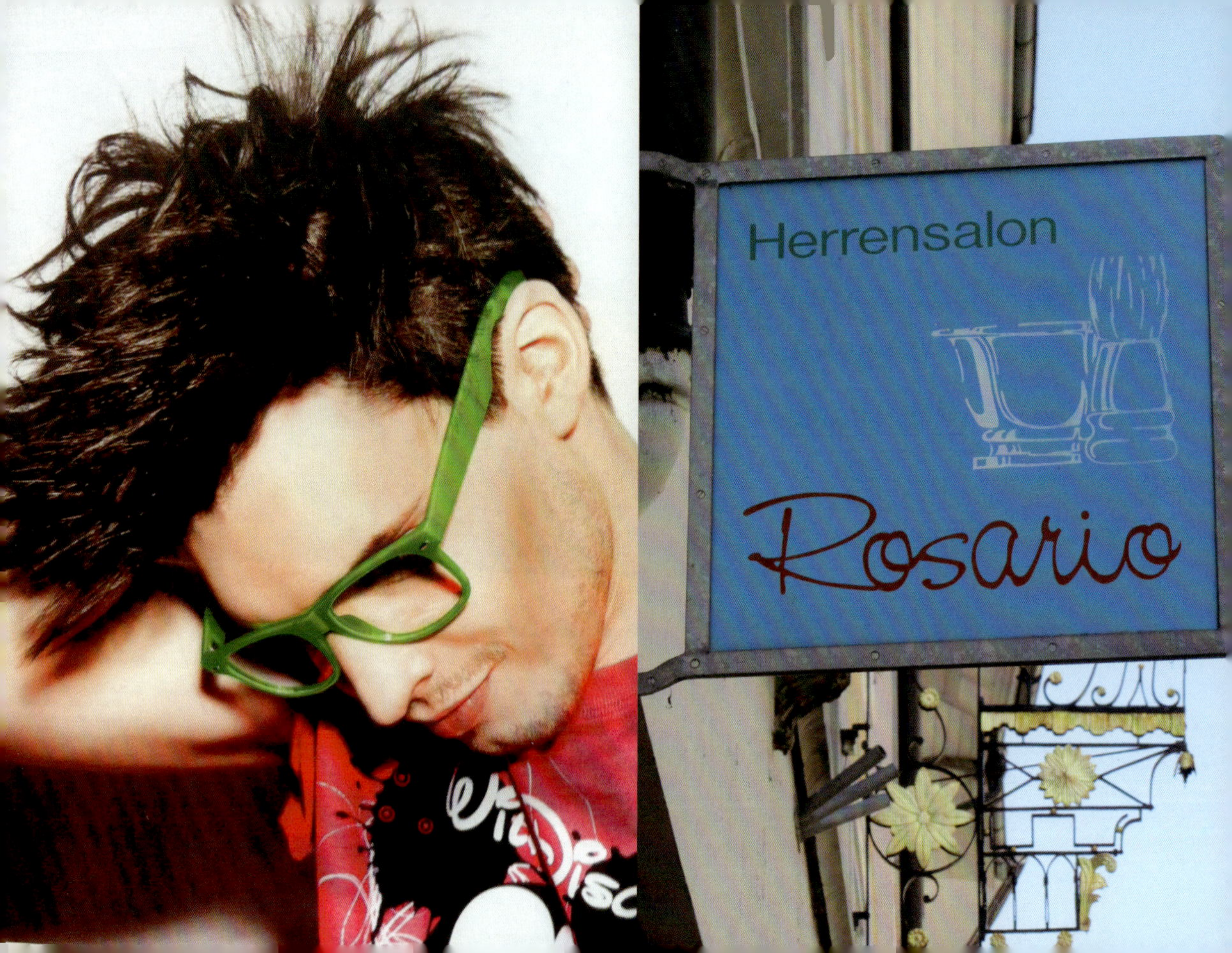
Herrensalon
Rosario

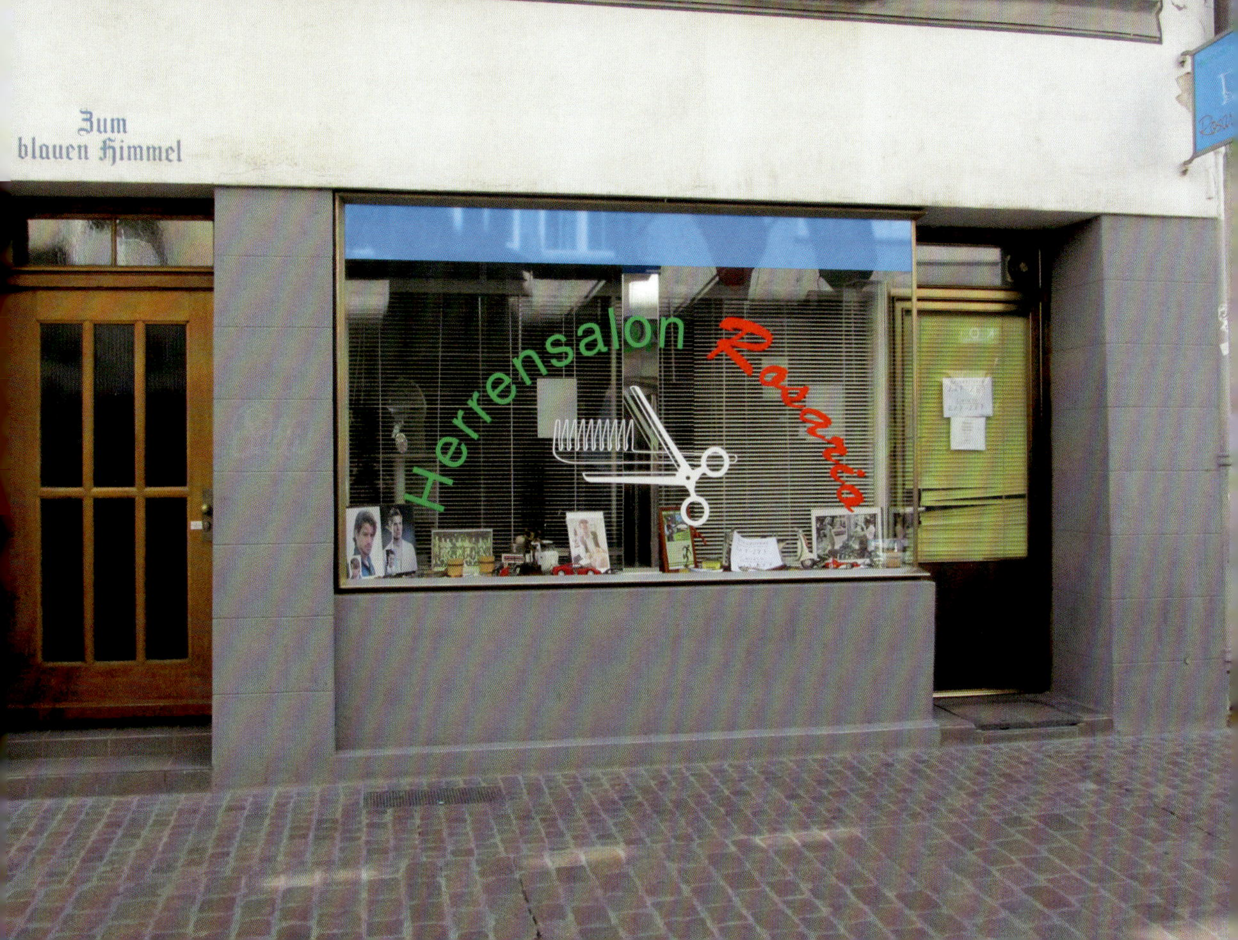
Zum
blauen Himmel
Herrensalon Rosaria

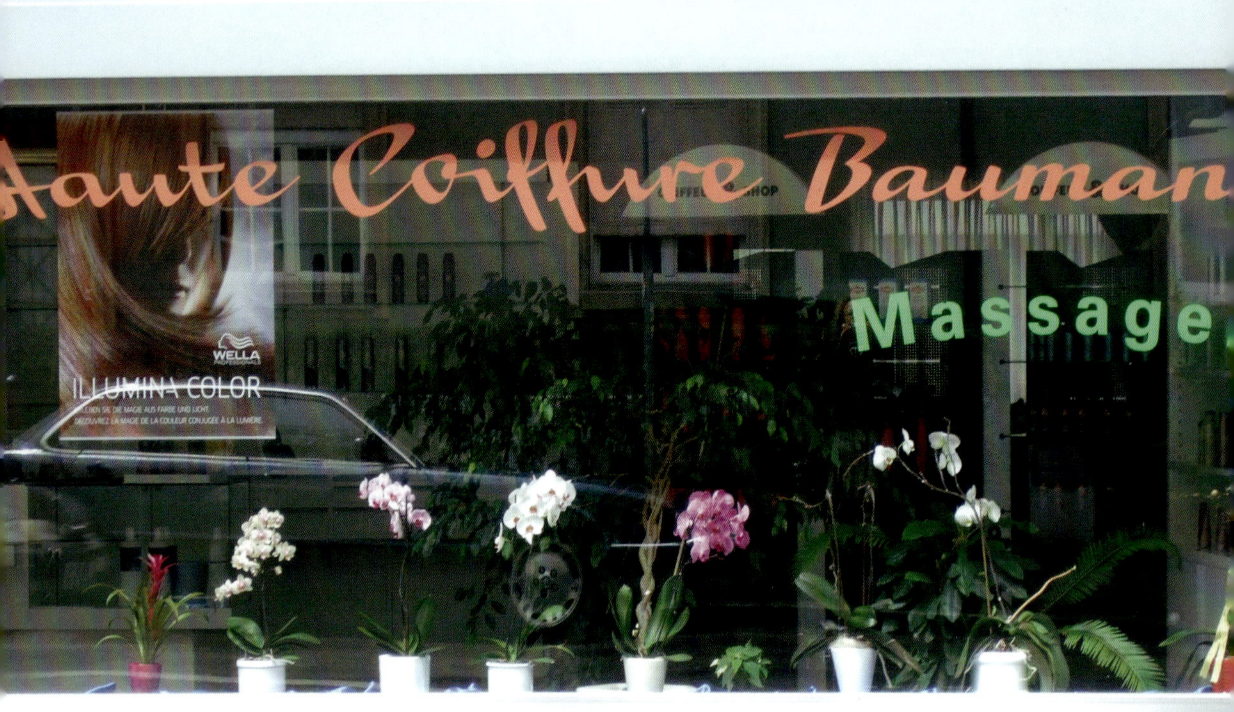

Haute Coiffure Bauman
Massage
WELLA
ILLUMINA COLOR

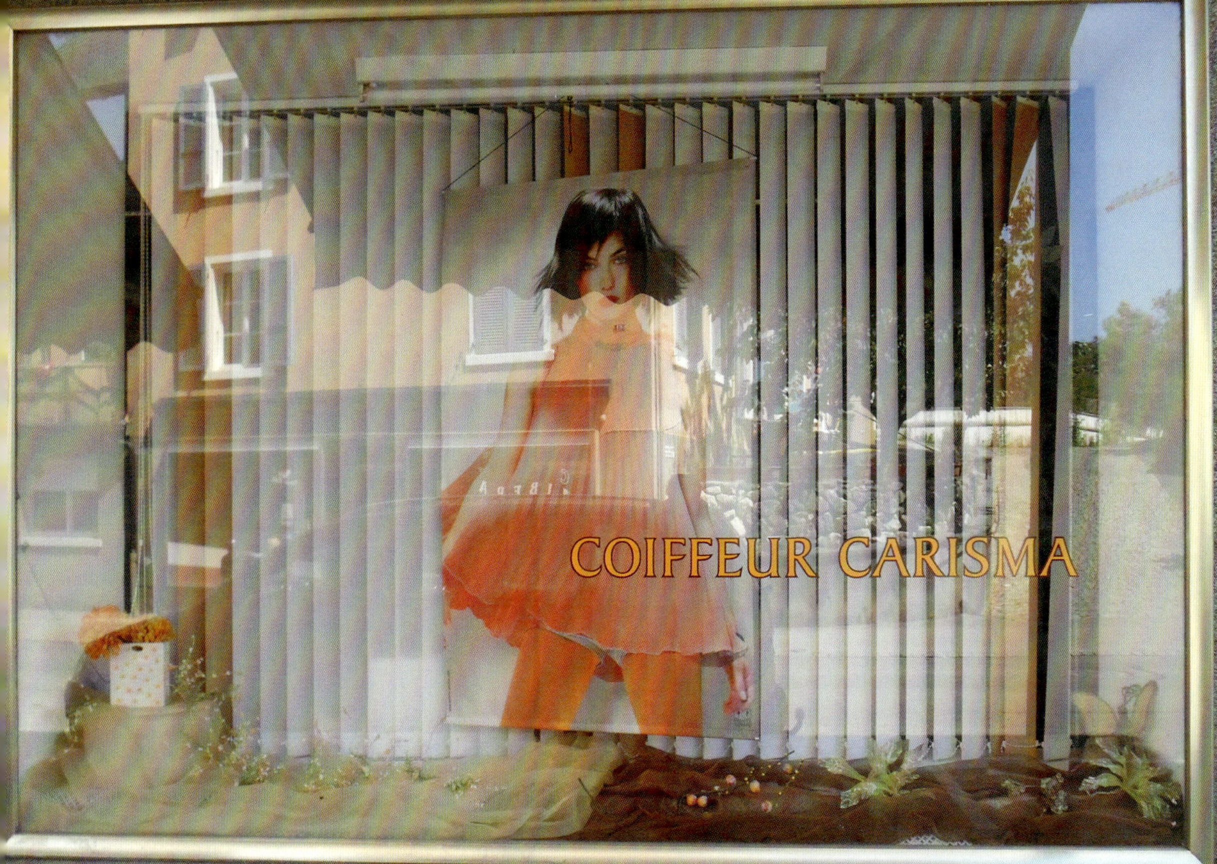
COIFFEUR CARISMA

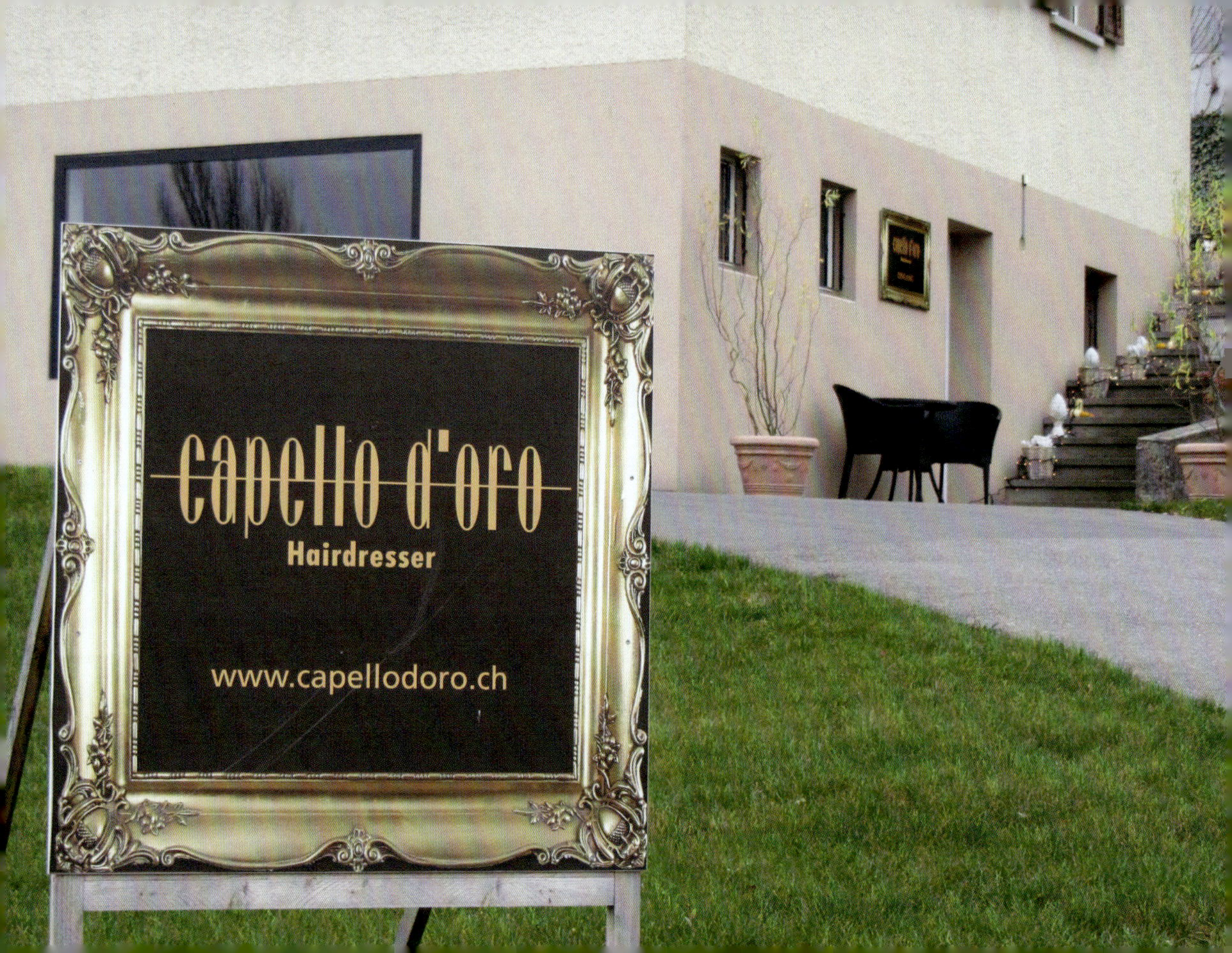
capello d'oro
Hairdresser
www.capellodoro.ch

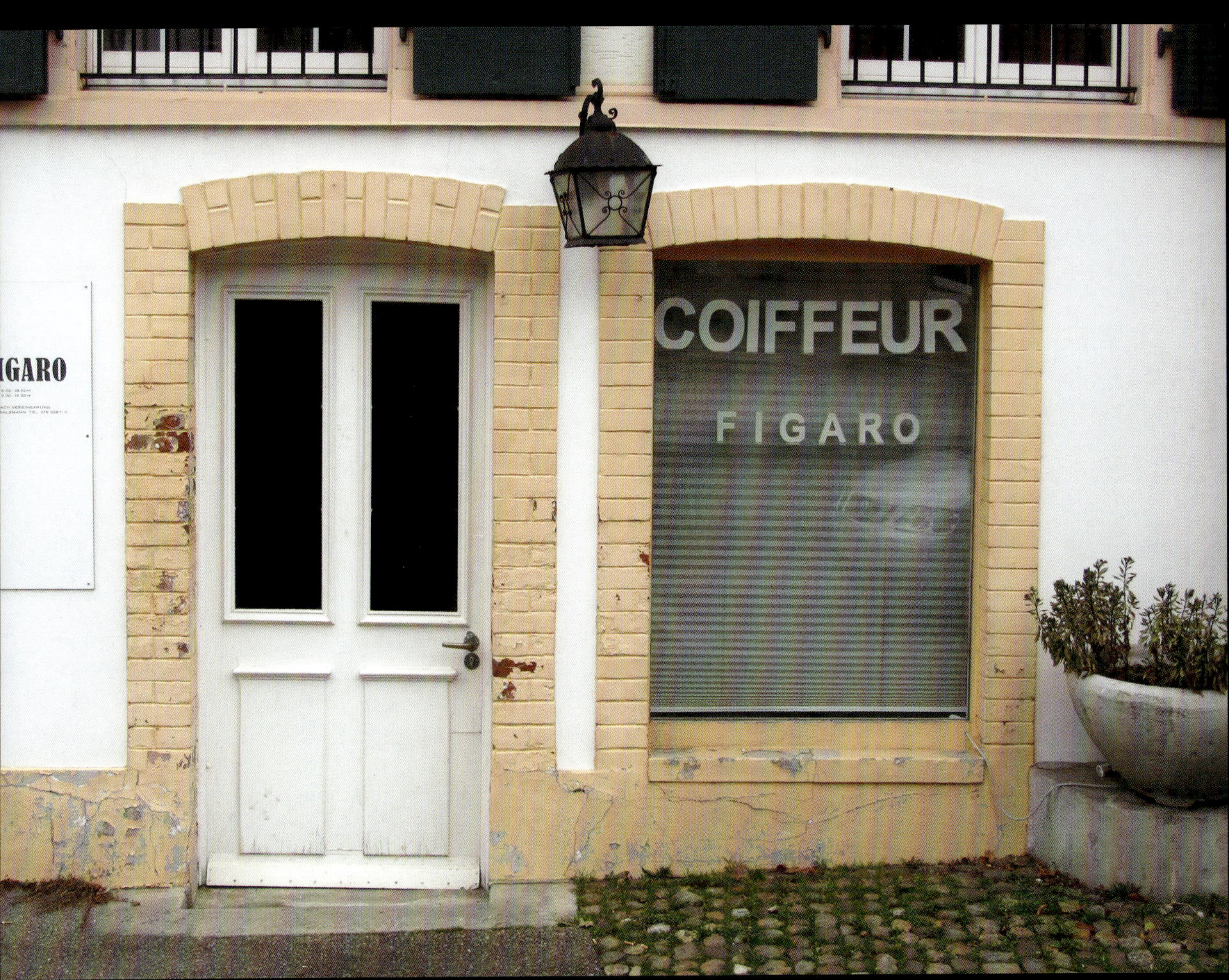
IGARO
COIFFEUR
FIGARO

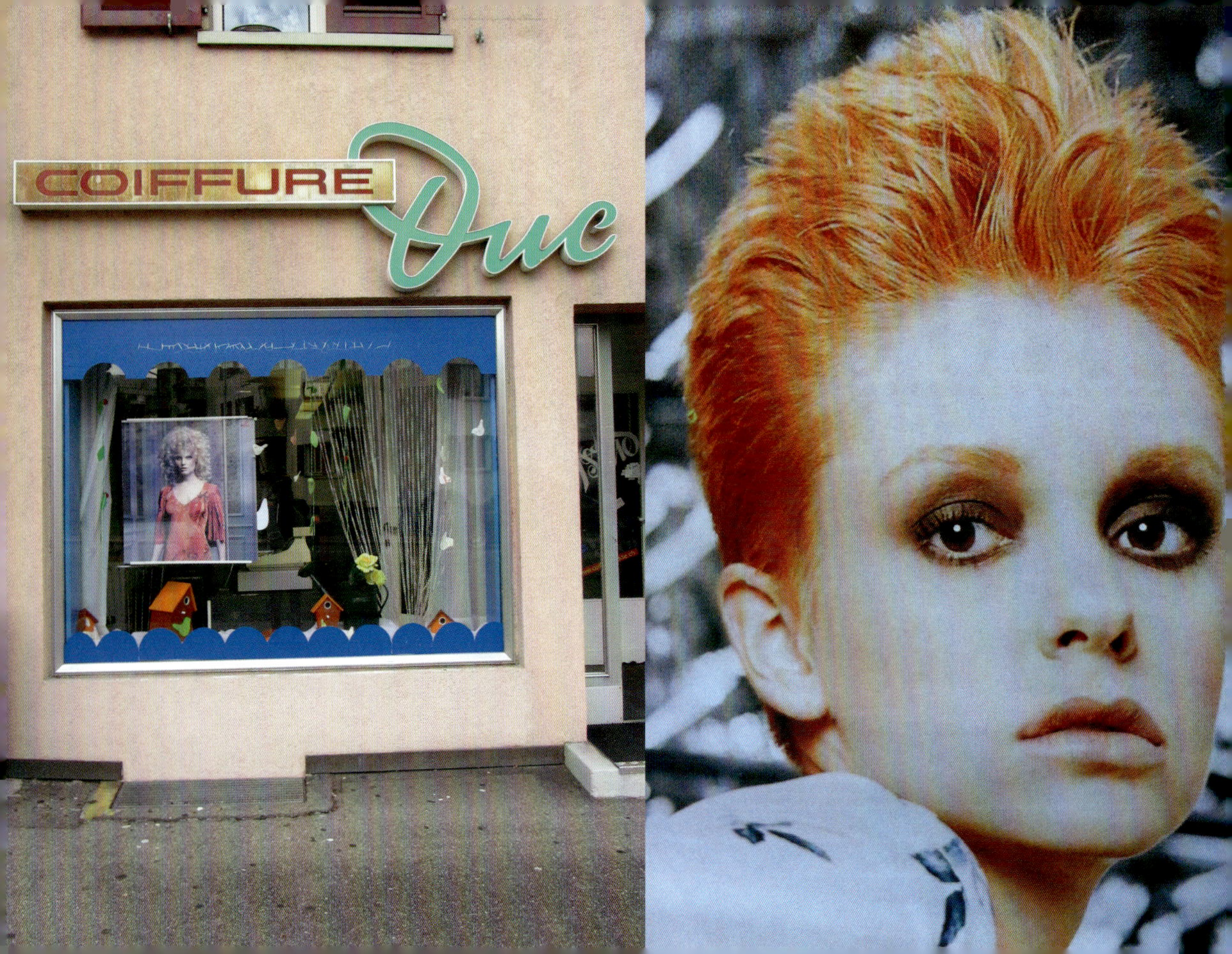
COIFFURE
Duc

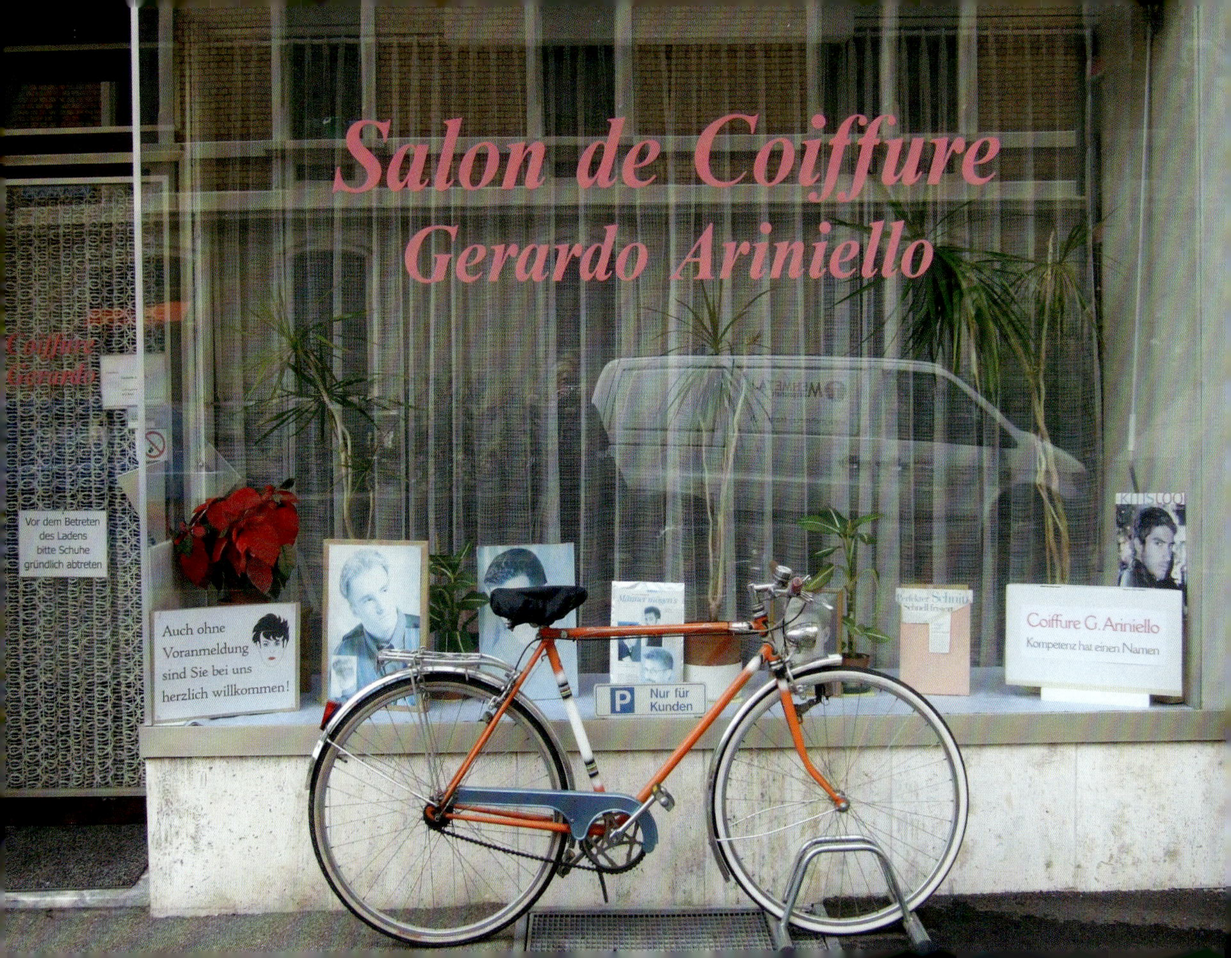

Salon de Coiffure
Gerardo Ariniello
Coiffure
Gerardo
Vor dem Betreten
des Ladens
bitte Schuhe
gründlich abtreten
Auch ohne
Voranmeldung
sind Sie bei uns
herzlich willkommen!
P Nur für
Kunden
Coiffure G. Ariniello
Kompetenz hat einen Namen

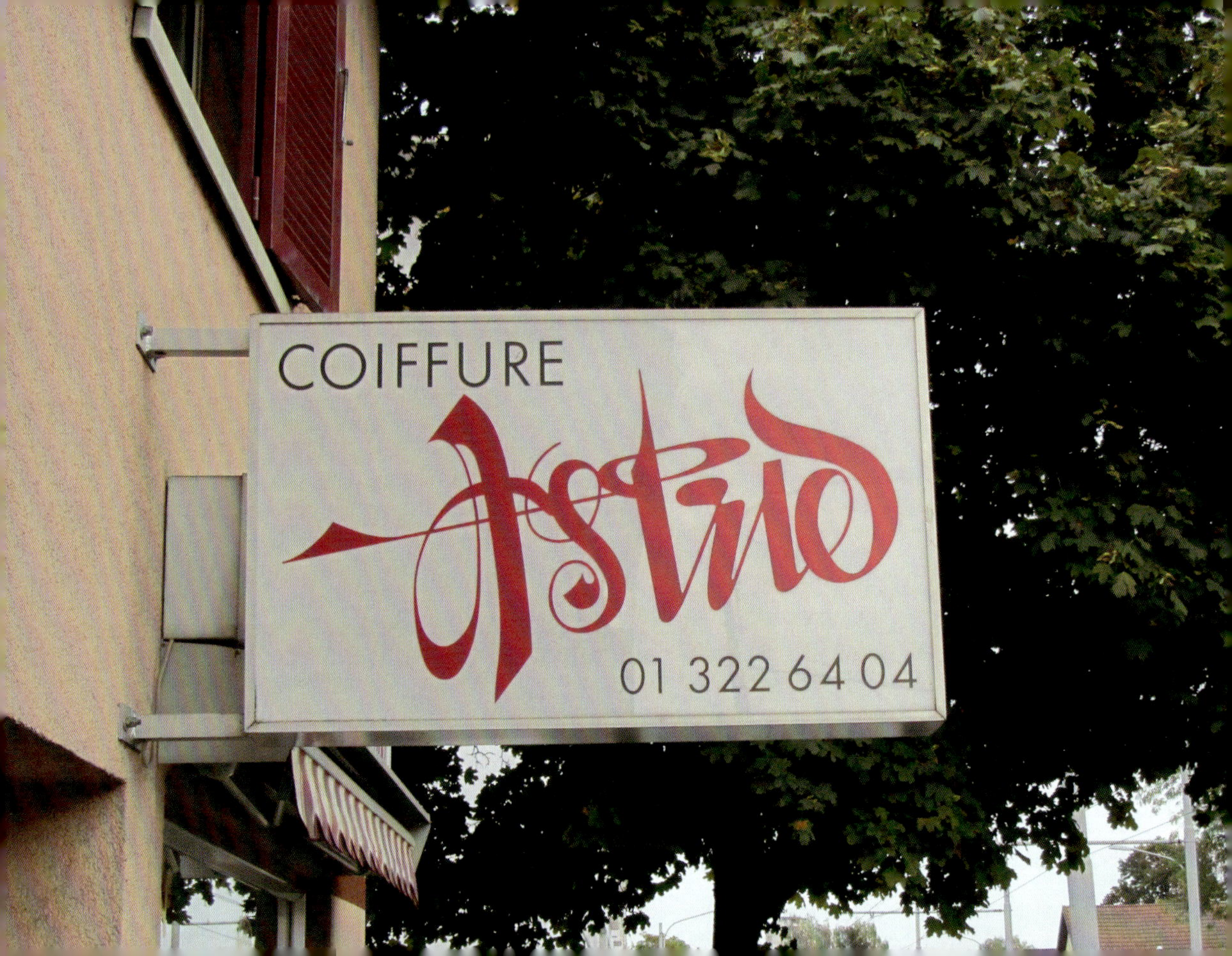
COIFFURE
Astrid
01 322 64 04

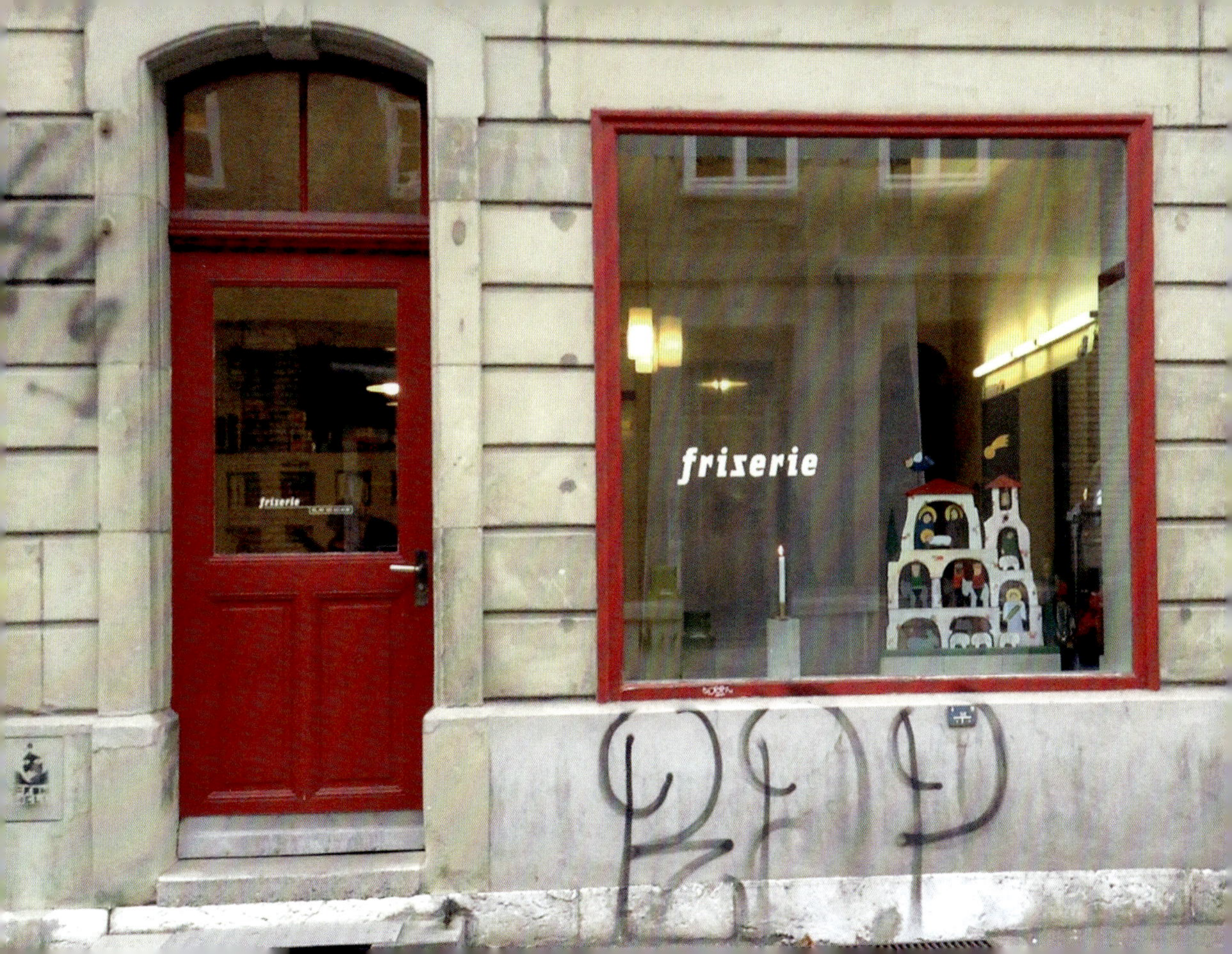

frizerie

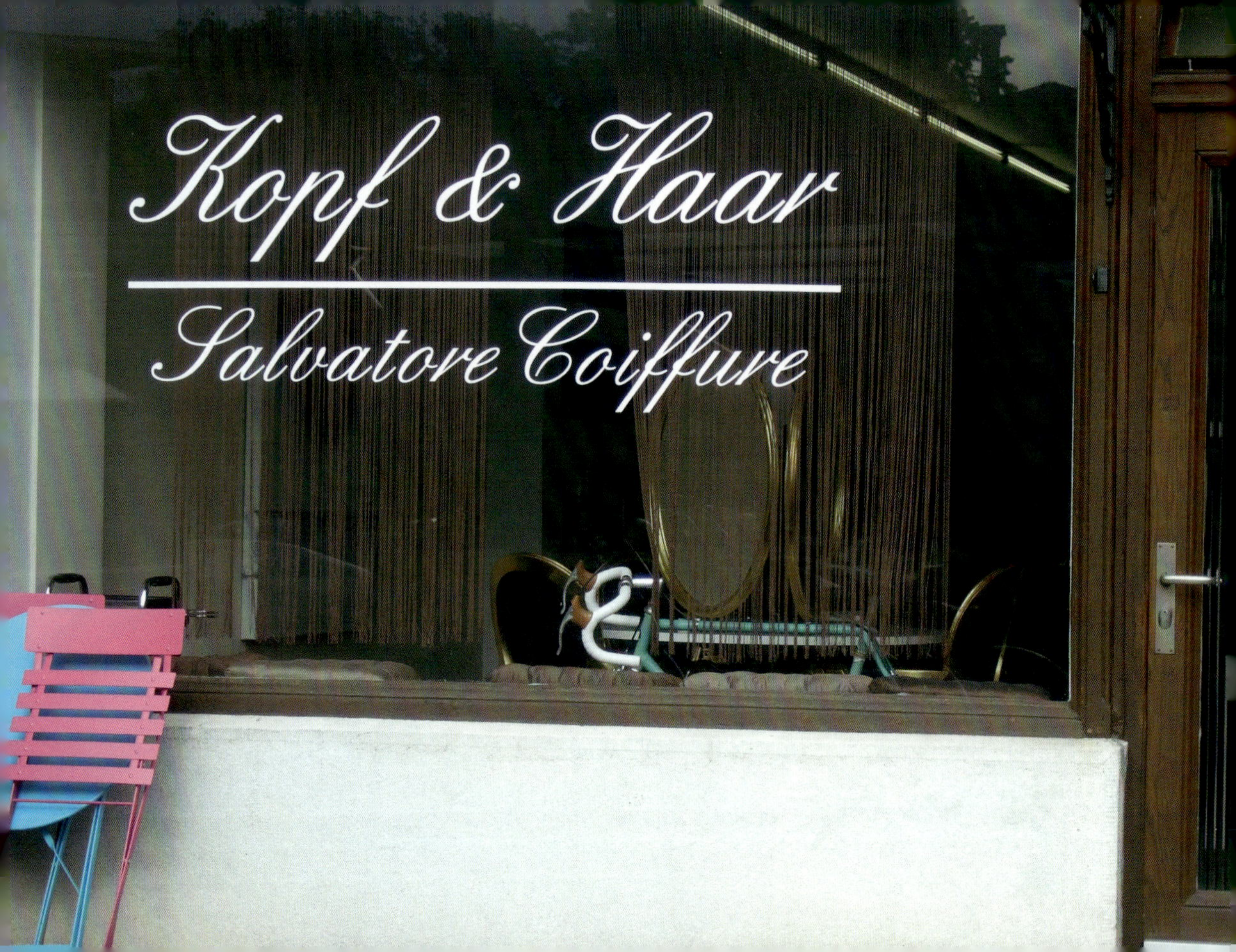
Kopf & Haar
Salvatore Coiffure

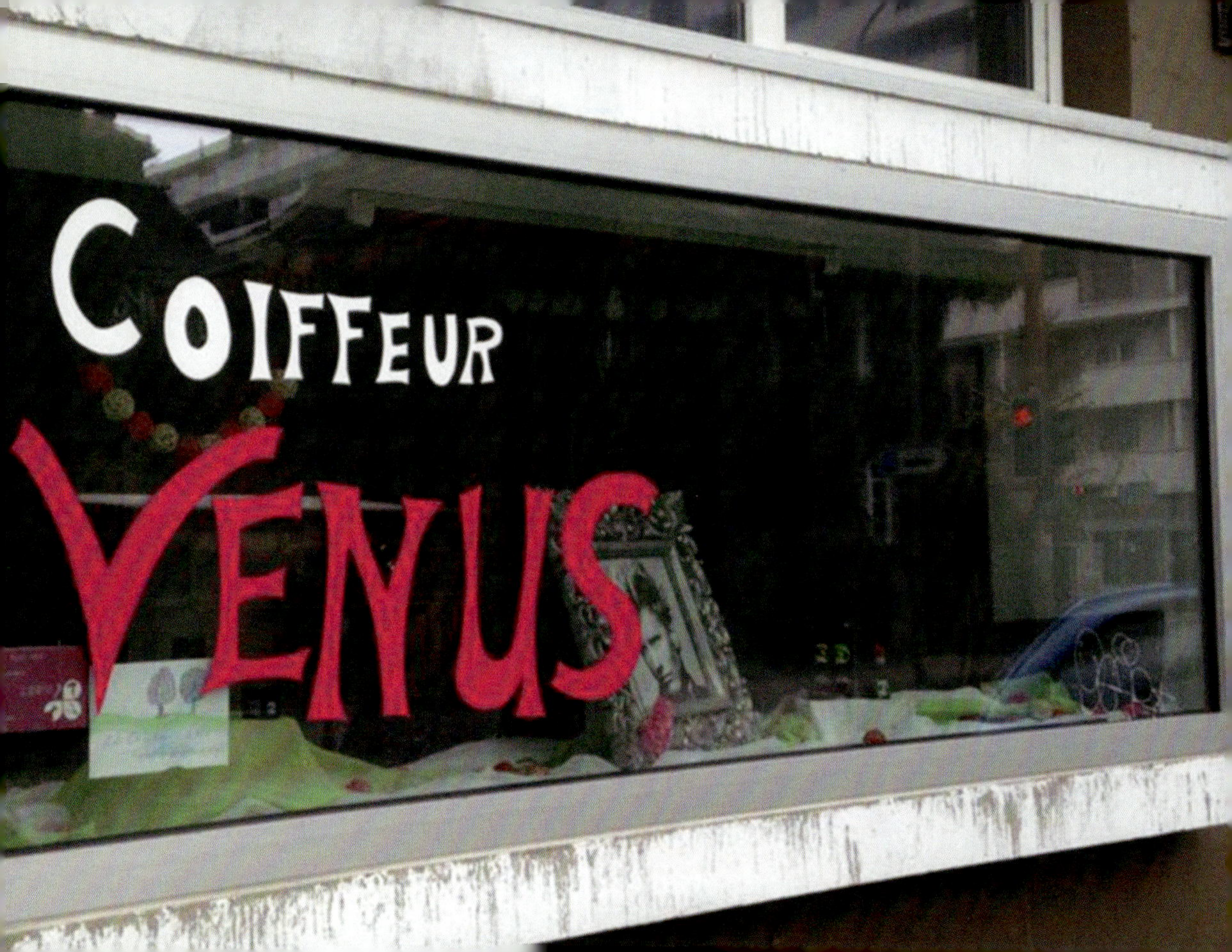
COIFFEUR
VENUS

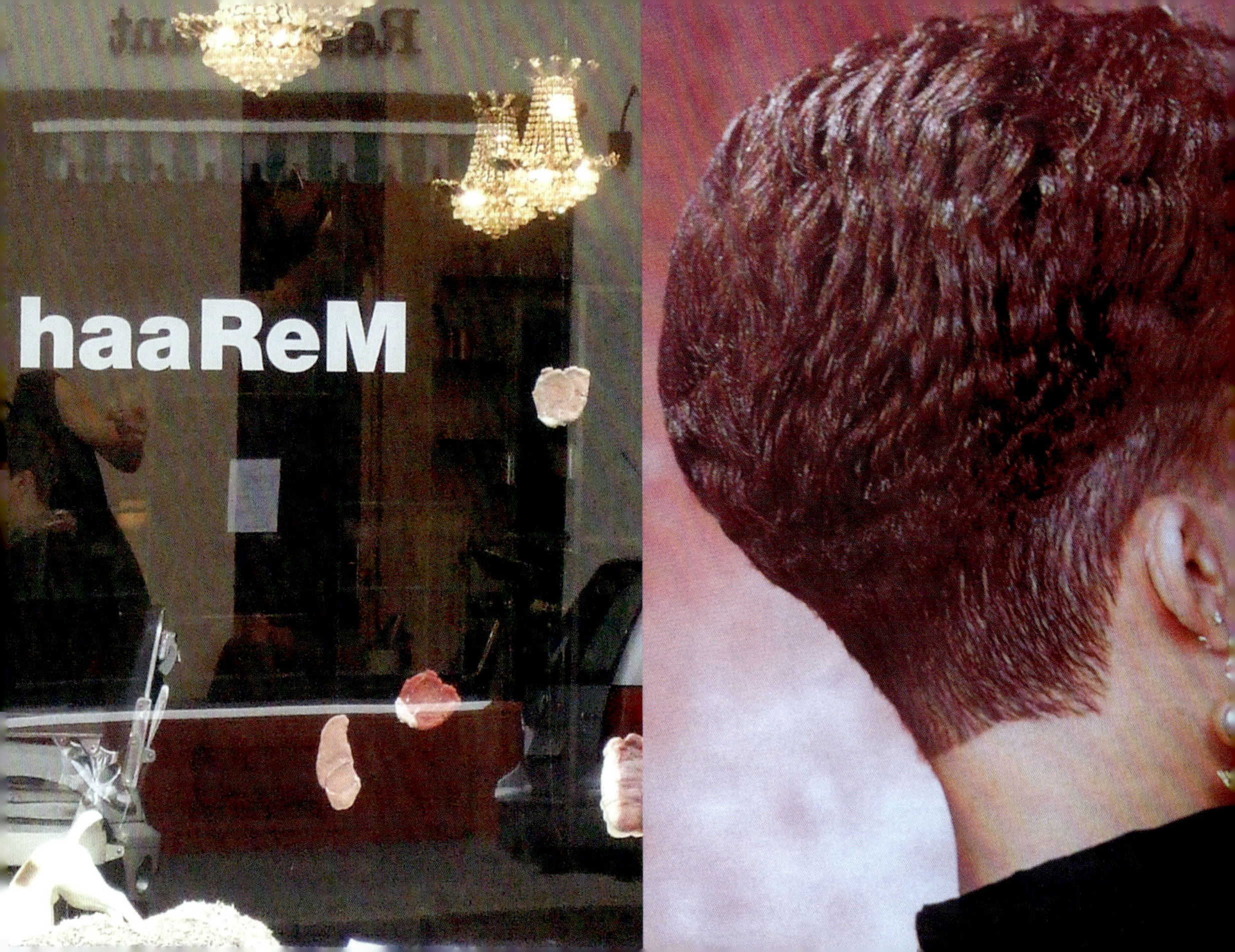
haaReM

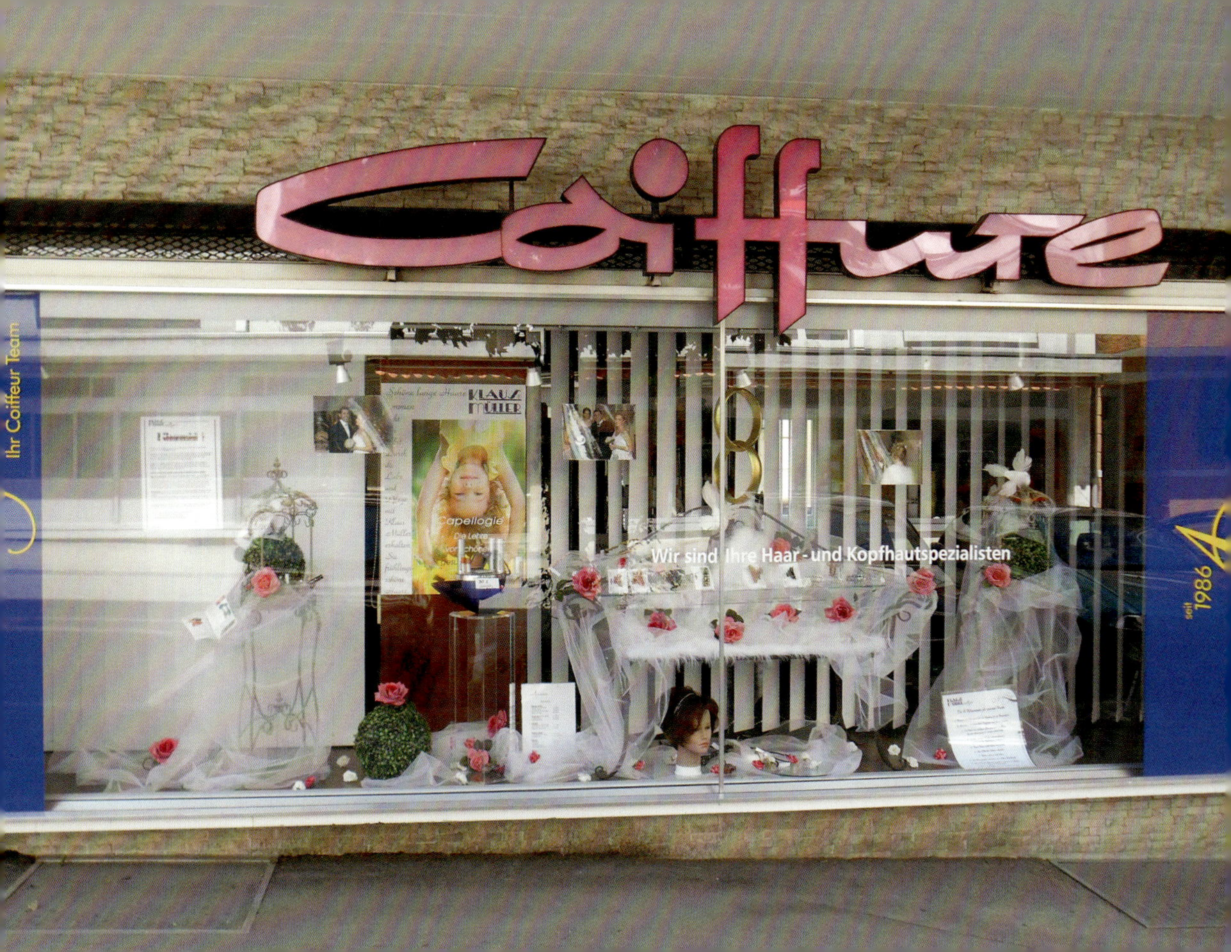
Coiffure
Ihr Coiffeur Team
seit 1986
KLAUS MÜLLER
Capellogie
Wir sind Ihre Haar- und Kopfhautspezialisten

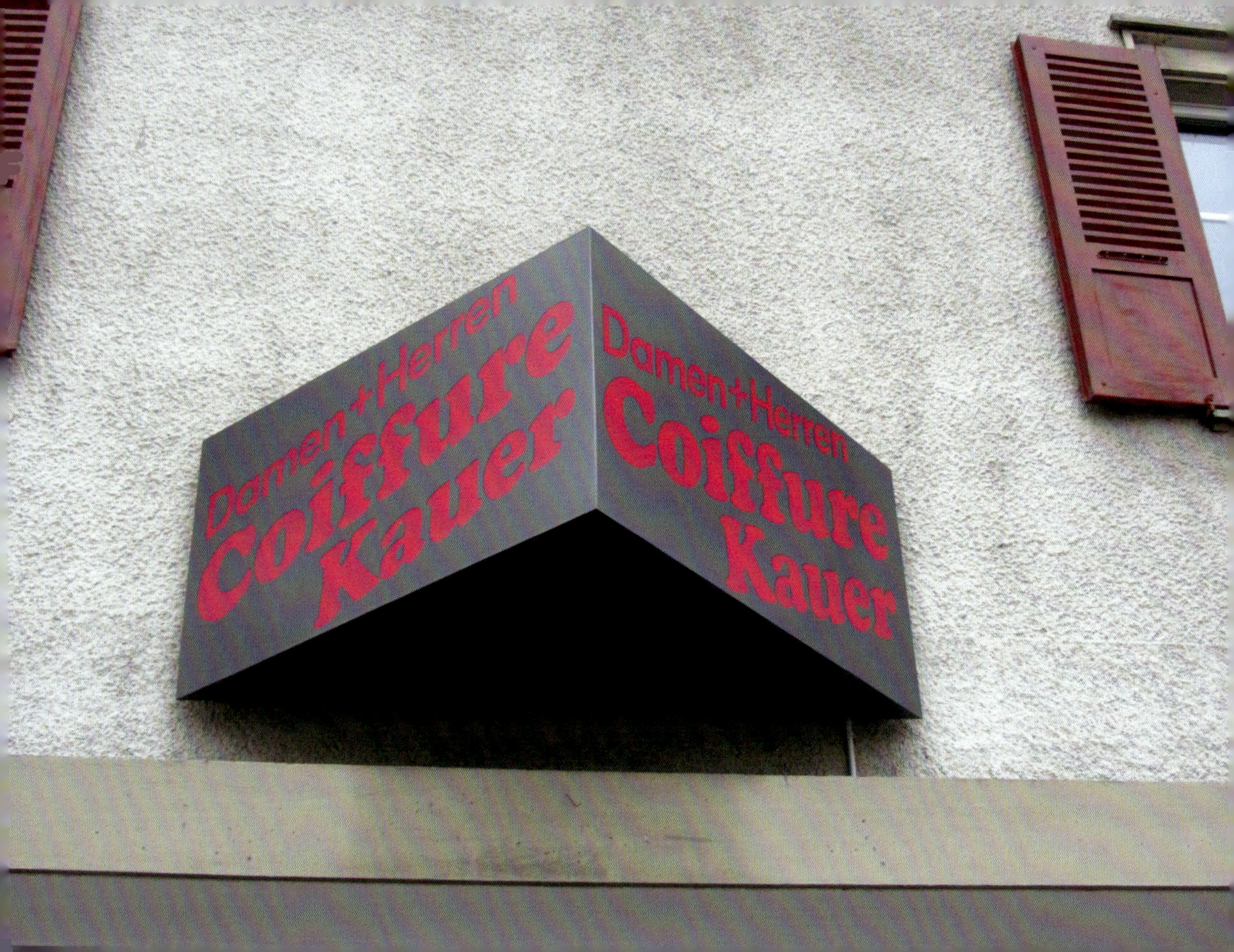
Damen+Herren
Coiffure
Kauer
Damen+Herren
Coiffure
Kauer

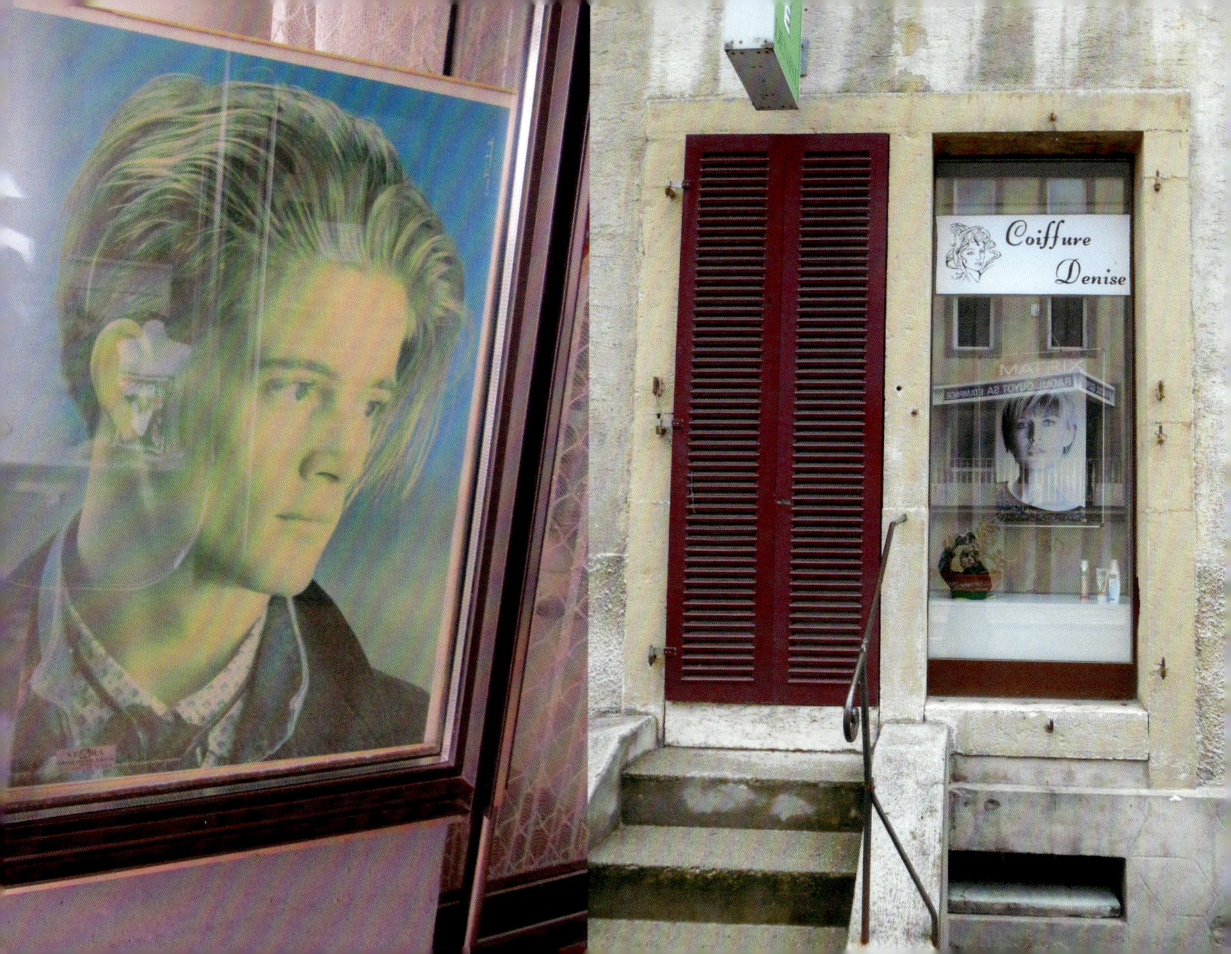
Coiffure
Denise

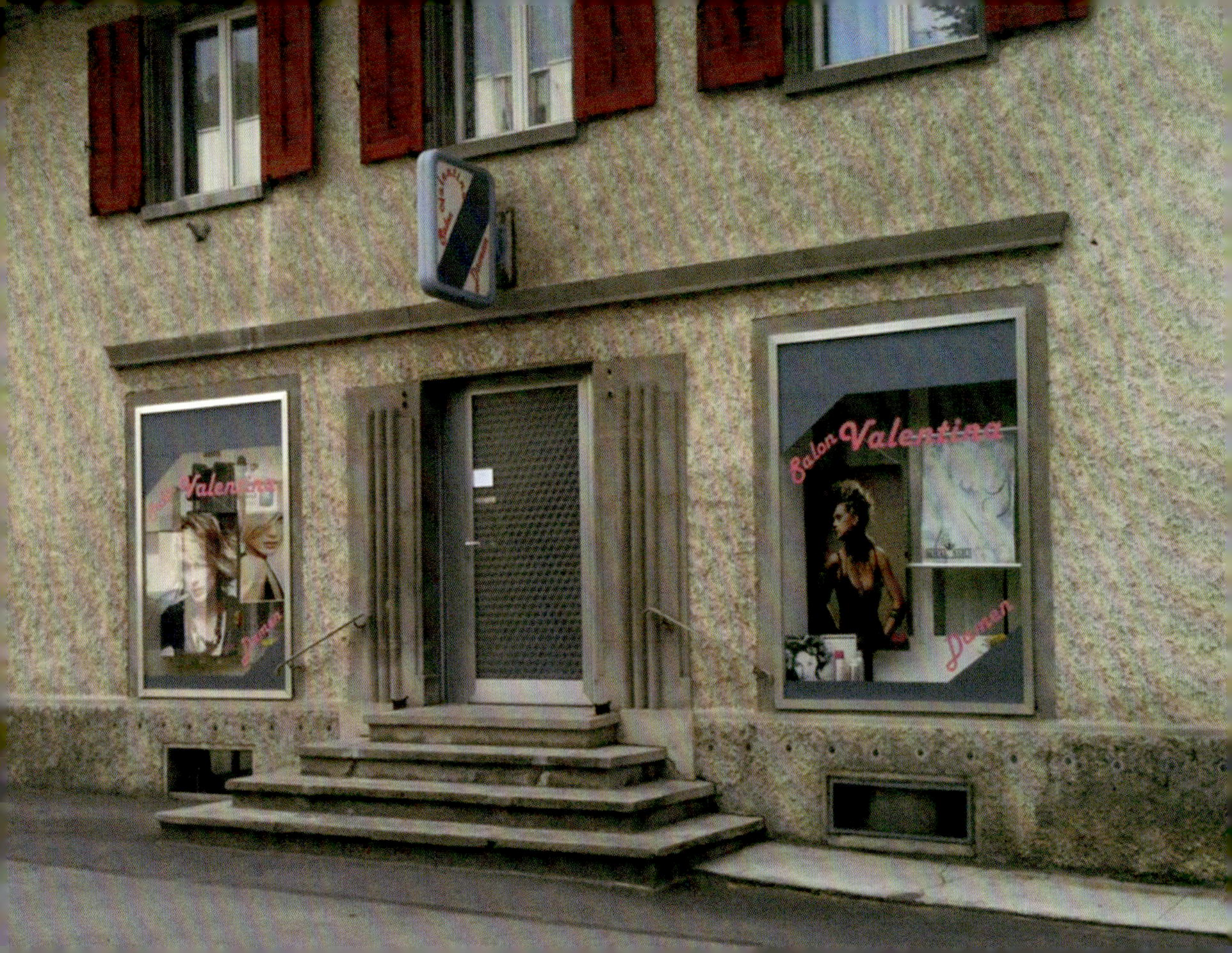
Valentina
Damen
Salon Valentina
Damen

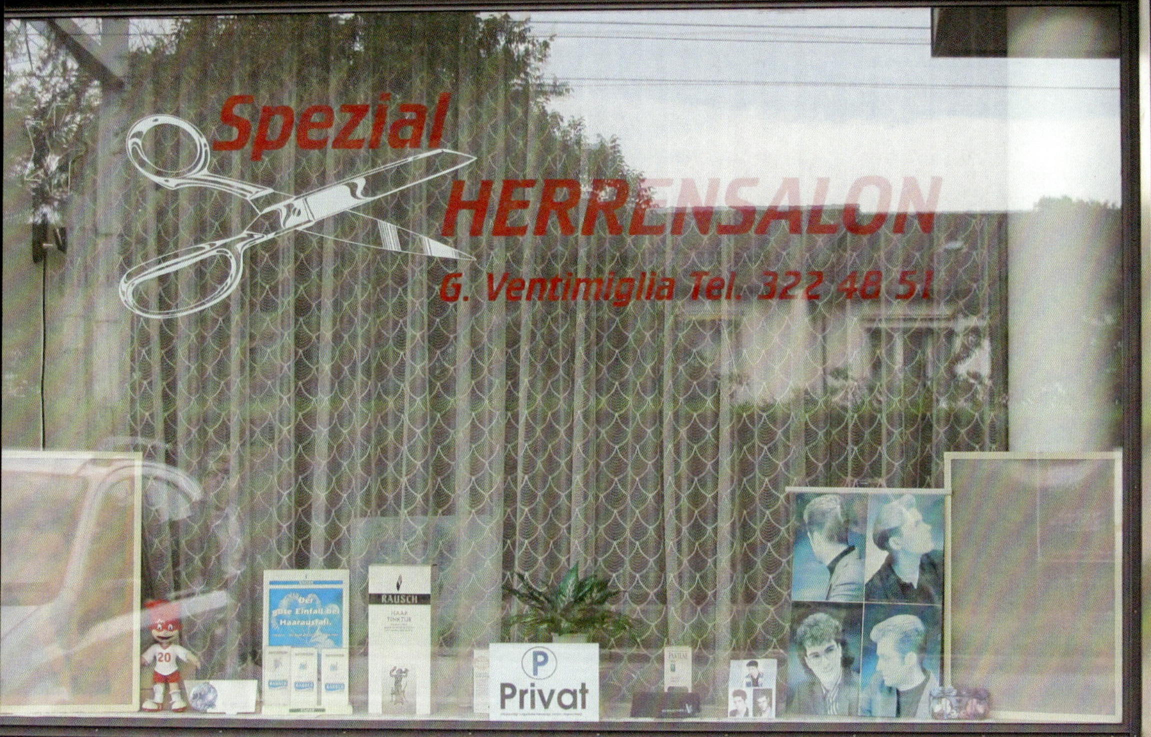
Spezial
HERRENSALON
G. Ventimiglia Tel. 322 48 51
RAUSCH
Privat
22

Coiffure Rosy
Damen & Herren
Tel. 951 18 60

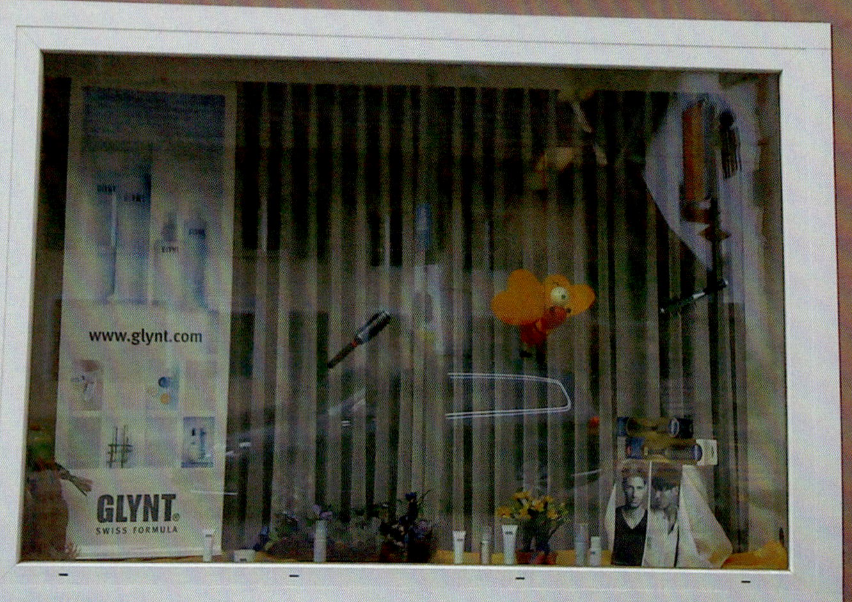

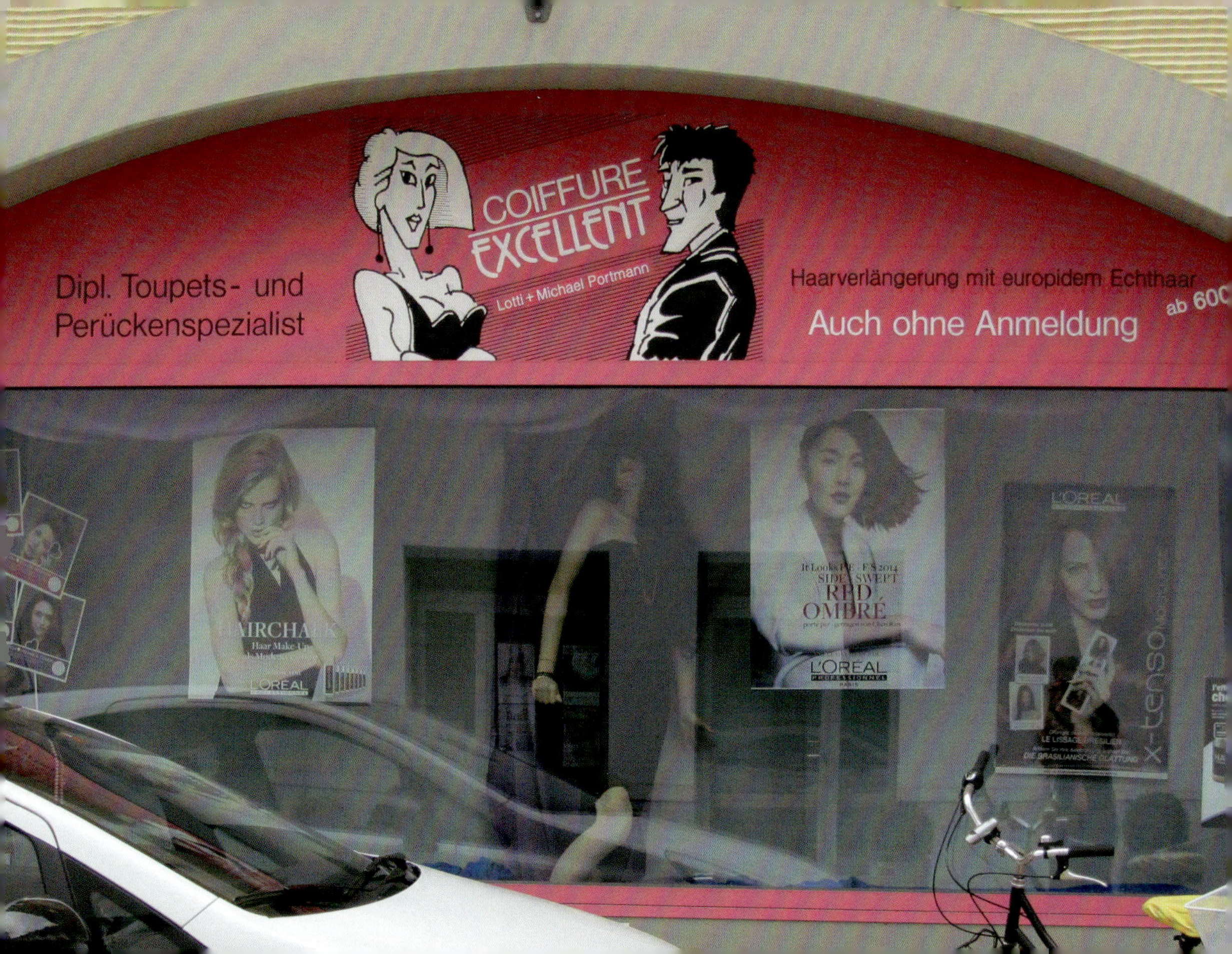

COIFFURE
EXCELLENT
Lotti + Michael Portmann

Dipl. Toupets- und
Perückenspezialist

Haarverlängerung mit europidem Echthaar
ab 600
Auch ohne Anmeldung

L'ORÉAL

SIDE SWEPT
RED
OMBRÉ

L'ORÉAL
PROFESSIONNEL
PARIS

L'ORÉAL

X-tenso

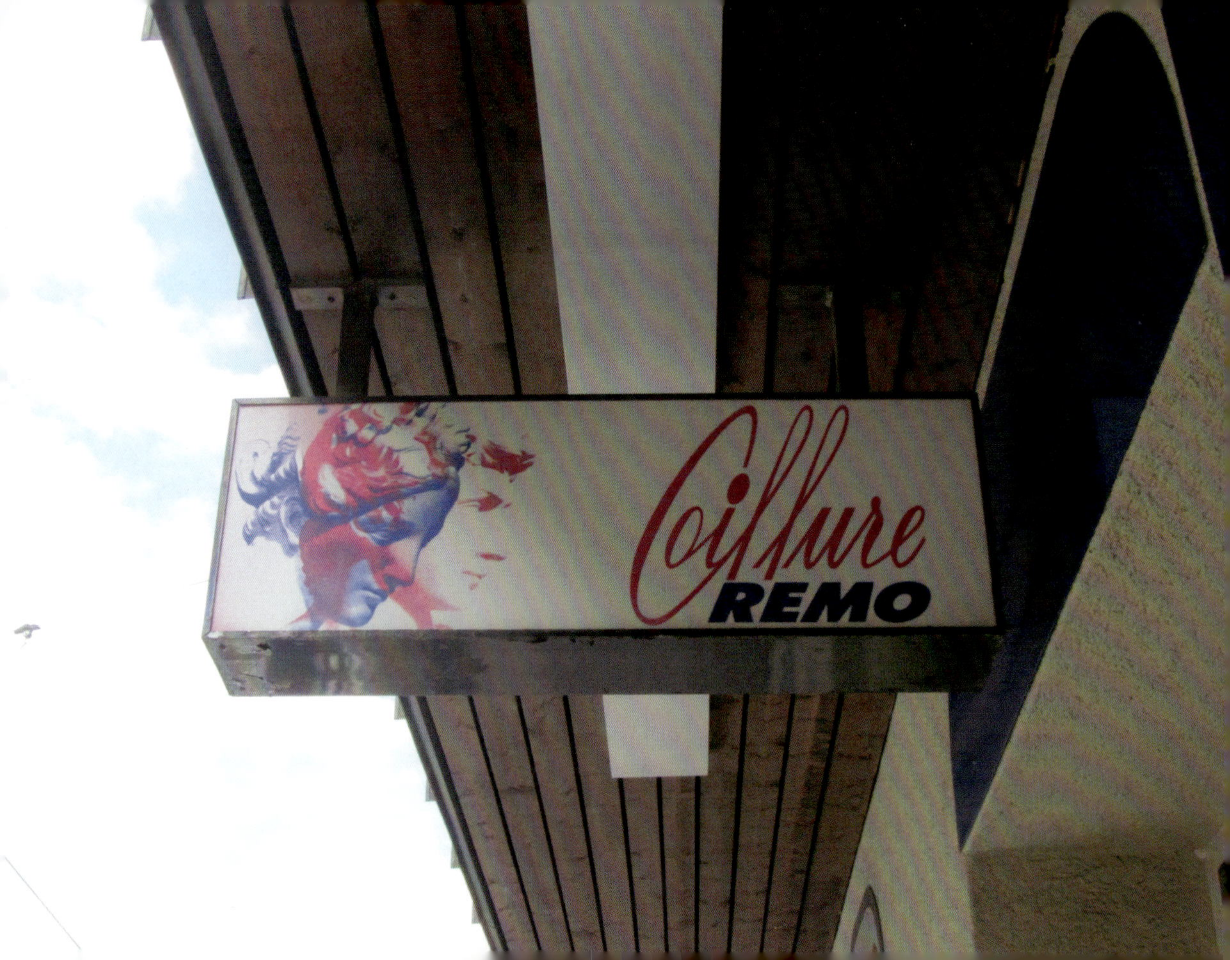
Coiffure
REMO

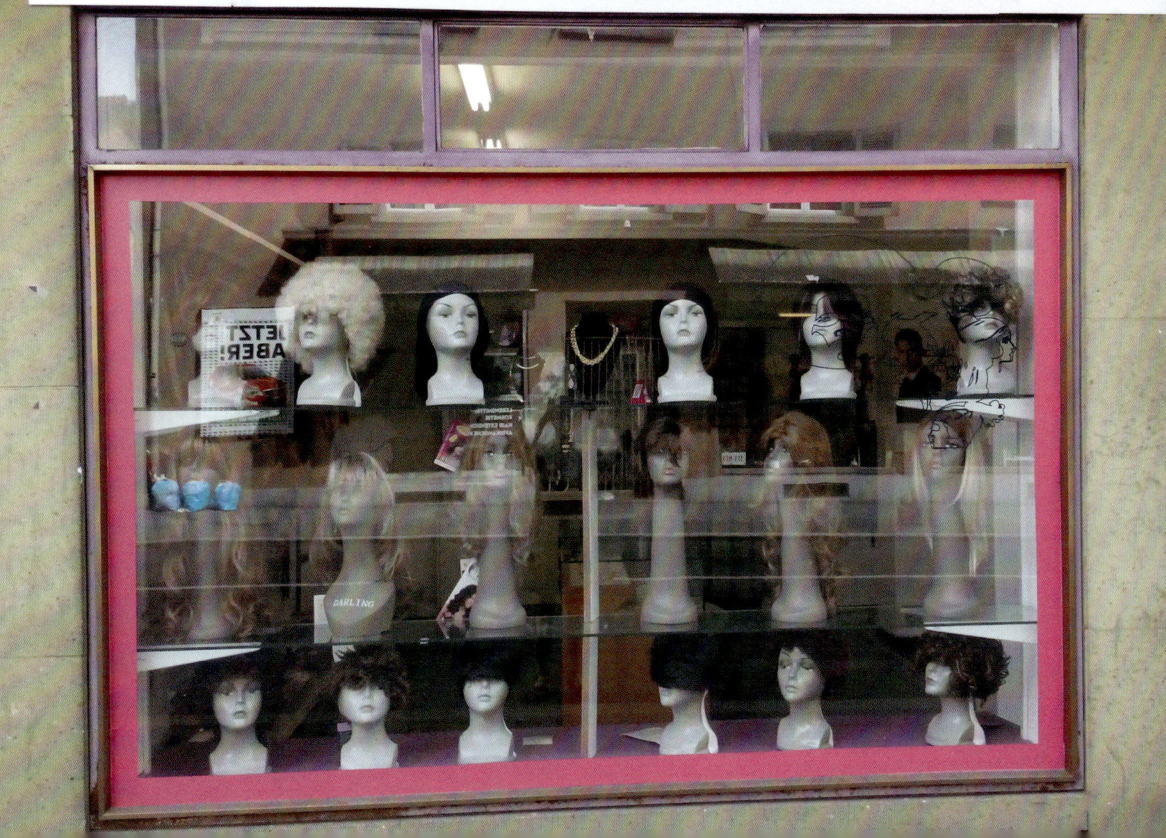
SALON AFRO-EUROPA
DARLING

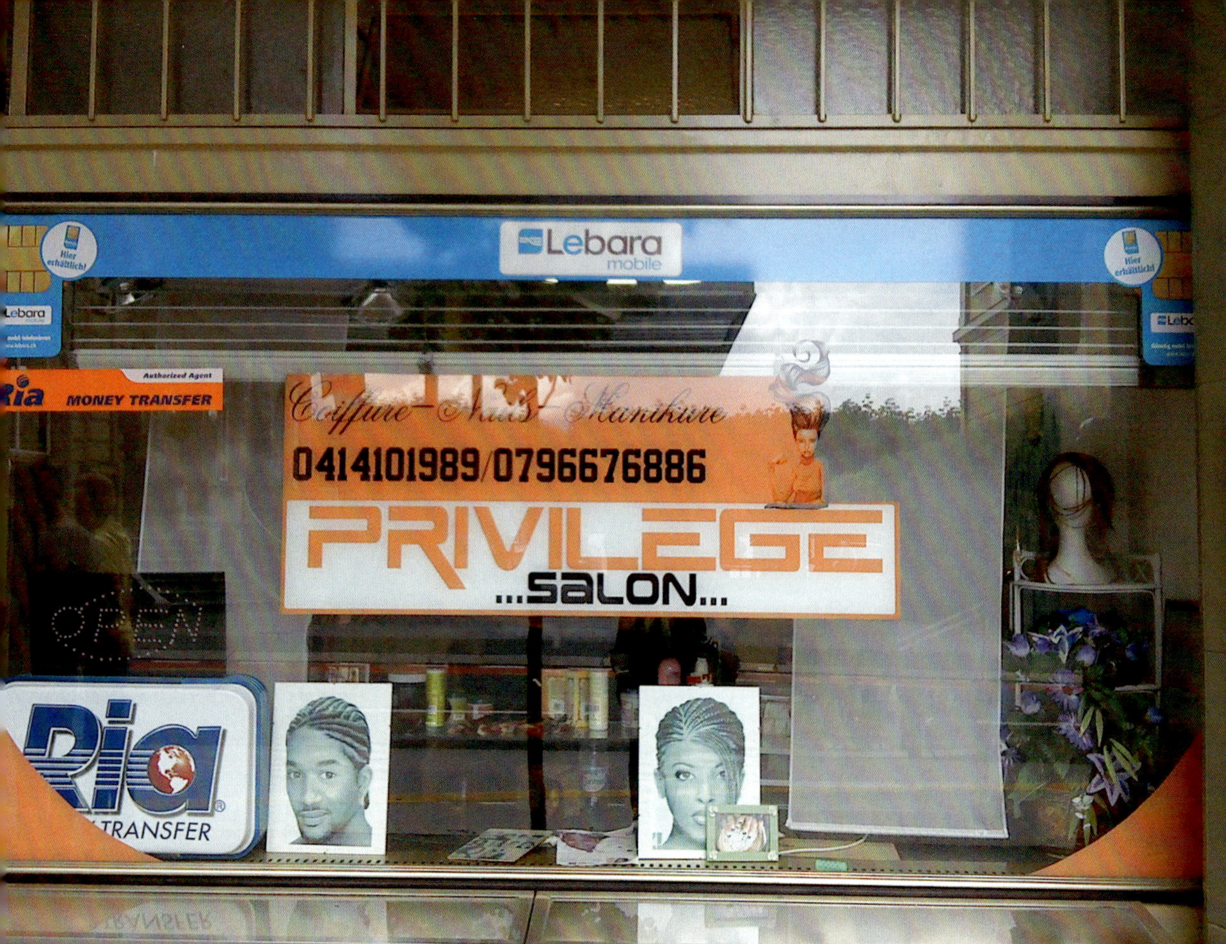
Lebara
mobile
Authorized Agent
Ria MONEY TRANSFER
Coiffure–Nails–Manikure
0414101989/0796676886
PRIVILEGE
...SALON...
Ria
TRANSFER

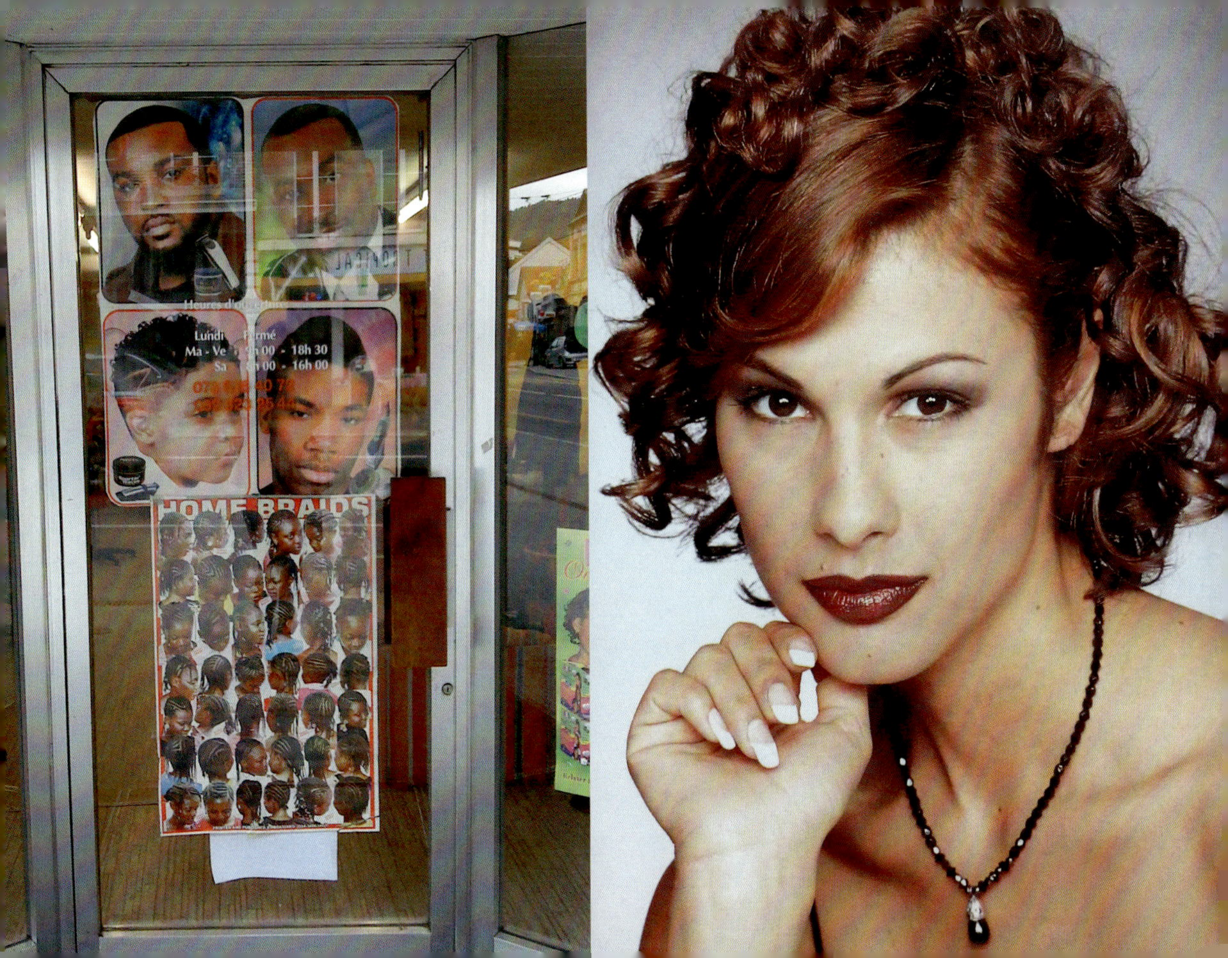
Lundi
Ma - Ve
18h 30
Sa
16h 00
HOME BRAIDS

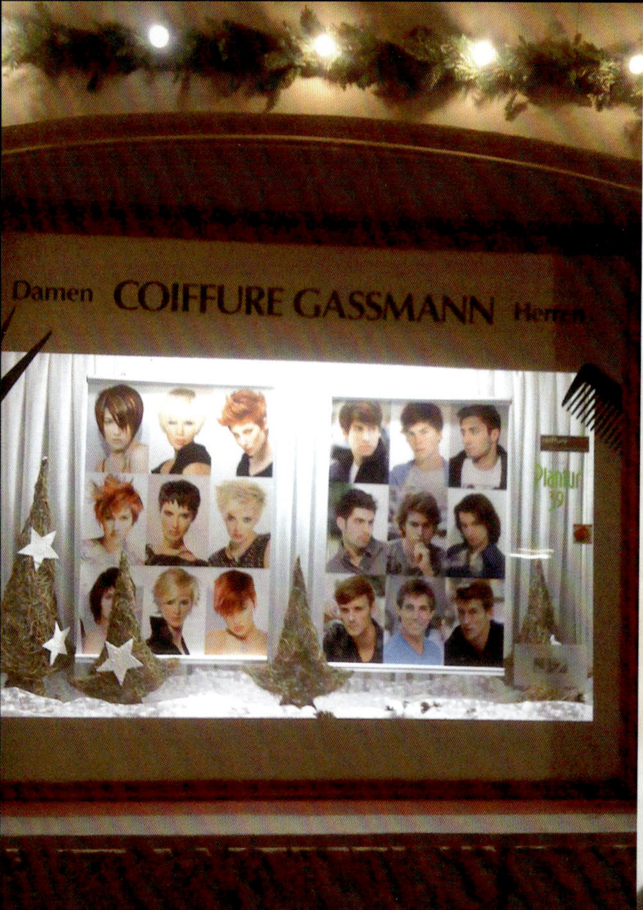

Damen COIFFURE GASSMANN Herren

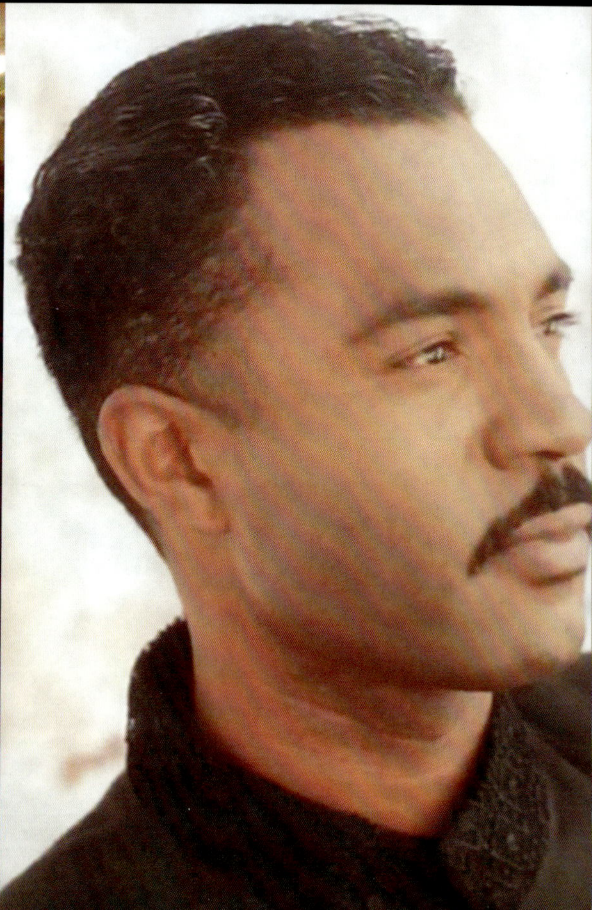

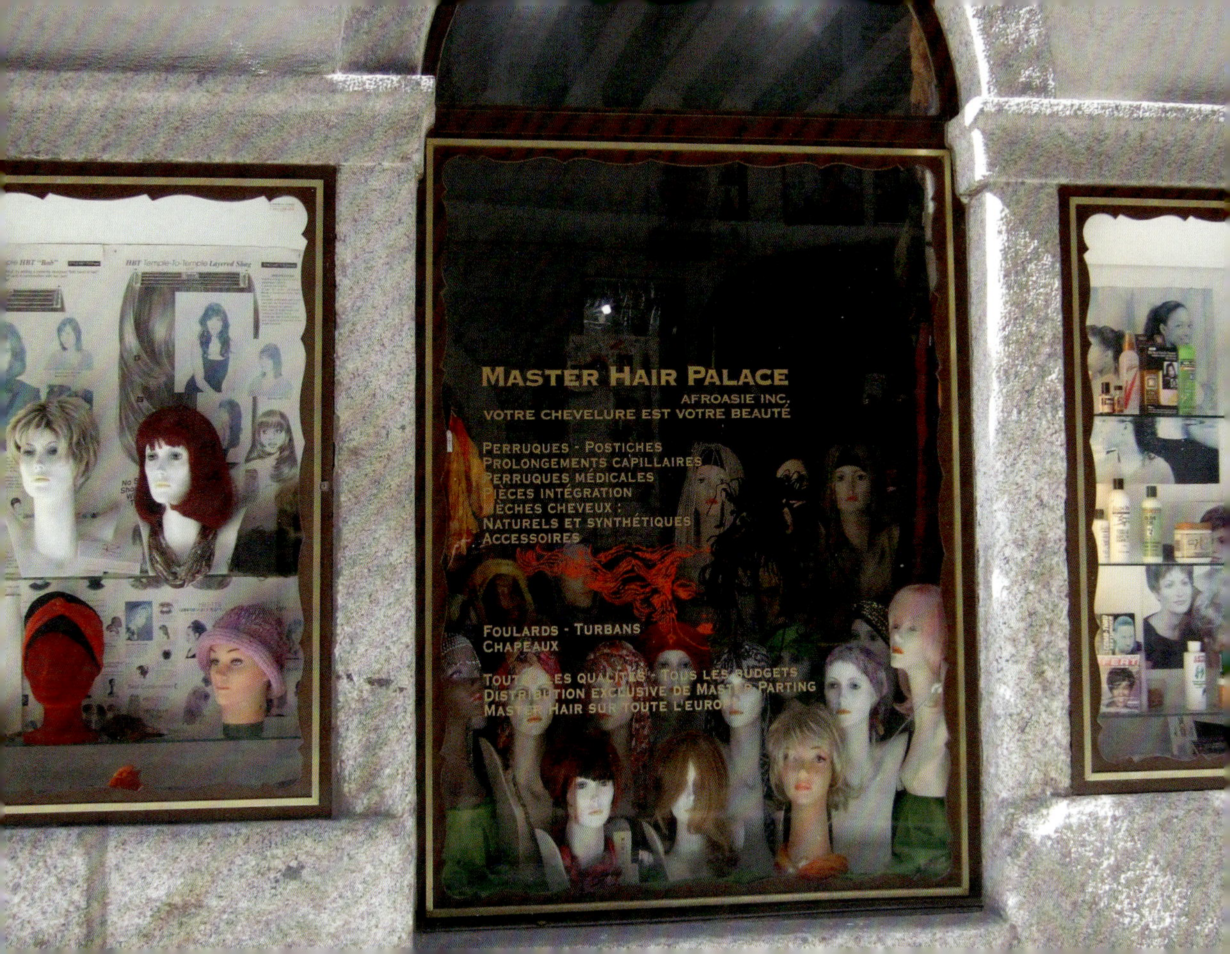
MASTER HAIR PALACE
AFROASIE INC.
VOTRE CHEVELURE EST VOTRE BEAUTÉ
PERRUQUES - POSTICHES
PROLONGEMENTS CAPILLAIRES
PERRUQUES MÉDICALES
PIÈCES INTÉGRATION
MÈCHES CHEVEUX :
NATURELS ET SYNTHÉTIQUES
ACCESSOIRES
FOULARDS - TURBANS
CHAPEAUX

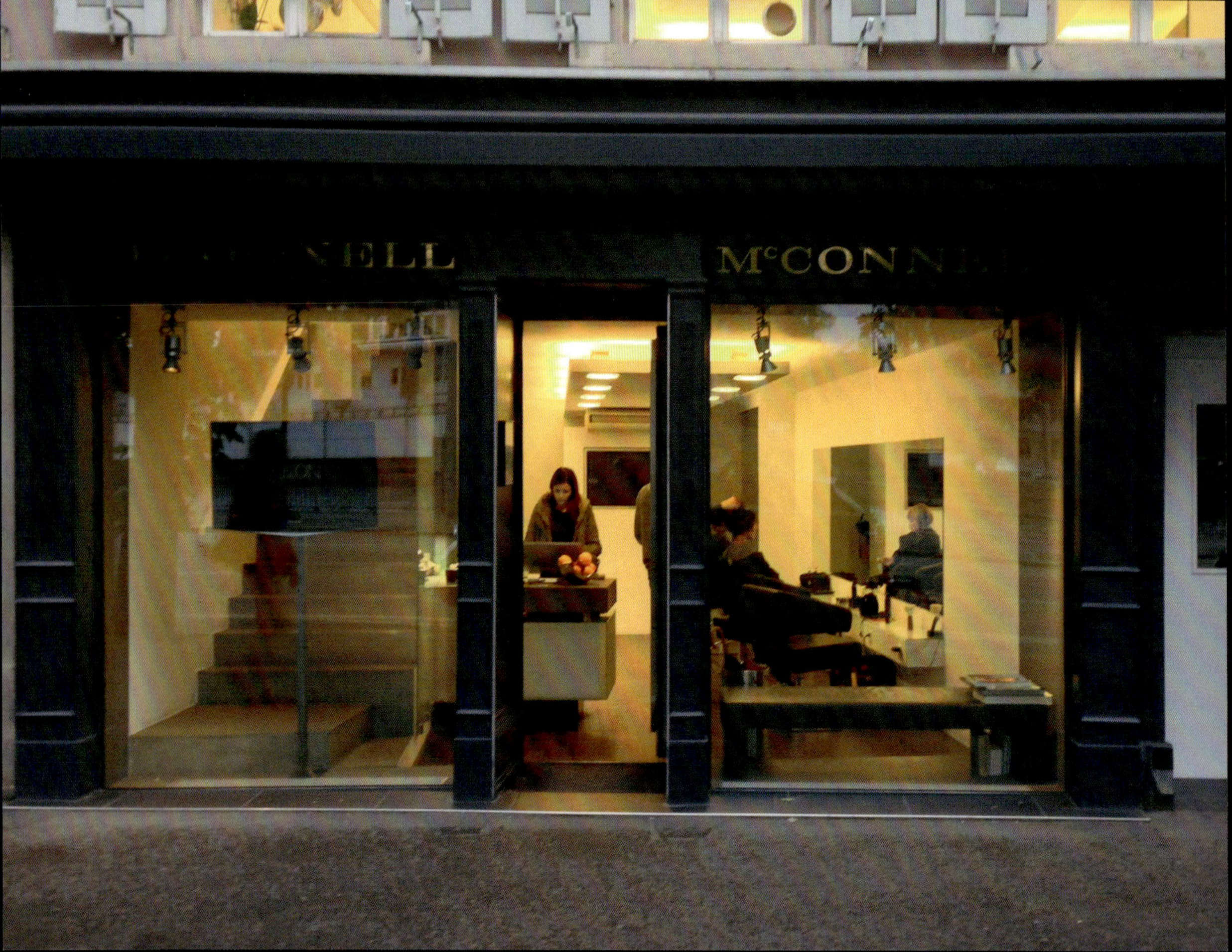

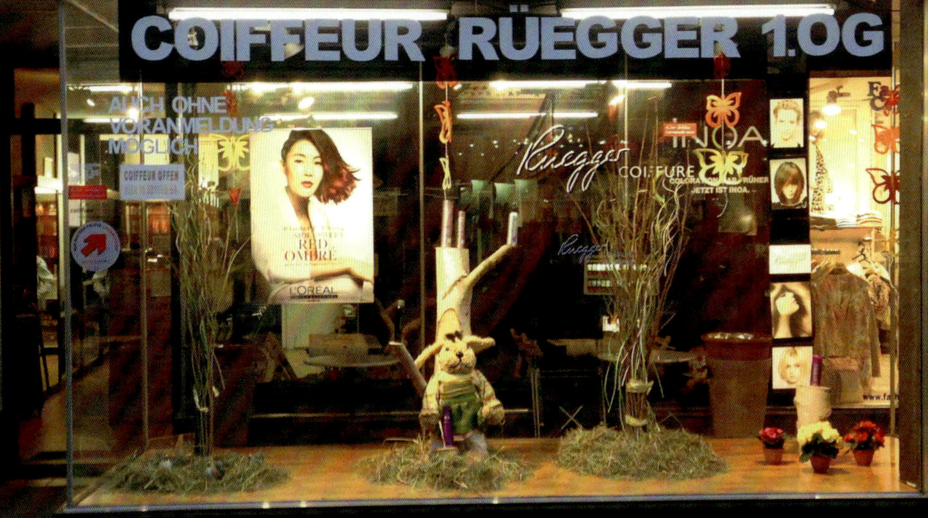
RUEGGER
COIFFEUR RÜEGGER 1.OG
AUCH OHNE
VORANMELDUNG
MÖGLICH
COIFFEUR OFFEN
Ruegger
COIFFURE
INOA
RED
OMBRE
L'OREAL

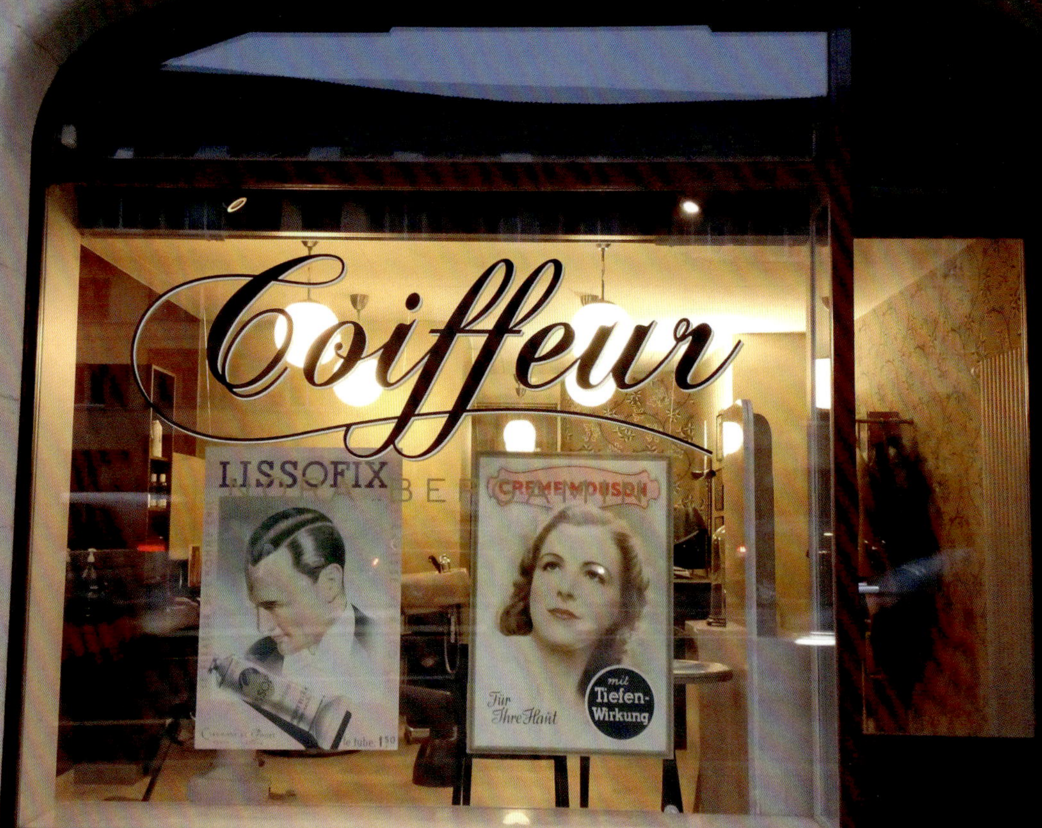
Coiffeur
LISSOFIX
CREME MOUSON
Für Ihre Haut
mit Tiefen-Wirkung

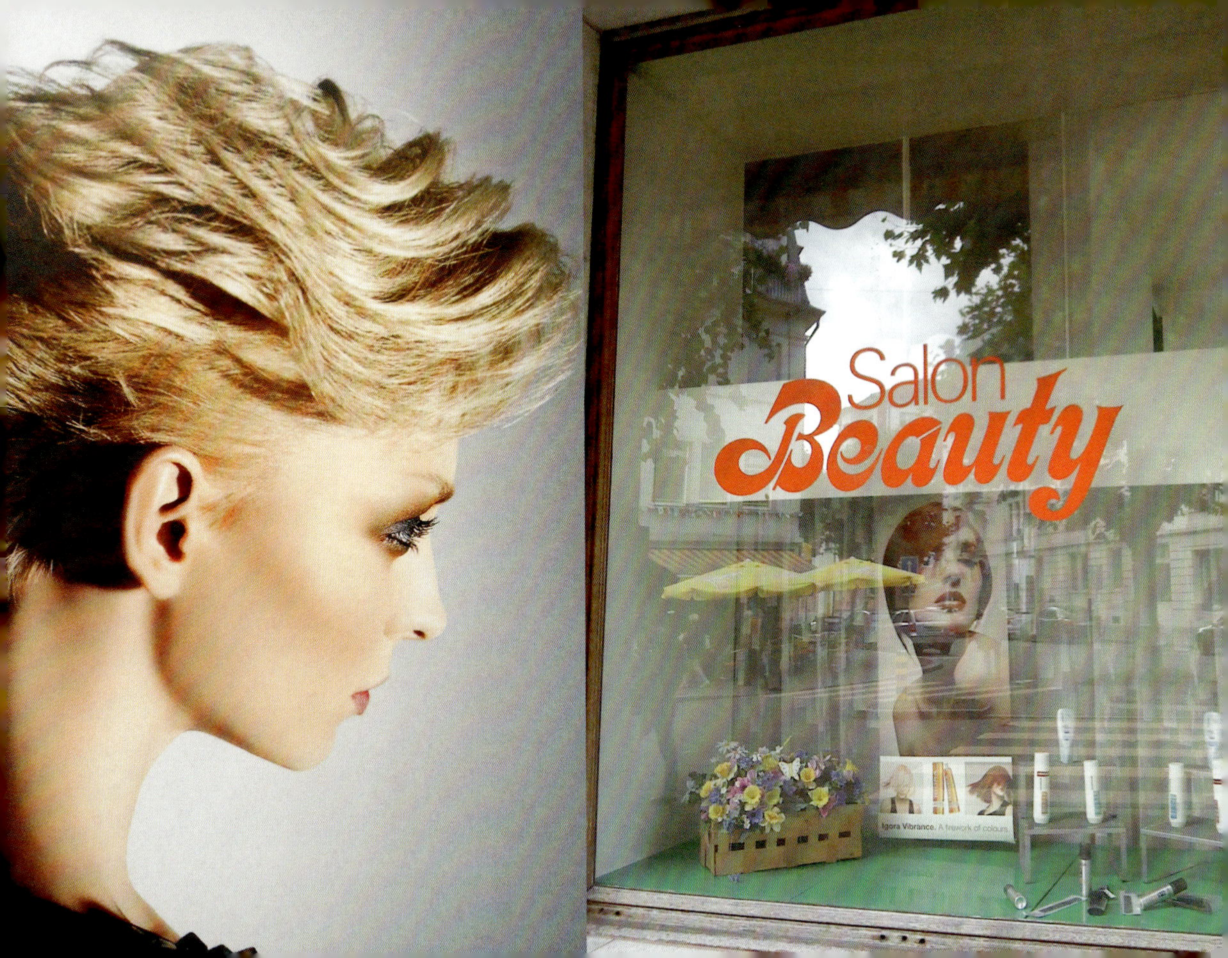

Salon
Beauty
Igora Vibrance.

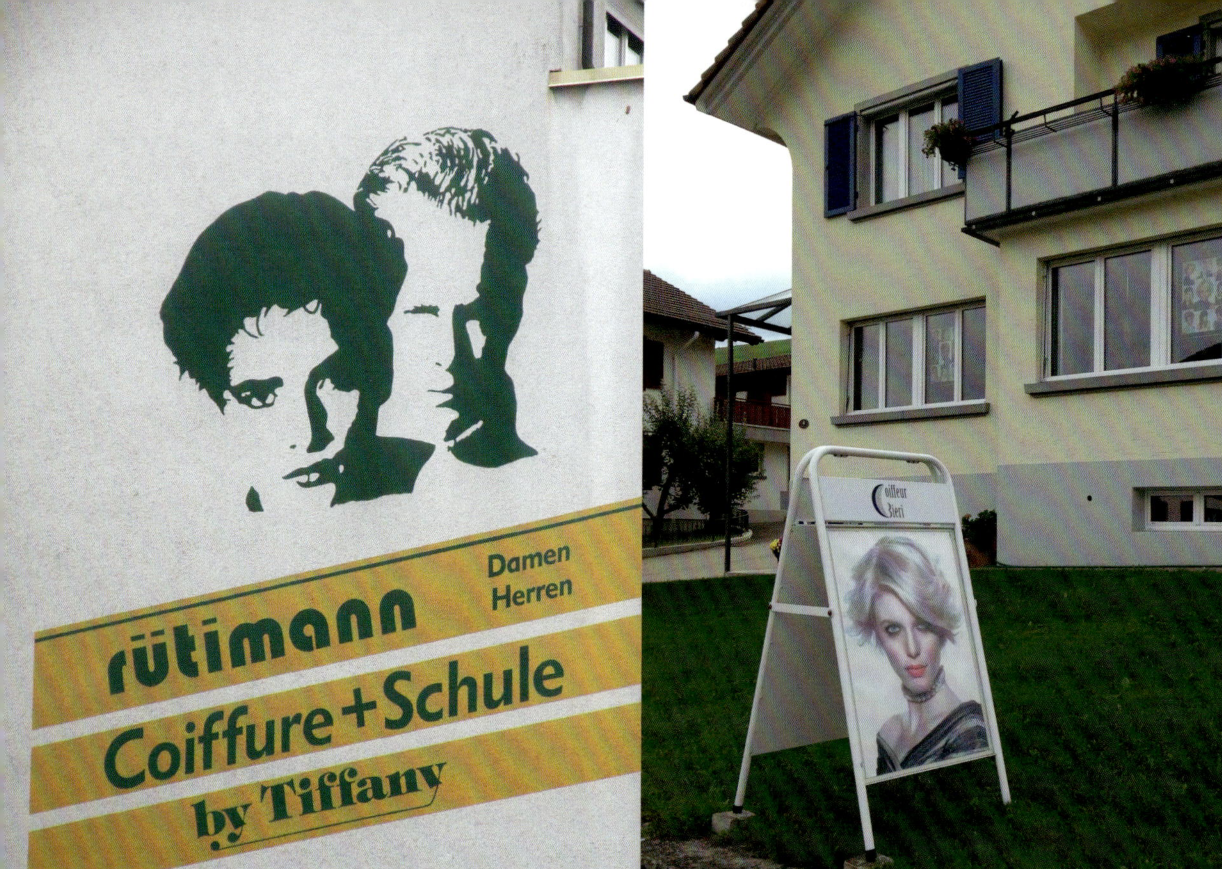
Damen
Herren
rütimann
Coiffure + Schule
by Tiffany
Coiffeur
Bieri

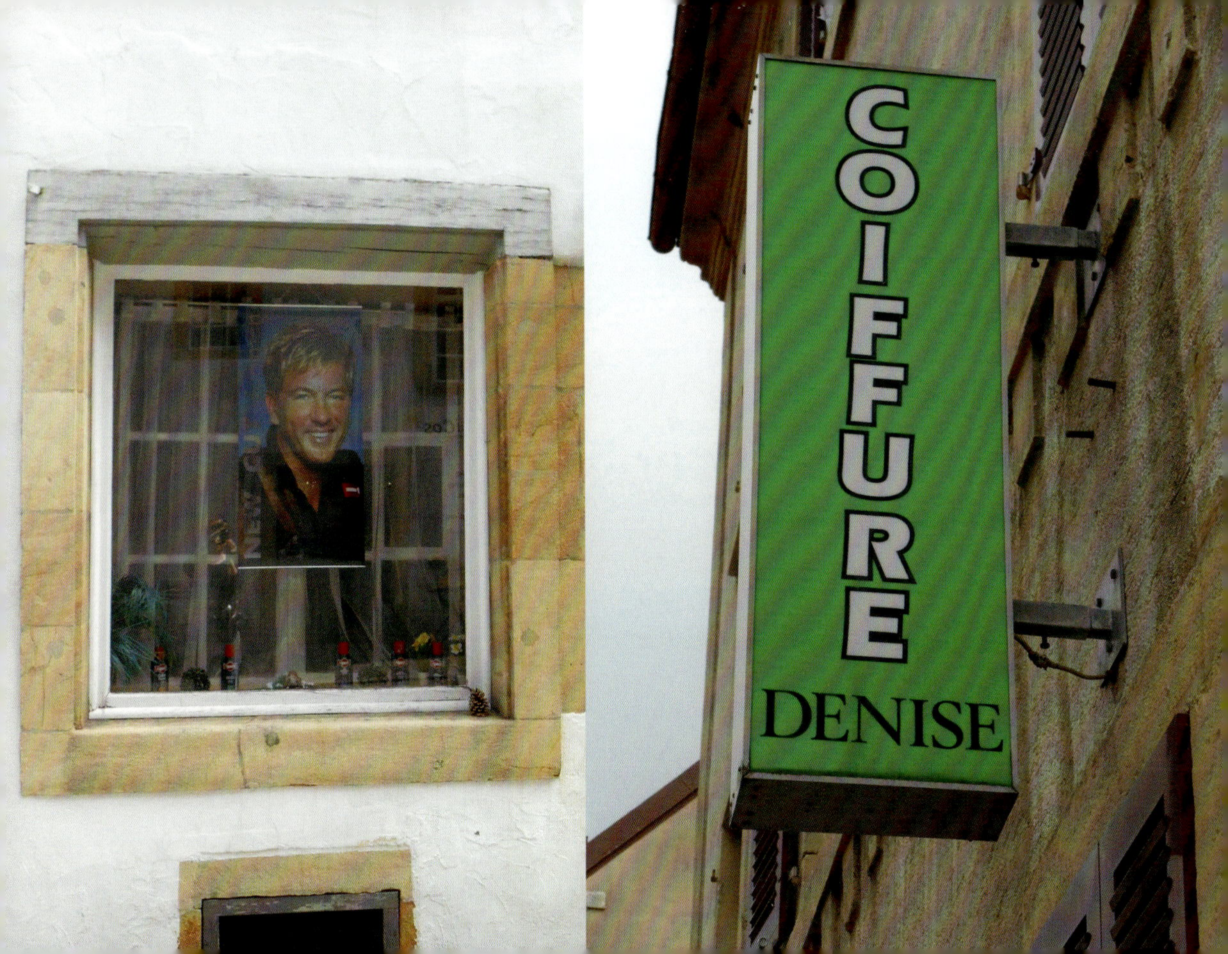
COIFFURE
DENISE

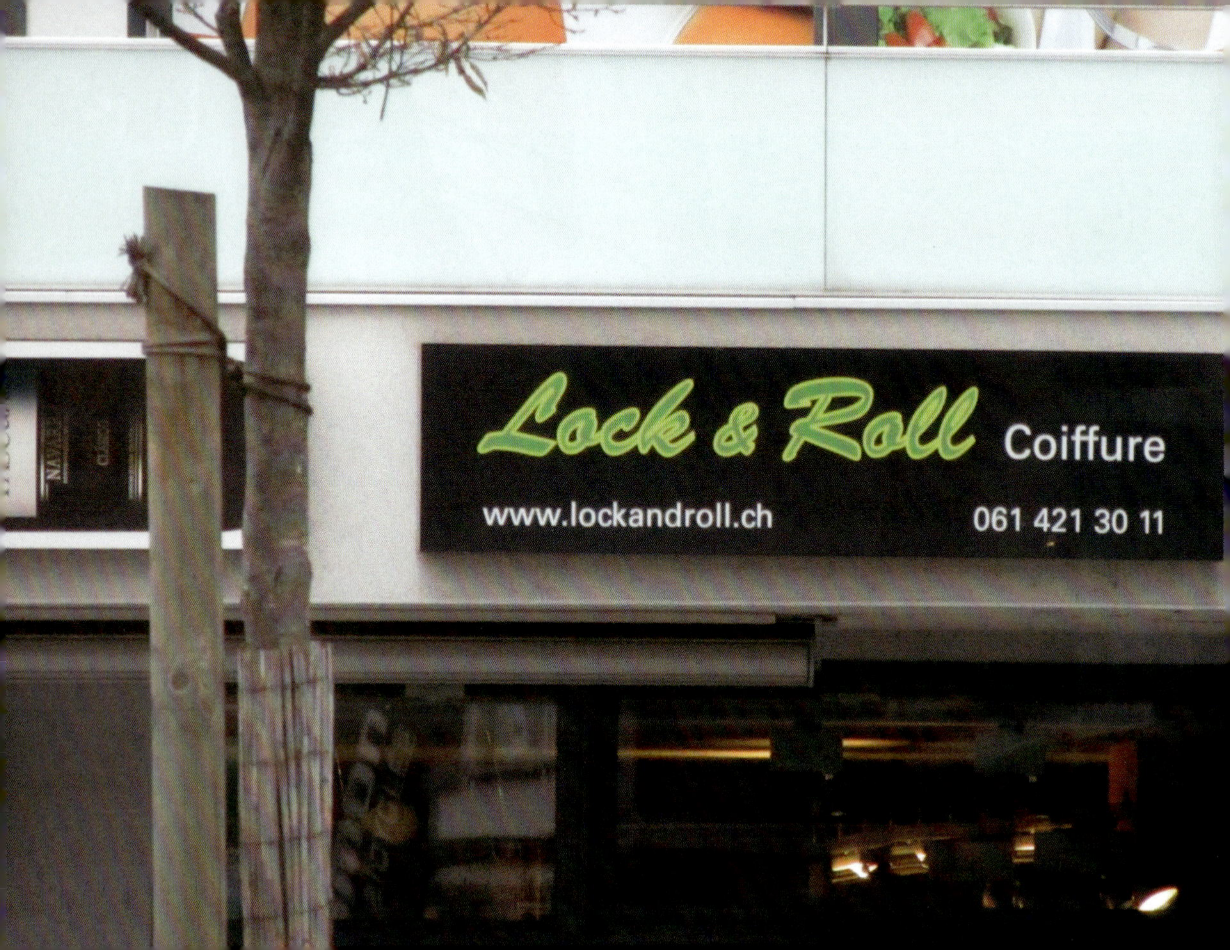
Lock & Roll
Coiffure
www.lockandroll.ch
061 421 30 11

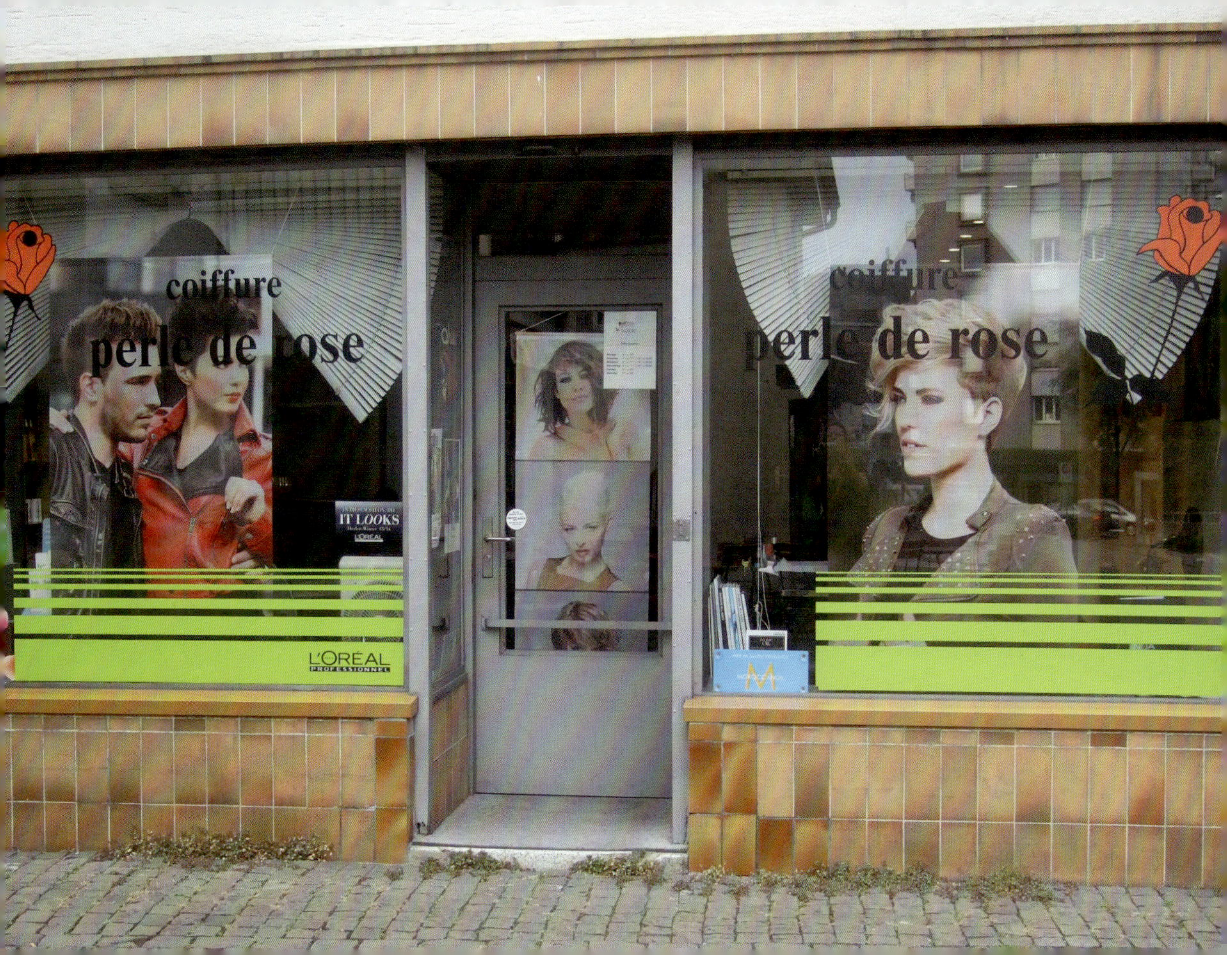

coiffure
perle de rose
IT LOOKS
L'ORÉAL
L'ORÉAL
PROFESSIONNEL
coiffure
perle de rose

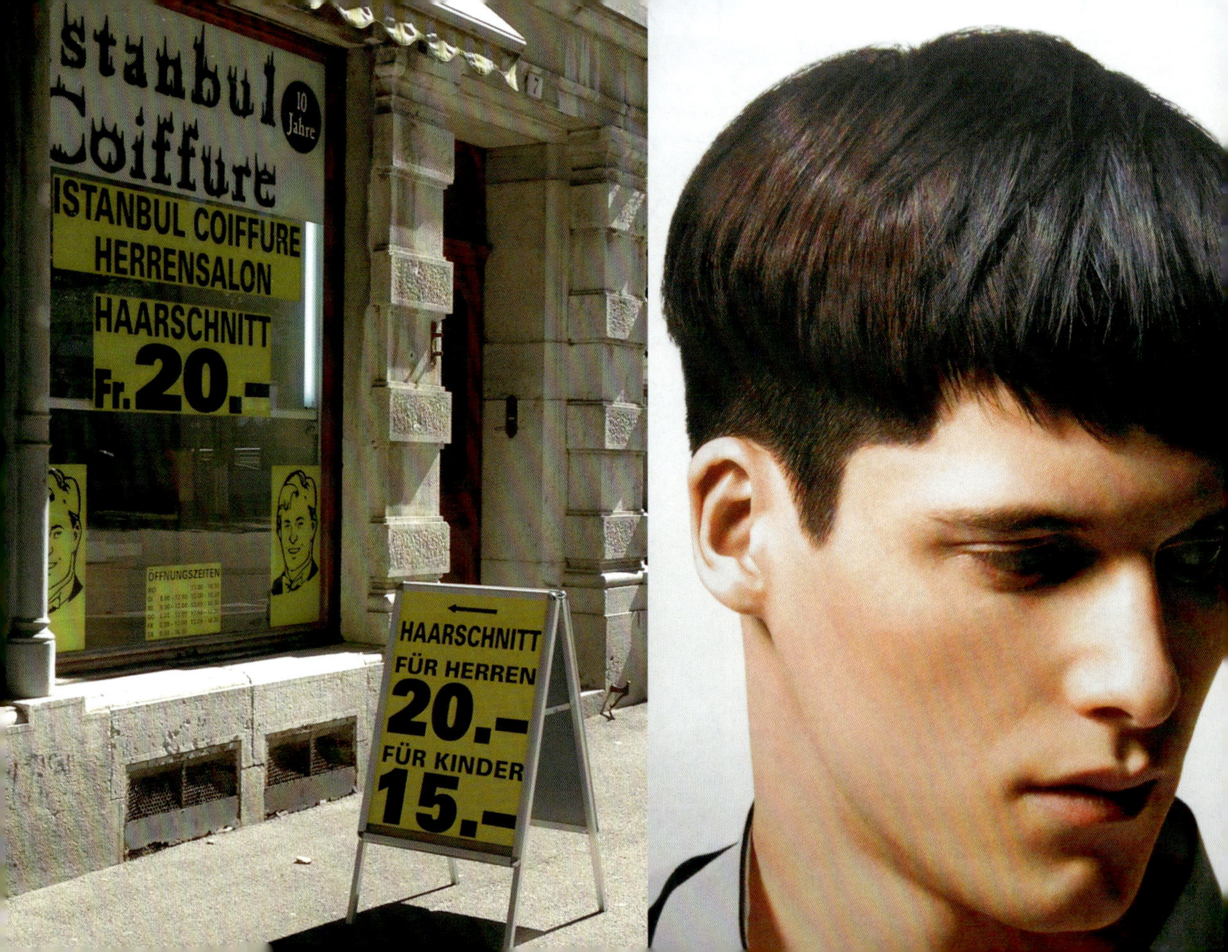
Istanbul Coiffure
10 Jahre
ISTANBUL COIFFURE
HERRENSALON
HAARSCHNITT
Fr. 20.–
HAARSCHNITT
FÜR HERREN
20.–
FÜR KINDER
15.–

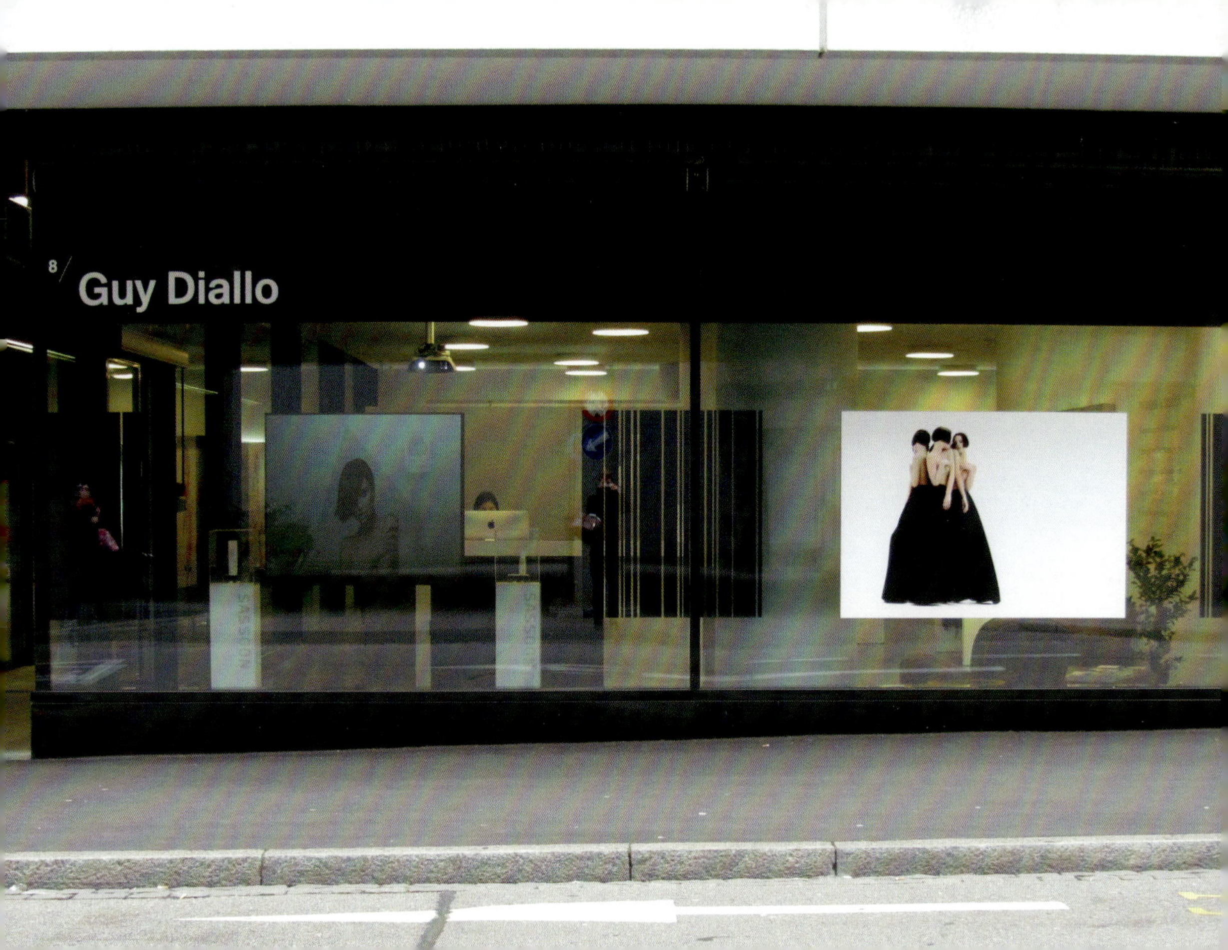
8 /
Guy Diallo

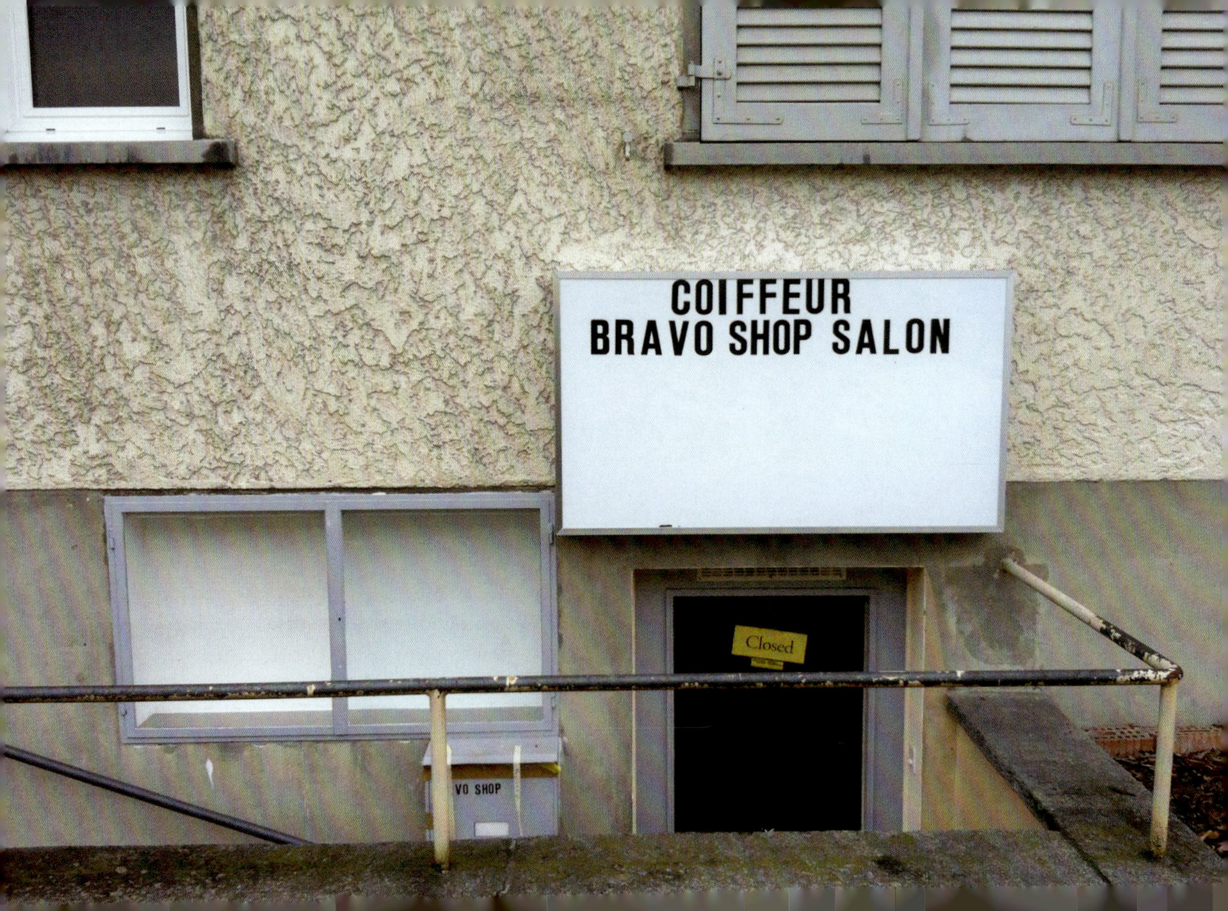
COIFFEUR
BRAVO SHOP SALON
Closed
VO SHOP

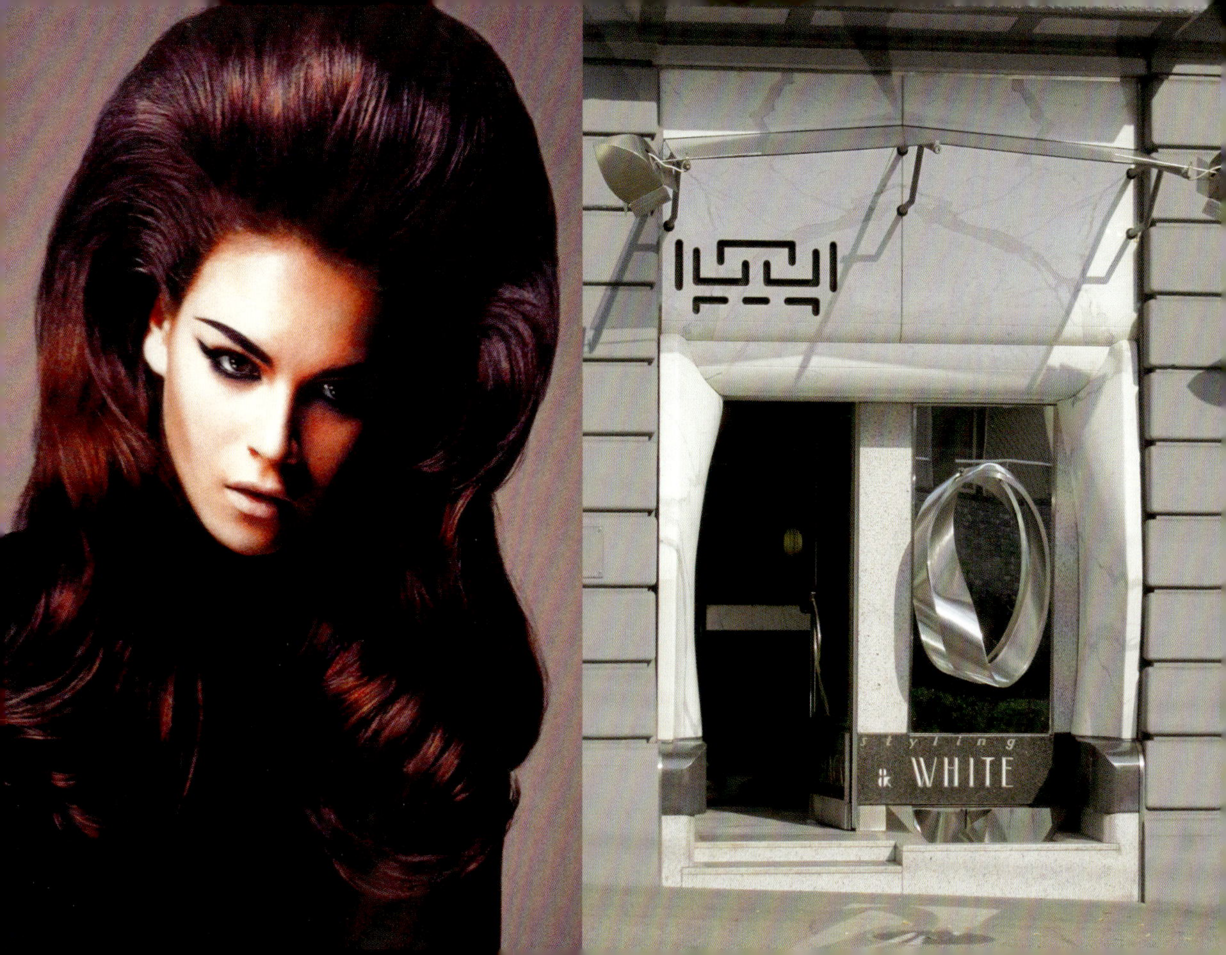
styling
WHITE

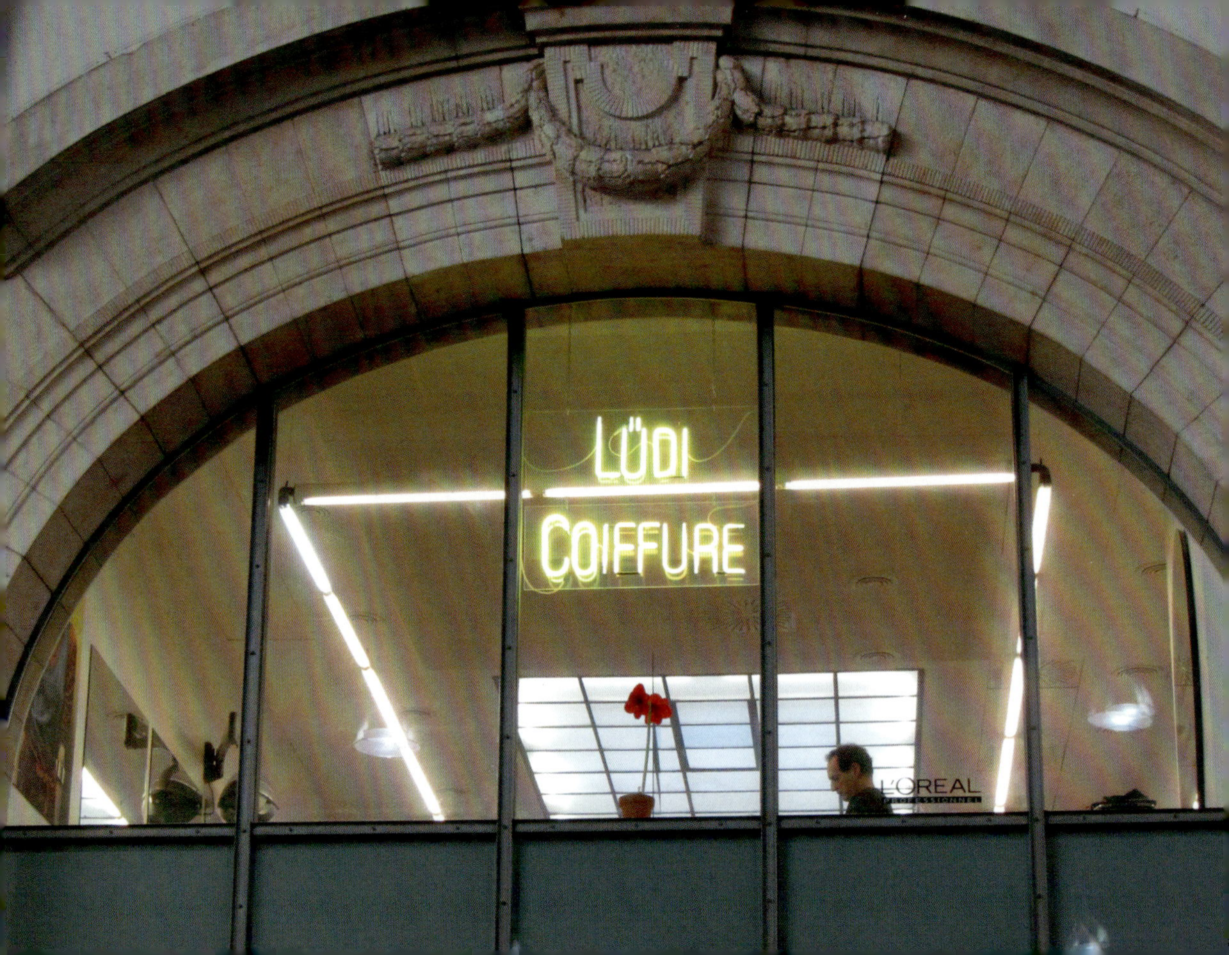
LÜDI
COIFFURE
L'OREAL

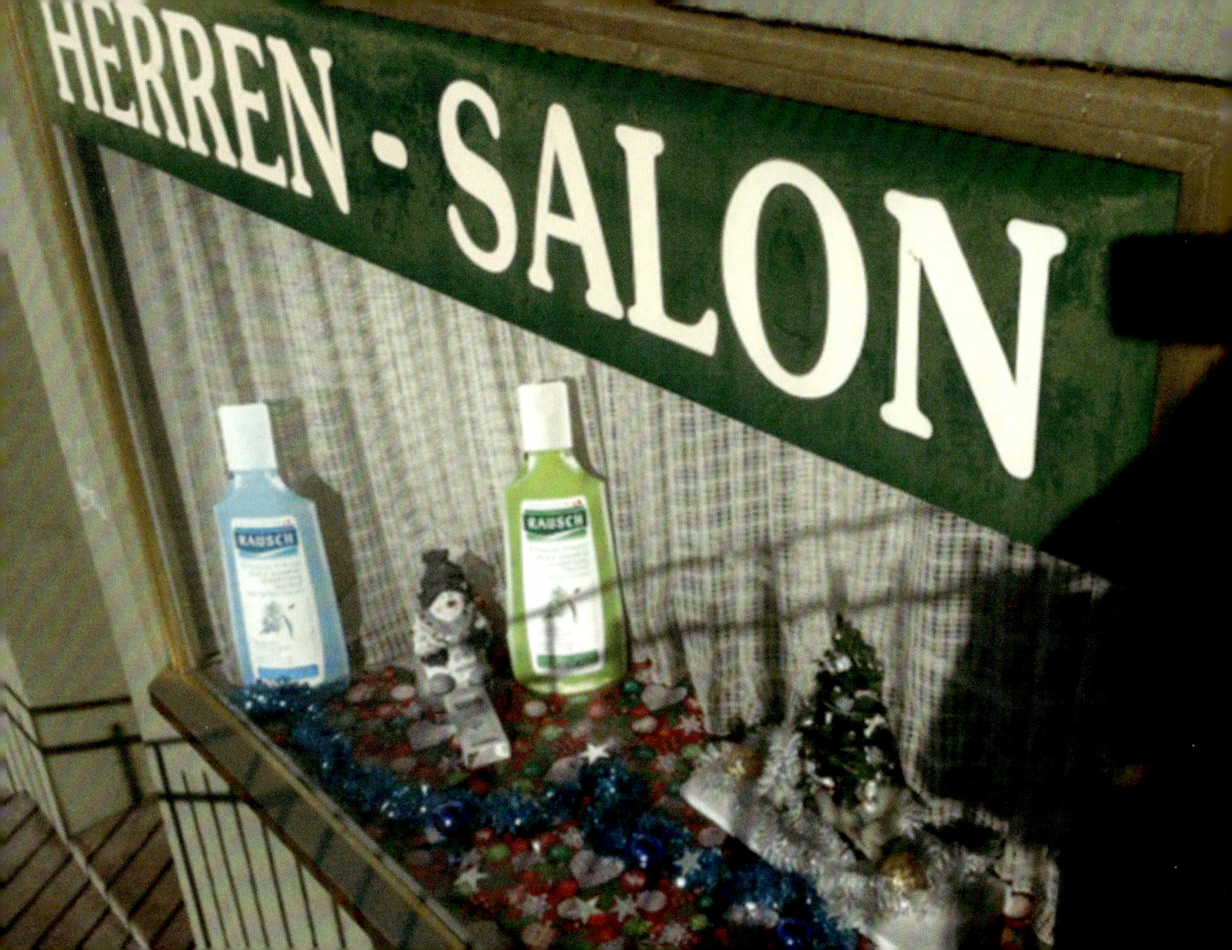
HERREN-SALON

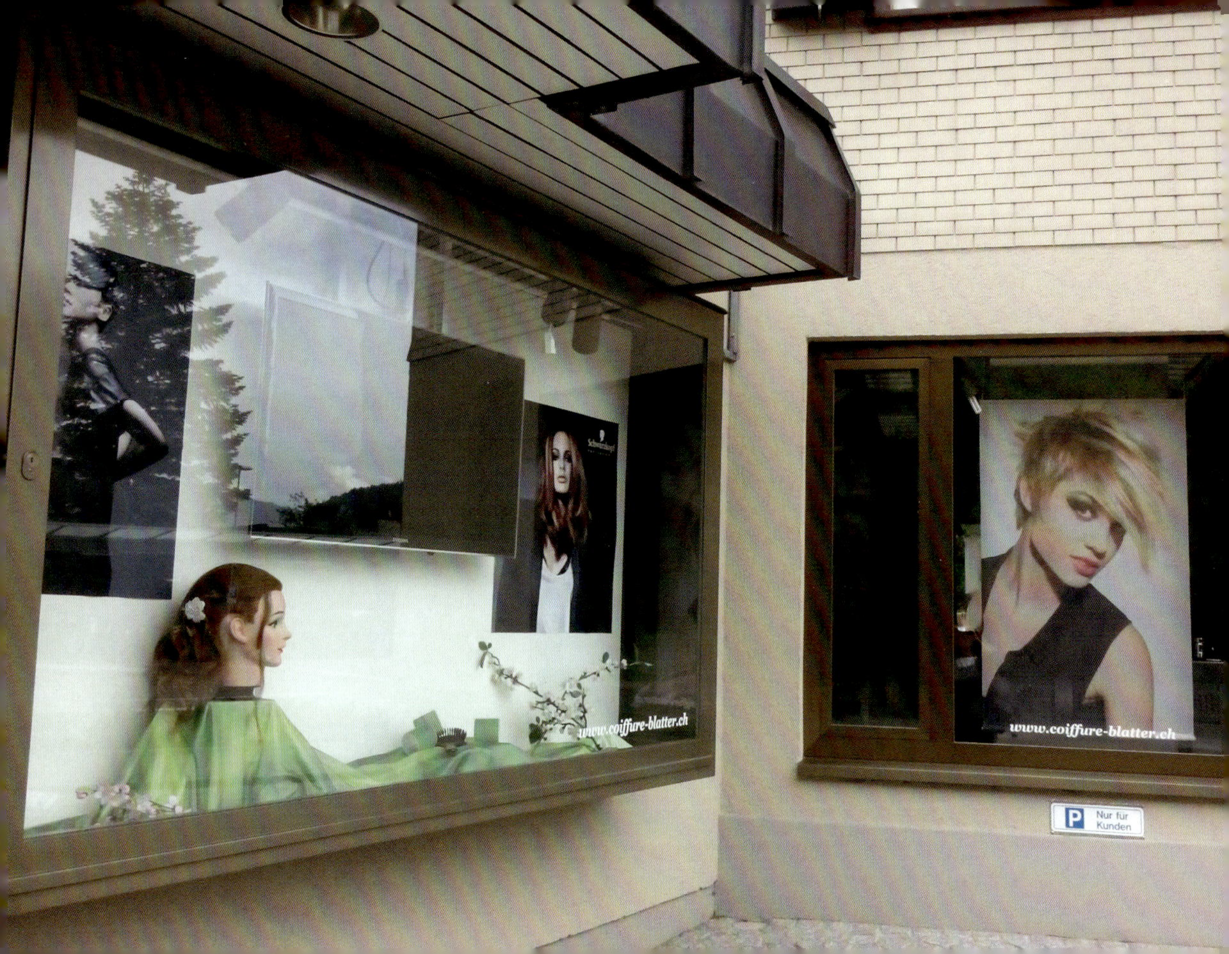
www.coiffure-blatter.ch
www.coiffure-blatter.ch
P
Nur für
Kunden

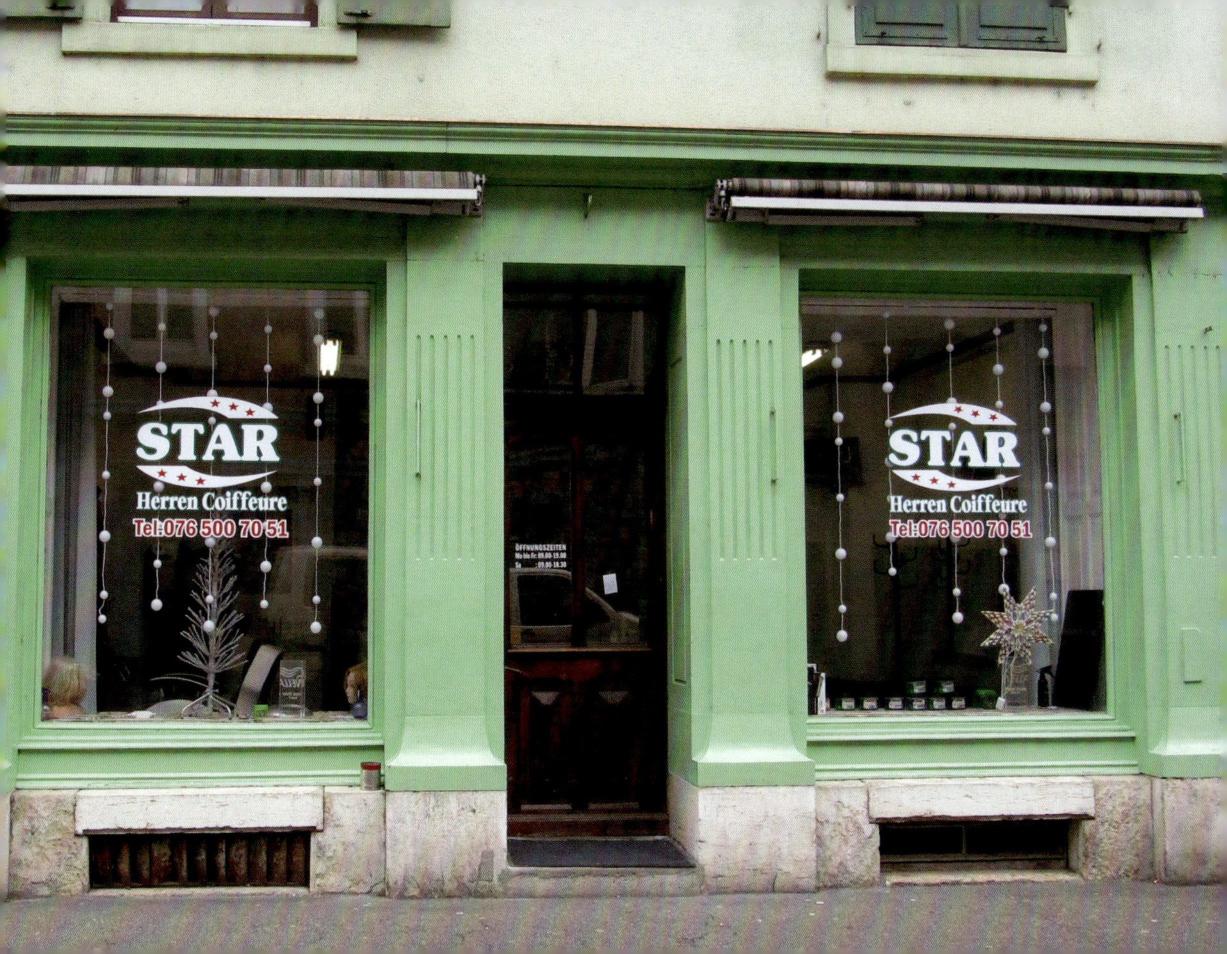
STAR
Herren Coiffeure
Tel:076 500 70 51
ÖFFNUNGSZEITEN
STAR
Herren Coiffeure
Tel:076 500 70 51

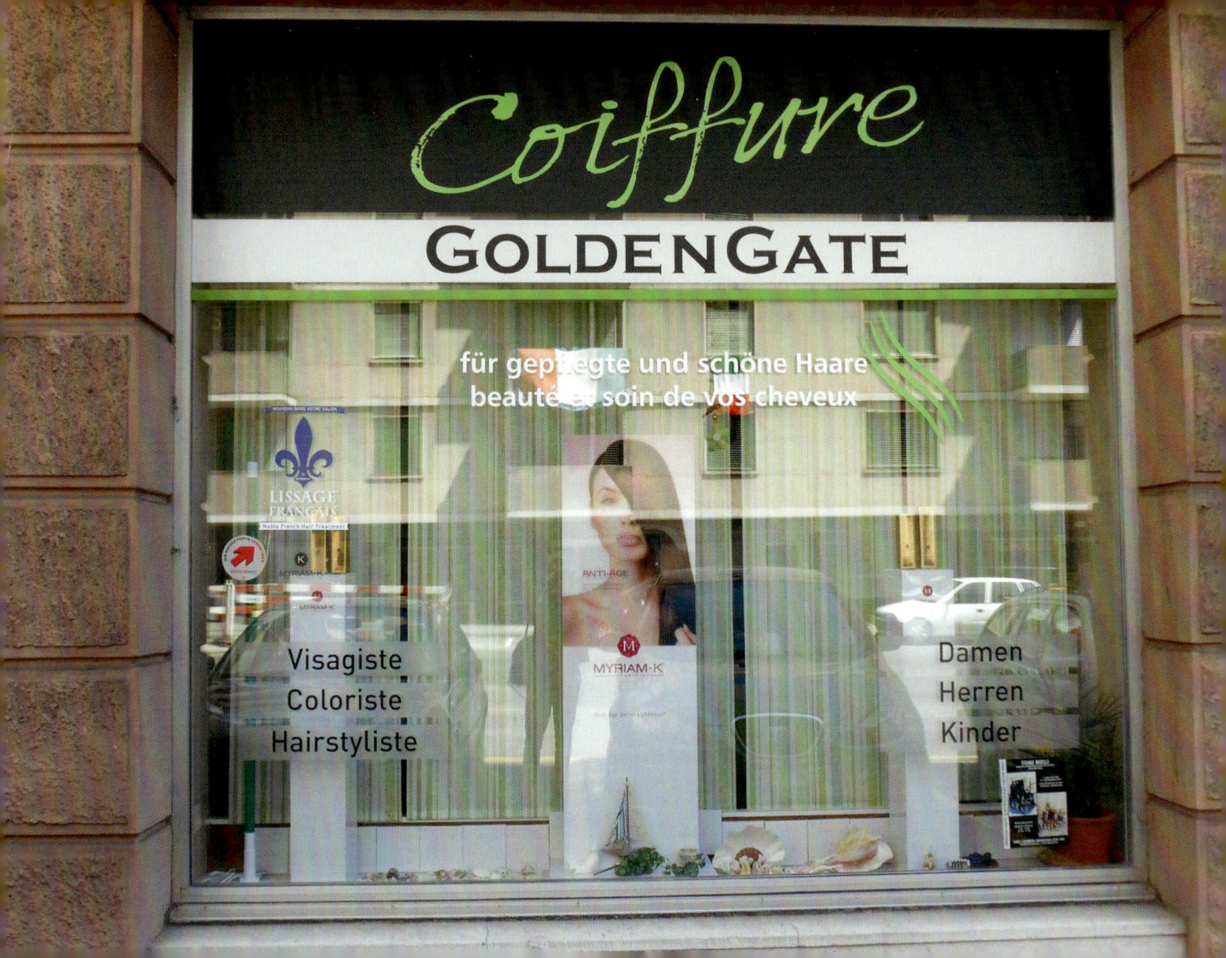

Coiffure

GOLDENGATE

für gepflegte und schöne Haare
beauté et soin de vos cheveux

LISSAGE FRANÇAIS
Noble French Hair Treatment

MYRIAM·K

ANTI-AGE

MYRIAM·K

Visagiste
Coloriste
Hairstyliste

Damen
Herren
Kinder

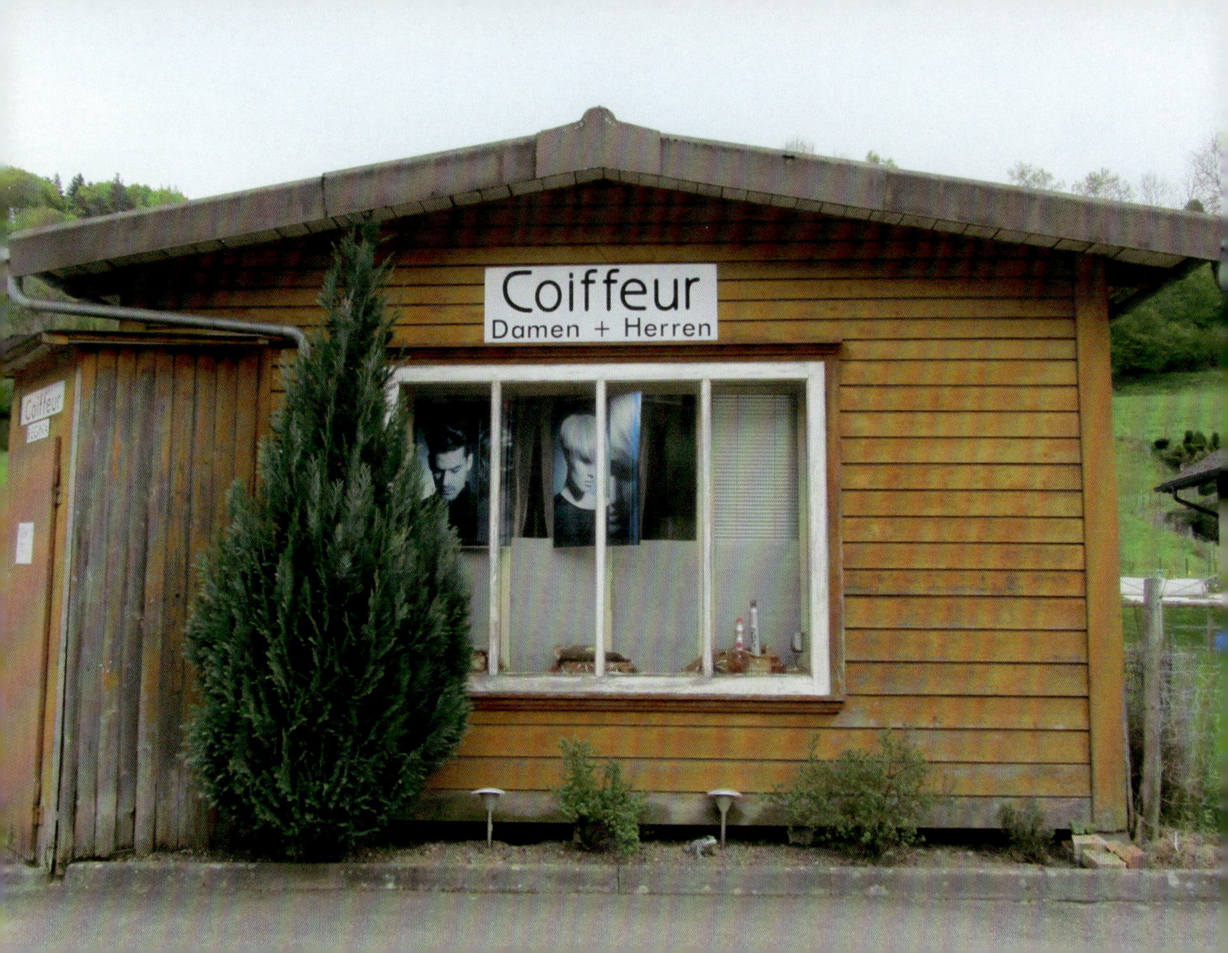
Coiffeur
Damen + Herren
Coiffeur

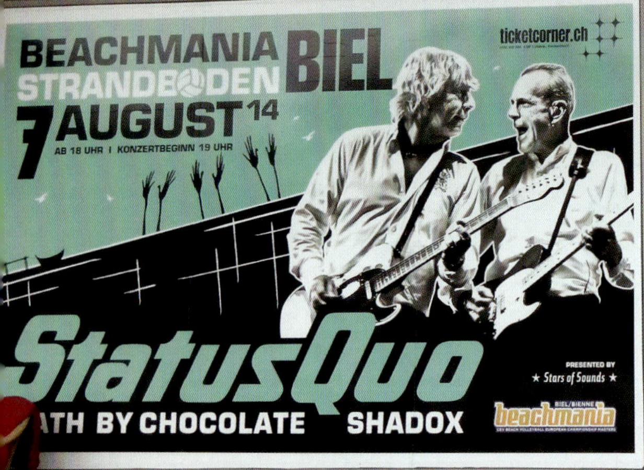
BEACHMANIA BIEL
STRANDBODEN
7 AUGUST 14
AB 18 UHR | KONZERTBEGINN 19 UHR
ticketcorner.ch
StatusQuo
ATH BY CHOCOLATE
SHADOX
PRESENTED BY
★ Stars of Sounds ★
BIEL/BIENNE
beachmania

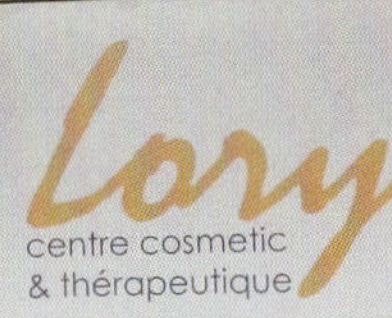
Coiffure
Lory
centre cosmetic
& thérapeutique
50 m
metabolic balance
EOSONIC
Silhouette Sculptor
drainage lymphatique manuel
réflexologie - aromathérapie
manucure - pose d'ongles
soin et massage du corps
soins esthétiques - IPL
extension des cils
rue de la gare 7 2502 bienne tel: 032 341 83 02
info@lorycentrecosmetic.ch - lorycentrecosmetic.ch

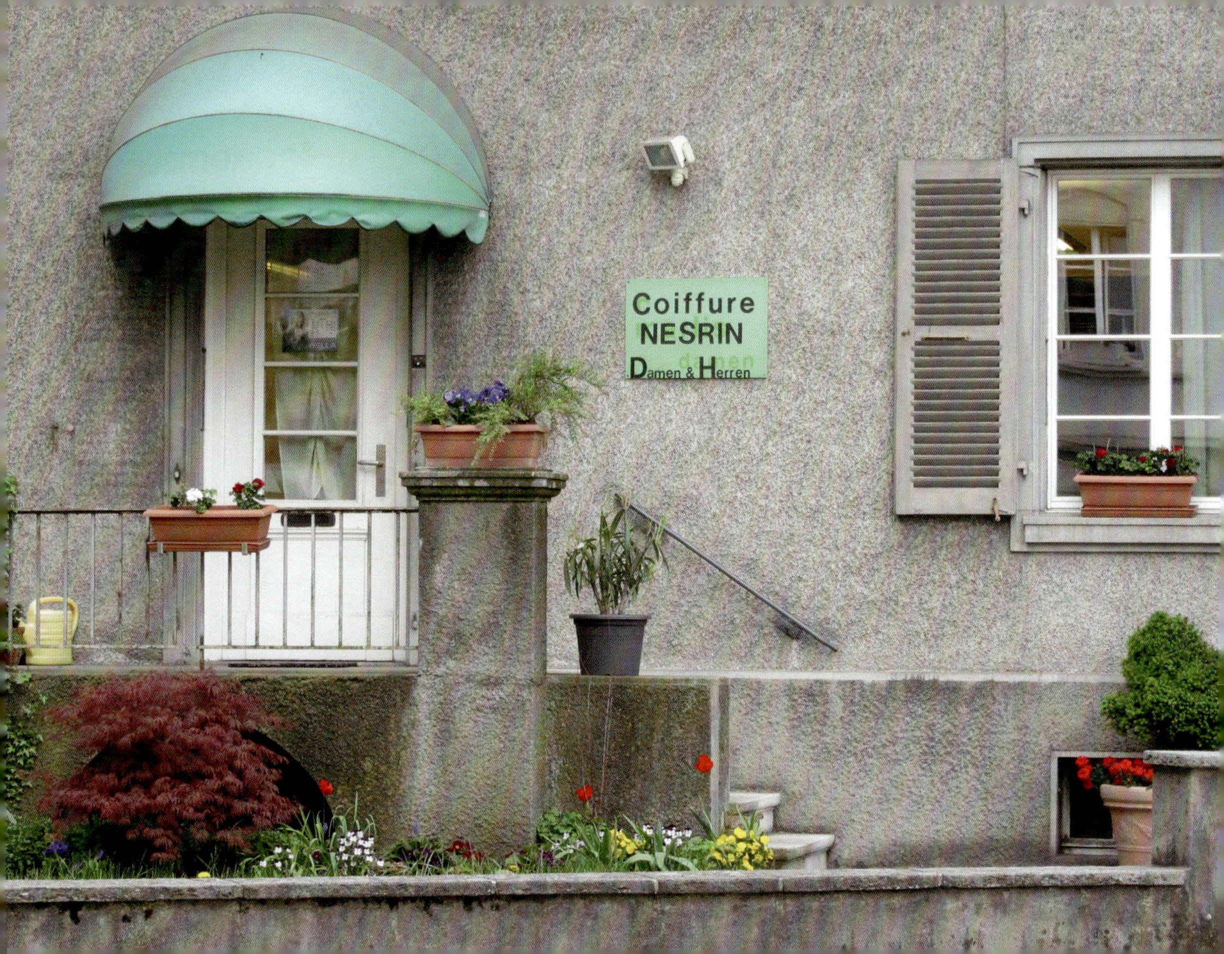
Coiffure
NESRIN
Damen & Herren

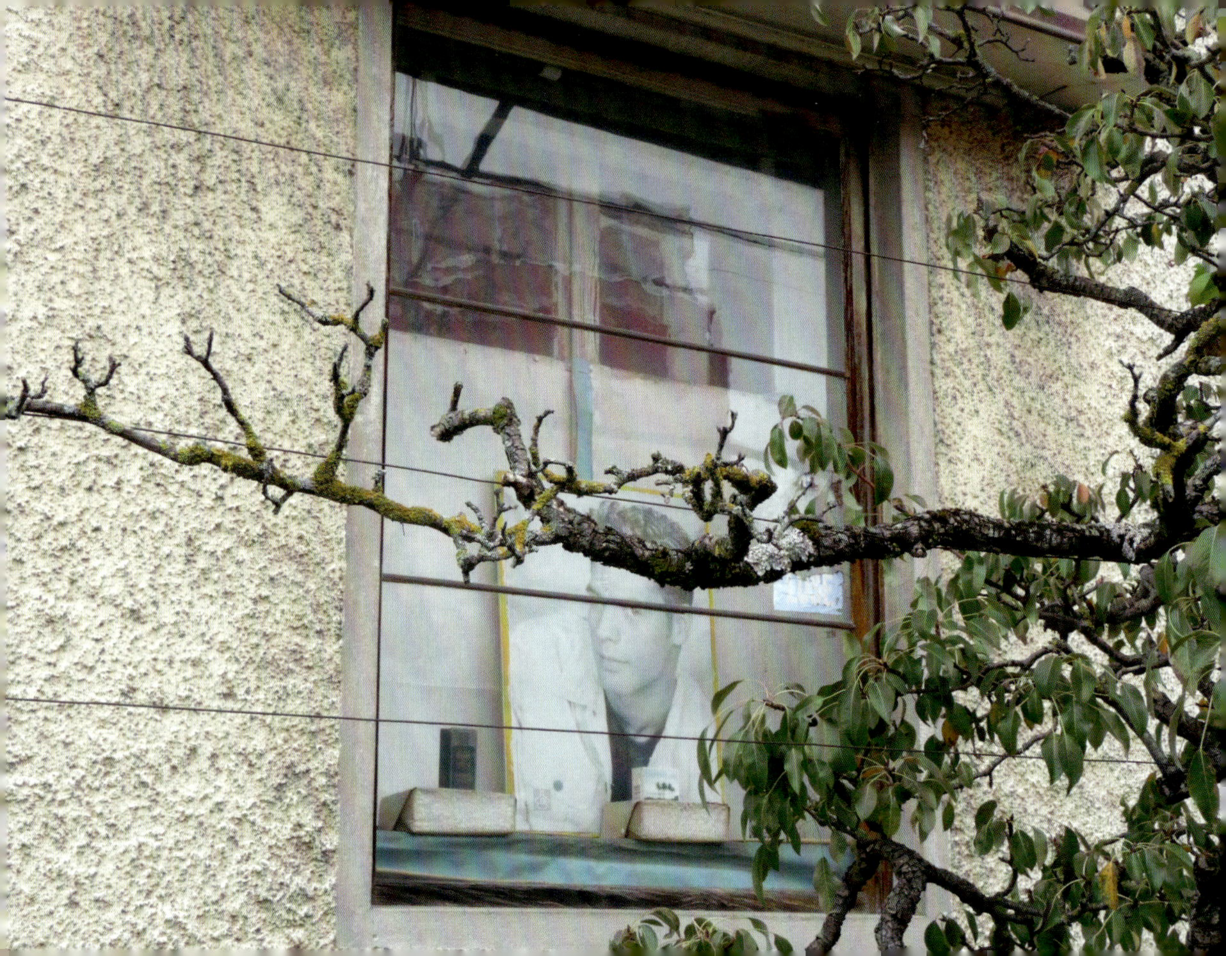

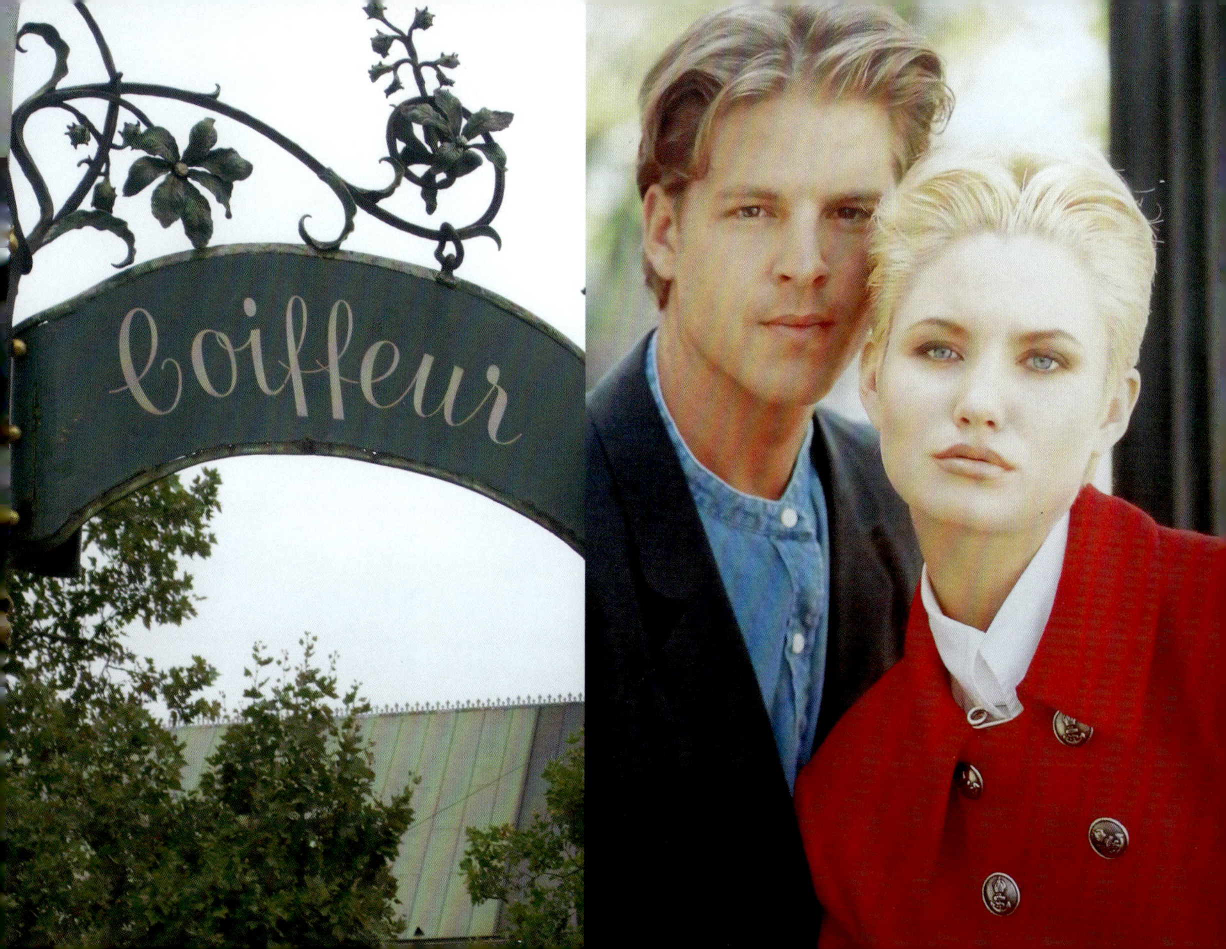
Coiffeur

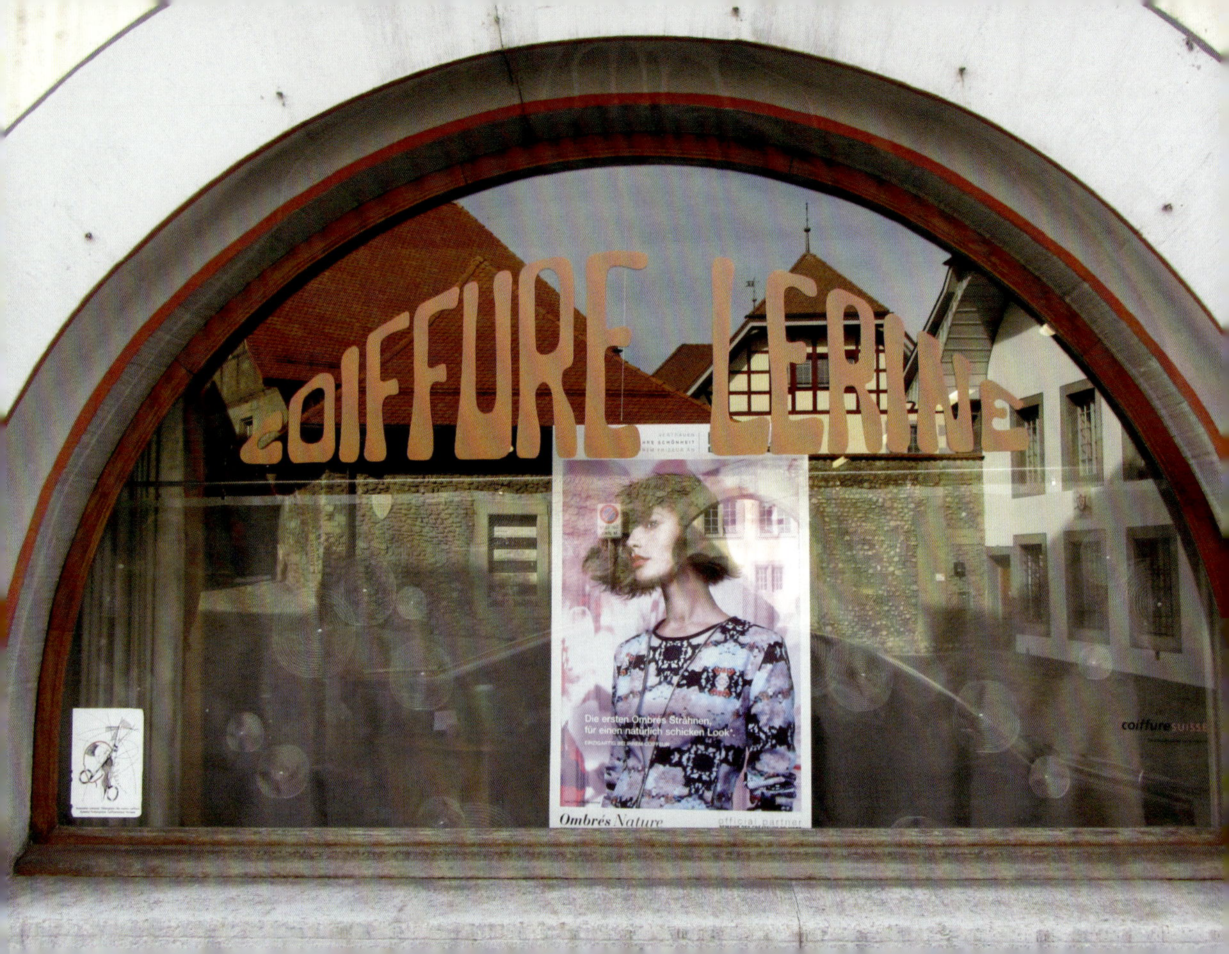
COIFFURE LERINE
Die ersten Ombrés Strähnen,
für einen natürlich schicken Look*.
Ombrés Nature
official partner
coiffureSUISSE

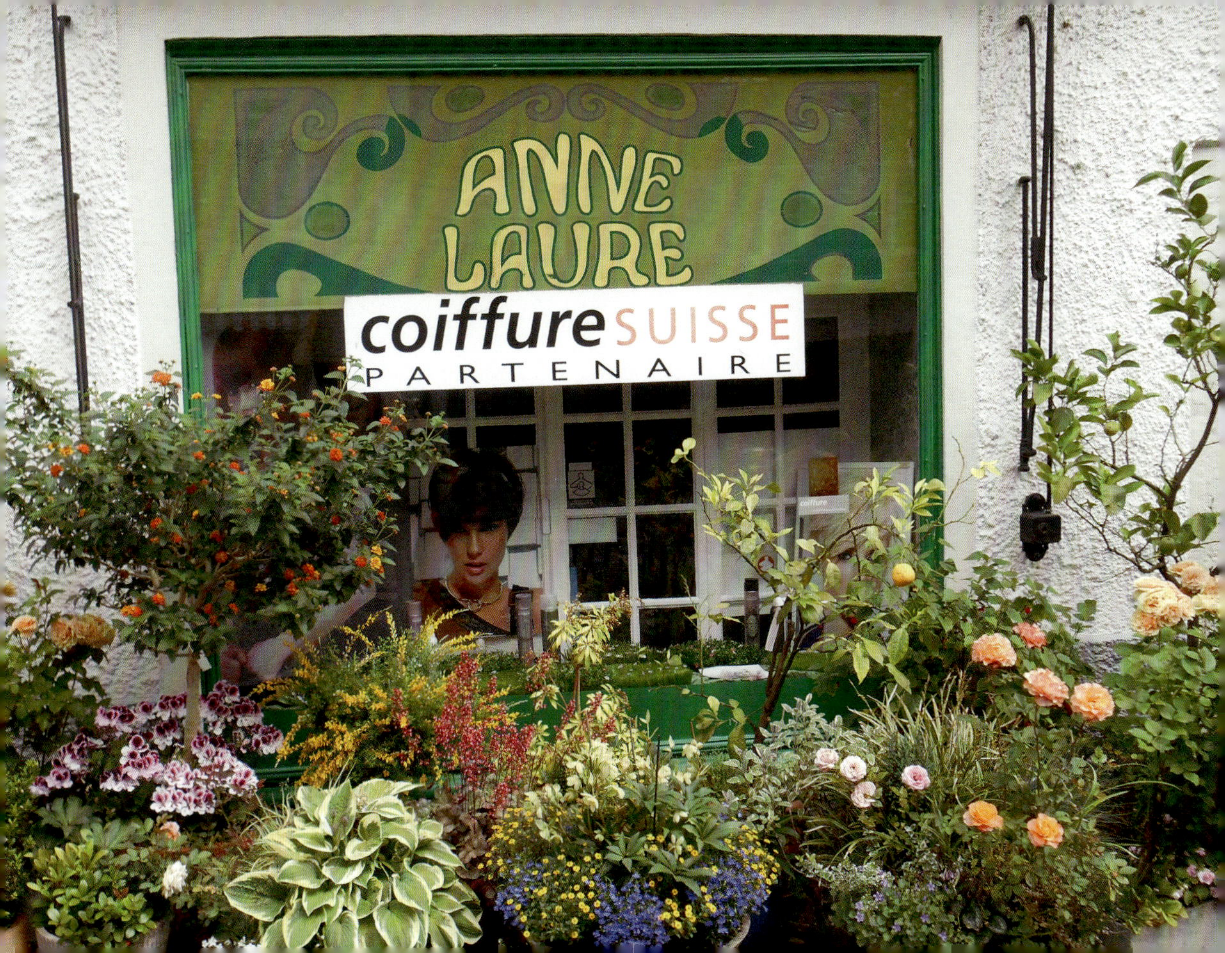
ANNE LAURE
coiffure SUISSE
PARTENAIRE

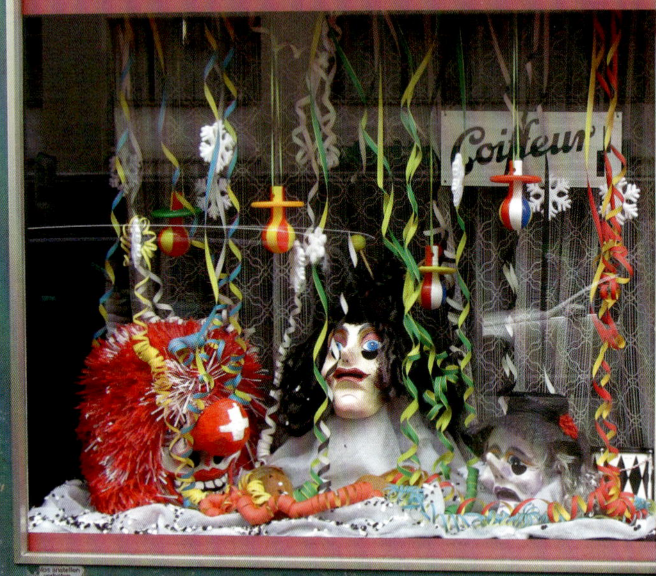
HERRENSALON
Coiffeur

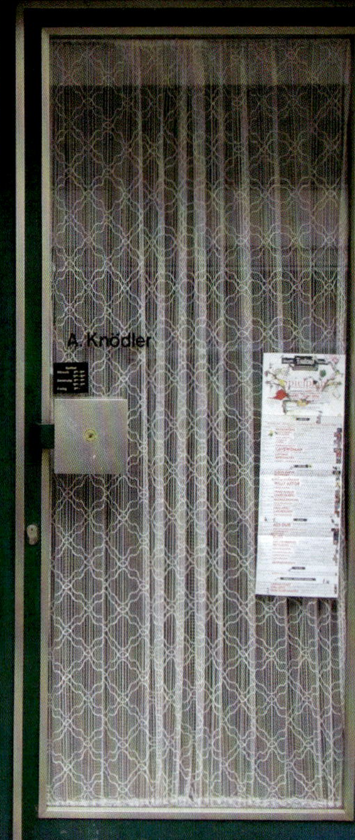
A. Knödler

Kopfsalat

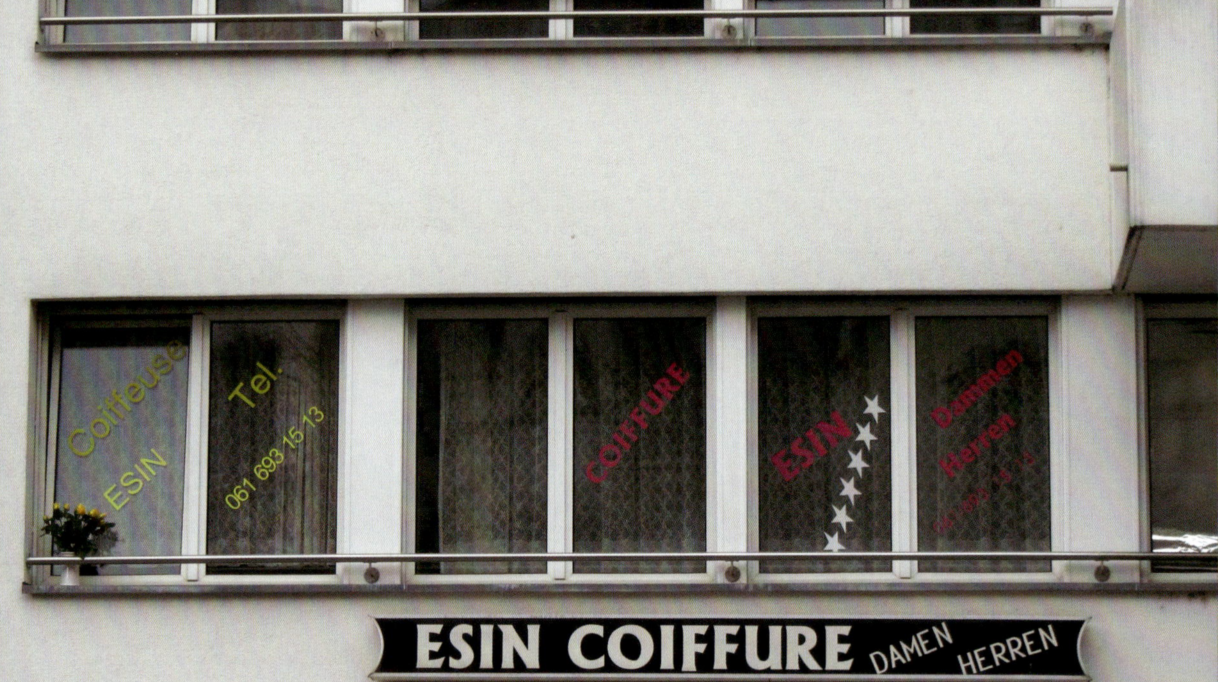
Coiffeuse
ESIN
Tel.
061 693 15 13
COIFFURE
ESIN
Dammen
Herren
ESIN COIFFURE
DAMEN
HERREN

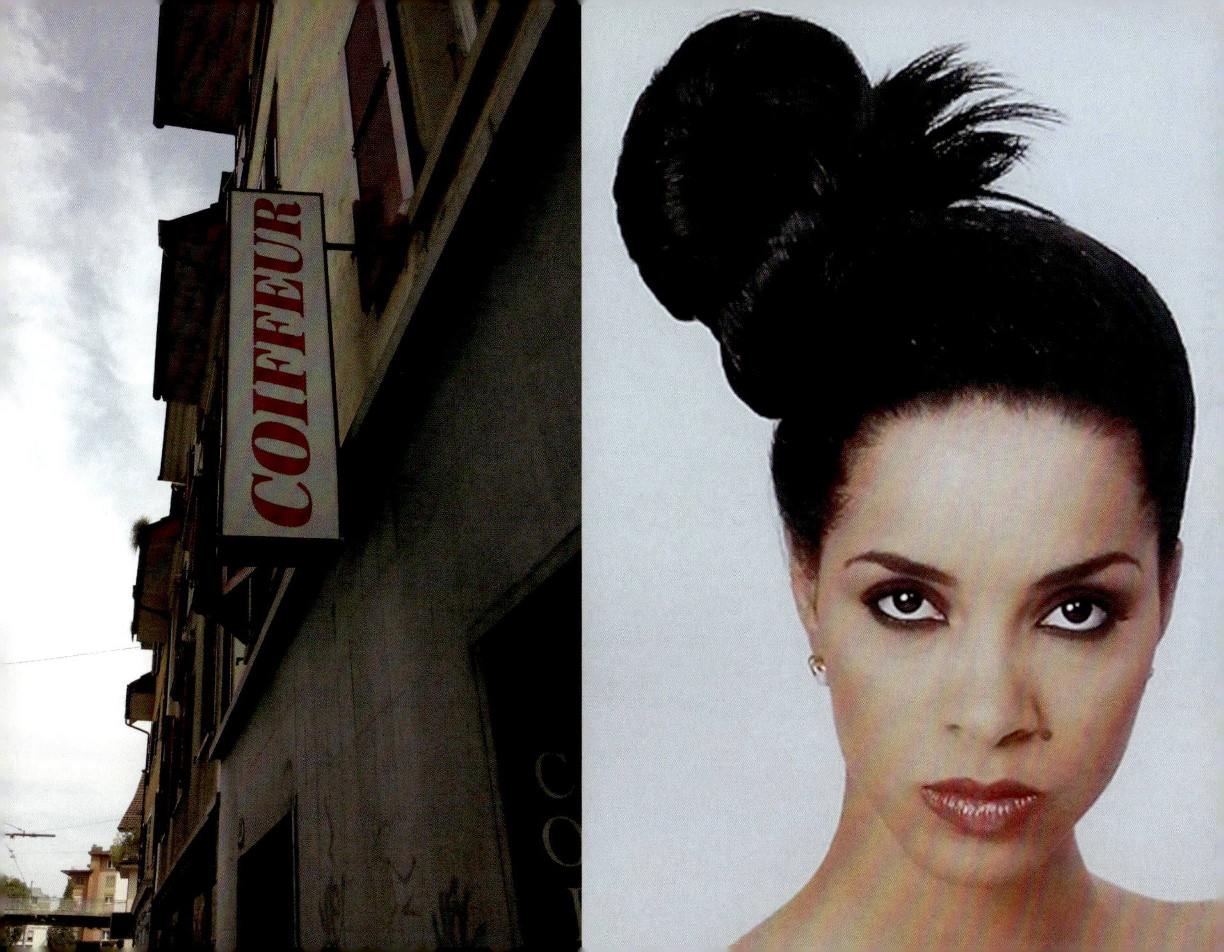
COIFFEUR

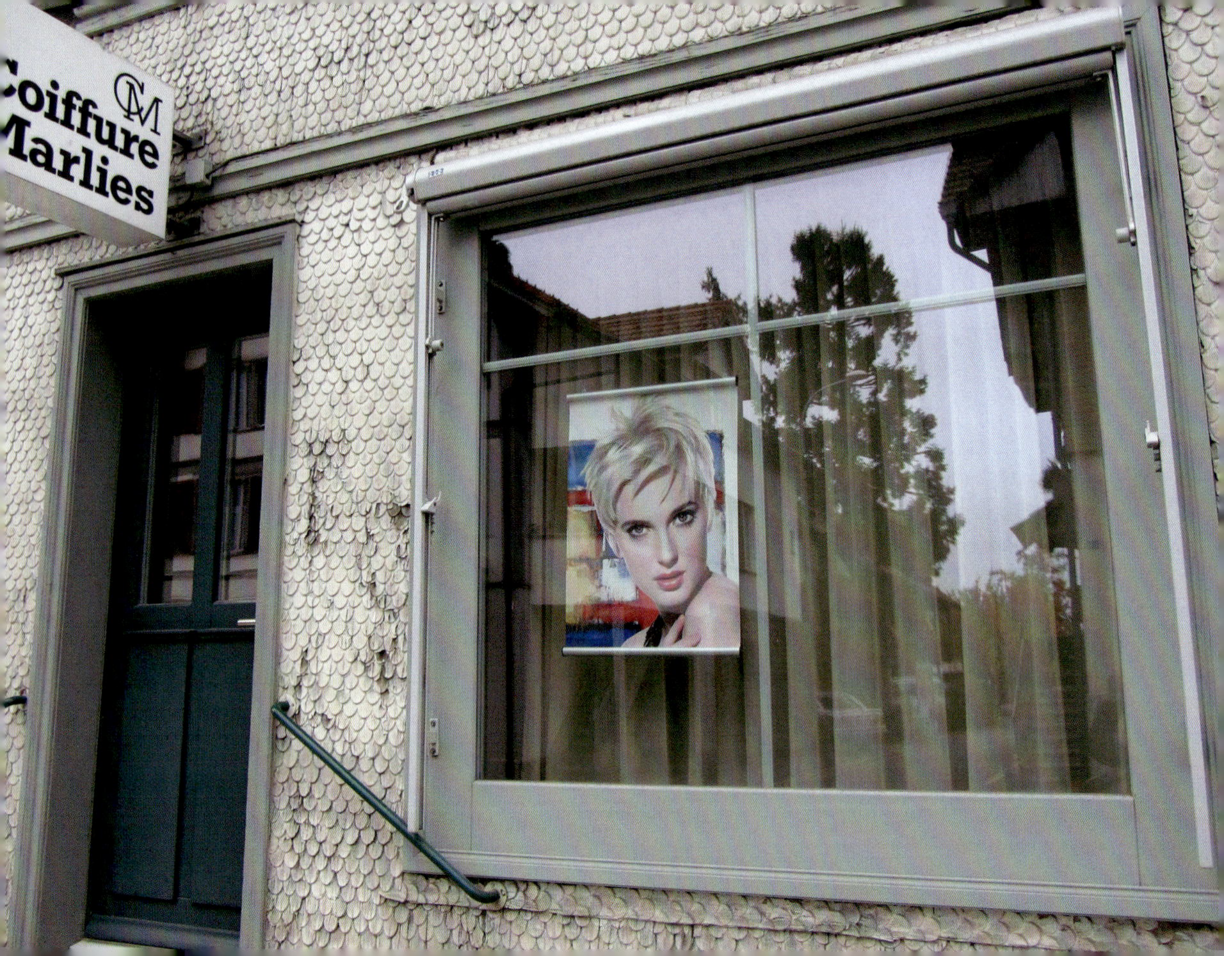
CM
Coiffure
Marlies

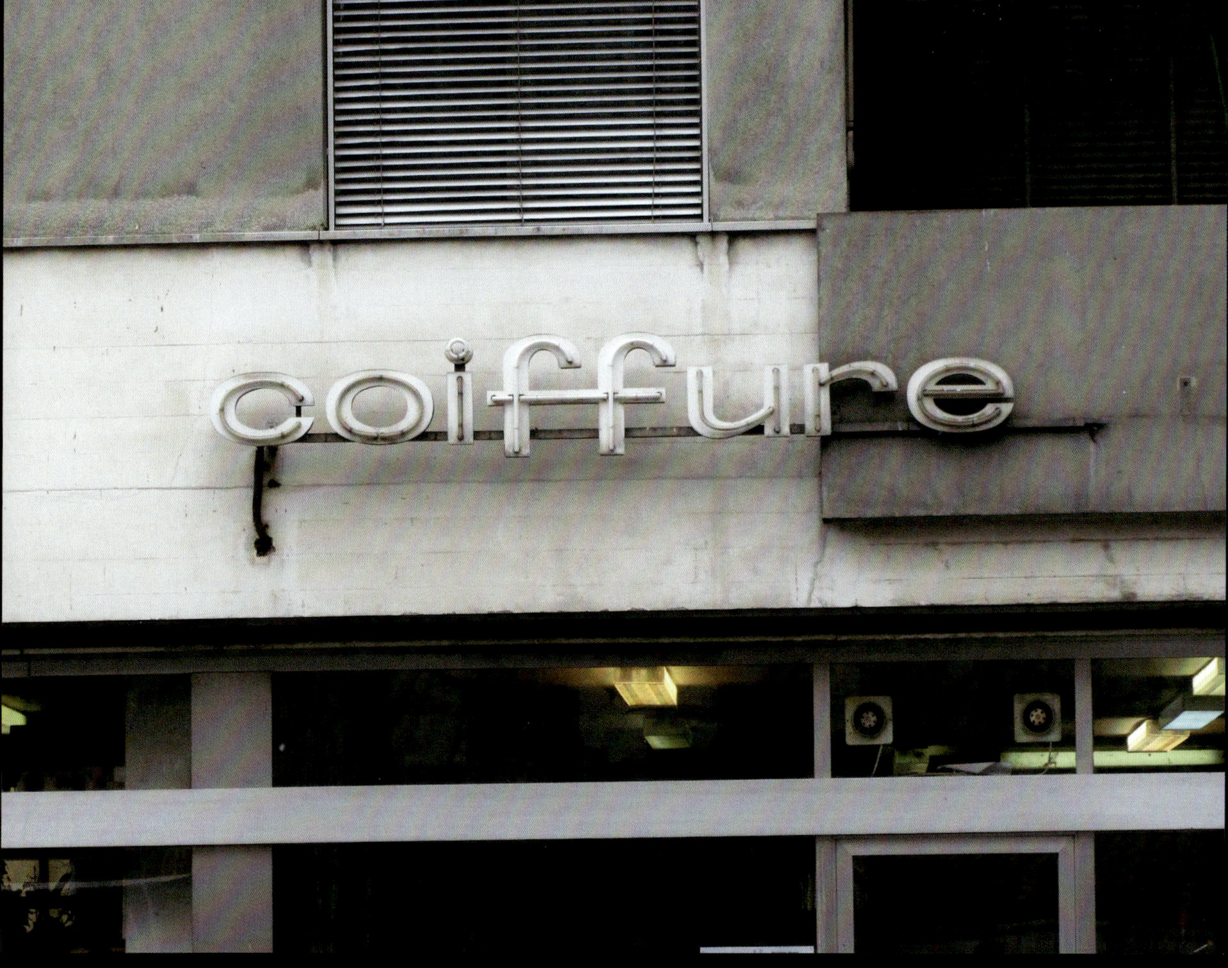
coiffure

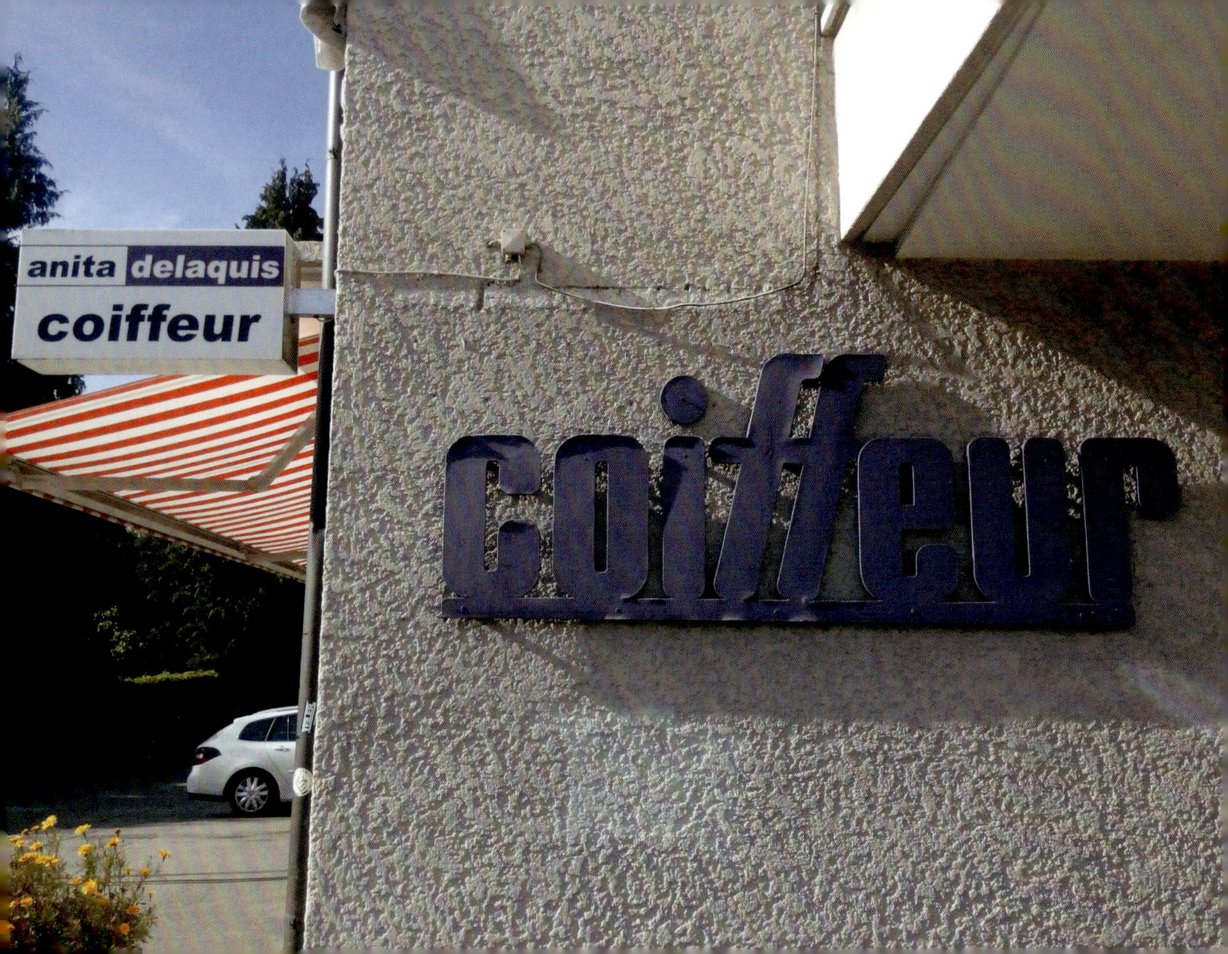
anita delaquis
coiffeur
coiffeur

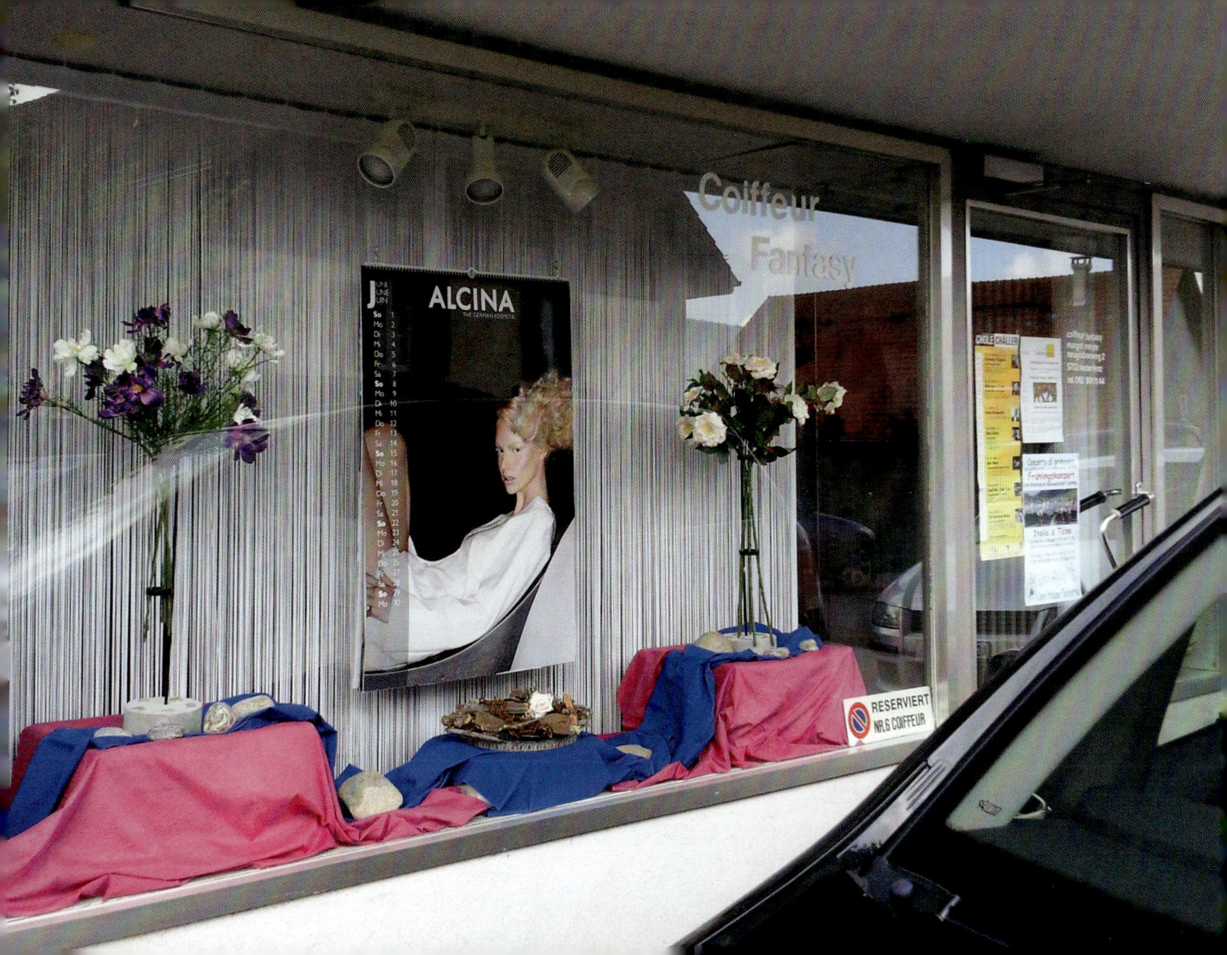
Coiffeur
Fantasy
ALCINA
RESERVIERT
NR.6 COIFFEUR

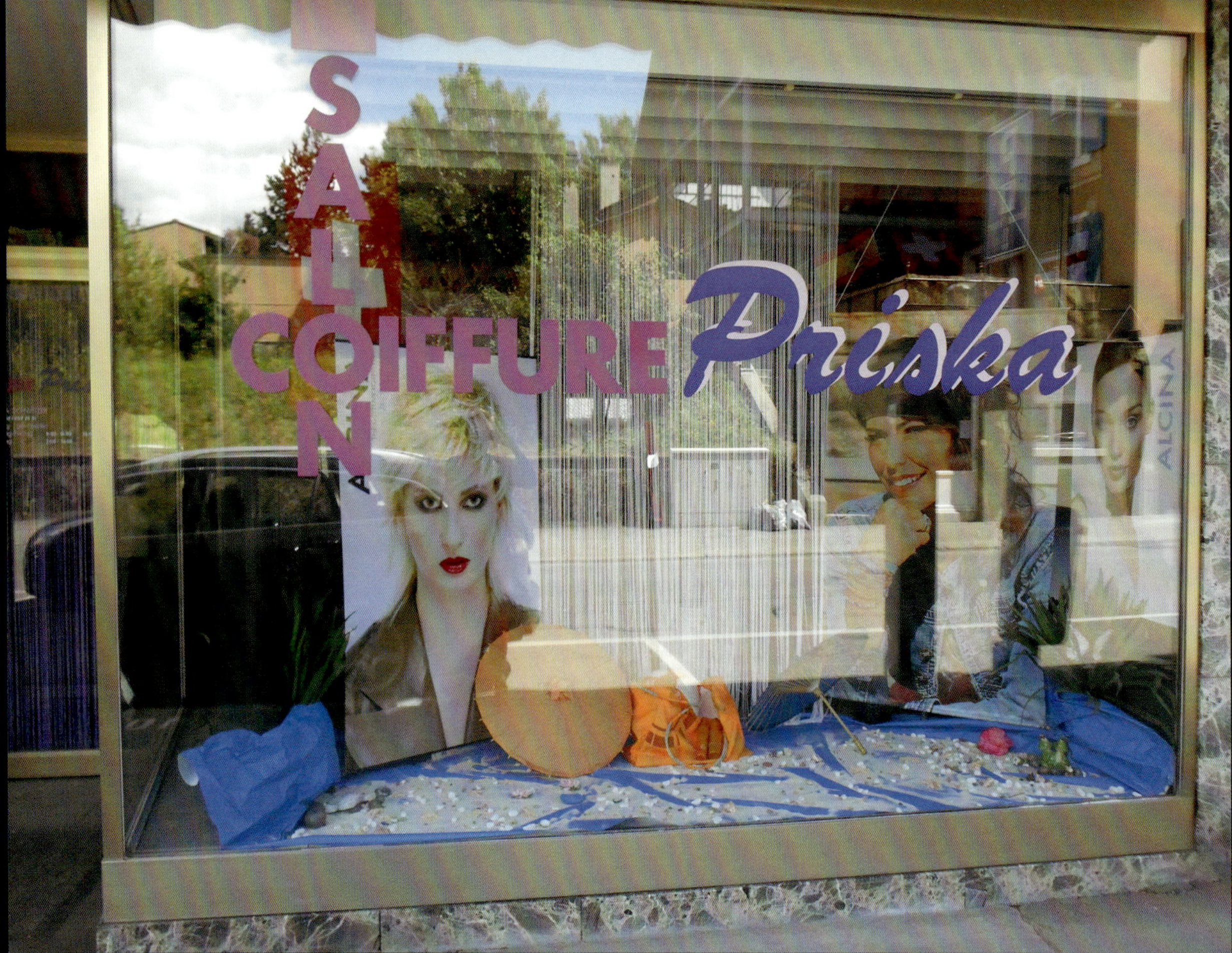
SALON
COIFFURE
Priska
ALCINA

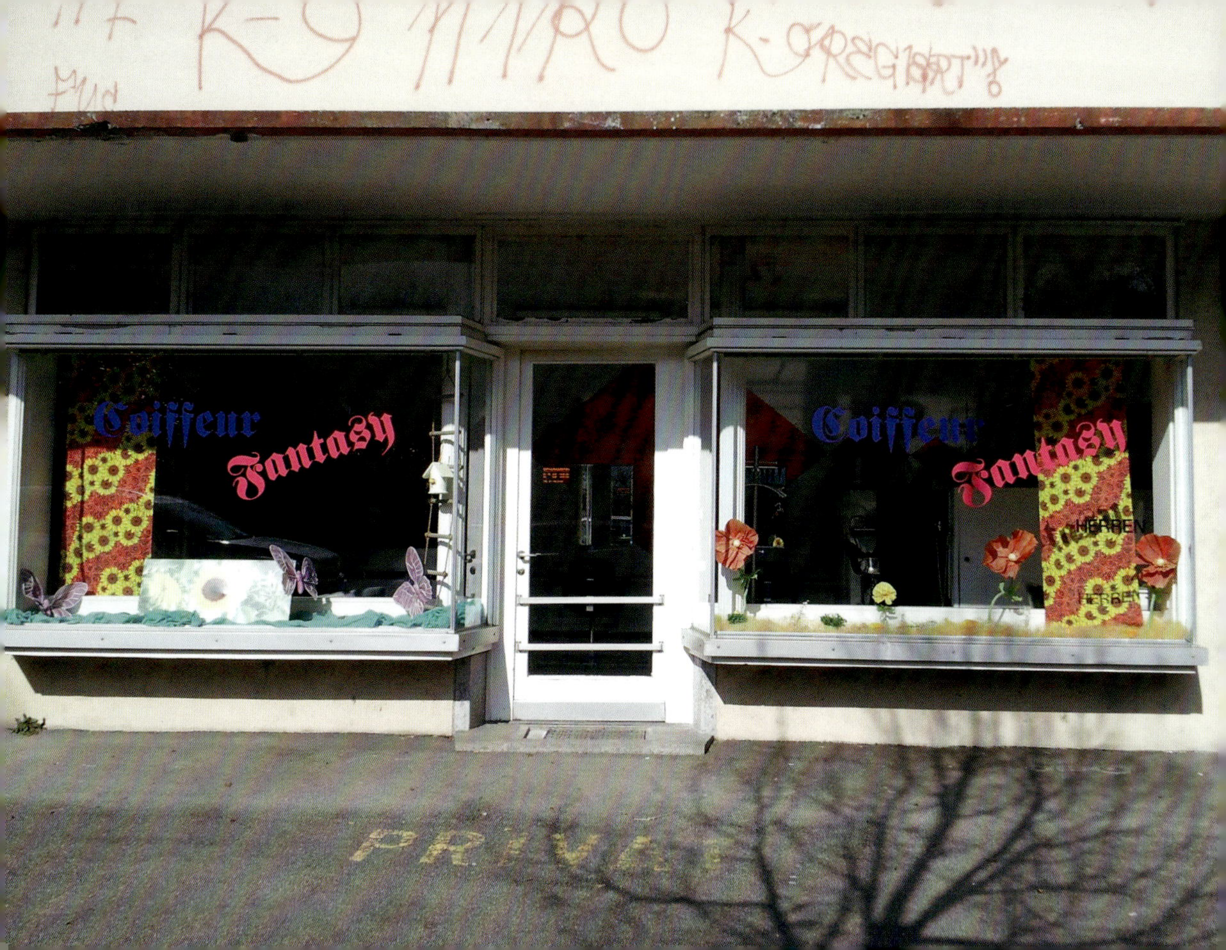
Coiffeur
Fantasy
Coiffeur
Fantasy
HERREN
HERREN

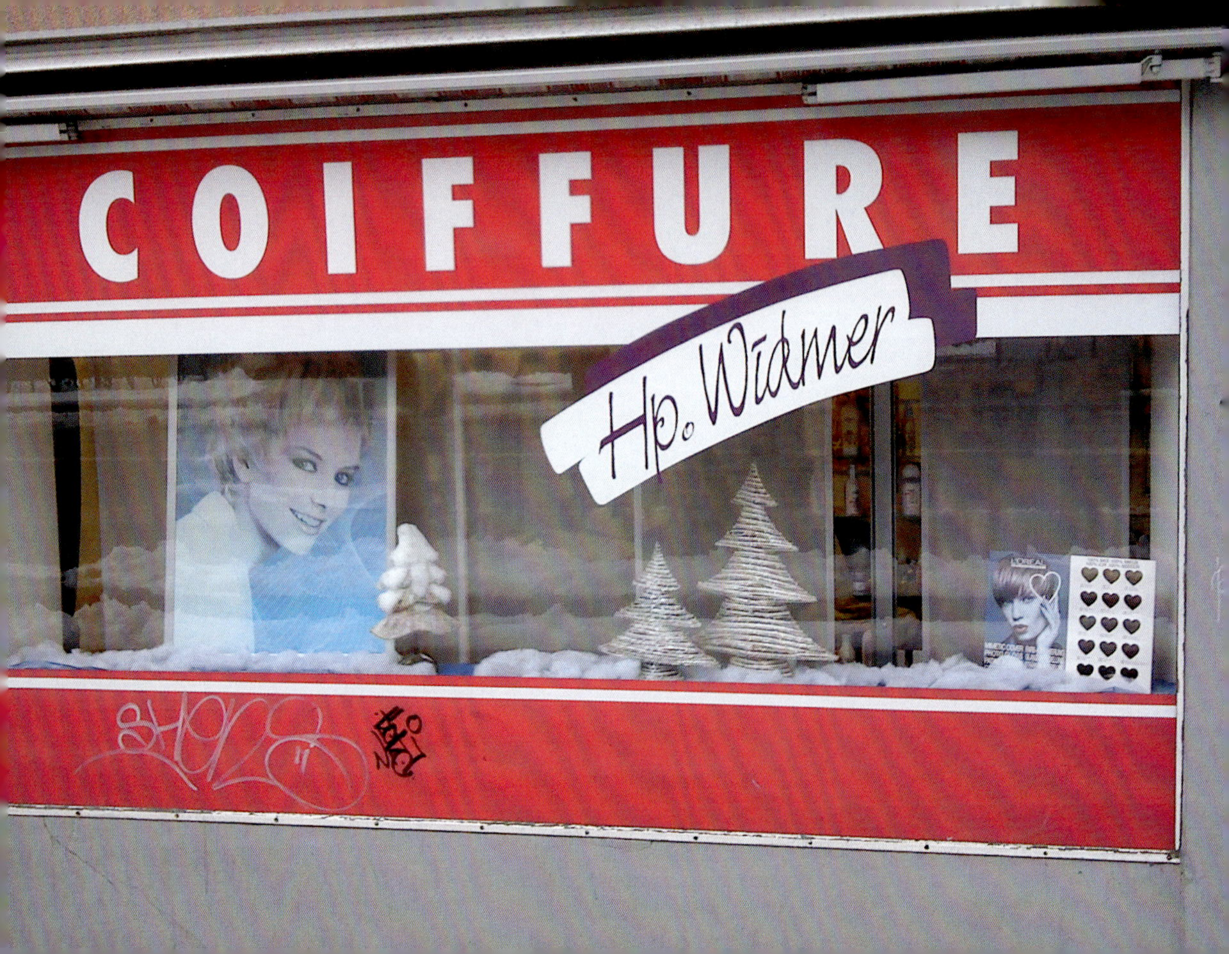

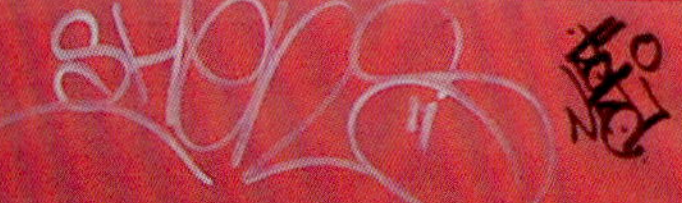
COIFFURE
Hp. Widmer

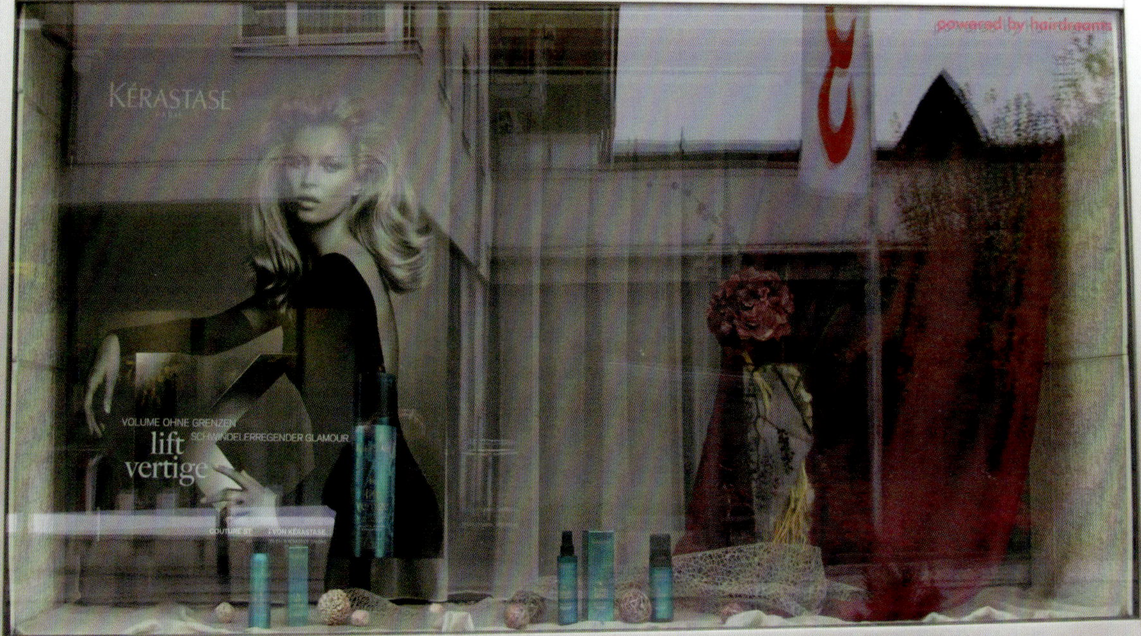
Haarverdichtung
powered by hairdreams
KÉRASTASE
VOLUME OHNE GRENZEN
lift
vertige
SCHWINDELERREGENDER GLAMOUR

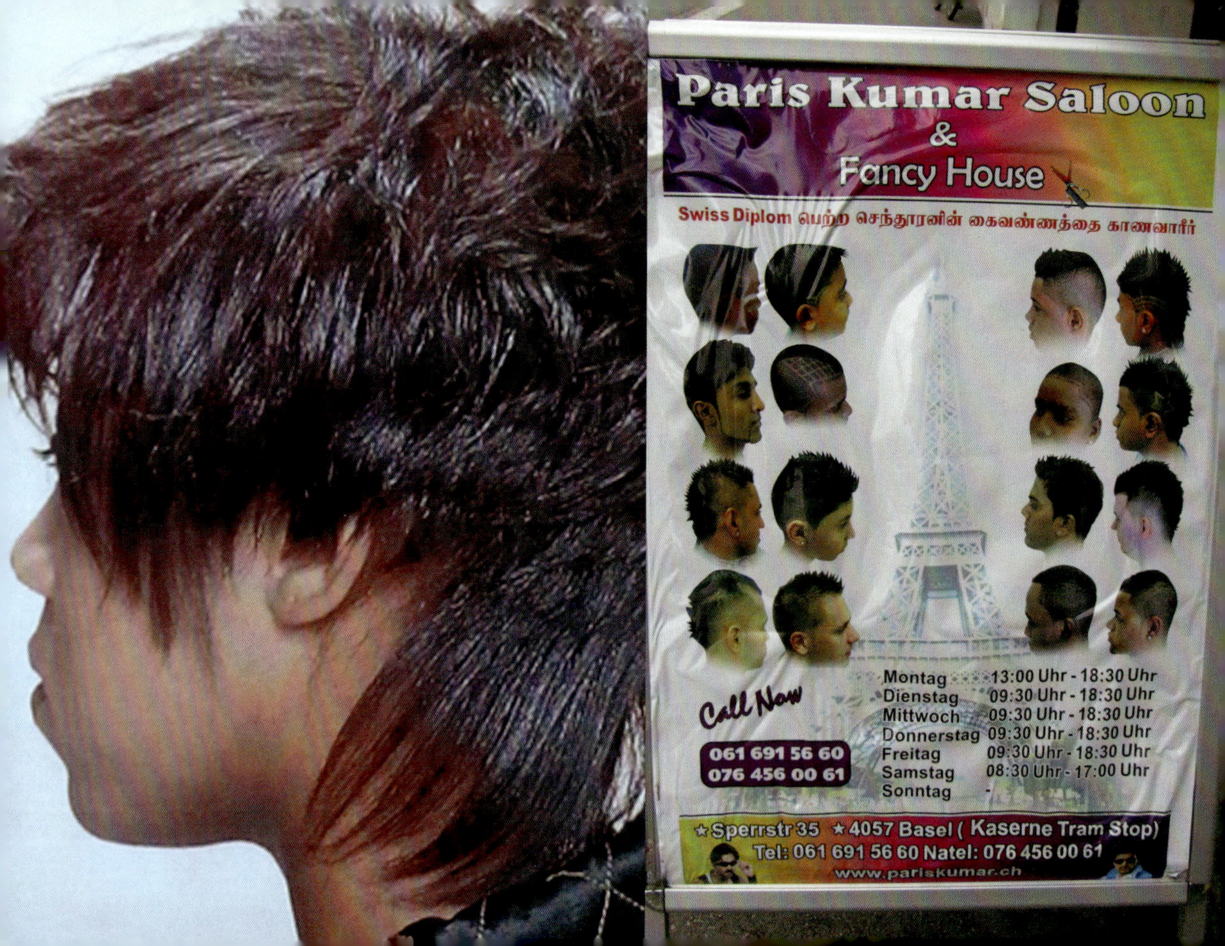

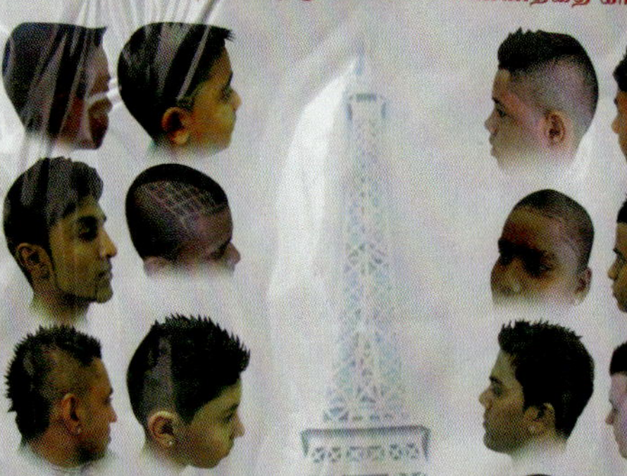

Paris Kumar Saloon
&
Fancy House
Swiss Diplom பெற்ற செந்தூரனின் கைவண்ணத்தை காணவாரீர்
Call Now
061 691 56 60
076 456 00 61
Montag 13:00 Uhr - 18:30 Uhr
Dienstag 09:30 Uhr - 18:30 Uhr
Mittwoch 09:30 Uhr - 18:30 Uhr
Donnerstag 09:30 Uhr - 18:30 Uhr
Freitag 09:30 Uhr - 18:30 Uhr
Samstag 08:30 Uhr - 17:00 Uhr
Sonntag -
★Sperrstr 35 ★4057 Basel (Kaserne Tram Stop)
Tel: 061 691 56 60 Natel: 076 456 00 61
www.pariskumar.ch

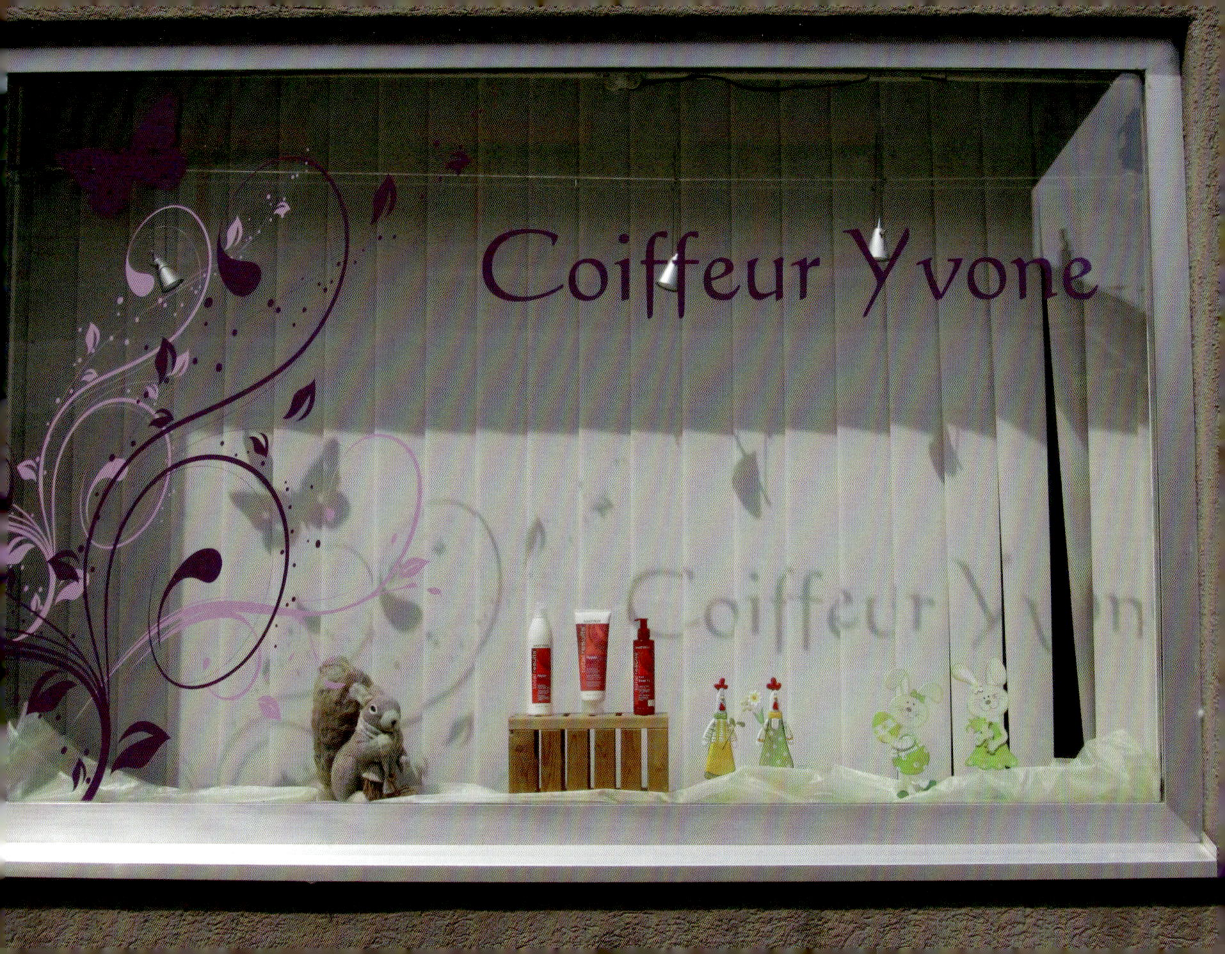

Coiffeur Yvone

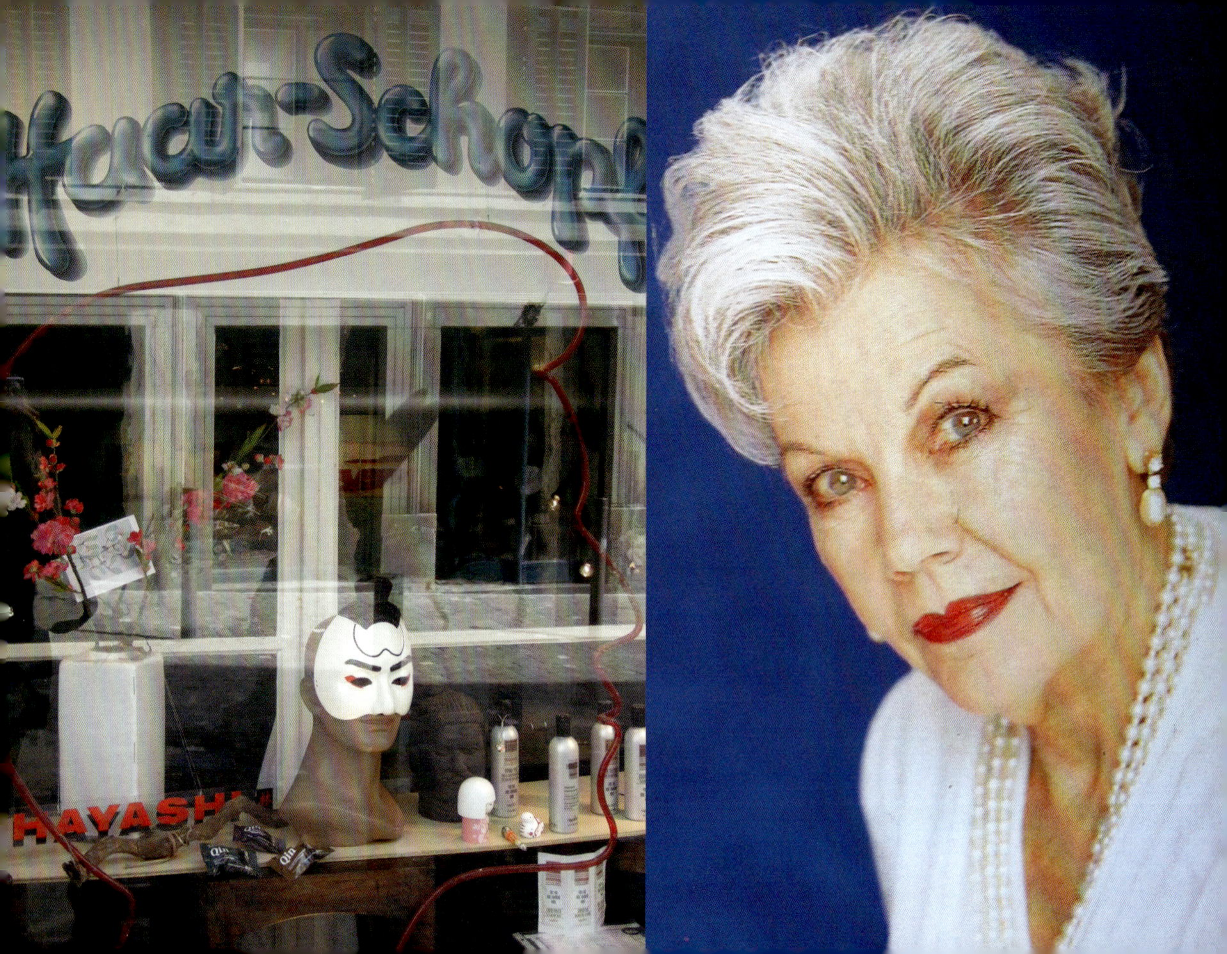
HAYASHI

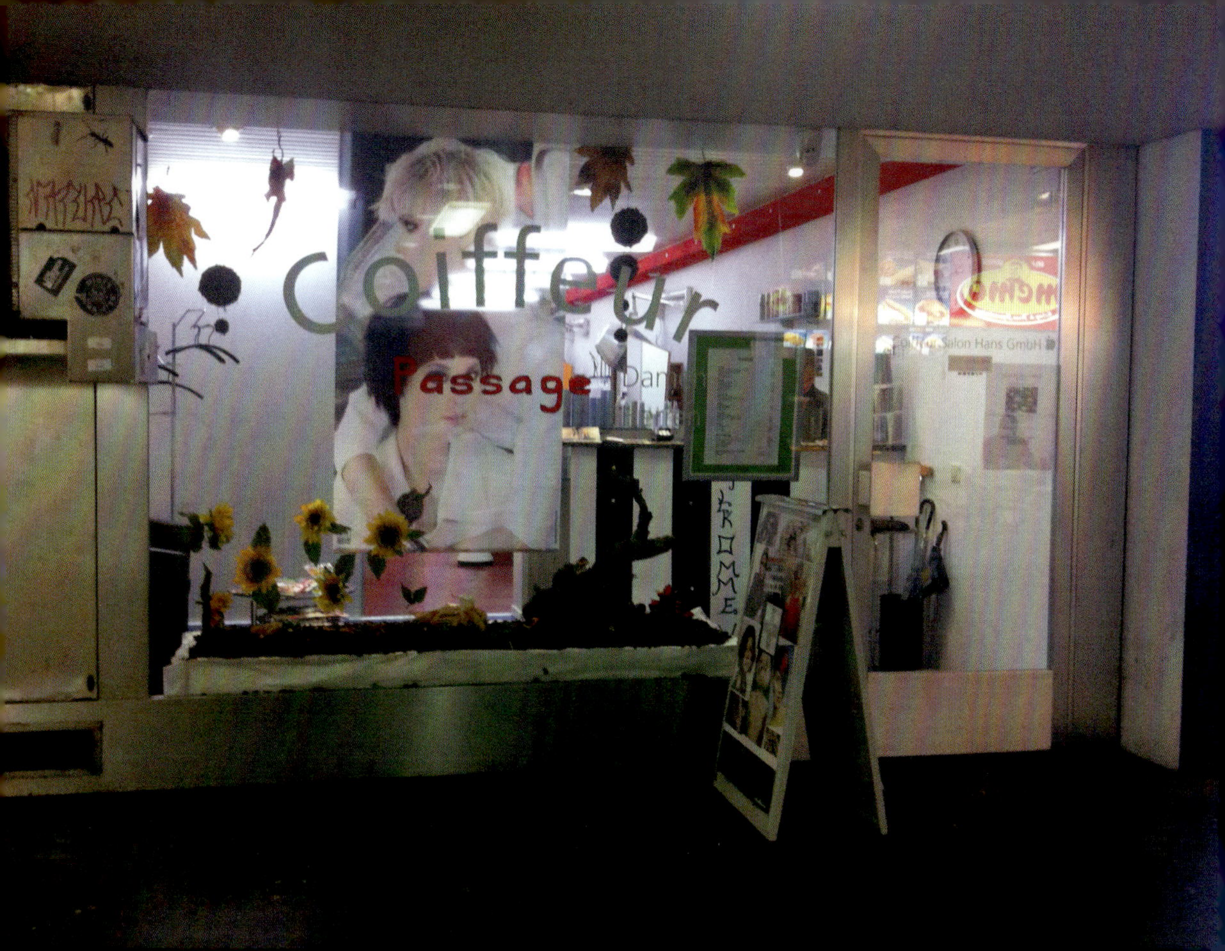
Coiffeur
Passage
Salon Hans GmbH

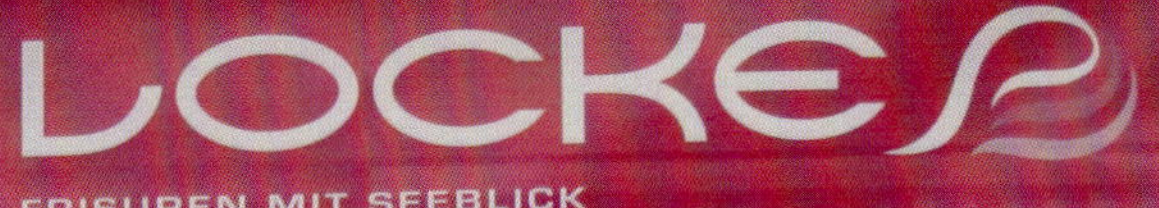

«Mein Ziel ist es, dass die **Kundin**
so zufrieden ist mit ihrer **Frisur**,
dass sie nicht mal
der **besten Freundin** verrät,
wer ihr **Friseur** ist!»

Di-Do: 8–18 Uhr • Fr: 8–20 Uhr • Sa: 8–13 Uhr • +41 33 654 12 12 • info@locke.ch • www.locke.ch

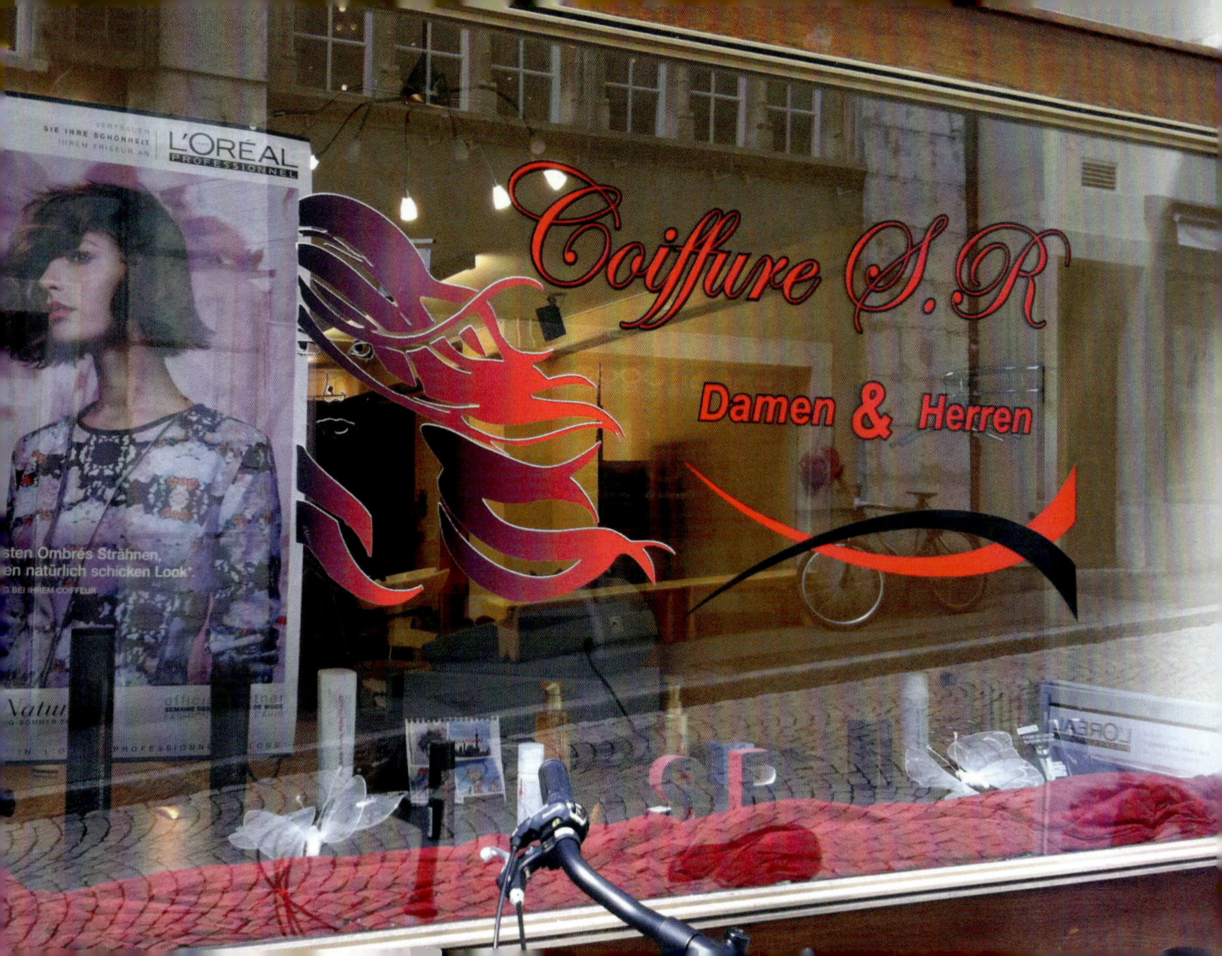
L'ORÉAL
PROFESSIONNEL
Coiffure S.R
Damen & Herren

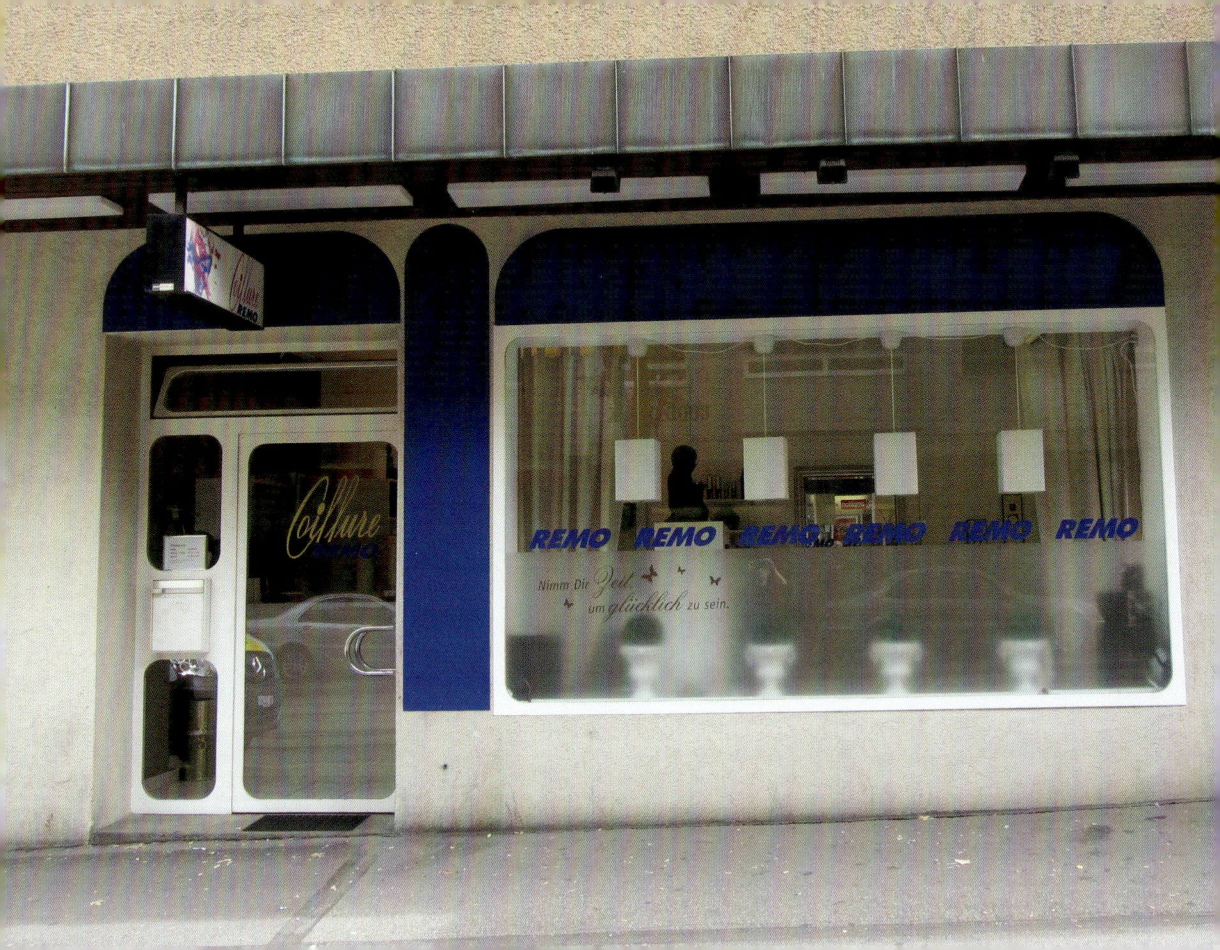
Coiffure
REMO
Coiffure
REMO
REMO
REMO
REMO
REMO
REMO
Nimm Dir Zeit
um glücklich zu sein.

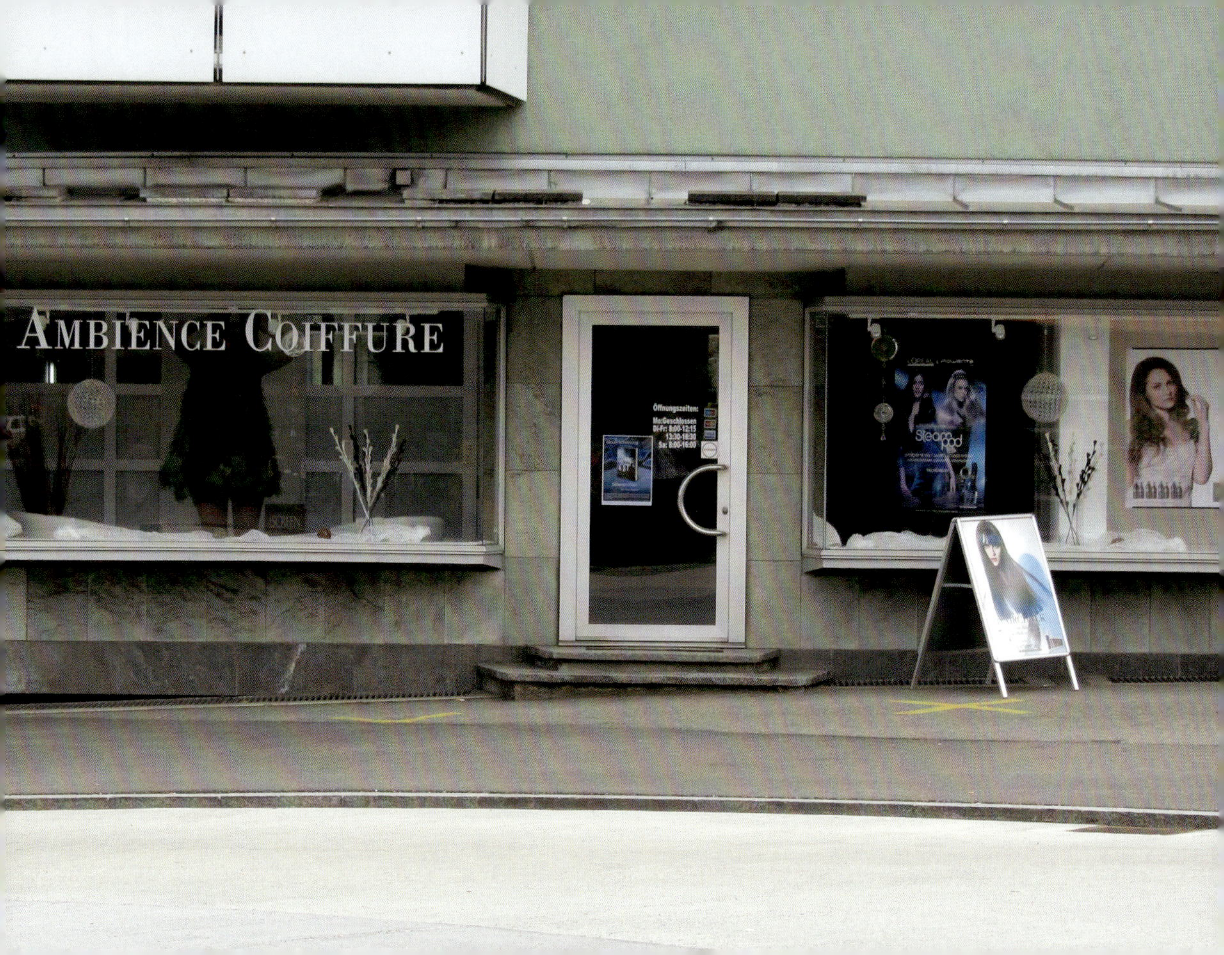
AMBIENCE COIFFURE
Öffnungszeiten:
Mo:Geschlossen
Di-Fr: 8:00-12:15
13:30-18:30
Sa: 8:00-16:00
Steampod

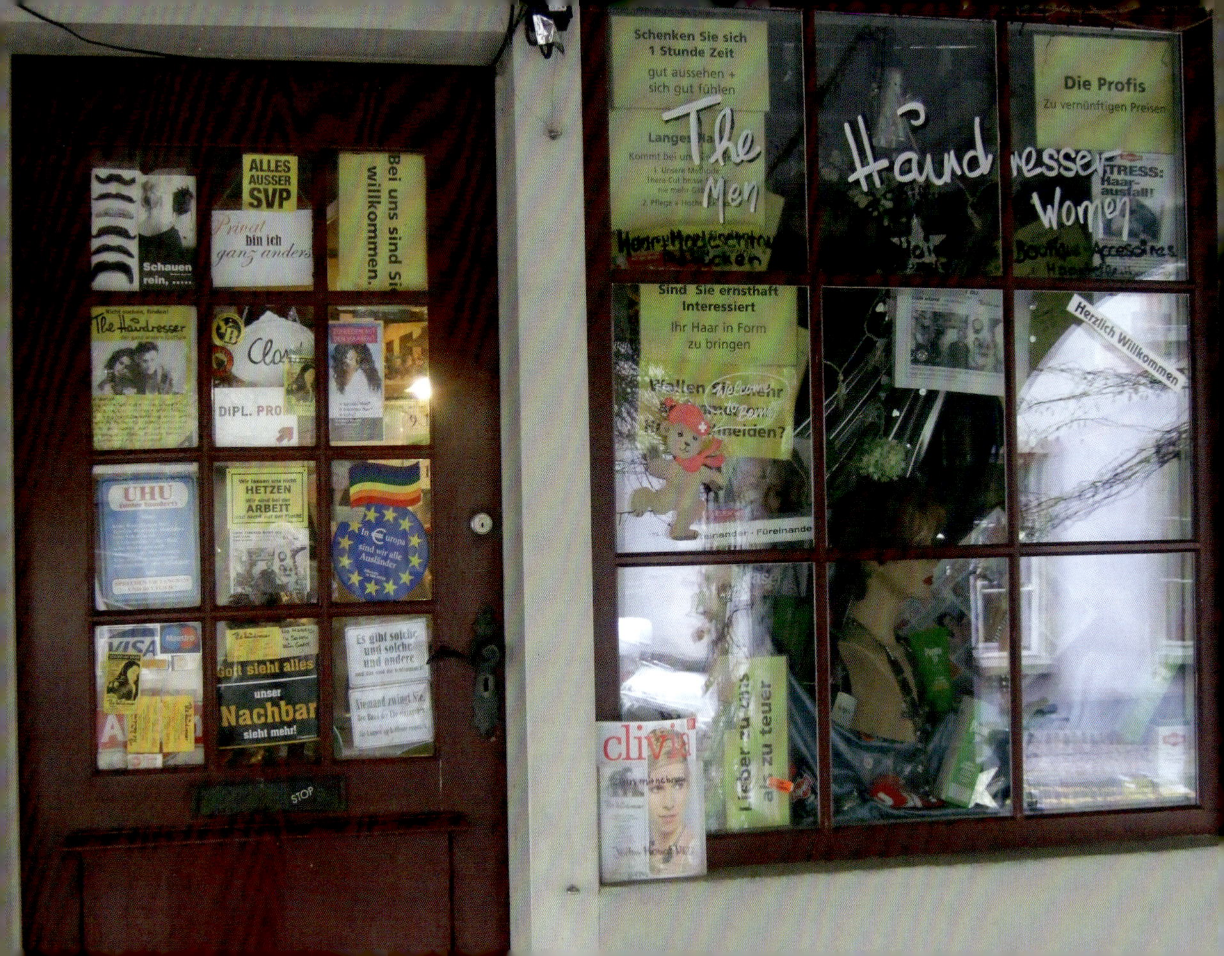

Schenken Sie sich
1 Stunde Zeit
gut aussehen +
sich gut fühlen

The Hairdresser
Men
Women

Die Profis
Zu vernünftigen Preisen

ALLES
AUSSER
SVP

Privat
bin ich
ganz anders

Bei uns sind Sie willkommen.

Schauen
rein, ...

The Hairdresser

DIPL. PRO

UHU

Wir lassen uns nicht
HETZEN
Wir sind bei der
ARBEIT

In Europa
sind wir alle
Ausländer

VISA

Gott sieht alles
unser
Nachbar
sieht mehr!

Es gibt solche
und solche
und andere

Niemand zwingt Sie

STOP

Sind Sie ernsthaft
Interessiert
Ihr Haar in Form
zu bringen

Herzlich Willkommen

Lieber zu zweit als zu teuer

clivia

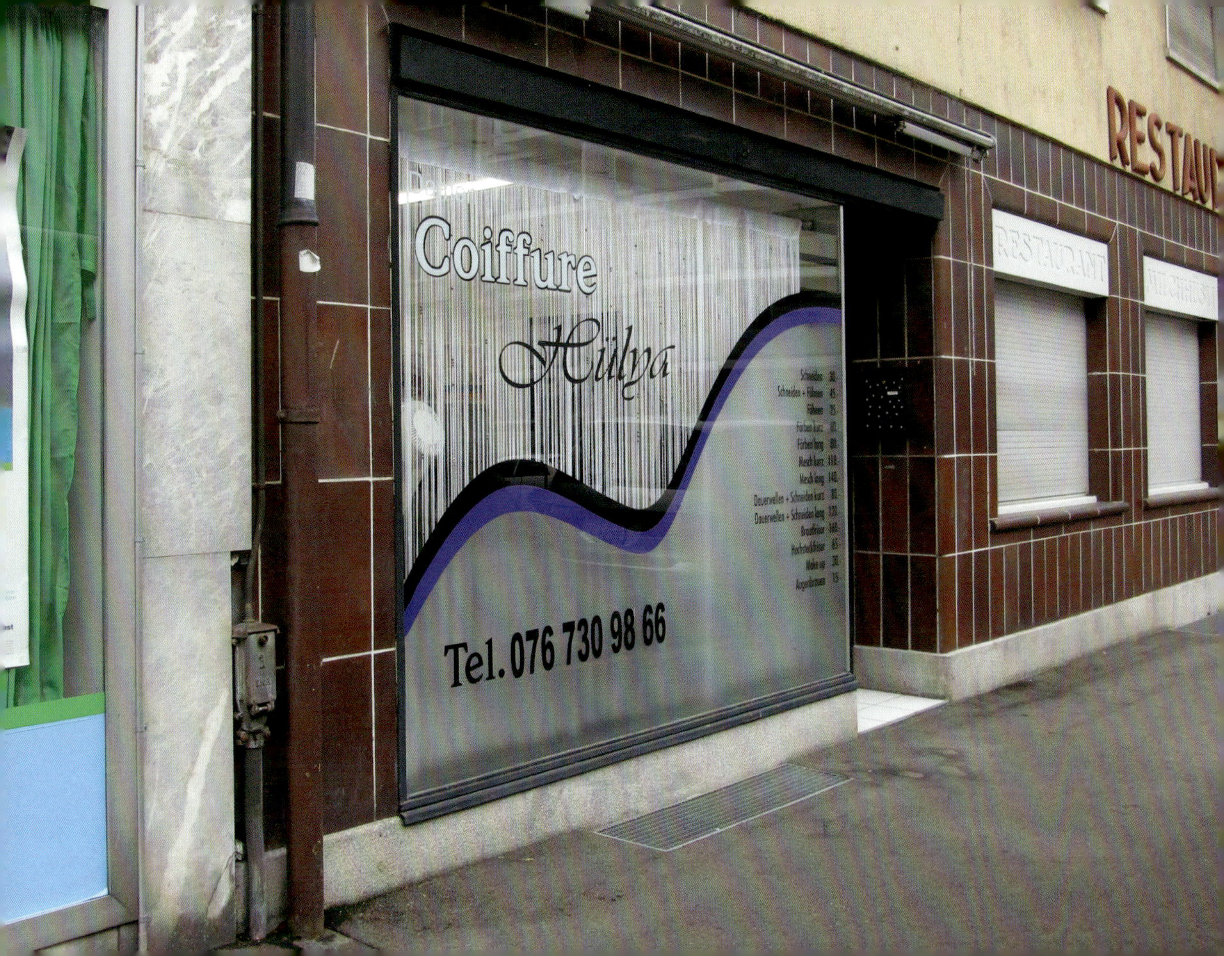
Coiffure
Hülya
Tel. 076 730 98 66
RESTAURANT

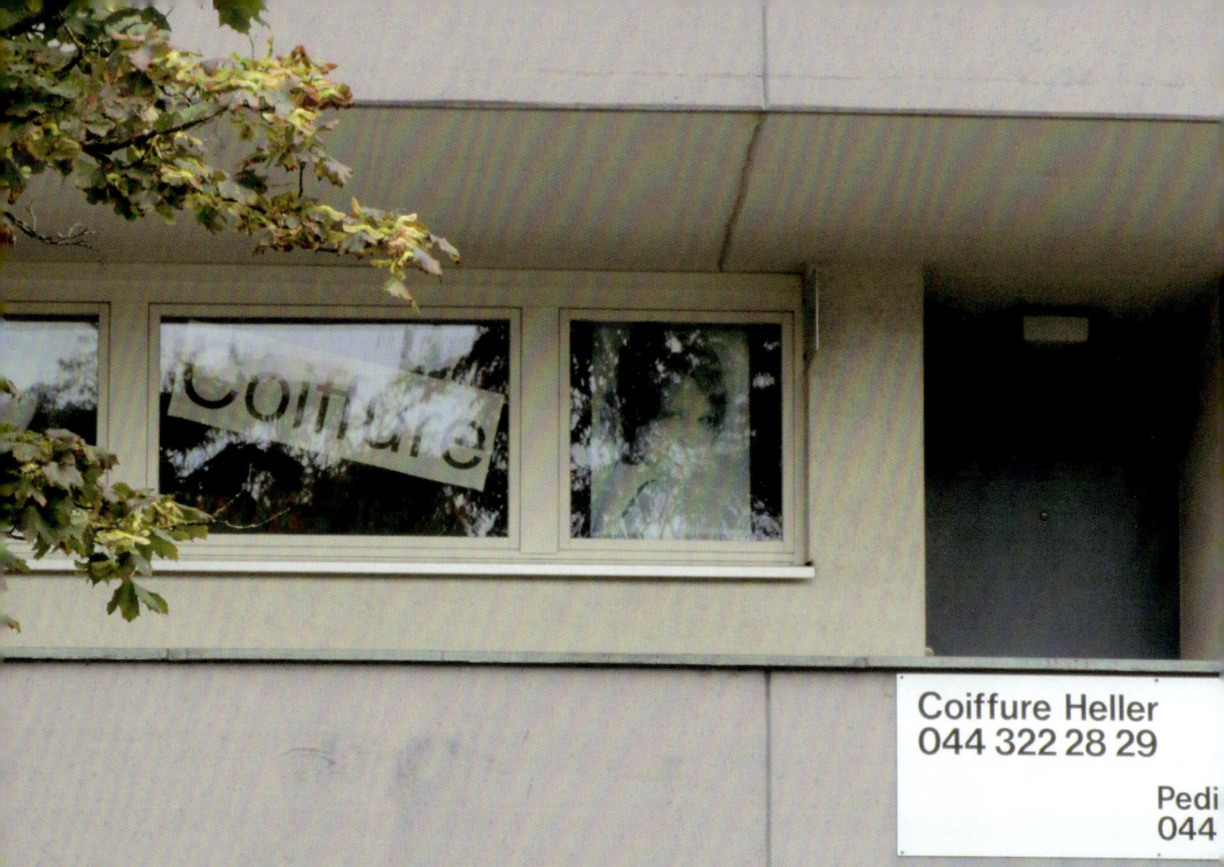
Coiffure
Coiffure Heller
044 322 28 29
Pedi
044

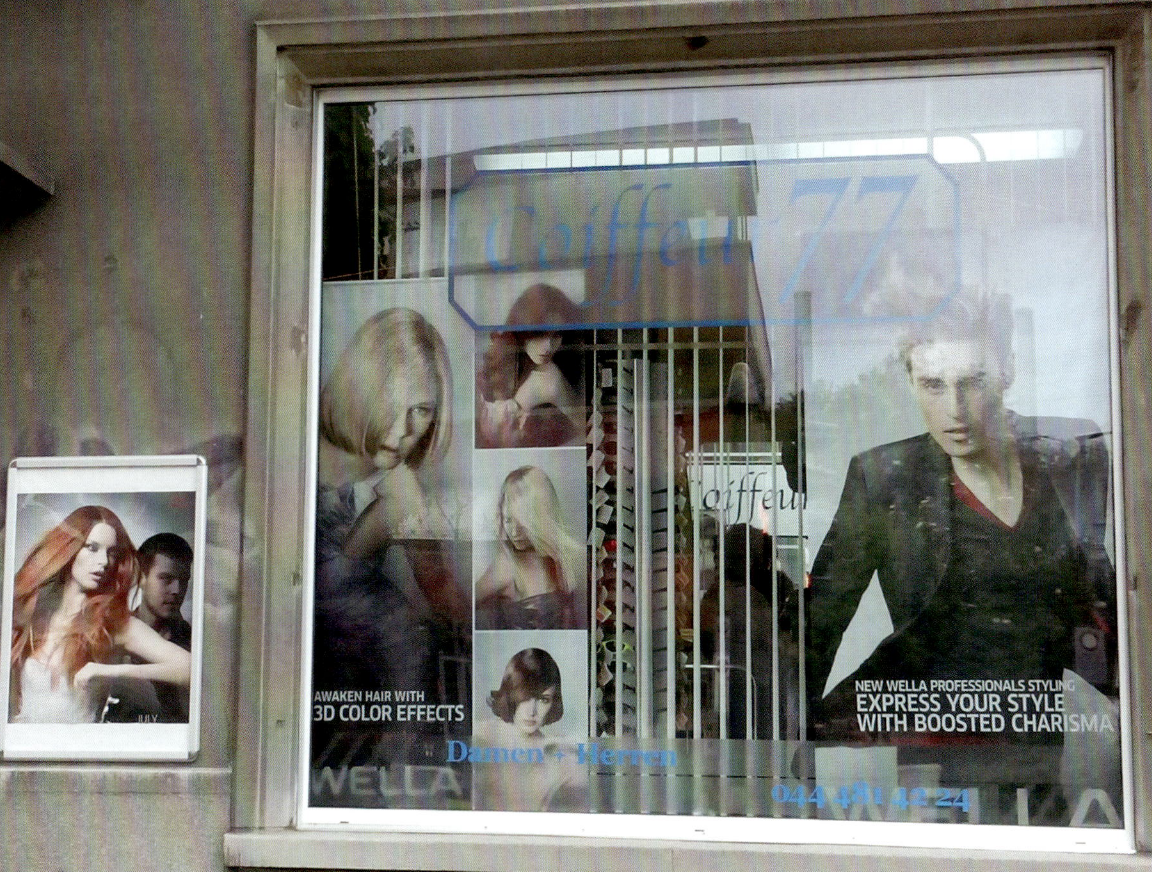
Coiffeur 77
Coiffeur
AWAKEN HAIR WITH
3D COLOR EFFECTS
NEW WELLA PROFESSIONALS STYLING
EXPRESS YOUR STYLE
WITH BOOSTED CHARISMA
Damen + Herren
WELLA
044 481 42 24
JULY

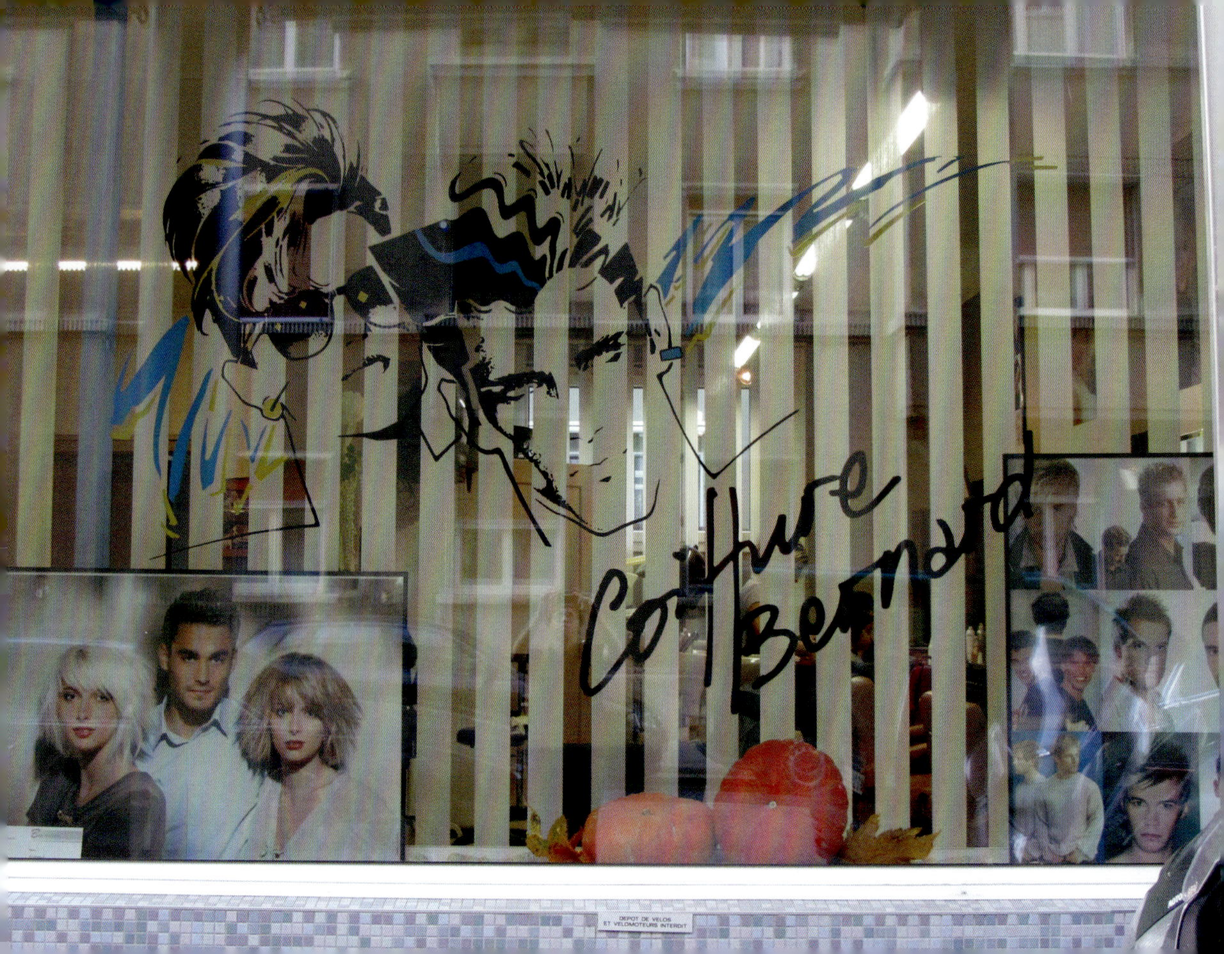
Coiffure Bernard
DEPOT DE VELOS
ET VELOMOTEURS INTERDIT

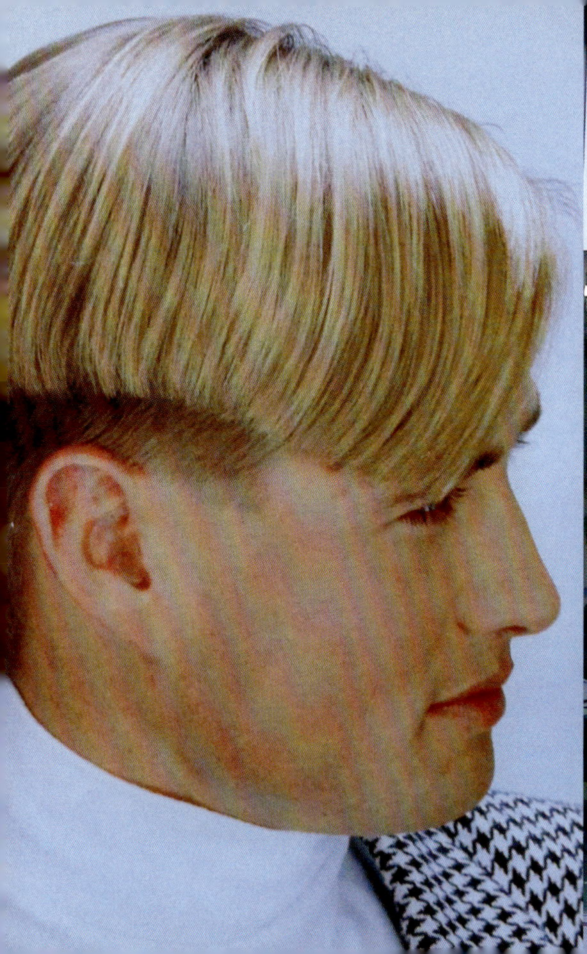

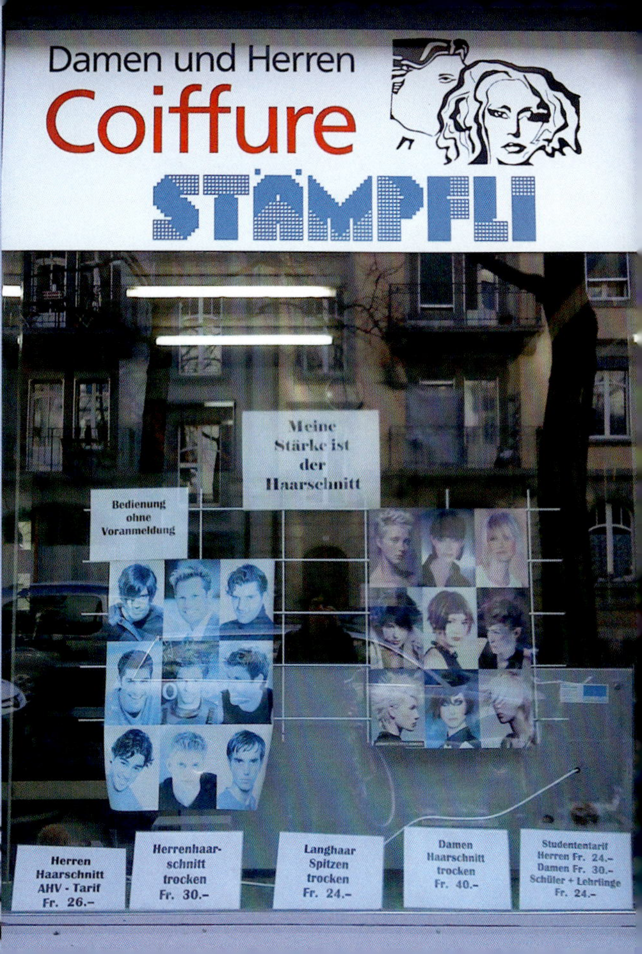

Damen und Herren
Coiffure
STÄMPFLI
Meine Stärke ist der Haarschnitt
Bedienung ohne Voranmeldung
Herren Haarschnitt AHV - Tarif Fr. 26.–
Herrenhaar-schnitt trocken Fr. 30.–
Langhaar Spitzen trocken Fr. 24.–
Damen Haarschnitt trocken Fr. 40.–
Studententarif Herren Fr. 24.– Damen Fr. 30.– Schüler + Lehrlinge Fr. 24.–

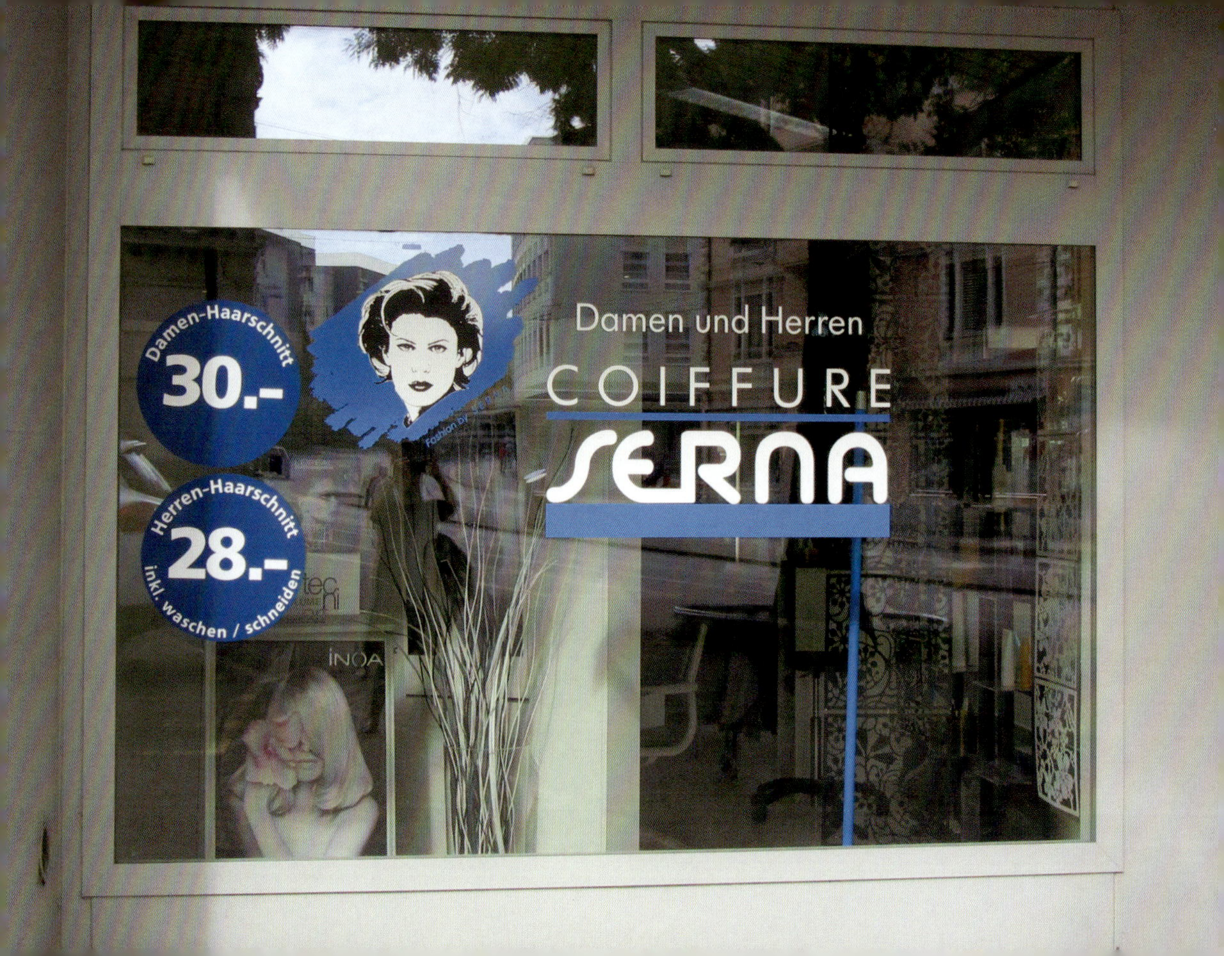

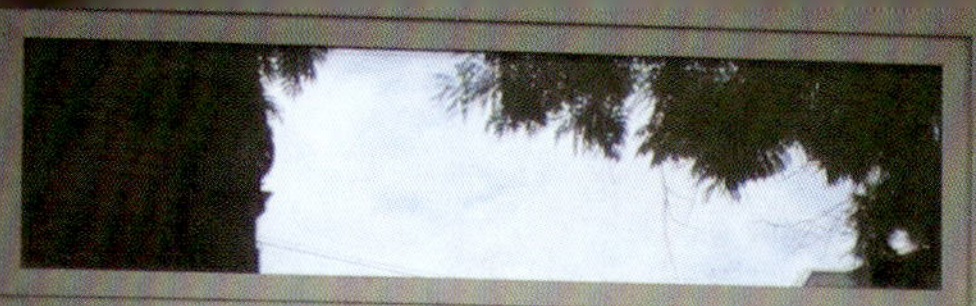

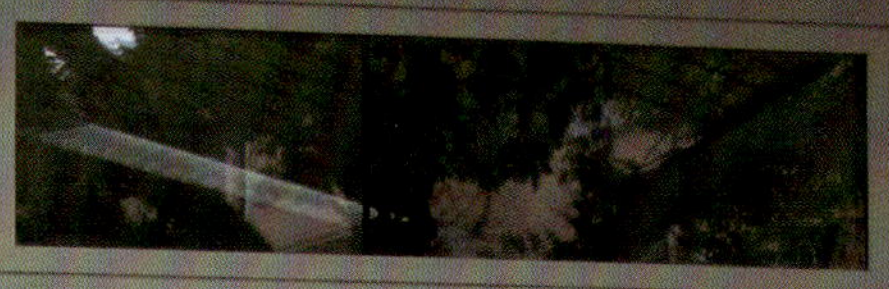
Damen-Haarschnitt
30.-
Herren-Haarschnitt
28.-
inkl. waschen / schneiden
Damen und Herren
COIFFURE
SERNA
INOA

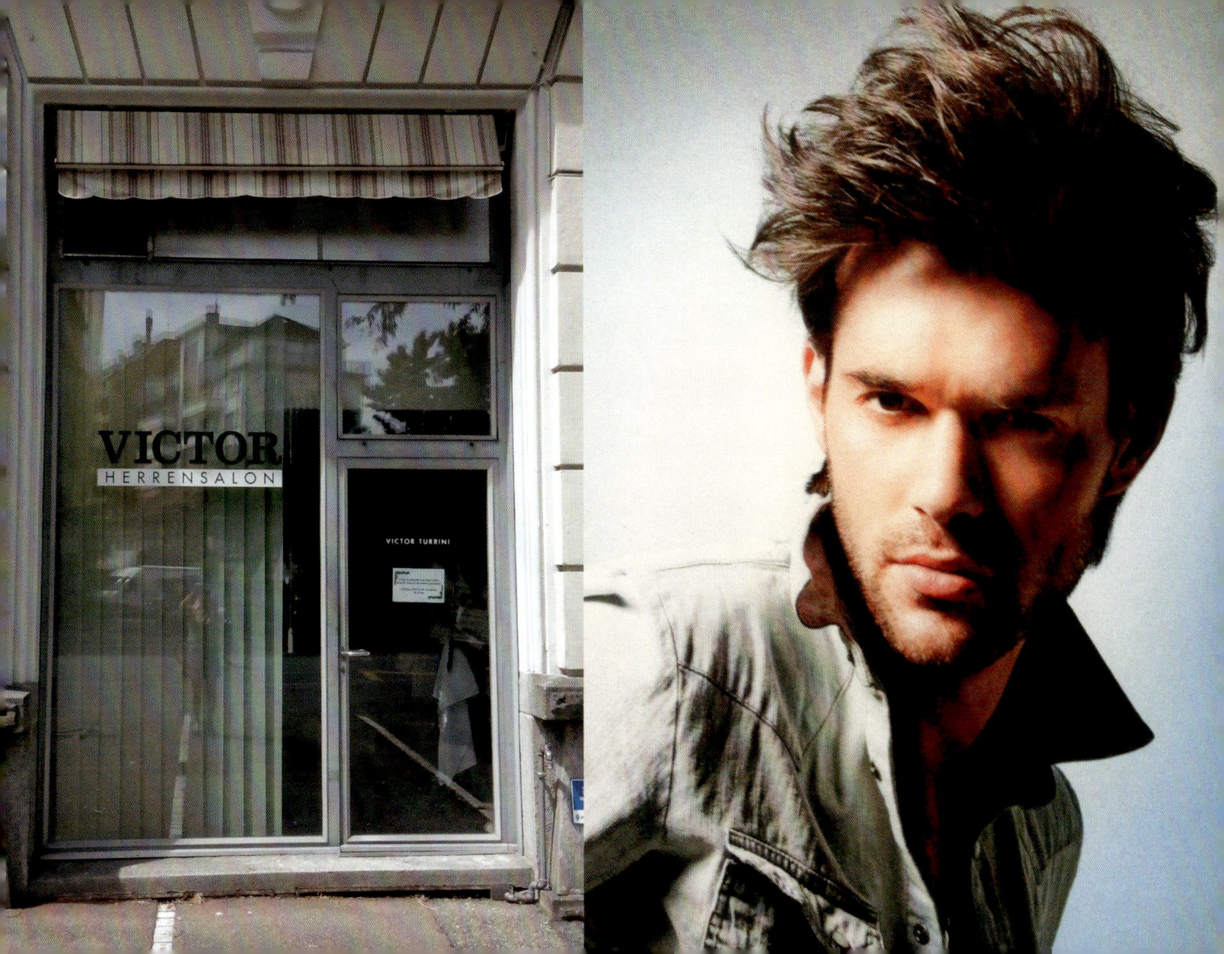
VICTOR
HERRENSALON
VICTOR TURRINI

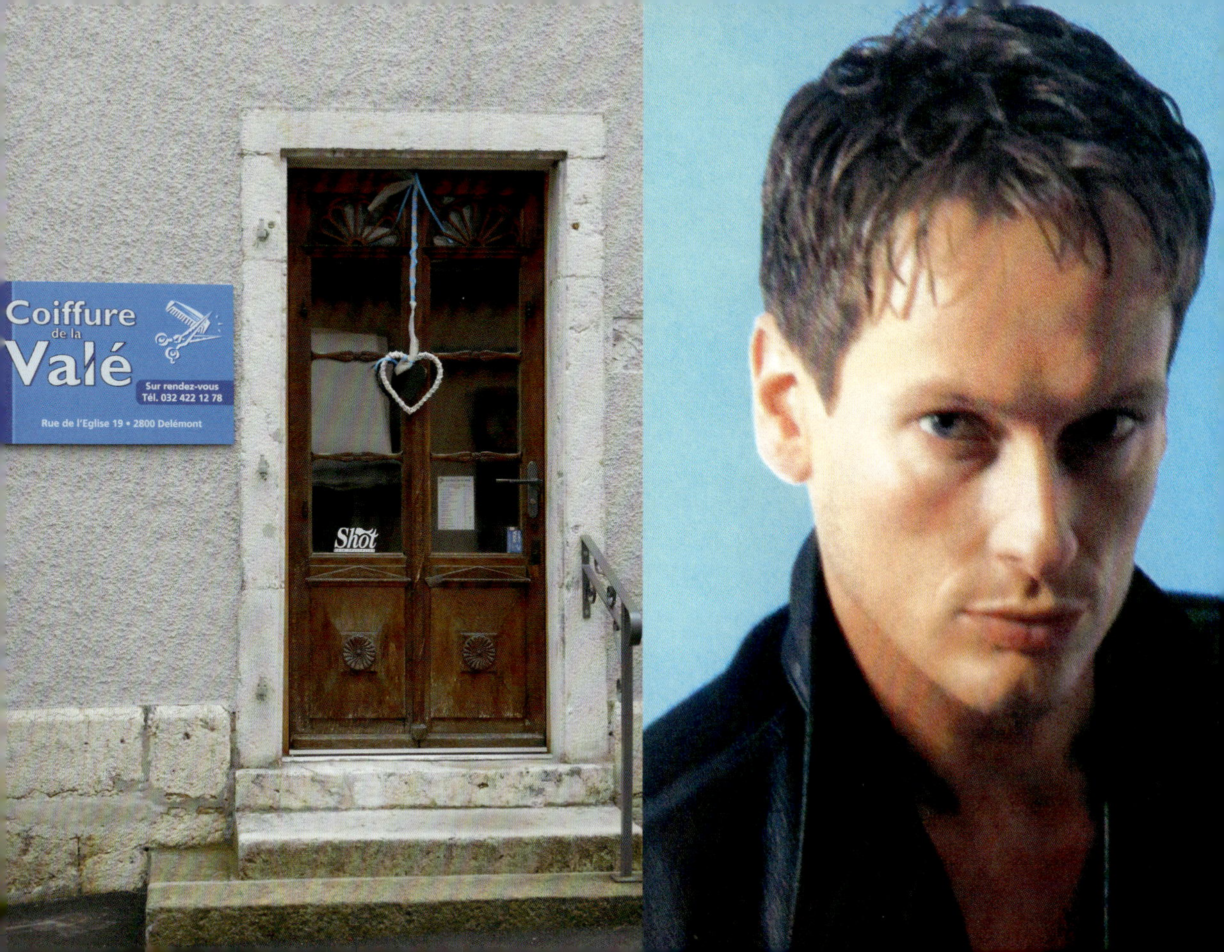
Coiffure
de la
Valé
Sur rendez-vous
Tél. 032 422 12 78
Rue de l'Eglise 19 • 2800 Delémont
Shot

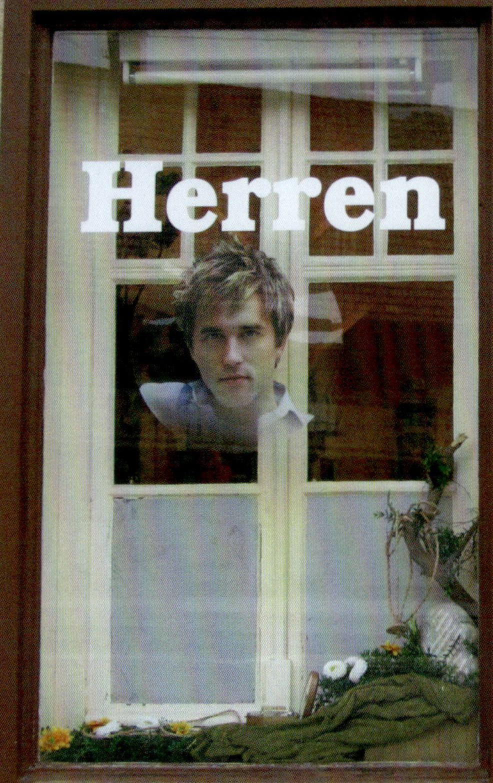
Herren

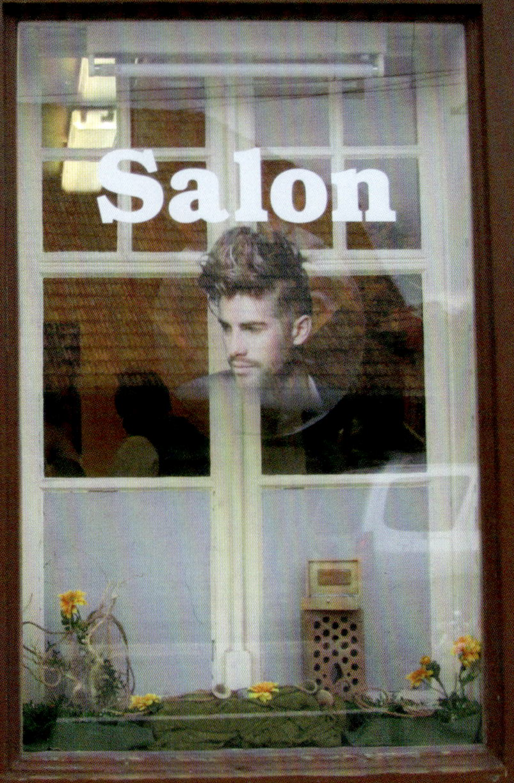
Salon

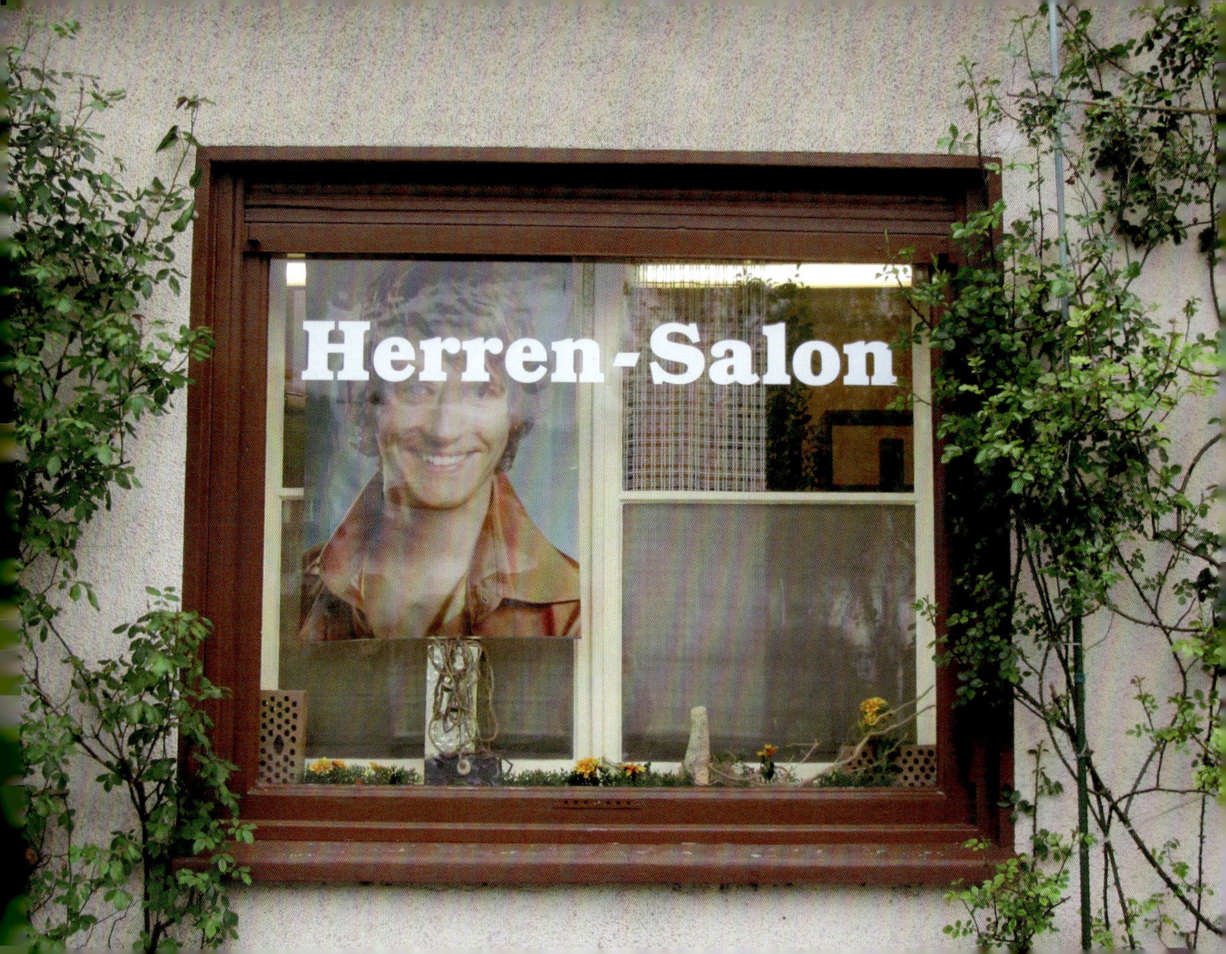
Herren-Salon

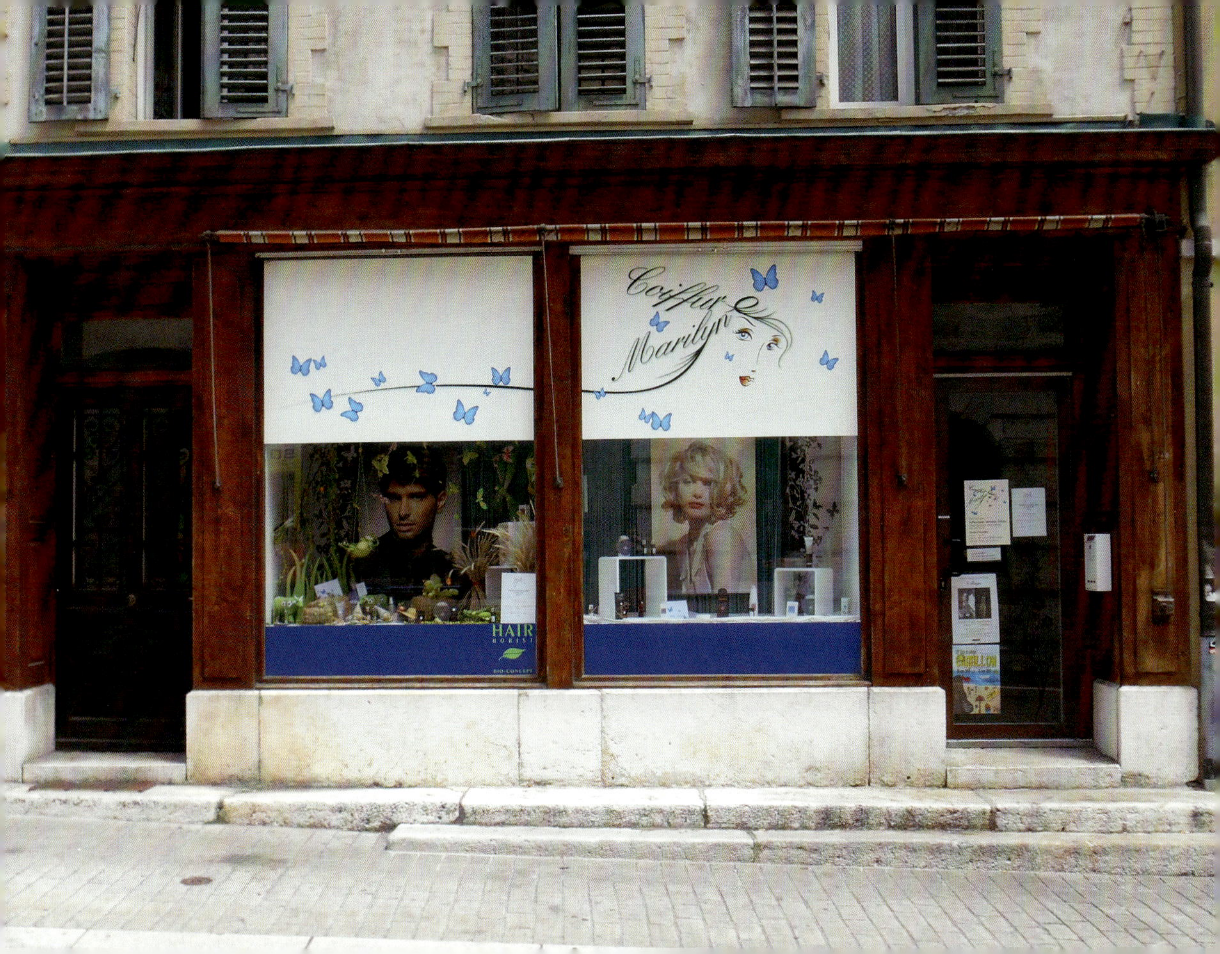
Coiffure
Marilyn
HAIR
BORIST
BIO-CONCEPT

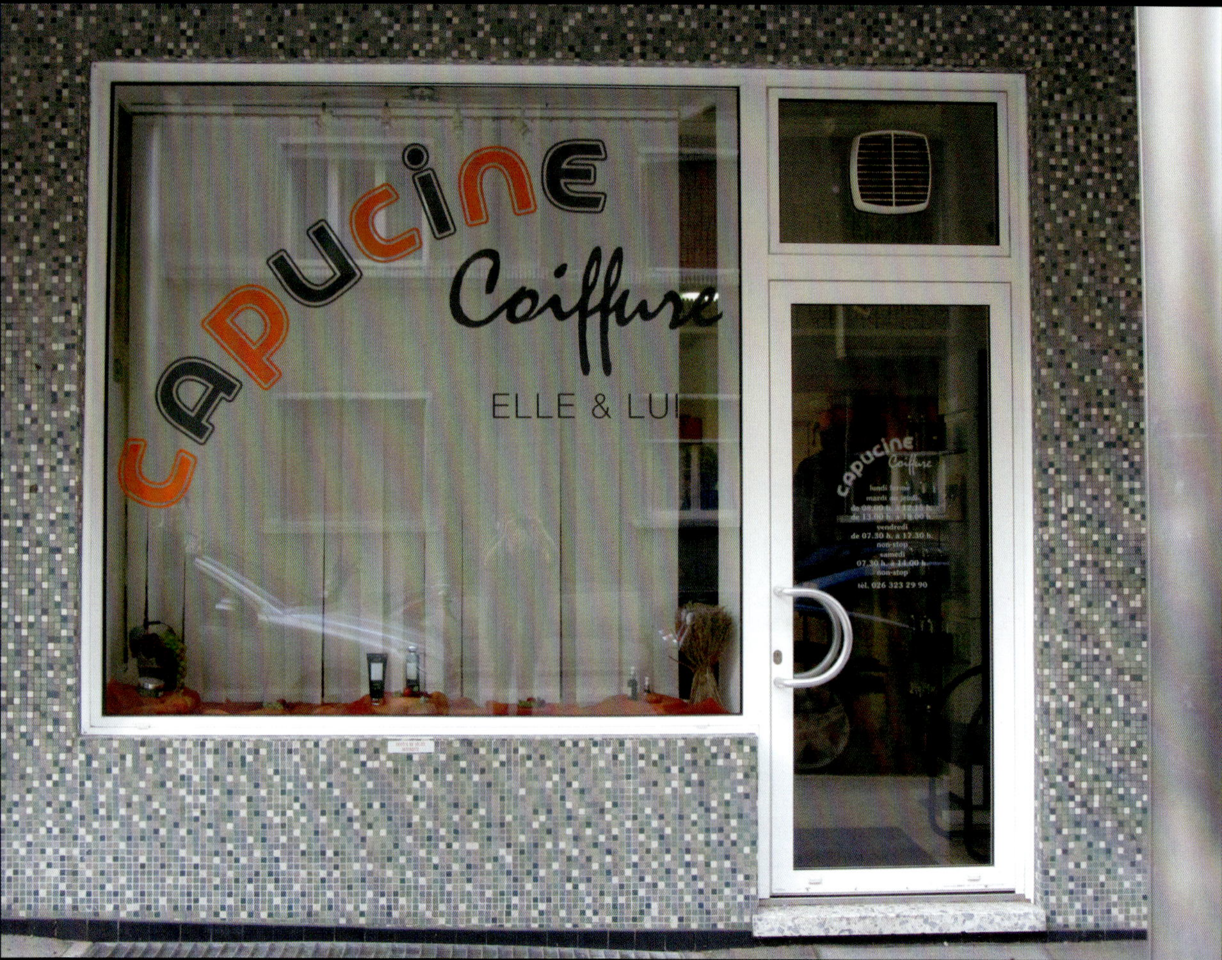

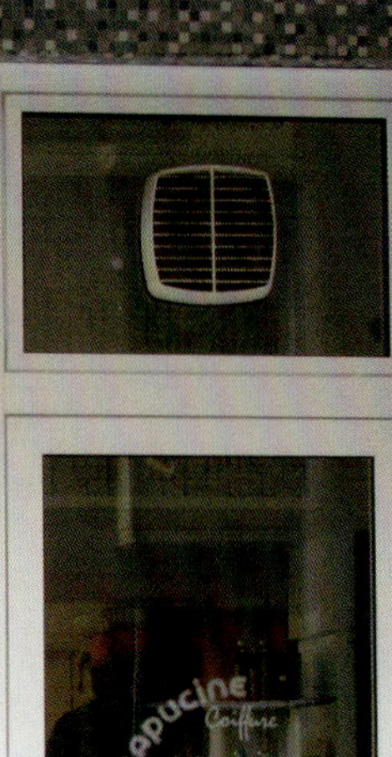
capucine
Coiffure

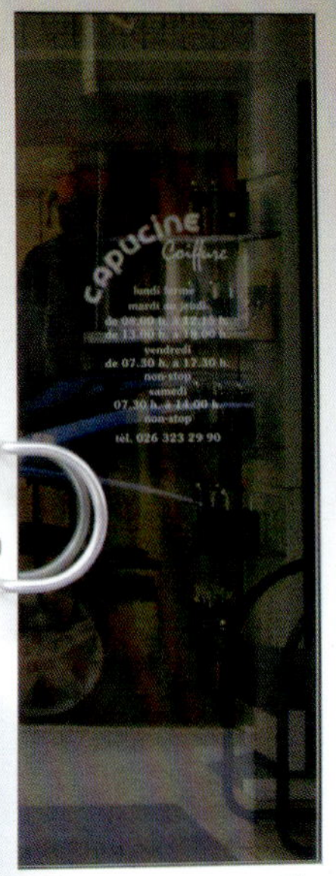
capucine
Coiffure
lundi fermé
mardi au jeudi
vendredi
de 07.30 h. à 17.30 h.
non-stop
samedi
07.30 h. à 14.00 h.
non-stop
tél. 026 323 29 90

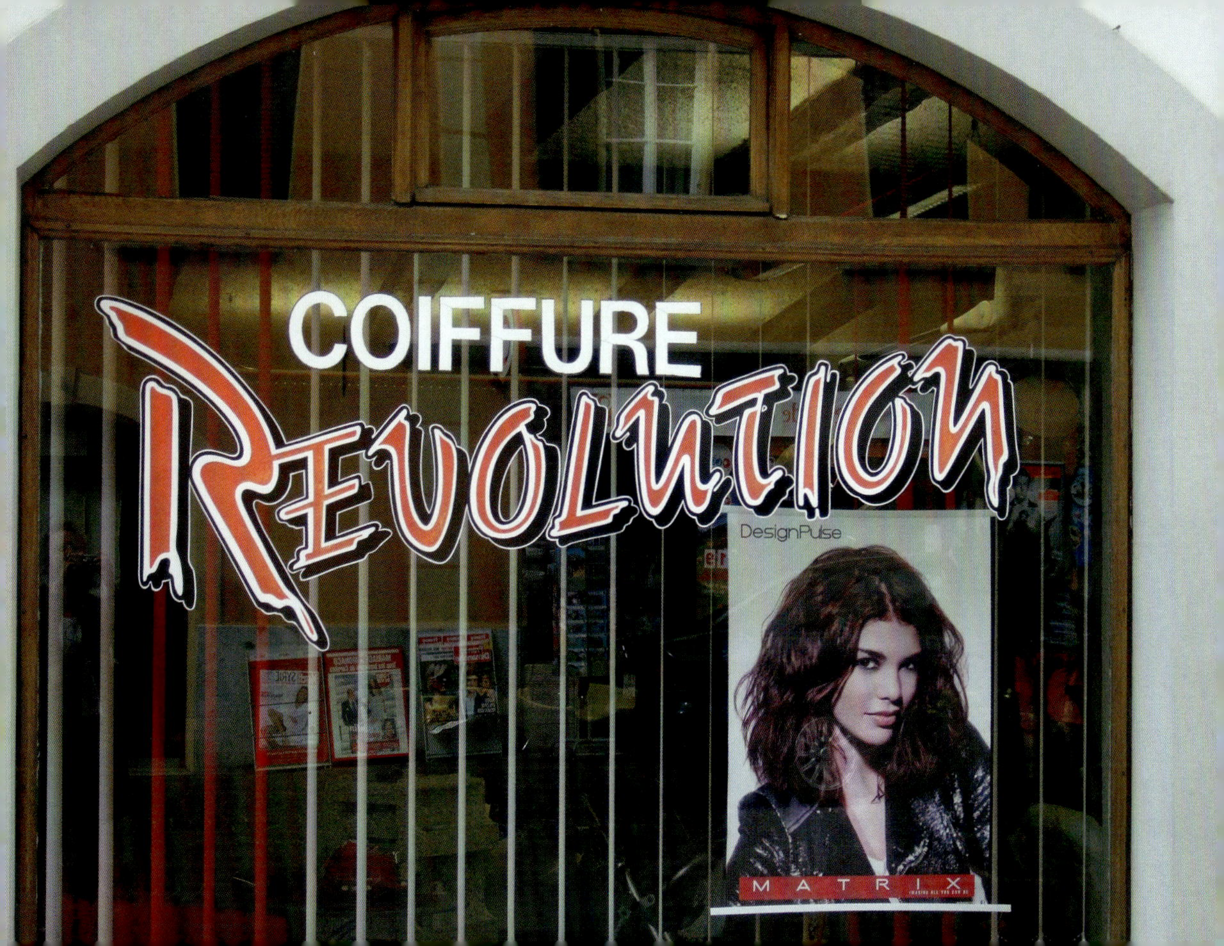
COIFFURE
REVOLUTION
DesignPulse
MATRIX

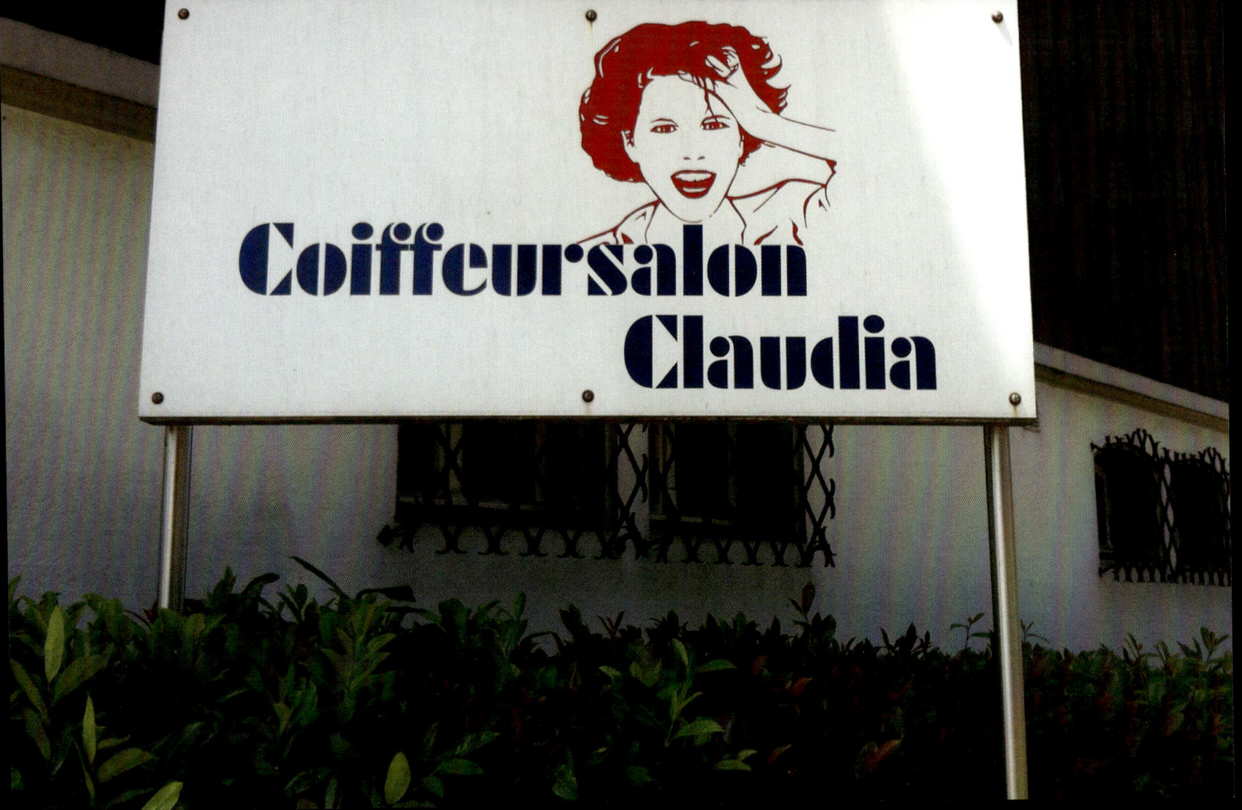
Coiffeursalon
Claudia

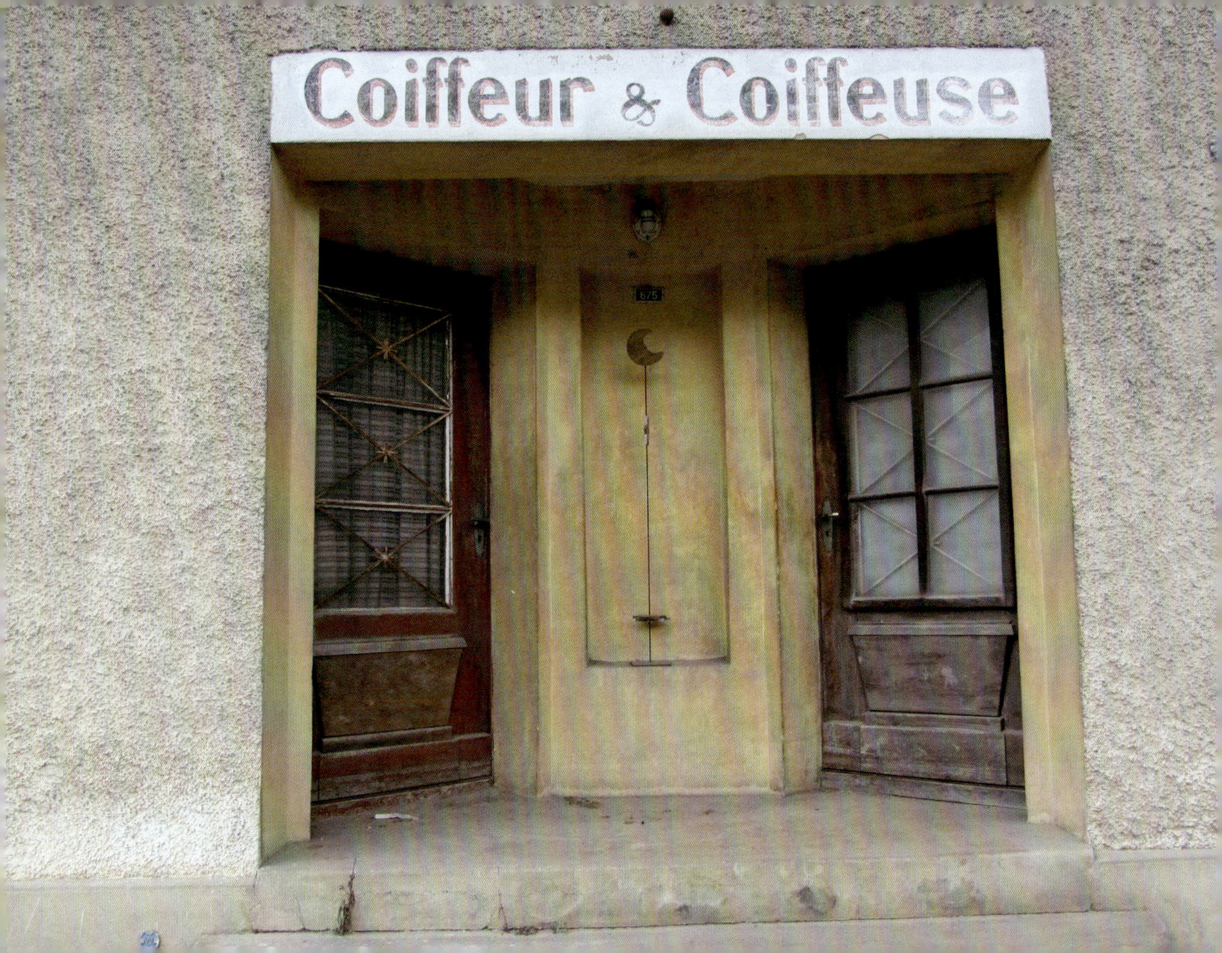

Coiffeur & Coiffeuse

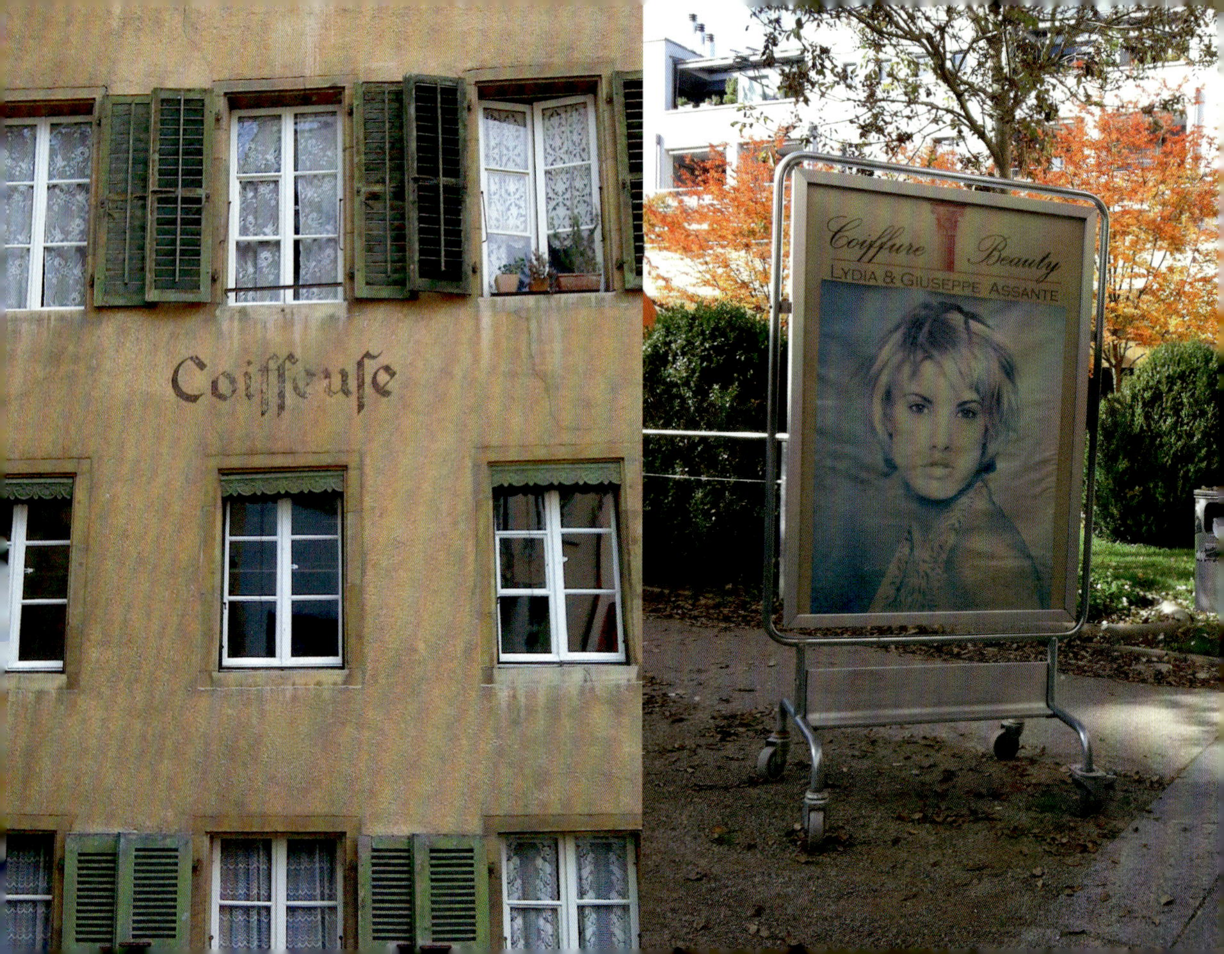
Coiffeuse
Coiffure Beauty
Lydia & Giuseppe Assante

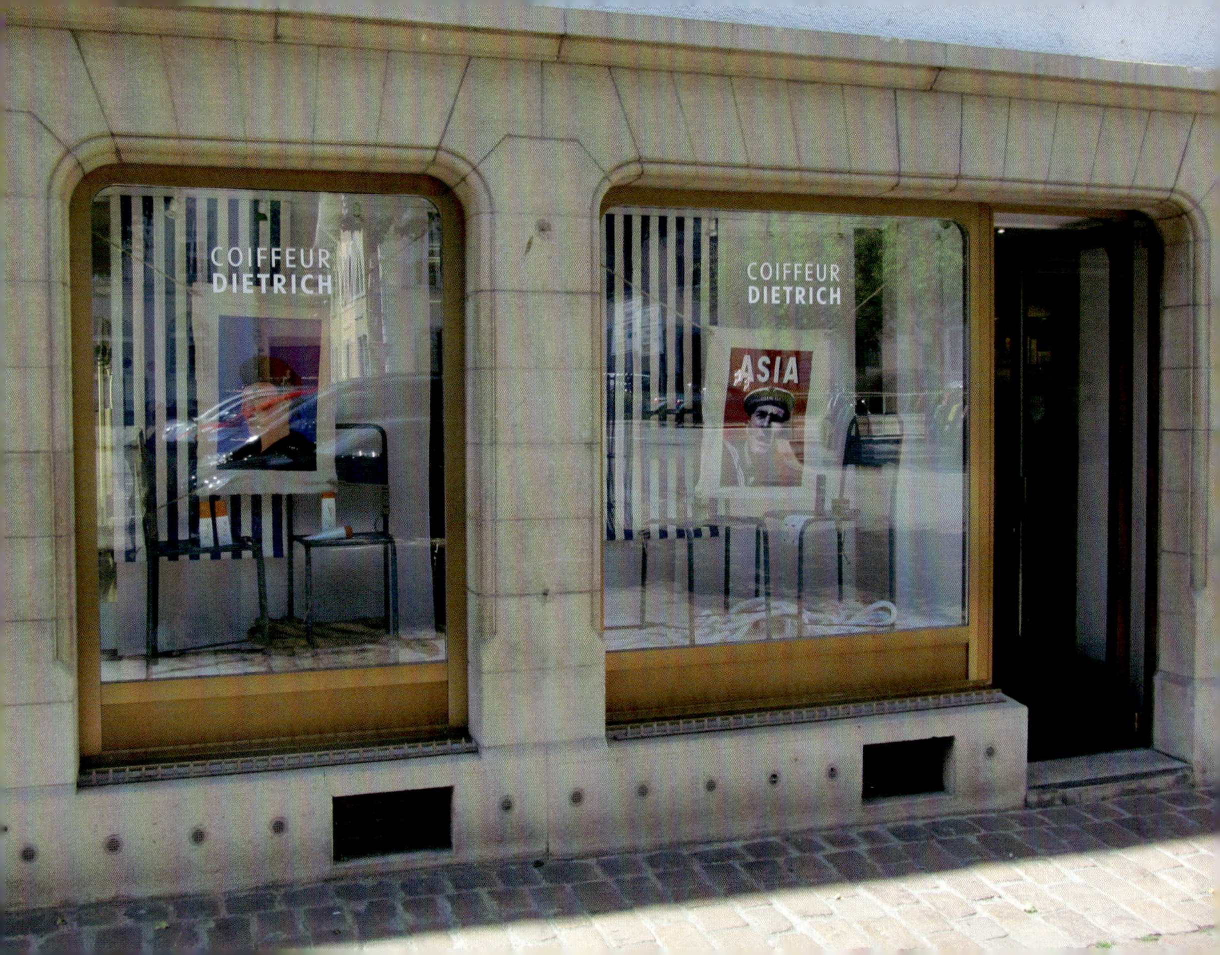
COIFFEUR
DIETRICH
COIFFEUR
DIETRICH
ASIA

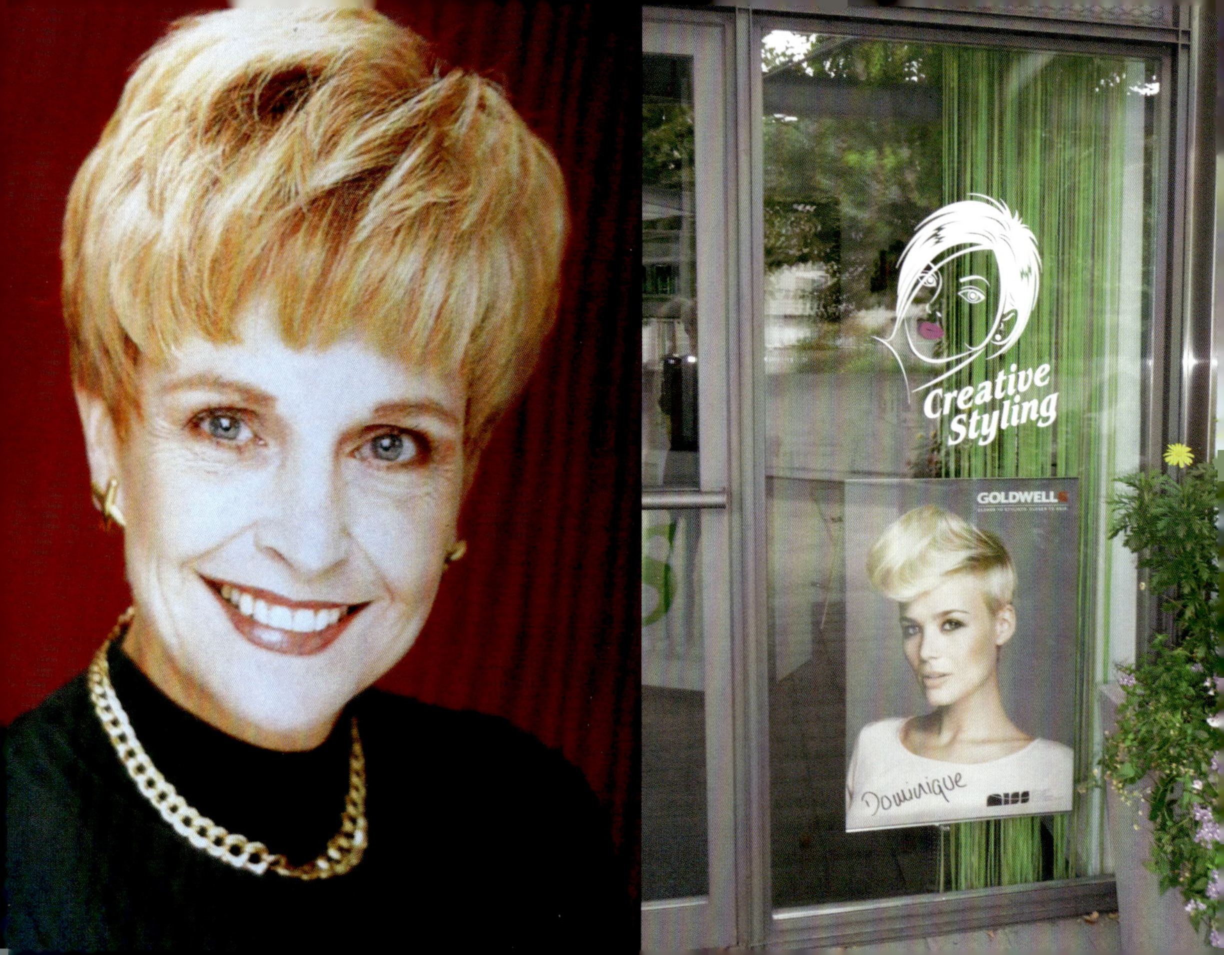
Creative
Styling
GOLDWELL
Dominique

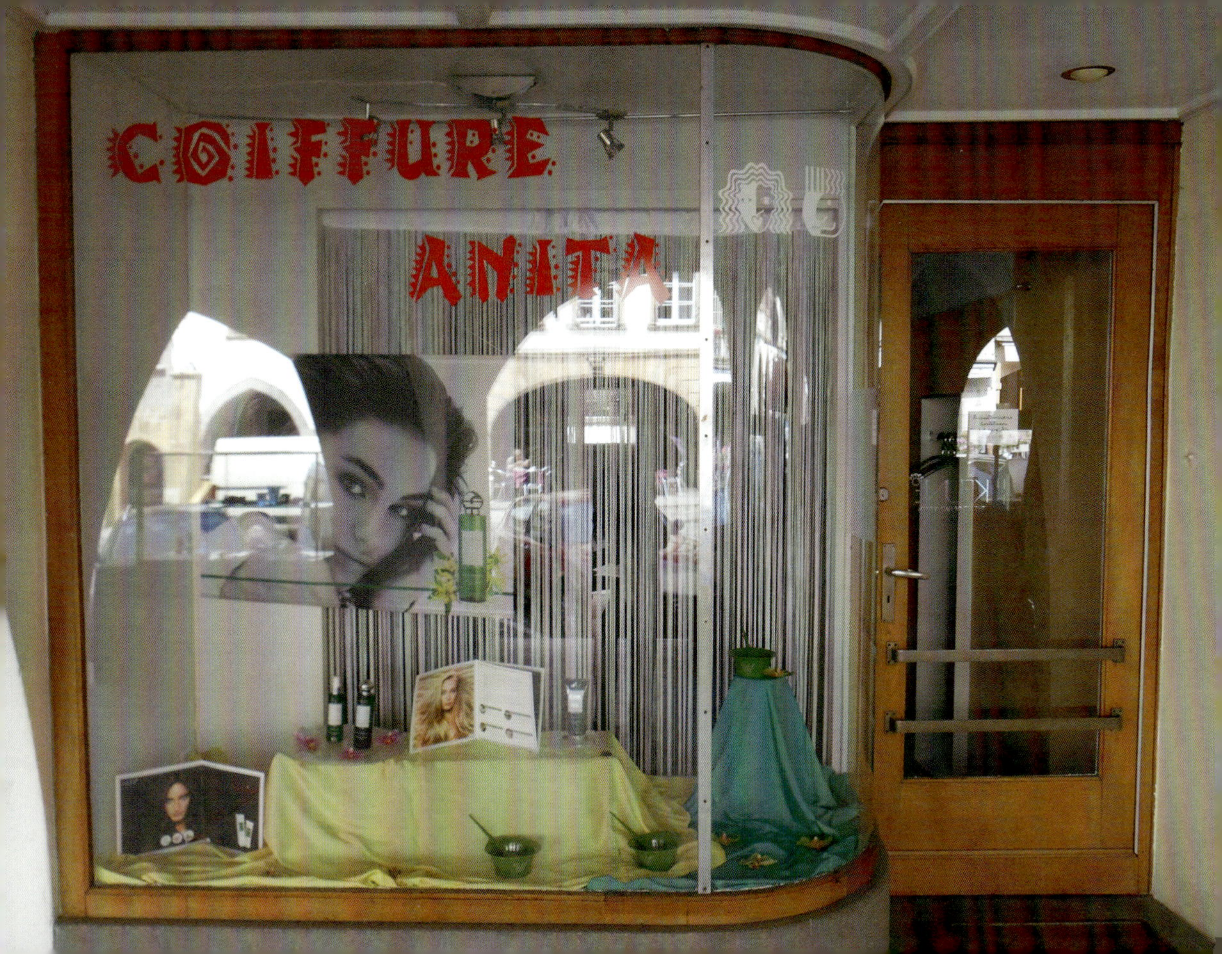

COIFFURE
ANITA

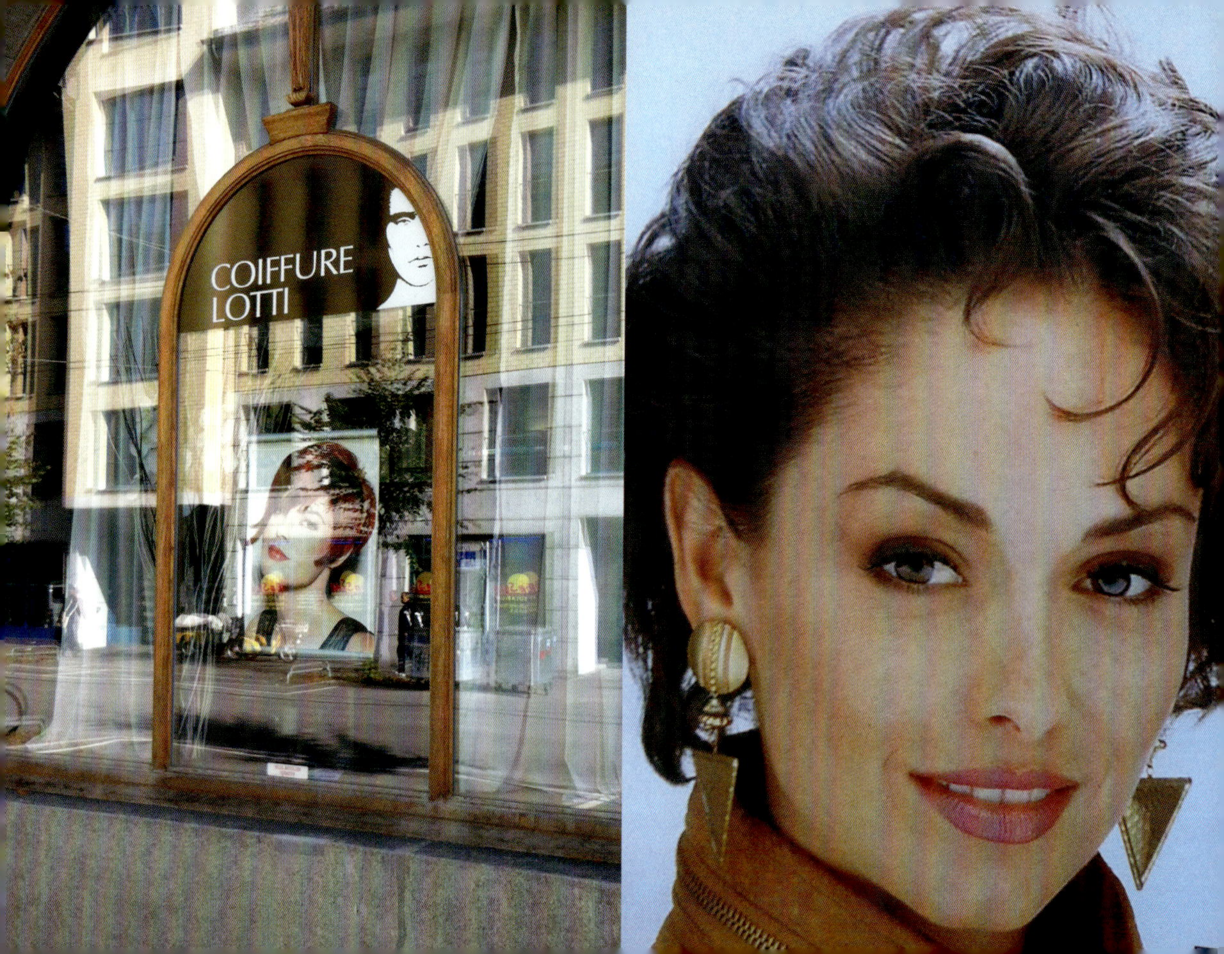
COIFFURE
LOTTI

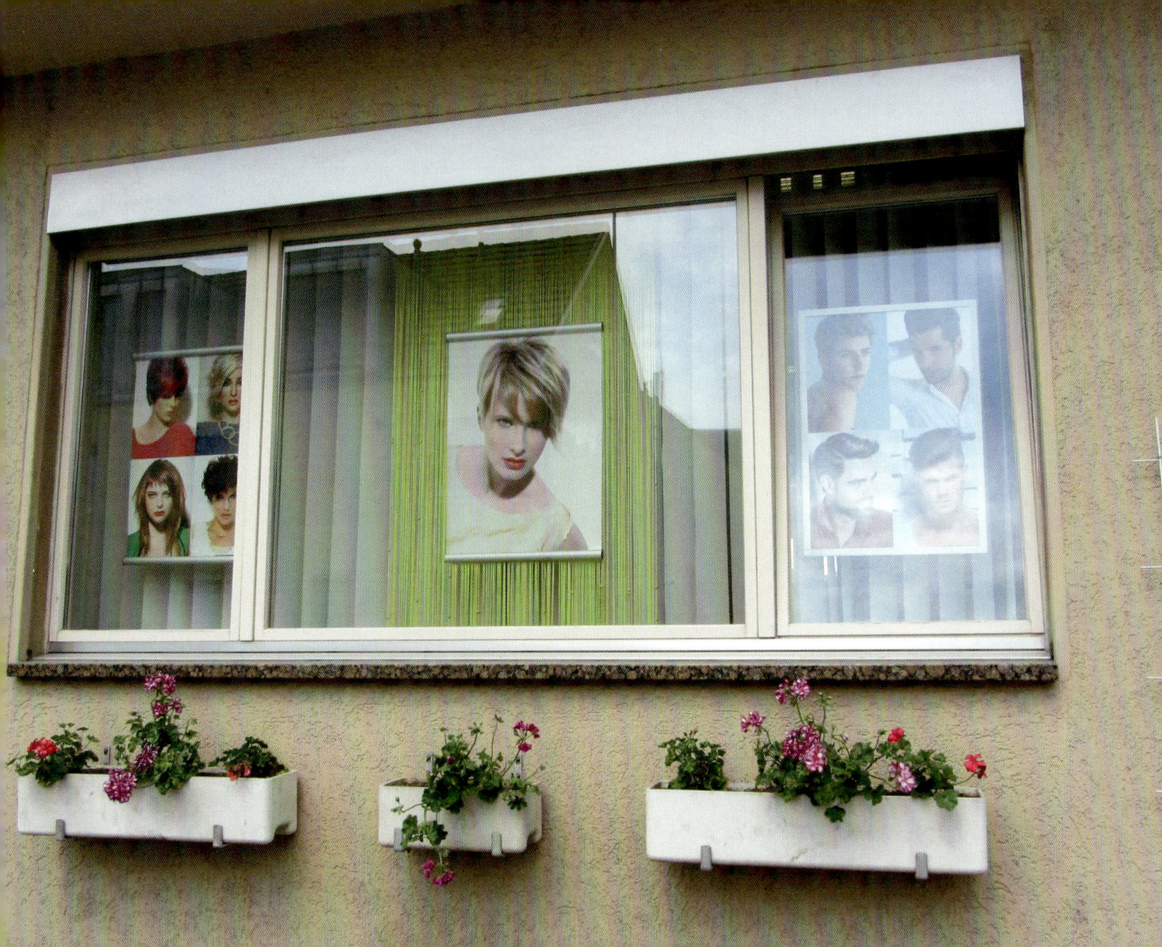

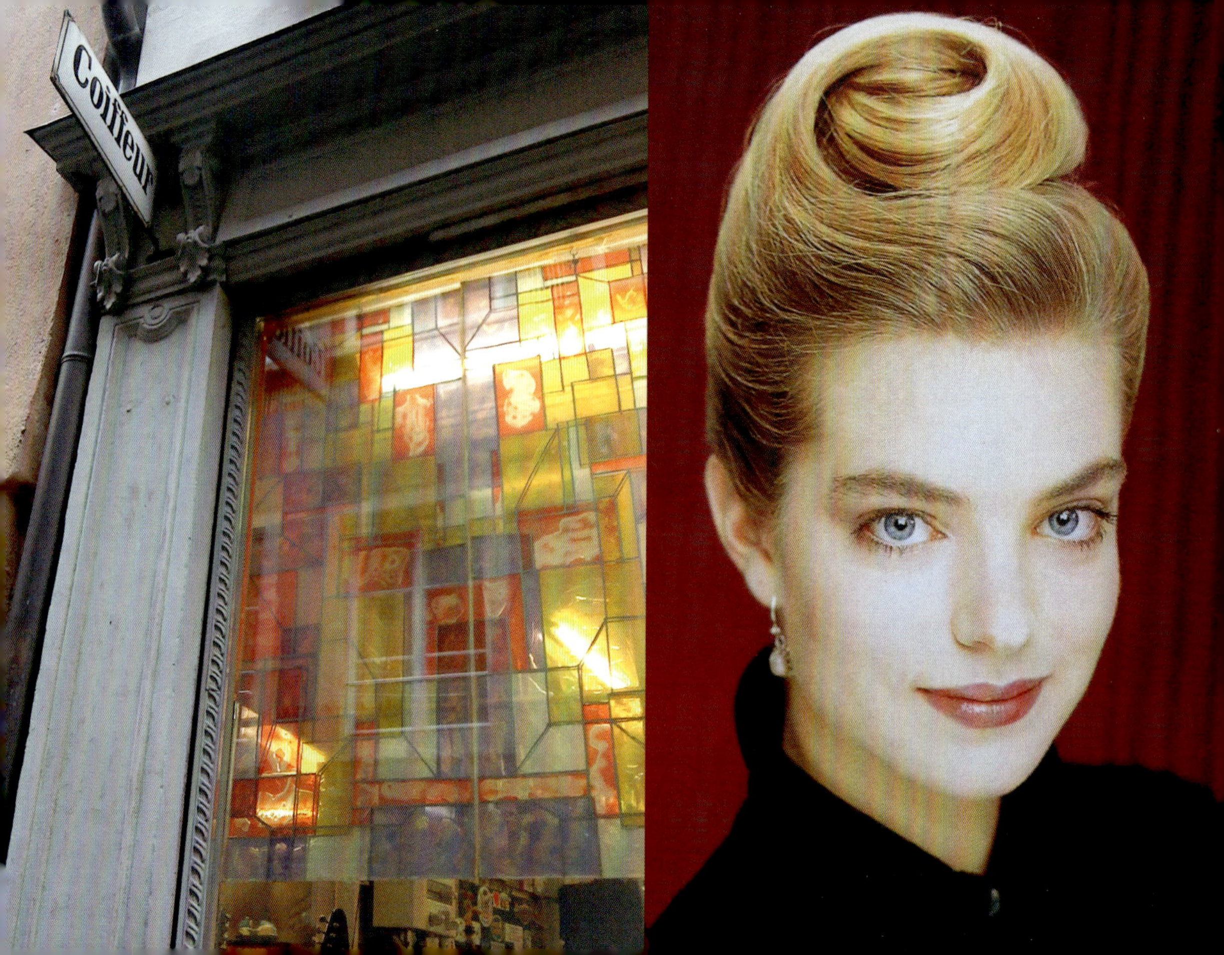
Coiffeur

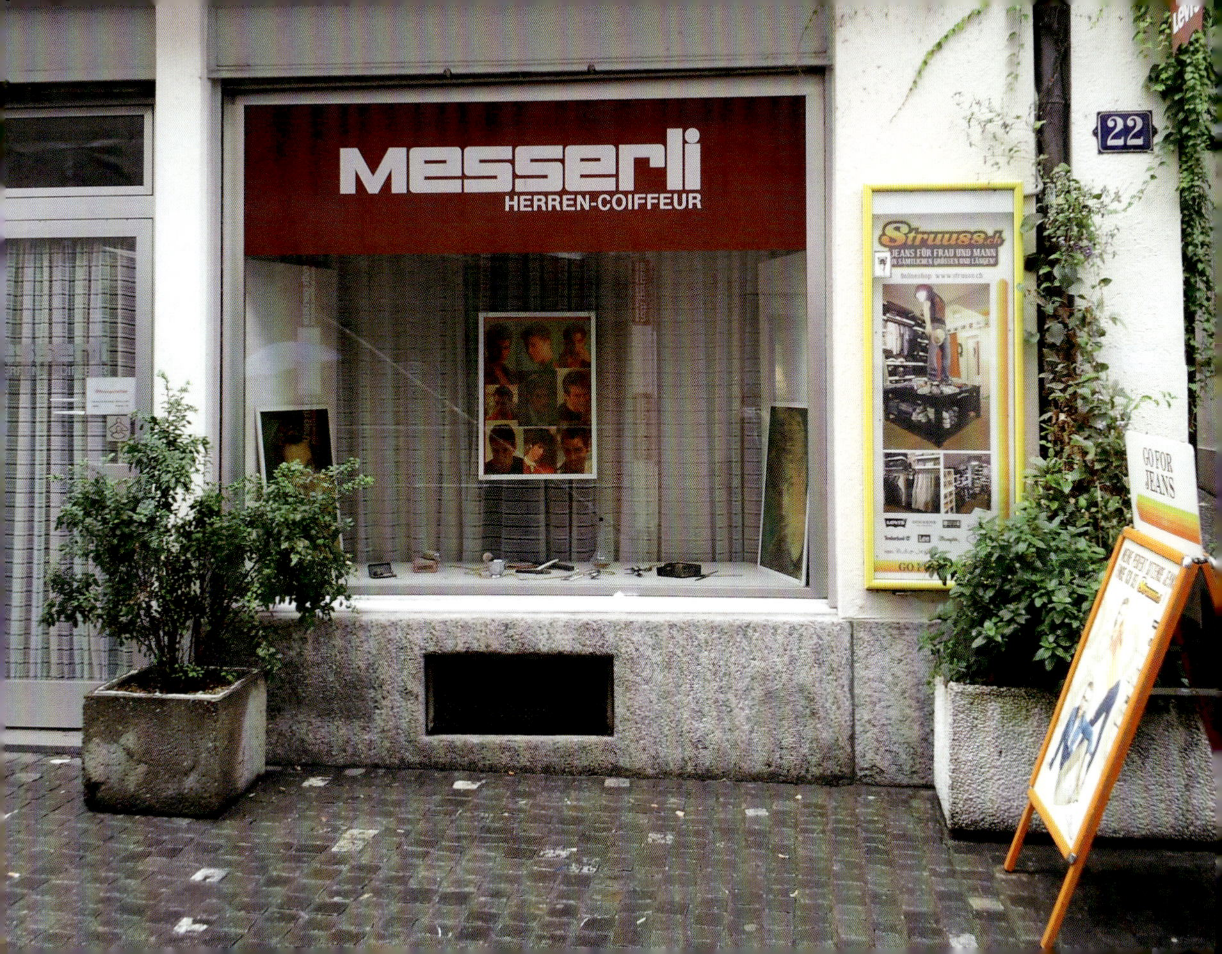

messerli
HERREN-COIFFEUR
22
Struuss.ch
JEANS FÜR FRAU UND MANN
IN SÄMTLICHEN GRÖSSEN UND LÄNGEN!
GO FOR
JEANS

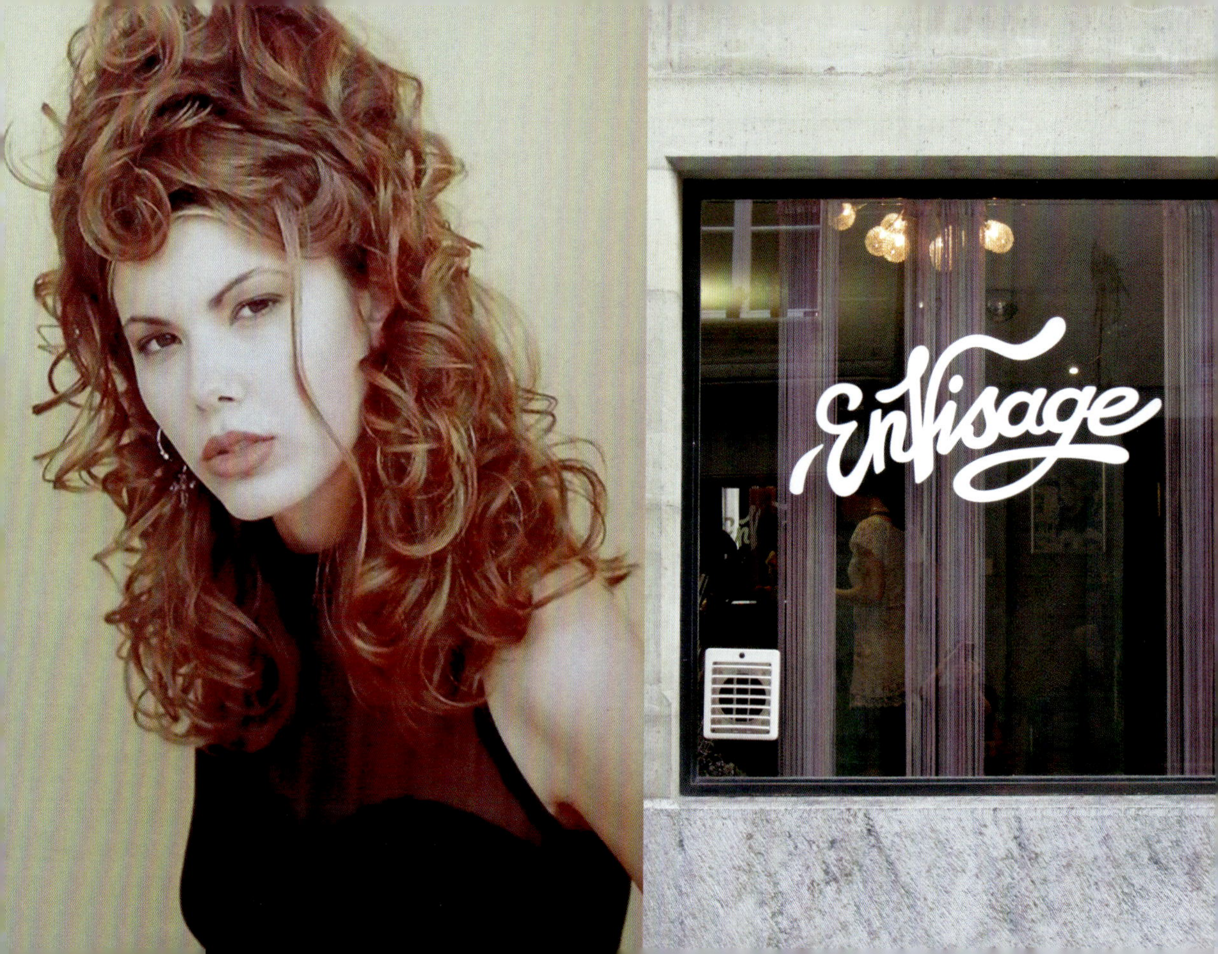
EnVisage

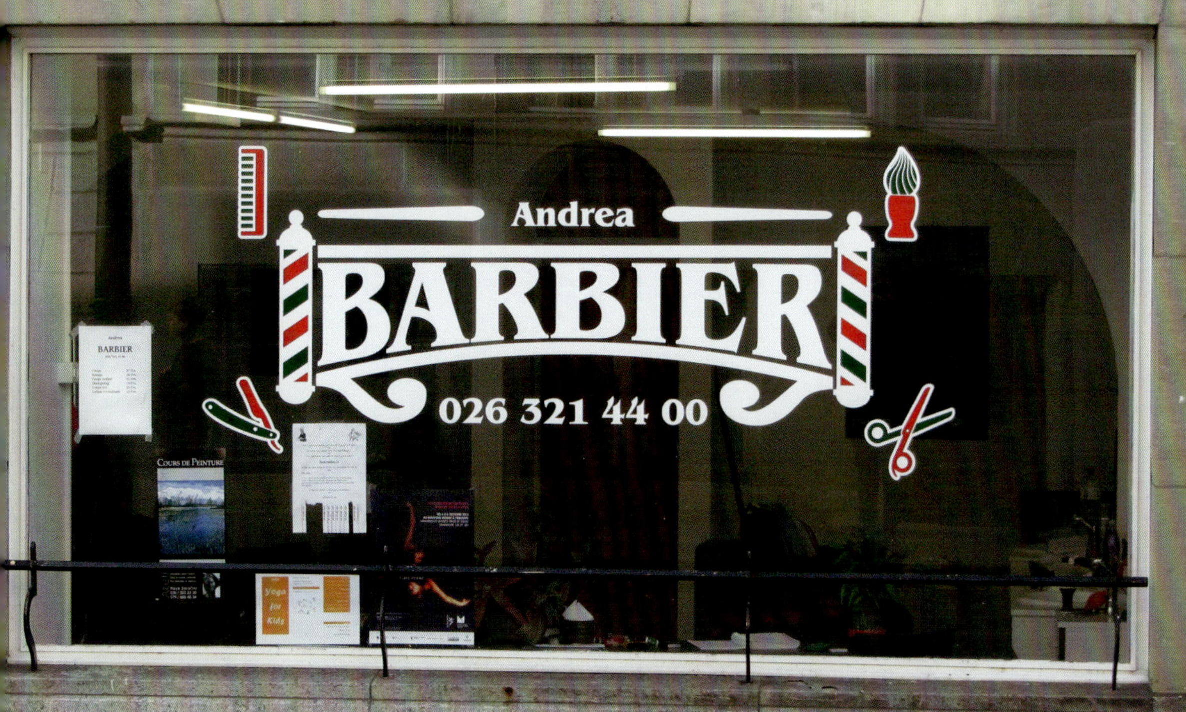
Andrea
BARBIER
026 321 44 00
Andrea
BARBIER
Cours de Peinture
Yoga for Kids

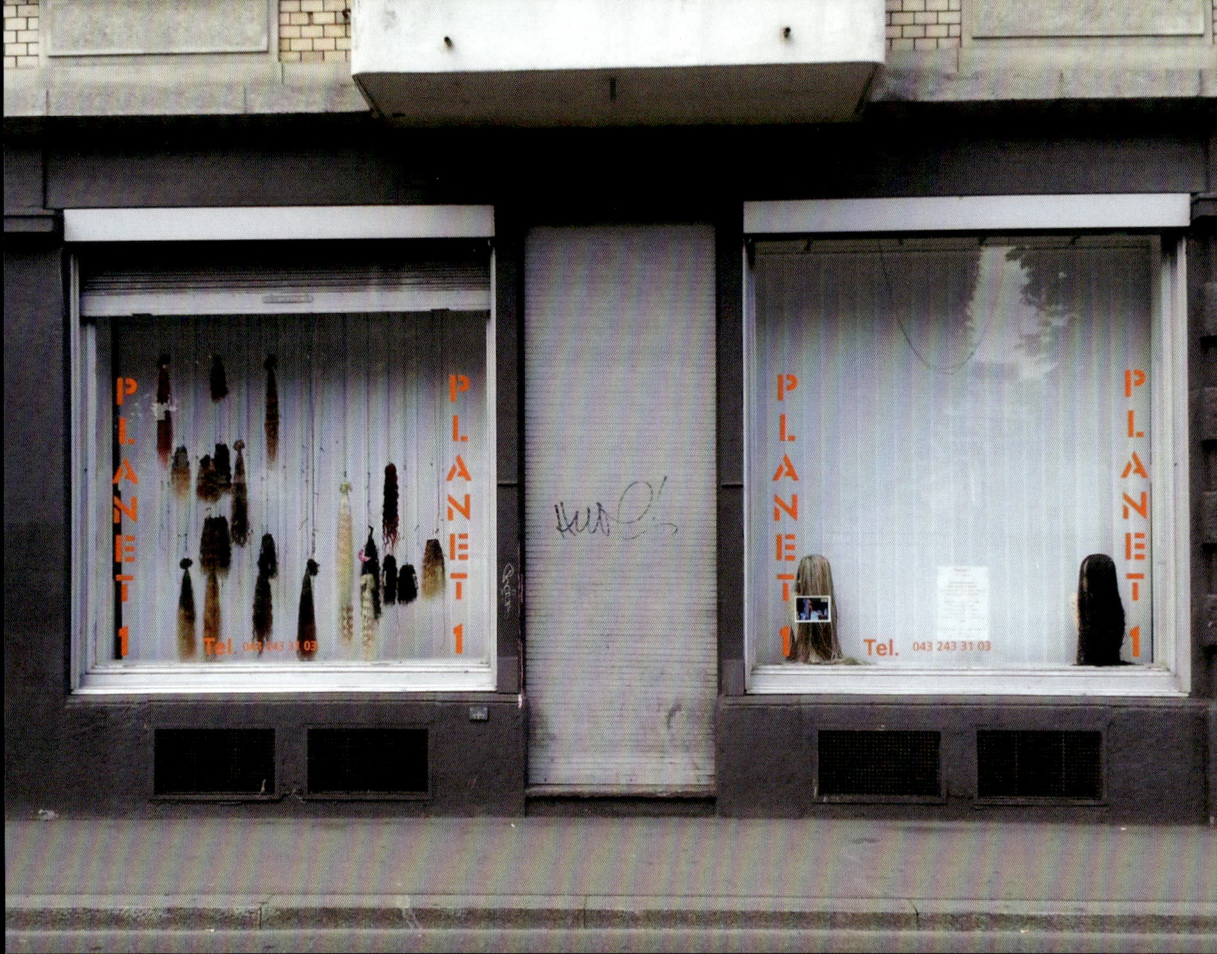
PLANET 1
Tel.
PLANET 1
PLANET 1
Tel. 043 243 31 03
PLANET 1

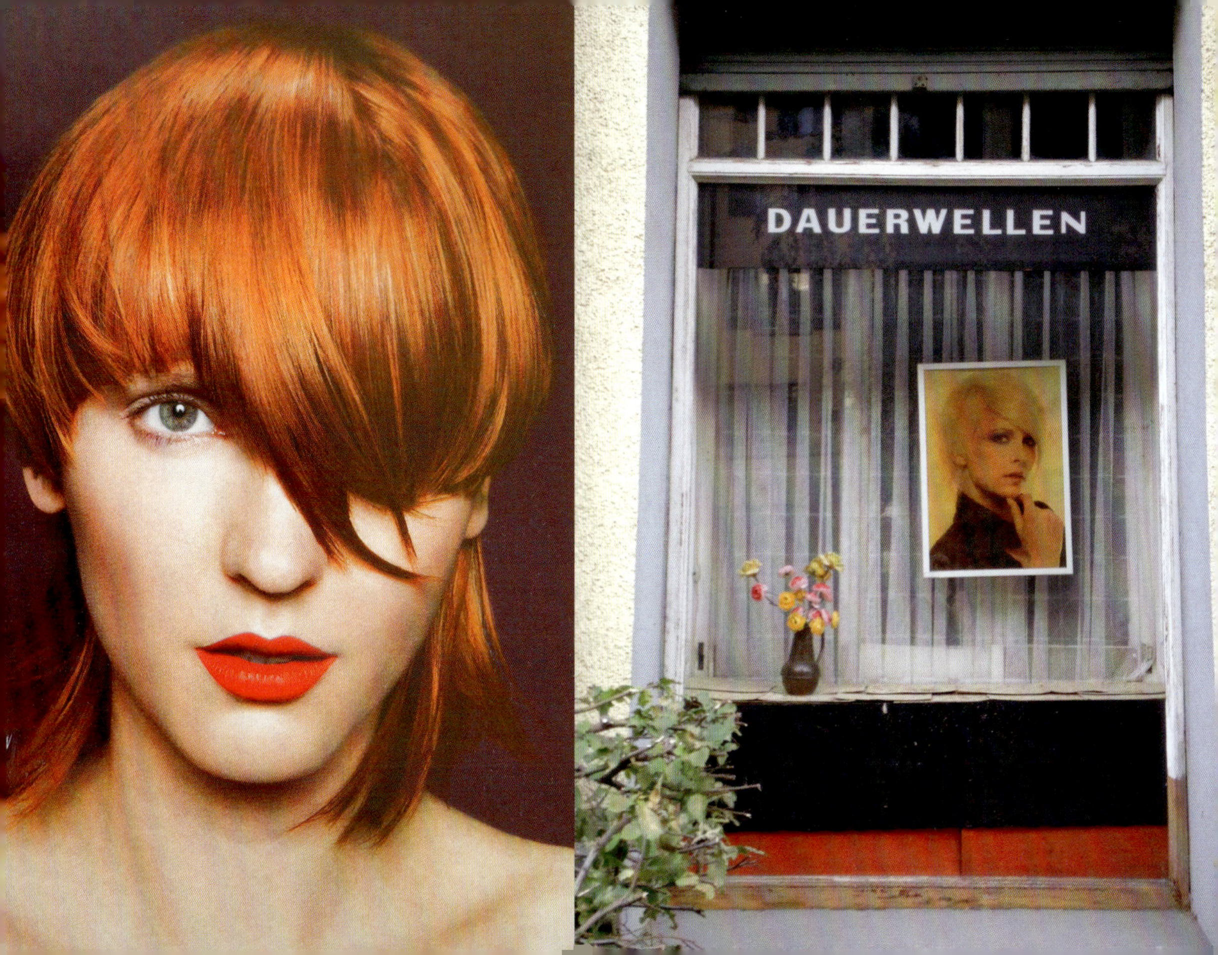
DAUERWELLEN

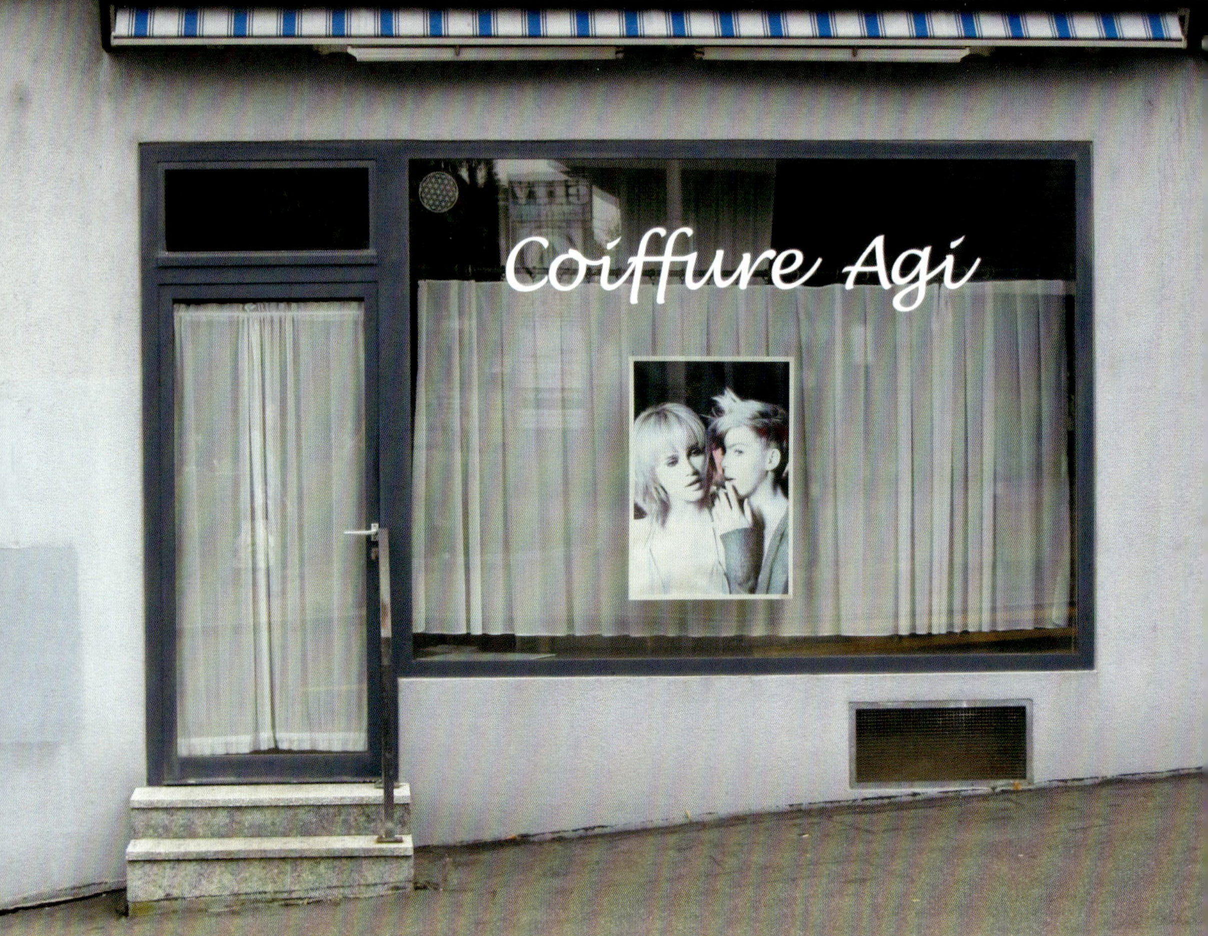
Coiffure Agi

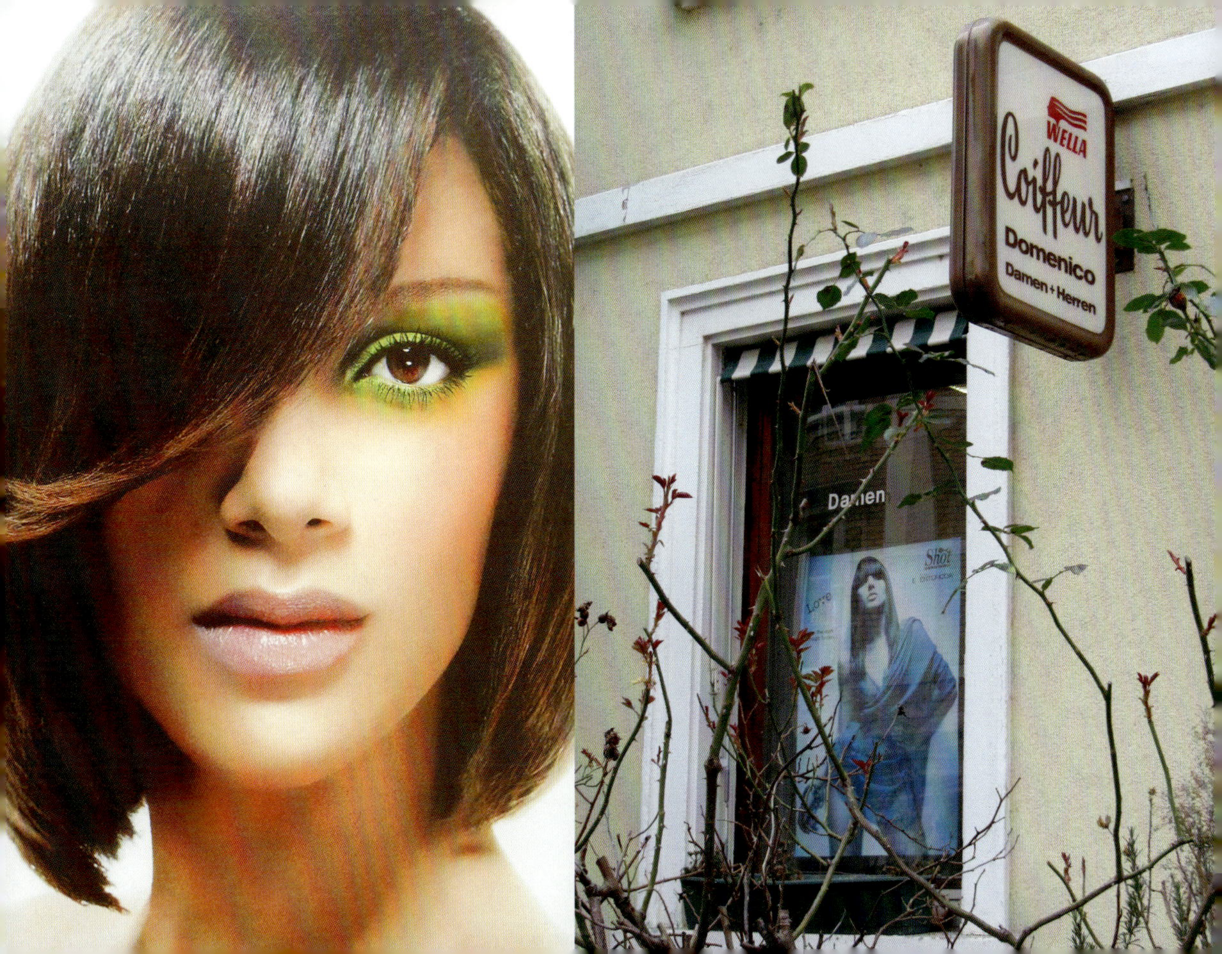
WELLA
Coiffeur
Domenico
Damen + Herren
Damen

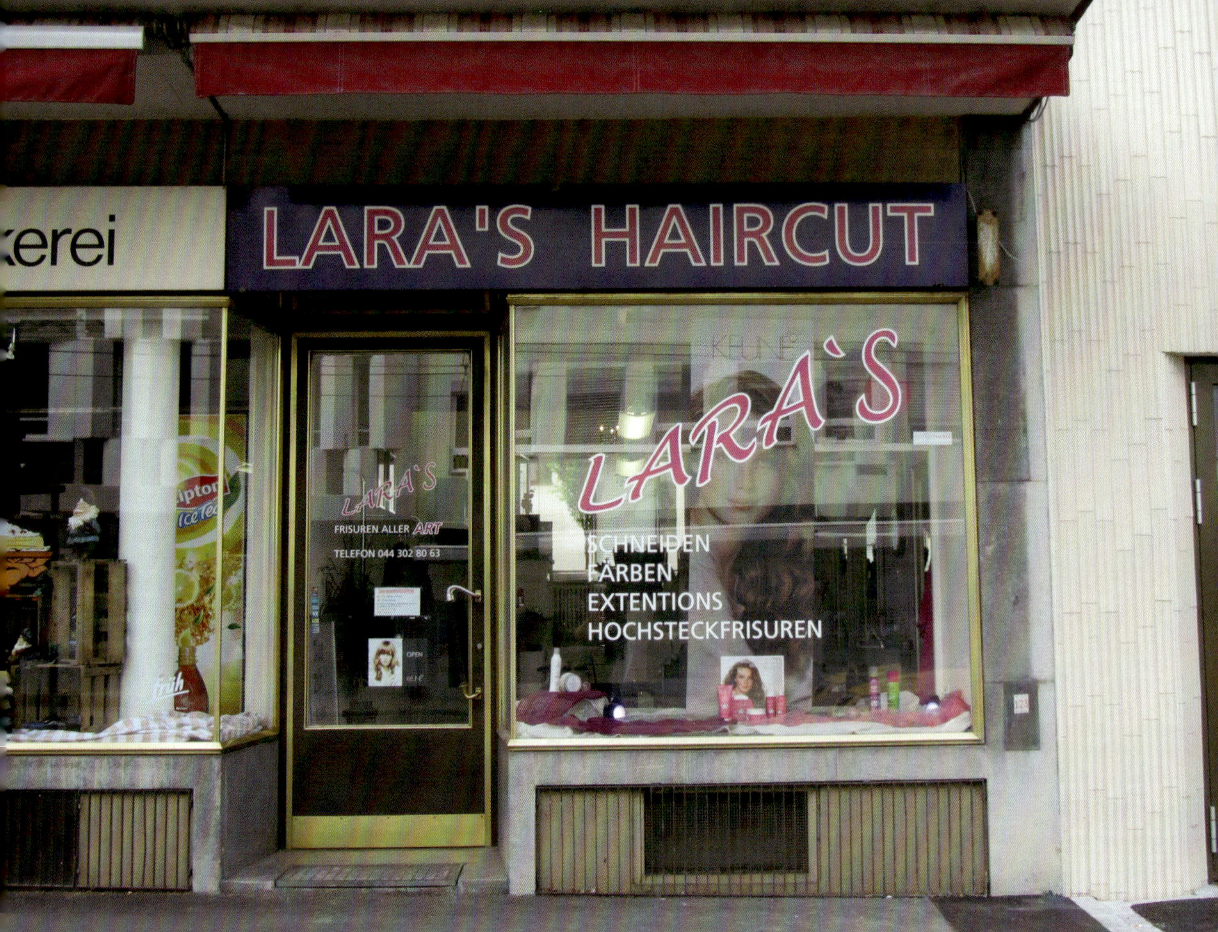

kerei
LARA'S HAIRCUT
LARA`S
FRISUREN ALLER ART
TELEFON 044 302 80 63
OPEN
LARA`S
SCHNEIDEN
FÄRBEN
EXTENTIONS
HOCHSTECKFRISUREN

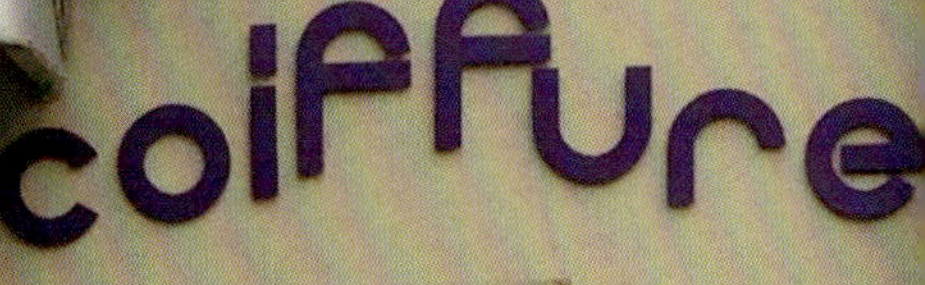
coiffure

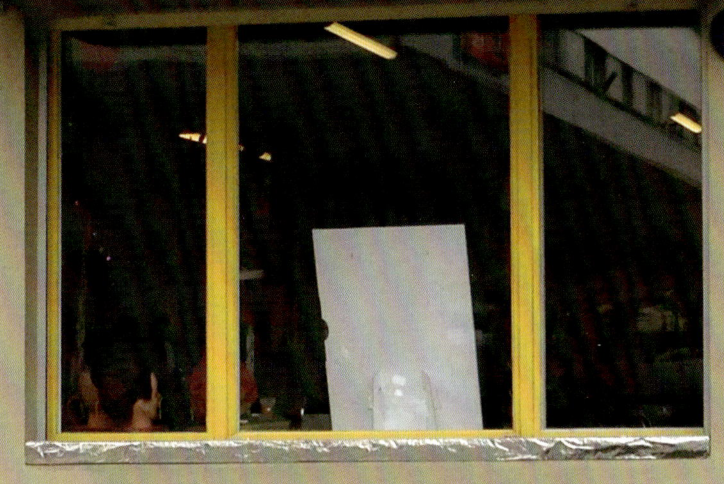
Damen Coiffure Herren

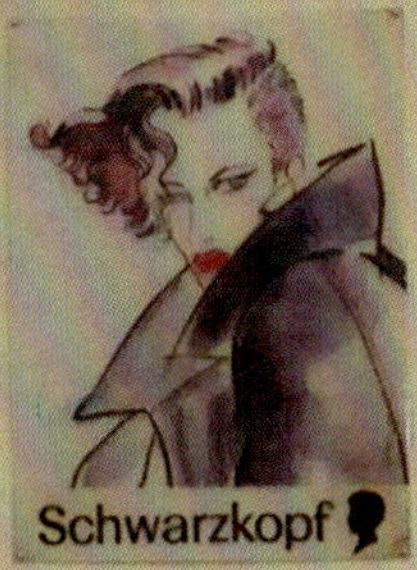
Schwarzkopf

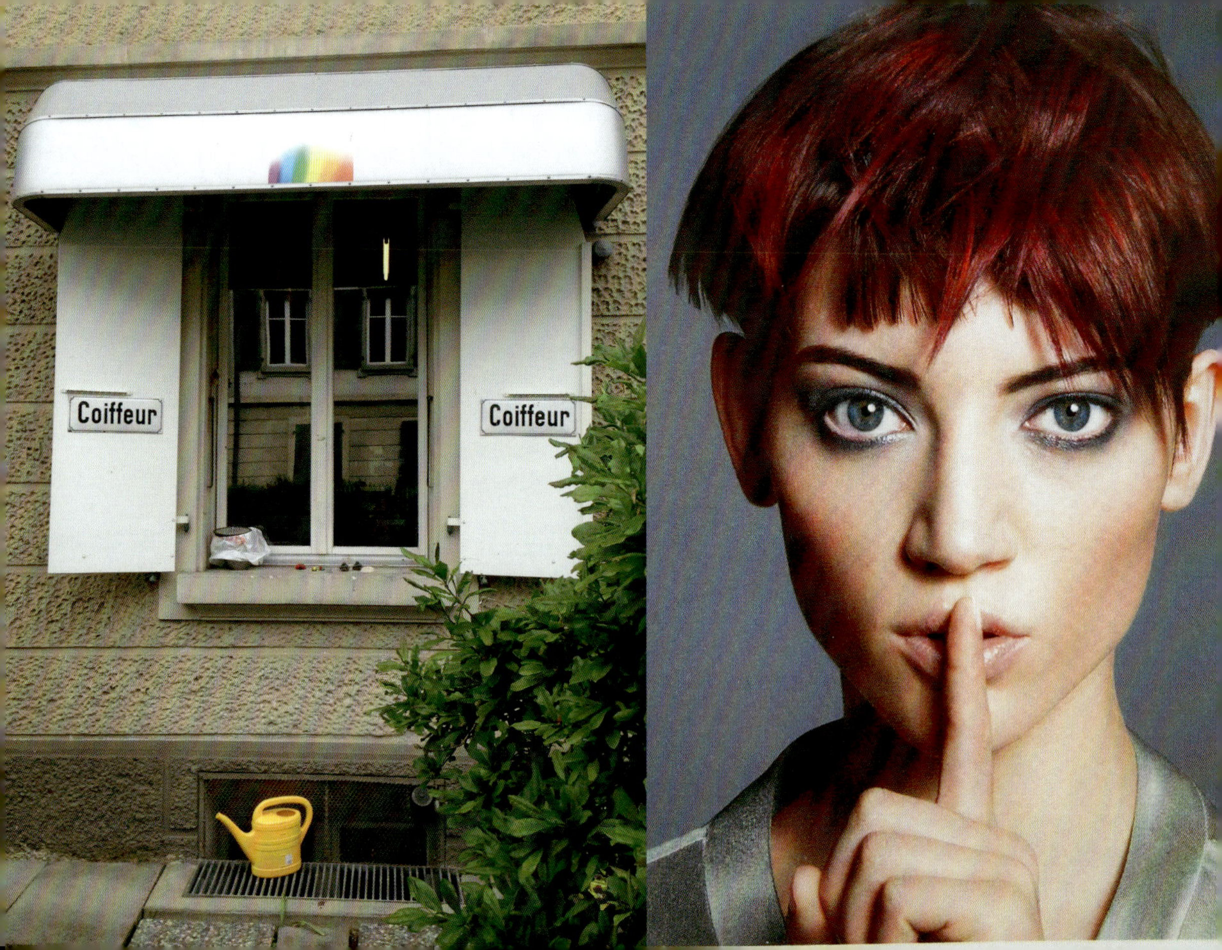
Coiffeur
Coiffeur

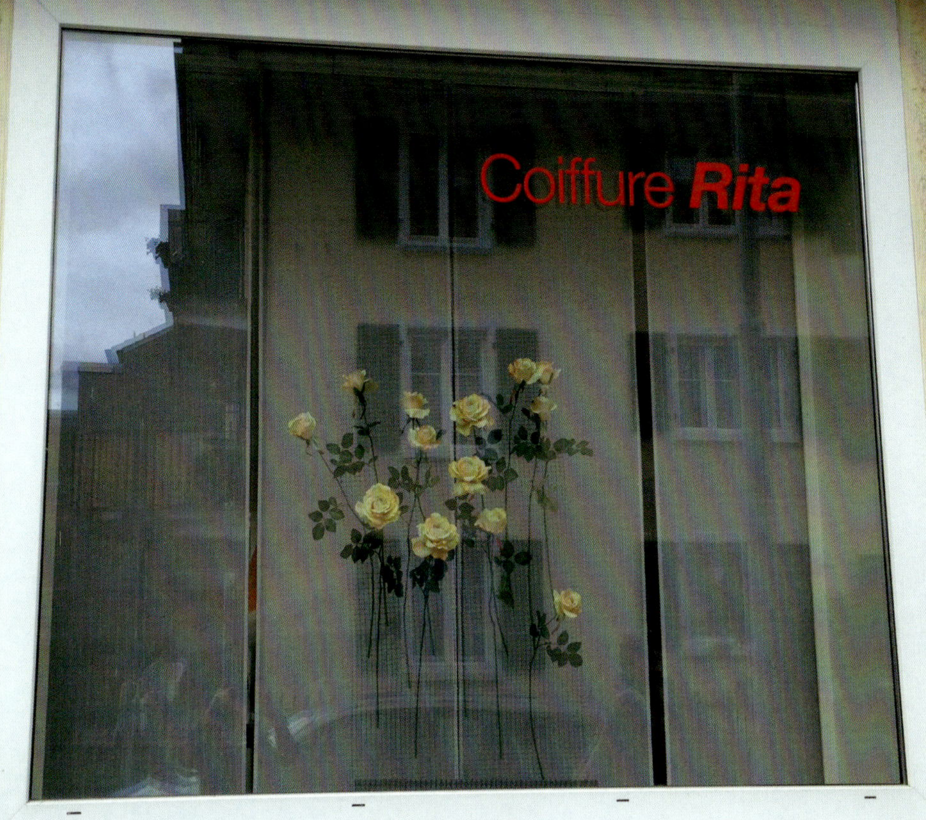
Coiffure Rita

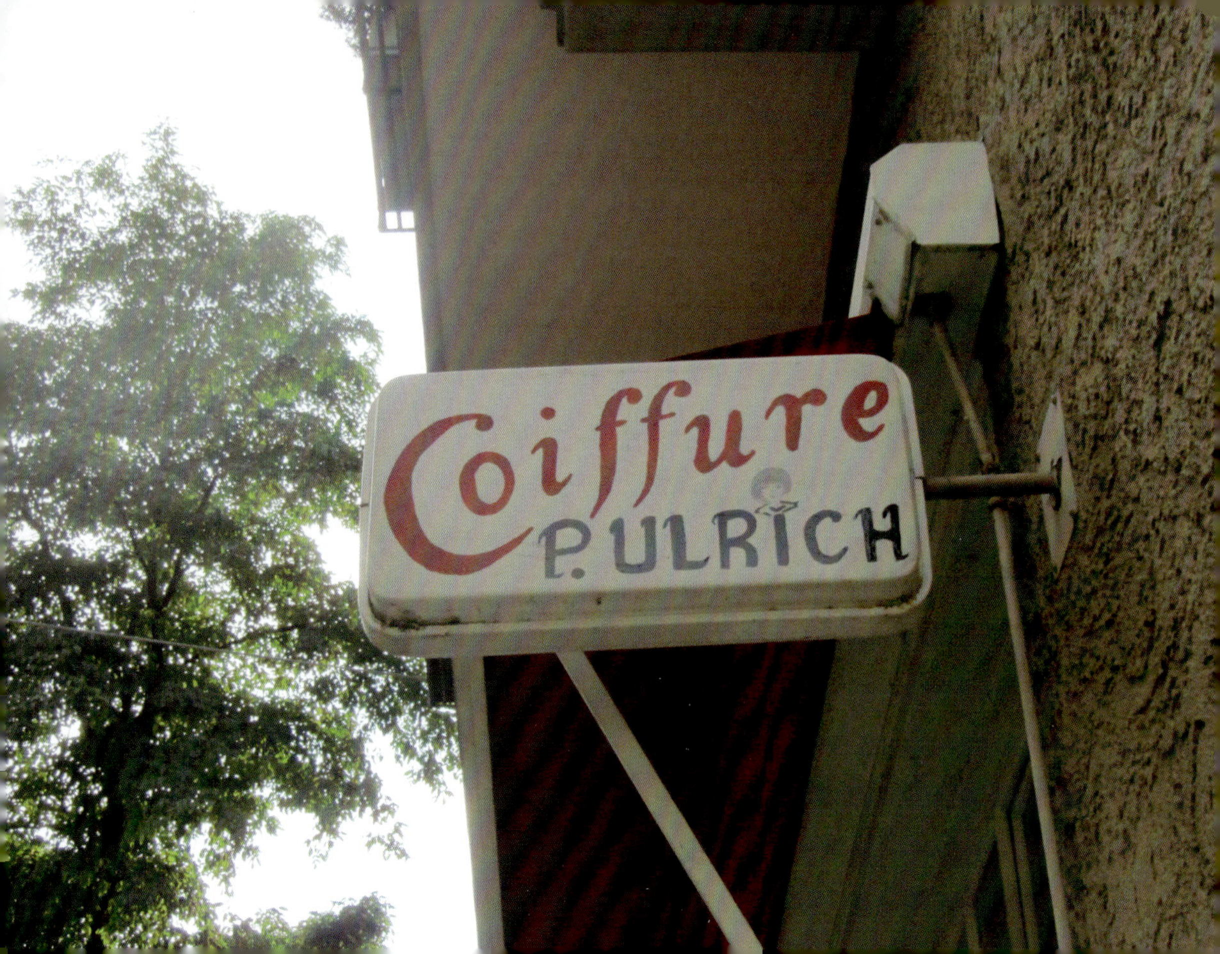
Coiffure
P. ULRICH

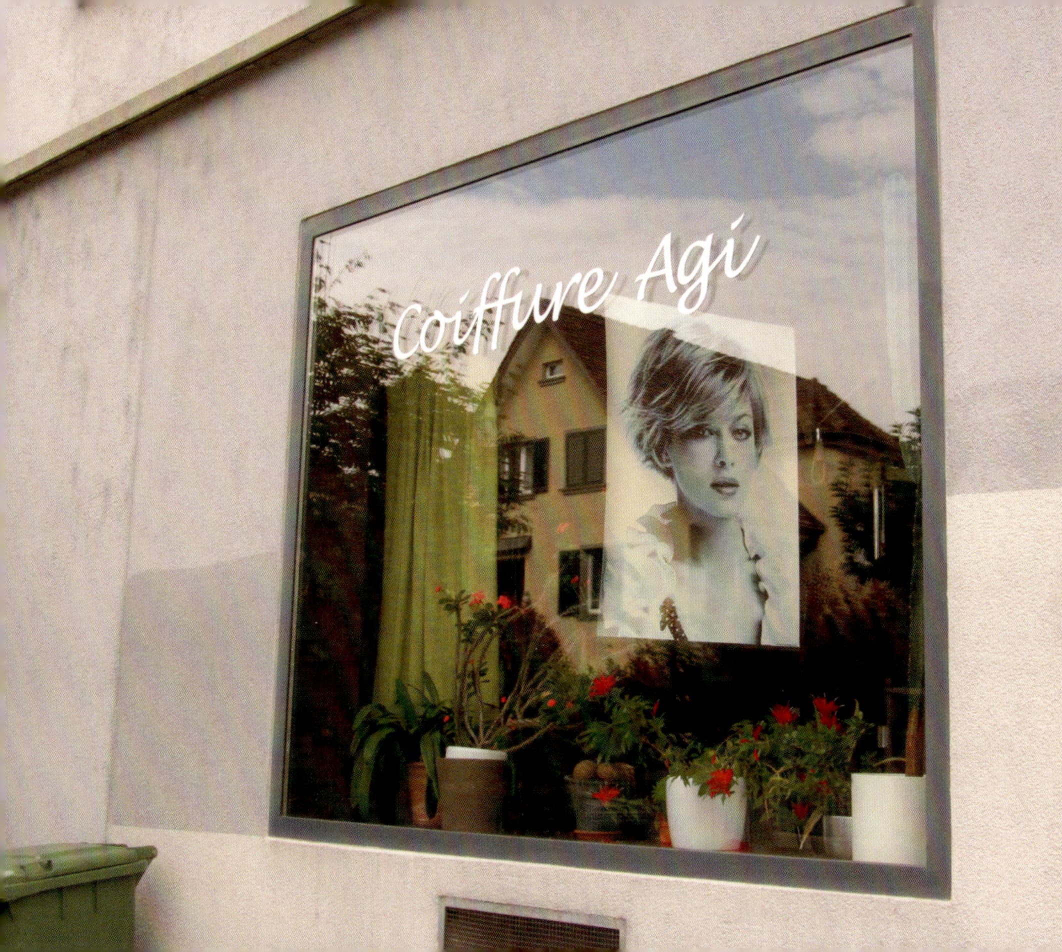
Coiffure Agi

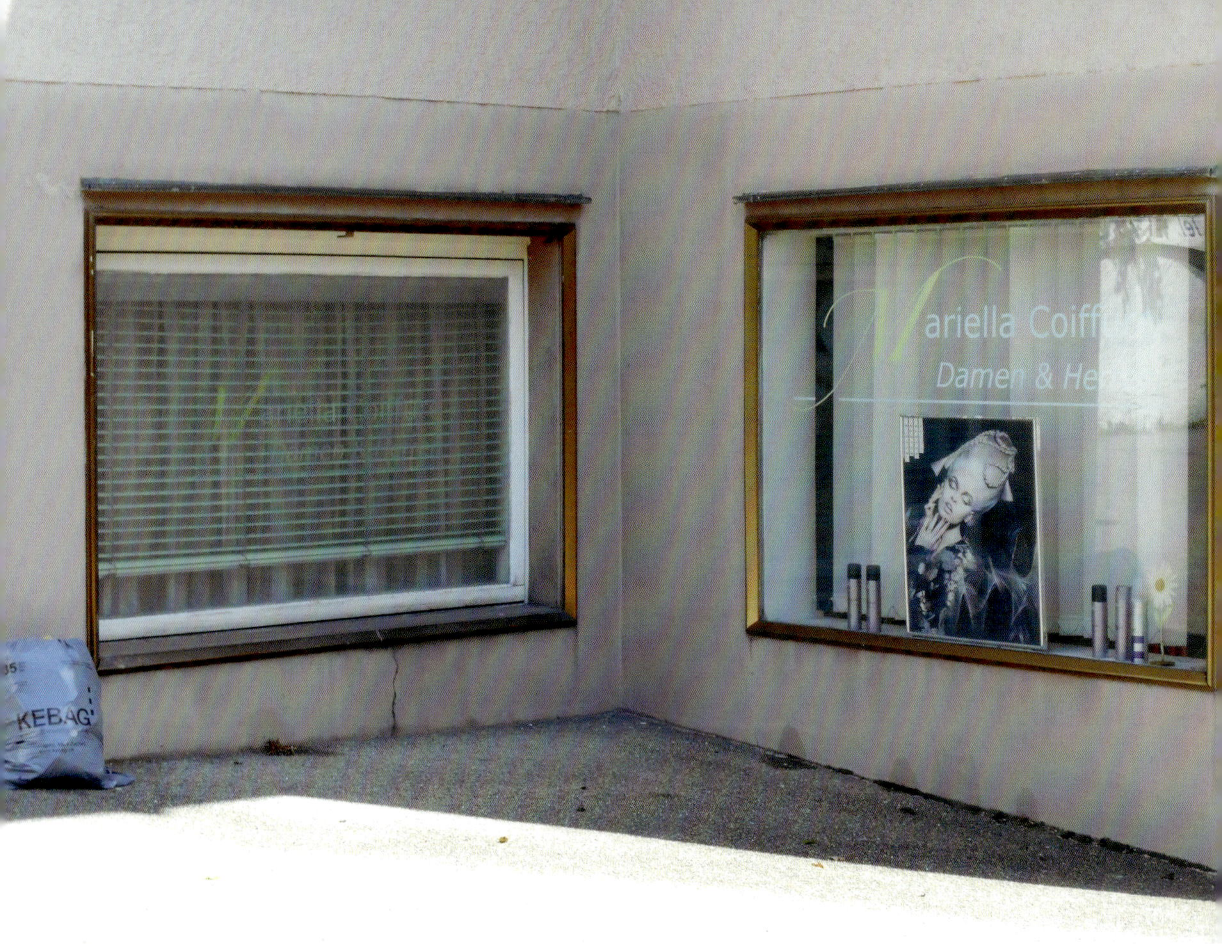
ariella Coiff
Damen & He
KEBAG

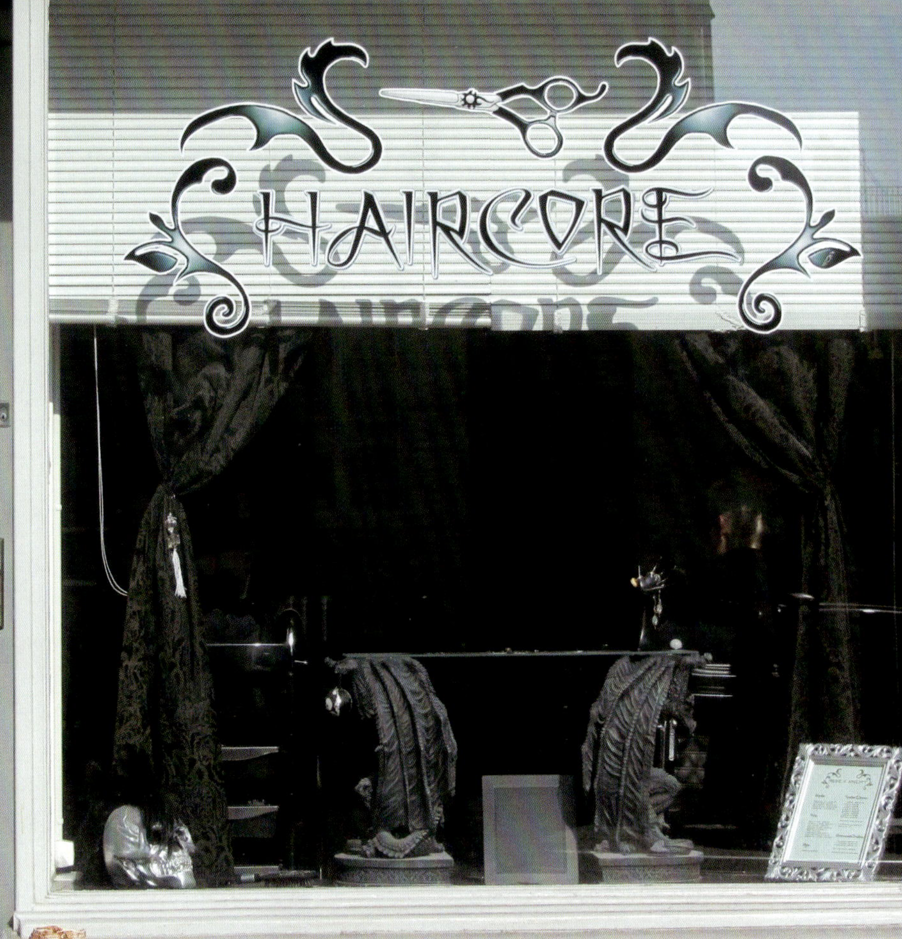
HAIRCORE
Mo geschlossen
Di + Fr 11.00-19.00
Mi 12.00-20.00
Do 11.00-17.00
Sa 10.00-16.00
078 847 30 61
haircore.ch

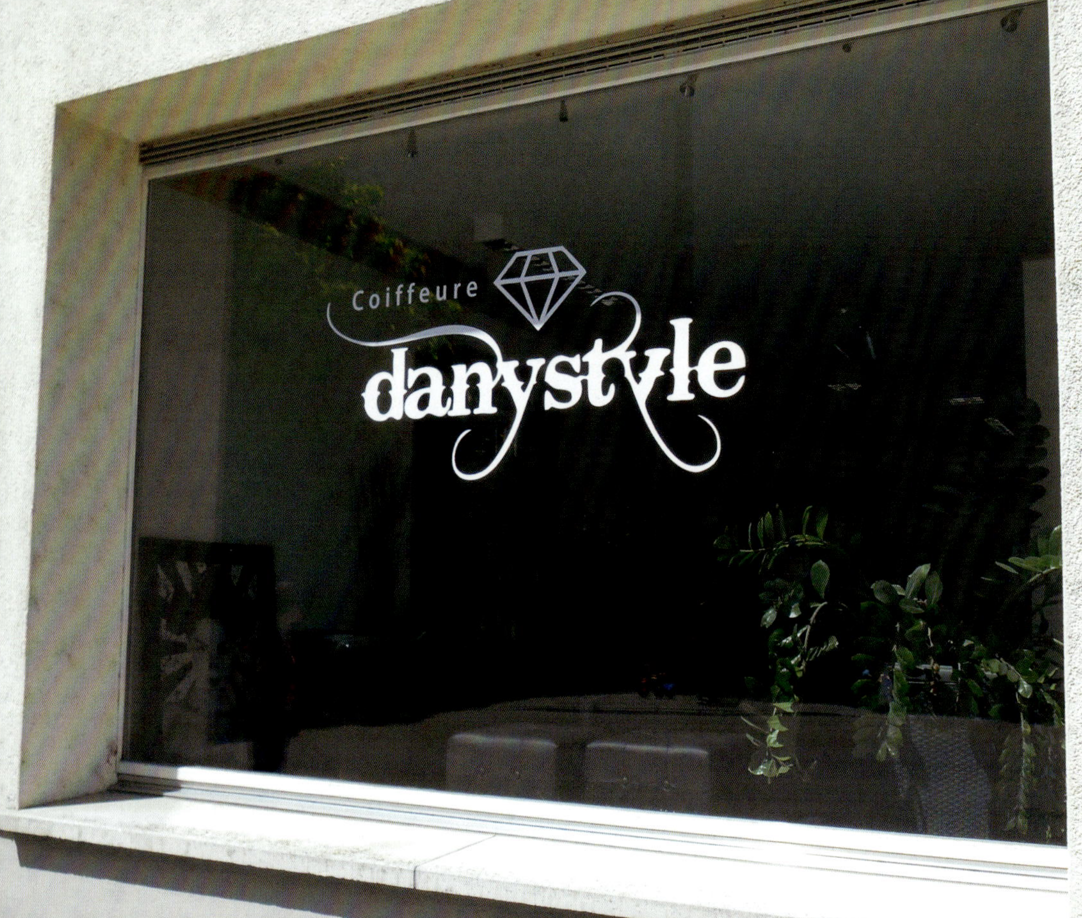
Coiffeure
danystyle

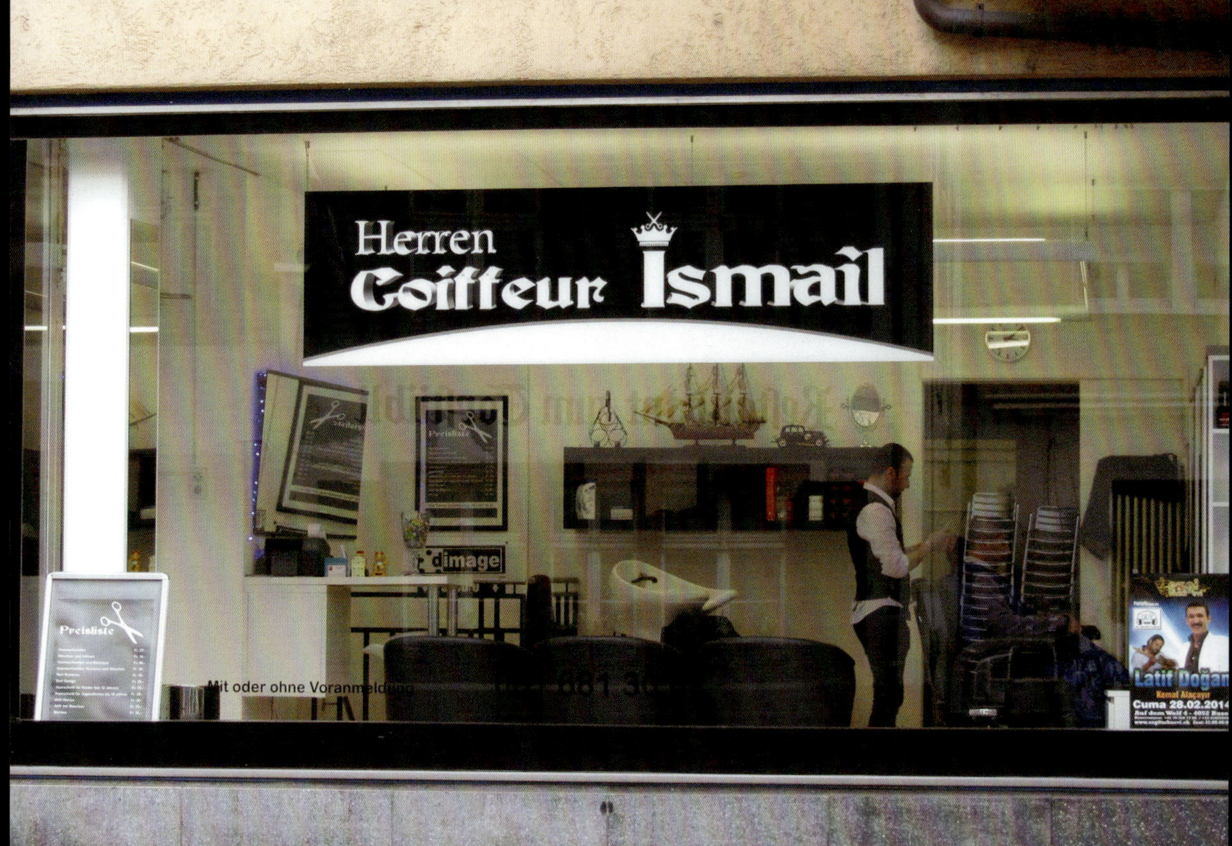

Herren
Coiffeur İsmail
dimage
Preisliste
Mit oder ohne Voranmeldung
Latif Doğan
Kemal Alaçayır
Cuma 28.02.2014

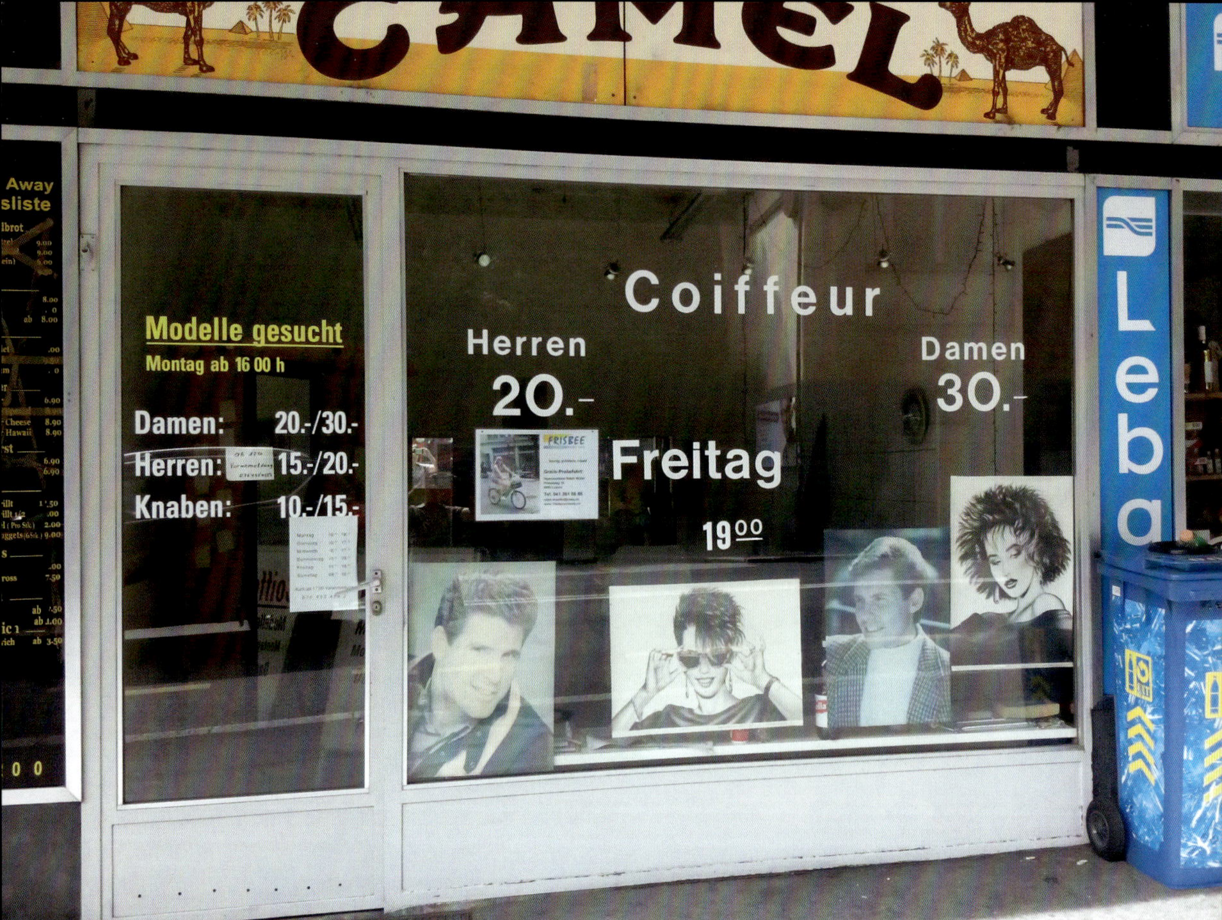

CAMEL
Modelle gesucht
Montag ab 16 00 h
Damen: 20.-/30.-
Herren: 15.-/20.-
Knaben: 10.-/15.-
Coiffeur
Herren
20.-
Damen
30.-
Freitag
19 00
FRISBEE

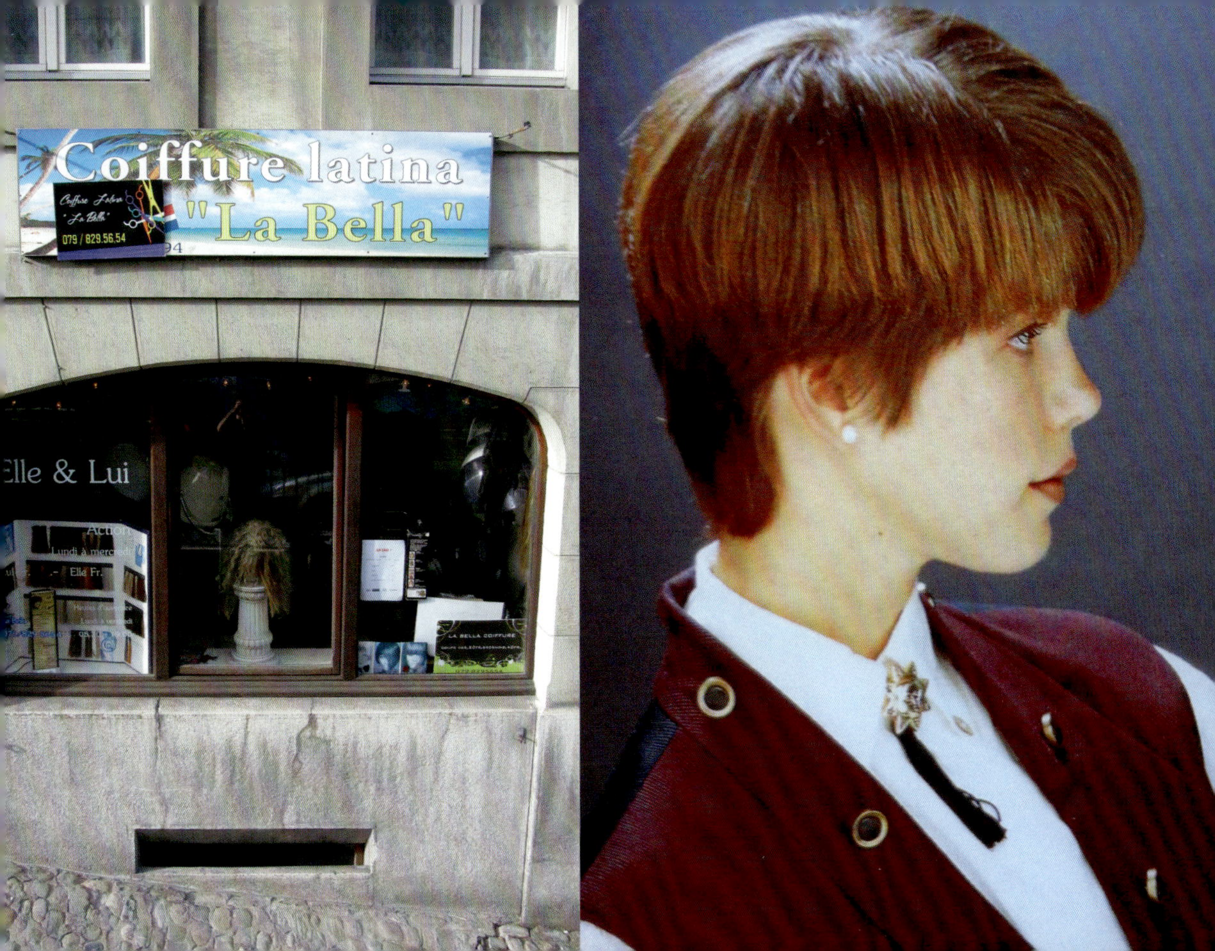

Coiffure latina
"La Bella"
079 / 829.56.54
Elle & Lui
LA BELLA COIFFURE

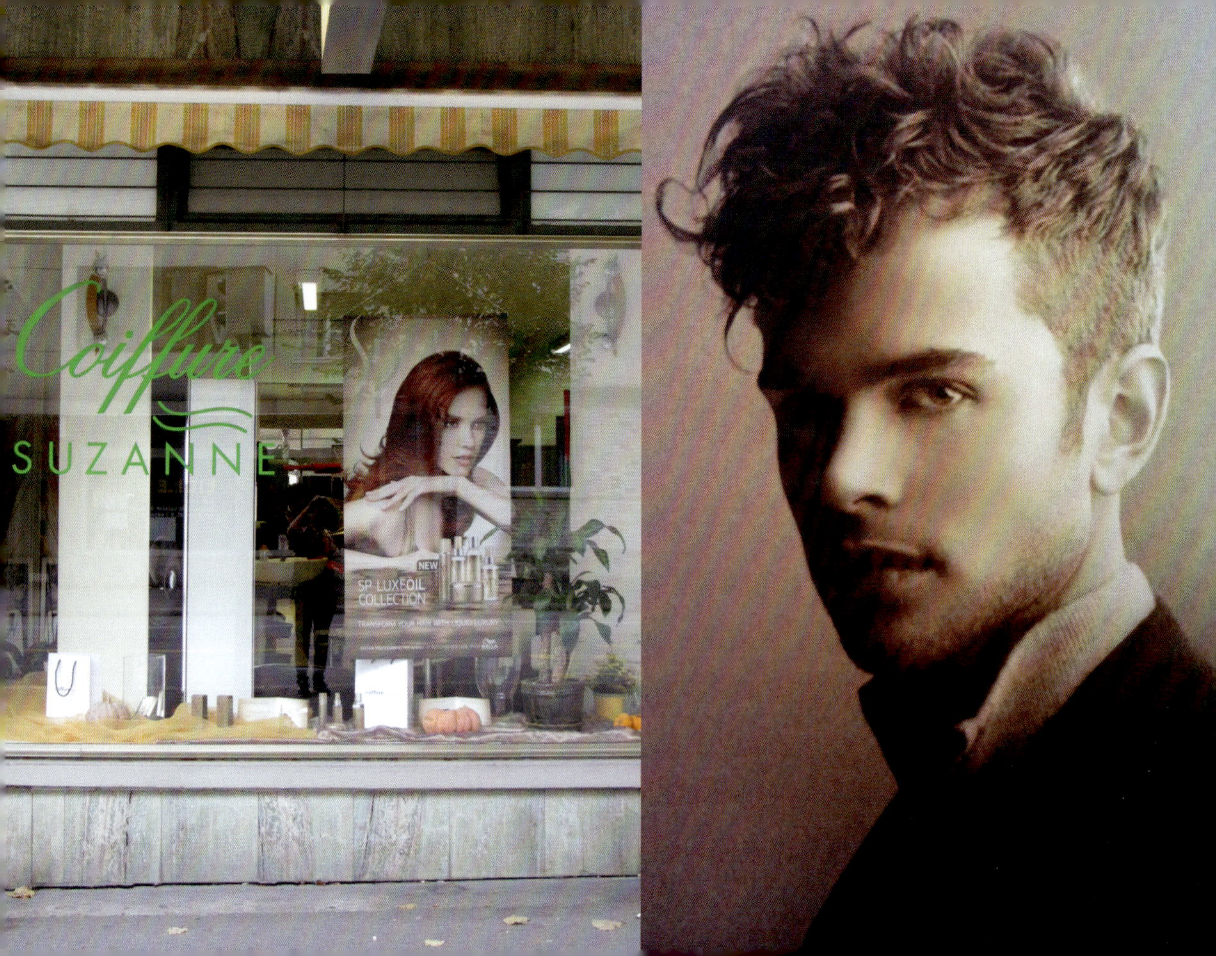
Coiffure
SUZANNE
NEW
SP LUXEOIL
COLLECTION

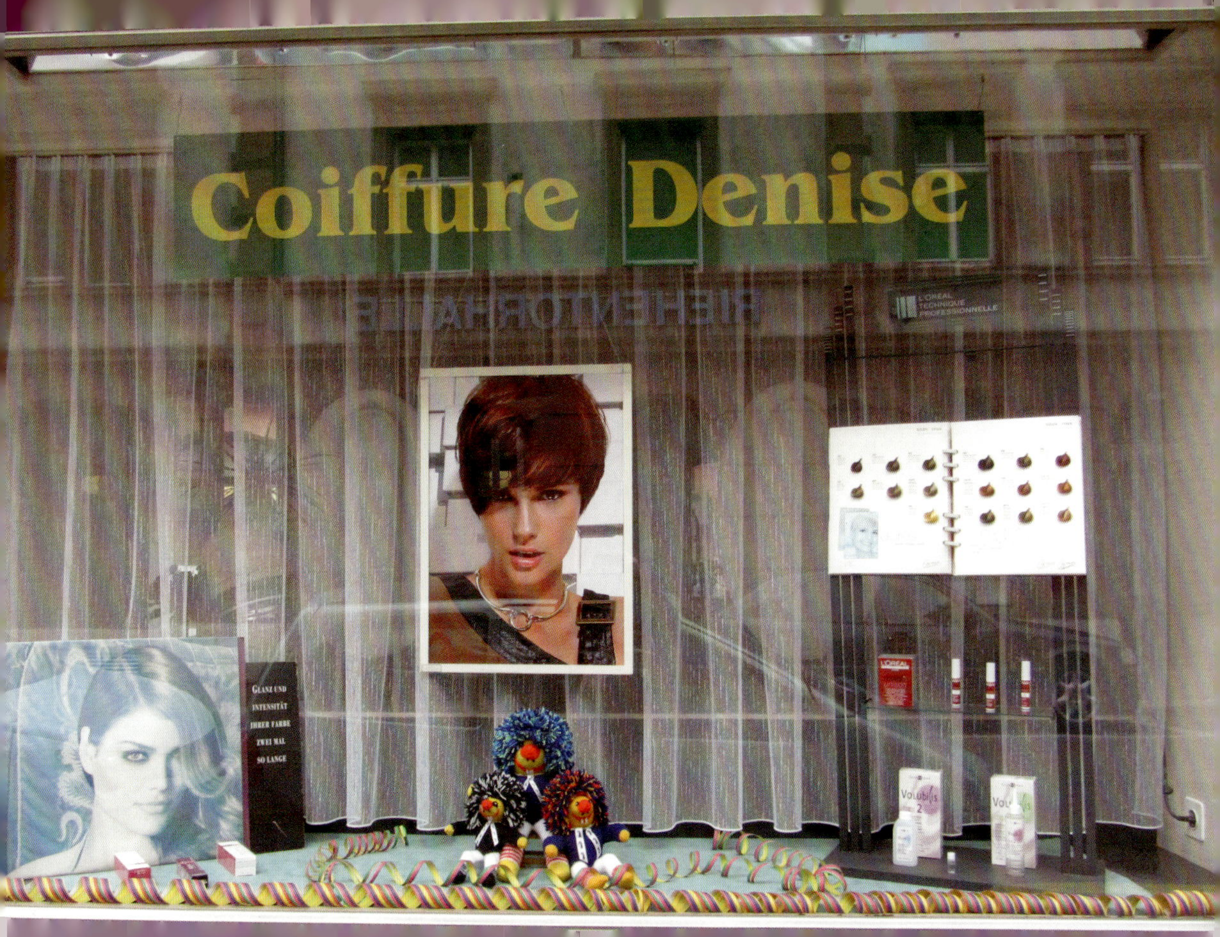
Coiffure Denise
L'ORÉAL TECHNIQUE PROFESSIONNELLE
GLANZ UND
INTENSITÄT
IHRER FARBE
ZWEI MAL
SO LANGE

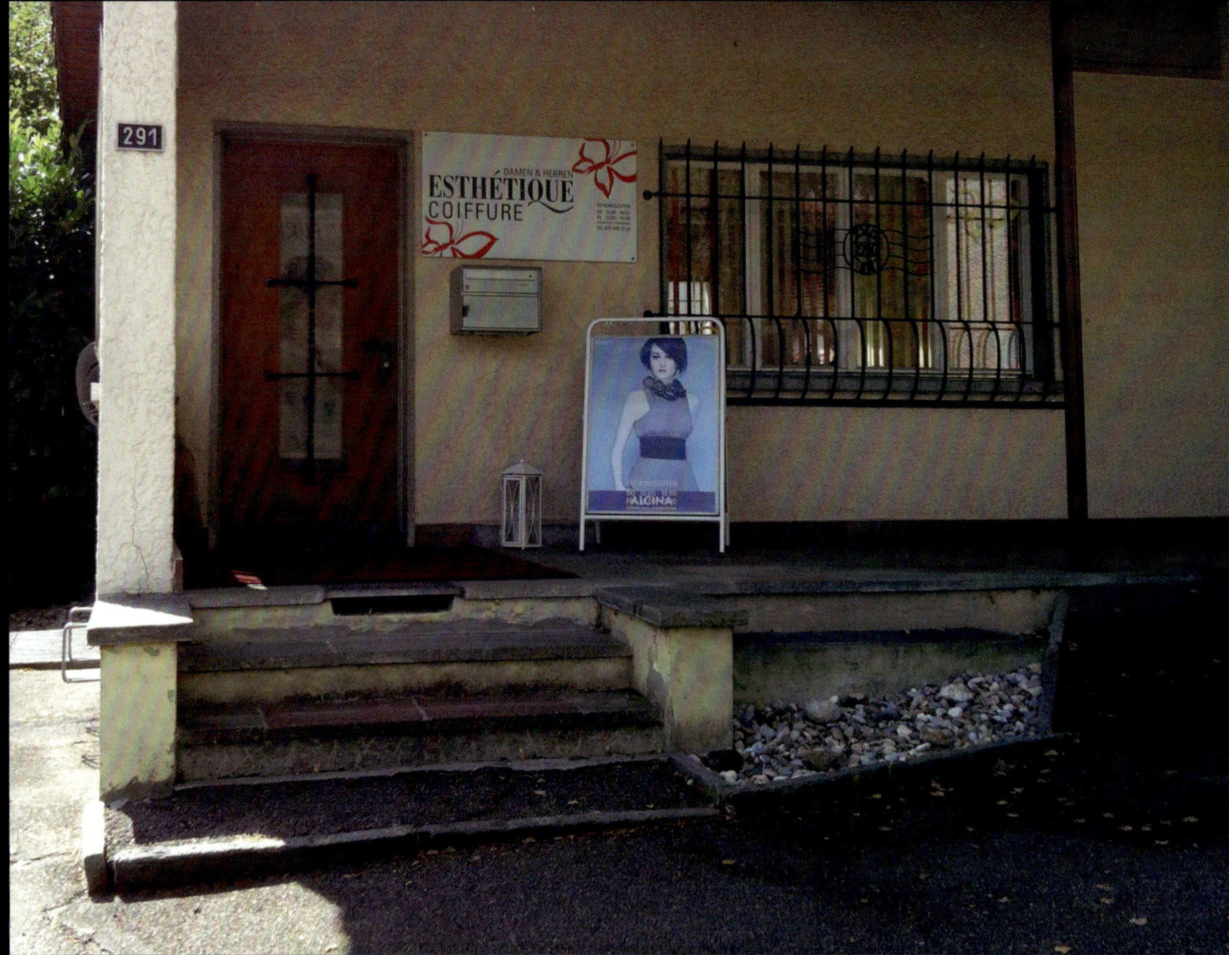
291
DAMEN & HERREN
ESTHÉTIQUE
COIFFURE
ALCINA

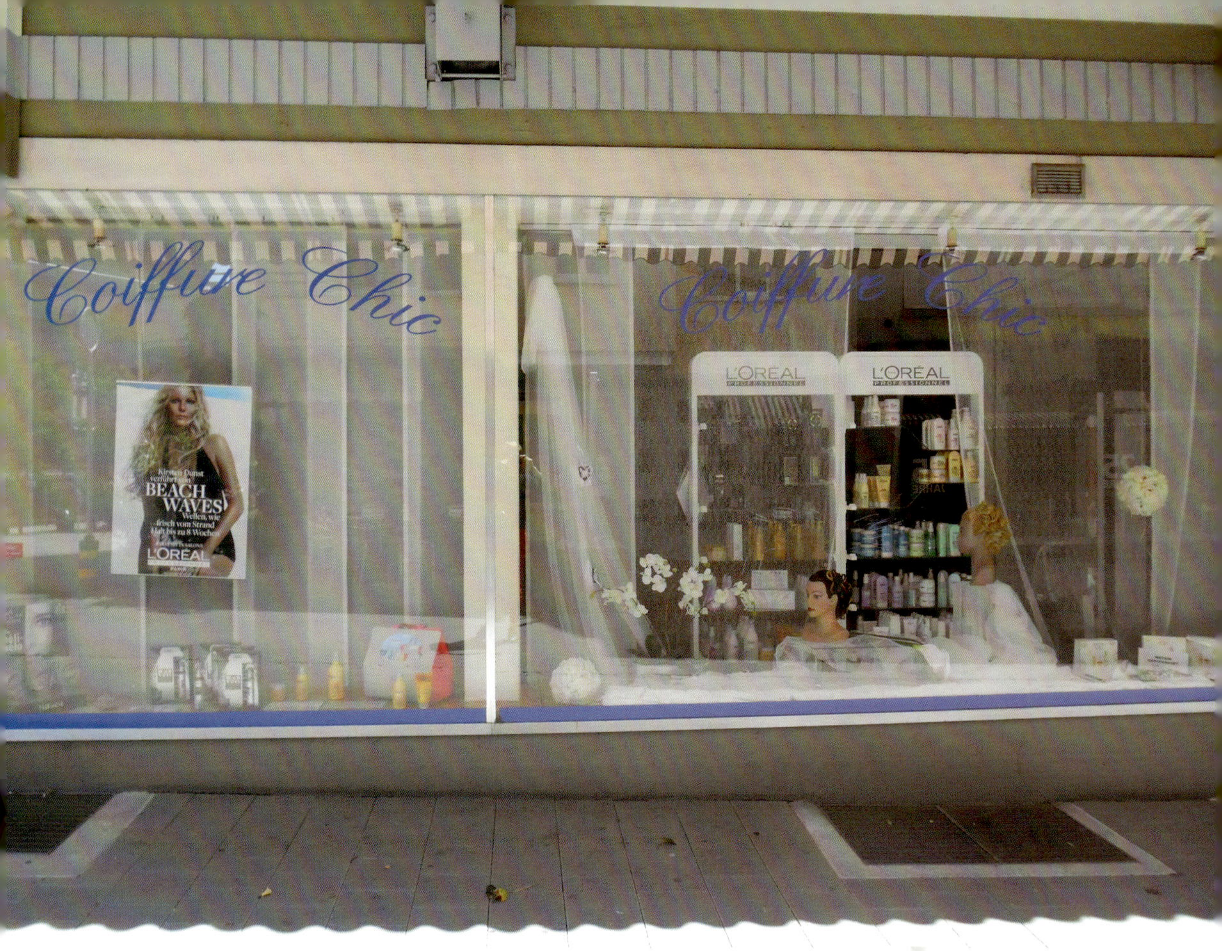
Coiffure Chic
BEACH
WAVES
L'ORÉAL
Coiffure Chic
L'ORÉAL
PROFESSIONNEL
L'ORÉAL
PROFESSIONNEL

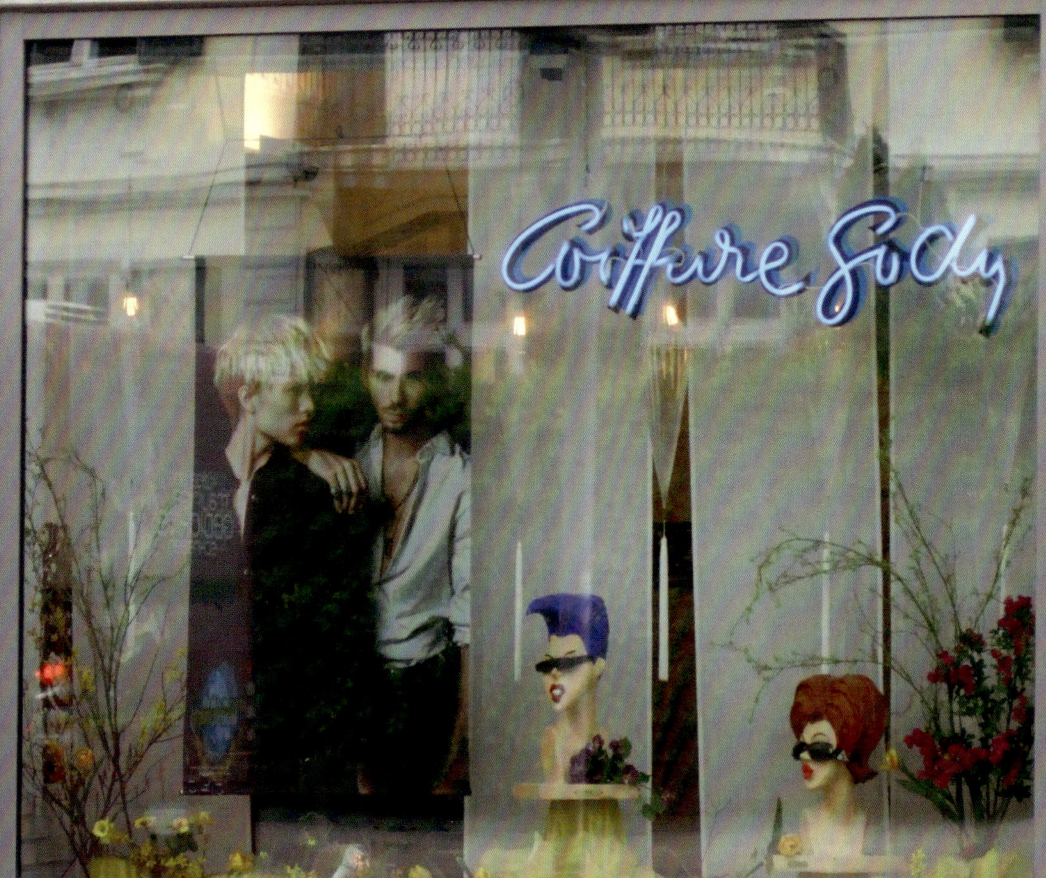
Coiffure Sody

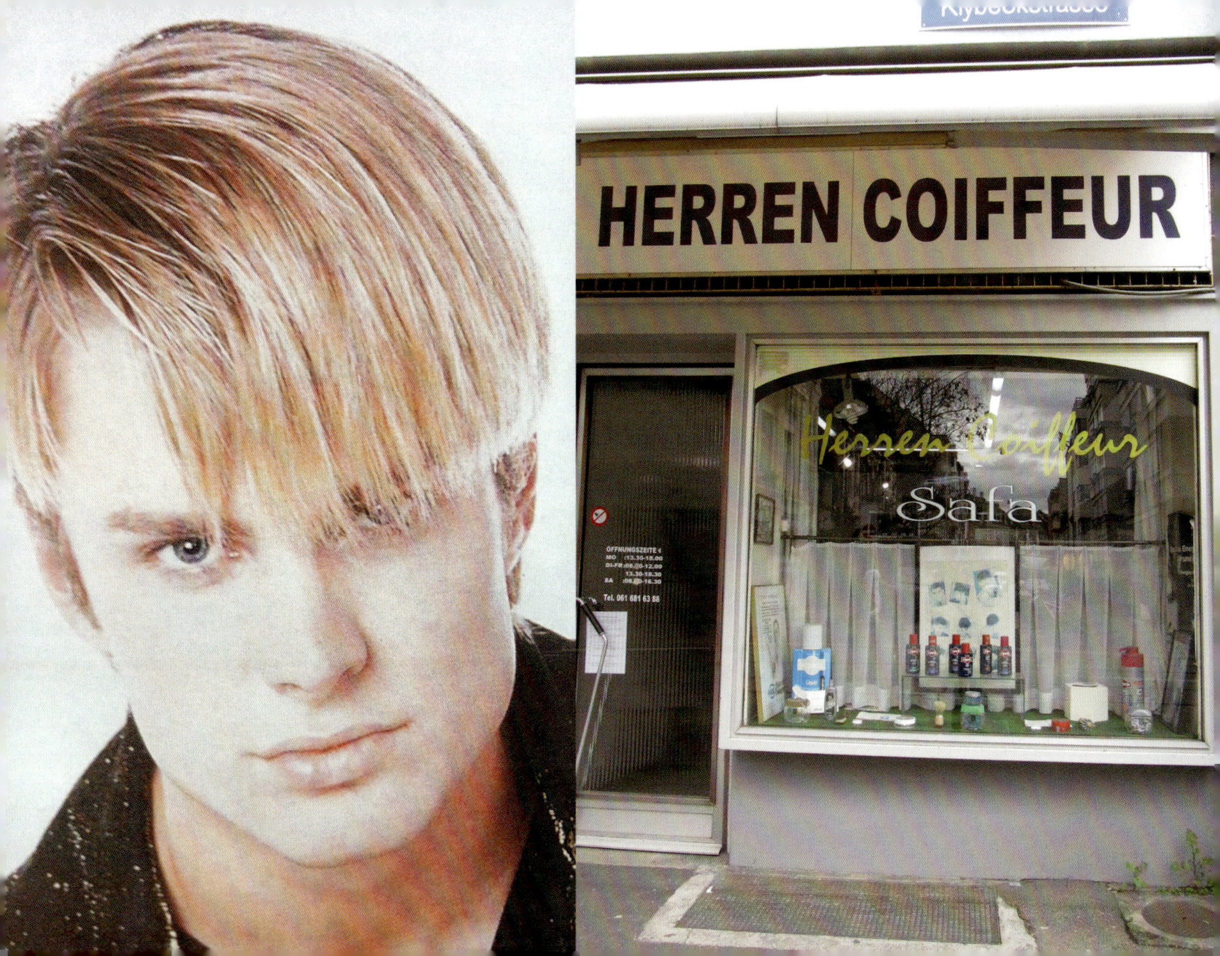
HERREN COIFFEUR
Herren Coiffeur
Safa

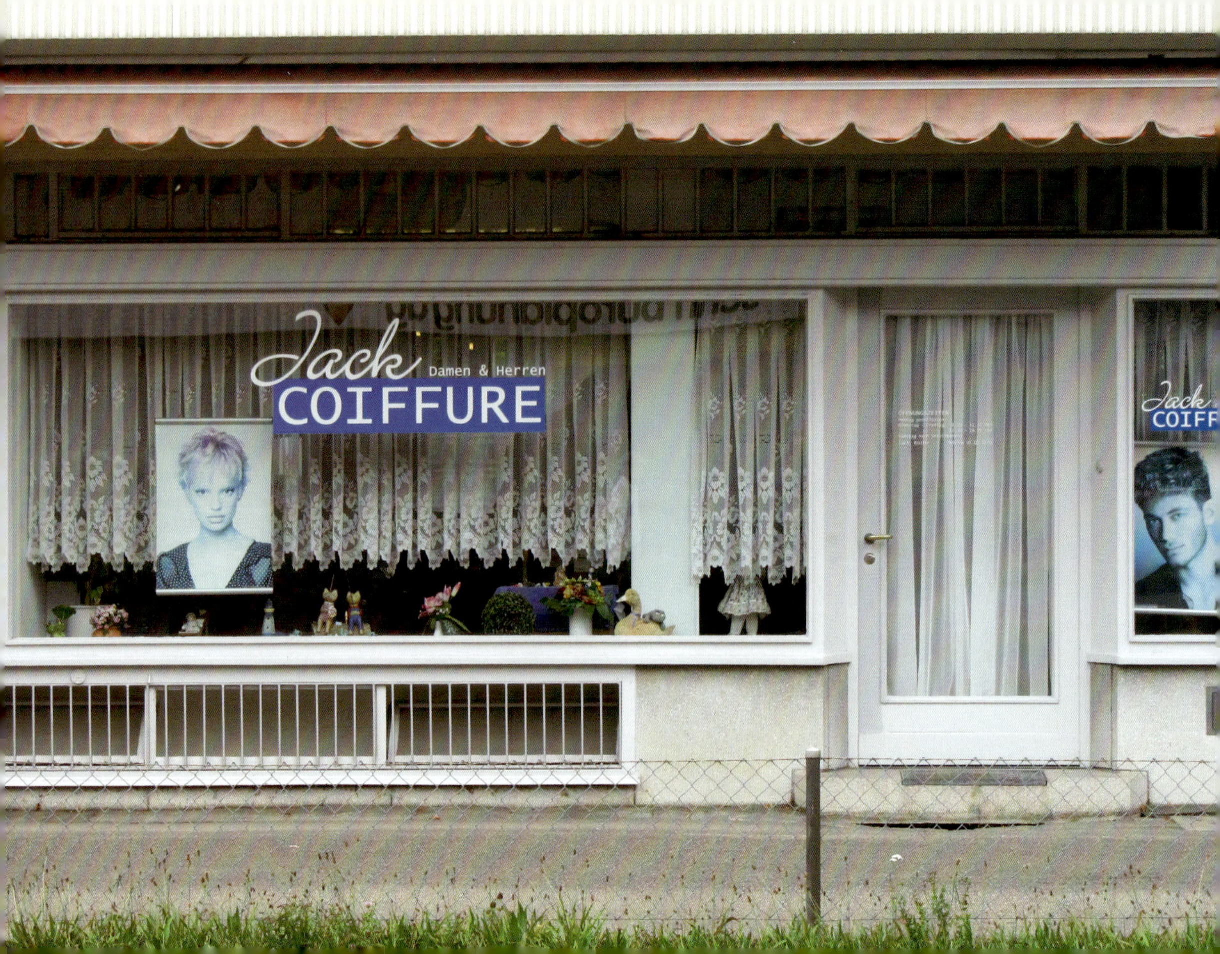
Jack
Damen & Herren
COIFFURE
Jack
COIFF

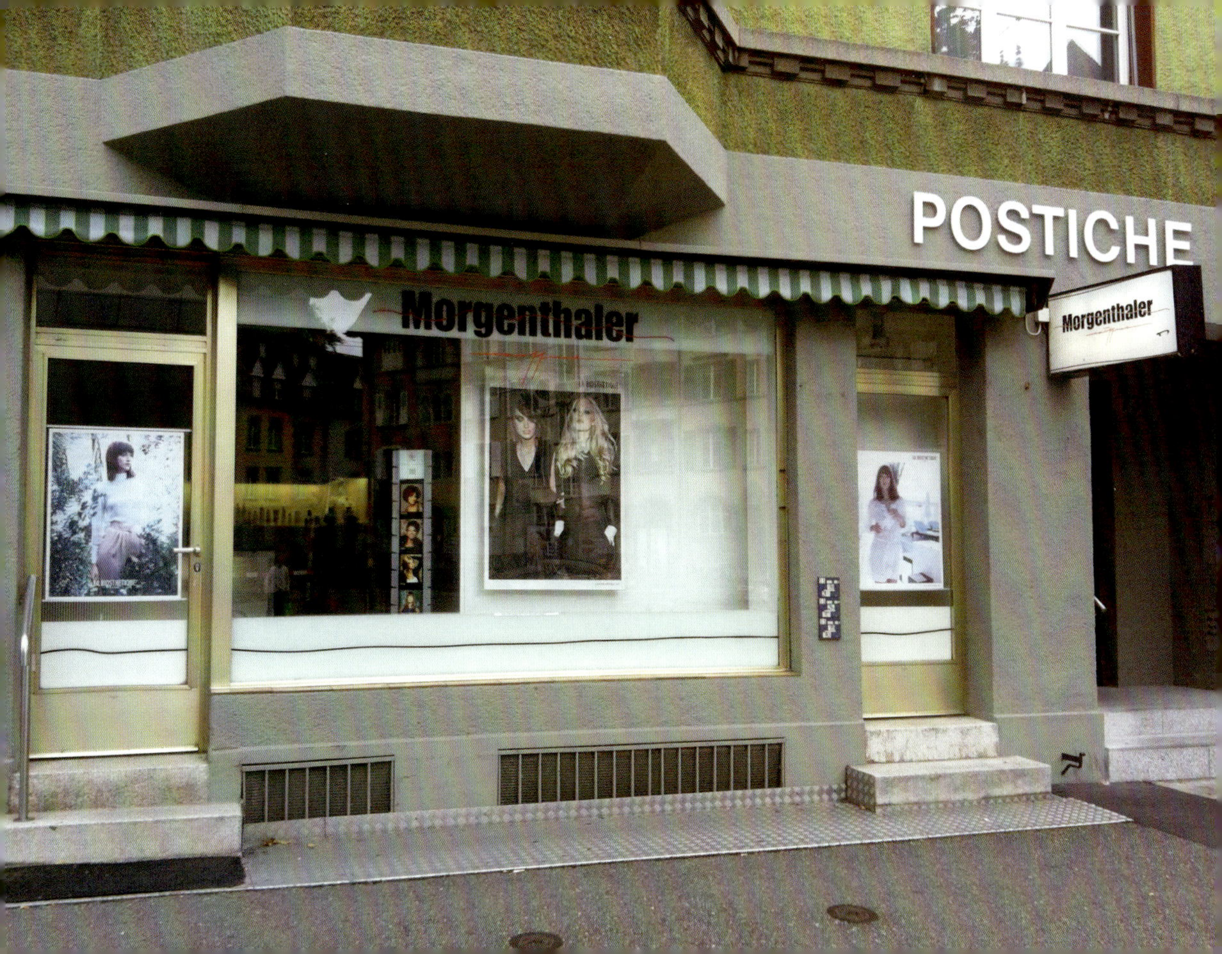
POSTICHE
Morgenthaler
Morgenthaler

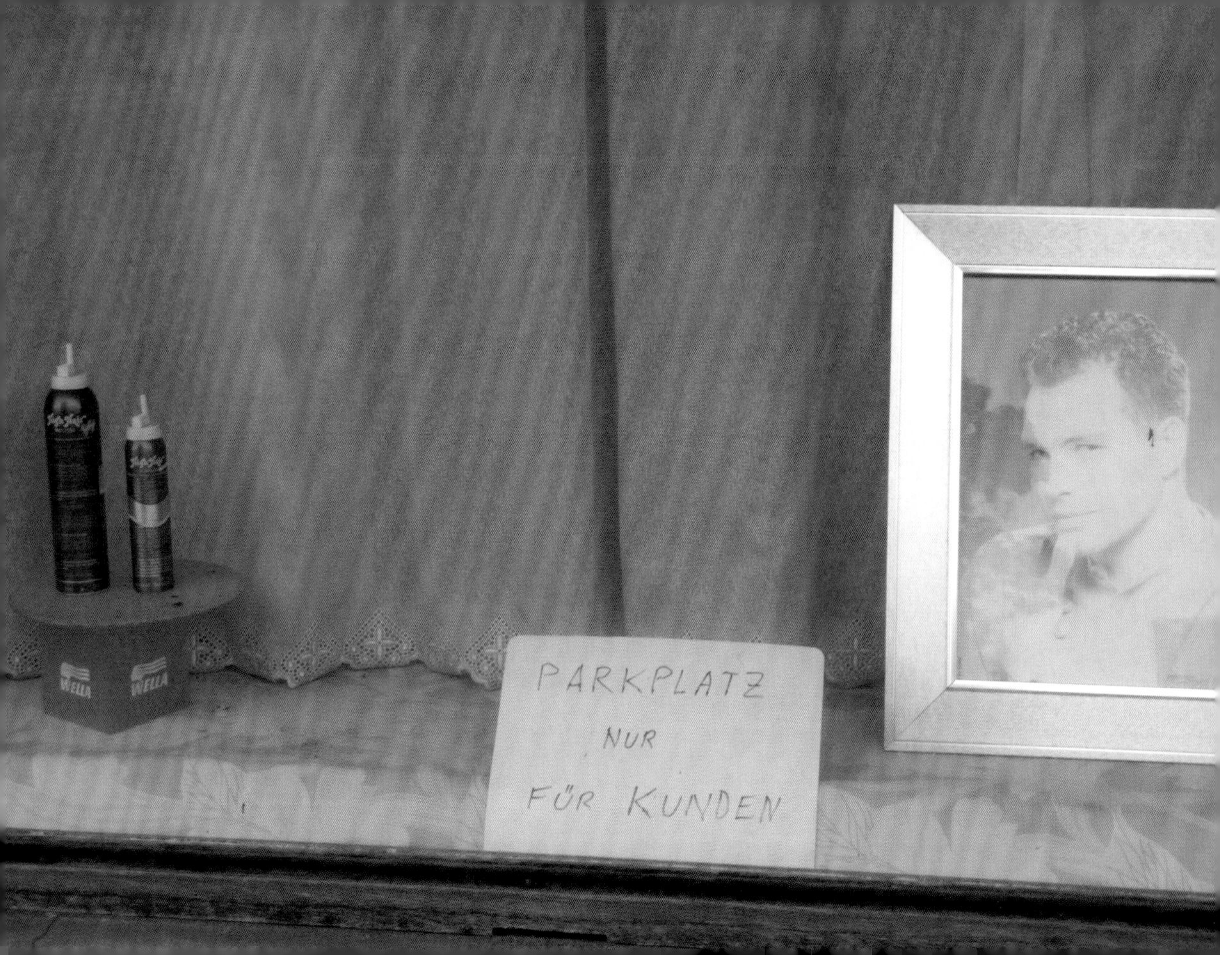
PARKPLATZ
NUR
FÜR KUNDEN

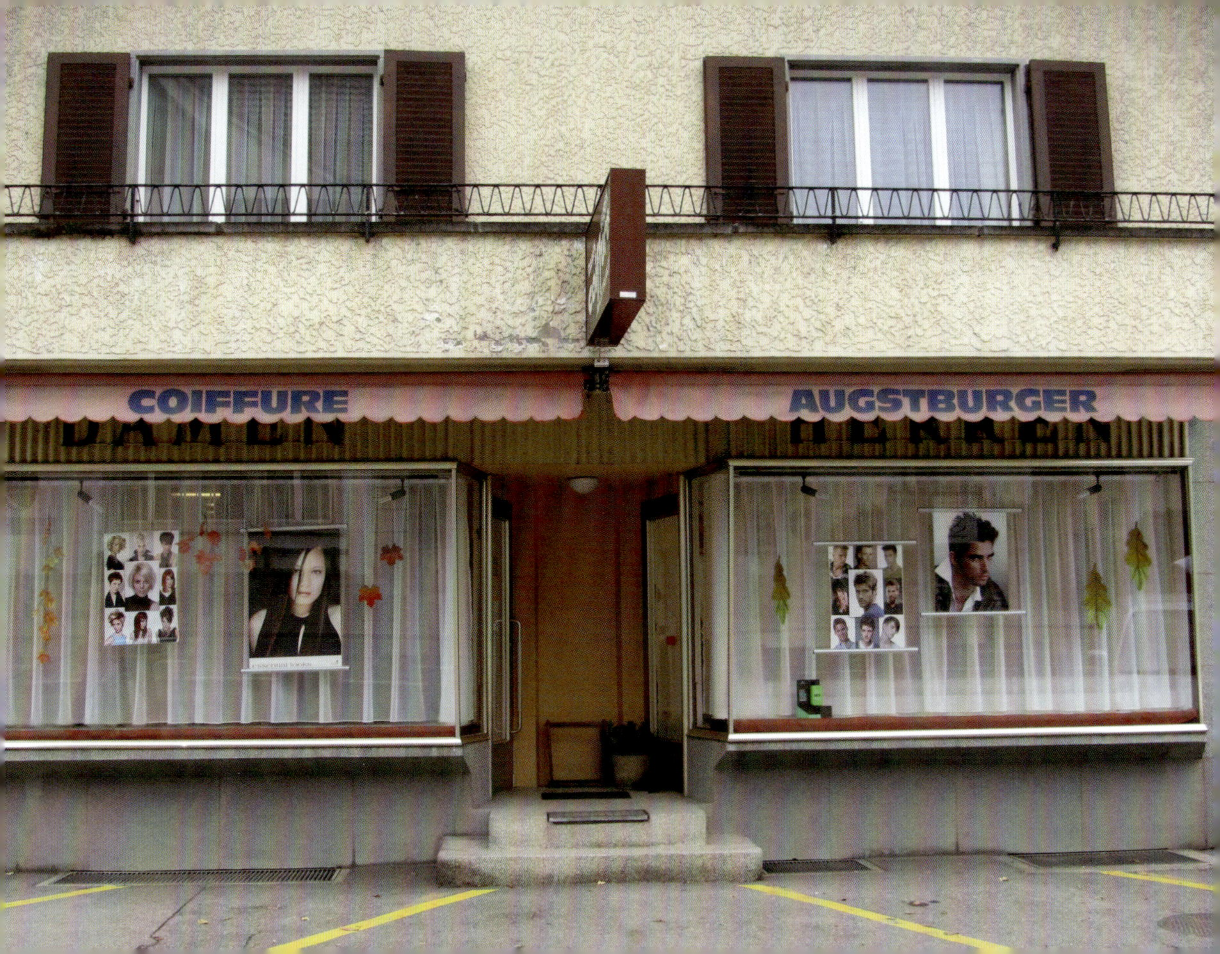
COIFFURE
AUGSTBURGER

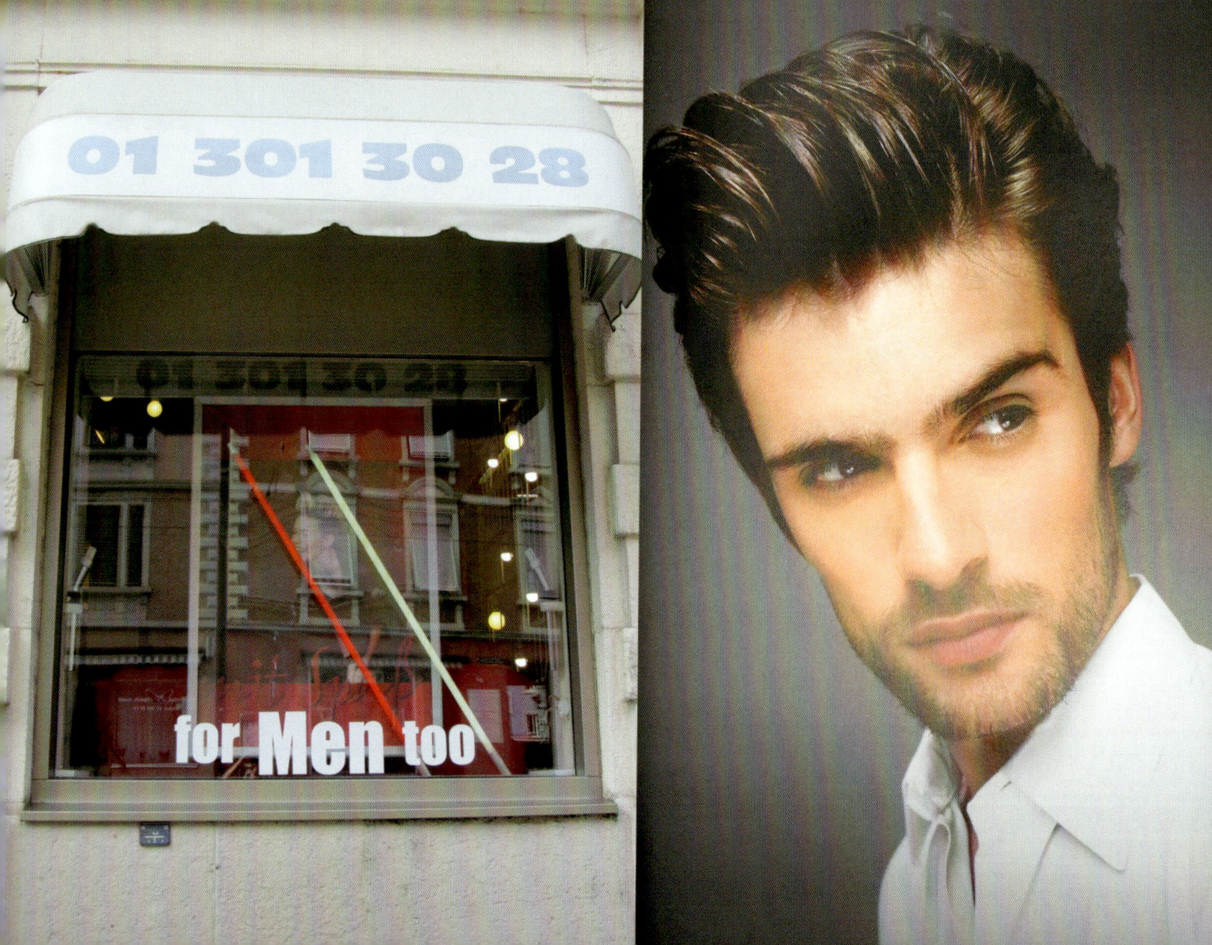
01 301 30 28
for Men too

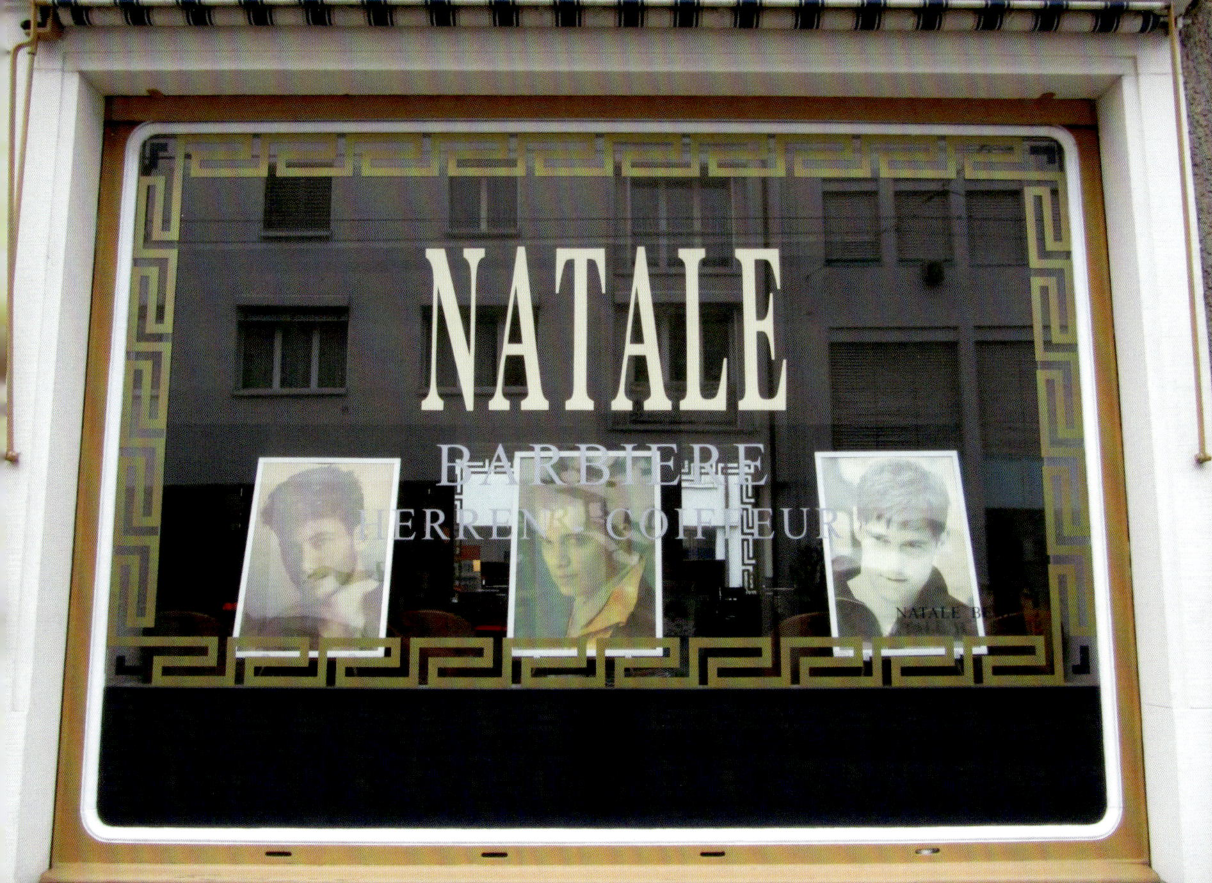
NATALE
BARBIERE
HERREN COIFFEUR

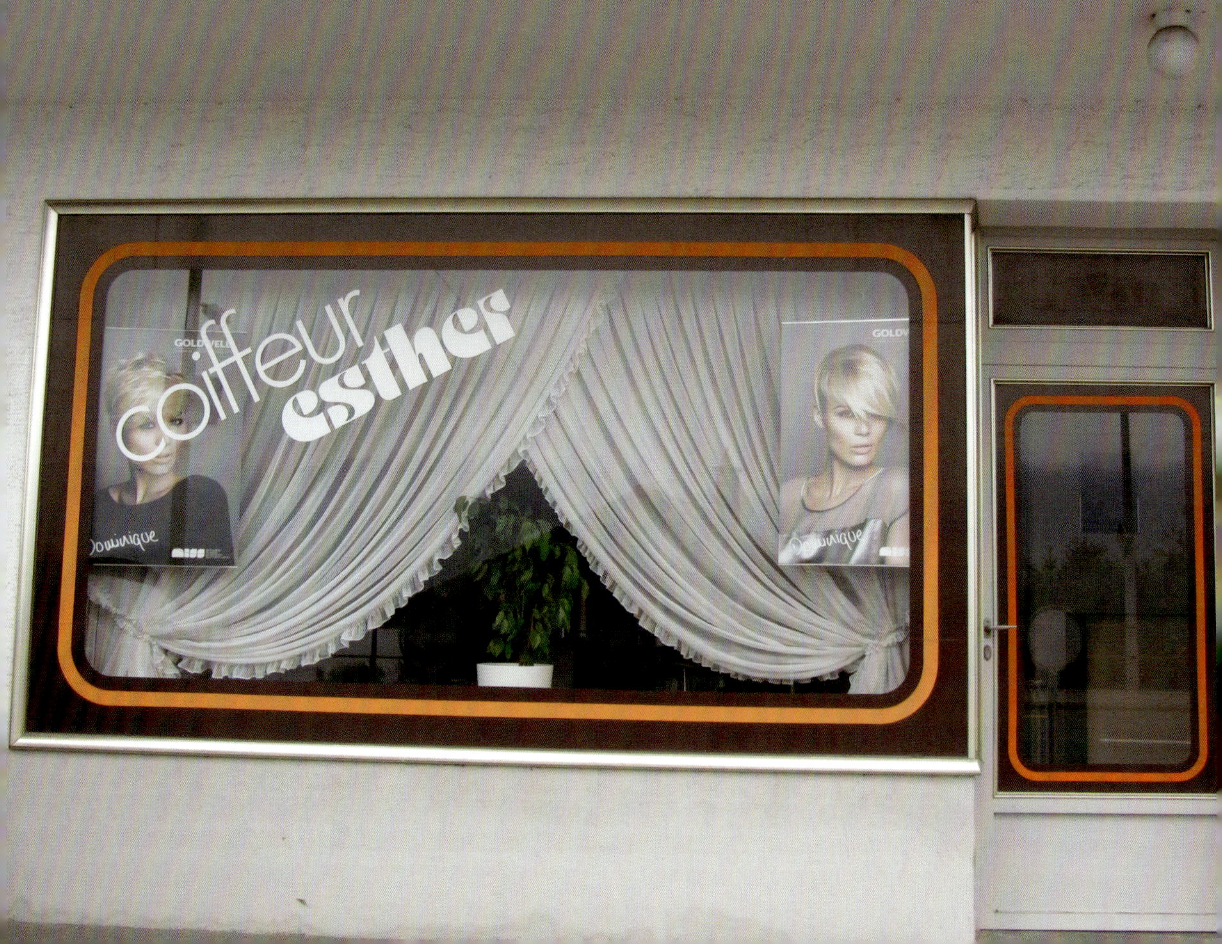
coiffeur
esther
Dominique
Dominique

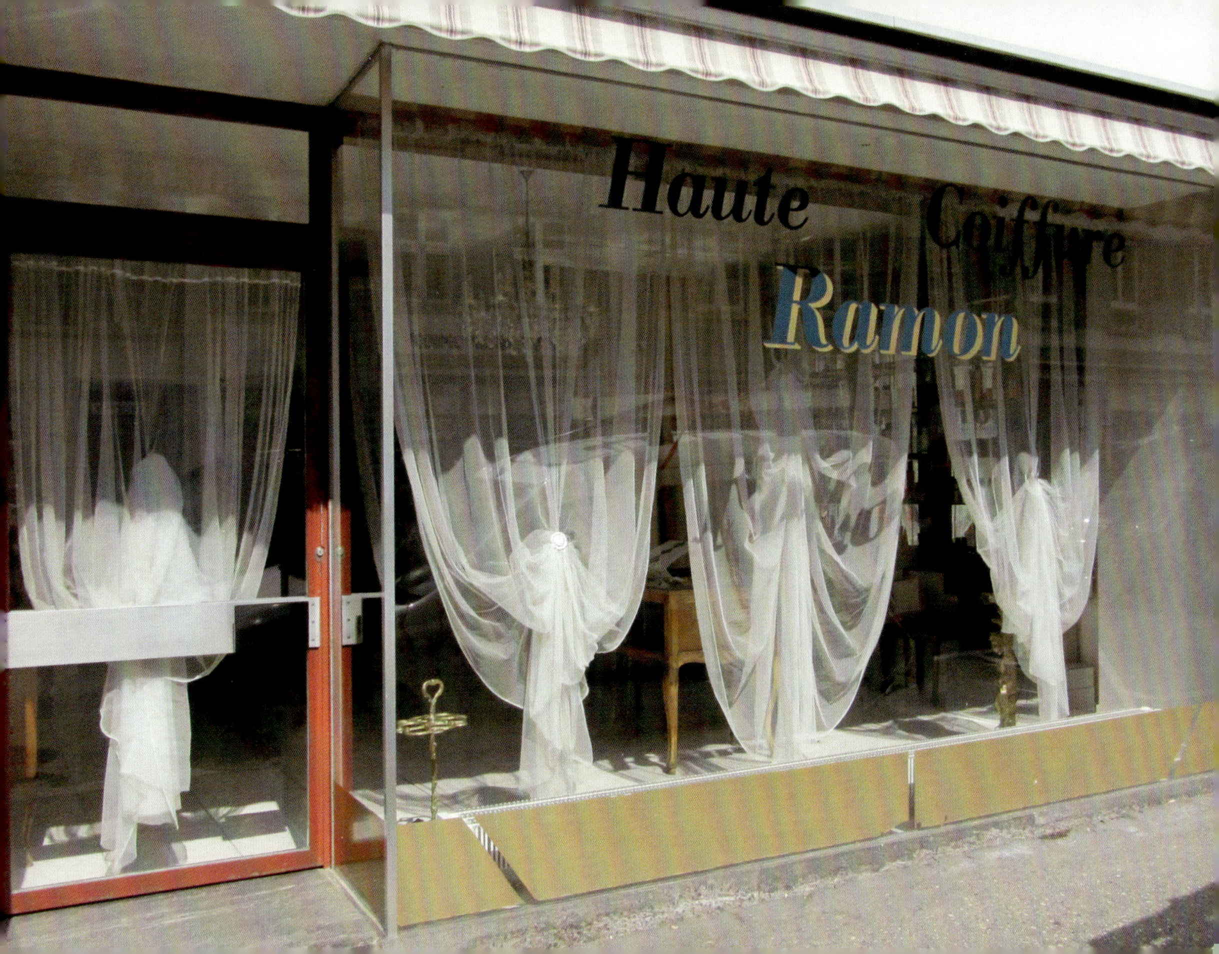
Haute Coiffure
Ramon

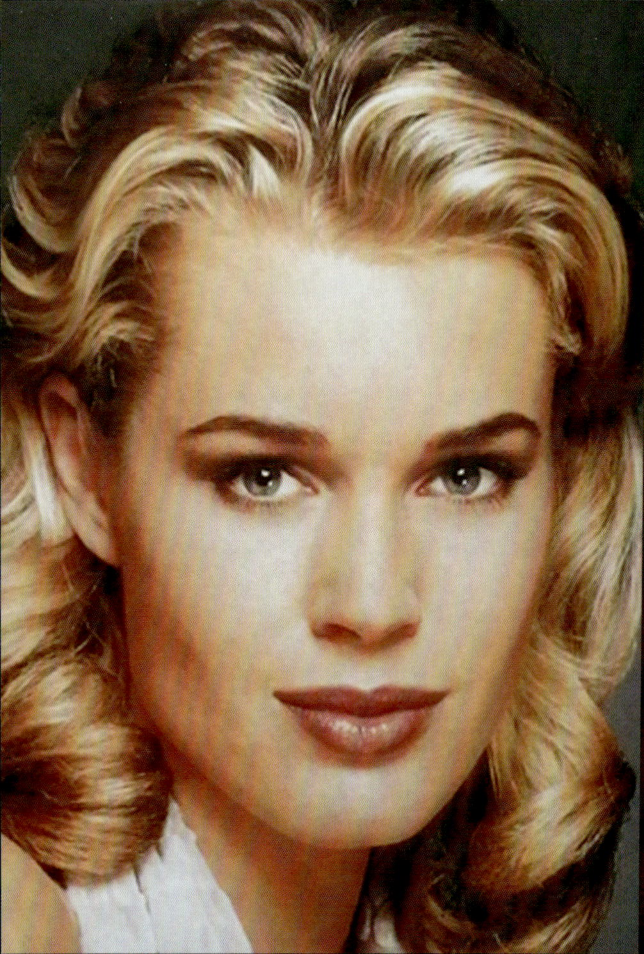

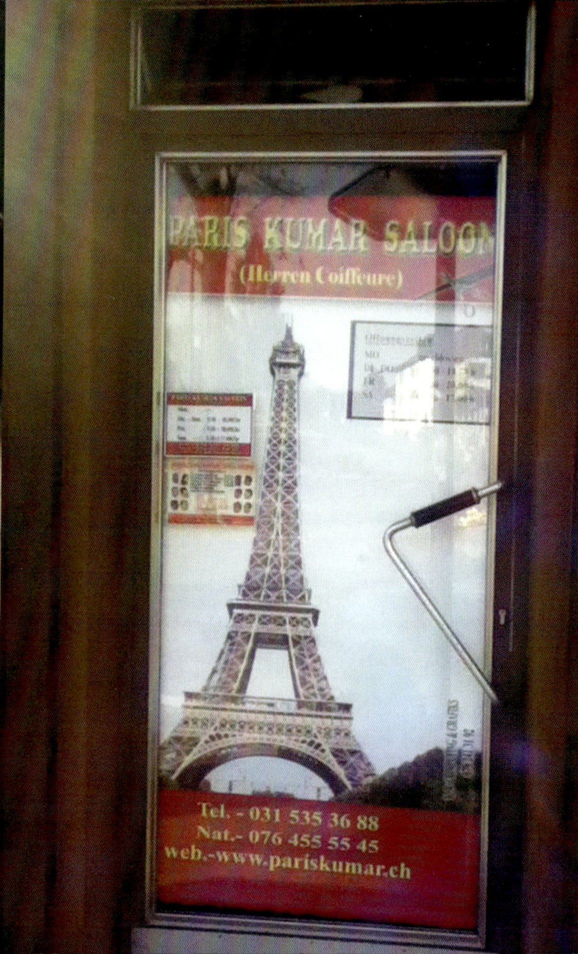

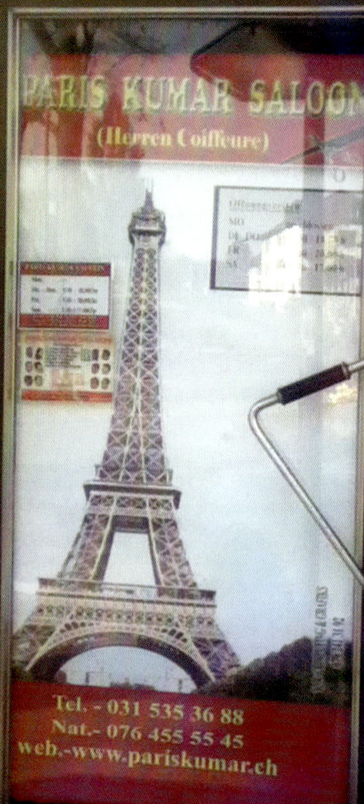
PARIS KUMAR SALOON
(Herren Coiffeure)
Tel. - 031 535 36 88
Nat.- 076 455 55 45
web.-www.pariskumar.ch

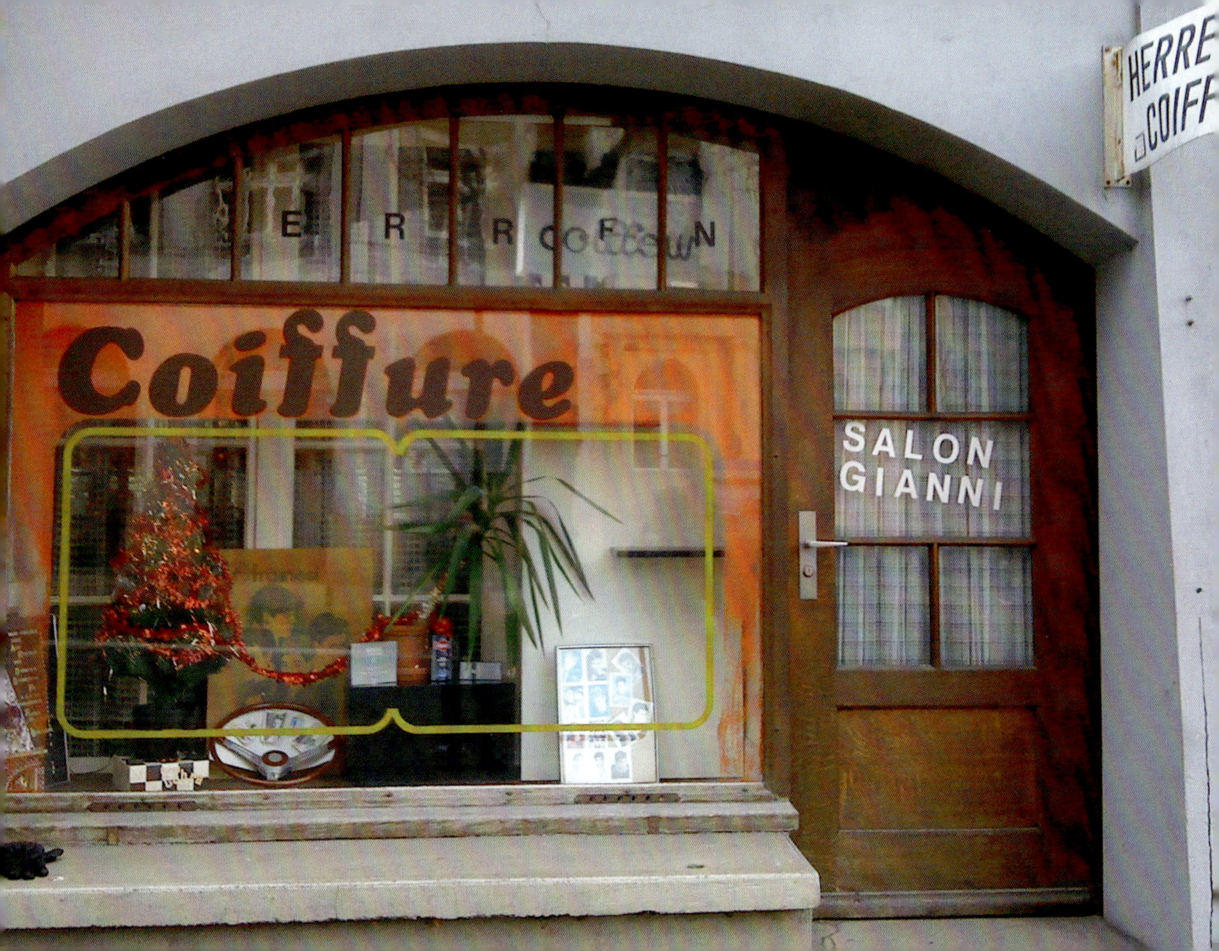
Coiffure
SALON
GIANNI
HERRE
COIFF

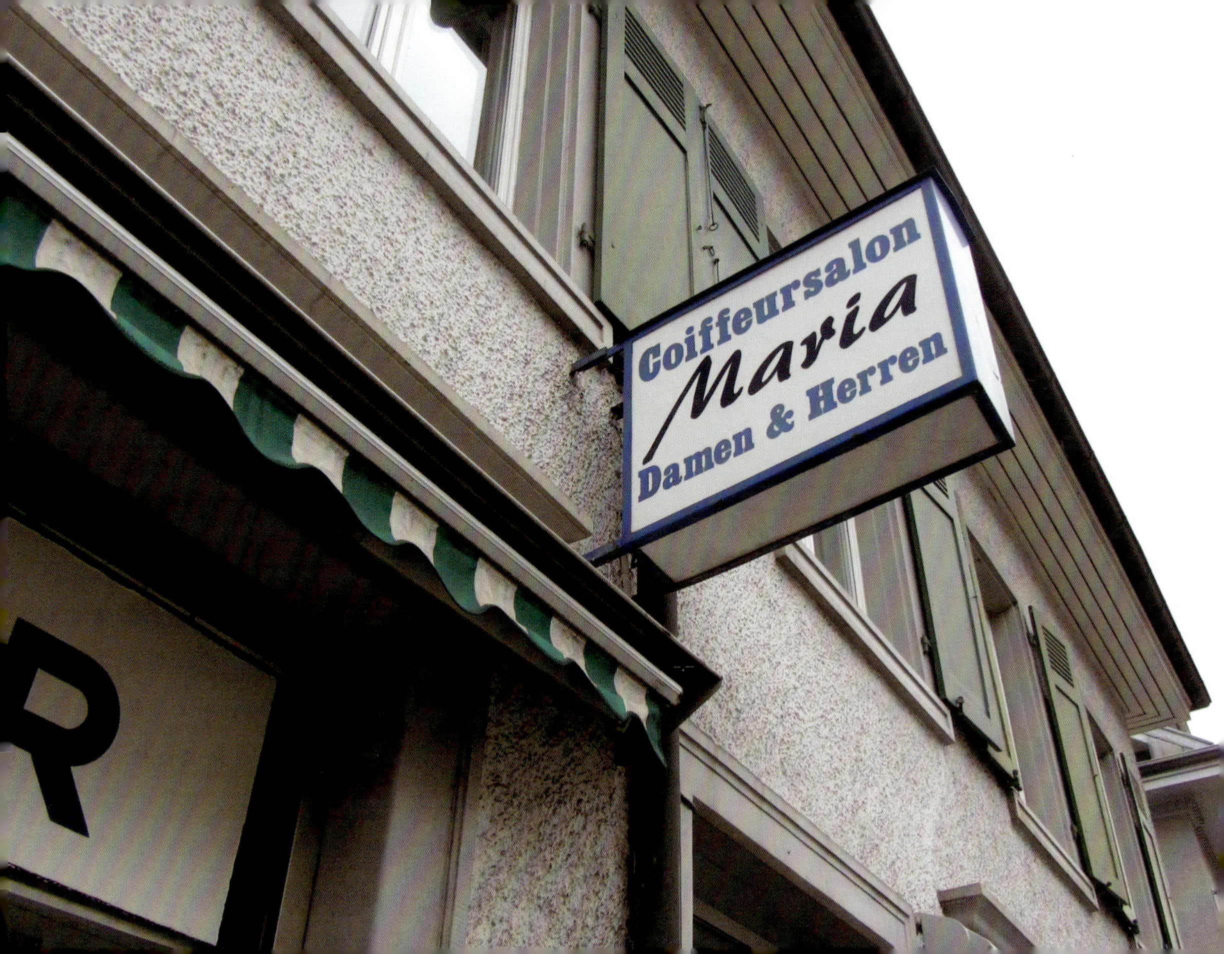
Coiffeursalon
Maria
Damen & Herren

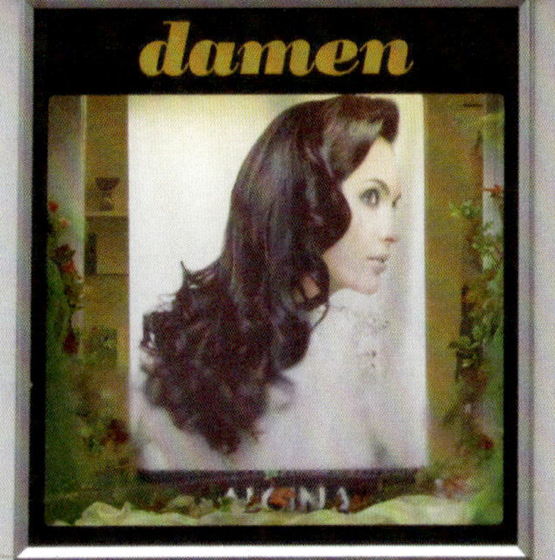
salon moderne
damen

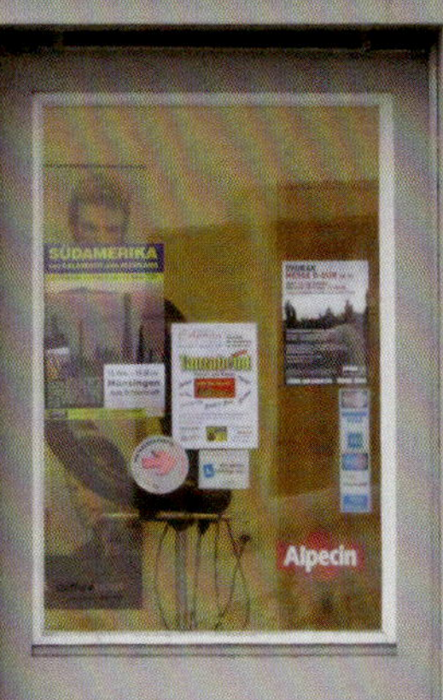
SÜDAMERIKA
Alpecin

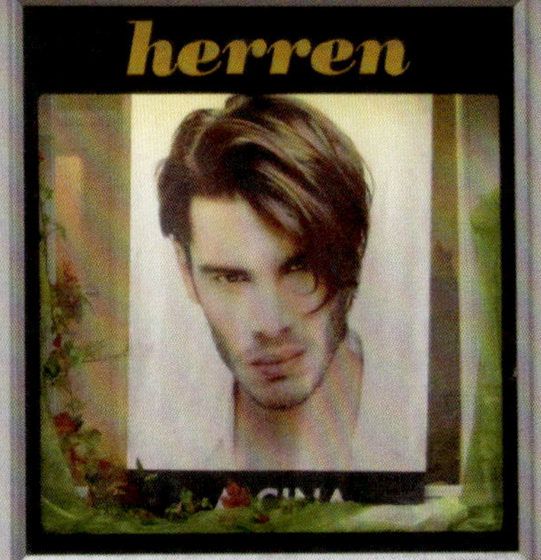
herren

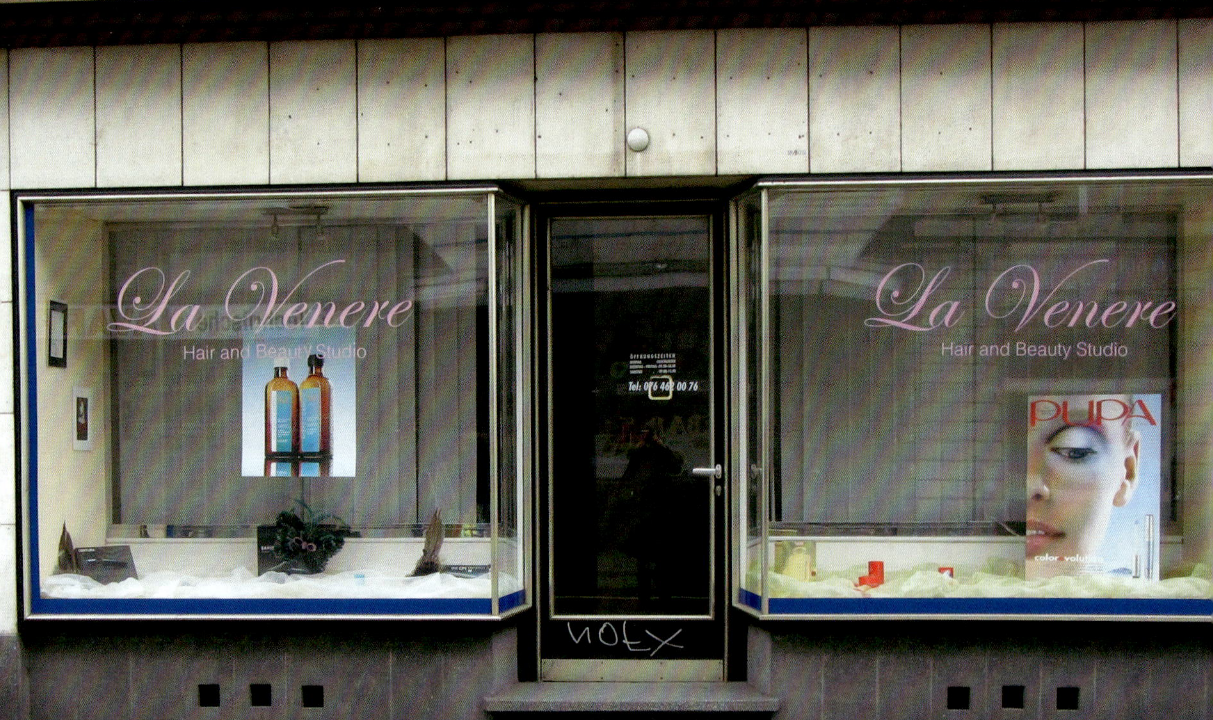
La Venere
Hair and Beauty Studio
Tel: 076 462 00 76
La Venere
Hair and Beauty Studio
PUPA

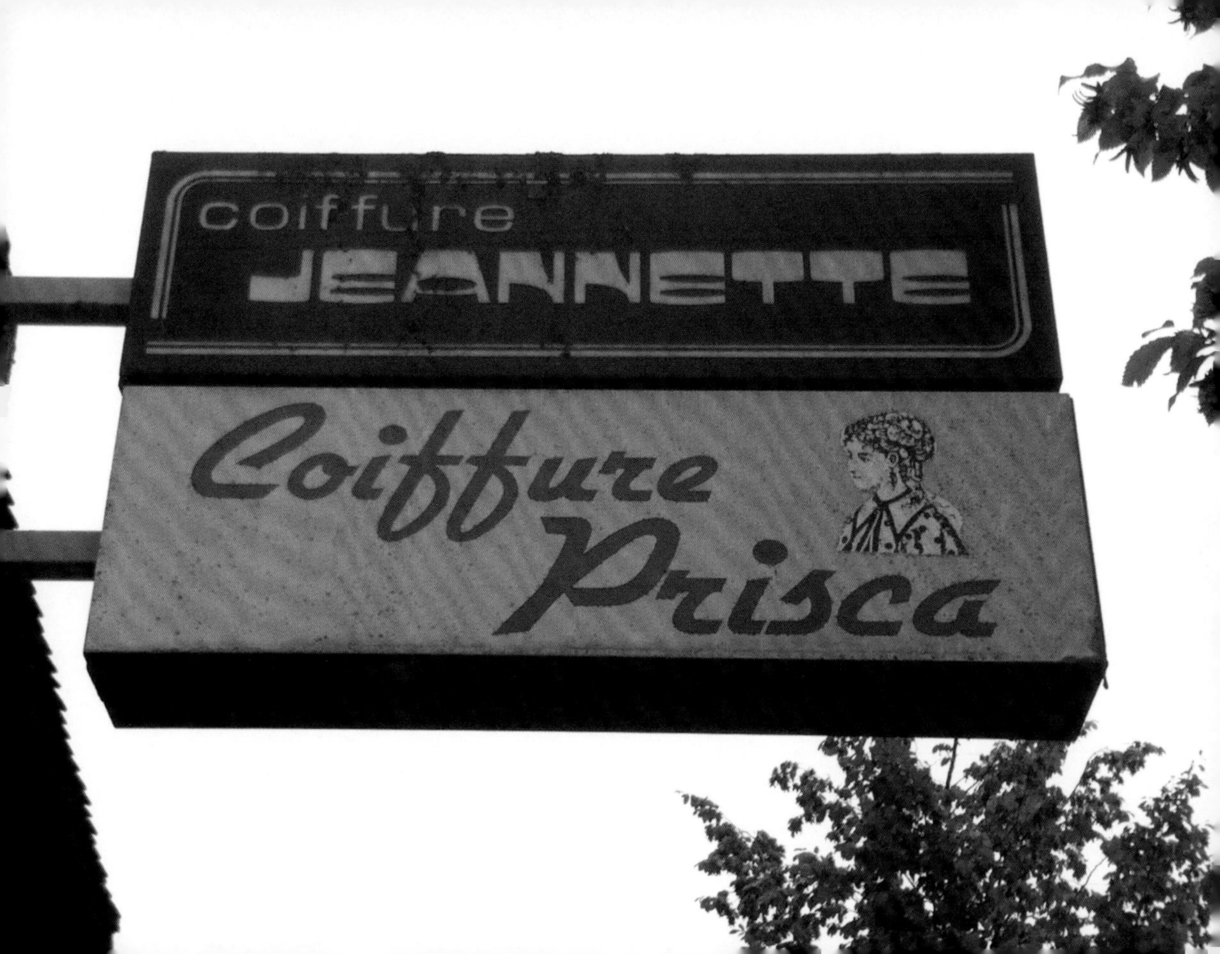

coiffure
JEANNETTE
Coiffure
Prisca

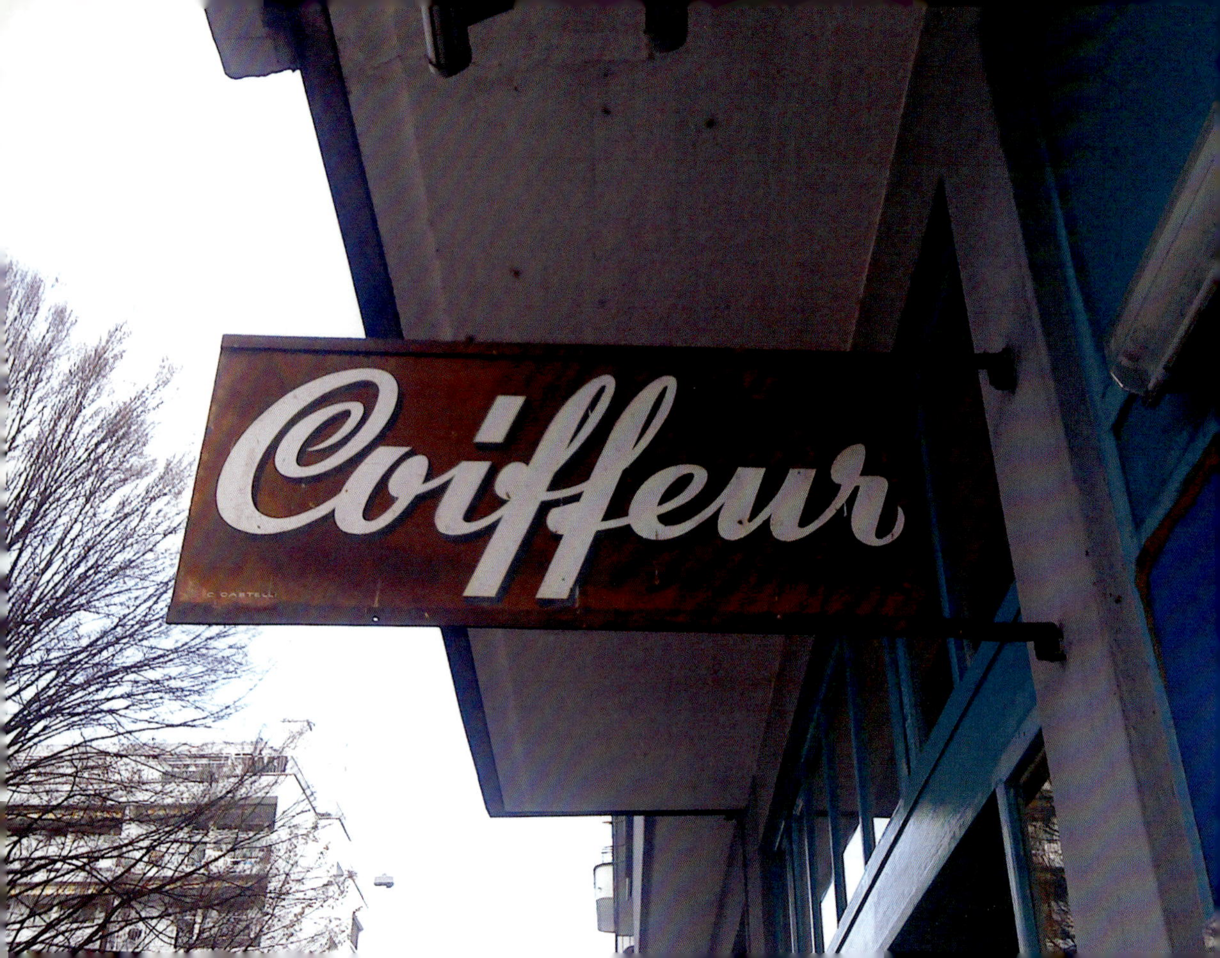
Coiffeur

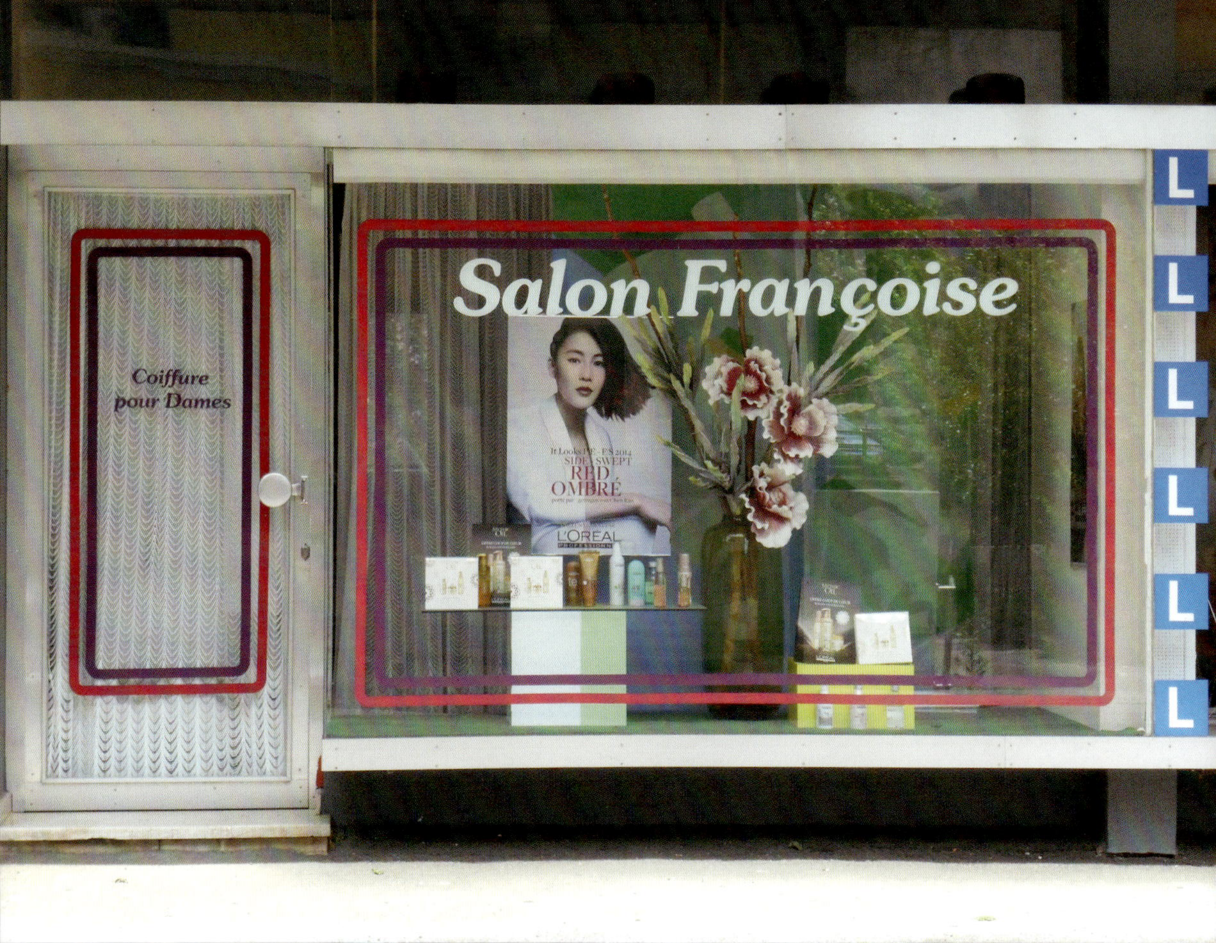

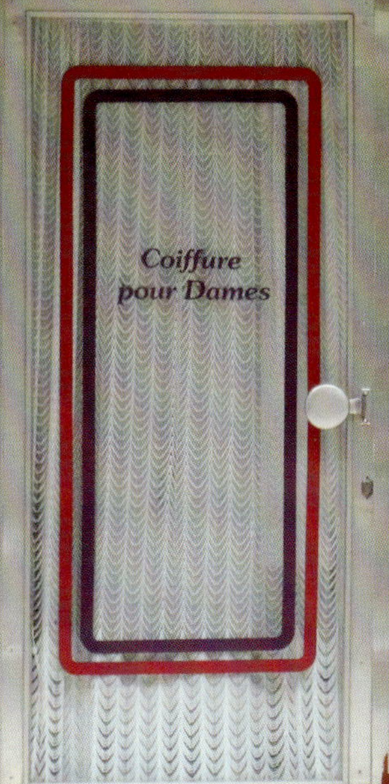
Coiffure
pour Dames
Salon Françoise
SIDE SWEPT
RED
OMBRÉ
L'OREAL

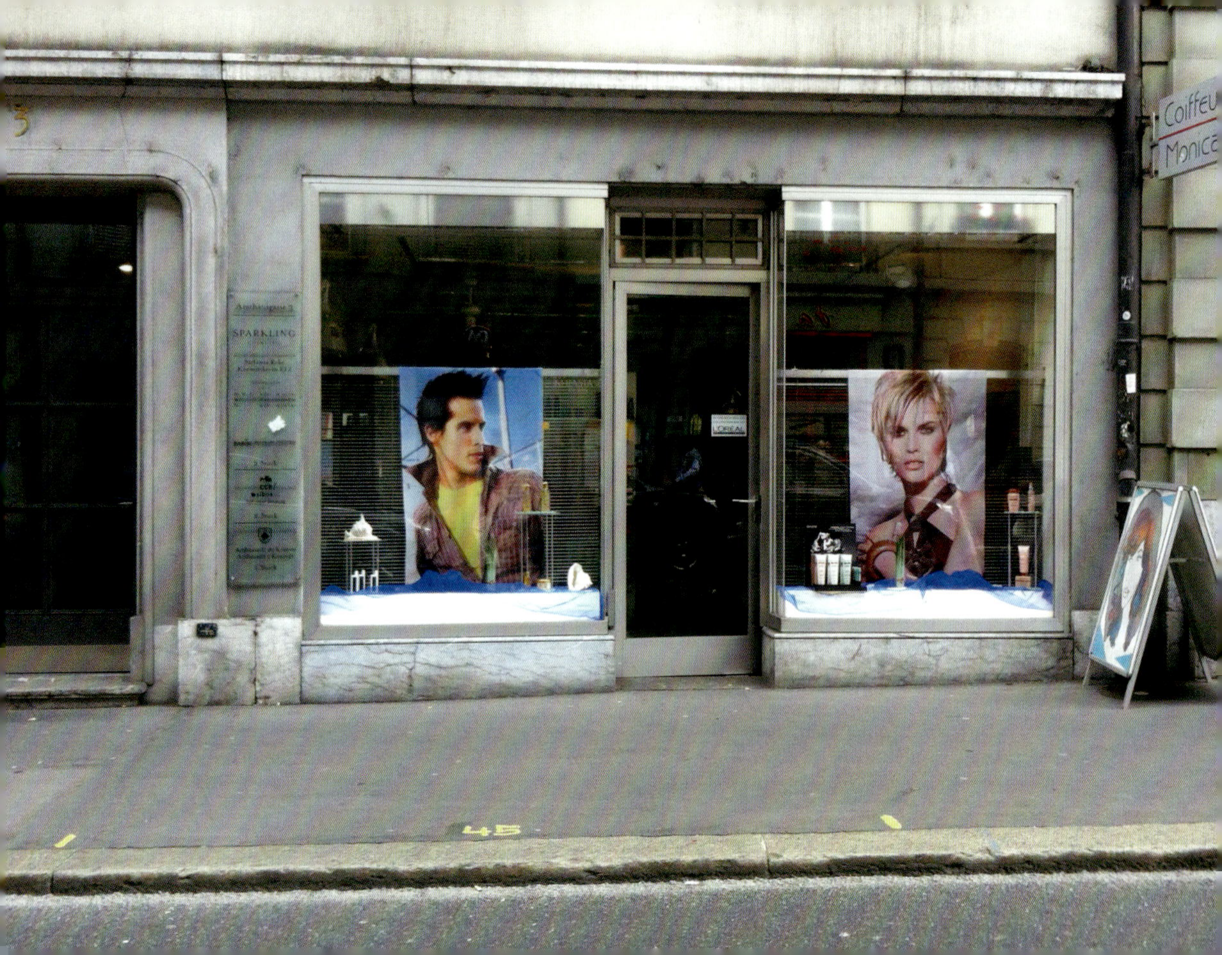
Monica
SPARKLING
L'ORÉAL
45

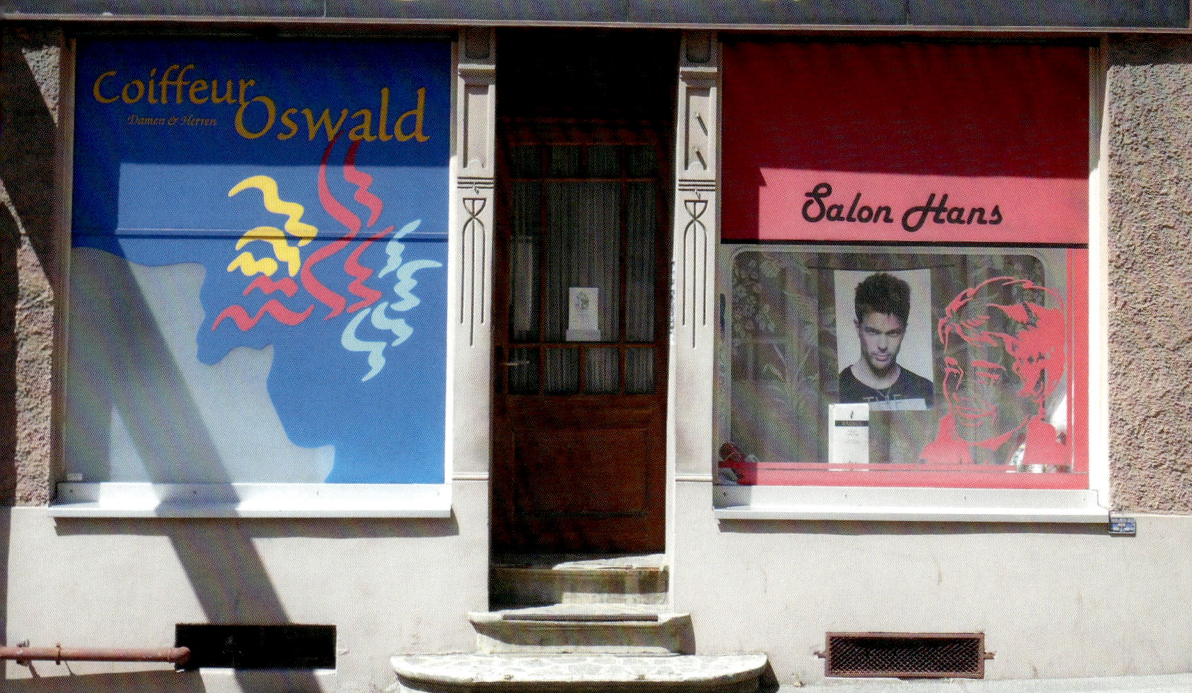
COIFFEUSE
Oswald
COIFFEUR
Coiffeur Oswald
Damen & Herren
Salon Hans

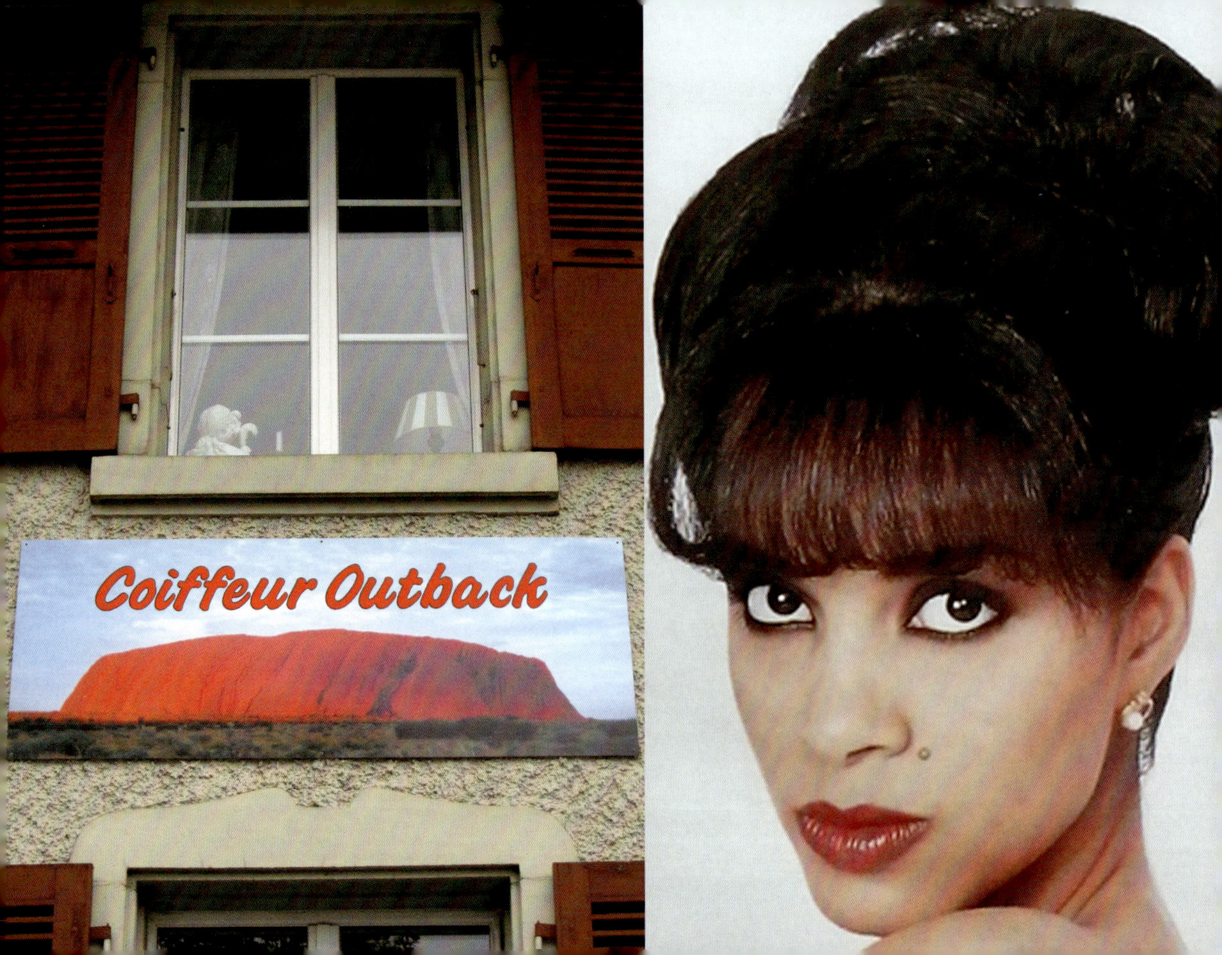
Coiffeur Outback

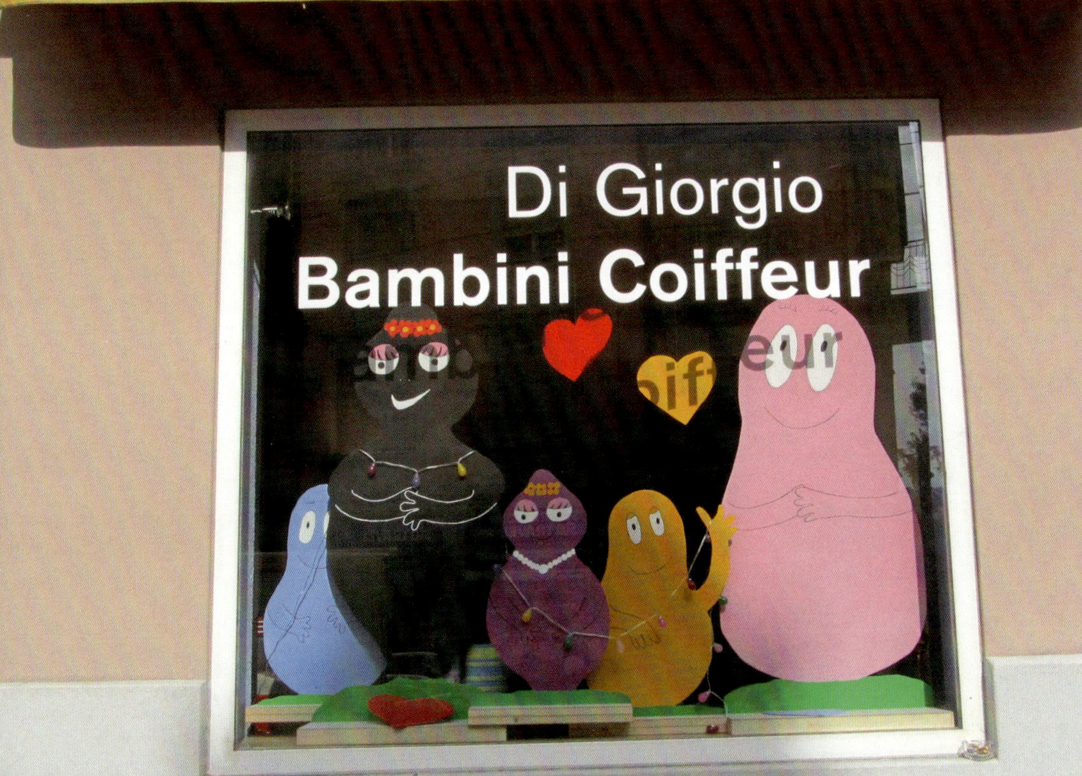
kindercoiffeurzuerich.ch
Di Giorgio
Bambini Coiffeur

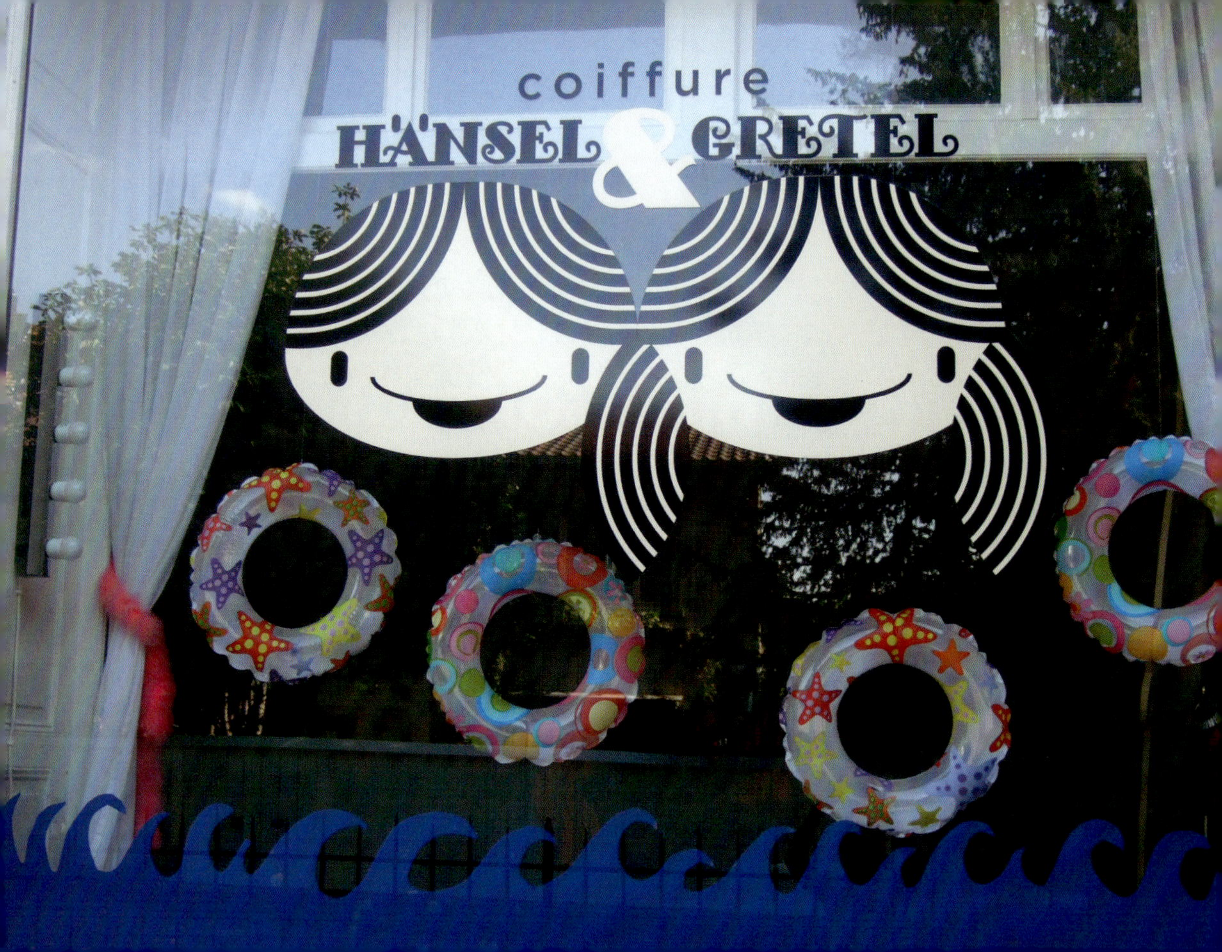
coiffure
HÄNSEL & GRETEL

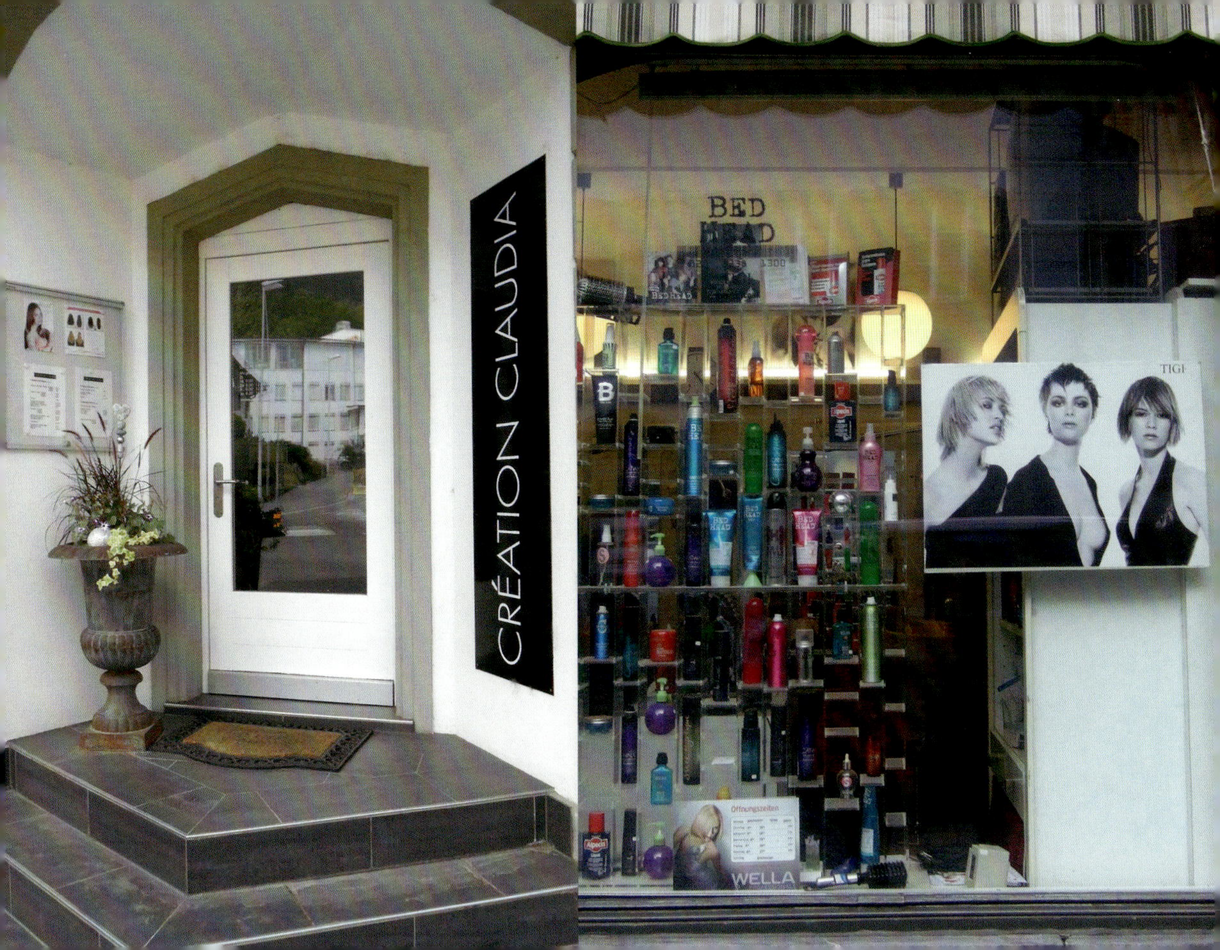
CRÉATION CLAUDIA
BED
TIGI
Öffnungszeiten
WELLA

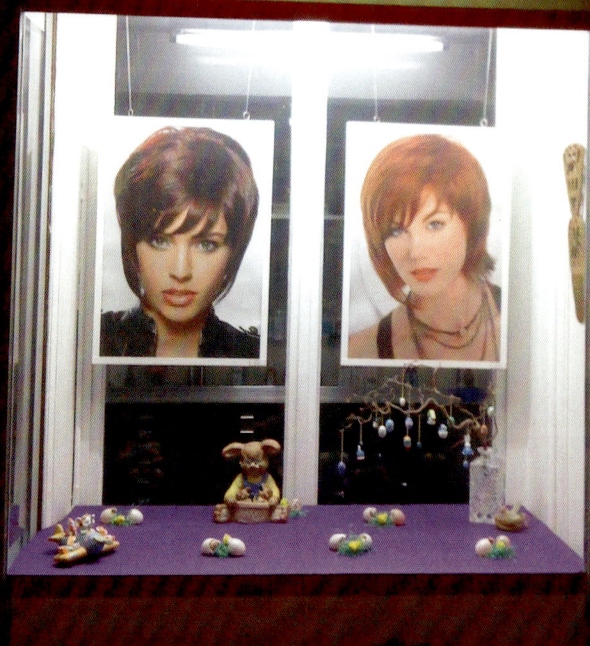
coiffure

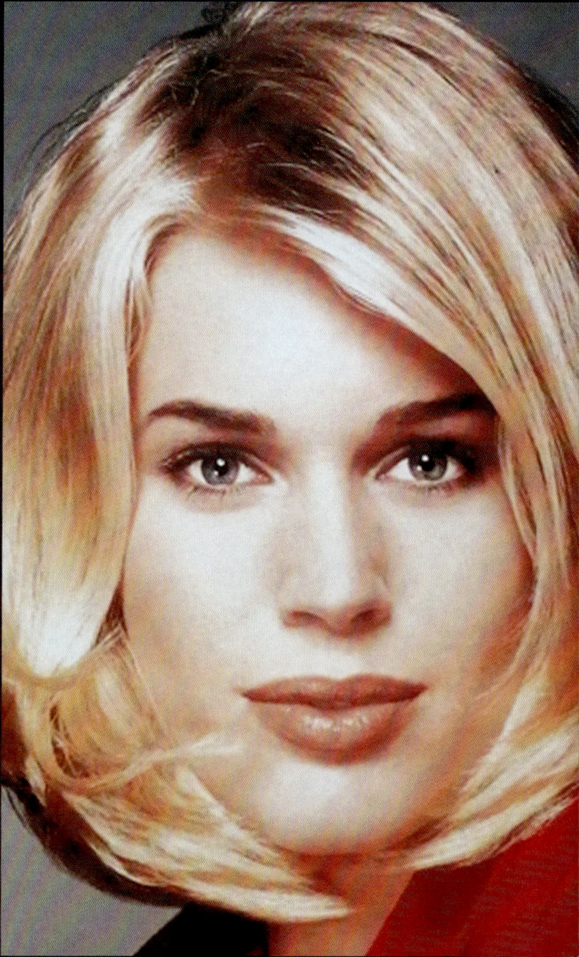

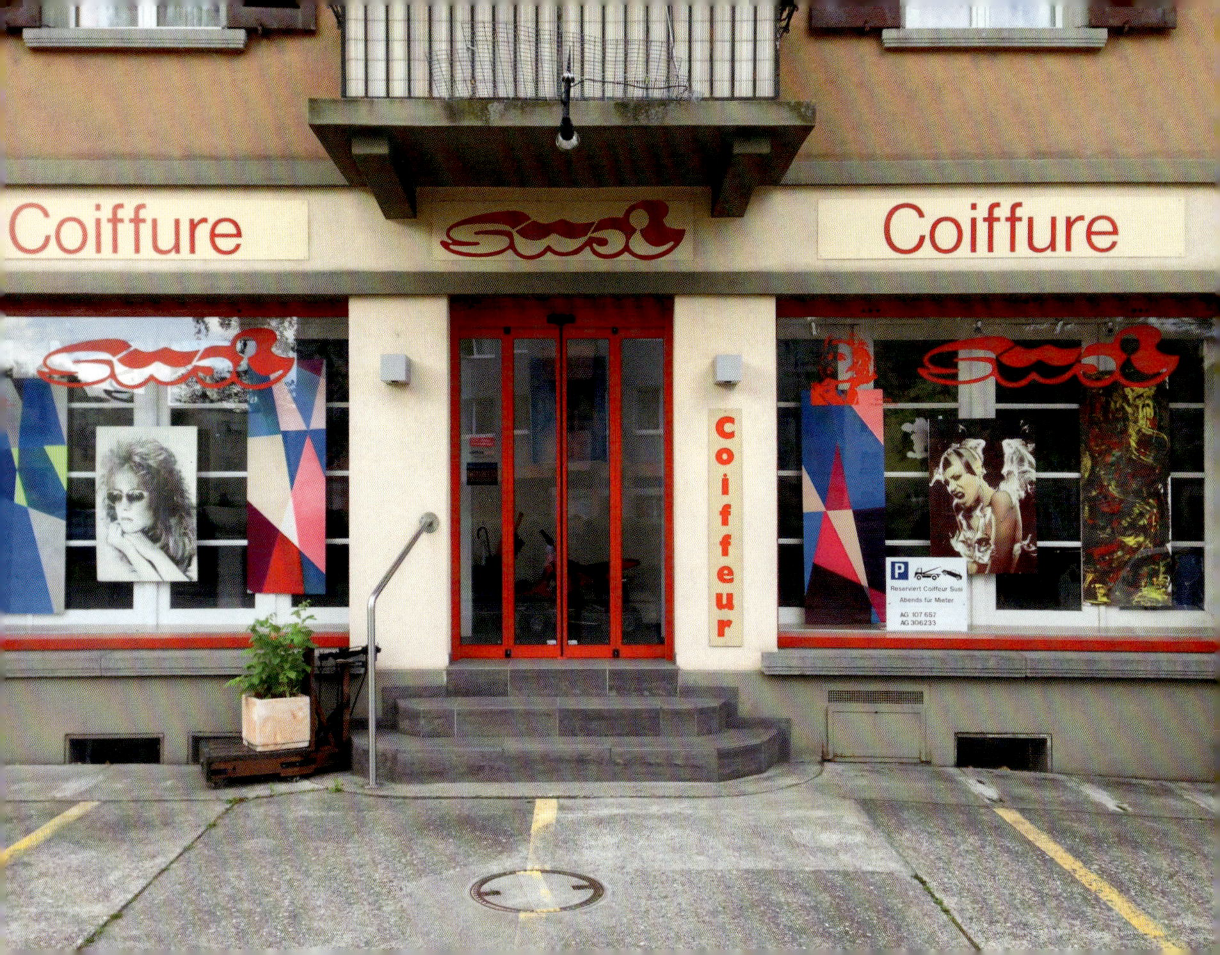
Coiffure
Susi
Coiffure
Susi
Susi
Coiffeur
P
Reserviert Coiffeur Susi
Abends für Mieter
AG 107 657
AG 306233

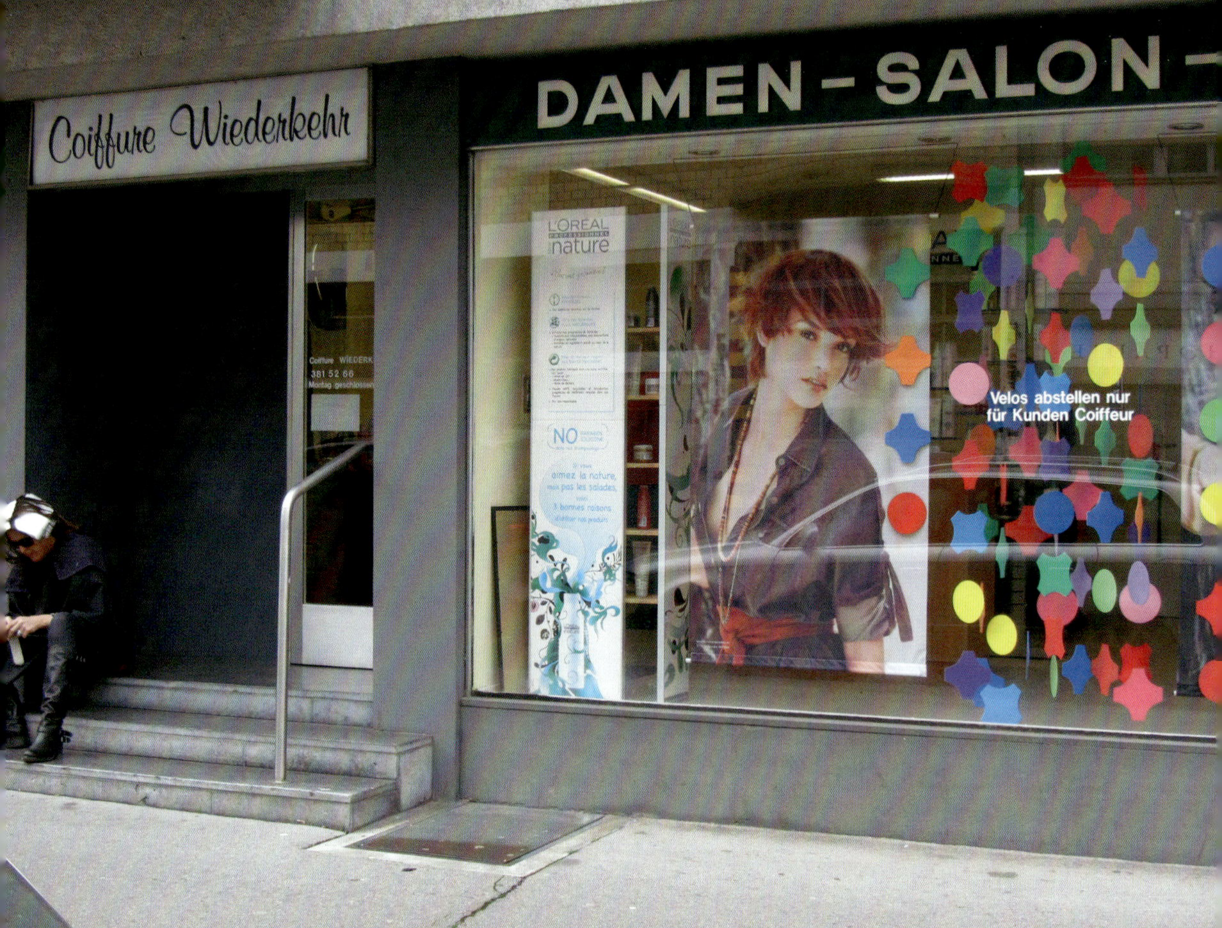
Coiffure Wiederkehr
DAMEN-SALON-
L'OREAL
nature
NO
Velos abstellen nur
für Kunden Coiffeur

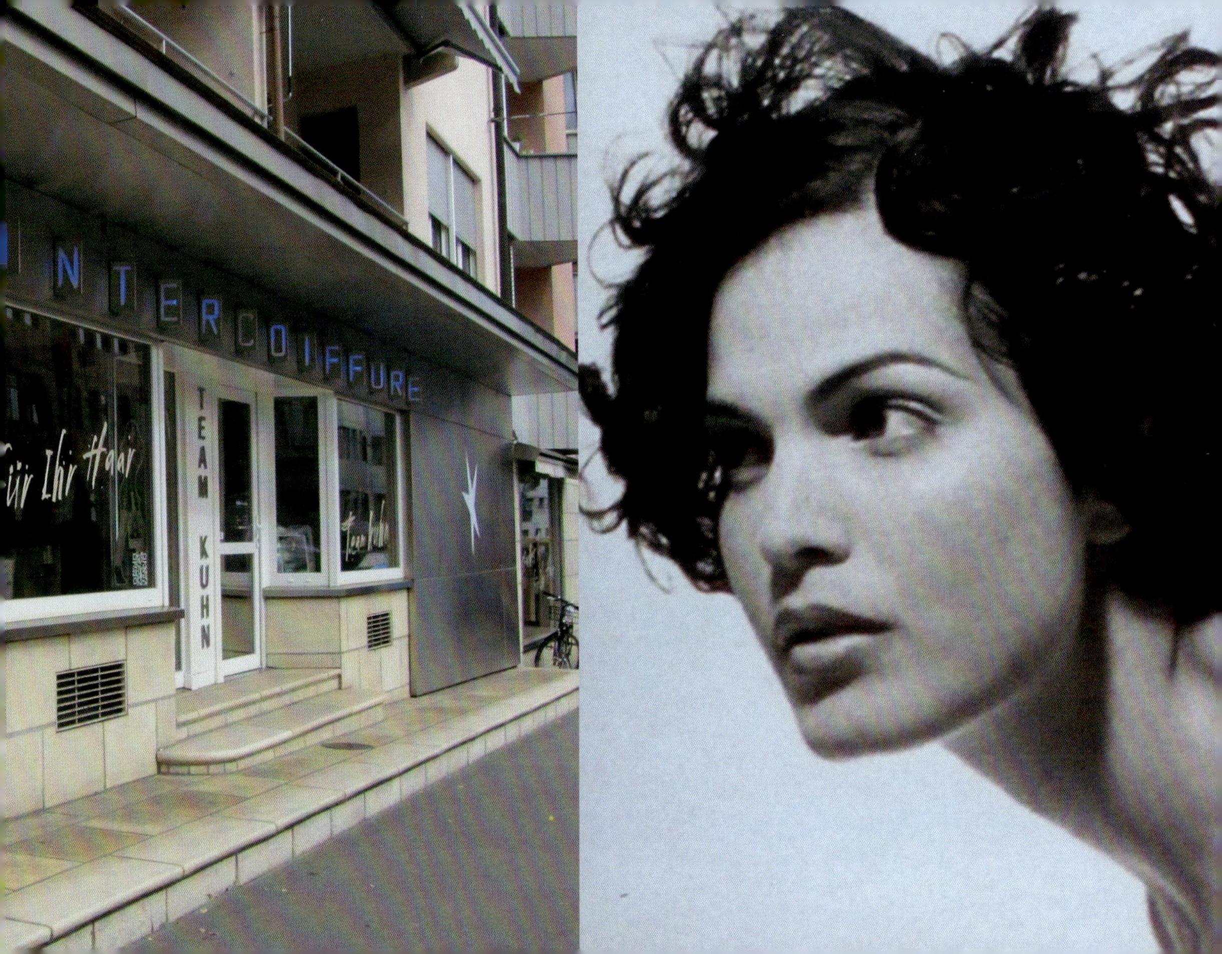
NTERCOIFFURE
TEAM KUHN
ür Ihr Haar

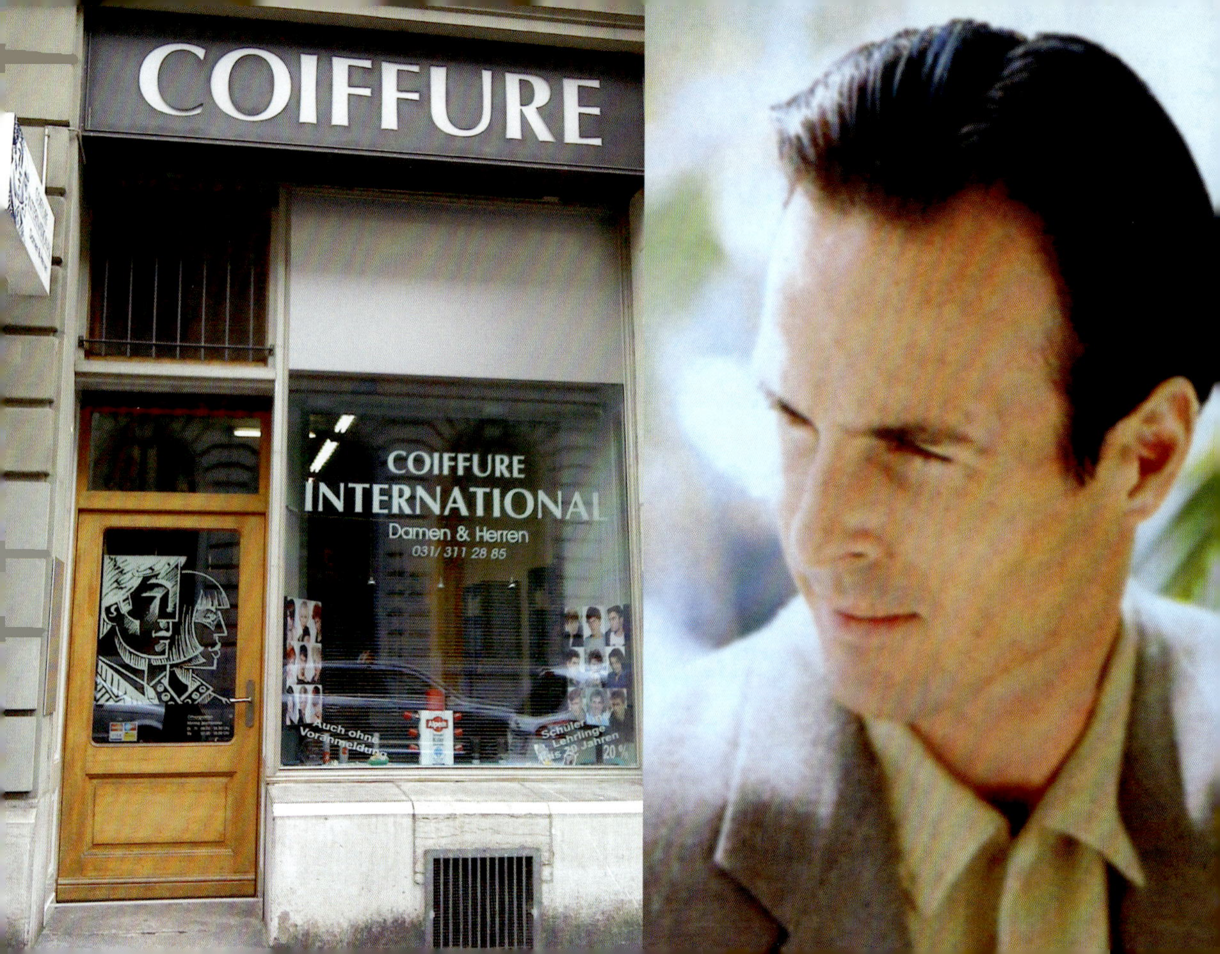
COIFFURE
COIFFURE
INTERNATIONAL
Damen & Herren
031/ 311 28 85
Auch ohne
Voranmeldung
Schüler
Lehrlinge
bis 20 Jahren
20 %

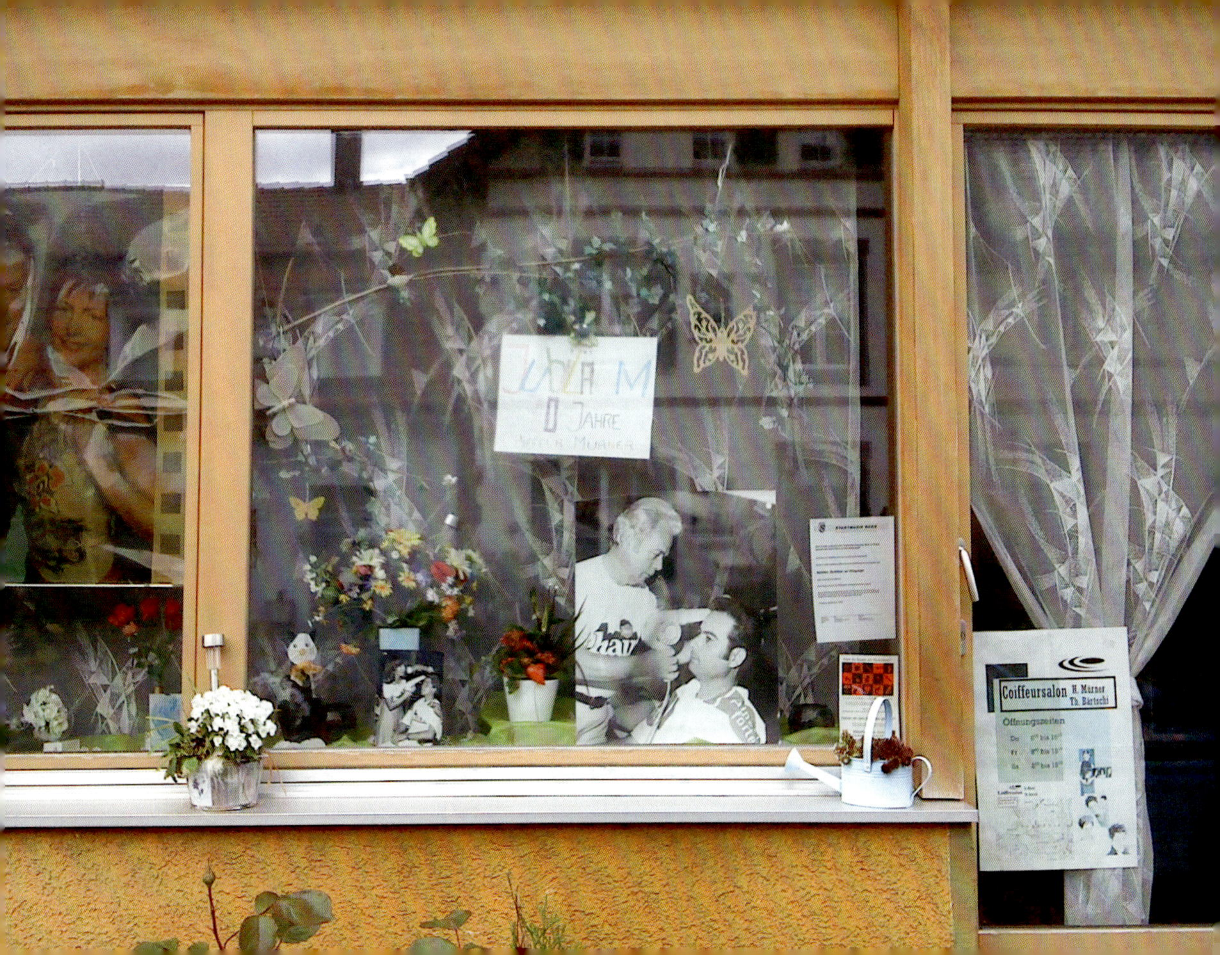

JAHRE
Coiffeursalon
H. Mürner
Th. Bärtschi
Öffnungszeiten

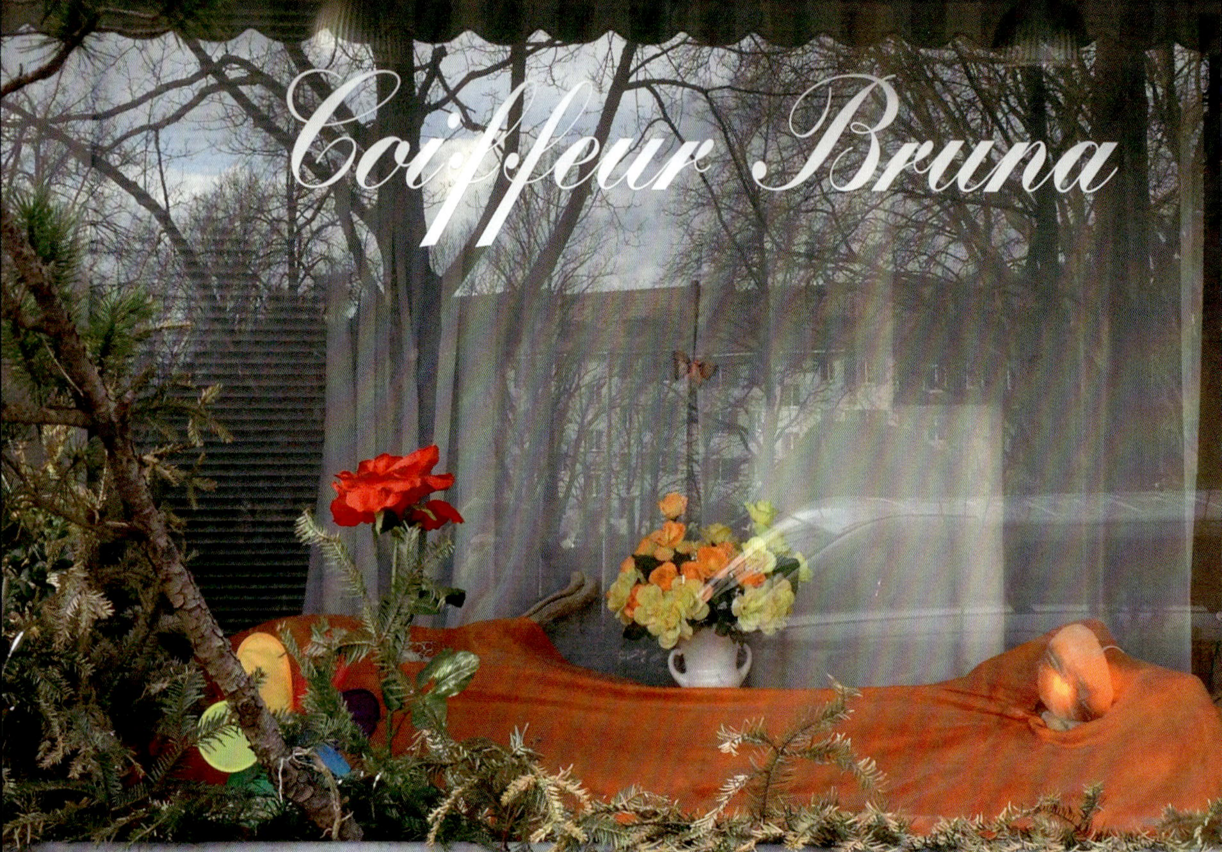
Coiffeur Bruna

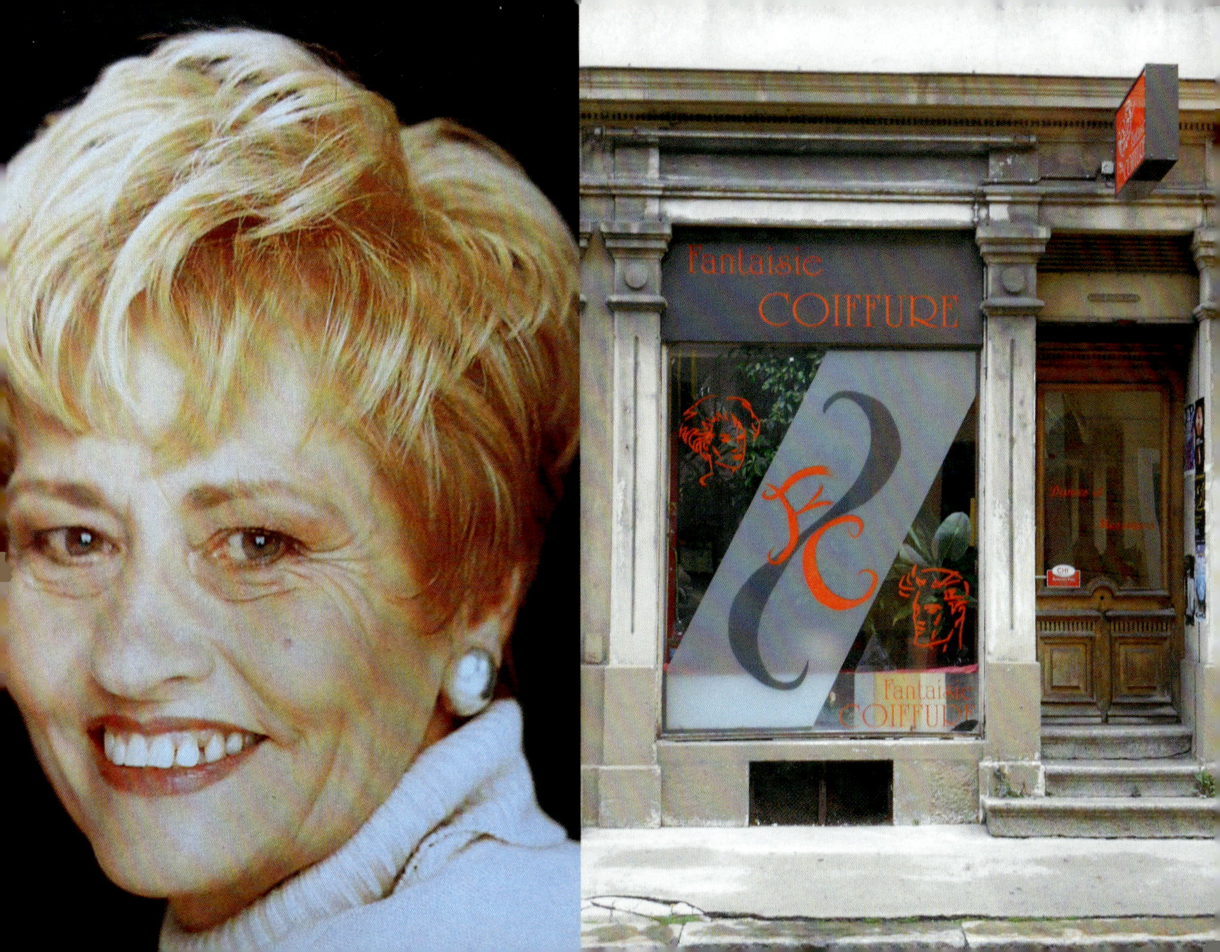
Fantaisie
COIFFURE
Fantaisie
COIFFURE

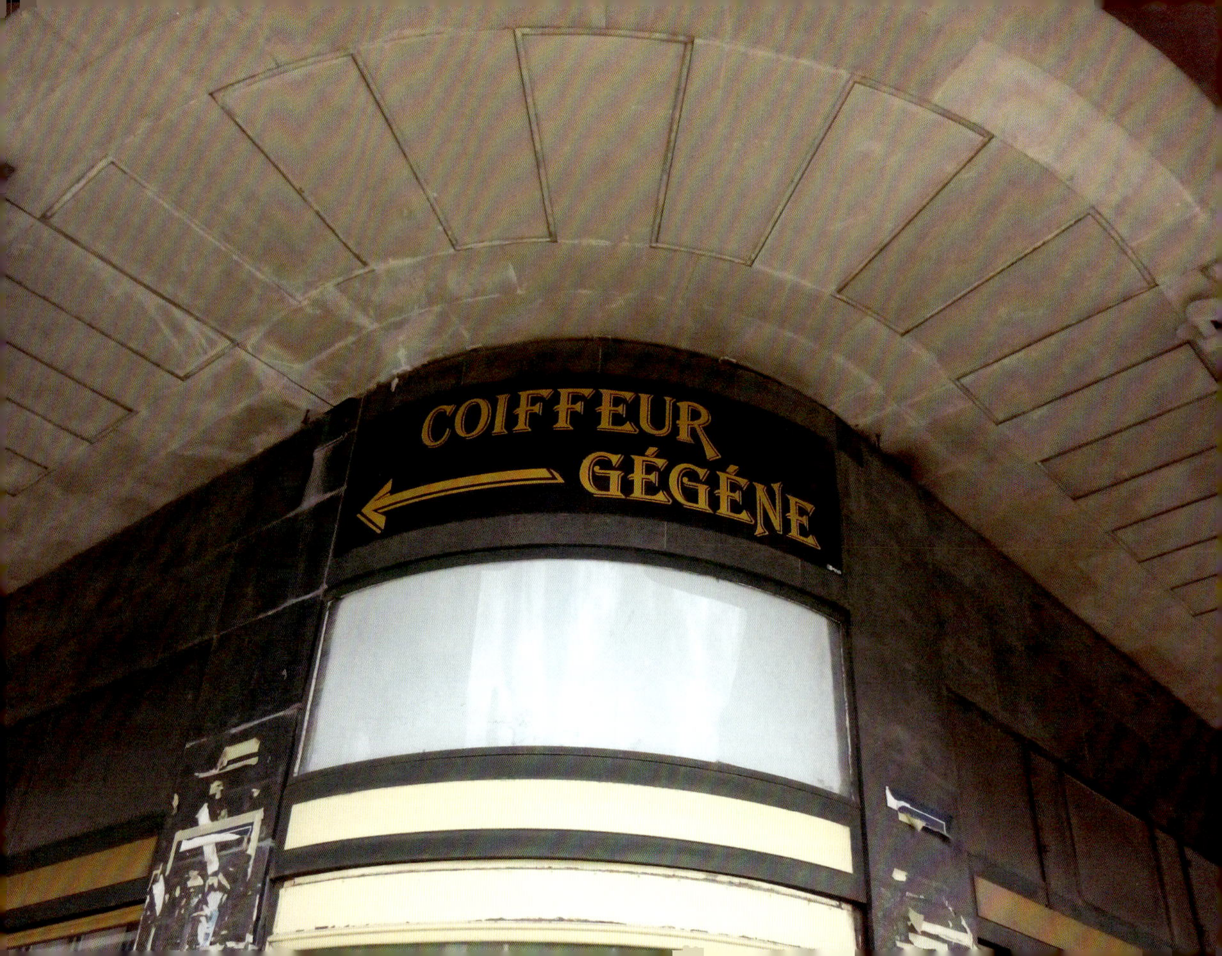
COIFFEUR
GÉGÉNE

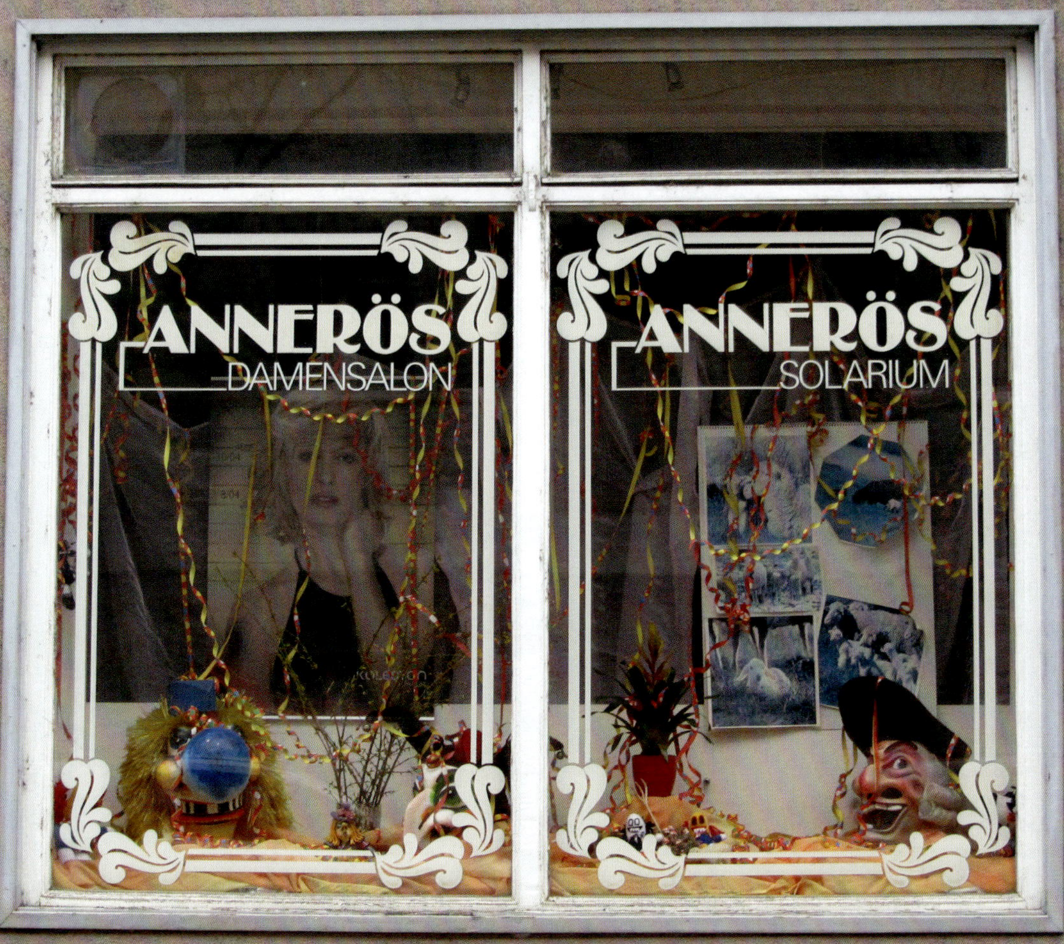
ANNERÖS
DAMENSALON
ANNERÖS
SOLARIUM

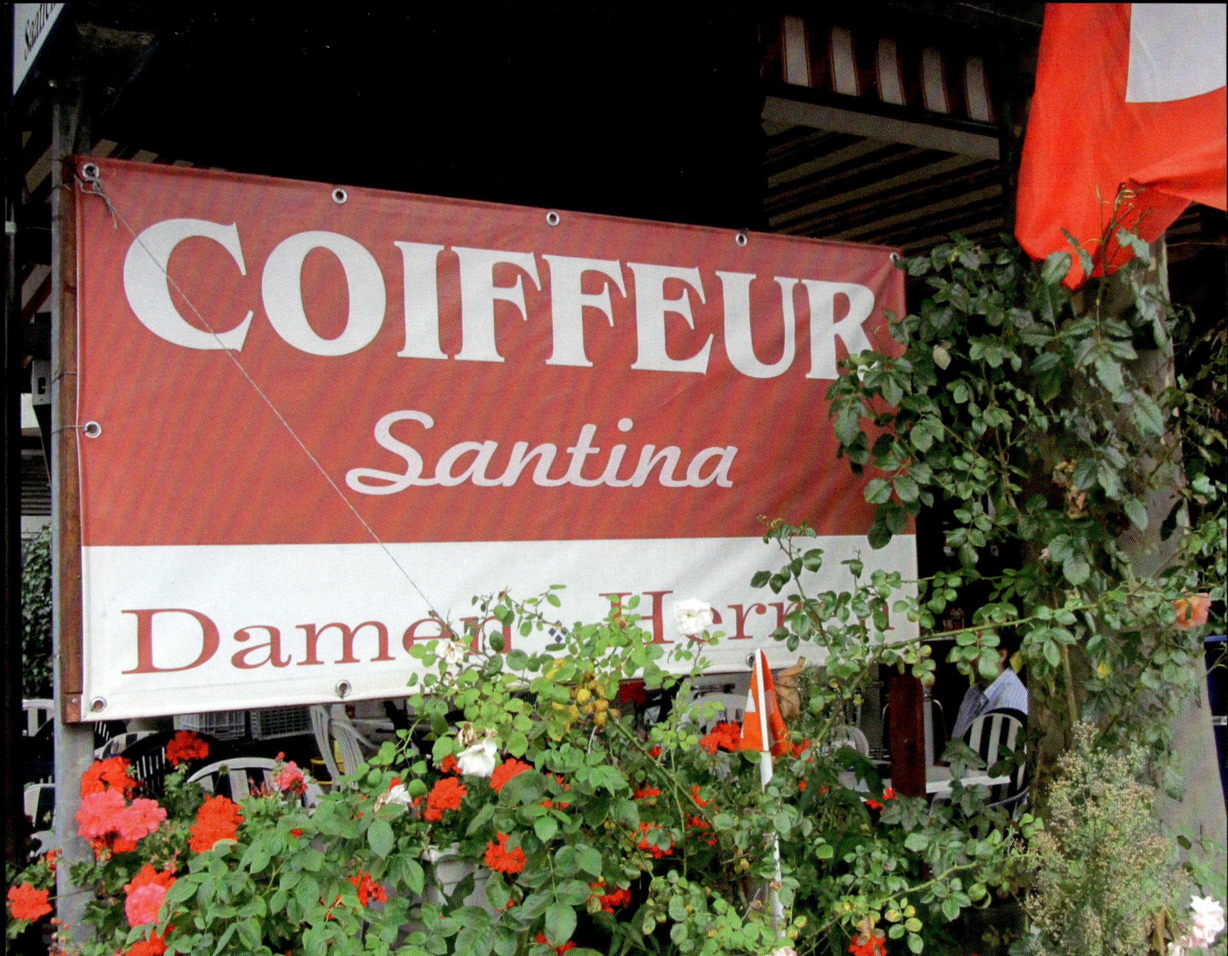
COIFFEUR
Santina

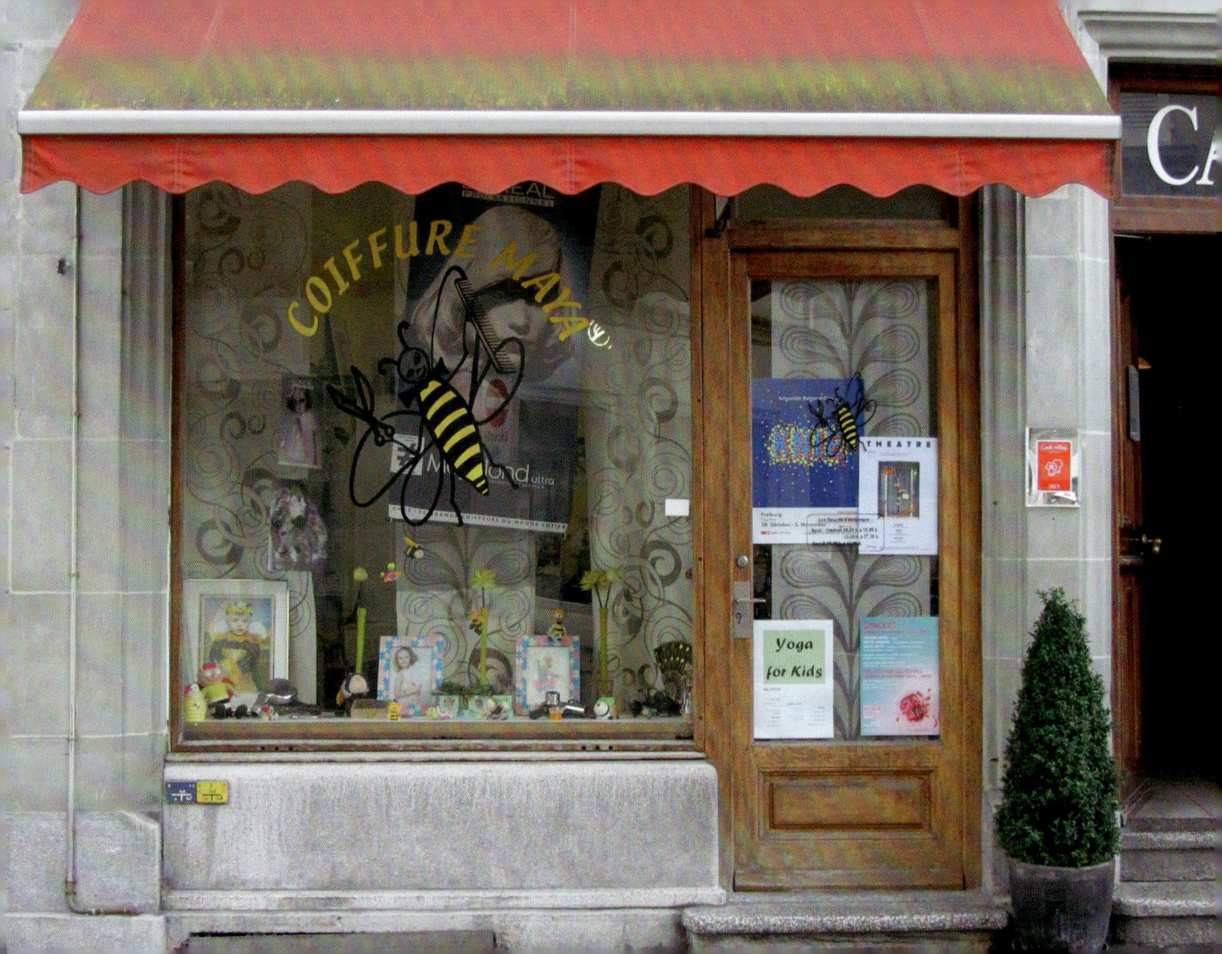
COIFFURE MAYA
THEATRE
Yoga
for Kids

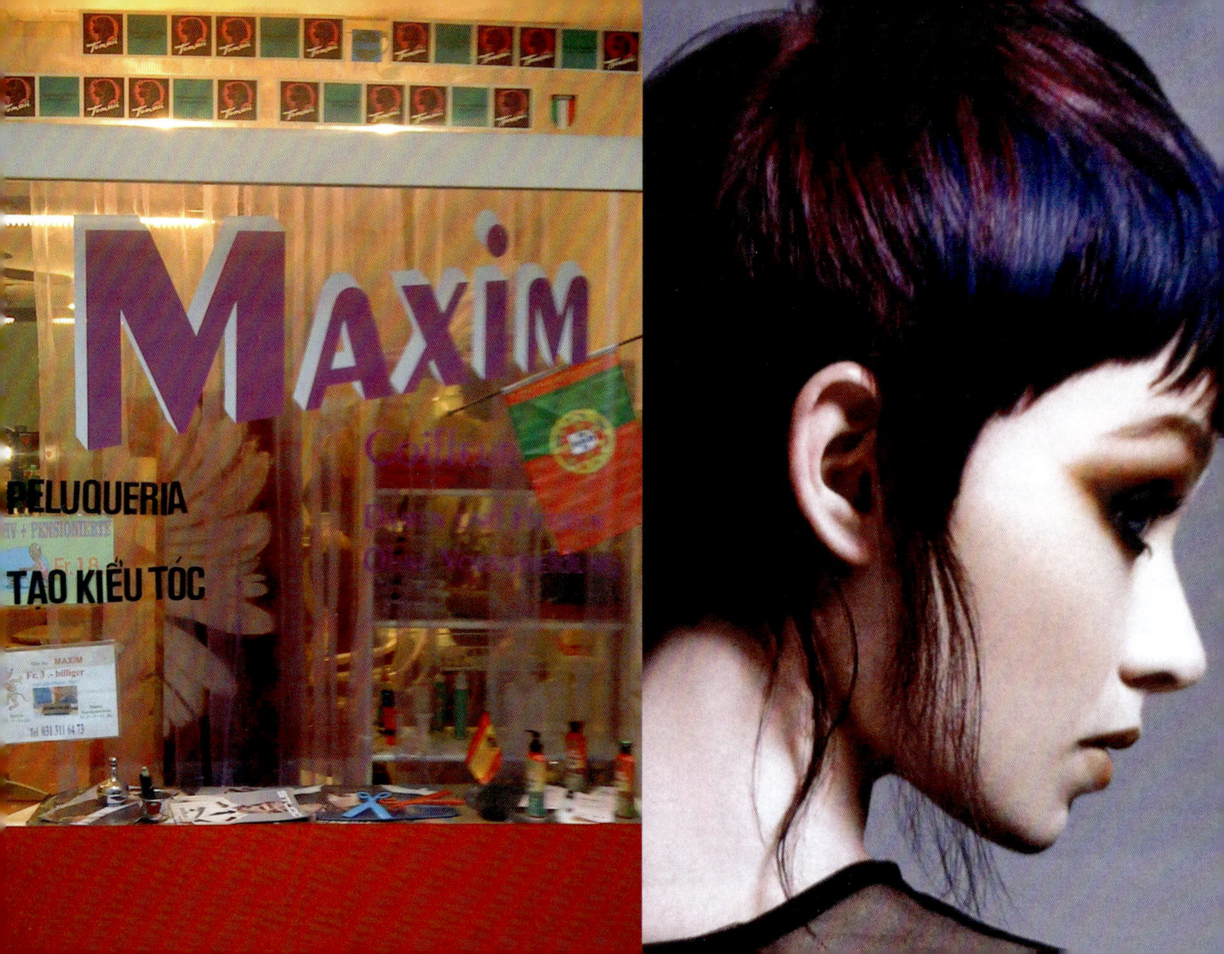
MAXIM
PELUQUERIA
TẠO KIỂU TÓC

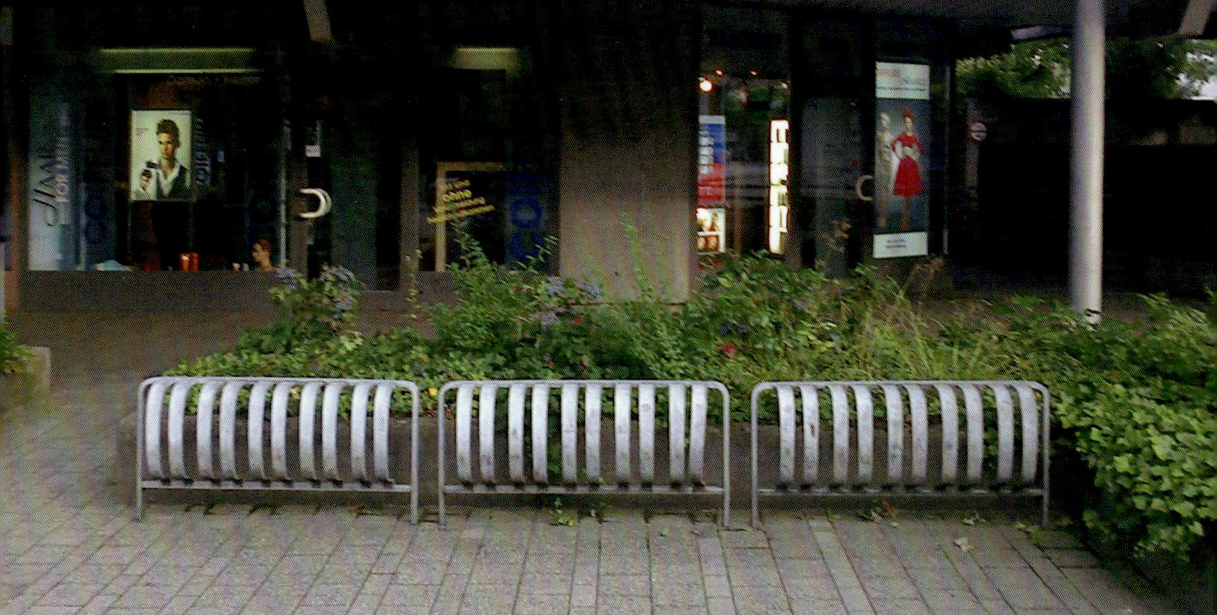
COIFFURE
HAARlekin

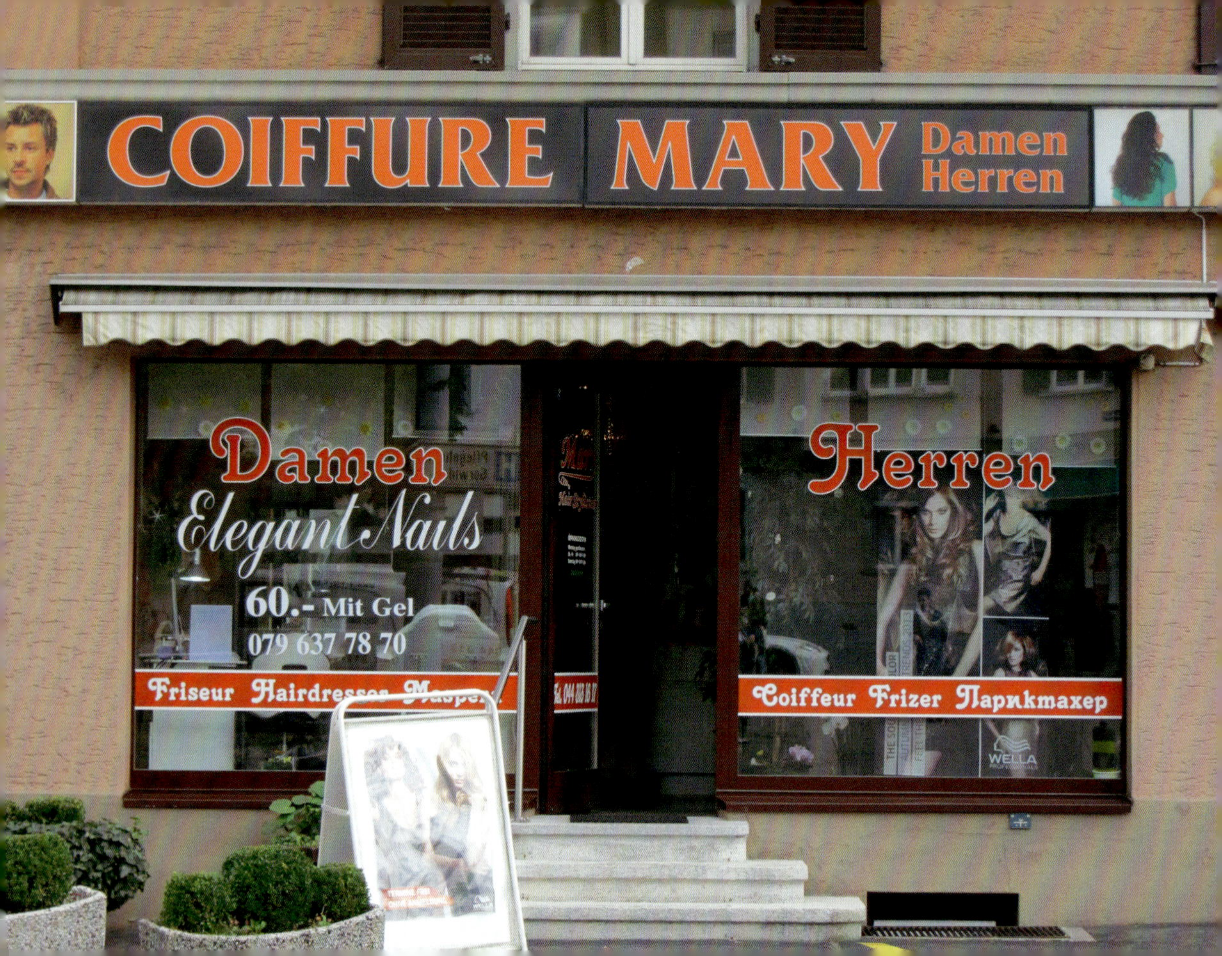

COIFFURE MARY
Damen
Herren
Damen
Elegant Nails
60.- Mit Gel
079 637 78 70
Herren
Friseur
Coiffeur Frizer Парикмахер
WELLA

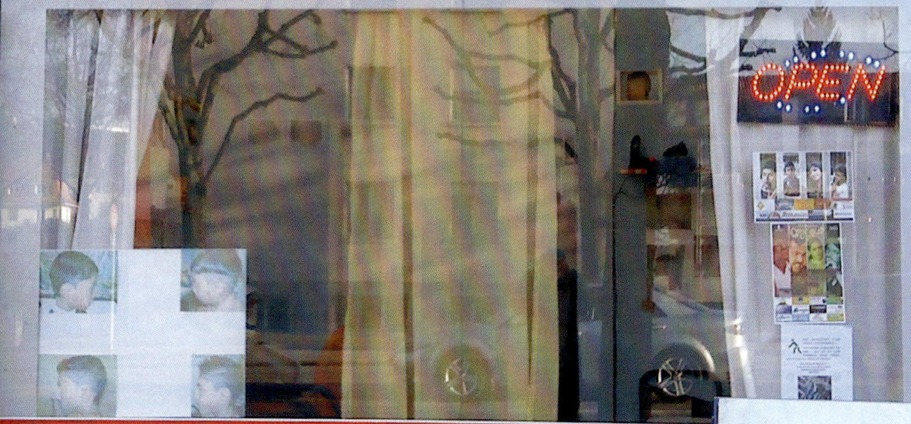
J.G.S Coiffure ஜெ.ஜி.எஸ் சலூான்
Herren K.S. Suntharam, Schlossstrasse 85B, 3008 Bern, Tel. 031 381 25 74, 076 294 52 84
OPEN
AVAILABLE HERE • HIER ERHÄLTLICH • AVAILABLE HERE • HIER ERHÄLTLICH
ortel MOBILE
J.G.S.Herrencoiffeur
Schlossstrasse 85 b
3008 Bern
Tel. 031 381 25 74
Öffnungszeiten:
Dienstag bis Samstag
10.00 - 19.00

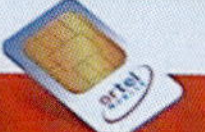

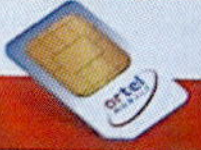

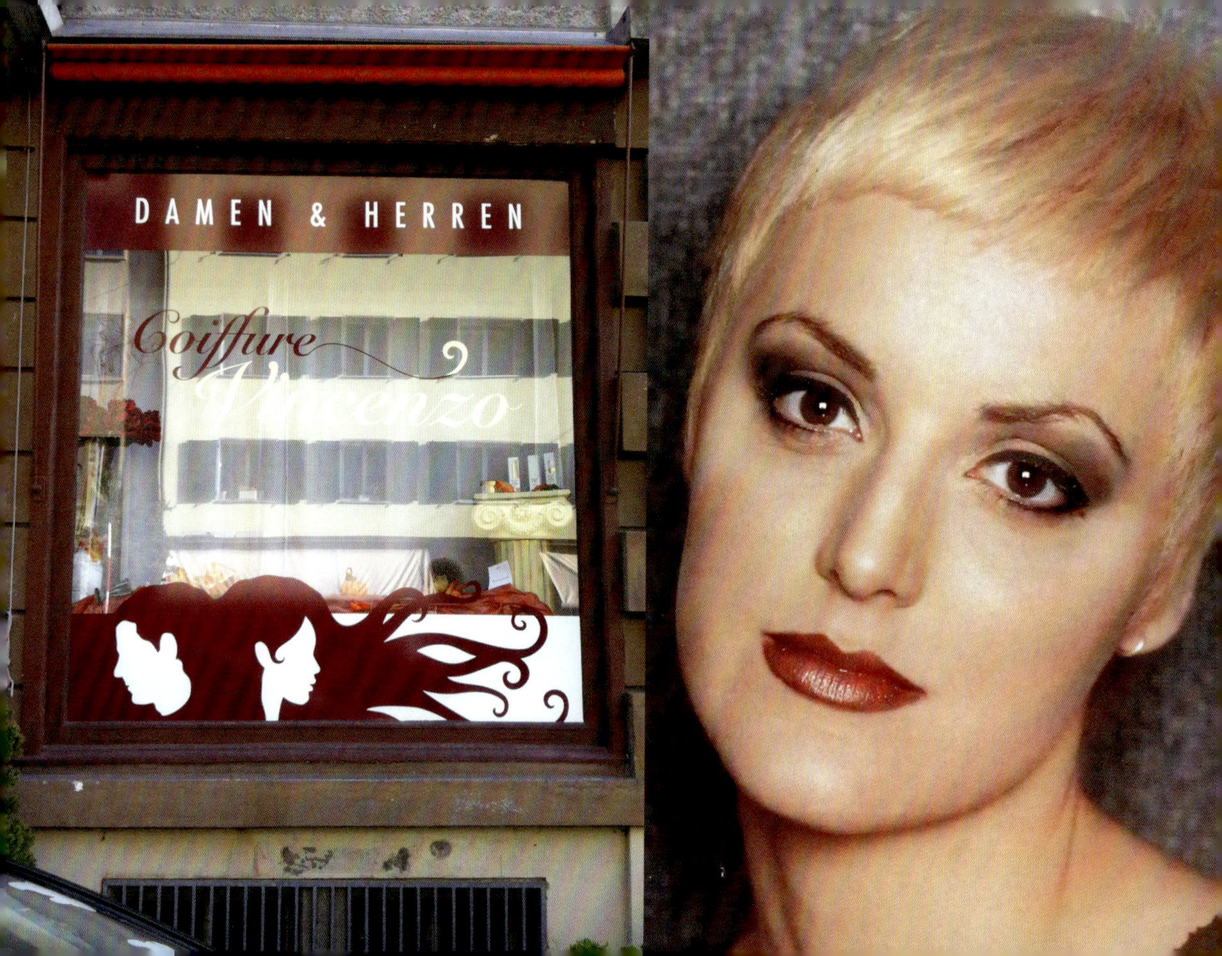
DAMEN & HERREN
Coiffure
Vincenzo

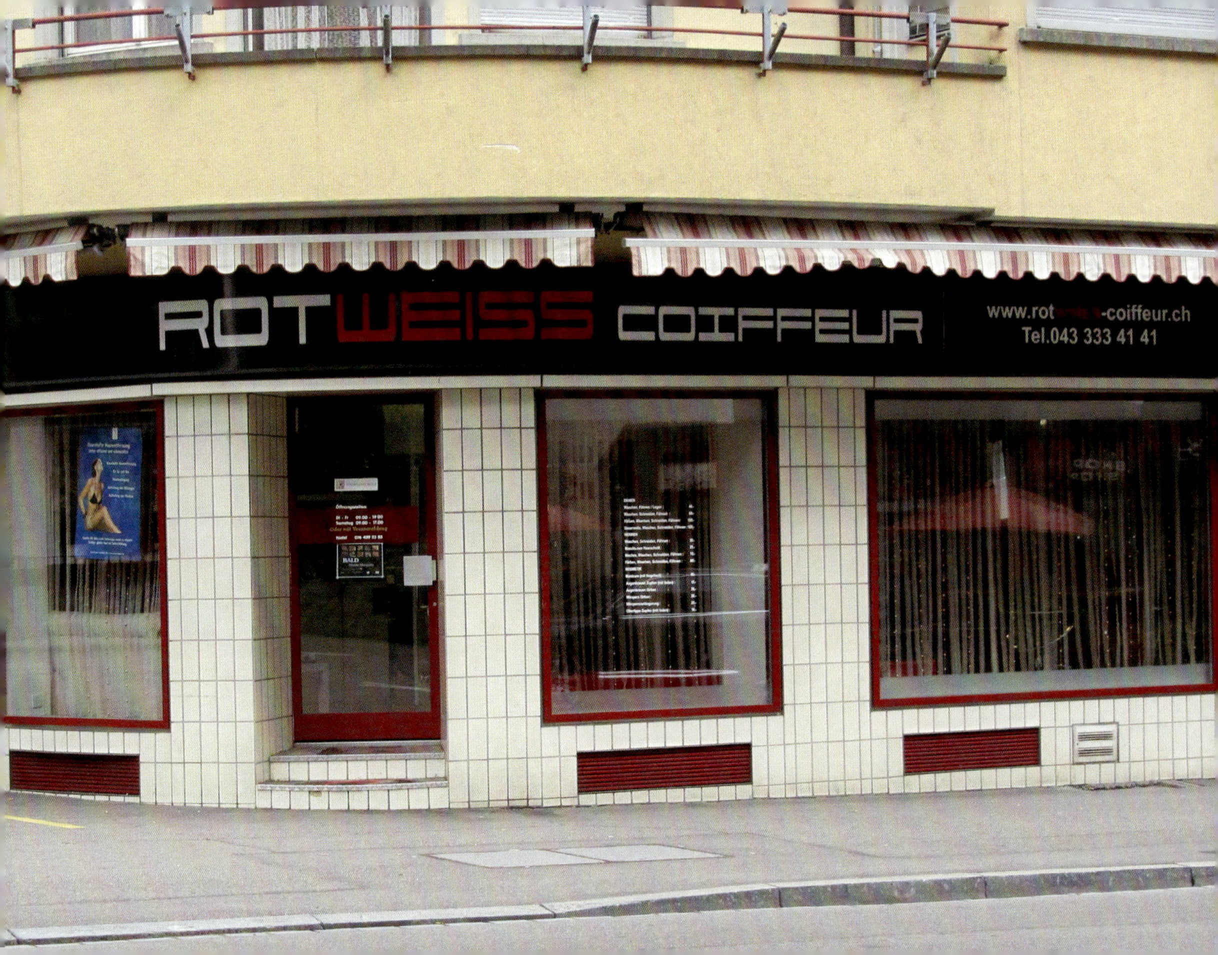
ROTWEISS COIFFEUR
Tel.043 333 41 41

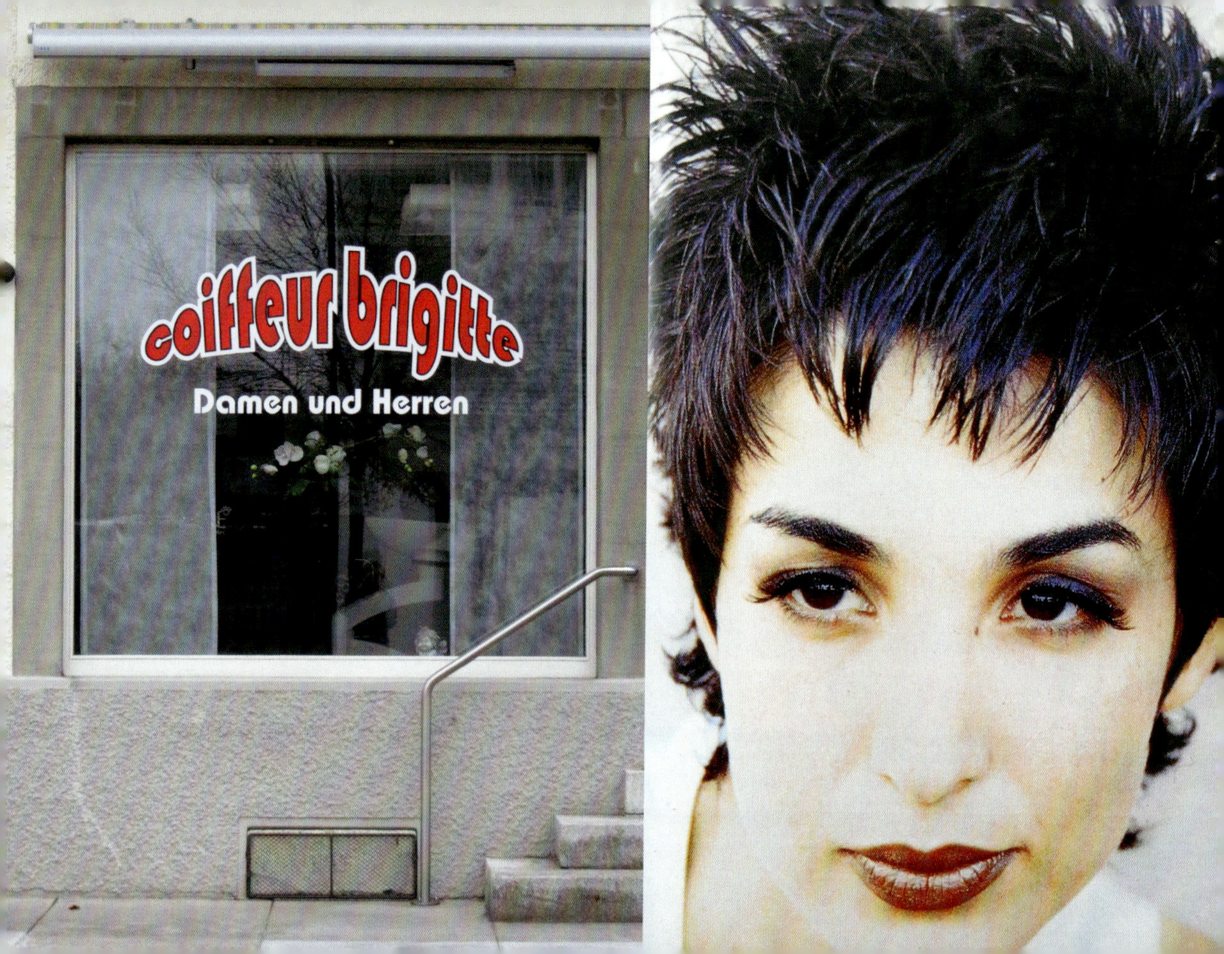
coiffeur brigitte
Damen und Herren

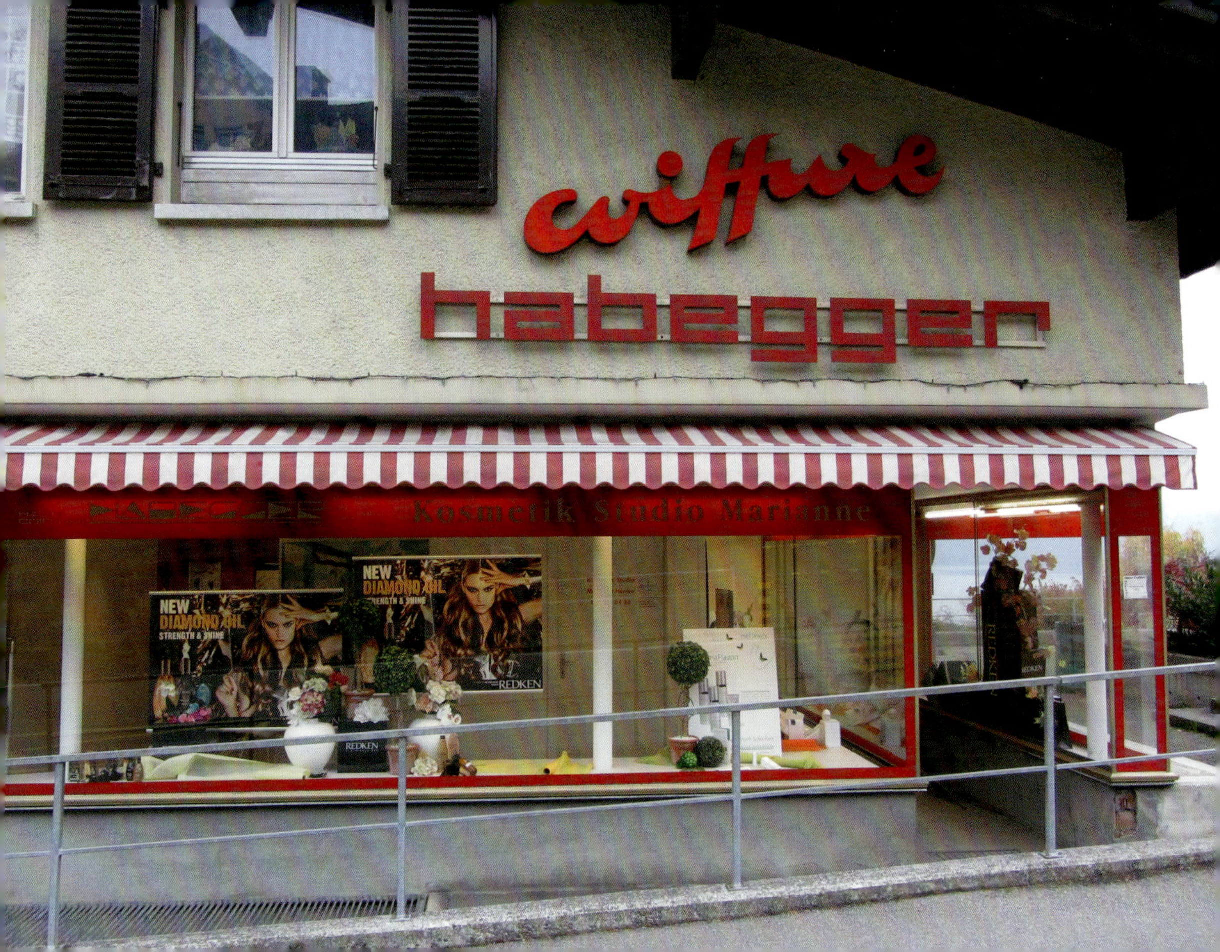
coiffure
habegger
Kosmetik Studio Marianne
NEW
DIAMOND OIL
STRENGTH & SHINE
REDKEN
NEW
DIAMOND OIL
STRENGTH & SHINE
REDKEN
REDKEN

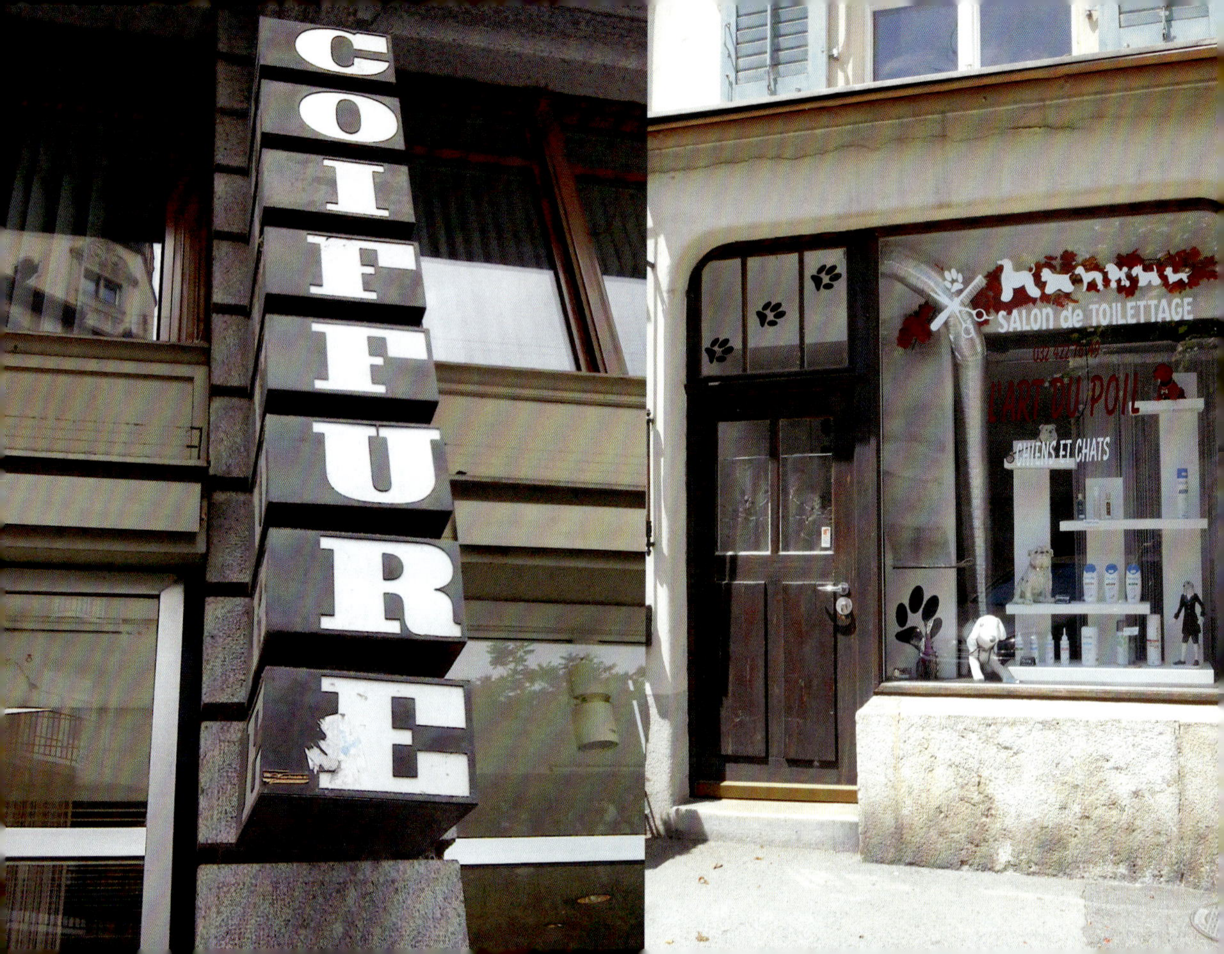

COIFFURE
SALON de TOILETTAGE
L'ART DU POIL
CHIENS ET CHATS

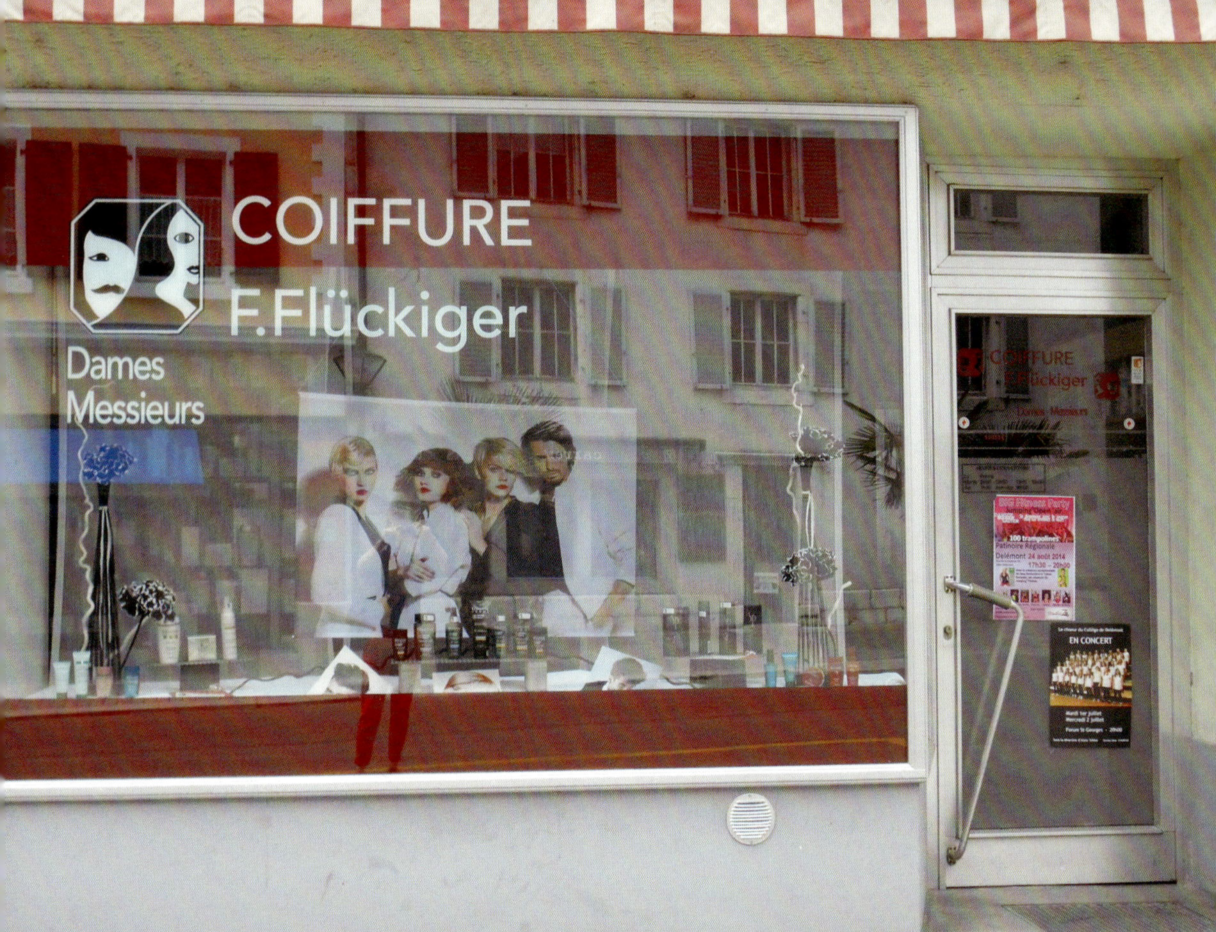
COIFFURE
F.Flückiger
Dames
Messieurs
COIFFURE
F.Flückiger
Dames Messieurs
100 trampolines
Patinoire Régionale
Delémont 24 août 2014
17h30 – 20h30
EN CONCERT

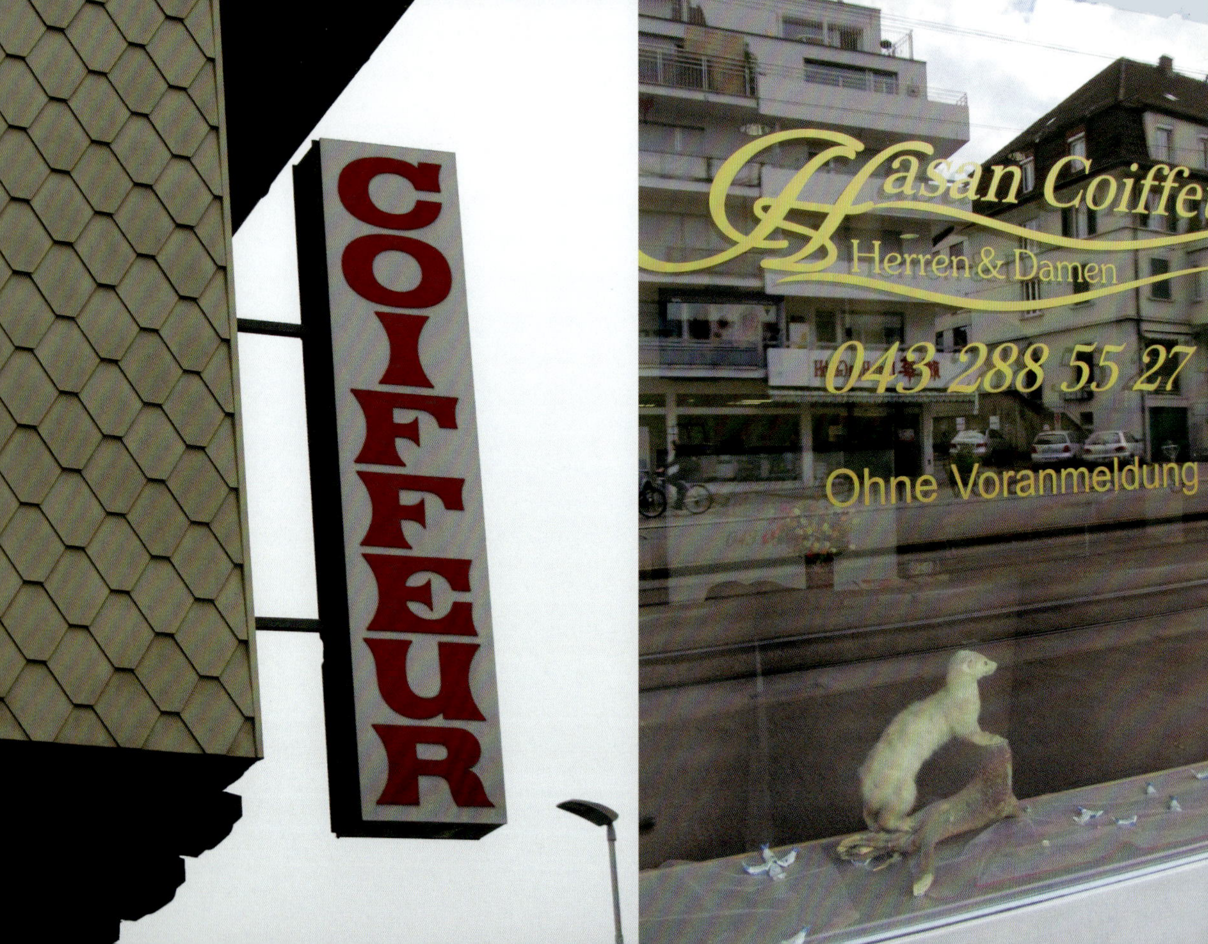
COIFFEUR
Hasan Coiffe
Herren & Damen
043 288 55 27
Ohne Voranmeldung

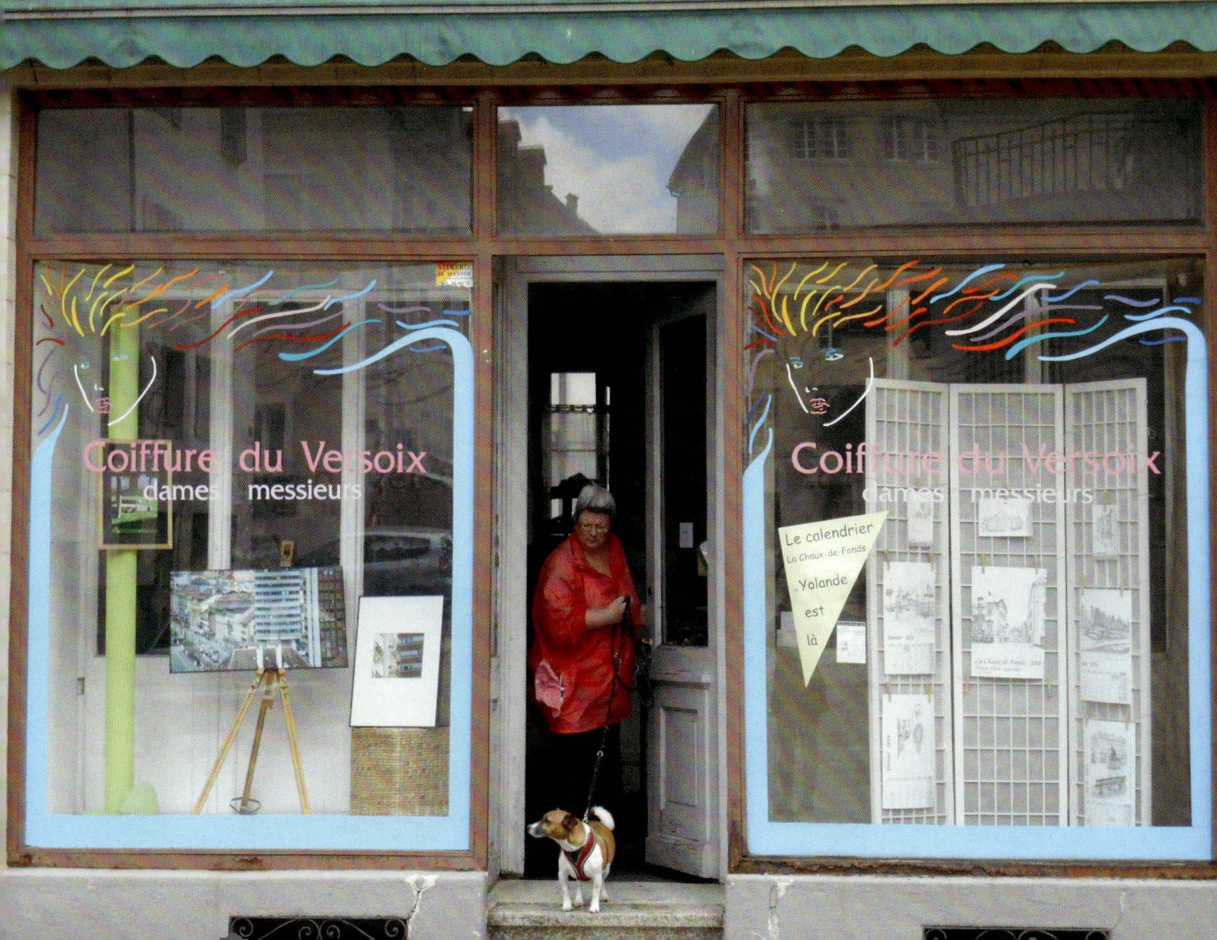
Coiffure du Versoix
dames messieurs
Coiffure du Versoix
dames messieurs
Le calendrier
La Chaux-de-Fonds
Yolande
est
là

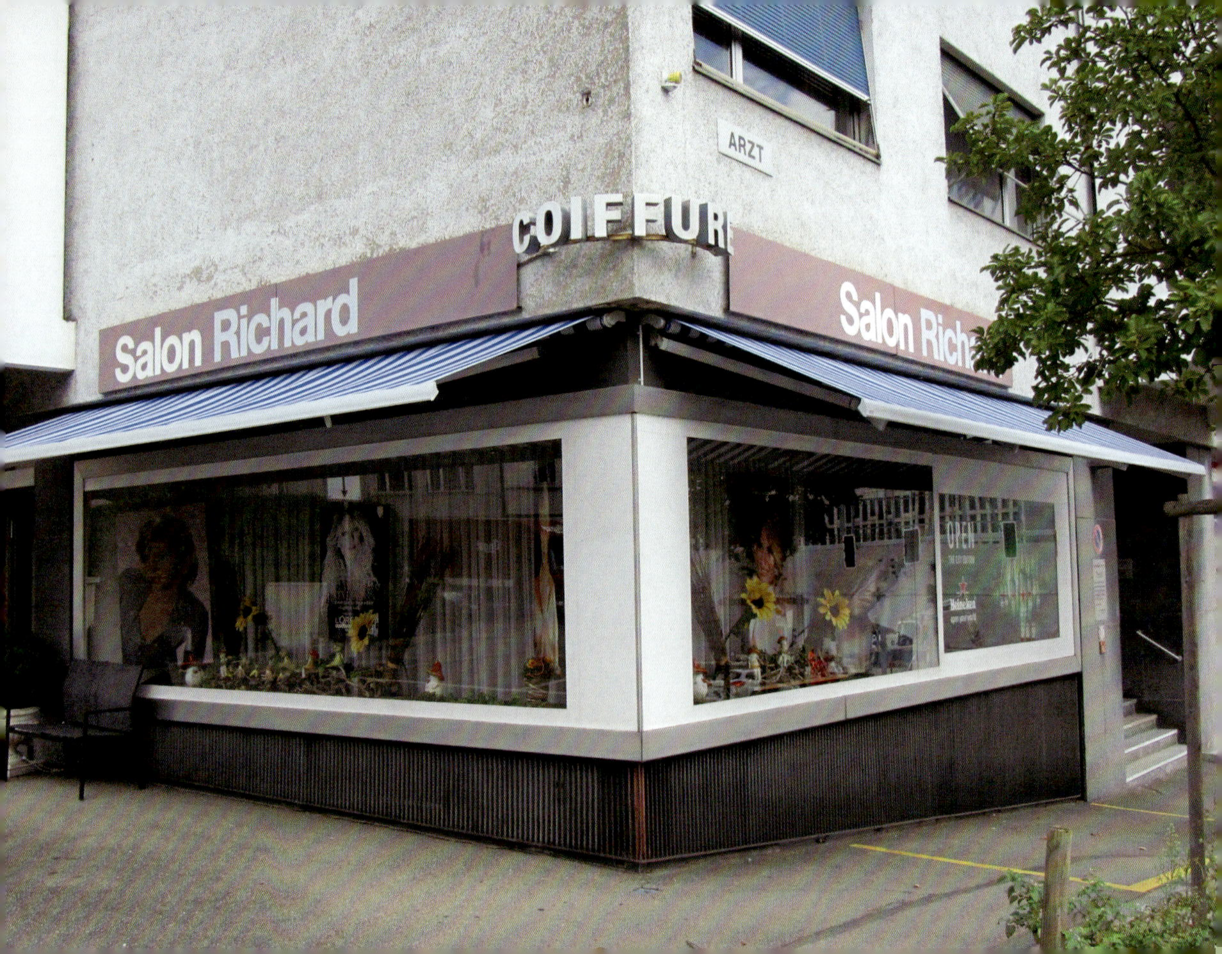
ARZT
COIFFURE
Salon Richard
OPEN

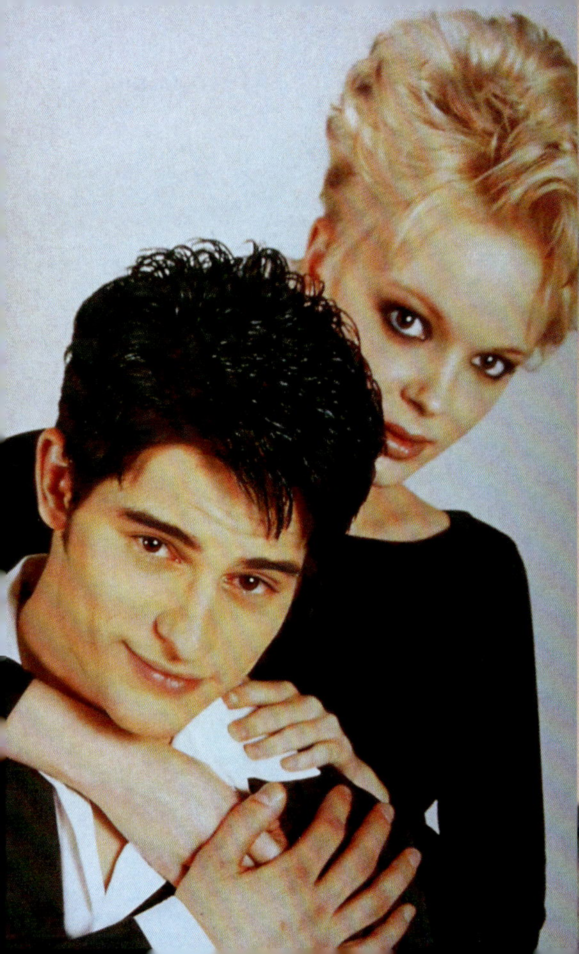

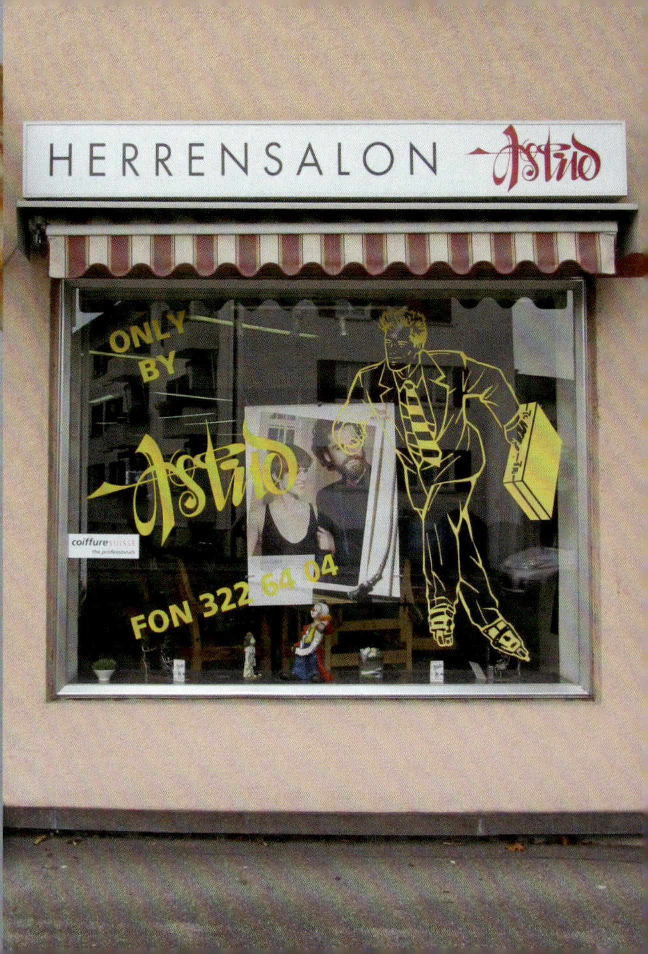

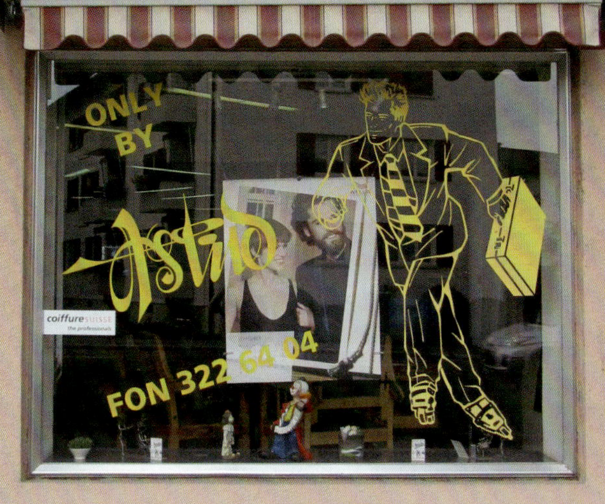
HERRENSALON
Astrid
ONLY BY
Astrid
coiffuresuisse
FON 322 64 04

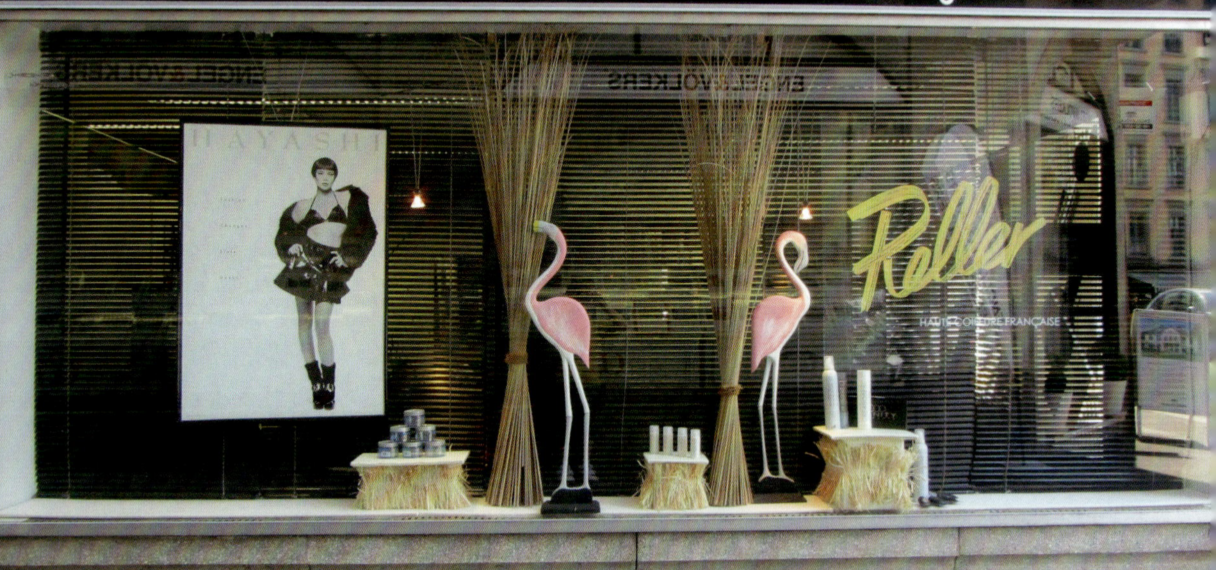
HAUTE COIFFURE FRANÇAISE
HAYASHI
Roller

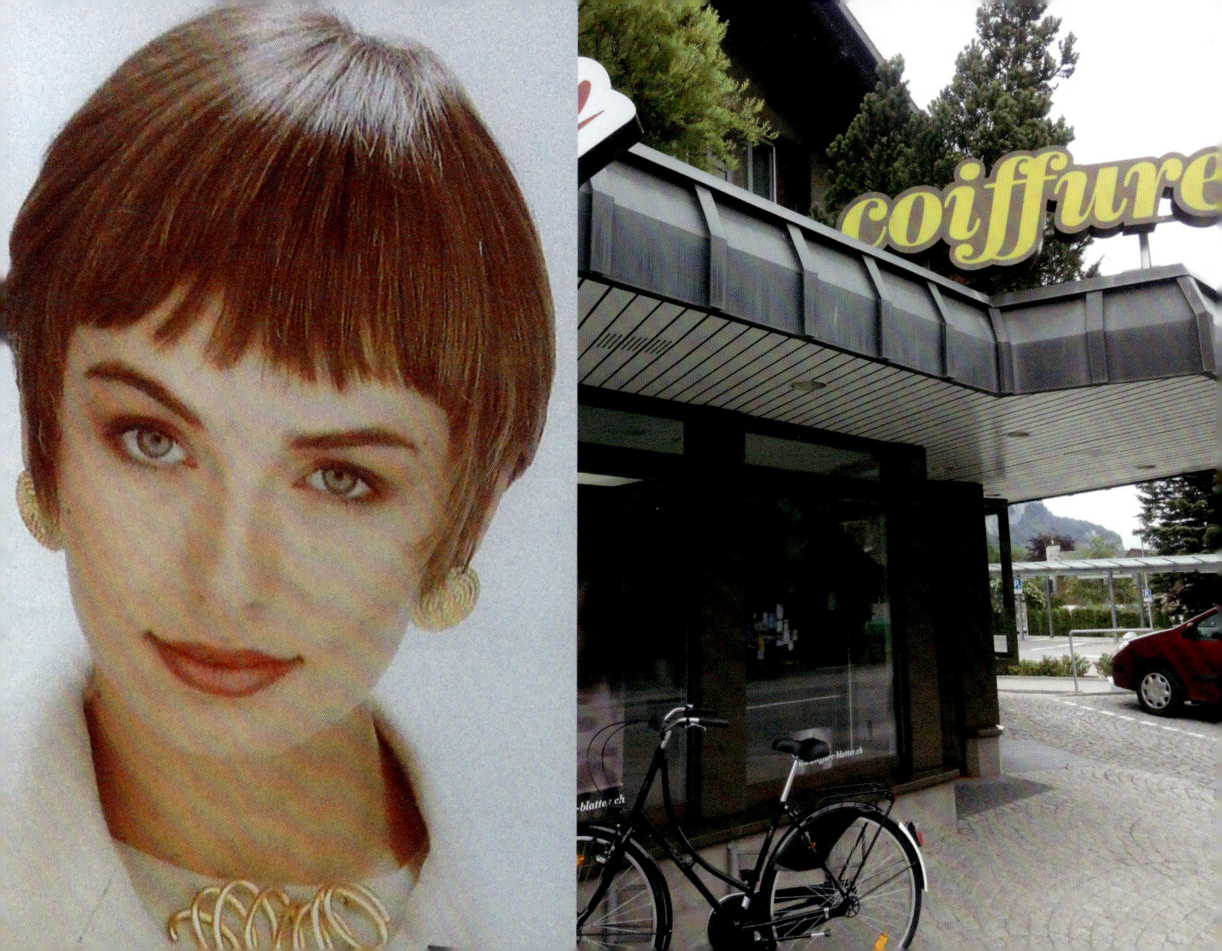
coiffure

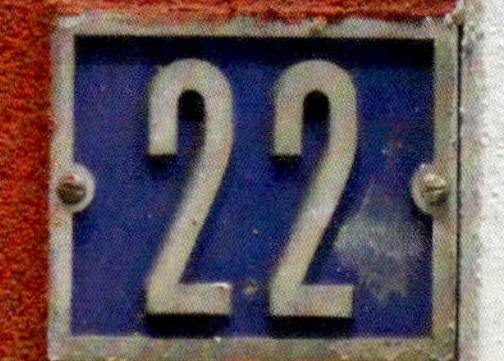

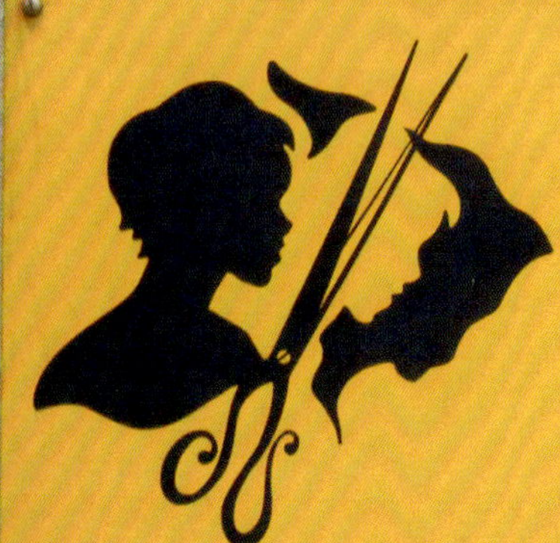

SALON DE COIFFURE

Raymond

DAMES MESSIEURS ENFANTS

Tél. 422 94 55 1er étage →

Mardi-vendredi 08.00-18.00 non-stop Samedi 07.00-16.00 non-st

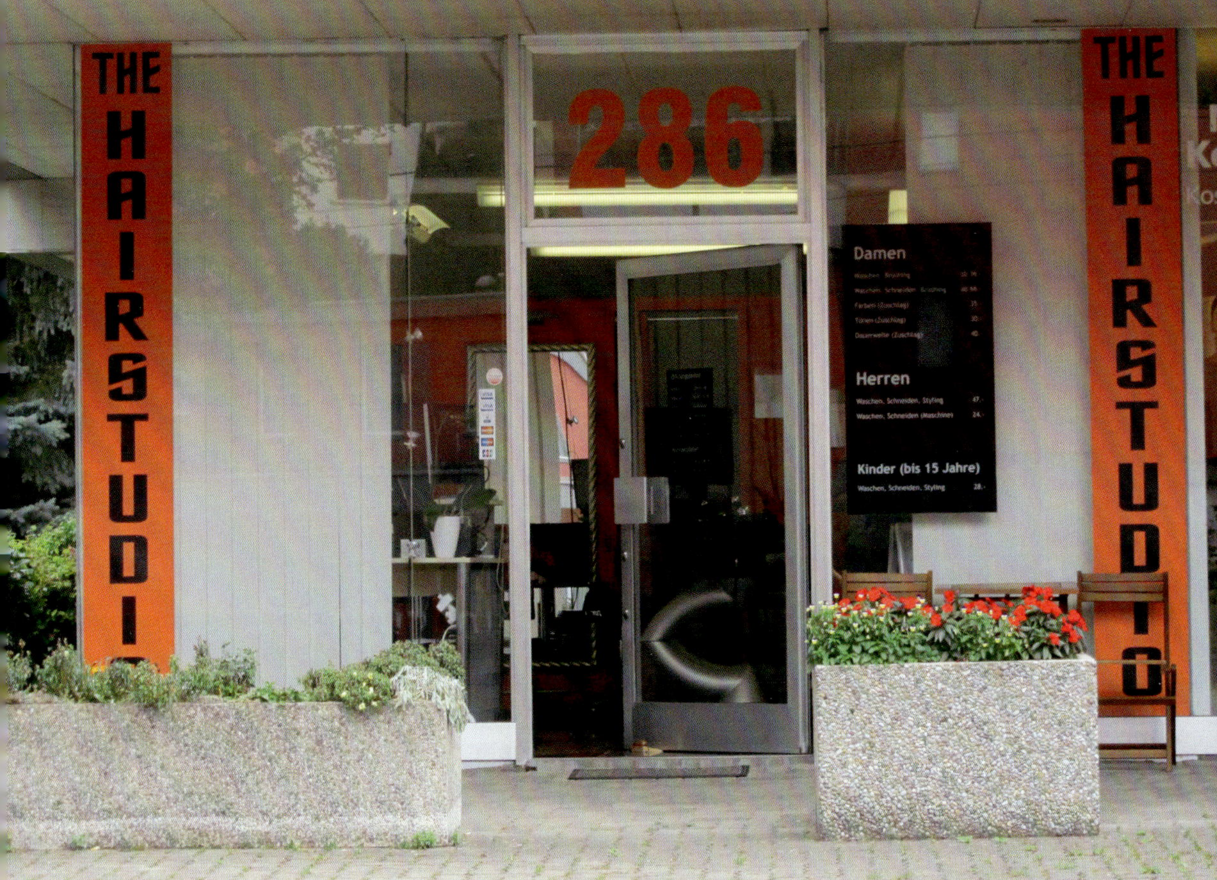
THE HAIRSTUDIO
286
Damen
Herren
Waschen, Schneiden, Styling 47.-
Waschen, Schneiden (Maschine) 24.-
Kinder (bis 15 Jahre)
Waschen, Schneiden, Styling 28.-
THE HAIRSTUDIO

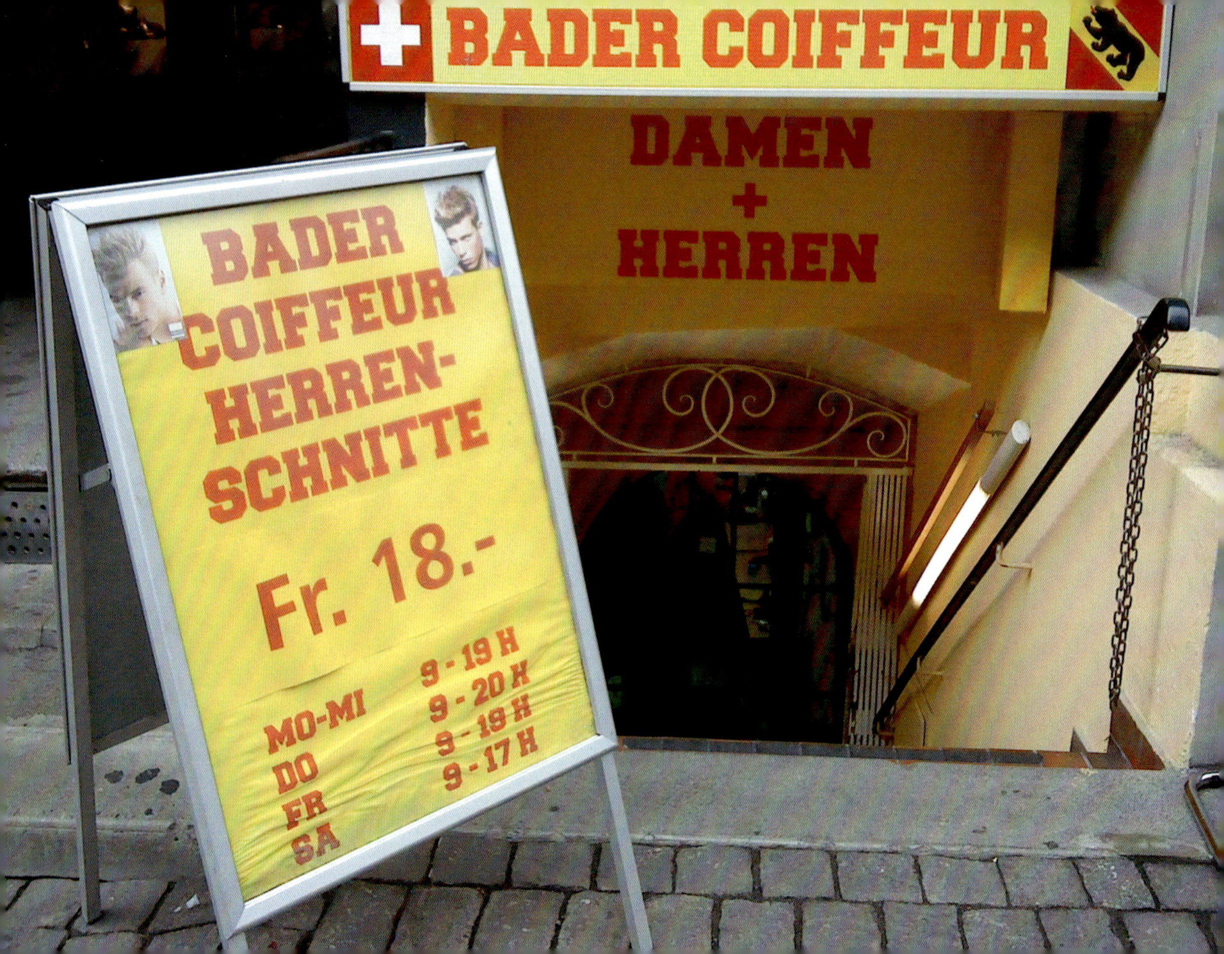
BADER COIFFEUR
DAMEN
+
HERREN
BADER
COIFFEUR
HERREN-
SCHNITTE
Fr. 18.-
MO-MI
DO
FR
SA
9 - 19 H
9 - 20 H
9 - 19 H
9 - 17 H

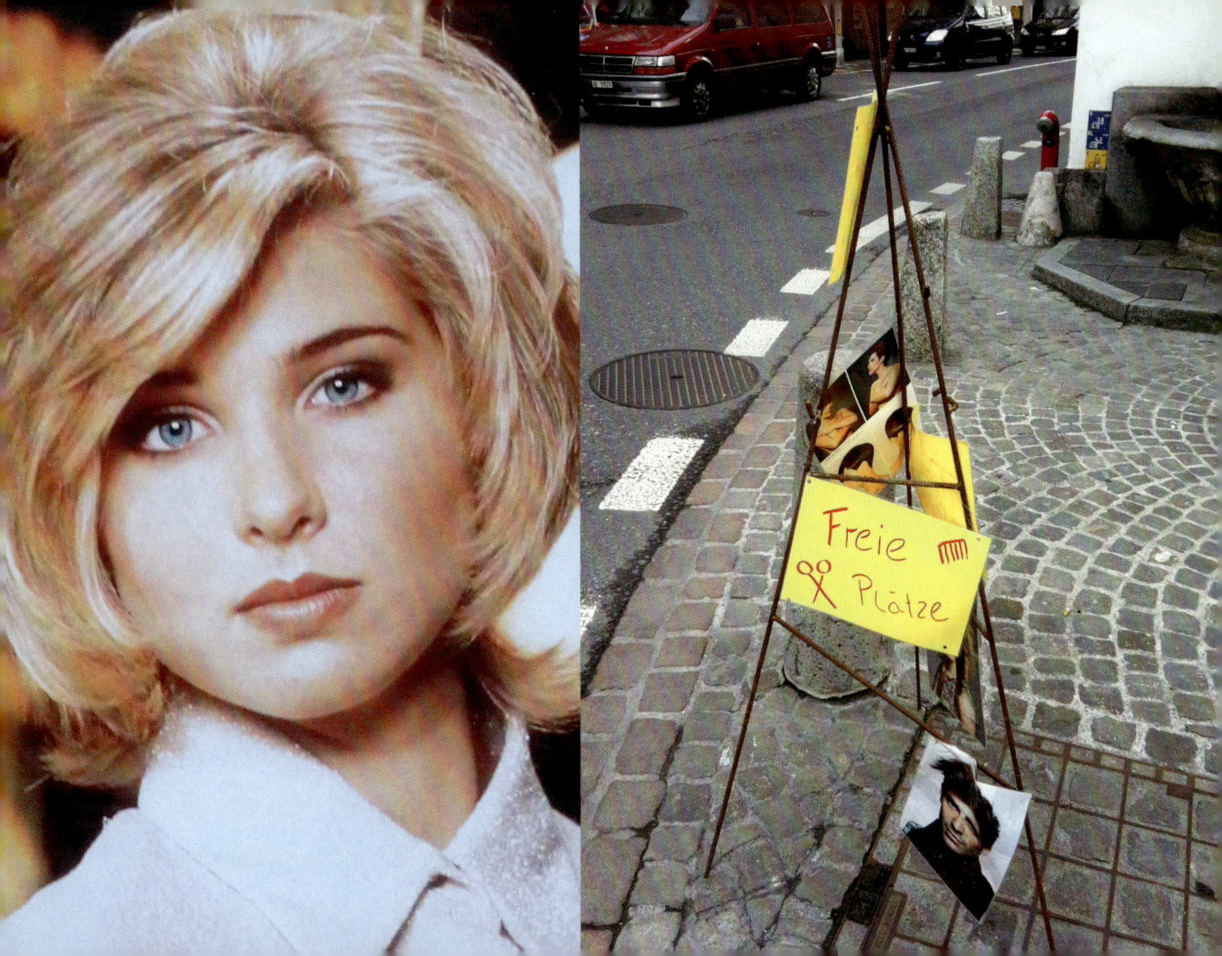
Freie
Plätze

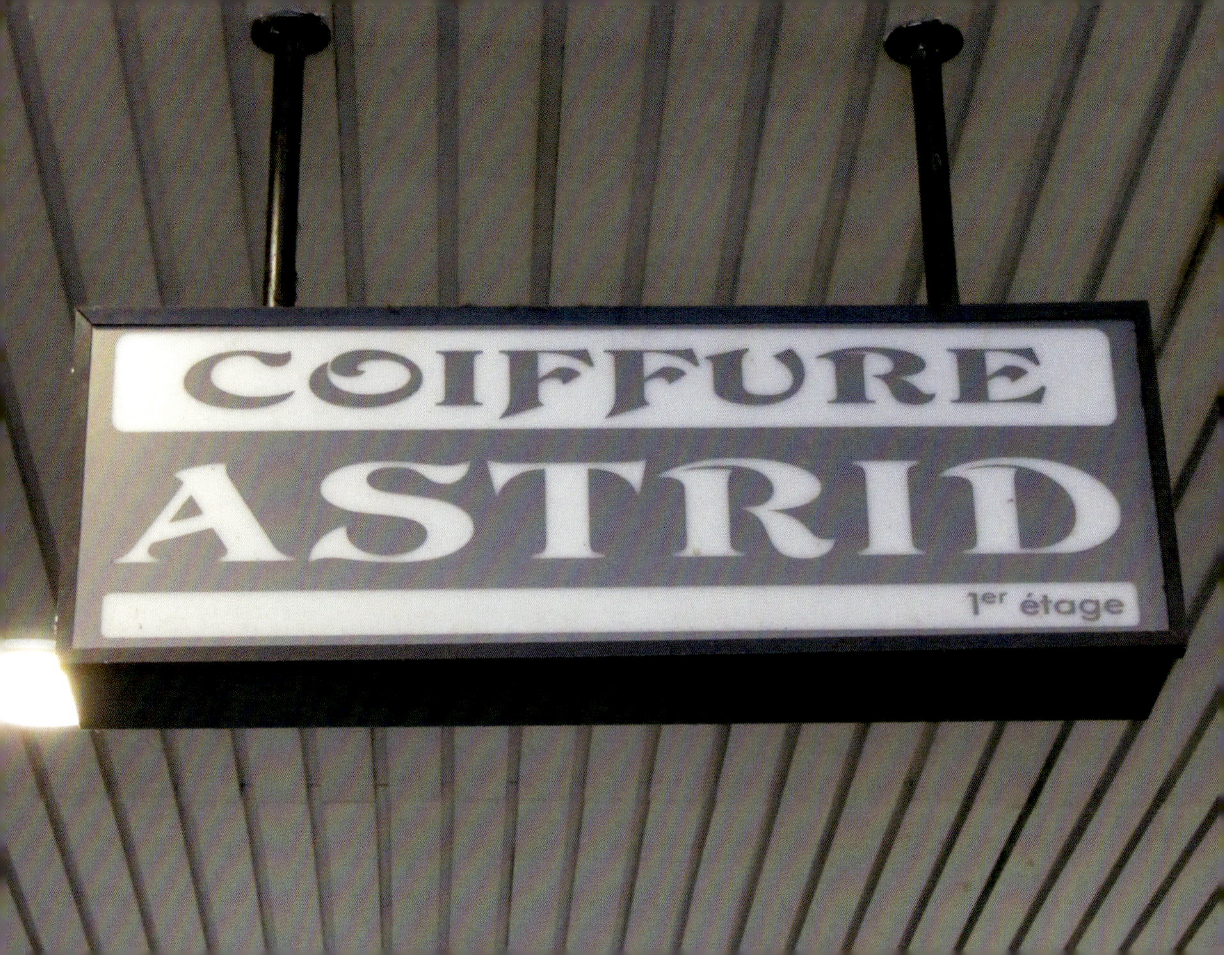

COIFFURE
ASTRID
1er étage

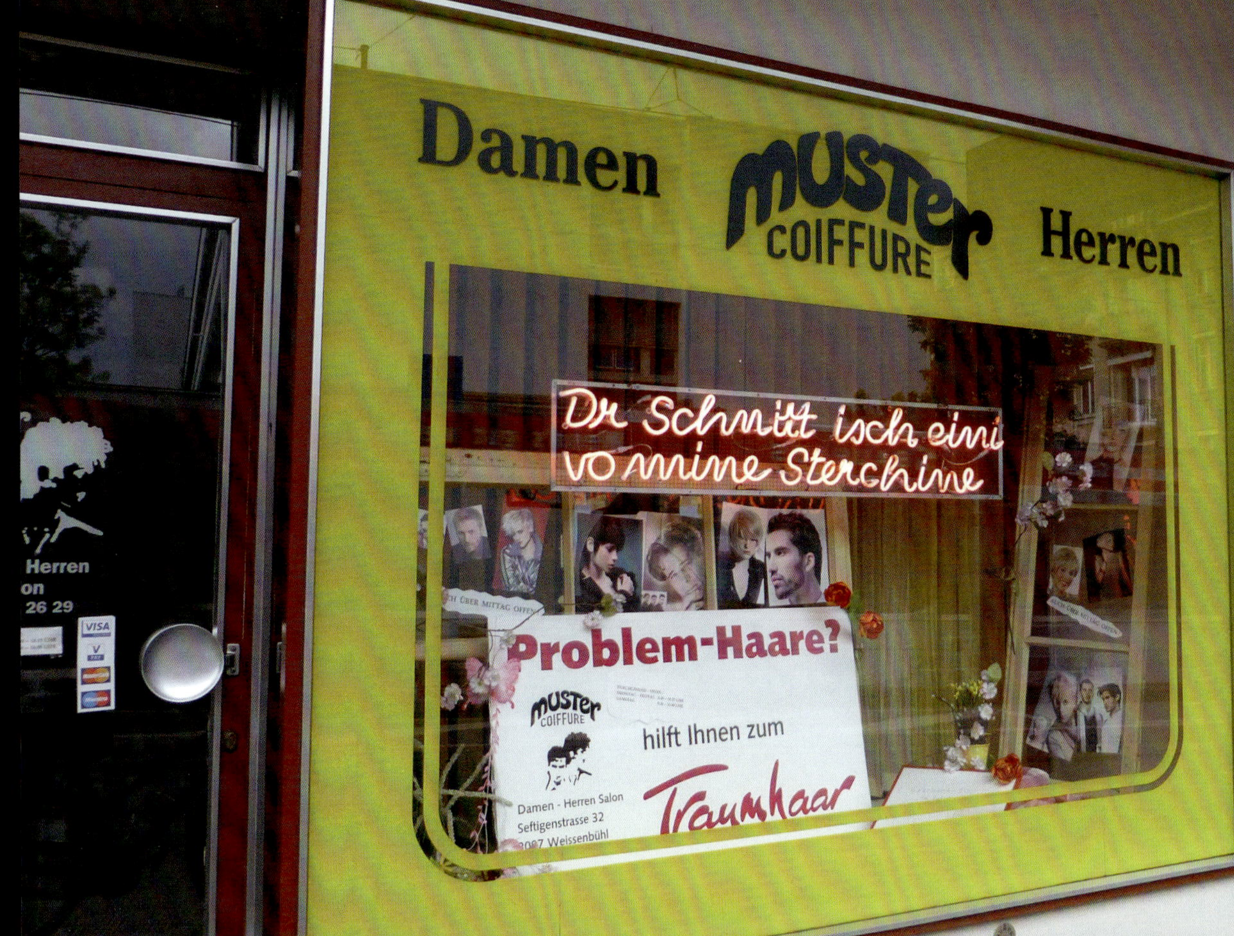
Damen
muster
COIFFURE
Herren
Dr Schnitt isch eini
vo mine Sterchine
Problem-Haare?
muster
COIFFURE
hilft Ihnen zum
Traumhaar
Damen - Herren Salon
Seftigenstrasse 32
Weissenbühl
Herren
on
26 29
VISA

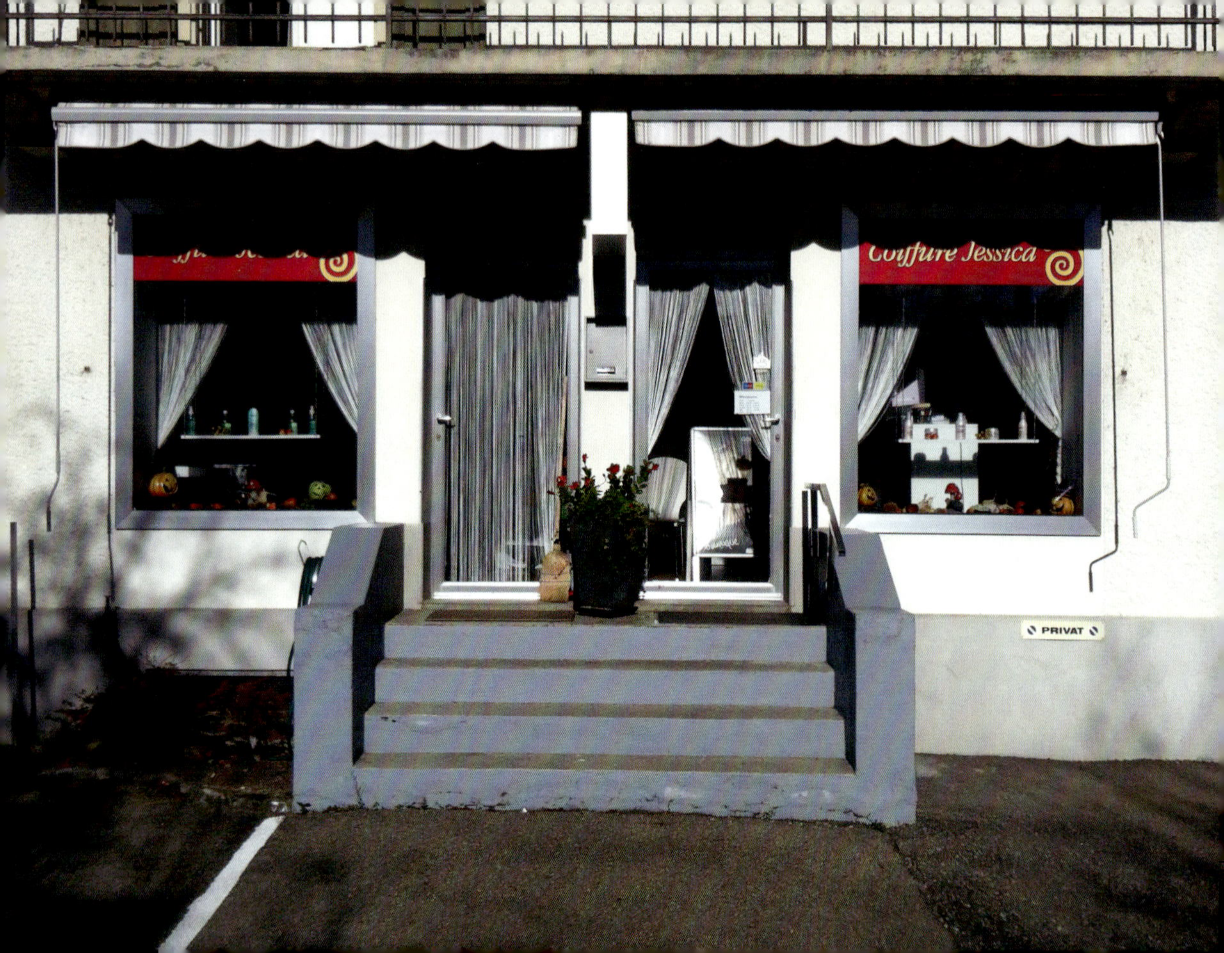
Coiffure Jessica
PRIVAT

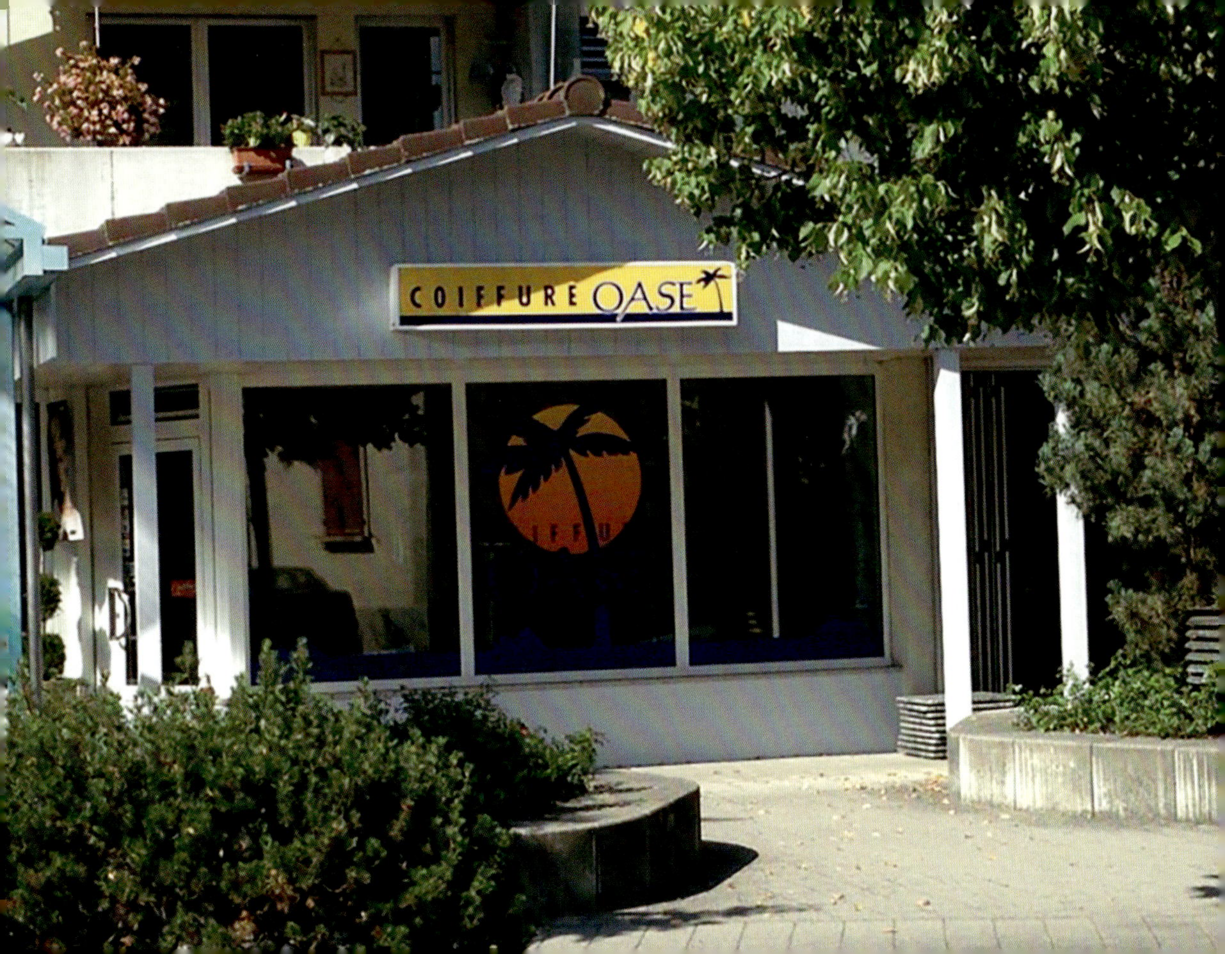
COIFFURE OASE

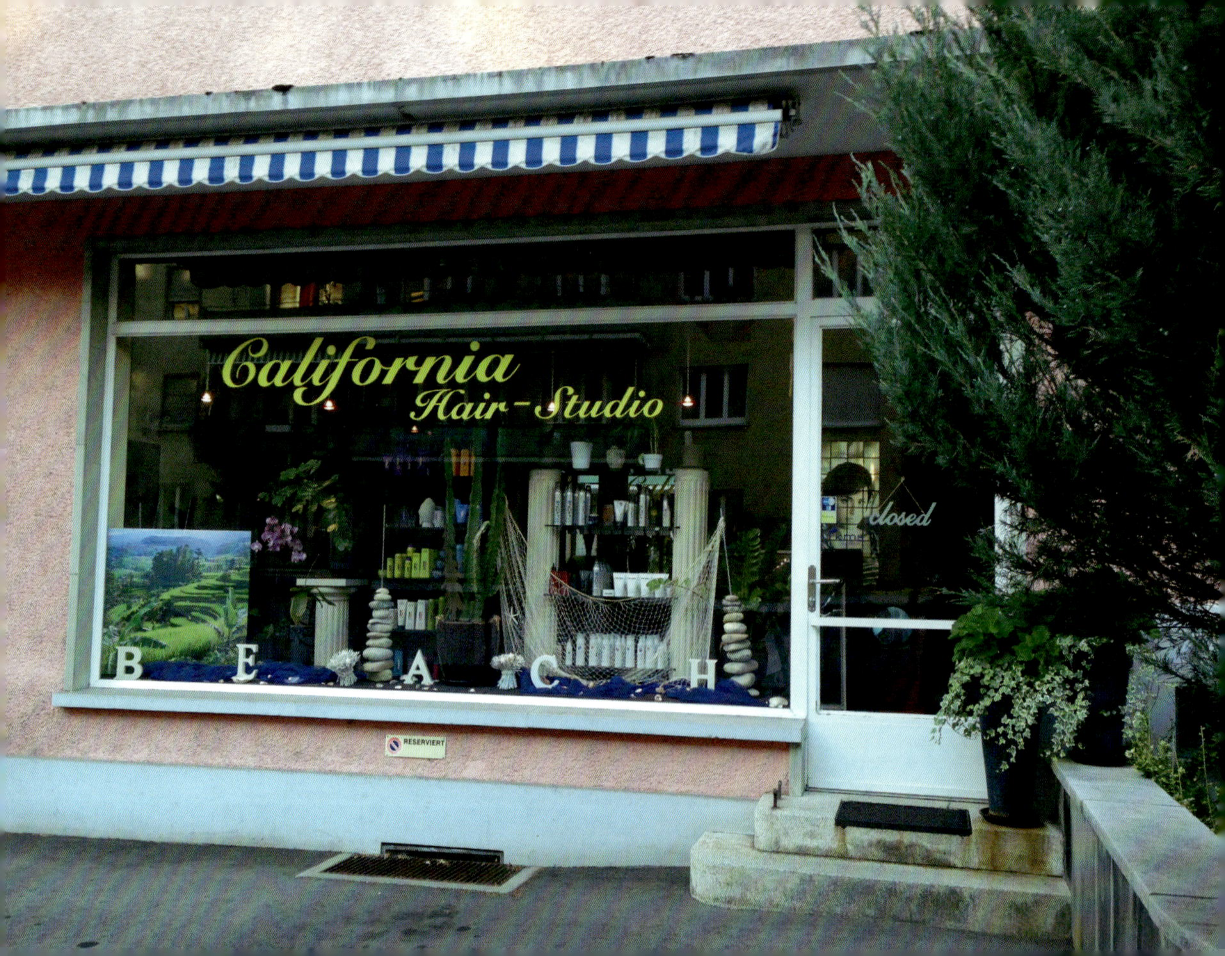
California
Hair-Studio
closed
B E A C H
RESERVIERT

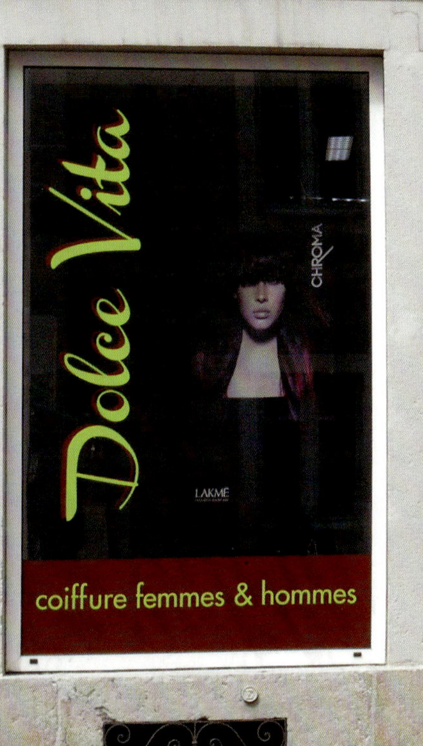
Dolce Vita
CHROMA
LAKMÉ
coiffure femmes & hommes

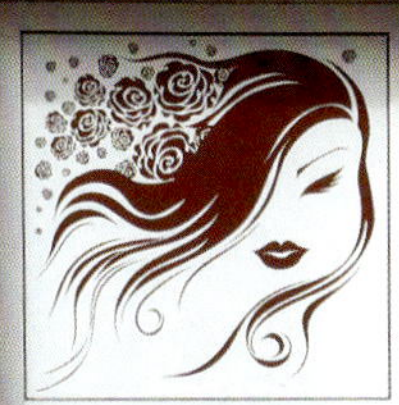

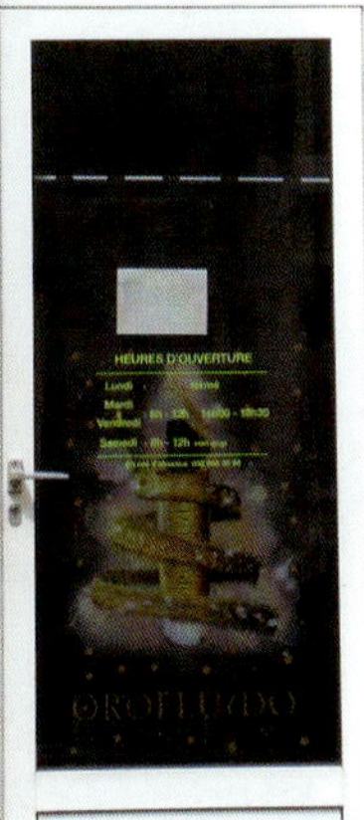
HEURES D'OUVERTURE

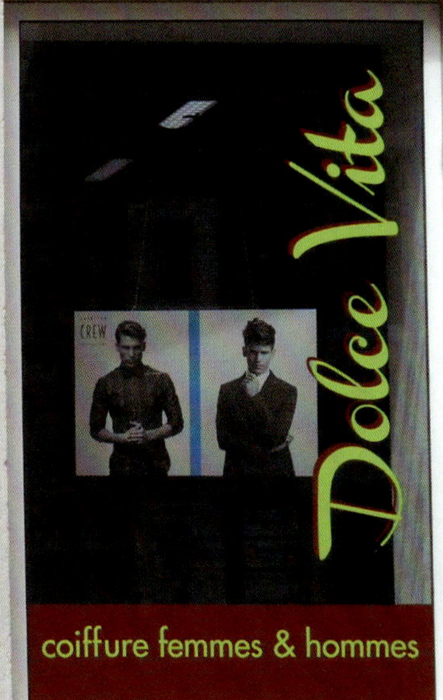
CREW
Dolce Vita
coiffure femmes & hommes

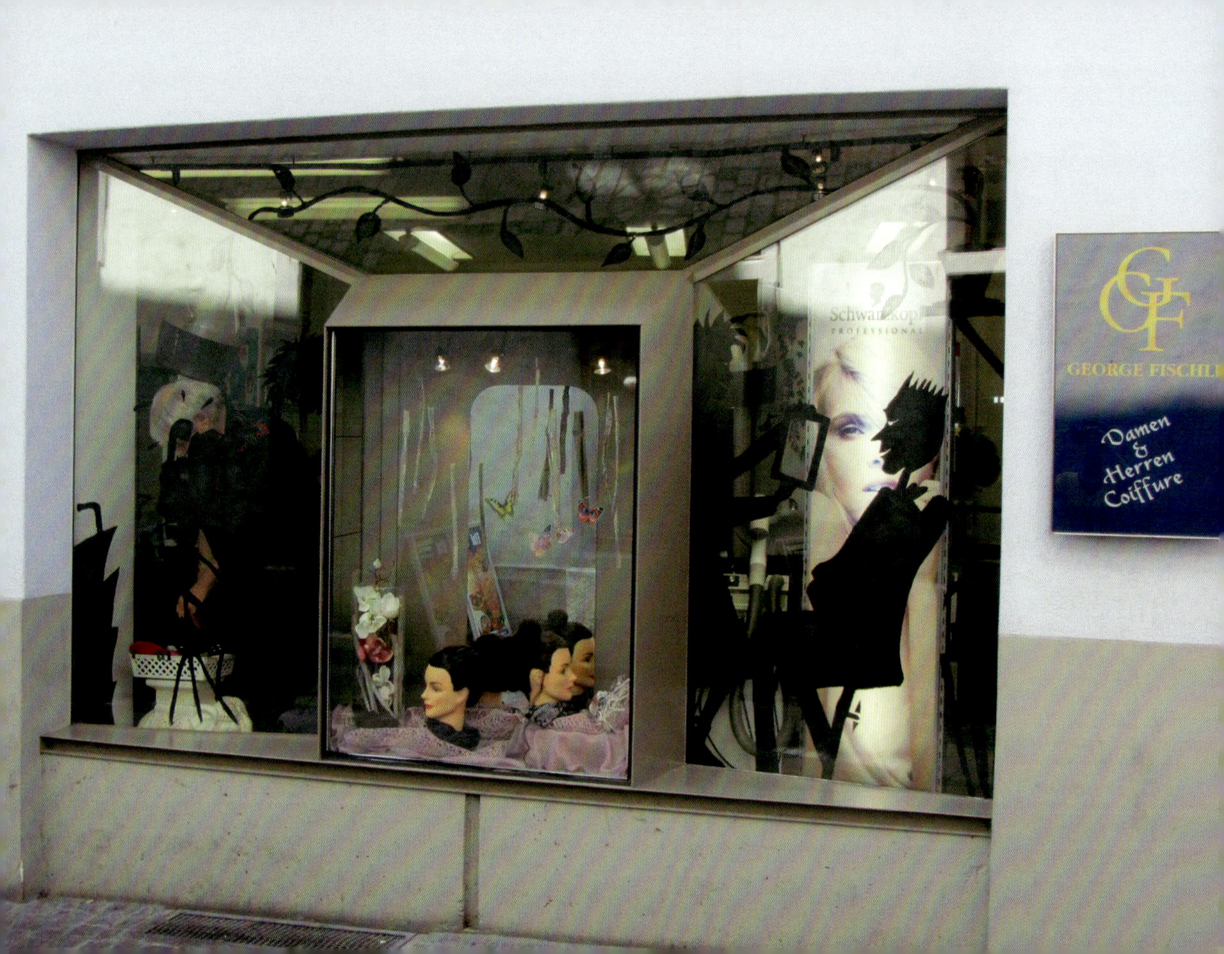

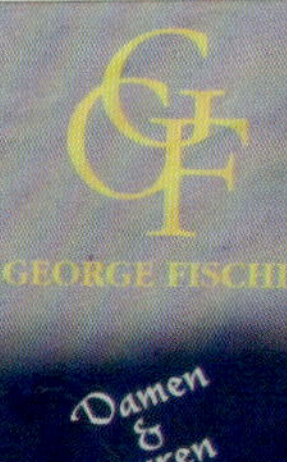
GF
GEORGE FISCHL
Damen
&
Herren
Coiffure

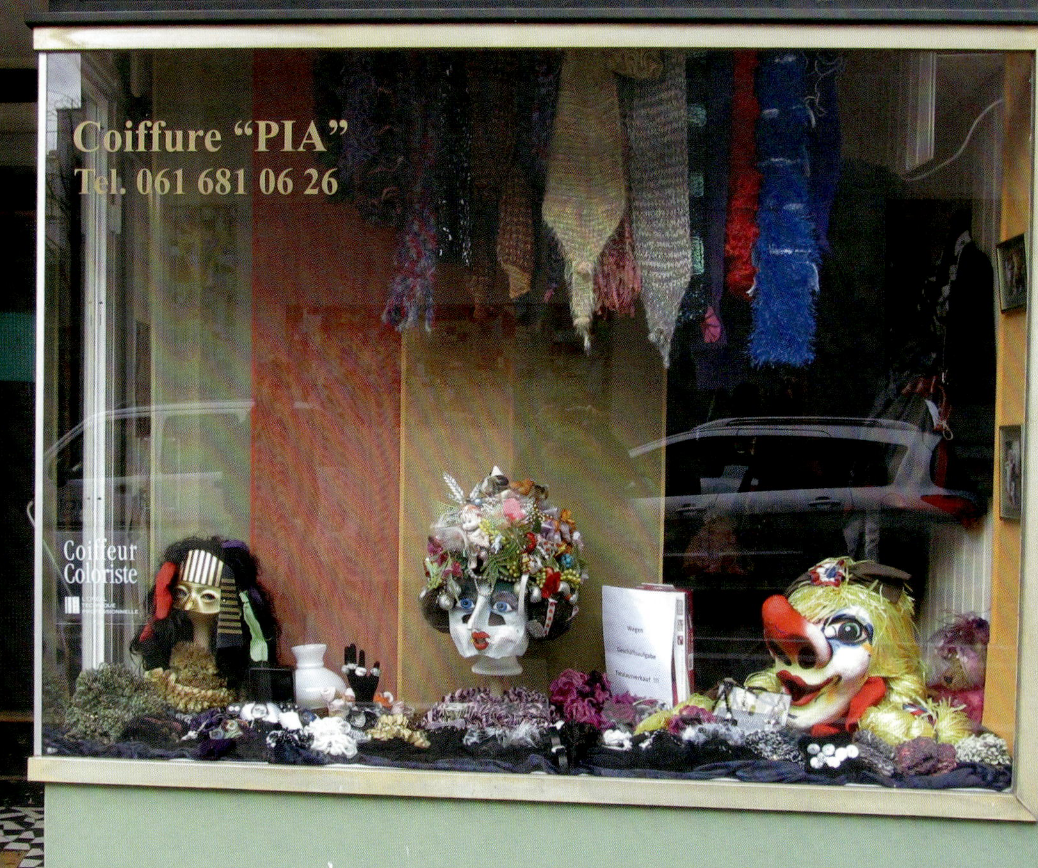
Coiffure “PIA”
Tel. 061 681 06 26
Coiffeur
Coloriste
Wegen

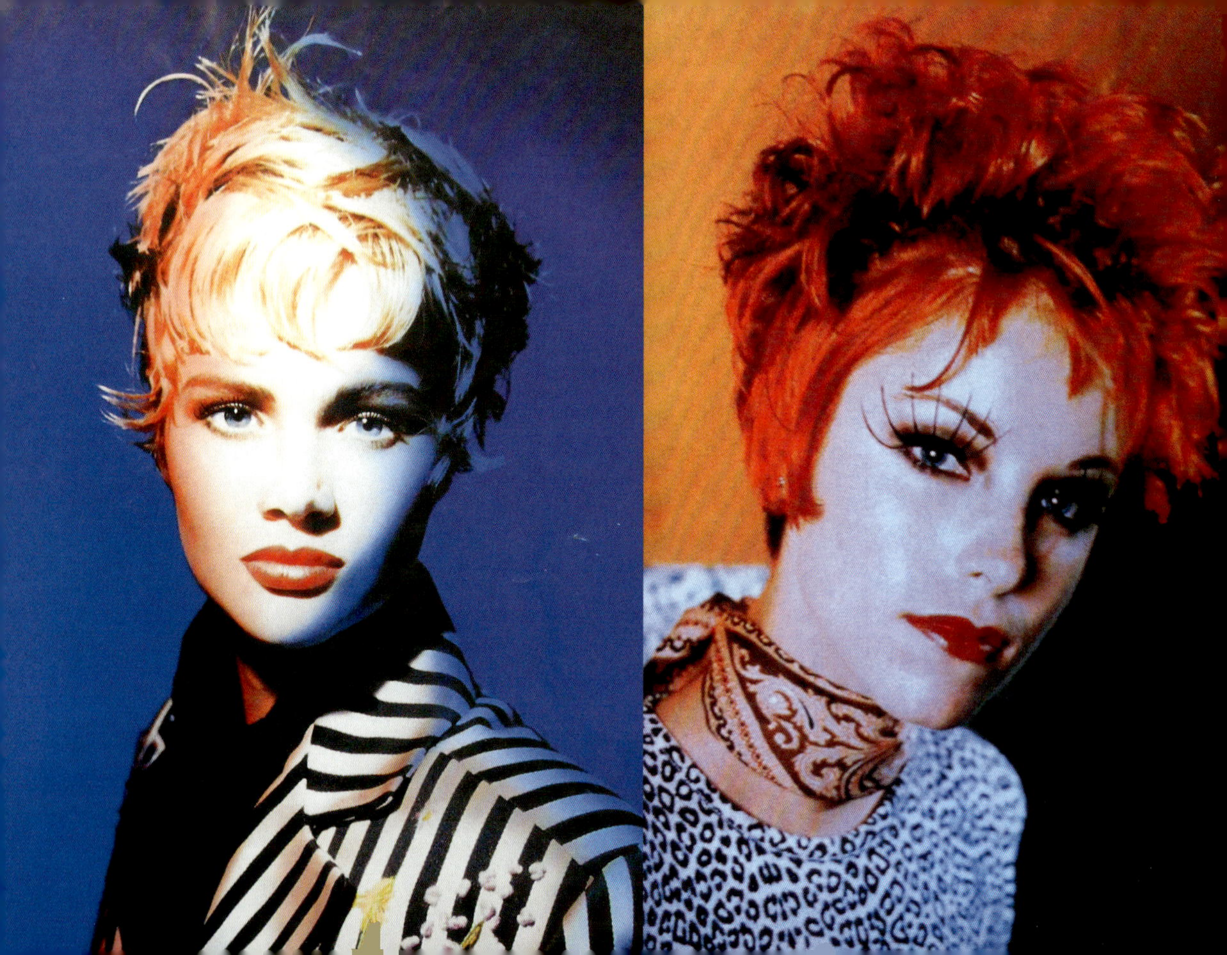

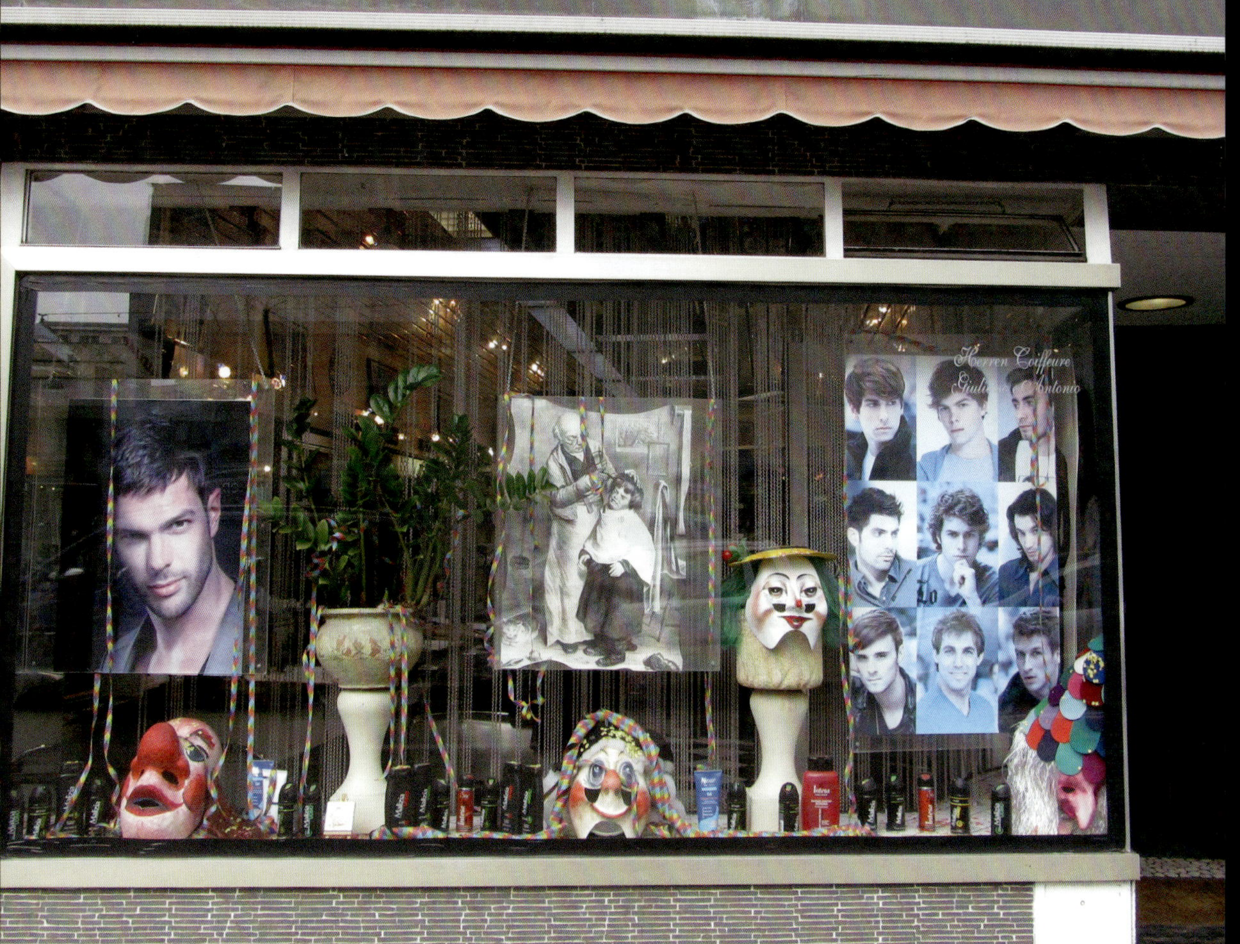
Herren Coiffeure
Antonio

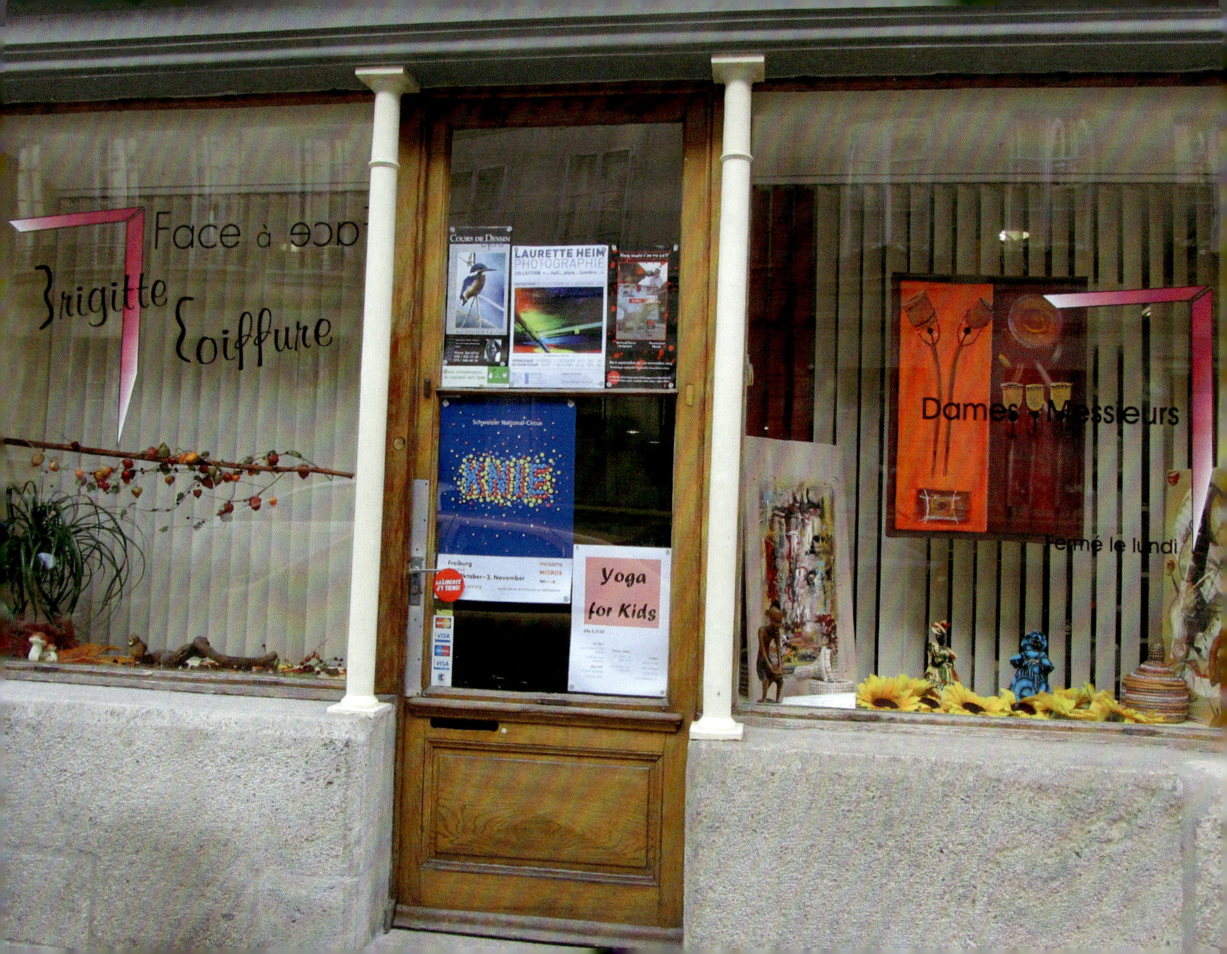

Face à
Brigitte
Coiffure
Cours de Dessin
LAURETTE HEIM
PHOTOGRAPHIE
Schweizer National-Circus
KNIE
Freiburg
Helsana
MIGROS
Yoga
for Kids
VISA
Dames Messieurs
Fermé le lundi

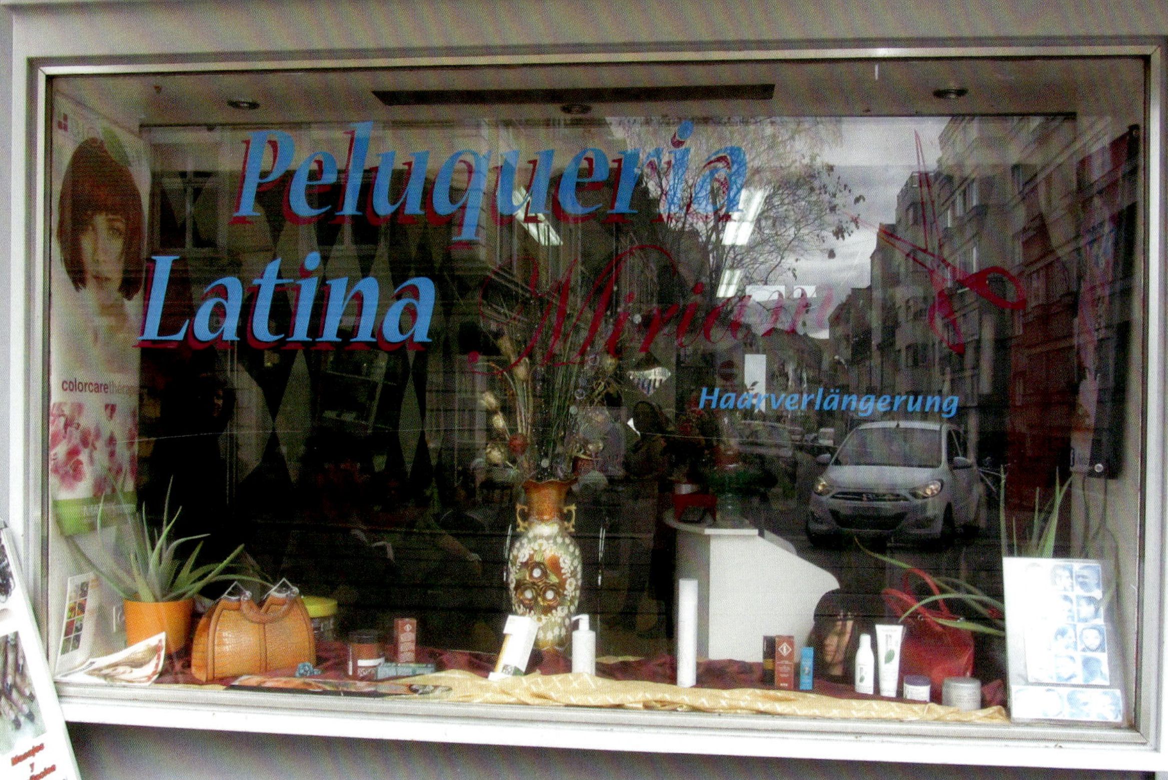
Peluqueria
Latina
Miriam
Haarverlängerung

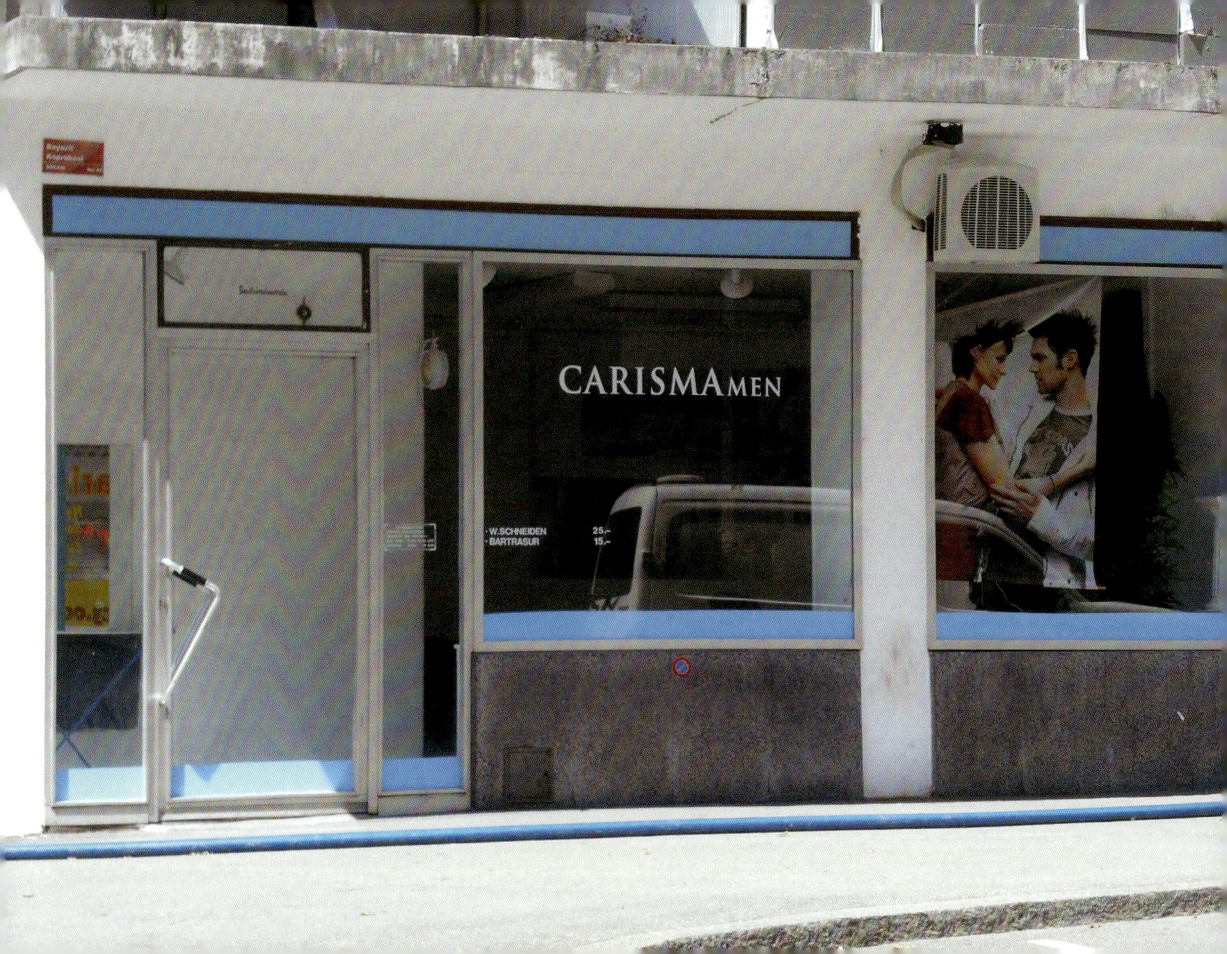
CARISMAMEN
W.SCHNEIDEN 25.–
BARTRASUR 15.–

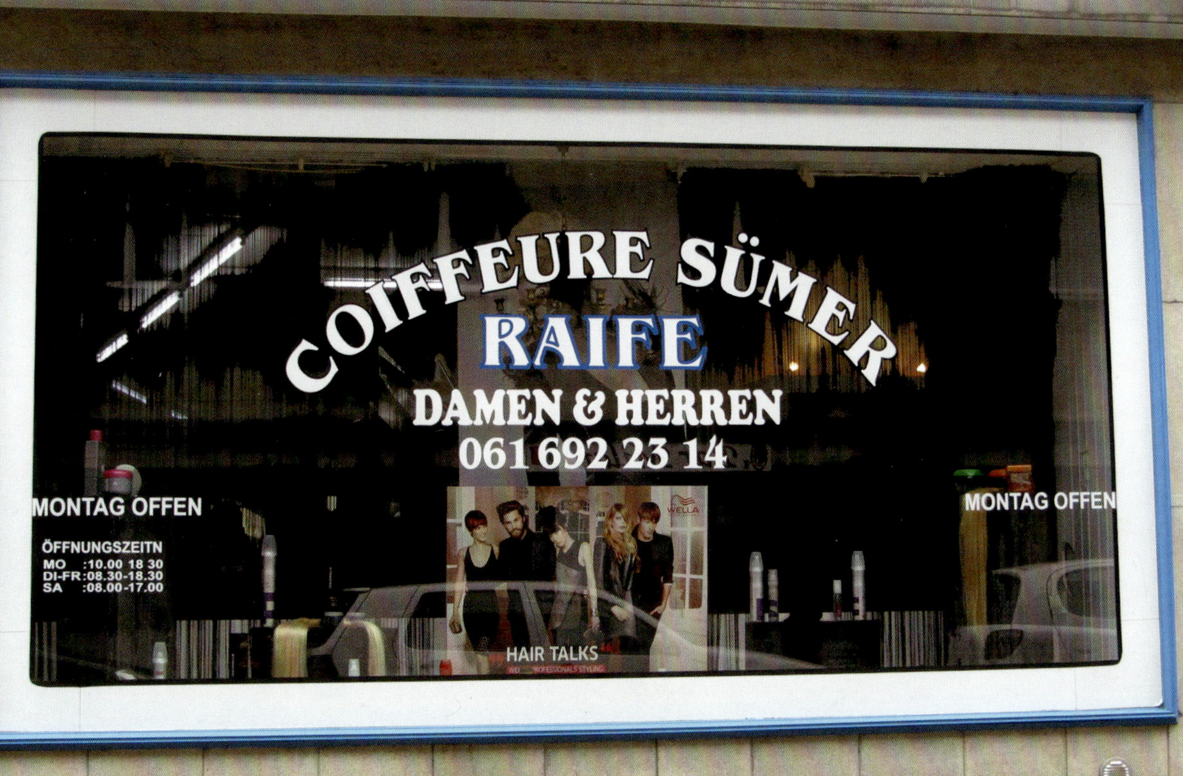
COIFFEURE SÜMER
RAIFE
DAMEN & HERREN
061 692 23 14
MONTAG OFFEN
MONTAG OFFEN
ÖFFNUNGSZEITN
MO :10.00 18 30
DI-FR:08.30-18.30
SA :08.00-17.00
WELLA
HAIR TALKS

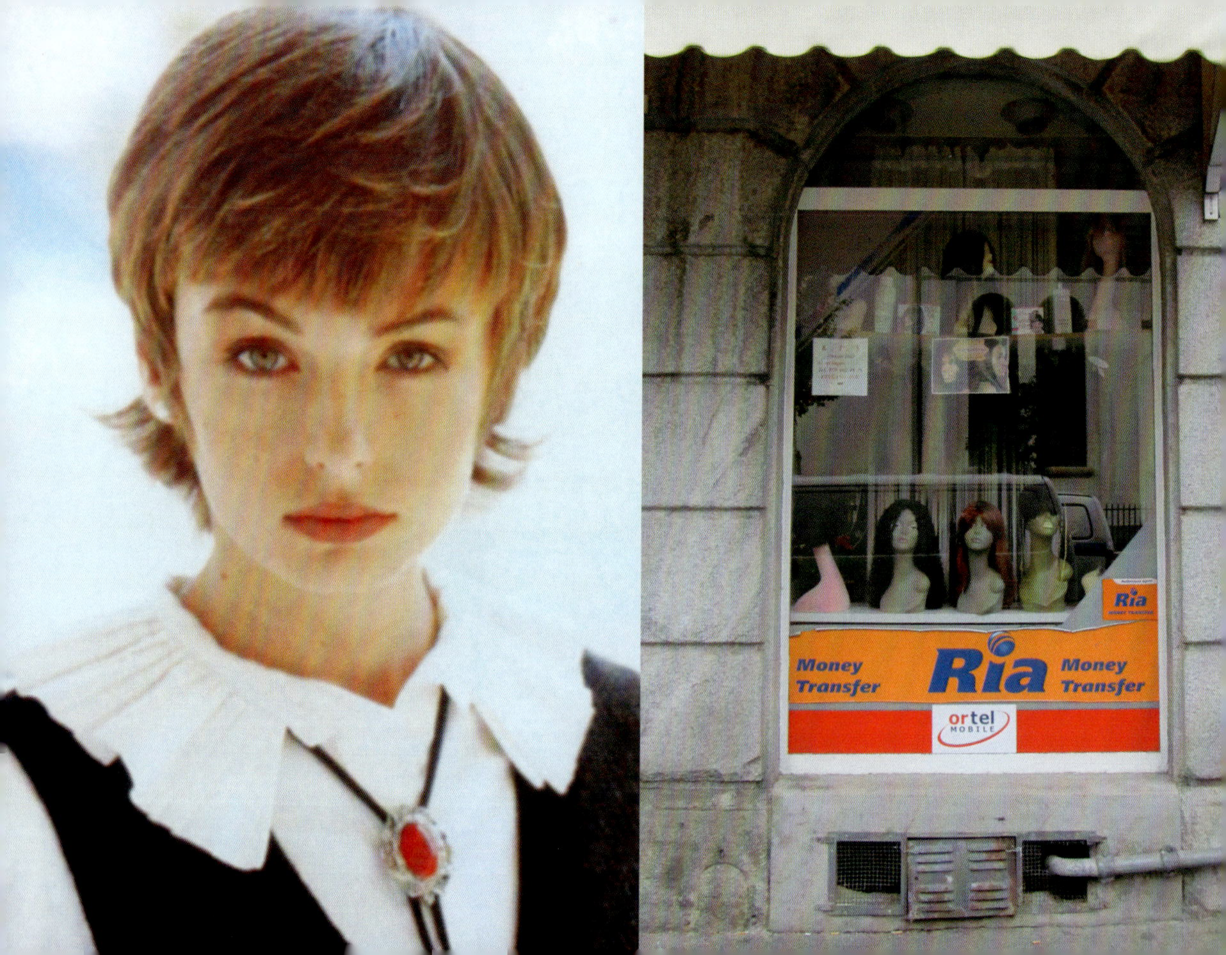
Money Transfer
Ria
Money Transfer
ortel MOBILE
Ria

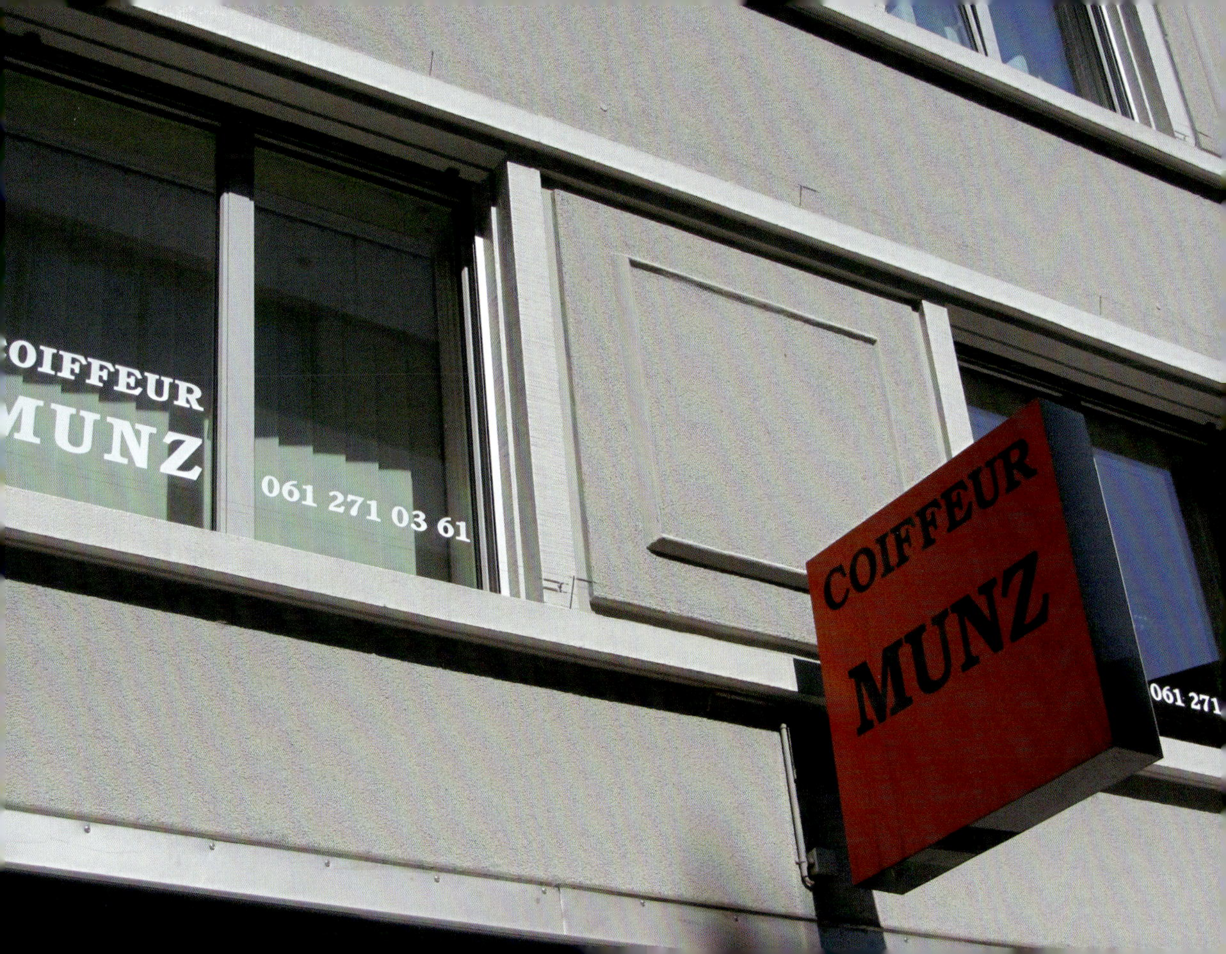
COIFFEUR
MUNZ
061 271 03 61

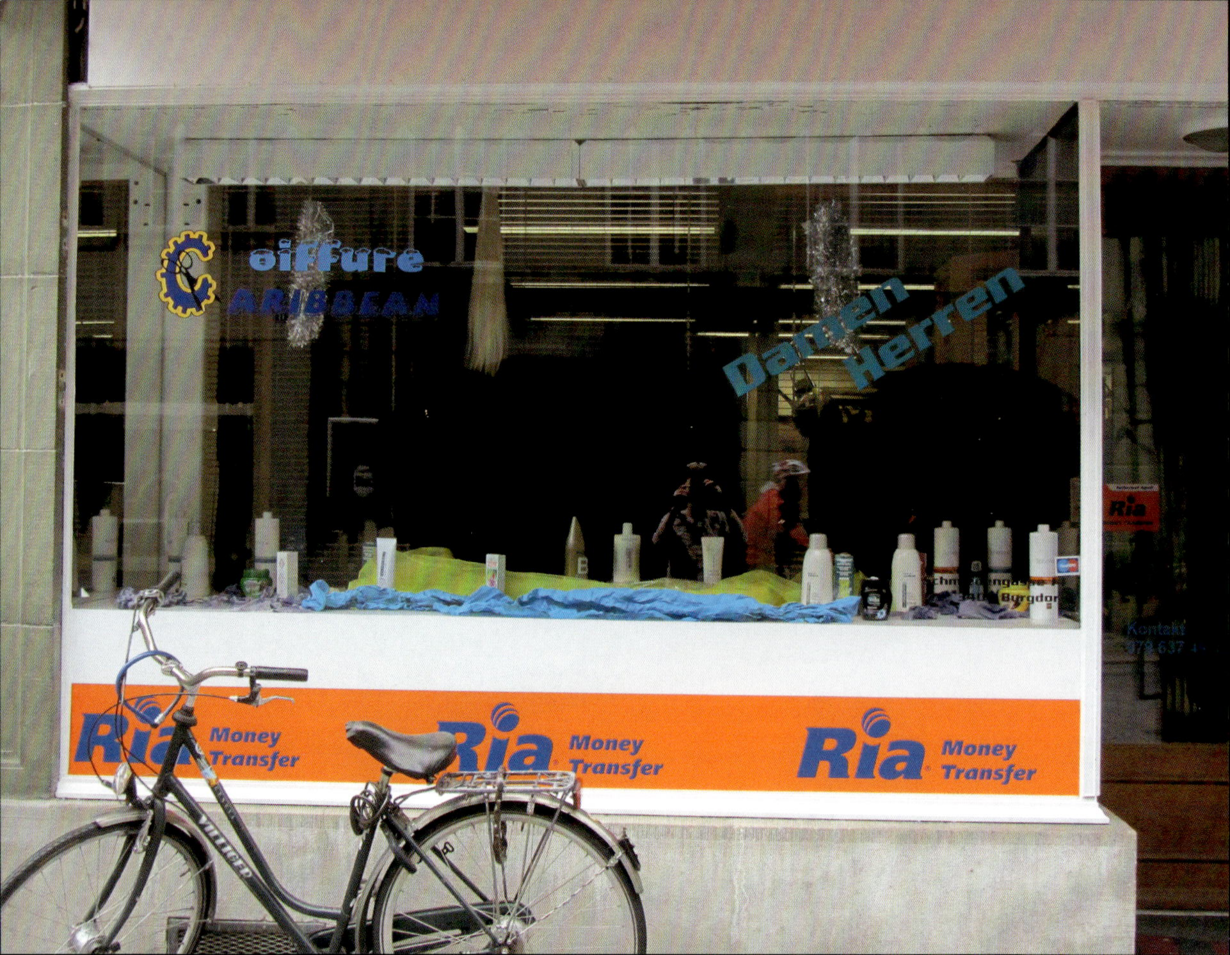
Coiffure
CARIBBEAN
Damen
Herren
Ria Money Transfer
Ria Money Transfer
Ria Money Transfer

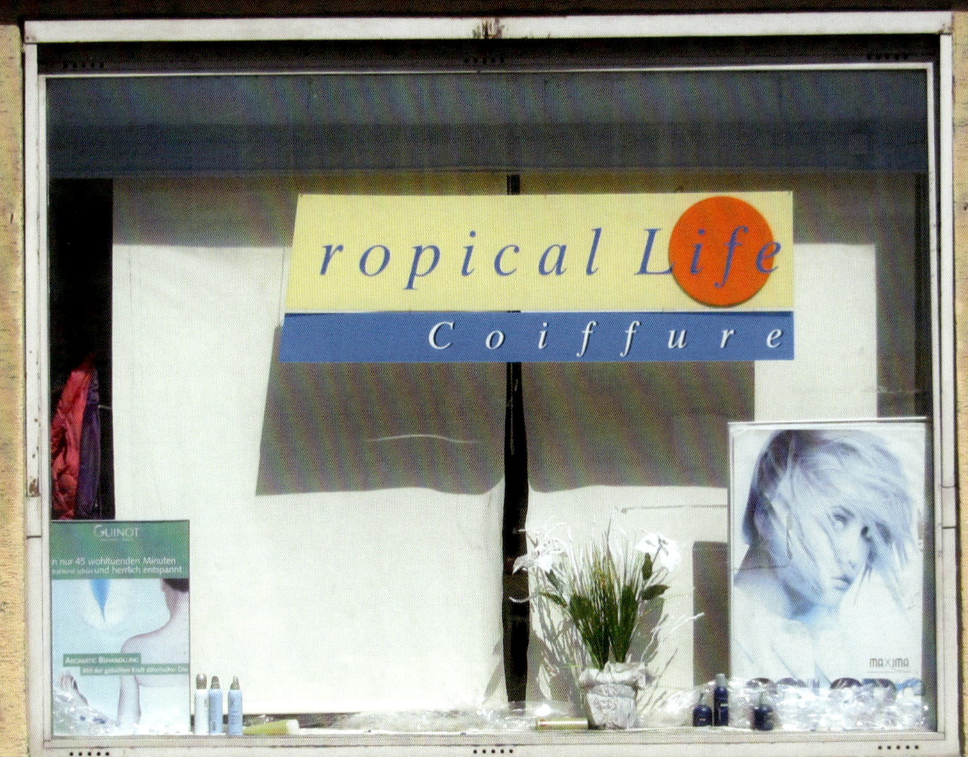
ropical Life
Coiffure
GUINOT
n nur 45 wohltuenden Minuten
und herrlich entspannt
MAXIMA

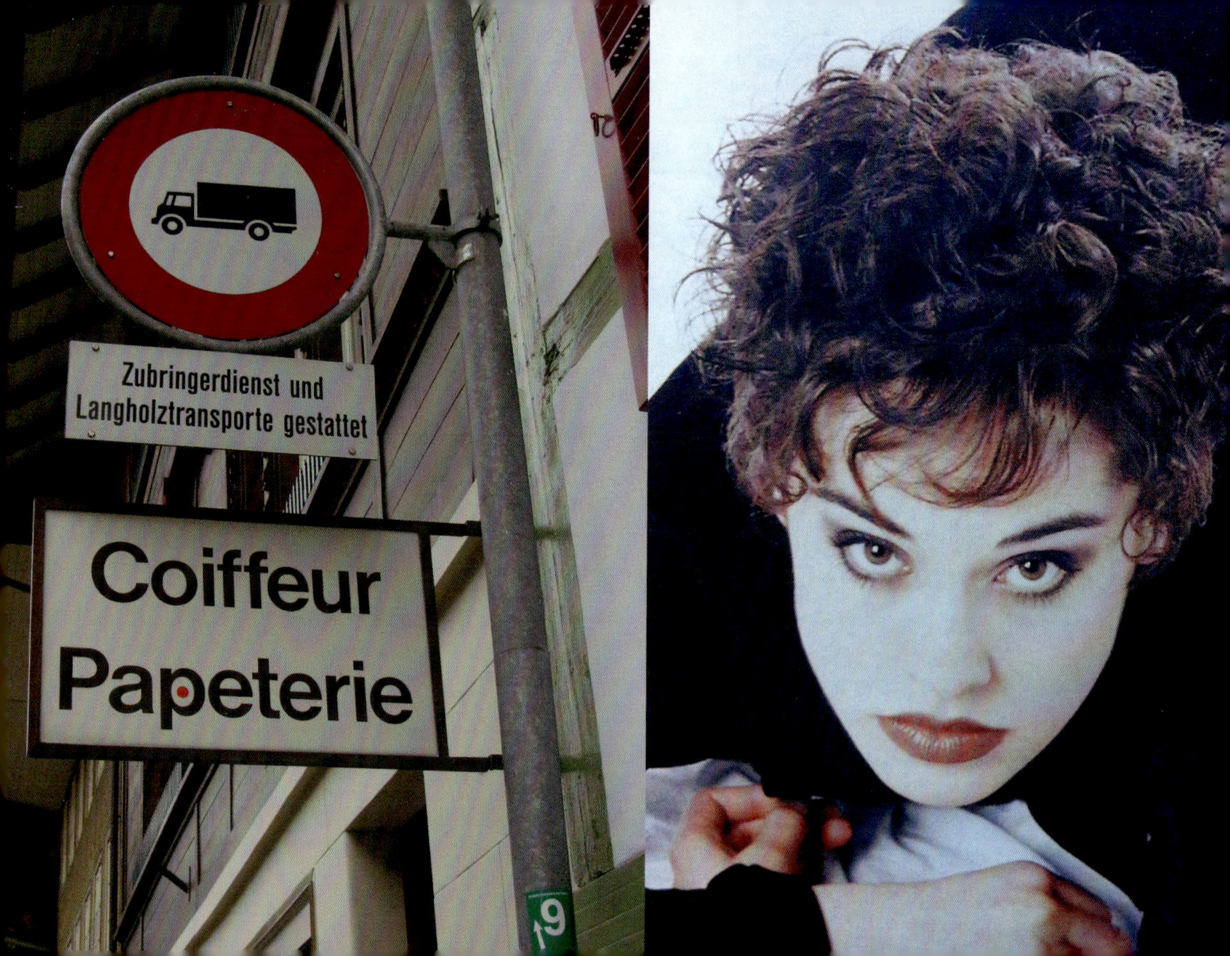
Zubringerdienst und
Langholztransporte gestattet
Coiffeur
Papeterie
9

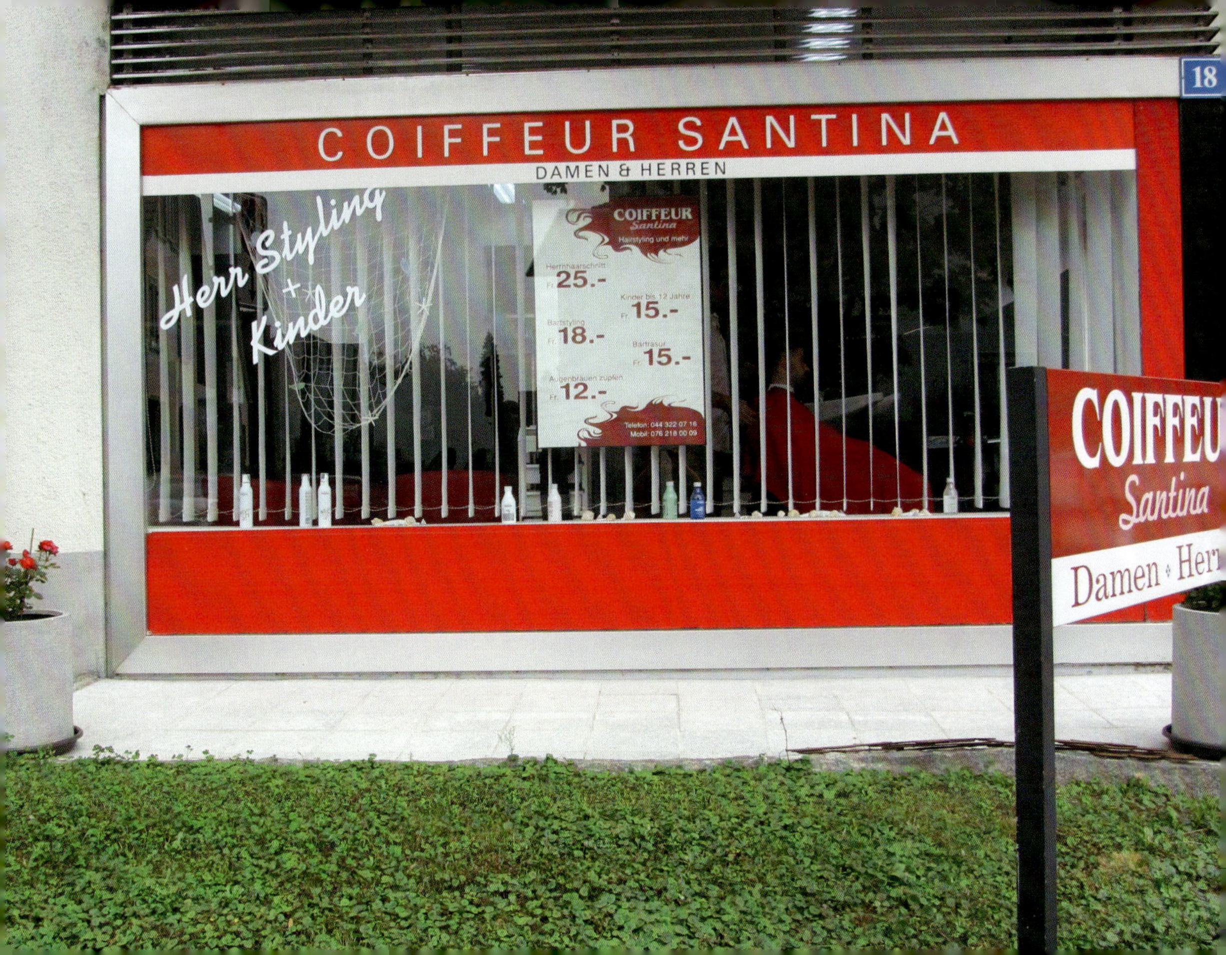
18
COIFFEUR SANTINA
DAMEN & HERREN
Herr Styling
+
Kinder
COIFFEUR
Santina
Hairstyling und mehr
Fr. 25.-
Kinder bis 12 Jahre
Fr. 15.-
Bartstyling
Fr. 18.-
Bartrasur
Fr. 15.-
Augenbrauen zupfen
Fr. 12.-
Telefon: 044 322 07 18
Mobil: 076 218 00 09
COIFFEU
Santina
Damen • Herr

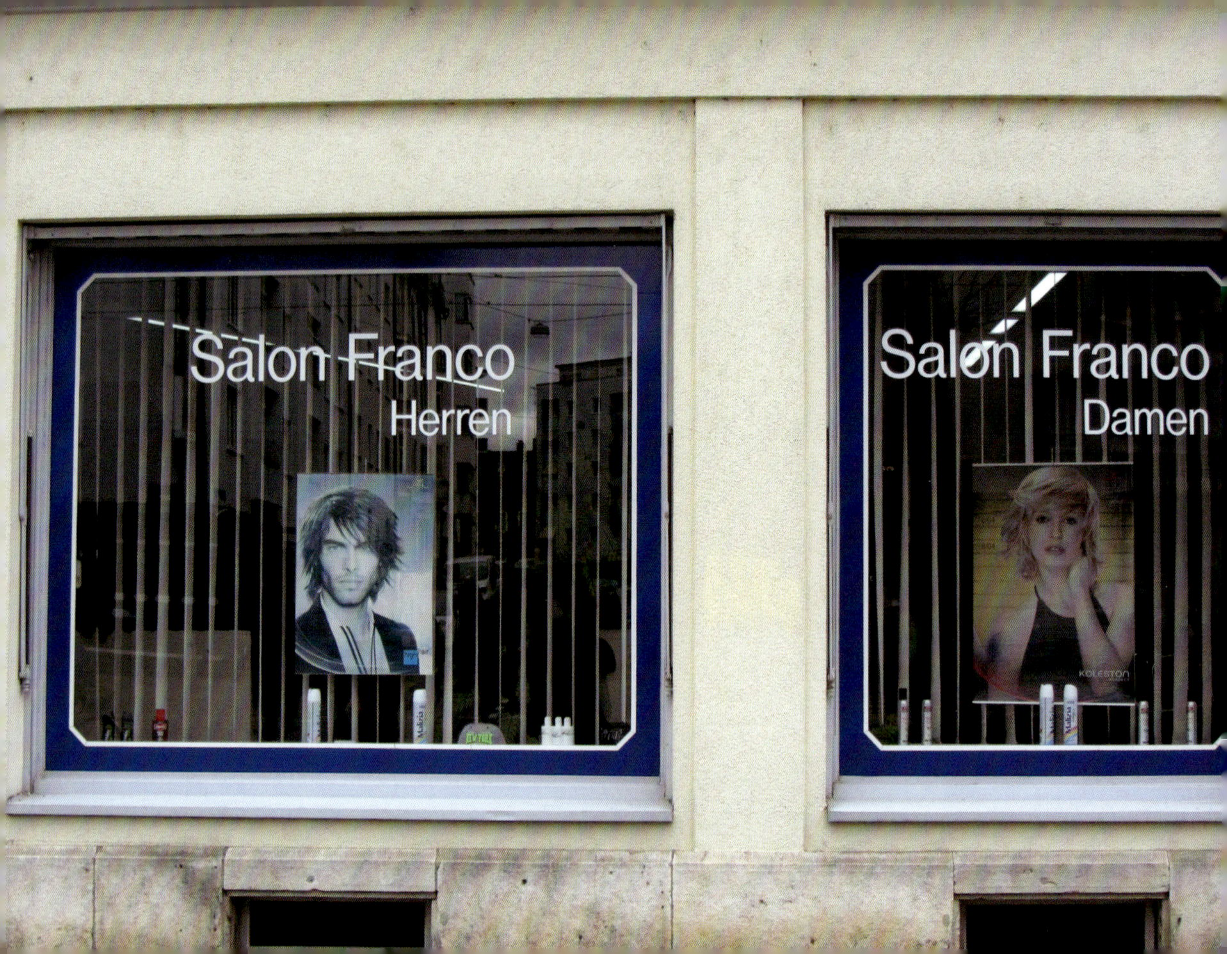
Salon Franco
Herren
Salon Franco
Damen
KOLESTON

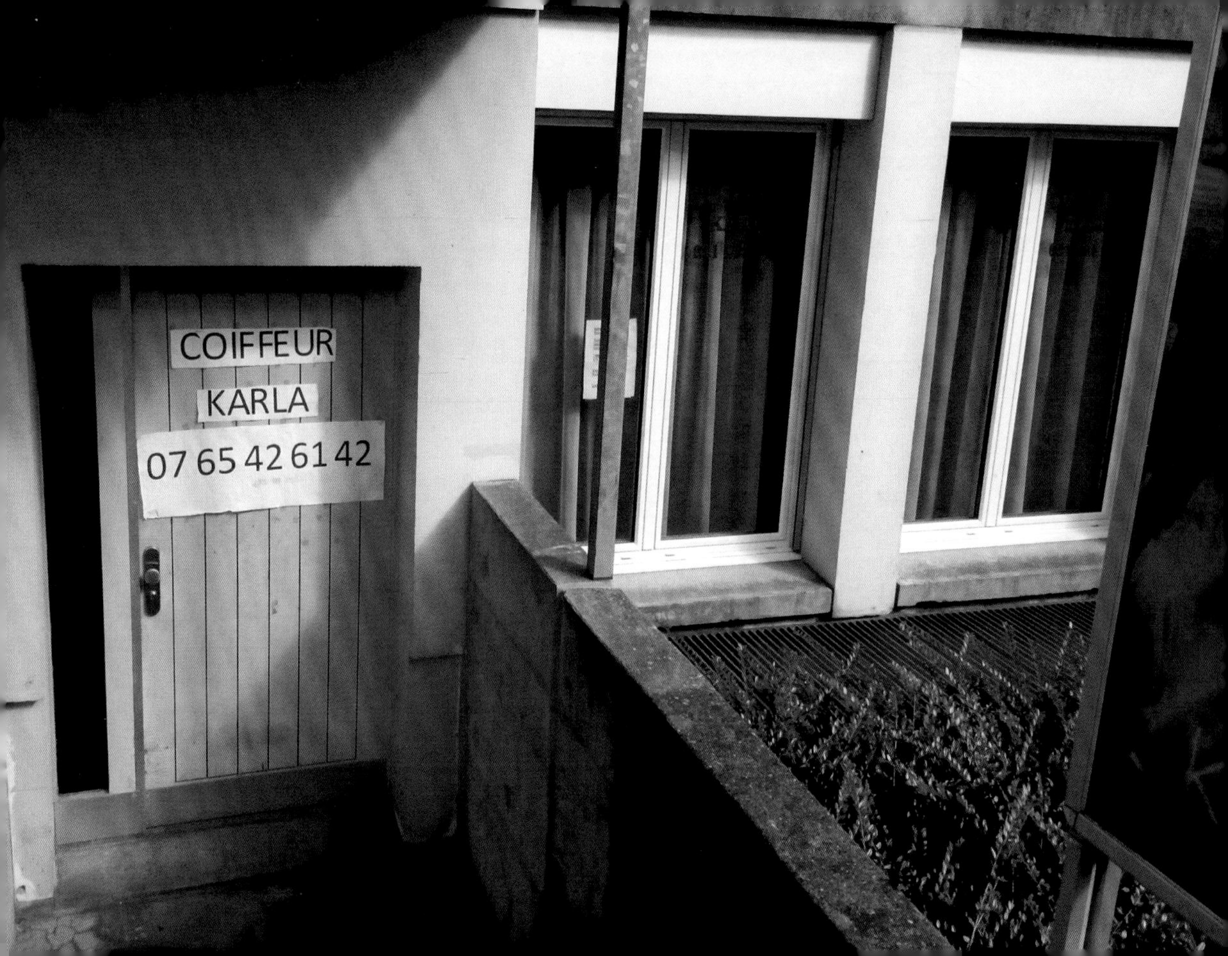
COIFFEUR
KARLA
07 65 42 61 42

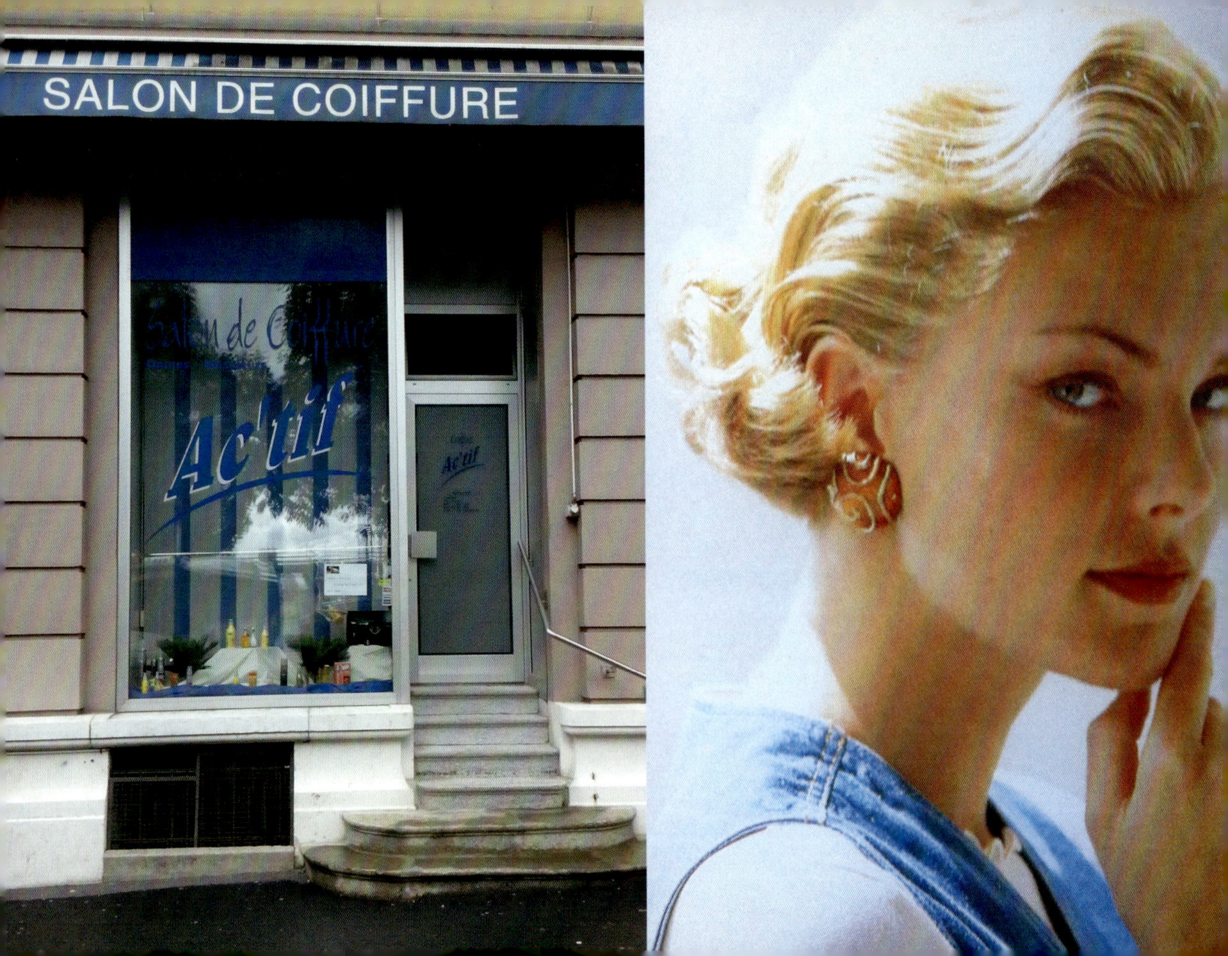
SALON DE COIFFURE
Salon de Coiffure
Ac'tif
Ac'tif

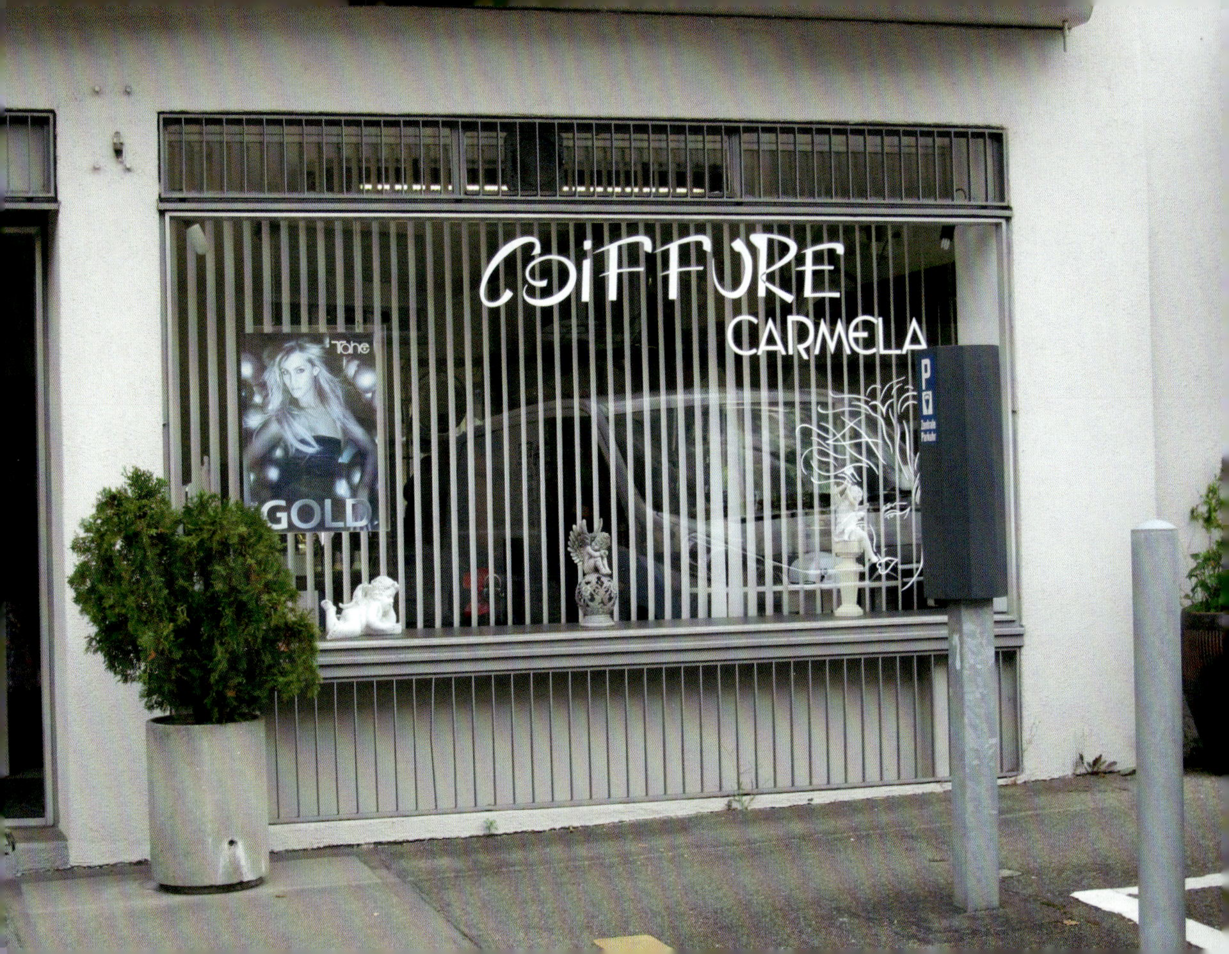
COIFFURE
CARMELA
GOLD
P

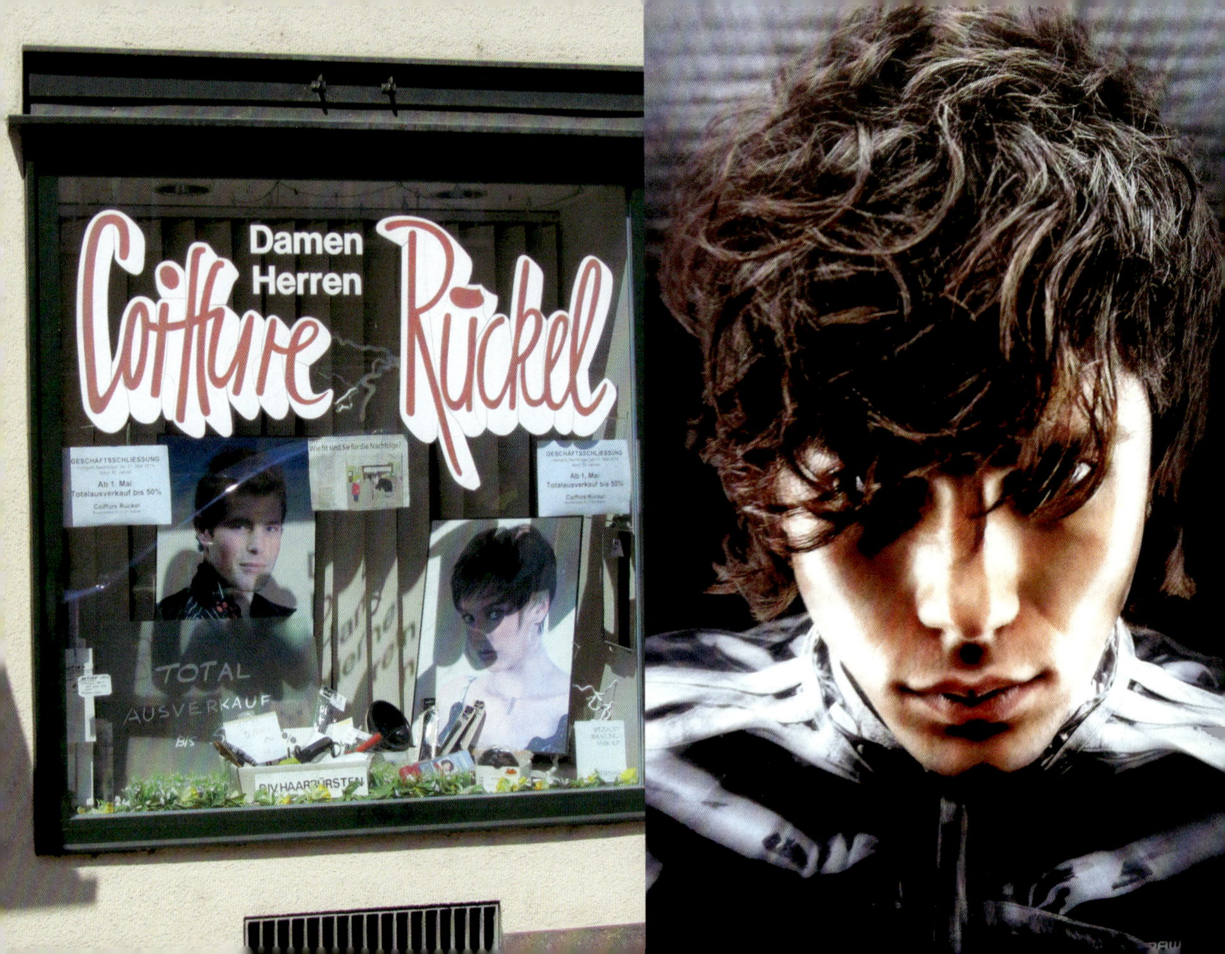
Damen
Herren
Coiffure Rückel
GESCHÄFTSSCHLIESSUNG
Ab 1. Mai
Totalausverkauf bis 50%
Coiffure Rucker
Wie fit sind Sie für die Nachfolge?
GESCHÄFTSSCHLIESSUNG
Ab 1. Mai
Totalausverkauf bis 50%
Coiffure Rucker
TOTAL
AUSVERKAUF
BIV HAARBÜRSTEN

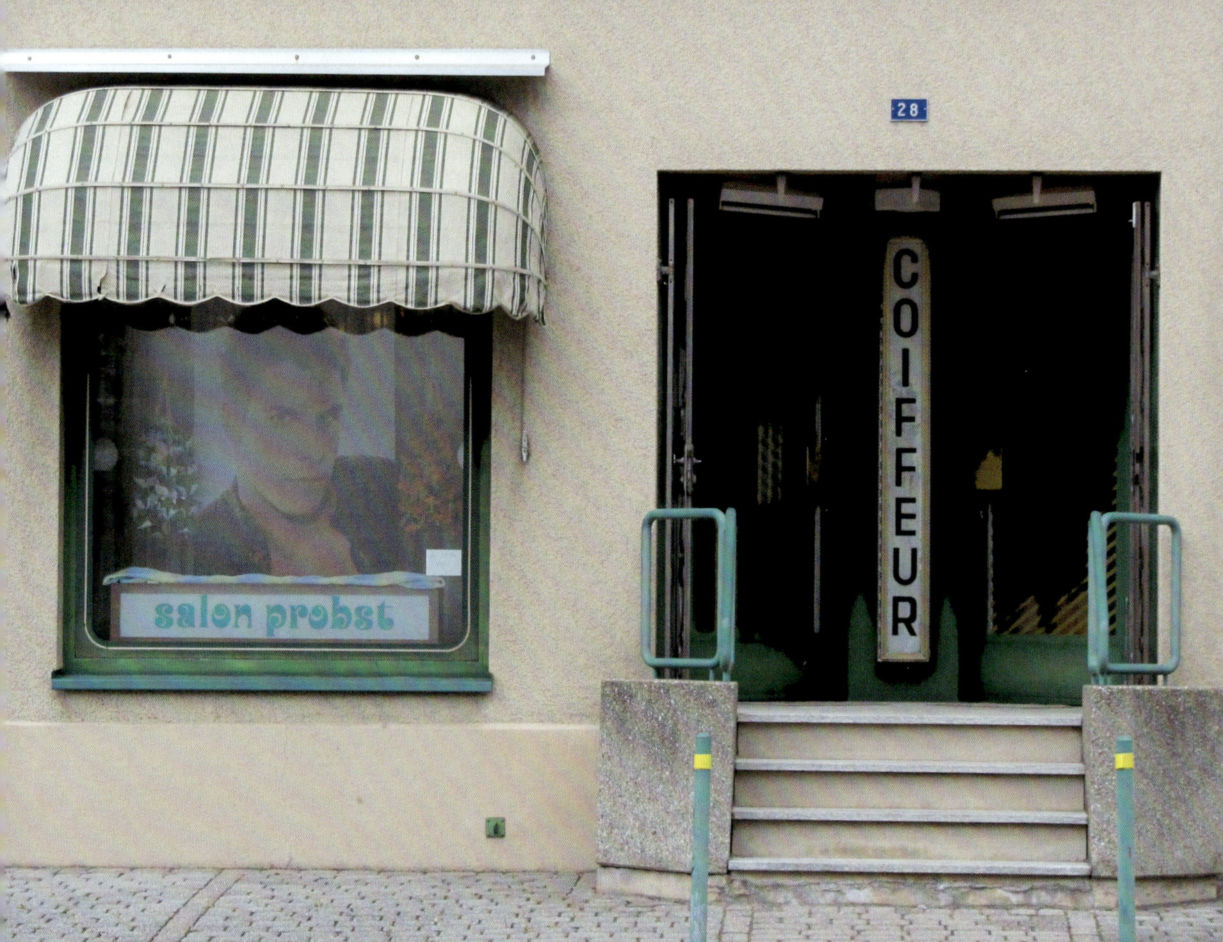
28
salon probst
COIFFEUR

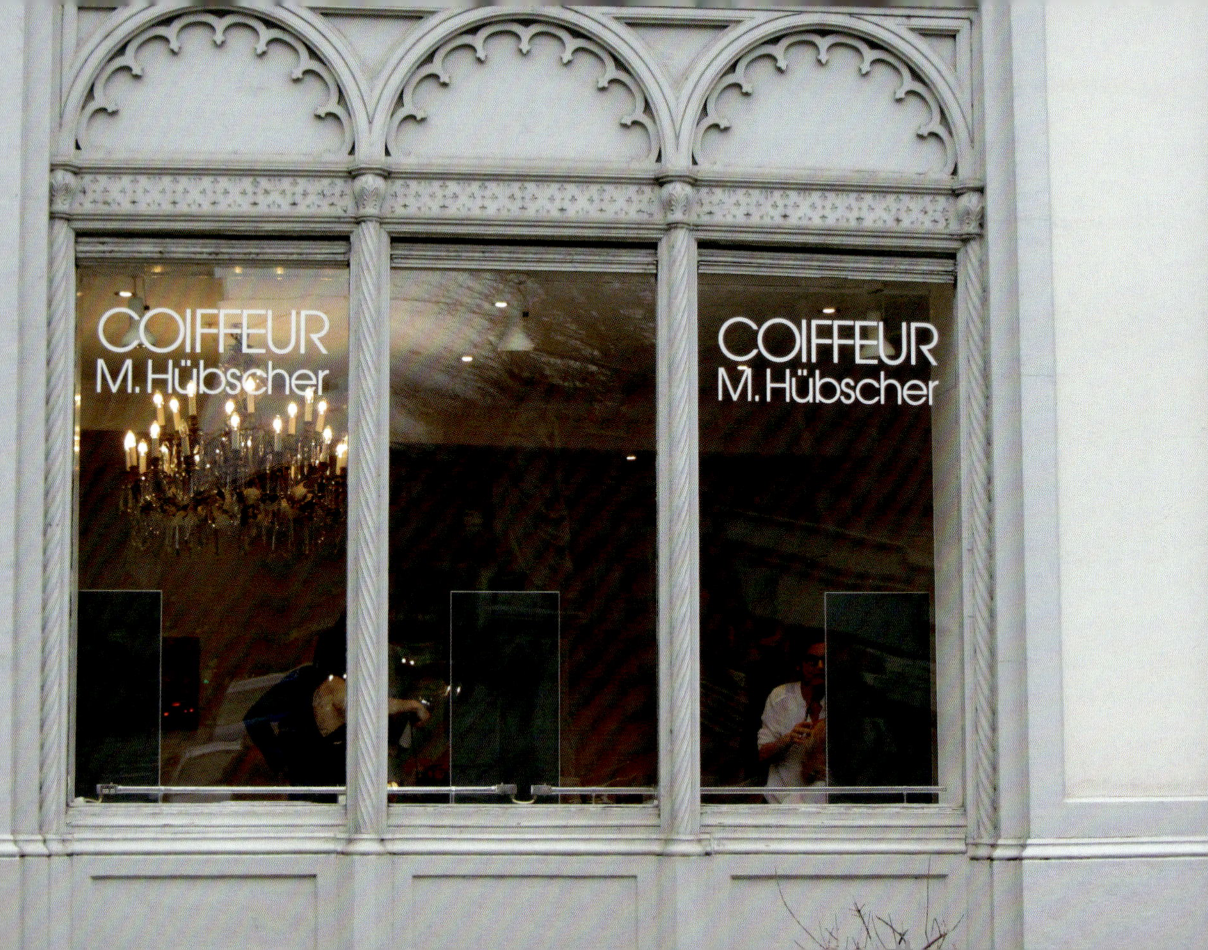
COIFFEUR
M. Hübscher
COIFFEUR
M. Hübscher

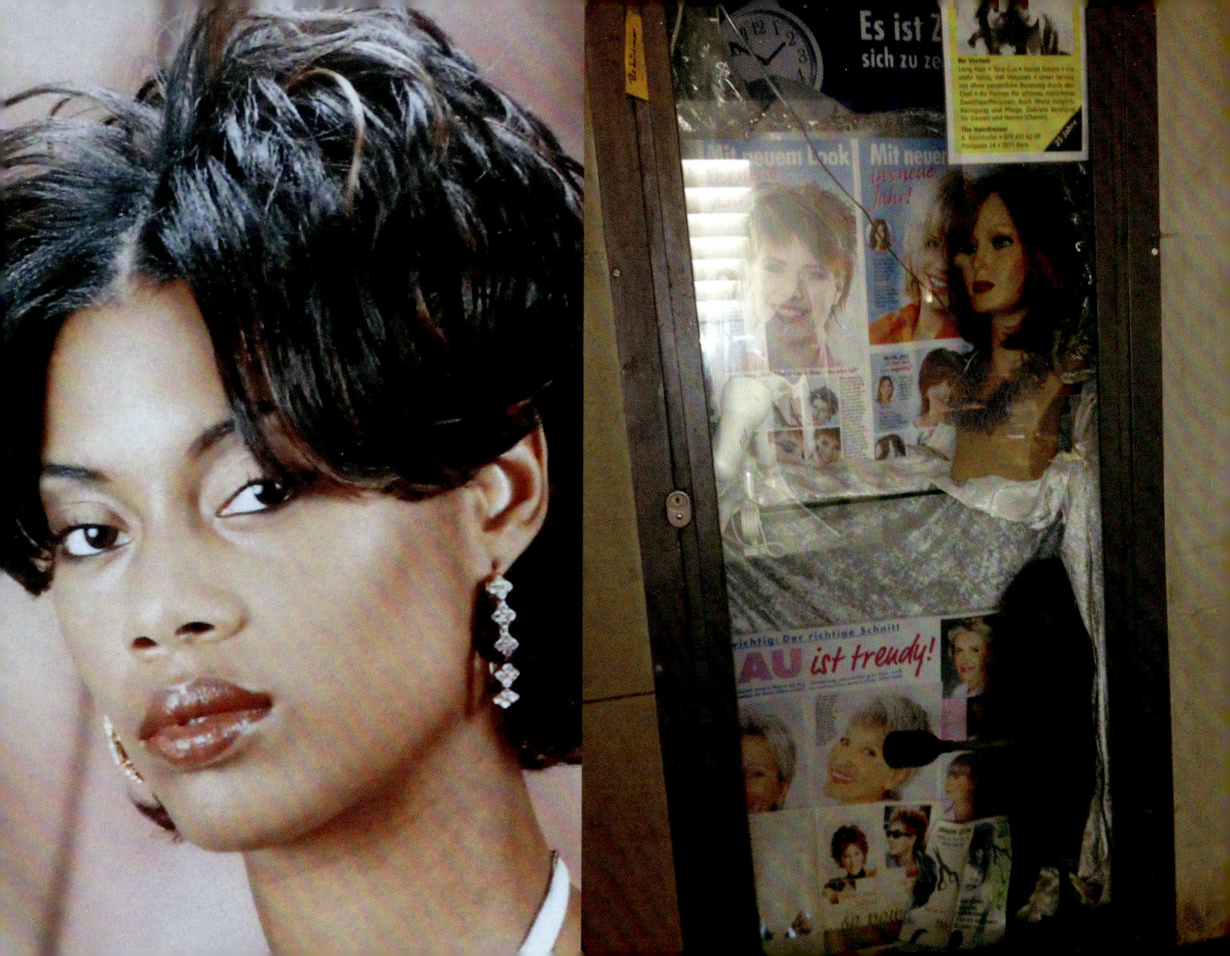
Mit neuem Look
ist trendy!

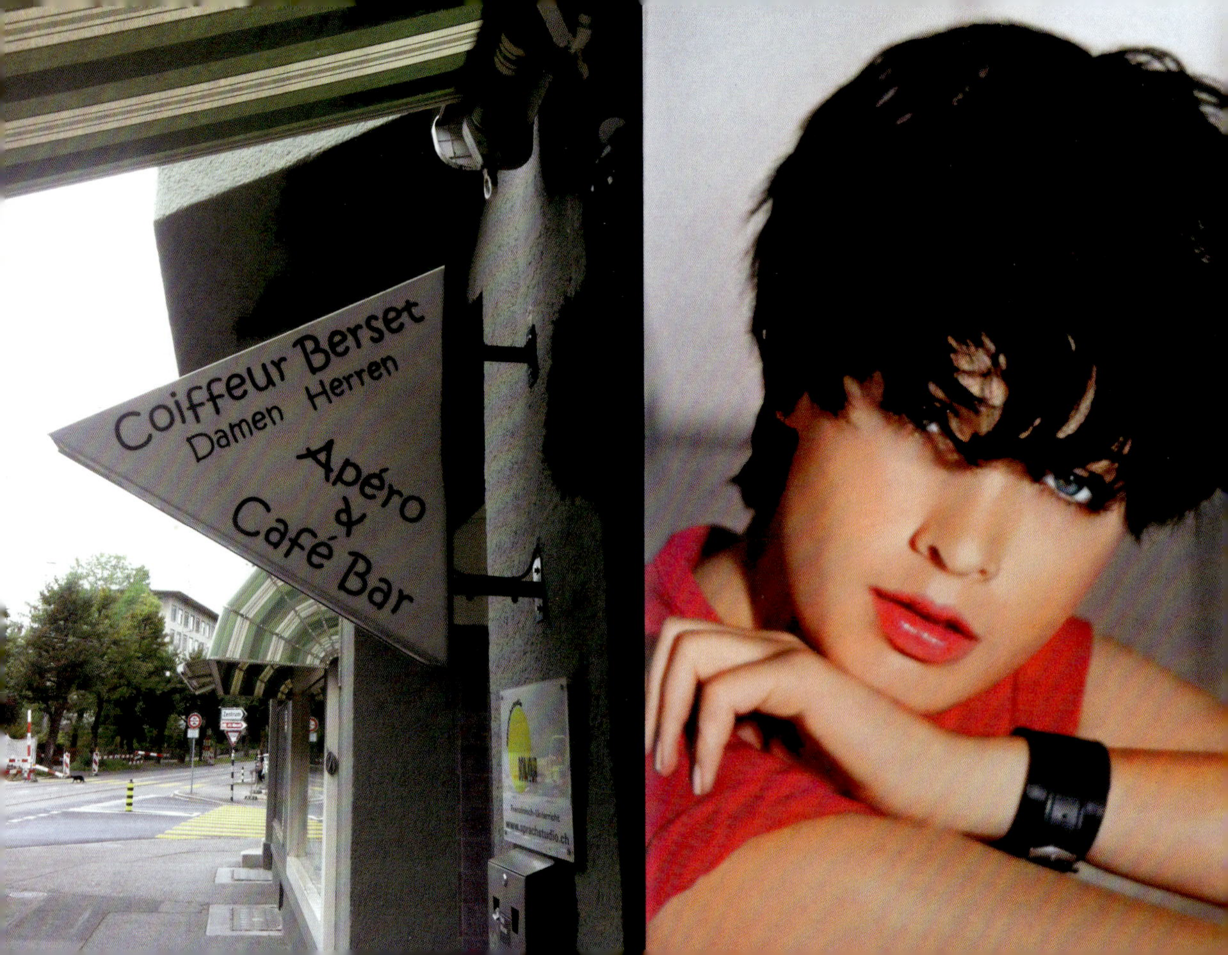
Coiffeur Berset
Damen Herren
Apéro
&
Café Bar

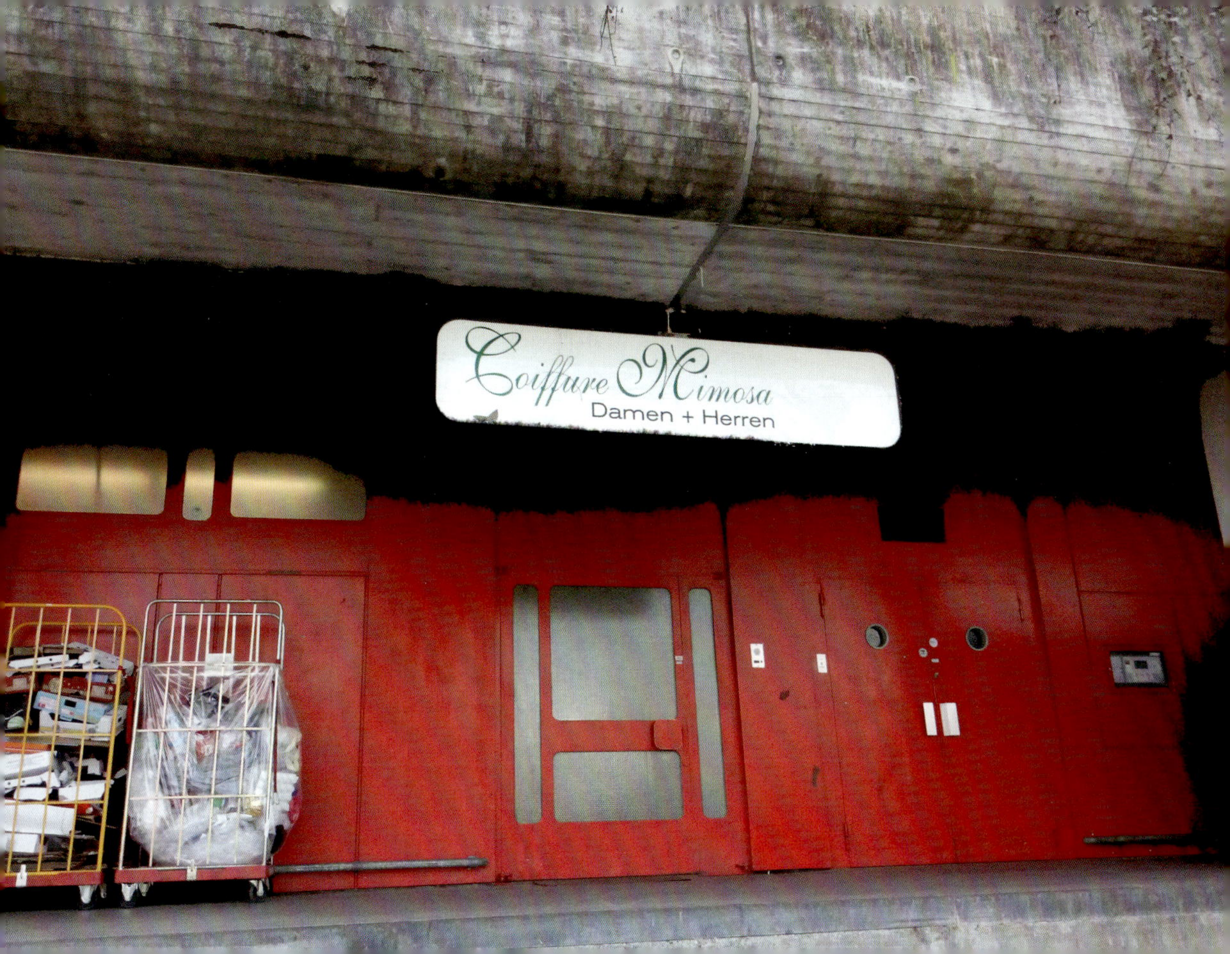
Coiffure Mimosa
Damen + Herren

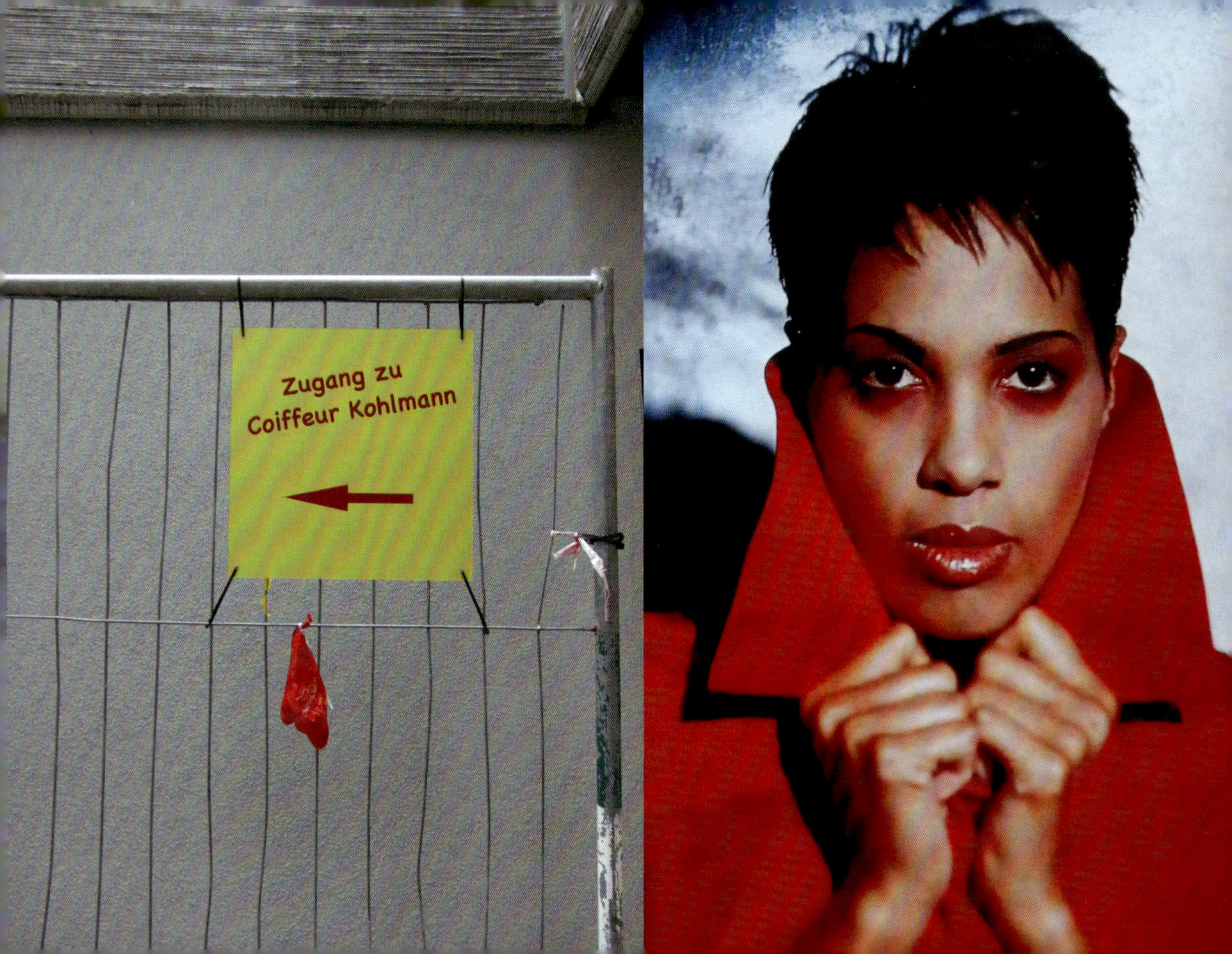
Zugang zu
Coiffeur Kohlmann

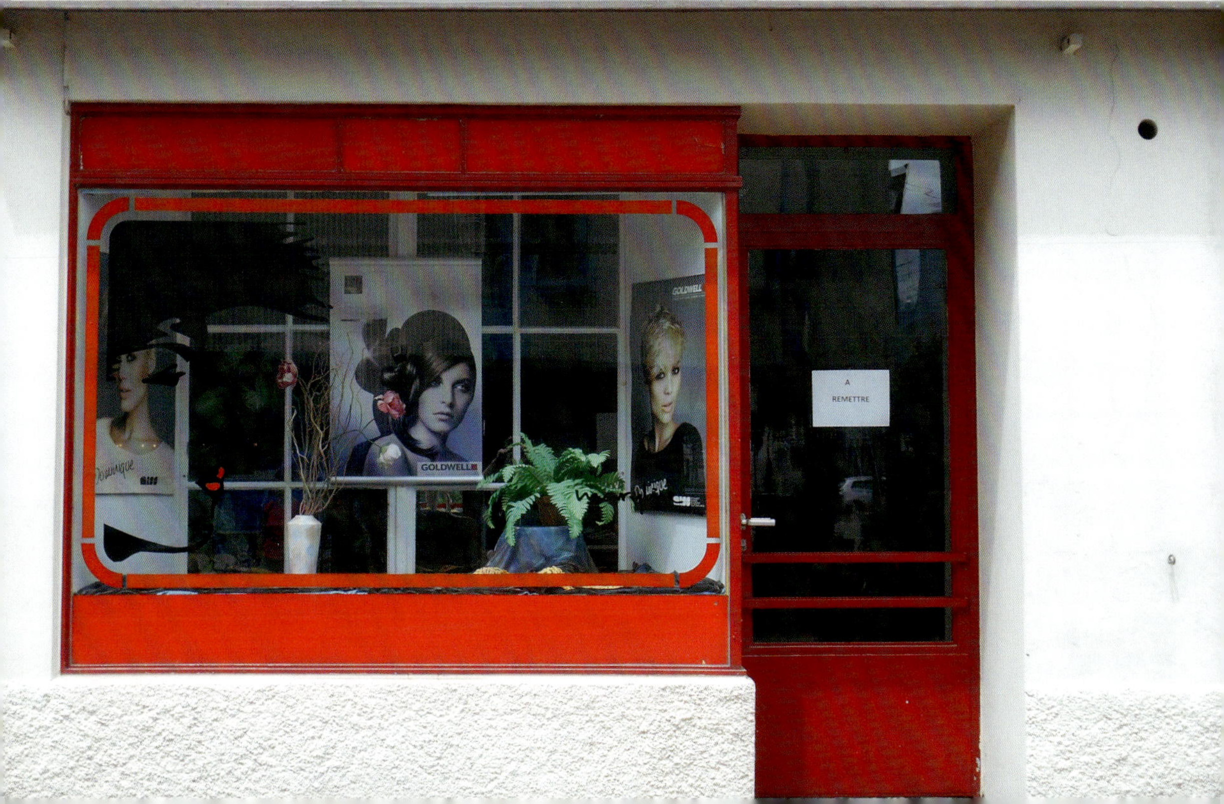
Coiffure POGGY
GOLDWELL
GOLDWELL
A
REMETTRE

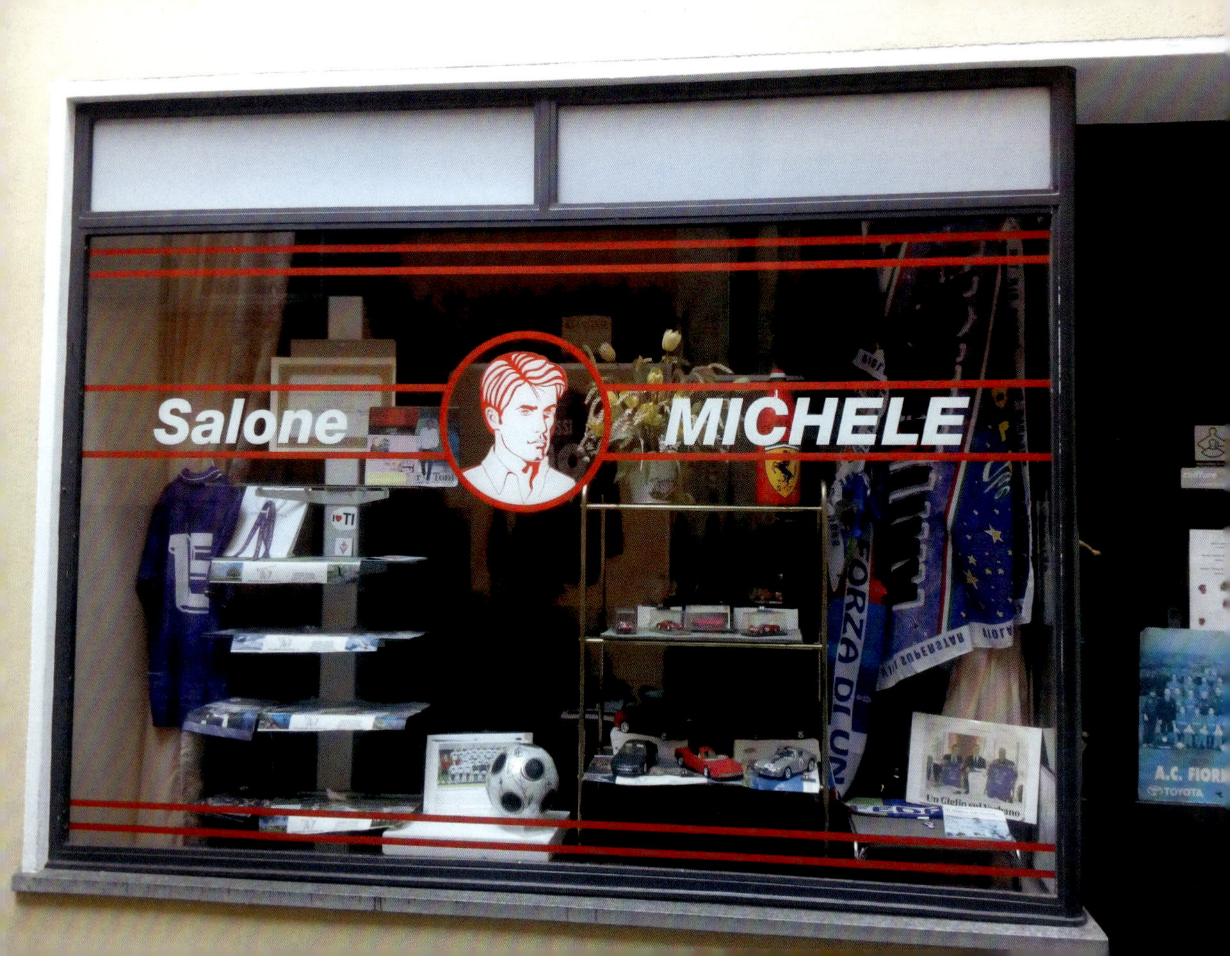

Salone
MICHELE

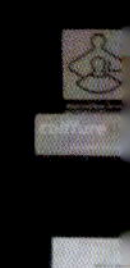

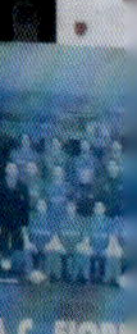

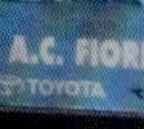
TOYOTA

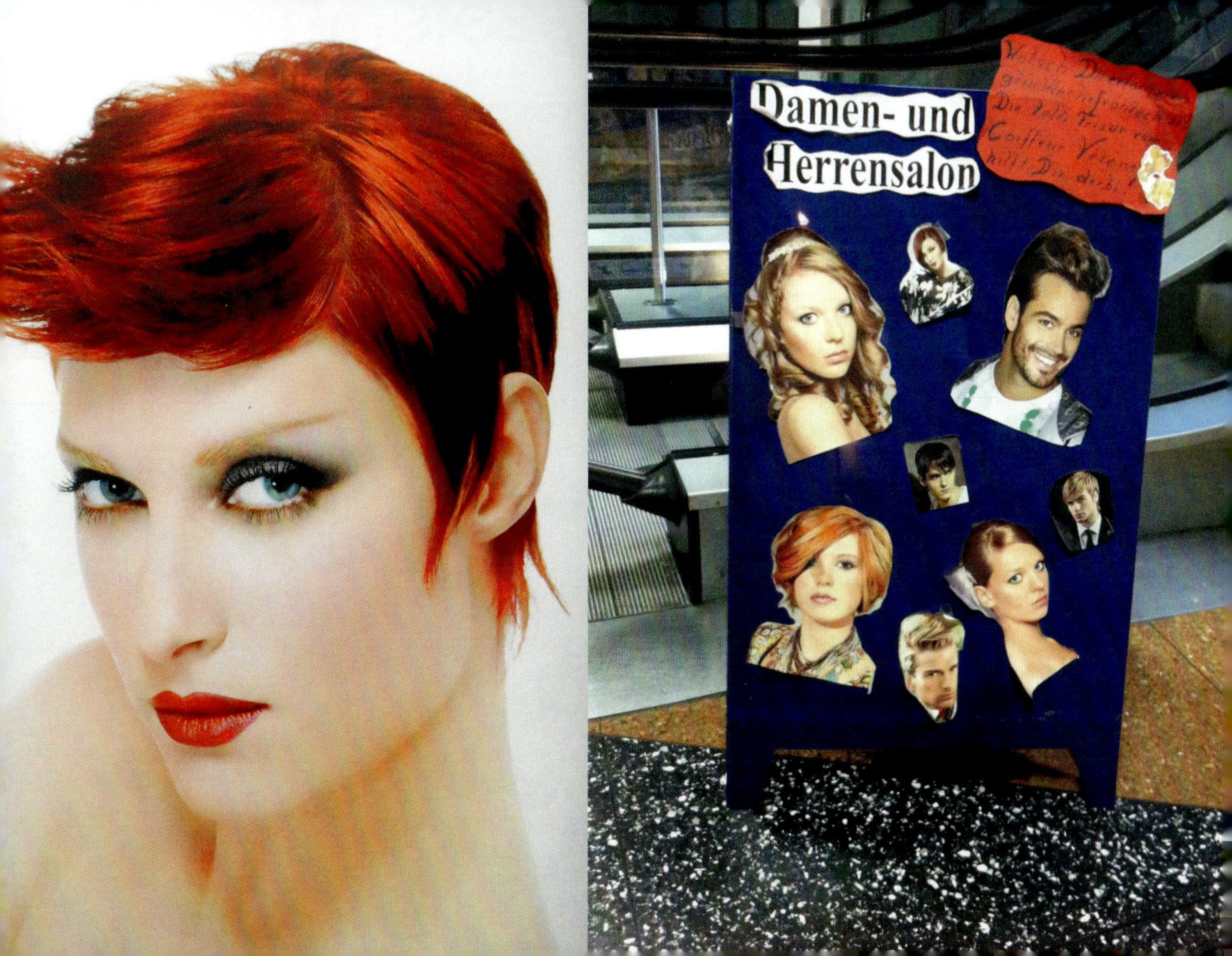
Damen- und
Herrensalon

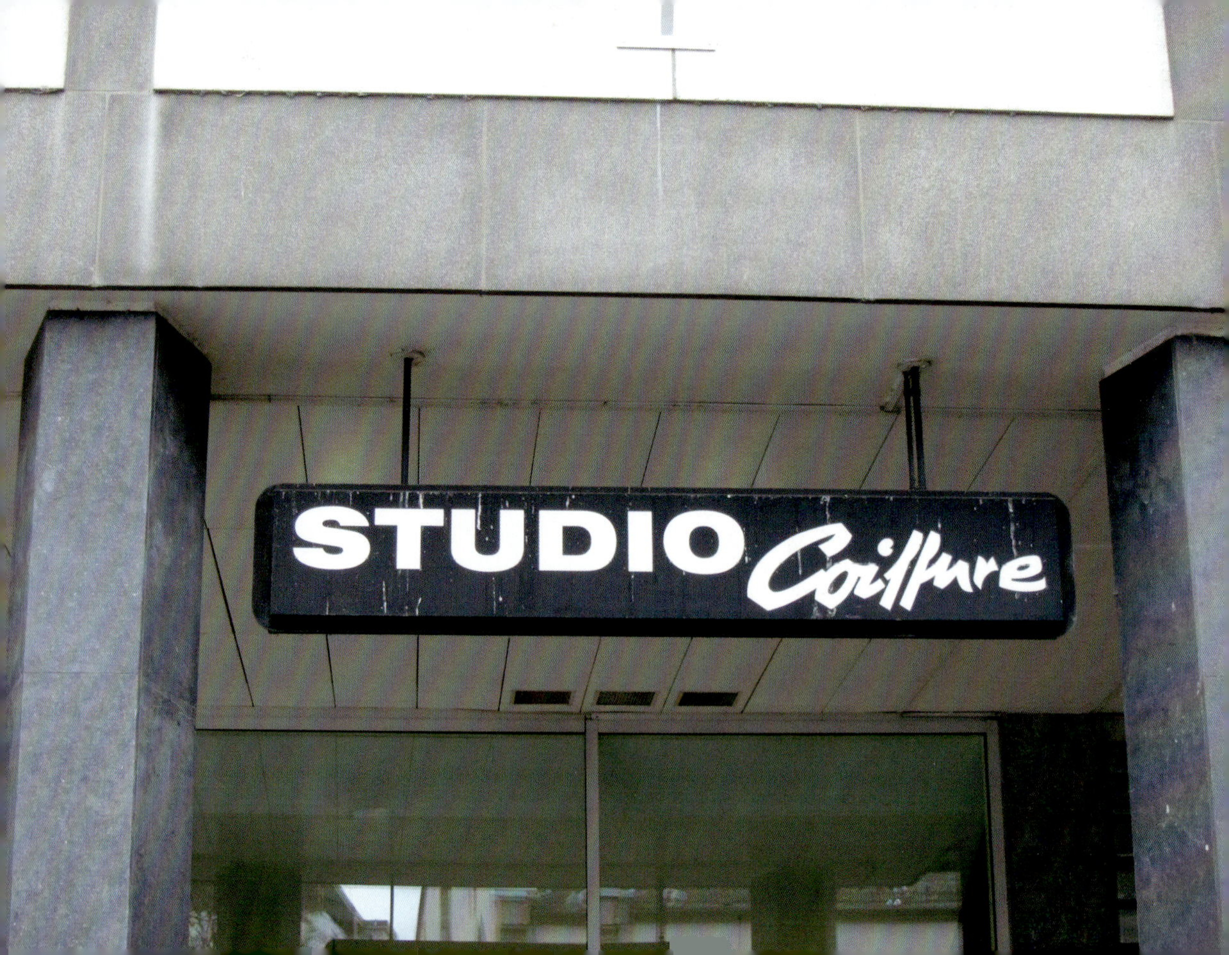

STUDIO Coiffure

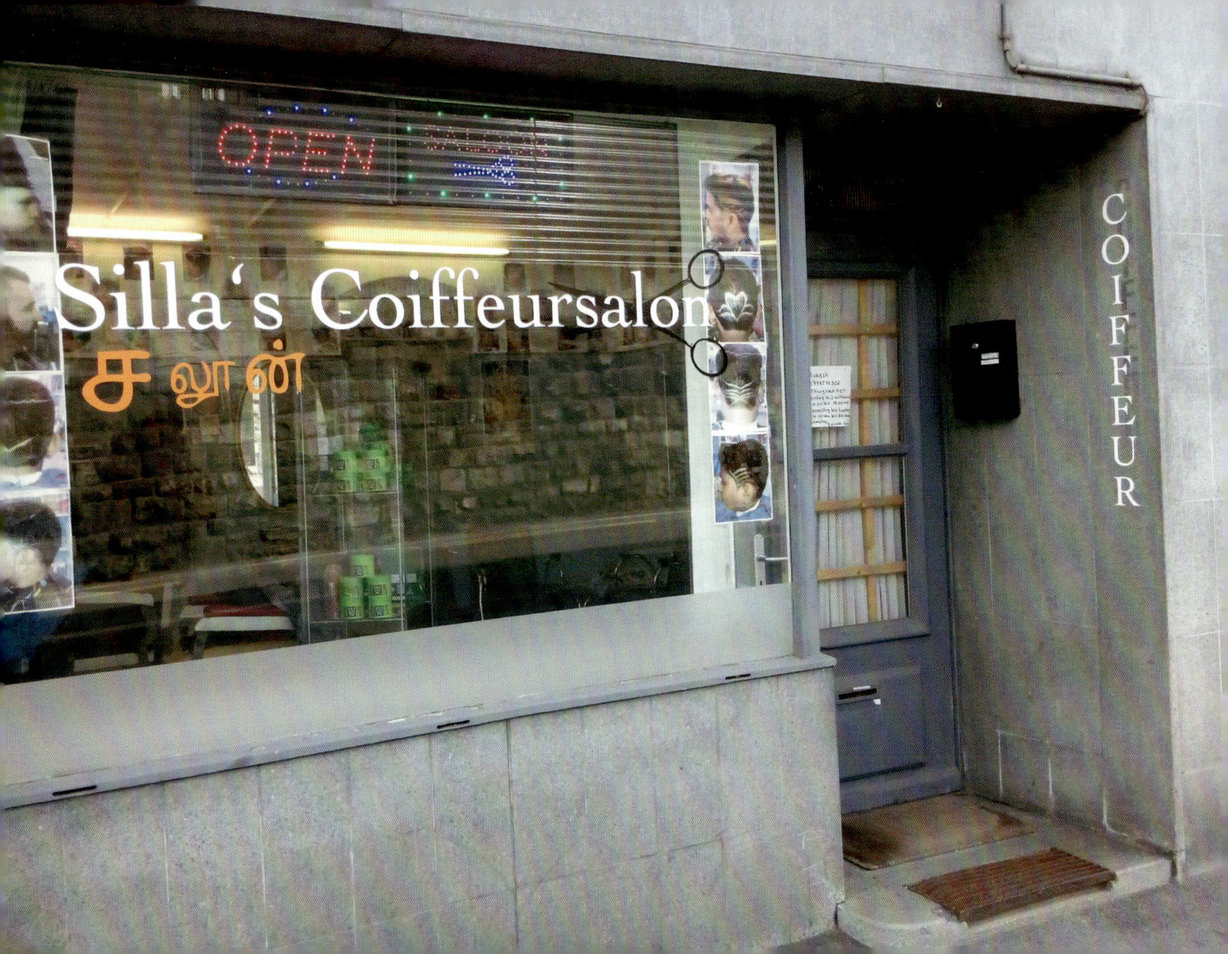
OPEN
Silla's Coiffeursalon
சலூன்
COIFFEUR

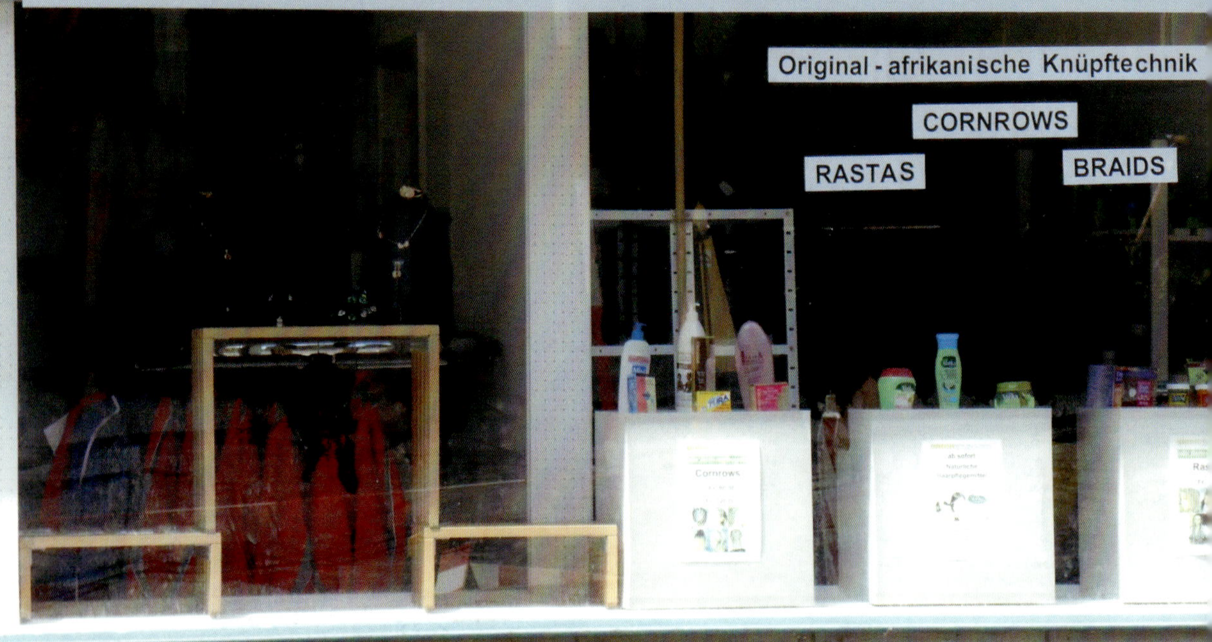
AFROHAIR_STYLING
Original - afrikanische Knüpftechnik
CORNROWS
RASTAS
BRAIDS
Cornrows

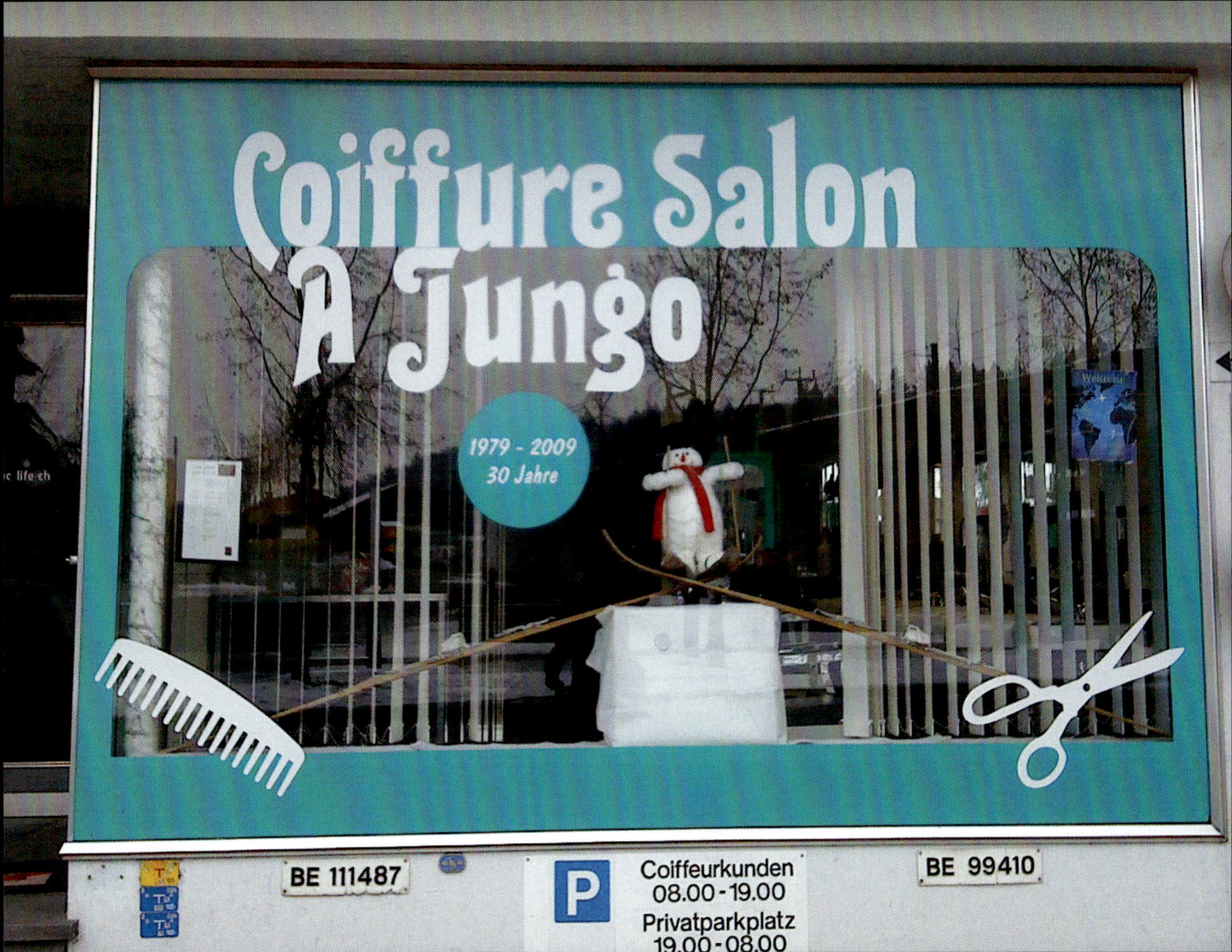

Coiffure Salon
A Jungo
1979 - 2009
30 Jahre
BE 111487
BE 99410

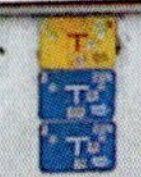

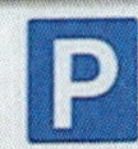
P
Coiffeurkunden
08.00 - 19.00
Privatparkplatz
19.00 - 08.00

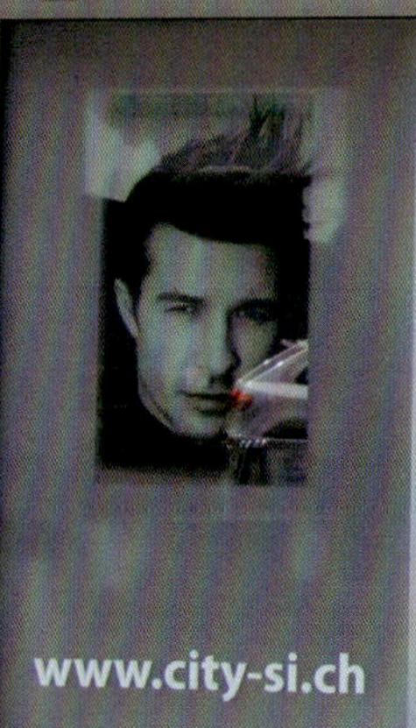
www.city-si.ch

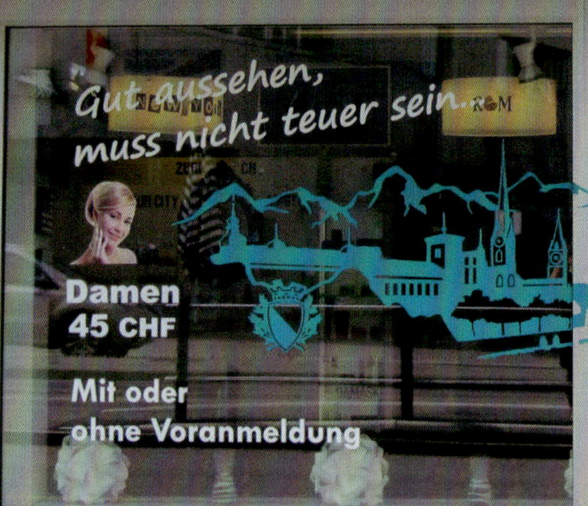
Herren 25 CHF
Gut aussehen,
muss nicht teuer sein...
Damen
45 CHF
Mit oder
ohne Voranmeldung

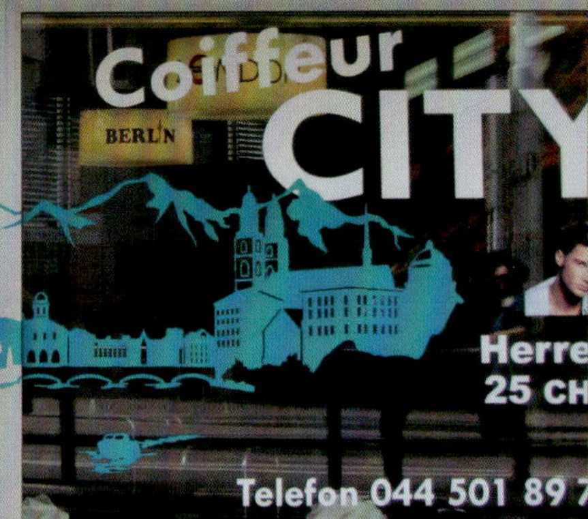
Damen 45 CHF
Coiffeur
CITY
NUR KUNDEN
COIFFEUR CITY

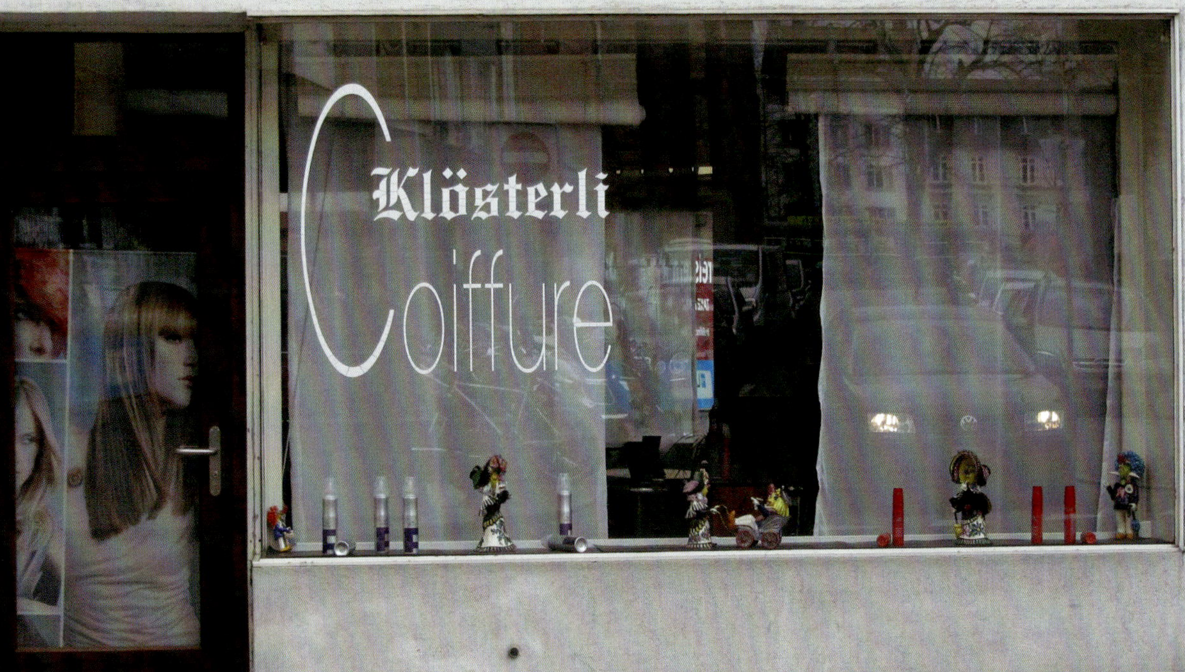
Klösterli
Coiffure

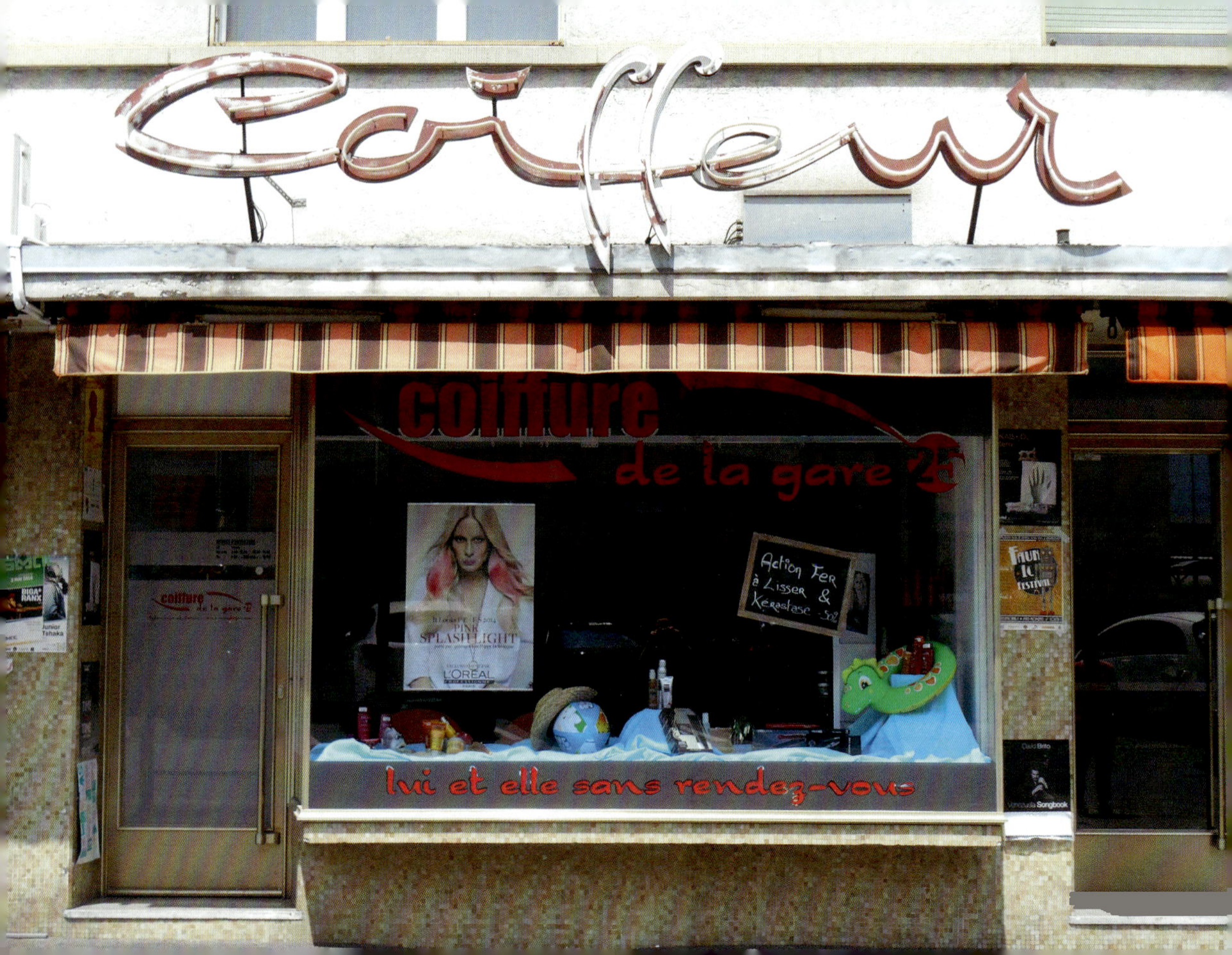
Coiffeur
coiffure
de la gare
lui et elle sans rendez-vous
Action Fer
à Lisser &
Kérastase -50%
PINK
SPLASHLIGHT
L'ORÉAL
FESTIVAL
David Brito
Venezuela Songbook

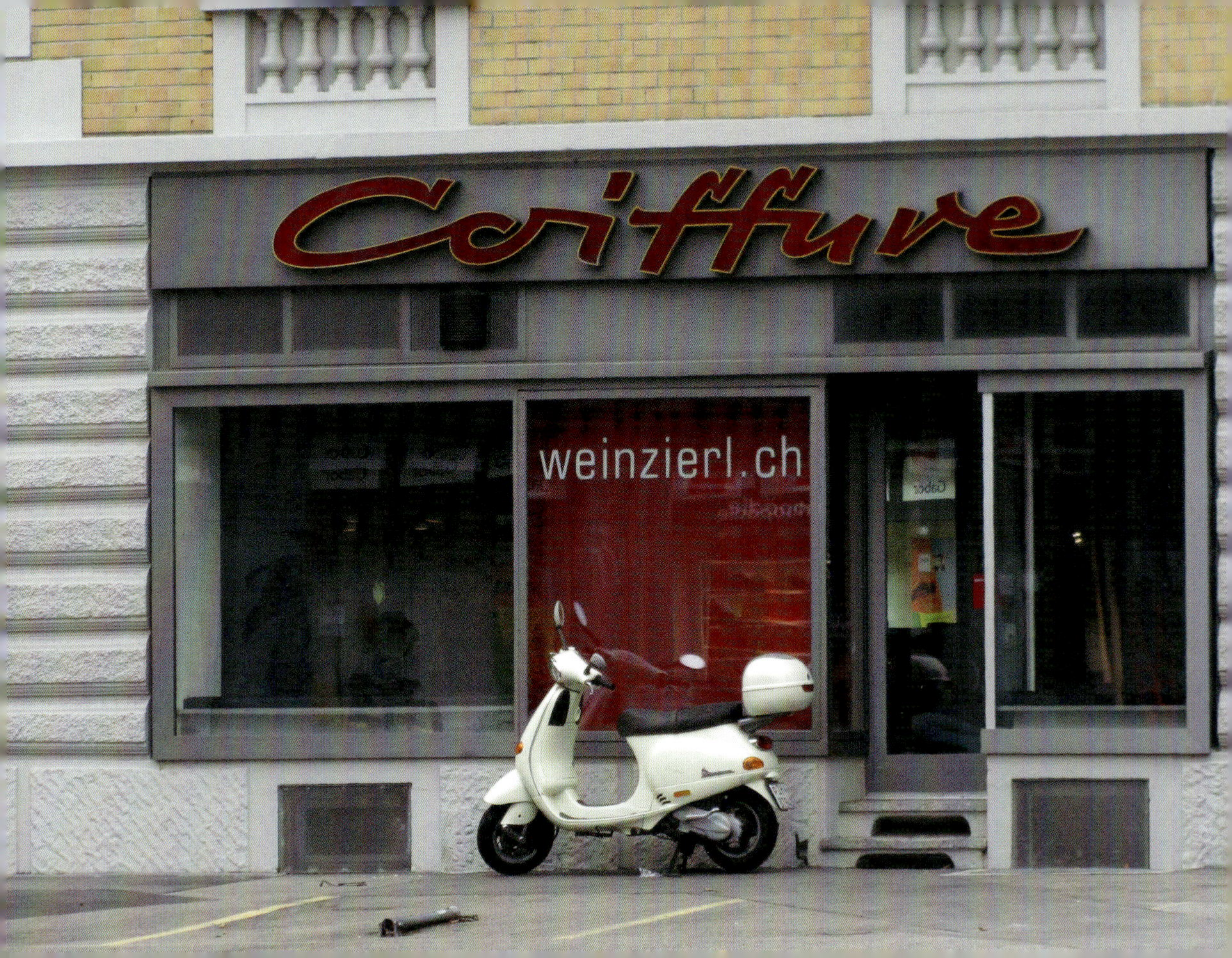
Coiffure
weinzierl.ch

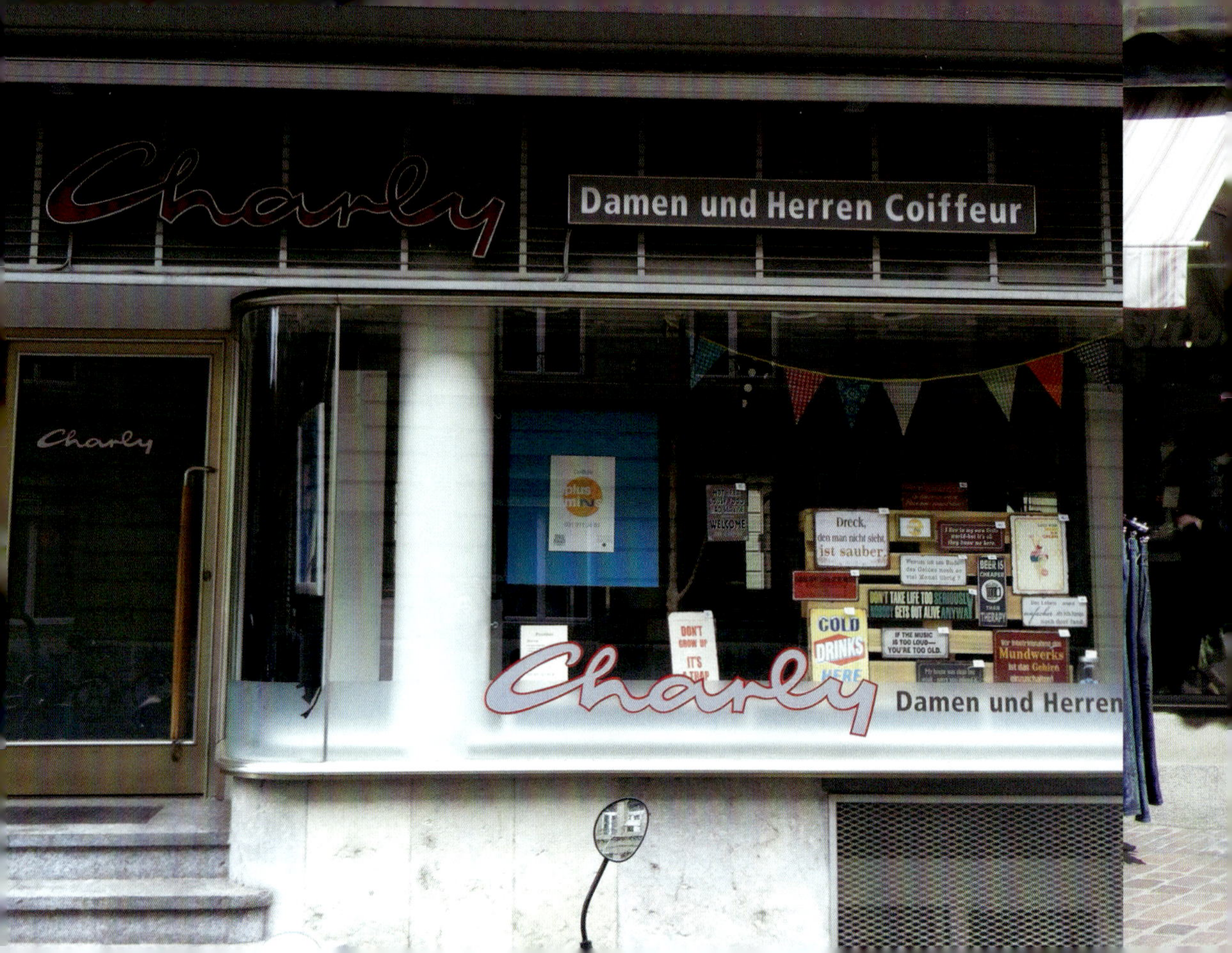
Charly
Damen und Herren Coiffeur
Charly
Dreck, den man nicht sieht, ist sauber.
BEER IS CHEAPER
THAN THERAPY
DON'T TAKE LIFE TOO SERIOUSLY NOBODY GETS OUT ALIVE ANYWAY
DON'T GROW UP IT'S
COLD DRINKS HERE
IF THE MUSIC IS TOO LOUD— YOU'RE TOO OLD.
Mundwerks
Charly
Damen und Herren

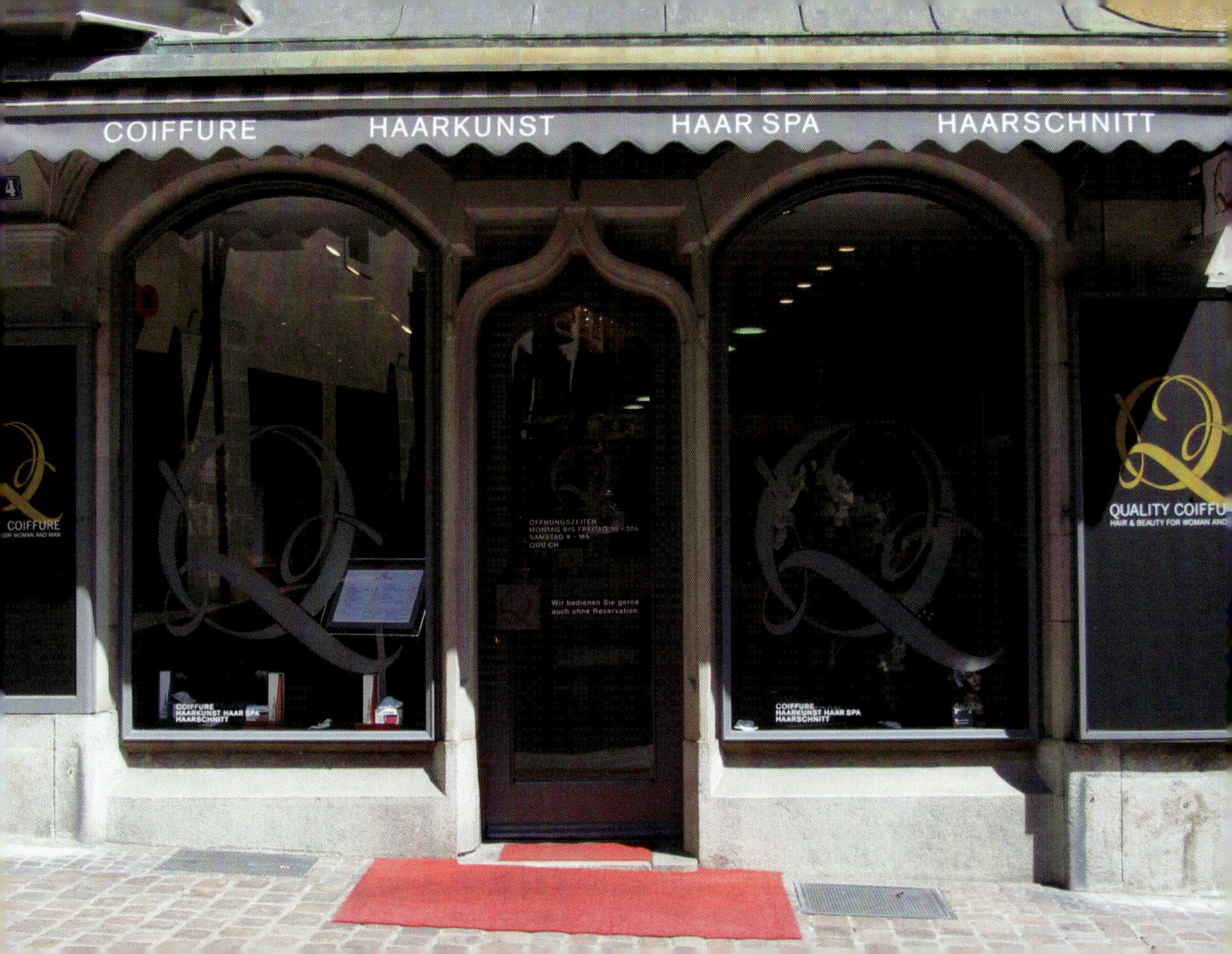
COIFFURE
HAARKUNST
HAAR SPA
HAARSCHNITT
COIFFURE
ÖFFNUNGSZEITEN
MONTAG BIS FREITAG 10 - 20h
SAMSTAG 9 - 18h
Wir bedienen Sie gerne
auch ohne Reservation.
QUALITY COIFFU
HAIR & BEAUTY FOR WOMAN AND
COIFFURE
HAARKUNST HAAR SPA
HAARSCHNITT
COIFFURE
HAARKUNST HAAR SPA
HAARSCHNITT

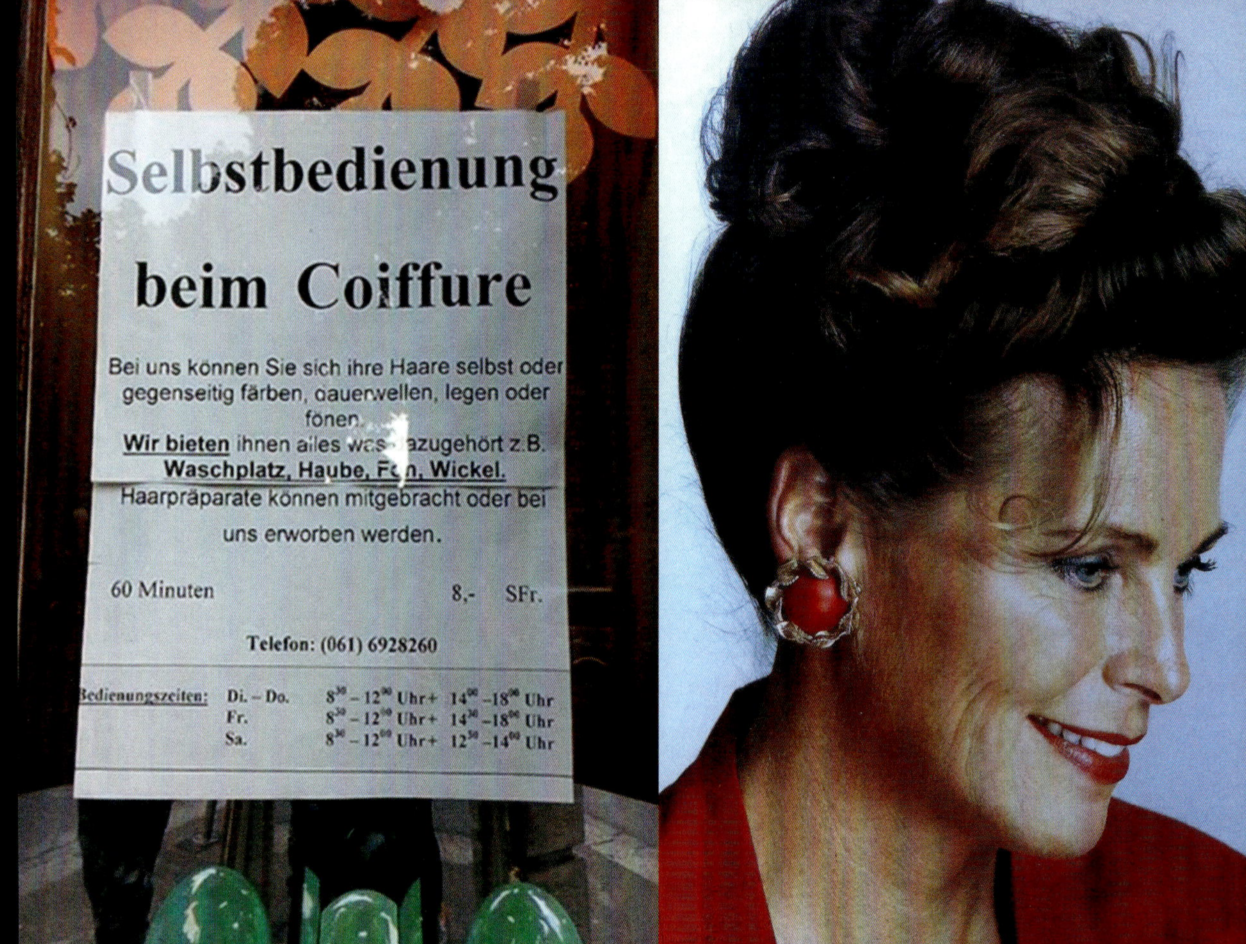
Selbstbedienung
beim Coiffure
Bei uns können Sie sich ihre Haare selbst oder gegenseitig färben, dauerwellen, legen oder fönen.
Wir bieten ihnen alles was dazugehört z.B.
Waschplatz, Haube, Fön, Wickel.
Haarpräparate können mitgebracht oder bei uns erworben werden.
60 Minuten 8.- SFr.
Telefon: (061) 6928260
Bedienungszeiten: Di. – Do. 8^{30} – 12^{00} Uhr + 14^{00} – 18^{00} Uhr
Fr. 8^{30} – 12^{00} Uhr + 14^{30} – 18^{00} Uhr
Sa. 8^{30} – 12^{00} Uhr + 12^{30} – 14^{00} Uhr

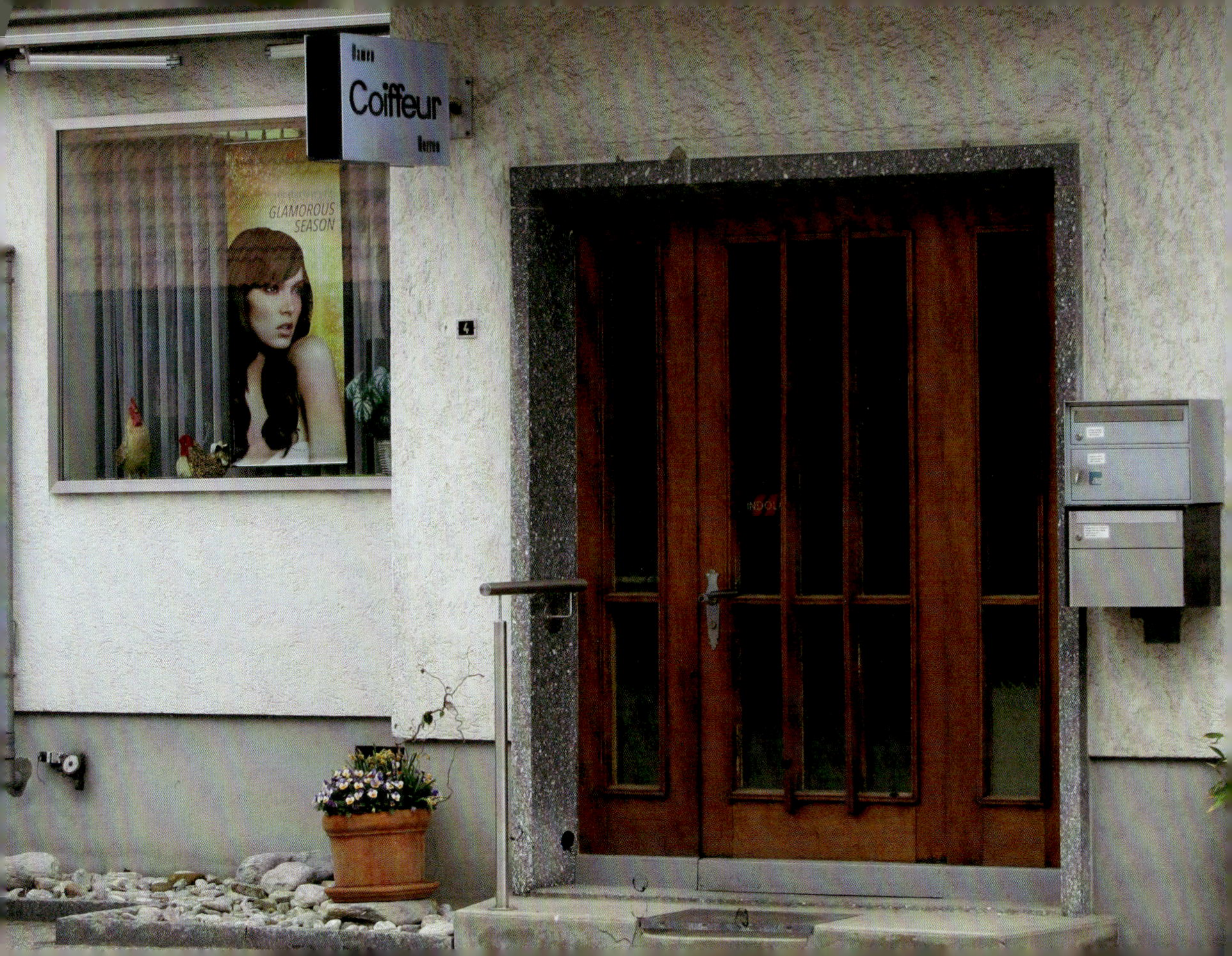
Coiffeur
GLAMOROUS
SEASON

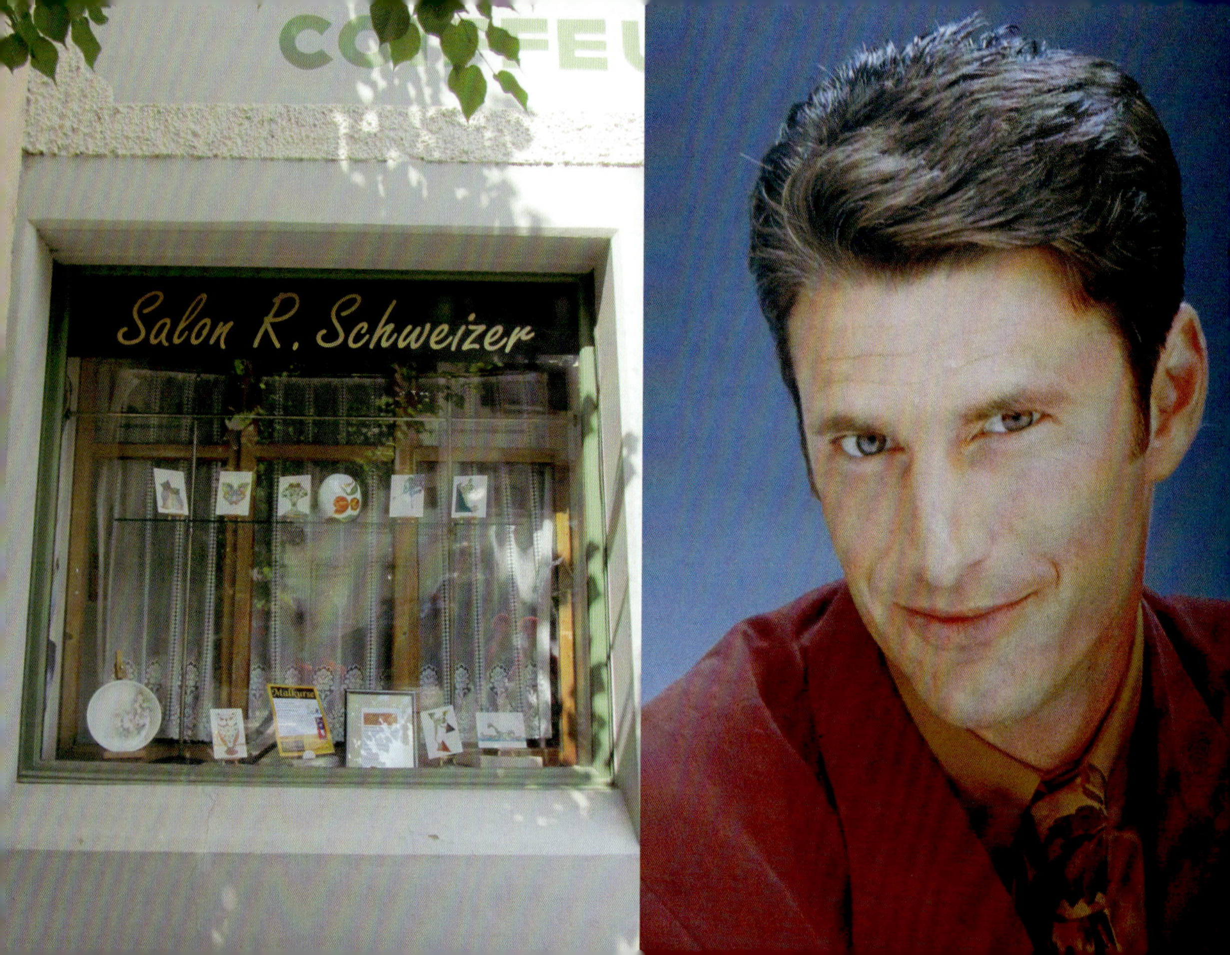
Salon R. Schweizer

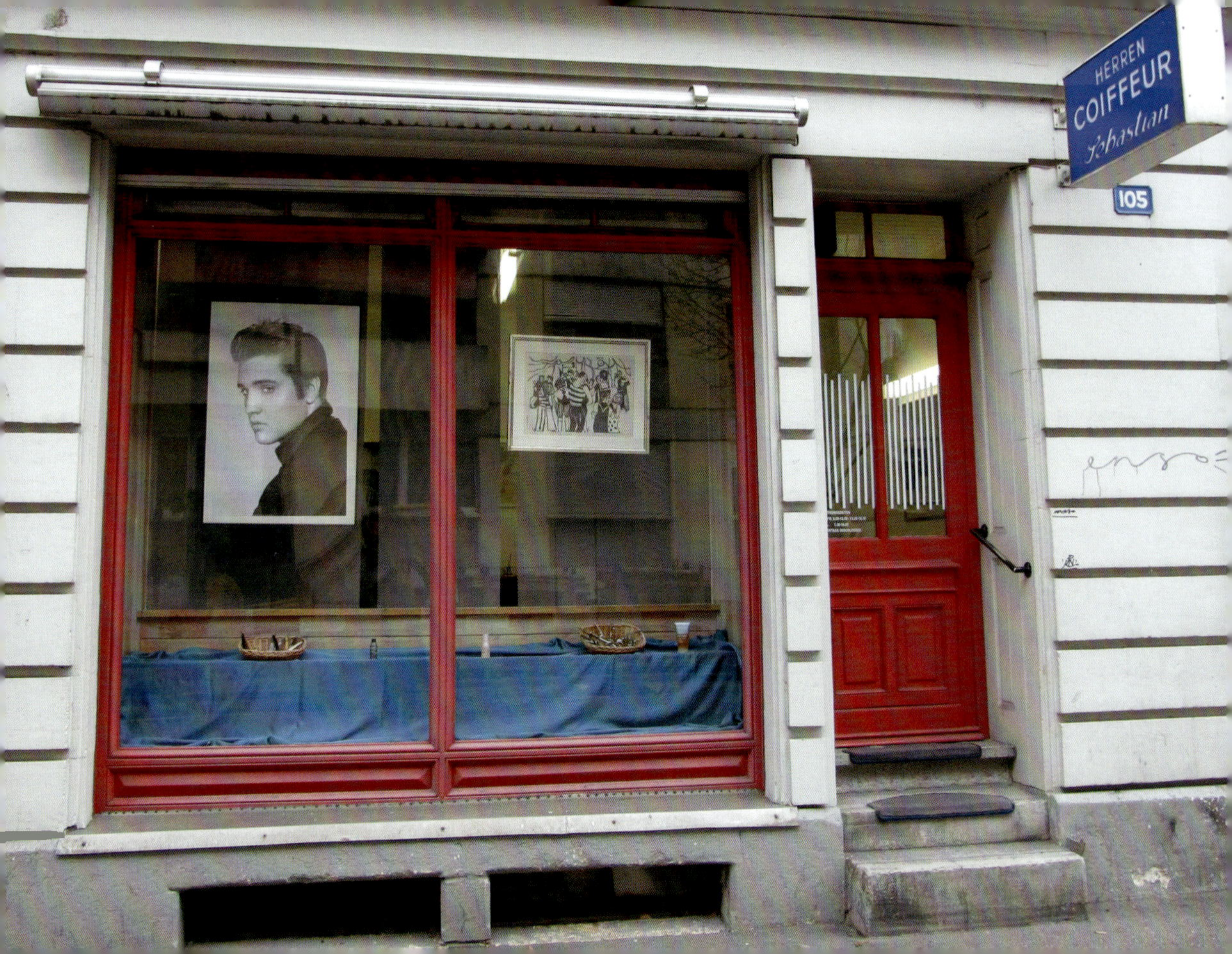
HERREN
COIFFEUR
Sebastian
105

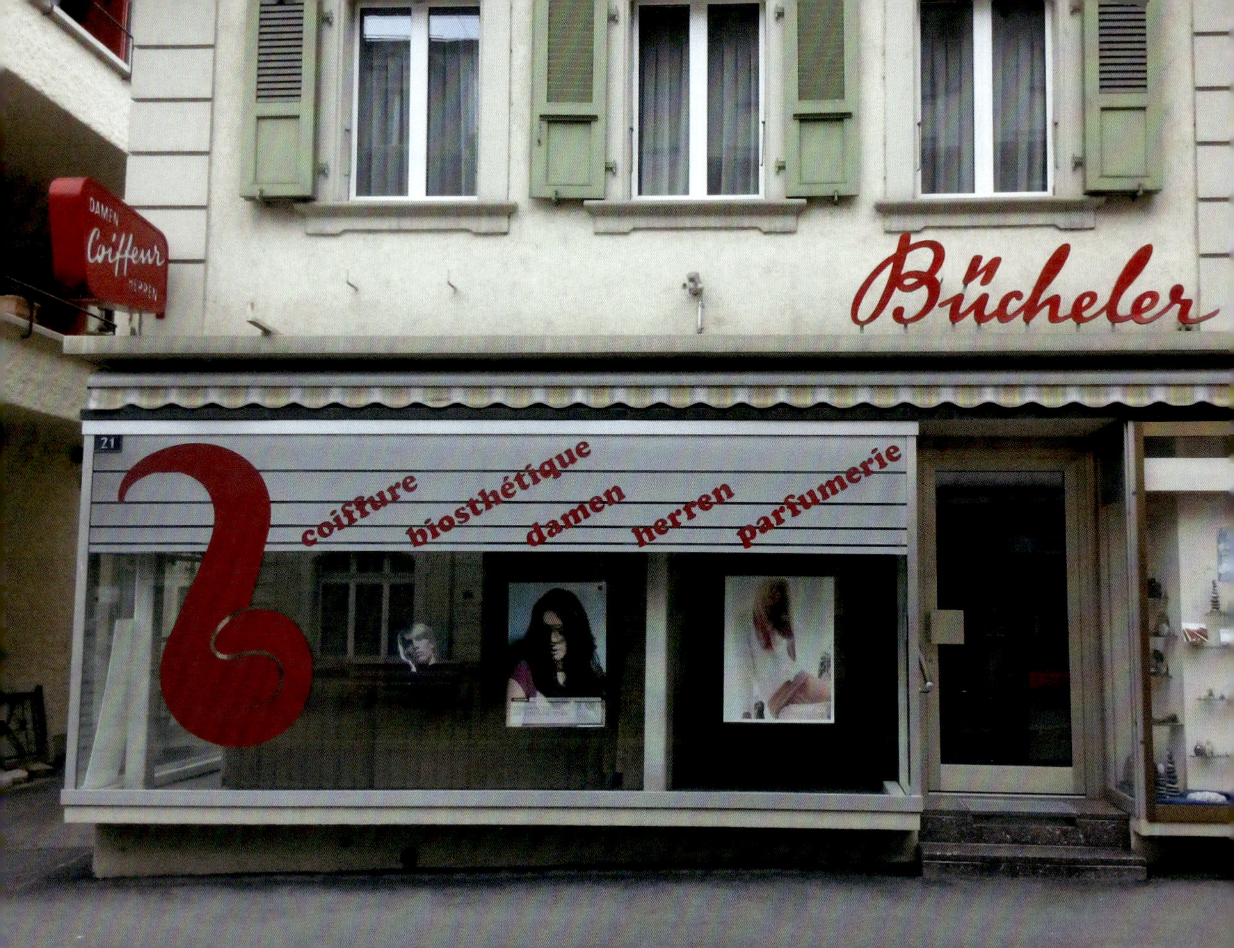
DAMEN
Coiffeur
HERREN
Bücheler
21
coiffure
biosthétique
damen
herren
parfumerie

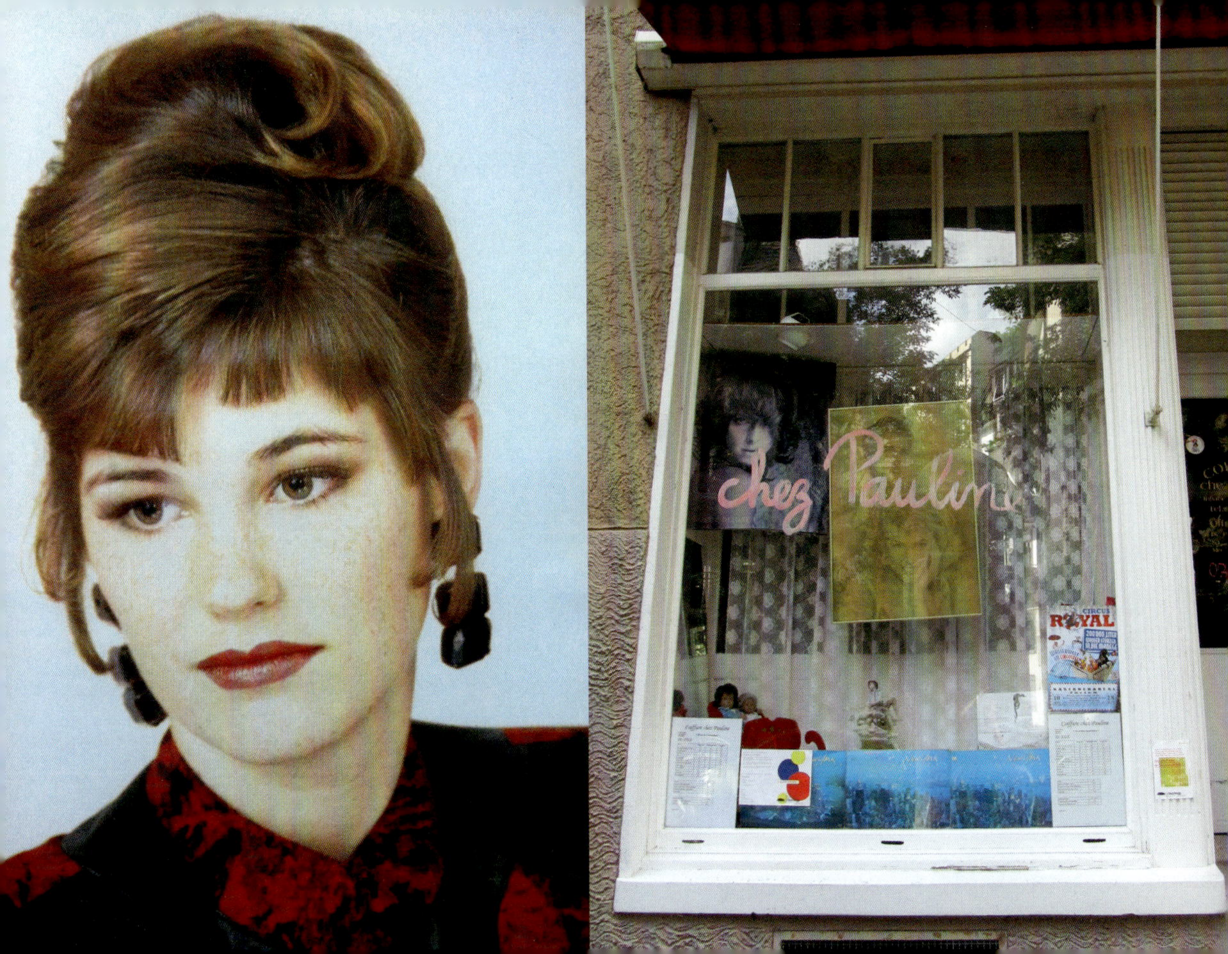

chez Pauline
CIRCUS
ROYAL

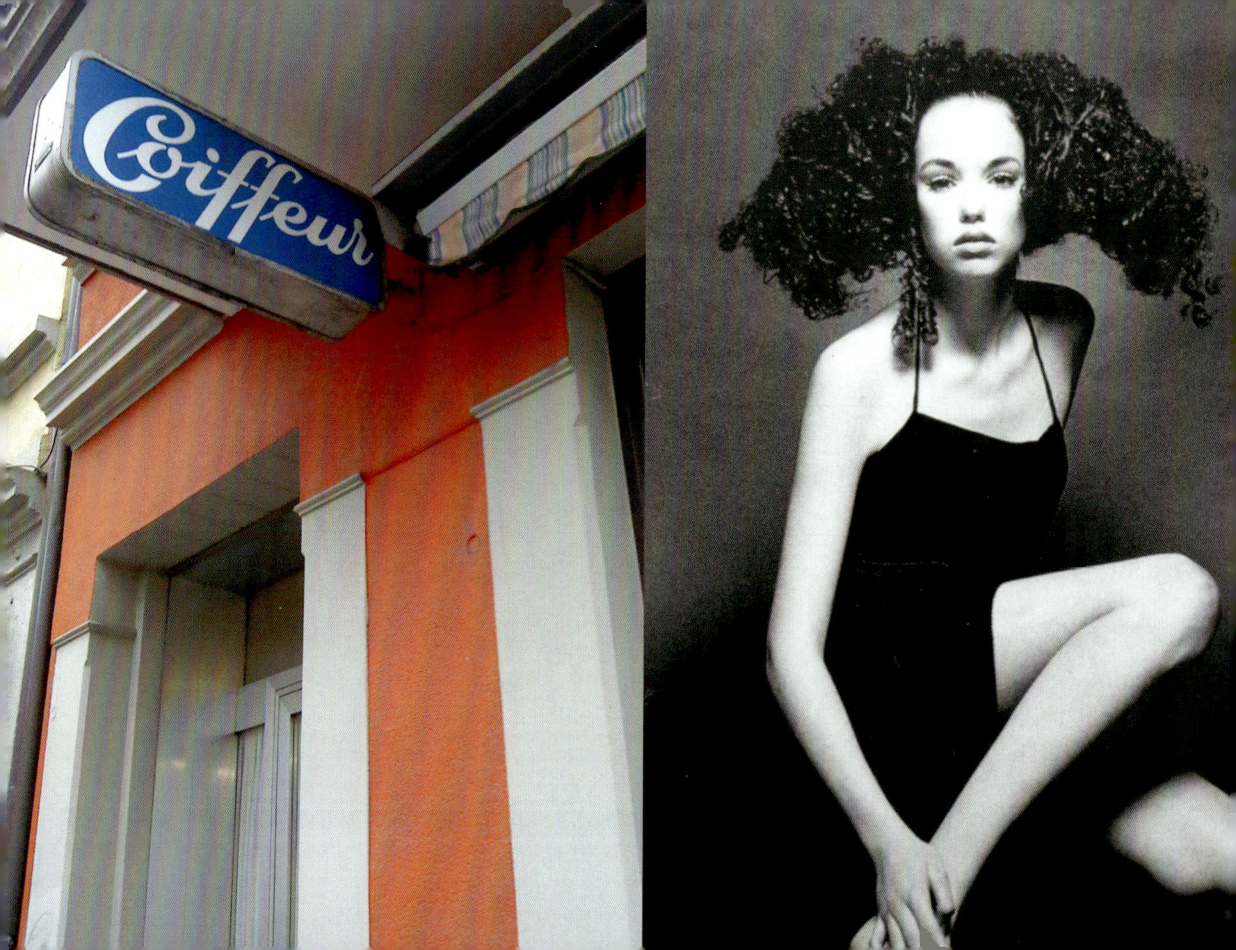
Coiffeur

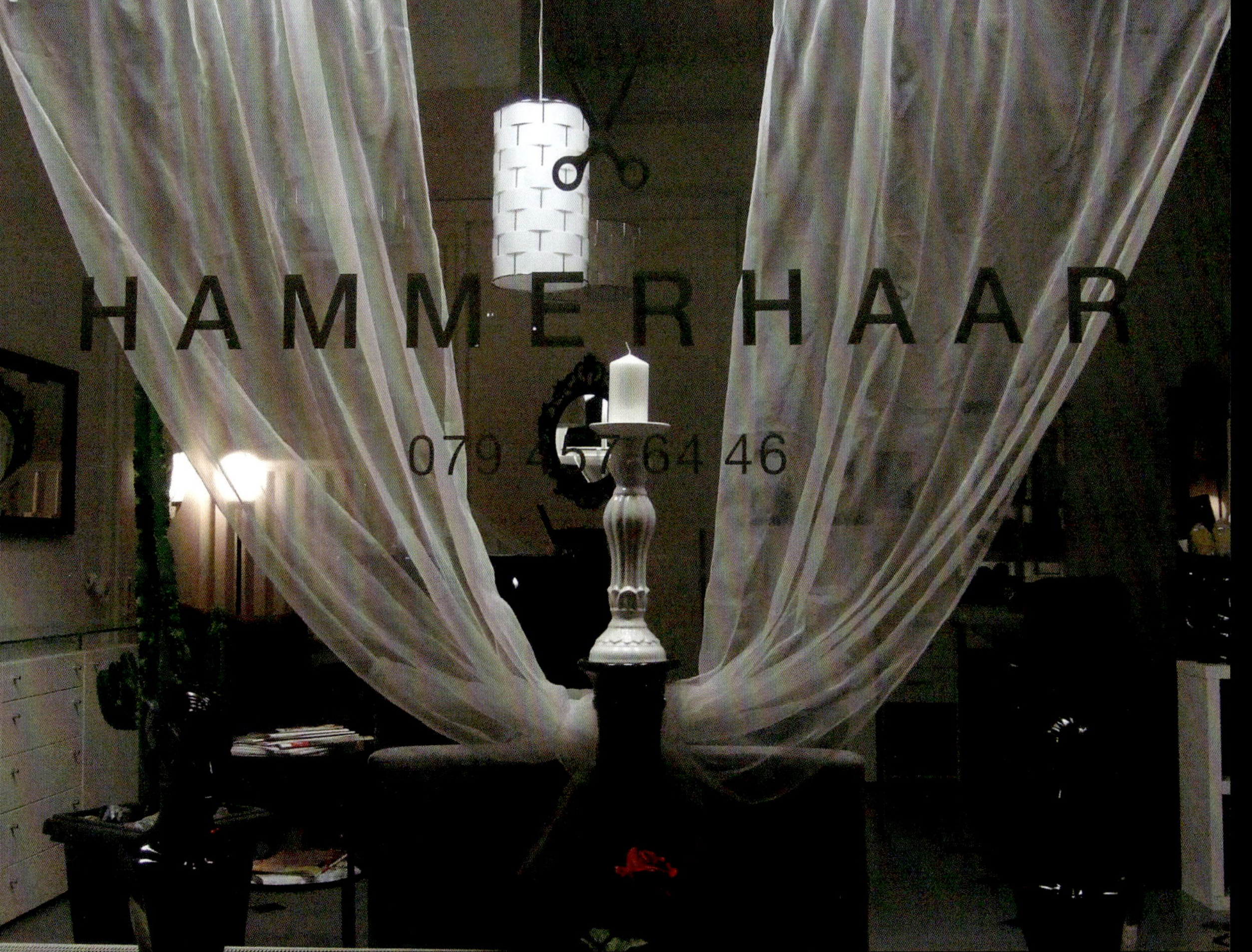
HAMMERHAAR
079 457 64 46

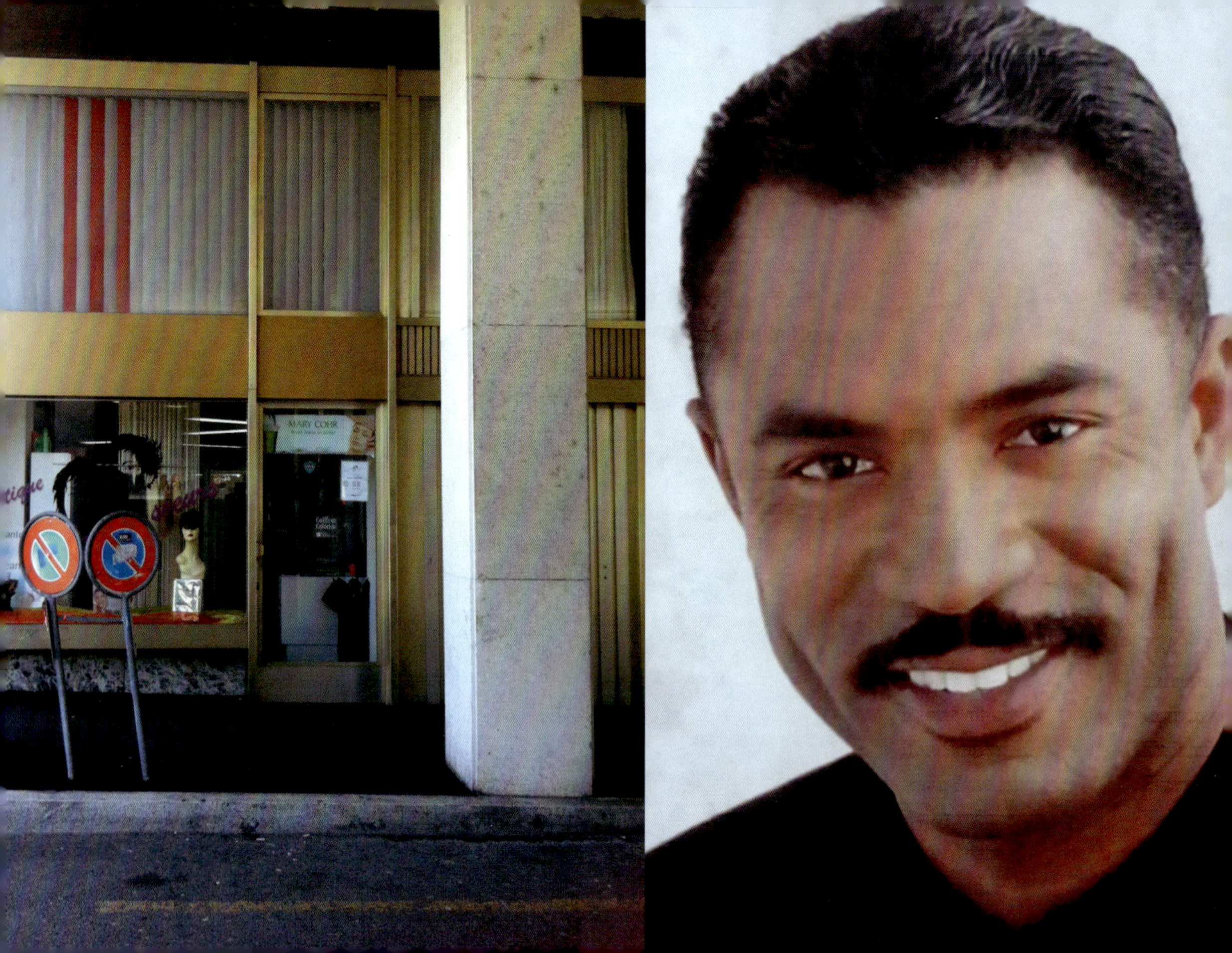
MARY COHR

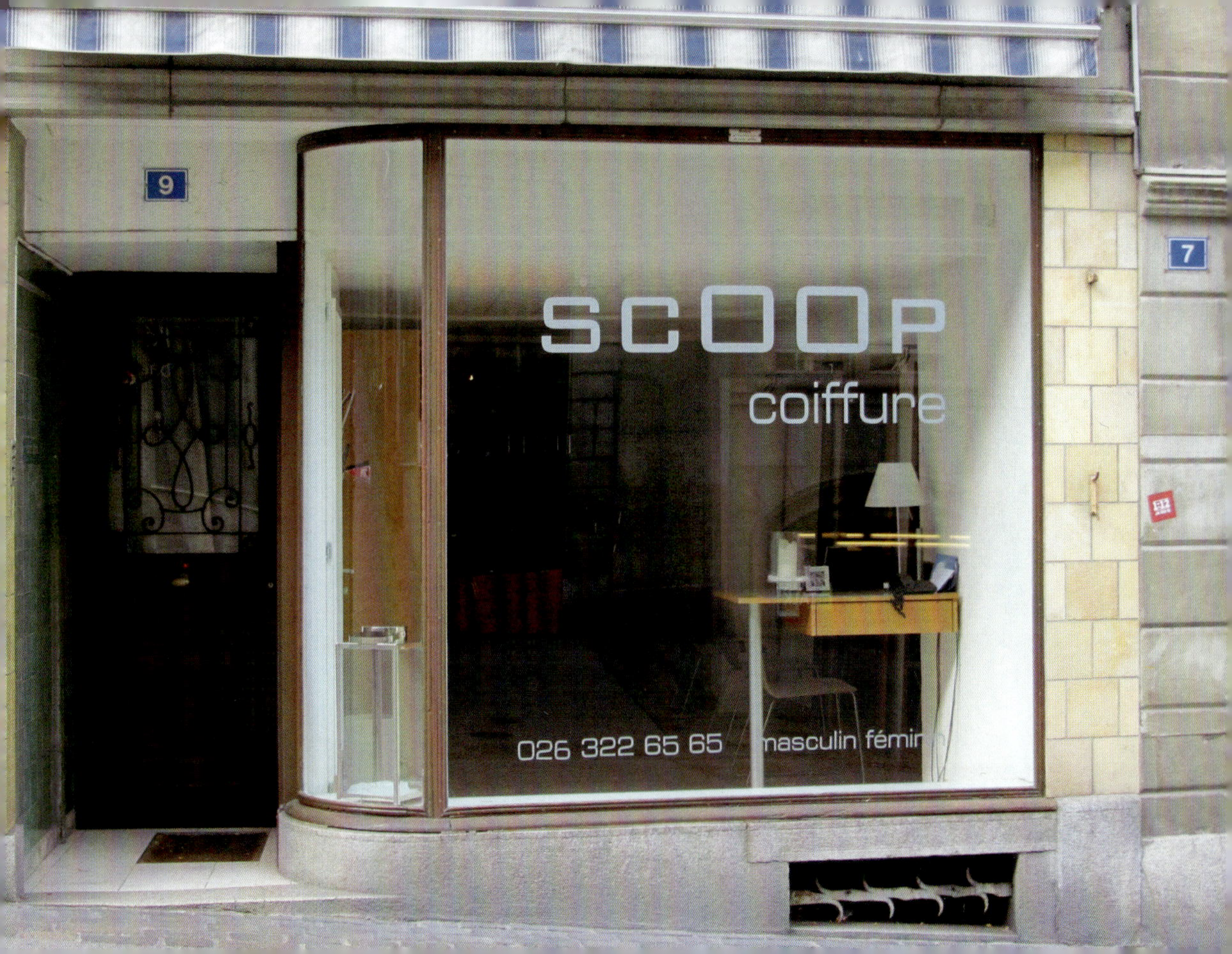
9
7
ScOOp
coiffure
026 322 65 65
masculin

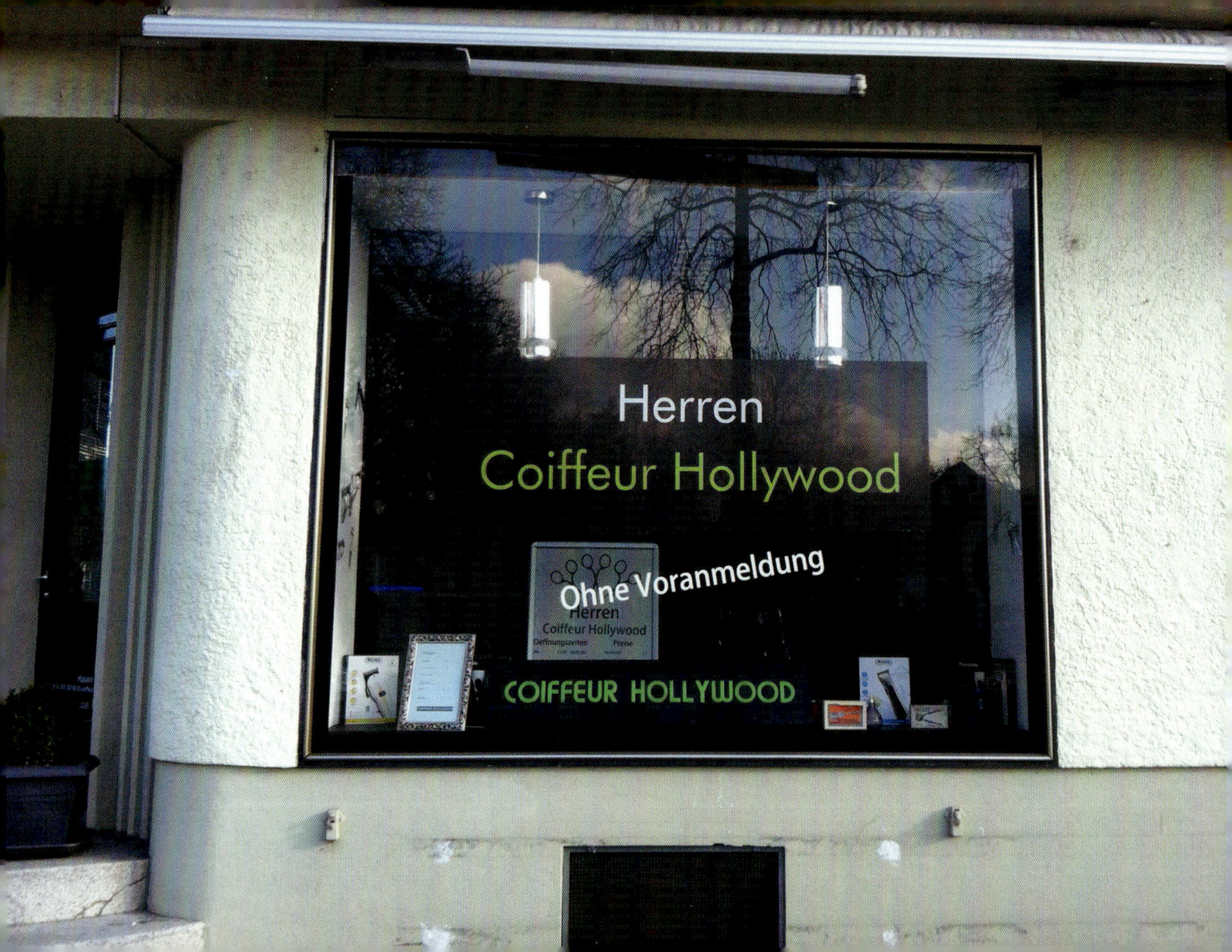
Herren
Coiffeur Hollywood
Ohne Voranmeldung
Herren
Coiffeur Hollywood
Öffnungszeiten
Preise
COIFFEUR HOLLYWOOD

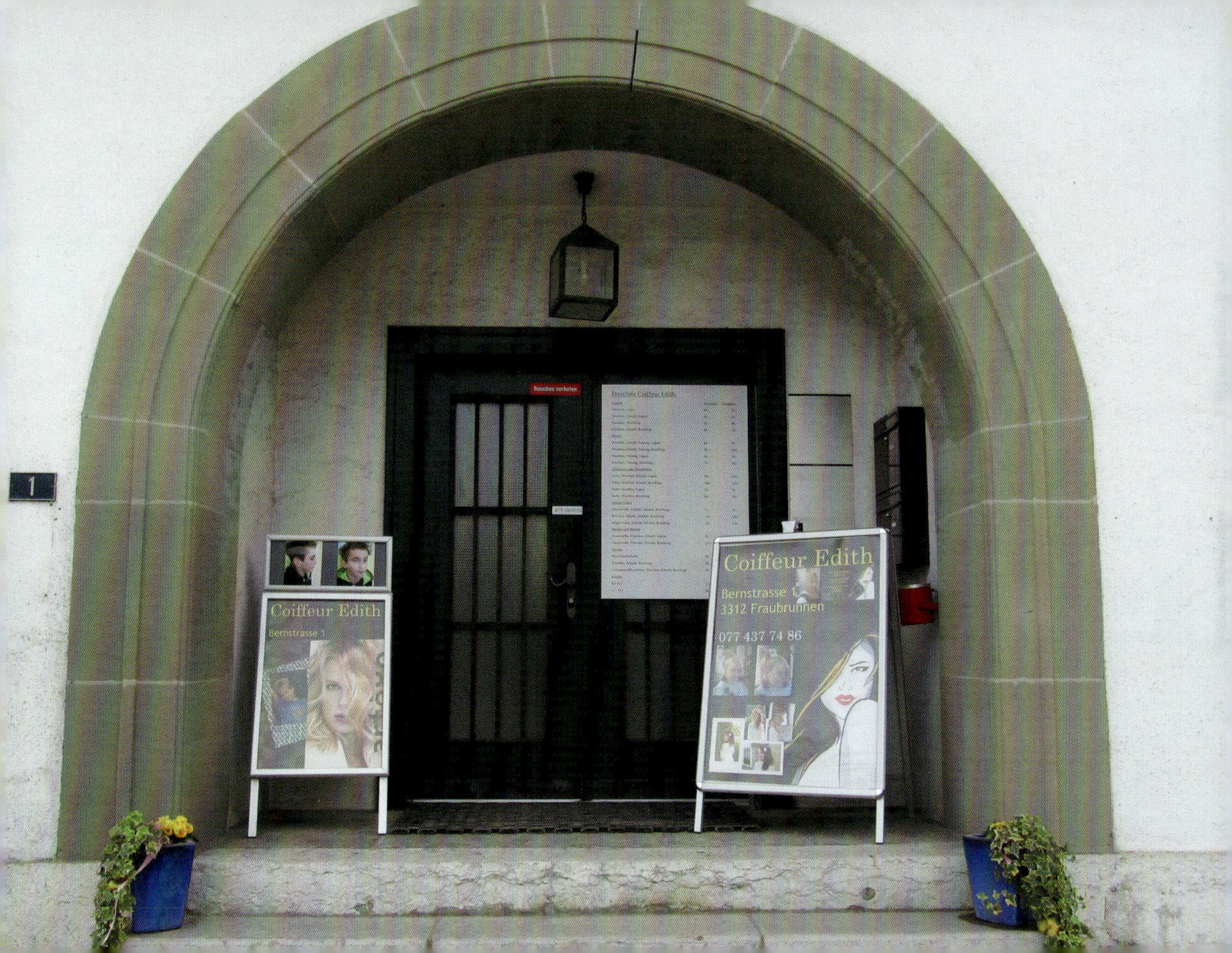
1
Coiffeur Edith
Bernstrasse 1
Coiffeur Edith
Bernstrasse 1
3312 Fraubrunnen
077 437 74 86

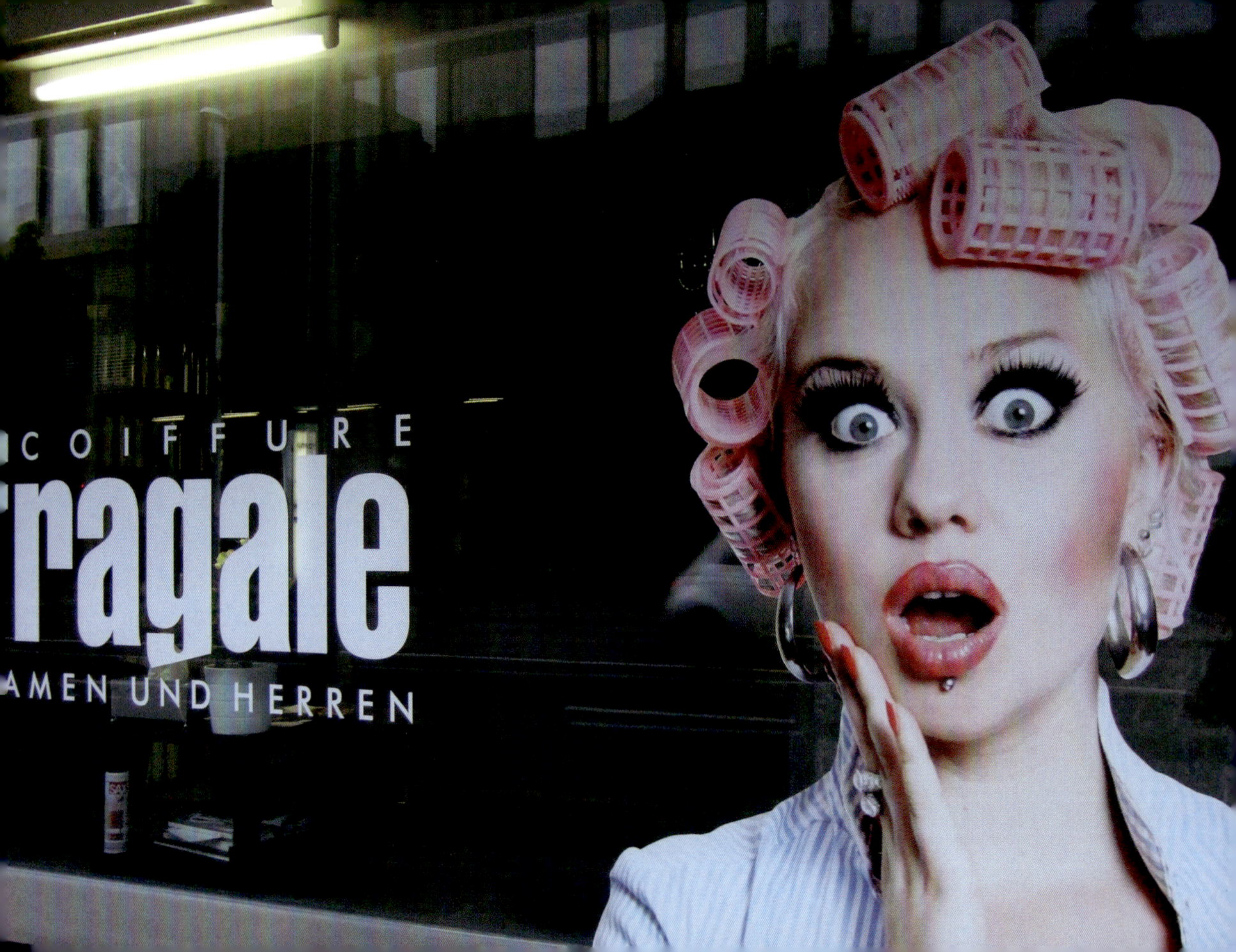
COIFFURE
ragale
AMEN UND HERREN

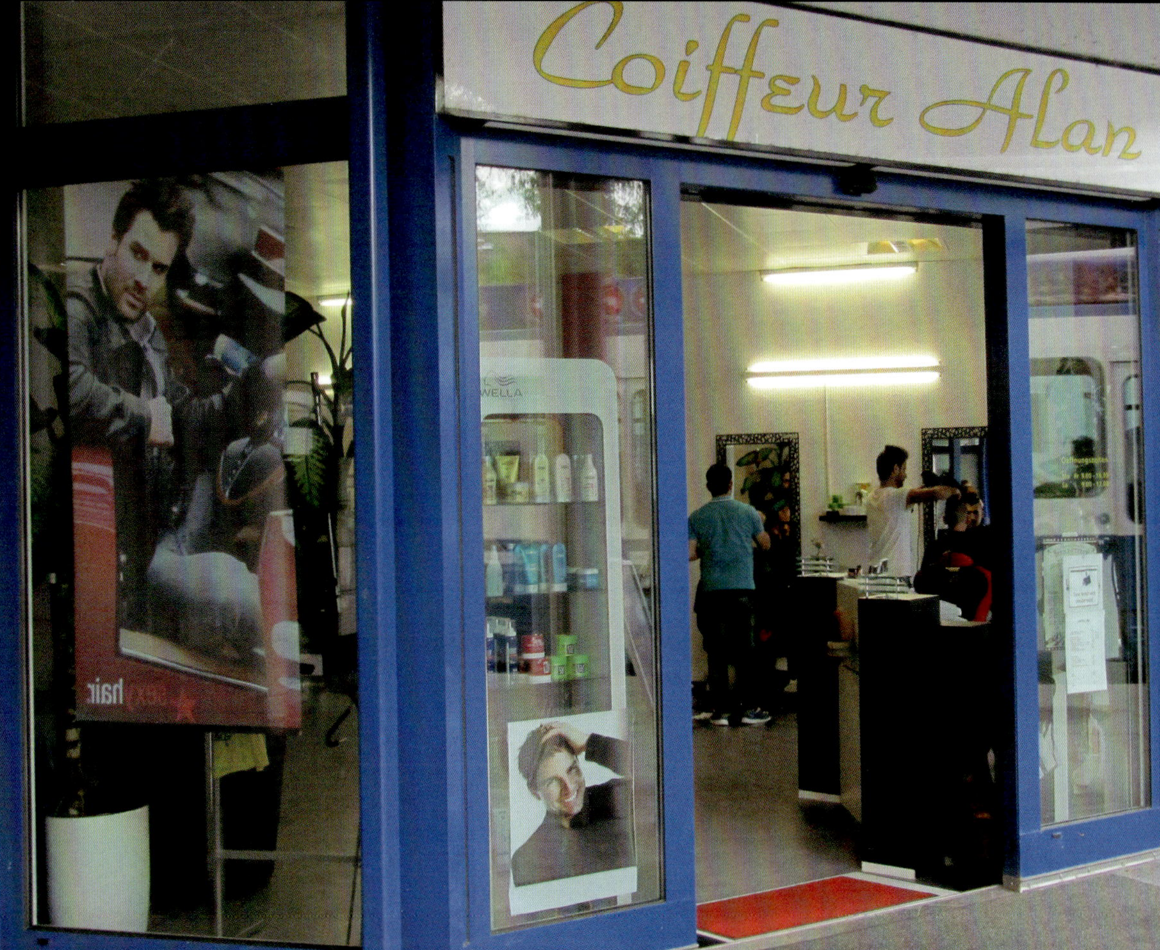
Coiffeur Alan

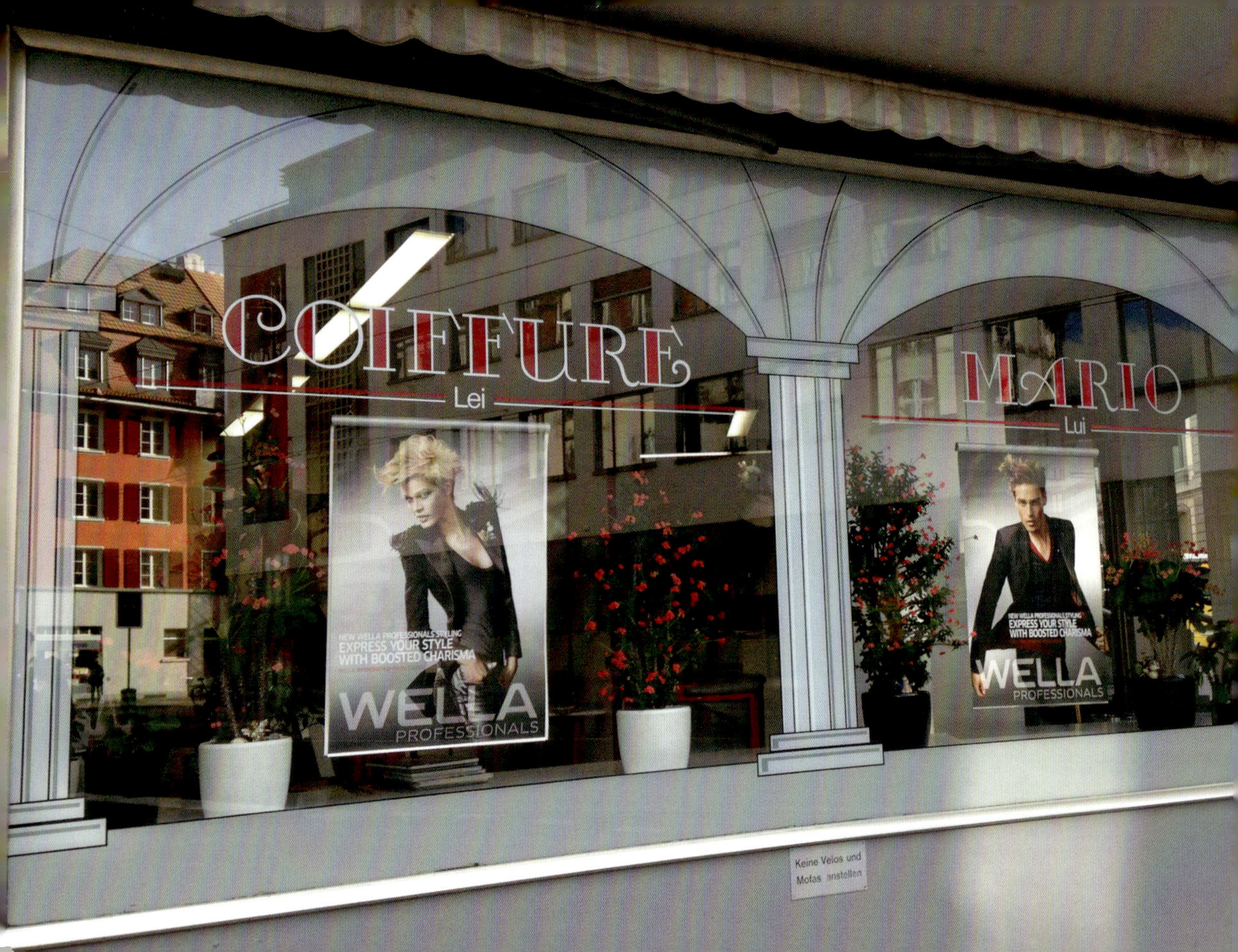
COIFFURE
Lei
MARIO
Lui
NEW WELLA PROFESSIONALS STYLING
EXPRESS YOUR STYLE
WITH BOOSTED CHARISMA
WELLA
PROFESSIONALS
NEW WELLA PROFESSIONALS STYLING
EXPRESS YOUR STYLE
WITH BOOSTED CHARISMA
WELLA
PROFESSIONALS
Keine Velos und
Mofas anstellen

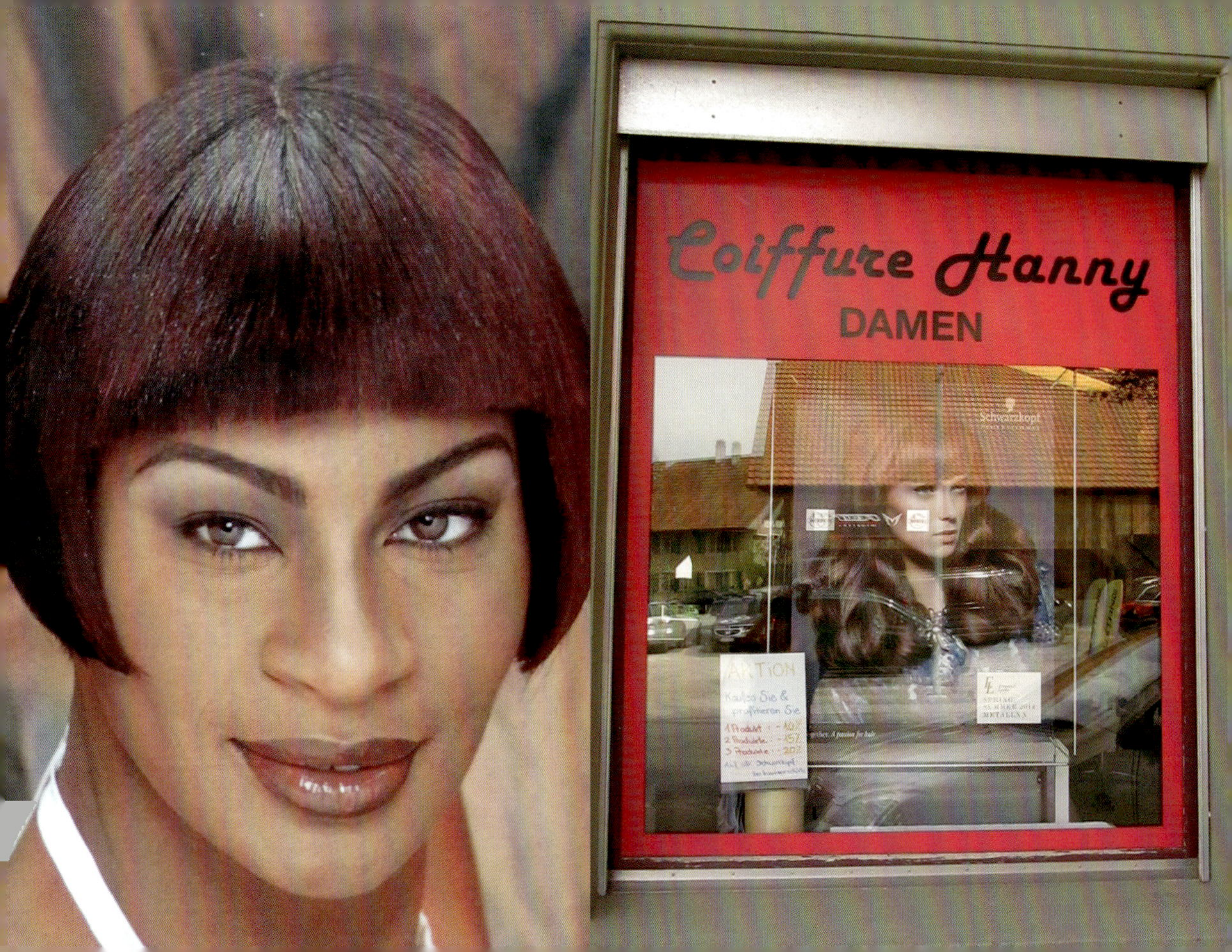
Coiffure Hanny
DAMEN
Schwarzkopf

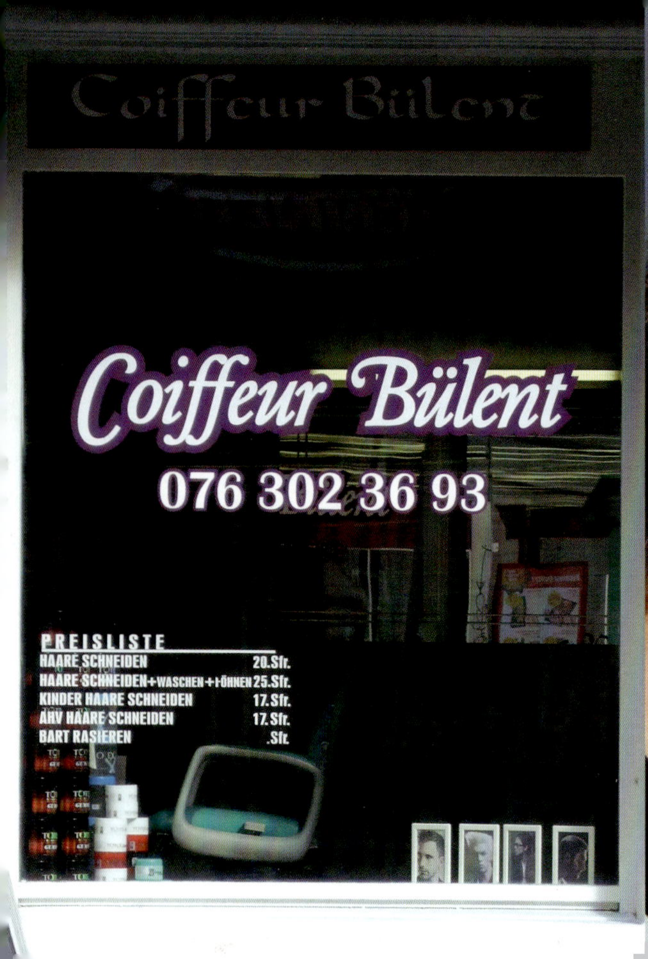

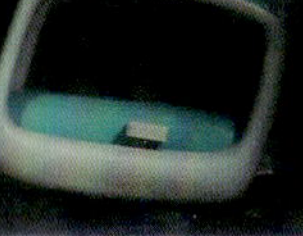

Coiffeur Bülent
Coiffeur Bülent
076 302 36 93
PREISLISTE
HAARE SCHNEIDEN 20.Sfr.
HAARE SCHNEIDEN+WASCHEN+FÖHNEN 25.Sfr.
KINDER HAARE SCHNEIDEN 17.Sfr.
AHV HAARE SCHNEIDEN 17.Sfr.
BART RASIEREN .Sfr.

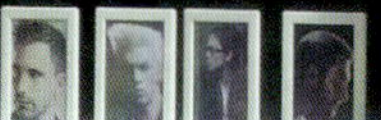

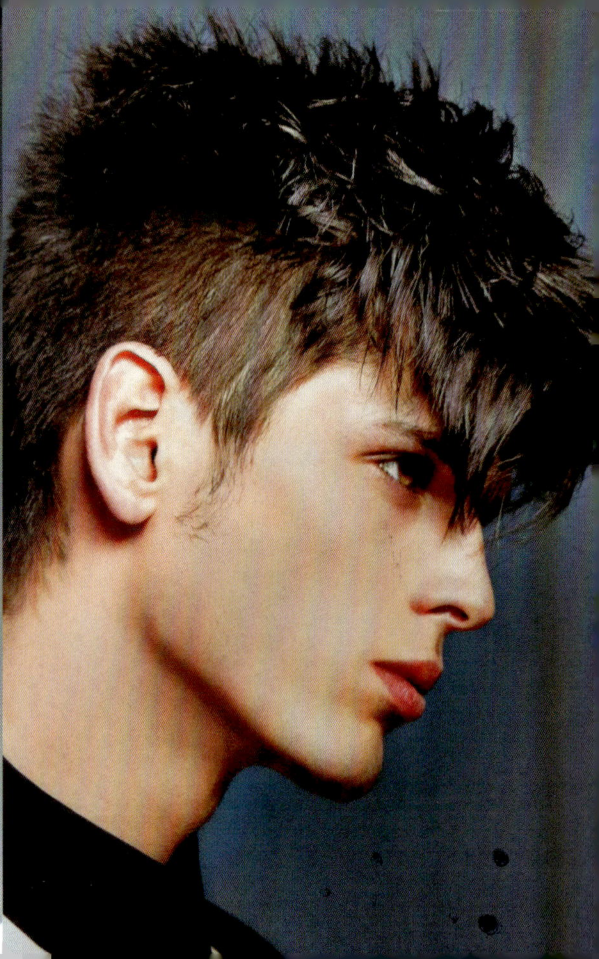

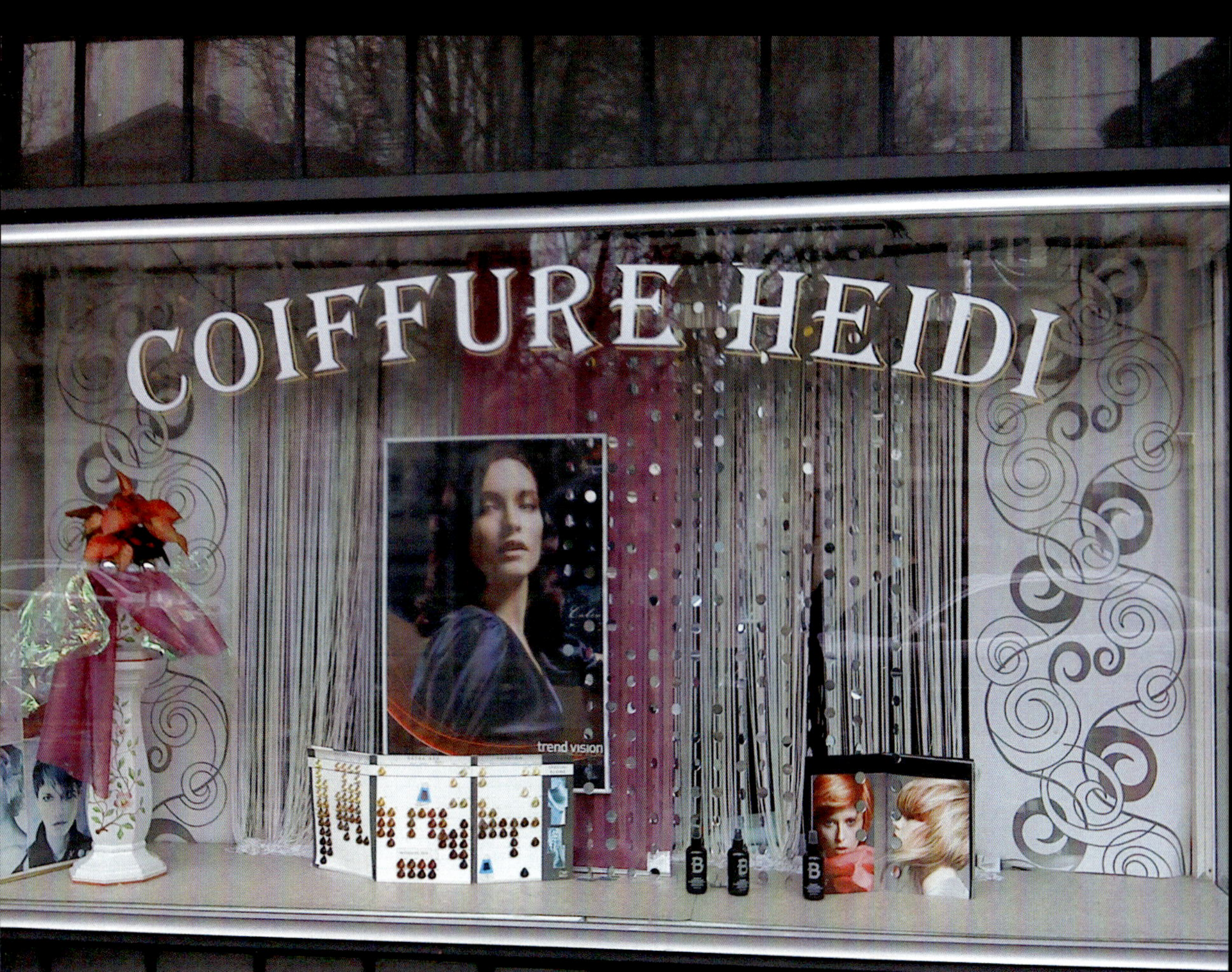

COIFFURE HEIDI
trend vision

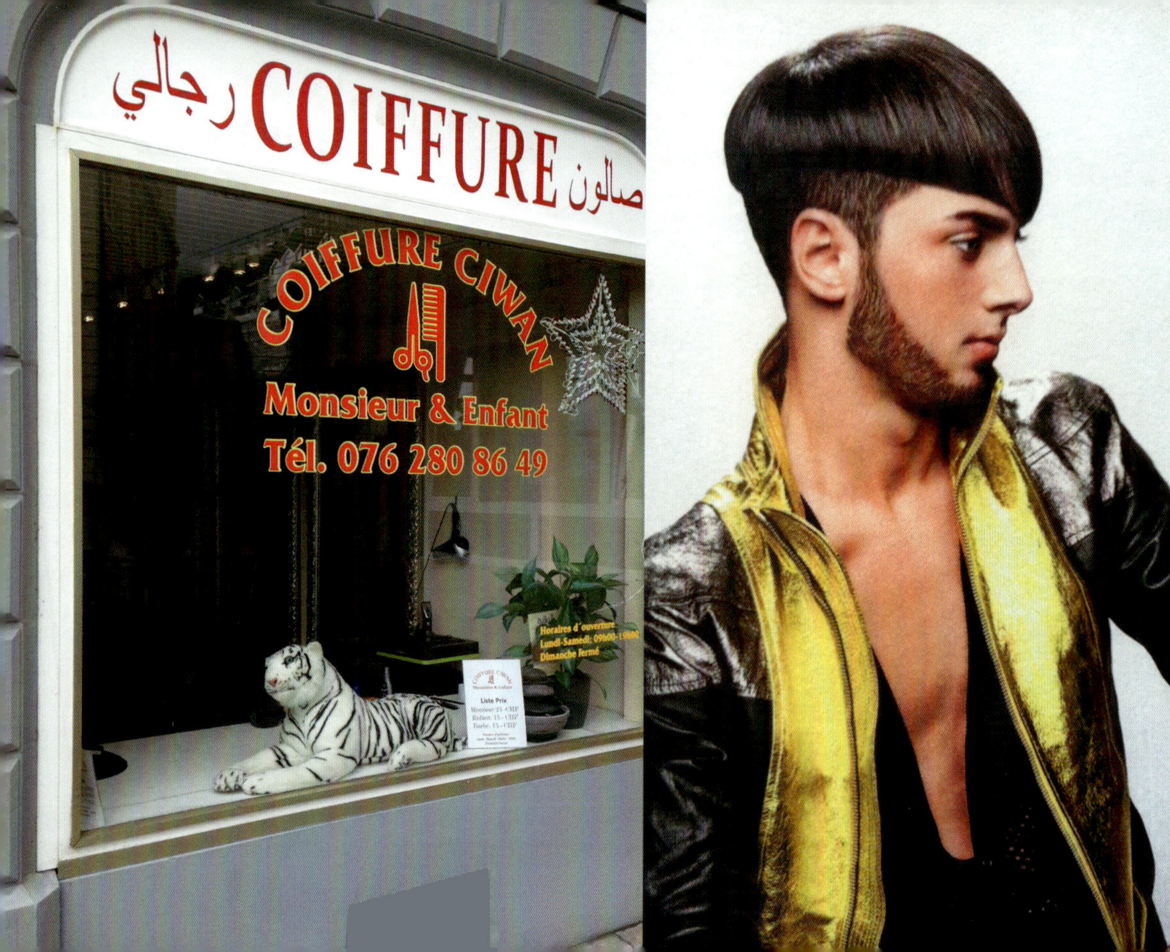
رجالي COIFFURE صالون
COIFFURE CIWAN
Monsieur & Enfant
Tél. 076 280 86 49
Horaires d´ouverture
Dimanche fermé
Liste Prix

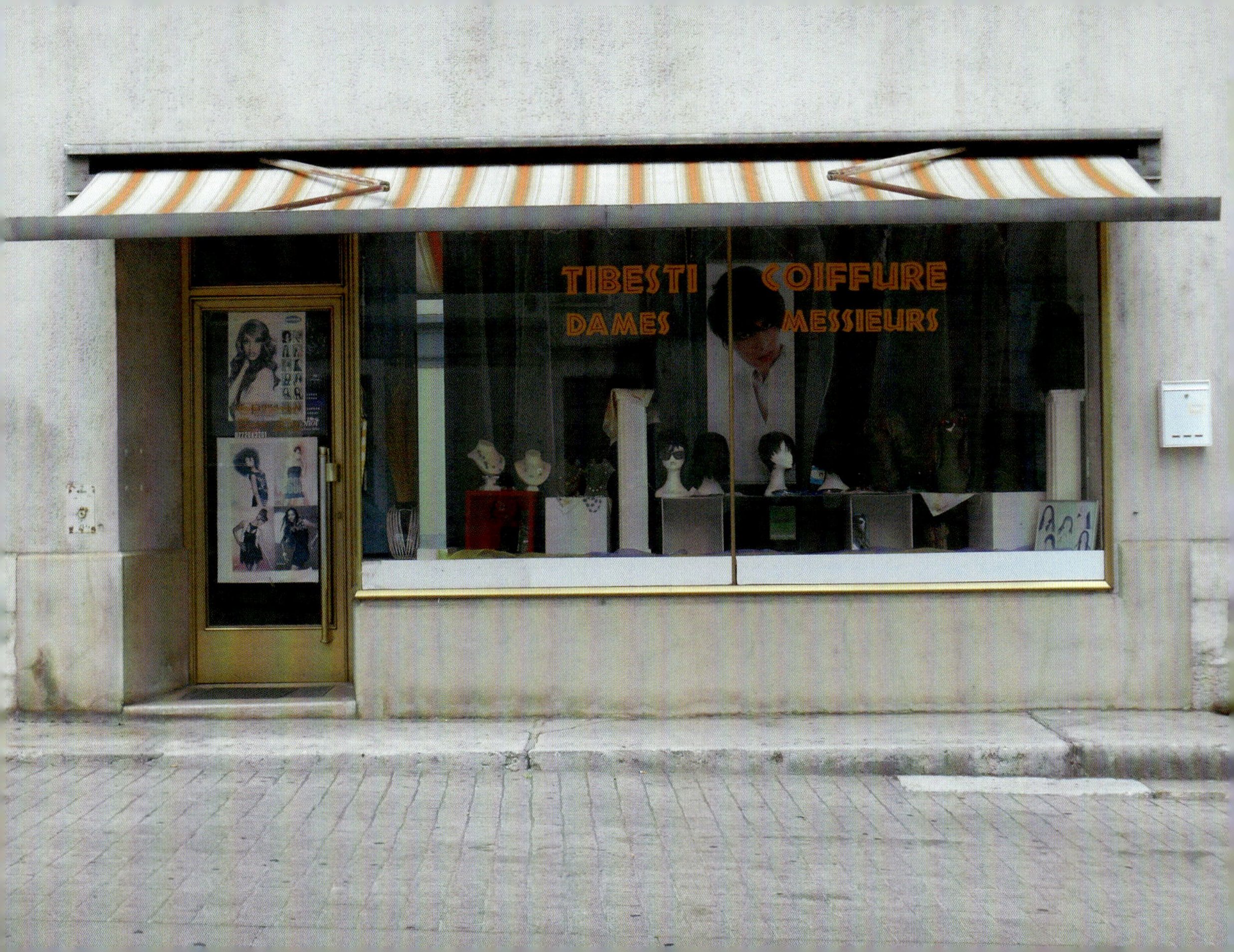
TIBESTI COIFFURE
DAMES MESSIEURS

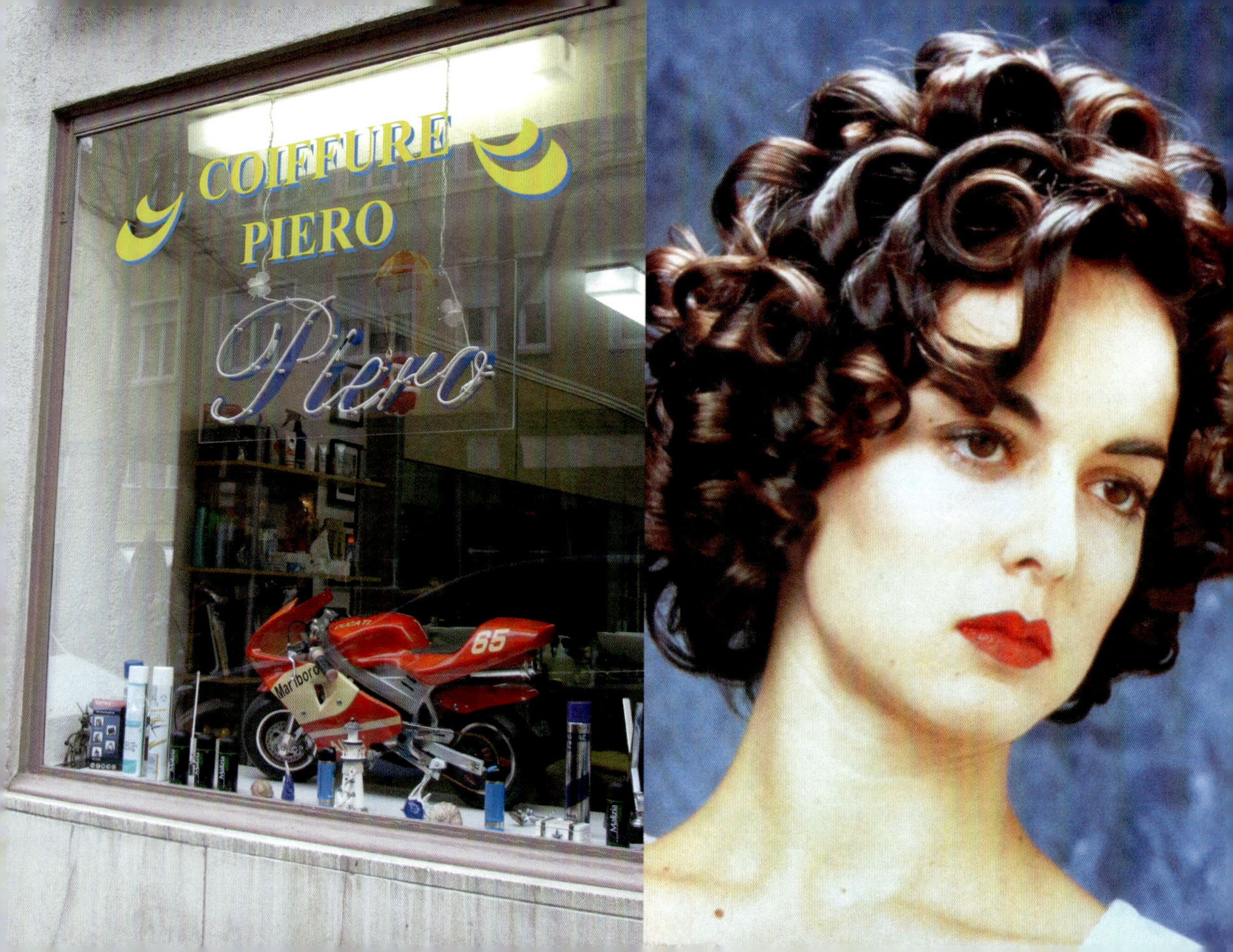
COIFFURE
PIERO
Piero
65

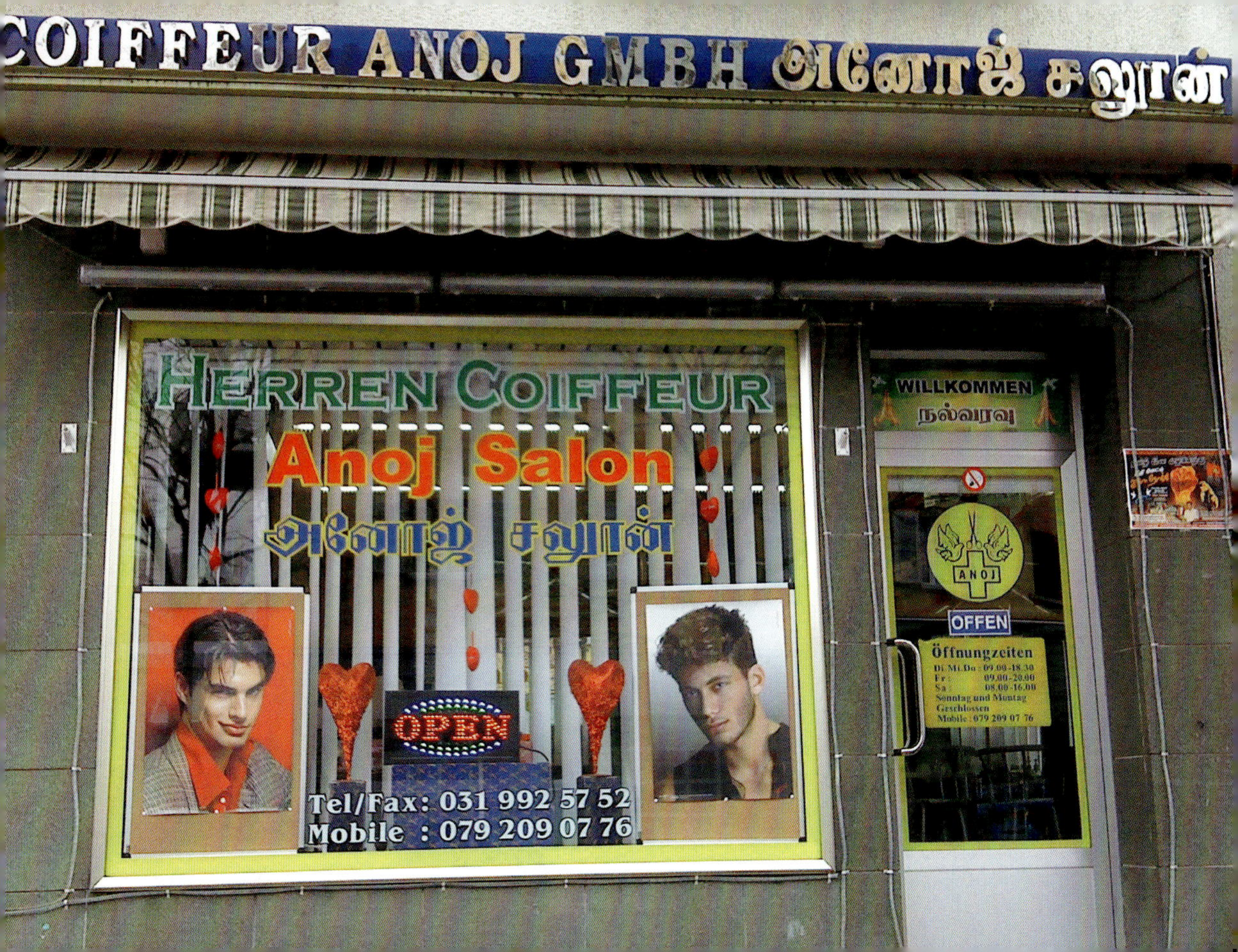
COIFFEUR ANOJ GMBH அனோஜ் சலூான்
HERREN COIFFEUR
Anoj Salon
அனோஜ் சலூான்
OPEN
Tel/Fax: 031 992 57 52
Mobile : 079 209 07 76
WILLKOMMEN
நல்வரவு
ANOJ
OFFEN
Öffnungzeiten
Di.Mi.Do : 09.00-18.30
Fr : 09.00-20.00
Sa : 08.00-16.00
Sonntag und Montag
Geschlossen
Mobile : 079 209 07 76

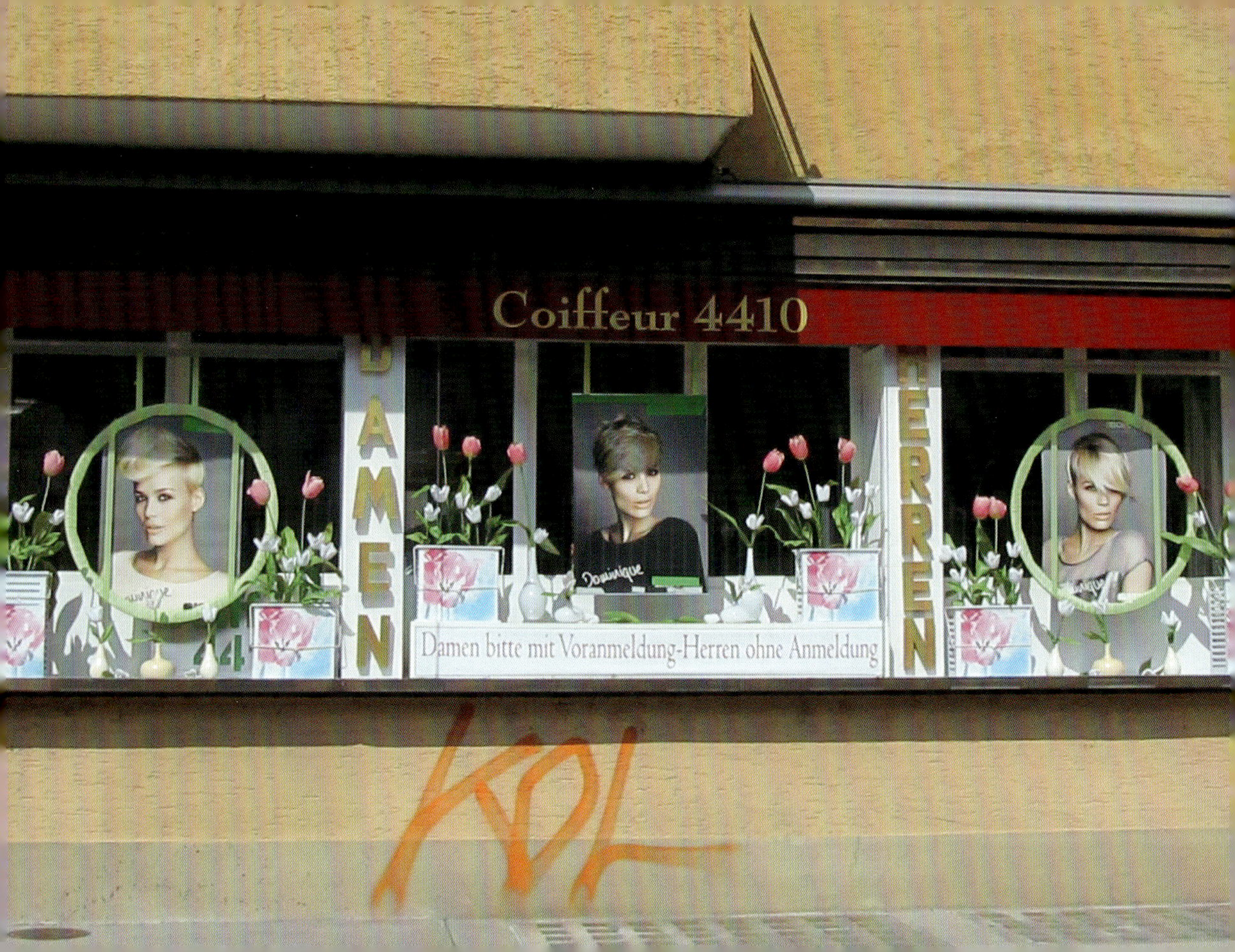
Coiffeur 4410
DAMEN
HERREN
Dominique
Damen bitte mit Voranmeldung-Herren ohne Anmeldung

Art on Hair
Atmosphair
Abschnitt B
Barb'hair shop
bel hair
Bulle d'hair
Changer d'Hair
Charakterchopf
Charisma Coiffeur
Coiffeur Usthair
Coiffure à Jour
Cosmetic Passage
Design am Kopf
ElementHaar
Elita Hair
Feinschnitt
Fit-Hair
Föhn-X
Friedhairich
Frizerie
Gerbhair
Global Hair
Glückssträhne
Haar ap
Haarbar

Haarbracadabra
Haarboutique Hairba
Haar Box
Haardepot
Haardieb
haaregge
Haare mobil
Haareszeiten
Haargenau
Haarklang
Haarkurve
Haar-Lay
Haarlekin
Haar-M.
Haarmonie
Haarpalast
Haarpracht
HAAR PUR
Haarscharf
Haar-Schopf
Haarspalterei
Haar-Station
Haarsträubend
Haarsturm
Haartraum

Haar und mehr
haar-werk
Haar 2-O
Hair2000
Hair Affair
Haircastle
Haircore
Hair-Corner
HairCool
Hair-damit
l'Hair de Plair
Haireinspaziert
hairfactory
Hairfeeling
Hairgate
Hairkules
Hair Lehmann
Hairlich
hairlounge
Hair meets Art
Hair mès coiffure
Hairness
Hairplay
HAIR POINT
Hair to Go

Hairtouch
Hair-X
hairxpress
Hairzblut
Hairzog
Hammerhaar
Happy Hair
Hauptsache
Hörlischnyder Gino
I Love Hair
Imagin'hair
Jennif'hair
Kaiserschnitt
Kopfsalat
k-haar-in
les ciseaux roulants
Lockeria
Lock & Roll
Love is in the Hair
Magisches Haar
Master Hair Palace
Mata Haari
MegaFön
Millennium Hair-Design
Millionhair

Miss'T'Hair
O'haara
Open Hair
PepHair
Plan B Hairstyling
Pfandhair
PompHair
Robhairto
Rocking Hair
Satisf'hair
Schneidwerk
Schnipp Schnapp
Schnitt-Art
Schnittstelle
Schnittwerk
SensHair
Sisters of Scissors
Strubelpeter
Taj Mahaar
Tête à Tête
Top Hair
United Haartists
Vision Hair
Vorhair Nachhair
wintHAIRthur

SALON MODERNE

Herausgegeben von Fabienne Eggelhöfer und Monica Lutz.
Wir bedanken uns bei allen, die uns ihre Fotografien zur Verfügung gestellt haben.

Book design: Judith Rüegger
Collaboration: Rolf Siegenthaler
Printed and bound by Kösel GmbH & Co. KG

Edition Patrick Frey, Limmatstrasse 268, CH–8005 Zurich
www.editionpatrickfrey.com
mail@editionpatrickfrey.ch

First edition: Edition Patrick Frey, 2015
ISBN 978-3-905929-92-8
Printed in Germany

Distribution:

Switzerland: AVA Verlagsauslieferung
CH–Affoltern am Albis, ava.ch

Germany, Austria: GVA Gemeinsame Verlagsauslieferung
D–Göttingen, gva-verlage.de

France, Luxembourg, Belgium: Les presses du réel
F–Dijon, lespressesdureel.com

United Kingdom: Antenne Books
GB–London, antennebooks.com

Japan: Marginal Press
JP–Tokyo, marginal-press.com

USA: RAM Publications and distributions
USA–Santa Monica, rampub.com

Australia, New Zealand: Perimeter Distribution
AU–Melbourne, perimeterdistribution.com

Rest of the world: Edition Patrick Frey
CH–Zurich, editionpatrickfrey.com